David Triesman
Ian Waitt

COLLEGE ADMINISTRATION

A HANDBOOK

SECOND EDITION

Published in association with
The National Association of
Teachers in Further and
Higher Education

natfhe

Longman

Professional Reference and Information Division
Longman Group UK Limited
6th Floor, Westgate House
The High
Harlow
Essex CM20 1NE
England

First edition published May 1980
Second edition published 1988

British Library Cataloguing in Publication Data
College administration — 2nd ed
1. Universities and Colleges — England — Administration
2. Universities and Colleges — England — Administration
I. Locke, Michael II. National Association of Teachers in Further and Higher Education
374'.942 LB2 341. 8. G7

ISBN 0-582-90117-0

ISBN 0-582-90117-0

Set by Tradeset Photosetting, Welwyn Garden City, Hertfordshire.
Printed in the United Kingdom by Biddles Ltd, Guildford and King's Lynn

CONTENTS

Section 2: The institutions and the staff

Section 3: Curriculum and students

Section 4: Buildings

INTRODUCTION

Michael Locke

The public sector of further and higher education is a system of extraordinary complexity. Indeed, it is not so much one system as the accumulation of many systems, overlaid upon each other.

Pieces of political and administrative reform have been introduced over the years, often with scant regard for their consistency or their impact on previous innovations. There isn't an underlying logic, other than the way in which people and institutions have continually been expected to respond – and actually have responded – to changes and to yet another piece of a system being added to the previous accretions.

This book is to help get to know the sector. It provides:

— information on how the systems work at present;
— understanding of what lies behind current systems;
— guidance on how to act in some of the everyday situations produced by the political and administrative systems.

The complexities of the system cannot be disentangled by, as it were, pulling on the knot in one place. There are different approaches appropriate for getting to grips with different problems. The material in this book is organised so that it can be used, as needed, for making management decisions, or for gaining a working knowledge of the system within which a reader works (whether to assist in implementing changes or simply to 'understand'), or for undertaking practical or academic research. It covers in its four main sections: the overall organisation of policies, law, institutions and major administrative systems; staff matters, including the national negotiating machinery introduced in 1987, employment law and the management of institutions' responses to external changes; the service – curriculum framework and issues for students; the buildings and their use. Each section includes a number of chapters written with specific expertise. It is of the nature of the different material in these chapters and of the different ways in which they are likely to be used that the writers have treated their subject matters with different emphases. All chapters can serve as a source of reference for further investigations.

This is the second edition of *College Administration*, the first having been published in 1980. Really, though, this is in most respects a new book. So much has changed since 1980, and all but a few pages of this book have been written afresh.

In 1980 it was not clear how much the new Conservative Government under Prime Minister Margaret Thatcher would change the environment in which staff and students in public sector further and higher education worked. It was clear – and had been for years too under the previous Labour Government – that the environment would get tougher, that there would be less money but more concern for "results" It was likely that the Manpower Services Commission would play a larger role in the sector and that a training and work experience programme for 16–19 year olds would take a more significant part of college provisions. It was likely that institutions of higher education would be subject to increasing centralised and detailed controls. But it was not clear how considerable would be the ideological shift the pressure on public services to perform to 'market' principles and be 'efficient' – though the sector had traditionally operated on entrepreneurial principles. The systems have become more complex and more restrictive to carry through these changes – and the need to understand the constraints and opportunities of these systems all the more important at all levels and in all parts of the service.

However, some of the developments since 1980 could, at first sight, appear divergent. Concern to promote equal opportunities in terms of sex, race, and physical ability (as well as in terms of class to which FE has always been dedicated) have taken root in the implementation of legislation and policy and in everyday practice. The improvement of 'access' especially to higher education, and of more open and individual learning modes have become characteristic of the sector. Whilst this is no time to be complacent about wider opportunities, the sector has built on its tradition of service and, in all the tensions produced by greater external pressures and fewer resources, the institutions and their staffs have learnt more about how to offer a human and responsive service. It is, in truth, unfair that FHE has not been consistently recognised at the level of national policy as capable of meeting whatever 'market' and social needs were put up. But all the more important is it therefore to improve the sector's knowledge of its own administration and of the administrative measures which have been imposed upon it. This books helps do that.

PREFACE BY THE EDITOR OF THE 1980 EDITION

Ian Waitt

The publication of the first edition of *College Administration* in 1980 marked a major departure in the study and practice of educational administration; and it coincided with a major shift in Government policies. The Government demanded different expressions of educational accountability and altered the resource base: on the one hand it encouraged vocational education and training, providing considerable funding, whilst on the other it restricted funding in order to promote institutional reform, responsiveness and relevance to perceived societal needs.

The prime use of the first edition therefore to many readers was as a source of objective reference – whether for the purposes of defence or attack, or simply the establishment of the rules of the game. In the context of changes in institutional and legal areas, *College Administration* was of immediate practical use to administrators, educationalists and students for its neutrality, accuracy and wealth of information.

The book made its focus that of *administration.* There is much dispute over whether 'management' or 'administration' takes precedence. The Book's standpoint was that 'administration' provided the more substantial intellectual foundation for action. 'Administration' represents the execution of societal authority and of institutional, collective and individual policy through documented, enforceable rules – around all of which are areas of discretion and interpretation – and the provision for accountability. Change can be effected only by understanding how the administrative provision expresses educational, financial and societal philosophy and what the barriers are. These barriers may be attitudinal, but they are nonetheless expressed somewhere in rule. On this basis *College Administration* presents the *facts* about the system and the changes since the first edition.

Some of the changes which have taken place in the years between the first and second editions of *College Administration* demonstrate the changes in the location of power. The fashionable hunt for the "responsive college", the attention given to marketing, the alterations in the structures of staff conditions of service, the slow growth of salaries, and the increase in student numbers—all illustrate the increase in the power of the client and the decrease in the power of institutional providers.

The second edition of *College Administration* has been comprehensively revised and rewritten to reflect these changes in provision and emphasis since 1980. The text is almost entirely new and reflects the massive changes in the structure of pay and conditions for staff in public sector further and higher education including aspects of staff appraisal as well as the shifts in college management to cope with an array of educational changes. The editorial team has been expanded, in order to benefit from the complementary perspectives of the team who are all active and respected practitioners, writers, and educationalists.

As the editor and main author of the first edition, it is a particular pleasure now to hand over the prime role to Michael Locke, and to strongly recommend the new approaches which have been successfully effected by him, David, Keith and Paula. Their work is perpetuating in its new form the essential message of original productions; know the administrative framework before assuming to understand the overall system.

NOTES AND ACKNOWLEDGEMENTS

NOTES AND REFERENCES

The system adopted for this book is that Notes are organised chapter by chapter and included at the end of each chapter, whereas References are – to avoid repetition – amalgamated at the back of the book. For some areas it has been appropriate to provide lists of addresses for further information or lists of specialist Further Reading, and such lists are included at the end of the relevant chapter.

ACKNOWLEDGEMENTS

The preparation of this new edition of *College Administration* has drawn on the knowledge and skills of many people. The writers, as 'by-lined' on the Contents page, have produced expert, clear and careful material. Members of the Advisory Board, which is set out at the back of the book, have contributed a wealth of expertise and close reading of draft chapters. Both writers and members of the Advisory Board have worked against often tight and continually shifting deadlines as we kept pace with changes in national policies, and the Editors are grateful not only for their expert contributions but for the good grace with which they coped with the pressures of producing this book at this time.

Specific thanks are also due to a number of individuals whose contributions may not otherwise be public, Keith Scribbins and David Triesman are indebted to Barry Fawcett and Joan Gordon for their advice on early drafts of the section on the Teachers Superannuation Scheme and helping them through the maze of regulations governing the Scheme. The preparation of Chapter 3.1 was assisted by contributions from Lucia Jones and Jean Bocock, Theresa Turner, Val Woolgar and Pat Davies of NATFHE staff helped with typing and general administration, Janet Evans, NATFHE librarian, assisted in compiling the list of references. The whole book owes much to the detailed comments and breadth of understanding which, above all others, David Bradshaw, Jackson Hall and Bob Morris gave in their comments on drafts.

The Editors are also grateful to colleagues who have helped and supported us in our three organisations, NATFHE, the Further Education Staff College and North London Polytechnic. Particular thanks are due to Mike Farmer, Ray Grace and Chris Minta of NATFHE's National Executive Committee.

The Editors are indebted to the Governing Body of the Further Education Staff College for the practical assistance in the production of this book and in particular for providing the services of Frank Walton in the preparation of chapters 2.4 and 2.7.

Michael Locke wishes to record his debt to Bea Pike in suffering with him the tensions and anxieties of editing a quarter of a million words into this book.

Janet Shuter prepared the Index.

We are grateful to the following for permission to reproduce copyright material:

Further Education Staff College for adaptation from Appendix by John Hunter

Scribbens & Walton 'Staff Appraisal in Further and Higher Education (8.9, 2.9); Health and Safety Executive for Appendix 1(2.7), Appendix 2(2.7);

The Controller of Her Majesty's Stationery Office for extracts from 'Statutory Instruments 1981, No 1086 Education, England and Wales. The Education (Schools of Further Education) Regulations 1981 *HMSO* 011 017086, Annex 1(1.2).

NOTE

Opinions and perspectives presented in this book are not necessarily those of NATFHE or of the Editors.

Section 1

THE ADMINISTRATIVE FRAMEWORK

1.1 THE DEVELOPMENT OF PUBLIC SECTOR FURTHER AND HIGHER EDUCATION

1 The public sector of further and higher education is not a unified system. The system is not defined by statute, though the system stems from the Education Act 1944 and is referred to by the corpus of Education Acts 1944–86 and other primary legislation and is regulated by statutory instruments (See **1.2**). It is a conglomerate of institutions and services. It includes colleges variously funded by local authorities and by central government, increasingly, with substantial contributions from the Manpower Services Commission and from employers and student fees, and with lesser amounts from voluntary and other sources. It includes different levels and forms of courses, from pre-vocational courses for 16–17 year olds to non-vocational adult education, to first and higher degrees, to mainstream vocational further education, in all subjects and by all modes. It includes teacher education, which until 1975 was a separate sector. What basically defines the *public* sector is its differentiation from the *private* sector of universities and from commercial organisations. But the different parts of the public sector became more closely identified in recent years and – at least until the 1987 White Paper (See below Appendix 1) – treated as parts of a whole in national policy.

2 Definitions within public sector further and higher education have developed to those that are recognised currently. The 1944 Act defined 'further education' in Section 41 as 'full-time and part-time education for persons over compulsory school age' and 'leisure-time occupation' in 'organised cultural training and recreative activities' (See **1.2** 14–17). As the system developed it became common to distinguish between 'further' and 'higher' education. 'Higher education' refers to courses of degree level and equivalent (i.e. requiring two GCE 'A' (Advanced) levels or equivalent for entry, broadly speaking[1]), and hence as a term could refer both to universities and to what came to be called 'public sector higher education' (PSHE). PSHE in these terms included HE both in colleges maintained by Local Education Authorities (LEAs) and in colleges funded by direct grant from central government. 'PSHE' would thus be synonymous with 'advanced further education' (AFE). On this definition 'further education' (FE) could be taken to refer only to 'non-advanced further education' (NAFE) (i.e. courses below degree level and equivalent). However, legalistically speaking under the 1944 Act, 'further education' embraces all, advanced and non-advanced.

3 The 1944 Act placed a duty on local education authorities to secure provision for further education for their areas. Before that many local authorities had made provision for what was then largely known as technical education but such provision was discretionary. After the 1944 Act and the end of World War II in 1945, provision of further education greatly increased but without much coherence in the system. Although LEAs were required to submit 'schemes of further education' (See **1.2** 14–16) to the Ministry and consult with other authorities in their region, they tended to act unilaterally. This resulted in a diverse pattern of provision varying from one LEA to the next. Moreover, the 1944 Act referred only to the duty of securing 'adequate facilities' for further education, a phrase capable of varying interpretations (See **1.2** 16 and 33–35). Other features of the 1944 Act, which would have contributed to a system of further education – proposals for county colleges and for universal provision for young people in the immediate post-school years – were never activated.

4 Public sector further and higher education experienced sustained growth from the 1944 Act for the next 25–30 years, shaped by major Reports and White Papers. The Percy Report of 1945 led to the establishment of the National Advisory Council on Education for Industry and Commerce and a nationwide pattern of Regional Advisory Councils. By 1956, a stratified pattern had developed based on regional, area, and local colleges and evening institutes. The Government's adoption of the proposals in the 1956 White Paper *Technical Education* institutionalised this stratification and created from large regional colleges ten Colleges of Advanced Technology (CATS), funded not by the LEAs but by direct grant from the Ministry of Education.

5 In the 1950s and 1960s there were several reports calling for expansion of non-advanced further education. The Crowther Report, *15–18* (1959) suggested that FE should be expanded as an alternative route for continuing education for all young people, encompassing technical and general education based on compulsory full-time or part-time education for all 16–17 year olds. Crowther led to the 1961 White Paper, *Better Opportunities in Technical Education*, which recommended the creation of courses for technicians, craftsmen and operatives, resulting in a shift away from evening-only study and the further development of local colleges. The Henniker–Heaton Report of 1964, *Day Release*, recommended that by 1969 there should be a doubling in the number of young employees released to attend day classes in the further education. This report was widely criticised for its omissions and did not produce any real expansion of release.

6 The Industrial Training Act 1964 recognised that for training to be effective it could not be left to the voluntary provision of industry, thus countermanding the Carr Report (1958) which recommended that industrial training should remain the responsibility of employers. The Act led to the creation of industrial training boards (ITBs) responsible for training in major sectors of industry. The ITBs varied in their effectiveness, and many companies complained that the financial burdens imposed, especially by the levy system, were irksome. The Employment and Training Act 1973 amended some provisions of the 1964 Act. Certain companies were exempted from the levy raised by the ITBs for the purpose of approved training. The 1973 Act also created the Manpower Services Commission (MSC) which took over the responsibilities for training of the Department of Employment and has played a steadily increasing role in further education (see below paragraph 24–31 and **1.7**). Meanwhile, higher education in the public sector developed somewhat separately.

7 The Robbins Report in 1963 *Higher Education* led to the conversion of the National Council for Technological Awards (set up in 1955) into the Council for National Academic Awards (CNAA) in 1964, empowered to award degrees in all subjects, not just technology. It also led to the granting of university status to the CATs. The 1966 White Paper *A plan for polytechnics and other colleges* recommended the concentration of advanced further education in a limited number of institutions. Here and in the 'Woolwich' (1965) and 'Lancaster' (1967) speeches by the Secretary of State, Anthony Crosland, a 'polytechnic policy' was set out for developing higher education with a more vocational orientation and broader access than had been associated with universities, thus distinguishing between university and public sector (FE) traditions, the so-called 'binary system'. This led to the designation from 1969 to 1973 of twenty-nine polytechnics in England and one in Wales.

8 The Report of the Haslegrave Committee on Technician Courses and Examinations in 1969 led to the establishment of the Technician Education Council in 1973 and the Business Education Council in 1974, for the development of courses and qualifications in their respective areas. TEC and BEC merged in January 1983 to form the Business and Technician Education Council (BTEC) (See **3.1** 44–49).

9 **Teacher education**

Teacher education developed for many years as a distinct sector of post-school education, originating in voluntary institutions and subsequently supplemented by LEA maintained colleges. Also, the sector has had close links with the universities and their departments of education through the Area Training Organisations (ATOs) set up following the 1944 McNair Report. The retitling of teacher training colleges, following the 1963 Robbins Report, as colleges of education was intended to enhance their status. The James Report (1971) and the White Paper *Education: A framework for expansion* in 1972, however, laid the basis for the integration of teacher education with the mainstream of public sector higher education. The Further Education Regulations 1975 included the sector in FE. The integration with the rest of the public sector could be said to have reached virtual completion on the reconstitution of the National Advisory Body for Public Sector Higher Education in 1985 to include the voluntary sector for planning and funding purposes (See **1.3** 54–65).

10 Since 1972, teacher education has gone through dramatic changes, having changed in a couple of years from rapid expansion to more rapid contraction of the sector, in response to the falling birthrate, Government policies opposing 'monotechnic' institutions in principle, and financial stringency. Teacher education in the public sector is now mostly provided in polytechnics and colleges (and institutes) of higher education, although a small number of monotechnic teacher education institutions still remain. The new pattern has been achieved partly by mergers of colleges and partly by diversification of colleges of education into a range of, primarily, humanities and social science courses. The teacher education system now faces new challenges in Government pressures to improve 'teaching quality' and the establishment of the Council for the Accreditation of Teacher Education (CATE) (See **3.1** Appendix 2), whilst student demand stagnates and the teaching profession suffers low morale and recruitment difficulties.

11 **Public sector higher education: the 1980s**

From the mid-1970s on there has been debate about the management and finance of higher education in the public sector, revolving around issues of central or local control and funding. The Oakes Report (1978) proposed a new national body to take responsibility for planning and costing the sector, together with new regional bodies; control of institutions was to continue to be vested in local authorities and existing institutional governing bodies. The Oakes proposals attracted considerable support, but while the debate was still ensuing the Conservative Government took office in May 1979 and rapidly sought more radical solutions, including greater degree of centralisation.

12 The new Government moved swiftly to impose a financial limit on (or 'cap') the Advanced Further Education Pool, the mechanism for the national funding of the sector (See **1.3**). This had hitherto been done on the basis of the aggregation of claims by providing LEAs, which was then apportioned to all

LEAs on the basis of a formula. This pooling system had been regarded with suspicion by central and local government for some time, since LEAs could spend on higher education in the knowledge that the cost of their spending would be borne by all authorities and by central government through the rate support grant. The Government pushed through what it admitted was a 'rough and ready' means of apportioning a capped pool and following the passage of the Education Act, 1980, with effect from the financial year 1980/81, the Advanced Further Education Pool has been capped. Since that date, the apportionment mechanism has been refined, particularly as a result of the Government's second innovation – the National Advisory Body (NAB).

13 In July 1981, the DES issued a consultative document, *Higher Education in England outside the universities: Policy, funding and management* (1981a), which posed two alternative models – one, based on proposals from the Council of Local Education Authorities (CLEA), retaining many of the features of the existing system with an 'Oakes' type national body; the other a highly centralised approach with a new sector of higher education financed directly by the Exchequer and severing the links with further education. The Government favoured the latter, centralist, model. After a considerable and heated period of debate, in which few supported the centralist proposal, the Government accepted a model of advice and control which was very close to the CLEA model, a body known first as the National Advisory Body for Local Authority Higher Education (NAB) (See **1.3** 54–65).

14 The establishment of NAB as an interim body was announced in December 1981, and its first meetings were held early in 1982. It was given a two-tier structure: A Board (chaired by Christopher Ball) which made recommendations to a Committee (chaired by the Parliamentary Under Secretary) which made recommendations to the Secretary of State on the allocation of the AFE pool (See **1.3** 49–53). Prior to its establishment a Committee chaired by a DES civil servant, Study Group on the Management of the AFE Pool, named after its chair, 'the Stephen Jones Group', had worked to resolve some of the technical problems arising from the distribution of the capped pool. NAB was able to build on this work, and has steered a course between the requirements of Government and the interests of local authorities and institutions. In January 1985, its success was reflected in the reconstitution of NAB. It ceased to be 'interim' and also took up new responsibilities for the voluntary sector. As a result it changed its title to 'National Advisory Body for Public Sector Higher Education', carrying forward the absorption of teacher education into the mainstream of PSHE. NAB operated principally through:

(i) Major planning exercises aimed at effecting a steer of the PSHE system as a whole in directions determined by Government and within resource levels set by Government, but in the context of advice from NAB itself. The Government has not consistently taken NAB's advice, for example on the pace and scale of cuts in teacher education provision or on the degree to which the 'unit of resource' (roughly, the financial support per student place) could be allowed to fall;

(ii) Sectoral studies aimed at changing the balance of provision in a particular subject area;

(iii) NAB has undertaken some transbinary planning with the University Grants Committee, with limited impact to date;

(iv) Strategic advice to the DES.

15 DES statistics[2] take a considerable time to collect and the basis of collection changes over the years, but the figures in Table 1 show the growth of PSHE. If all students are included – full-time, sandwich, and part-time – the PSHE has a significantly larger student population than the universities: for example, in Great Britain in 1983, there were 460,700 home students in PSHE compared with 370,300 in the universities.

Table 1
Public Sector Higher Education Student Numbers

1954/55	1962/63	1969/70	1974/75	November 1984
34,400	85,750	190,200	210,230	410,000
England and Wales				(England only)

These figures include CATs up to the time at which they became universities, and the colleges of education.

Table 2
Public Sector Higher Education Enrolments by Qualification Aim

	1980	*1983*	*1984*	*1985 (Prov)*
All Year Enrolments				
Full-time and Sandwich				
Postgrad/Higher Degree	11.0	9.9	10.6	11.0
1st Degree/Degree Equivalent	120.3	155.1	160.5	163.9
Other	55.6	65.6	67.0	70.0
Total	186.9	230.7	238.1	244.0
Part-time Day and Evening only				
Postgrad/Higher Degree	11.4	13.3	14.4	15.6
1st Degree/Degree Equivalent	24.2	27.8	28.0	29.2
Other	123.2	131.7	129.5	139.3
Total	158.8	171.9	171.9	184.1
All Modes (Number)				
Postgrad/Higher Degree	22.4	23.2	25.0	26.6
1st Degree/Degree Equivalent	144.5	182.1	188.5	193.1
Other	178.8	197.3	196.5	208.3
Total	345.7	402.6	410.0	427.9
All Years – Full-time Equivalent				
All Modes (Full-time Equivalent)				
Postgrad/Higher Degree	14.7	14.3	15.5	16.4
1st Degree/Degree Equivalent	124.9	160.0	165.6	169.4
Other	97.4	110.4	111.3	116.7
Total	236.9	284.7	292.4	302.5

16 The planning of future numbers of students in PSHE, or in higher education as a whole, has proved a difficult and controversial issue, requiring a balance of factors including demographic trends, entry qualifications and participation rates, as well as official policies on access and on the resources available and their distribution. For some years DES statisticians have been concerned about the impact of the demographic downturn which will reduce the size of the 18 year old age group (traditionally the largest group of entrants to higher education) by 40% from maximum in 1982–83 to minimum in the mid-1990s. Successive Governments have produced different forecasts. In 1978 DES discussion document, *Higher Education into the 1990s*, included a model which would have used the spare capacity by the fall in the 'traditional' age group to accommodate a modest increase in 'non-traditional' entrants, and this was widely welcomed in higher education. However, since then, official projections[3] envisaged a fall in student numbers more or less in line with the demographic downturn, although a wide range of objections on educational and statistical grounds led the DES to revise its projections upwards. Also, buoyant demand for higher education in spite of the demographic downturn made it difficult to cut provision to the extent which the Government has wished. Even so, the cuts and other pressures imposed by Government increased competition for entry and restricted choices of subjects for many entrants.

17 Meanwhile, there were moves toward institutions taking greater responsibility for their own qualifications. This relates particularly to the degrees awarded by CNAA, since PSHE offers a wide range of courses examined or validated by other bodies, including professional bodies. In April 1984, the Government established a Committee of Enquiry into the Academic Validation of Degree Courses in Public Sector Higher Education, under the Chairmanship of Sir Norman Lindop. The Lindop Report, published in April 1985, advocated a spectrum of validation arrangements reflecting the 'maturity' of each institution. After consultation, the CNAA announced in February 1987 that it would accredit some institutions, delegating powers to validate qualifications. (See **3.1** 54–59.)

18 The Government issued a Green Paper, *The development of higher education into the 1990s* in May 1985, which expressed the Government's concern to steer the higher education system further towards the perceived needs of the economy and industry. The Green Paper also suggested continued contraction of the size of the higher education system, including a narrower redefinition of the Robbins Principle on access to higher education. The reaction to the Green Paper was generally one of disappointment at its negative tone. A development of potential significance was the Further Education Act 1985, which set out to regulate and facilitate commercial activities in further education institutions (See **1.2**) though at time of writing its impact has not been very evident.

19 During 1985 and 1986 NAB undertook an inquiry into the much debated issues of the management and finance of public sector higher education. The inquiry on 'Good Management Practice' investigated management processes and governmental systems (See **2.8** 30). In doing so it revived questions which echoed back to Anthony Crosland's 'Woolwich' speech in 1965 and its assertion of a 'binary system', about the place of institutions of higher education in the local authority system. The Committee of Directors of Polytechnics

(CDP) took the opportunity to reemphasise their wish for legal autonomy (corporate status) for their institutions and for independence from LEAs.

20 In April 1987 Secretary of State Kenneth Baker published a White Paper *Higher Education: Meeting the Challange*, which proposed fundamental and controversial changes in the structure of both public and university higher education. For the public sector, the largest proposed changes included the removal of major higher education providers from local education authority control, according to these institutions corporate status and placing them under a new Polytechnics and Colleges Funding Committee; and funding them on a 'contract' basis, with the expectation that they would acquire a growing proportion of their resources elsewhere than from the public purse. The Conservative Government proceeded after its reelection in June 1987 to introduce legislation to implement the White Paper. (See below Appendix 1.)

21 **Non-advanced further education: the 1980s**

Non-advanced further education is a vast system with over 1.6 million students in major establishments (1984 figures), plus a similar number of students in adult institutes (See paragraphs 22–24) – a total of more than 3 million students. The system is as diverse as it is large, with a wide range of vocational, academic, leisure and remedial courses and a variety of modes of study. The size of the student population in NAFE is still rising in the long-term, partly boosted by new groups of students on MSC schemes, although the number of students in adult and continuing education has fallen significantly as a direct result of policies on resources and fee levels. The NAFE student numbers have included an increasing number of students on MSC-related schemes – particularly the Youth Training Scheme (YTS) (See **1.7** 3–11) and its predecessor the Youth Opportunities Programme (YOP). The Government statistics also include, from 1984, Open and Distance Learning courses supported by further education establishments. Over 25% of the age group 16–18 are enrolled in NAFE. The majority of students enrolled in NAFE are women (860,000 women compared with 760,000 men in November 1984). Over 75% of students in NAFE are on some type of part-time course. Nearly 90% of students aged 16–20 and 45% of older students are taking courses leading to qualifications. 25% of full-time and 17% of part-time students in NAFE in 1984 are studying for GCE O and A levels, compared with 47% (full-time) and 33% (part-time) studying for BTEC, City and Guilds, or RSA qualifications (1984 figures). The demographic downturn mentioned earlier had a major impact on non-advanced further education, as on schools, and many LEAs are reviewing their provision for 16–19 year olds in the light of the fall in numbers of this age group.

22 The range of provision in NAFE is thus very wide, and meets diverse student and employer needs. The sector has grown in response to demand rather than as a result of central direction. Since 1979, however, central government has taken for the first time a close interest in NAFE, and has adopted policies which have sought to increase the direct intervention of central government and its agencies to meet national policies and perceived market needs. This change of policy has been fuelled by concern about Britain's poor economic performance and the education system's part in it; the desire to foster a stronger vocational/industrial culture; and financial stringency and the pursuit of 'value for money'.

Table 3

Enrolments on Non-advanced Courses in FE Establishments and Adult Education Centres analysed by Mode of Attendance: November 1974 and 1978 to 1984

England								*Thousands*
	1974	*1978*	*1979*	*1980*	*1981*	*1982*	*1983*	*1984*
FE Establishments								
Full-time and sandwich	218	288	288	296	328	355	344	337
Part-time day								
With release from employment	464	452	455	419	351	313	352	368
Other part-time day	155	173	156	166	216	241	247	272
All part-time day	619	625	611	585	566	554	600	640
Evening only	728	660	583	573	573	596	635	642
All modes (Numbers)	1,566	1,572	1,482	1,455	1,468	1,505	1,578	1,619
All modes (Full-time equivalent)[2]	(431)	(493)	(486)	(484)	(501)	(521)	(524)	(526)
YTS/YOP[1] included above (Numbers)	–	2	5	8	18	32	104	114
Adult Education Centres								
Part-time day	–	358	347	316	334	365	429	429
Evening only	–	1,519	1,391	1,227	1,181	1,169	1,199	1,148
All modes (Numbers)	1,720	1,878	1,738	1,543	1,516	1,534	1,628	1,577
All modes (Full-time equivalent)[2]	–	(235)	(217)	(193)	(190)	(192)	(204)	(197)

Source: DES Statistical Bulletin 5/86. Enrolments on Non-Advanced courses of further education – November 1984 (March 1986).

NB: [1]Youth Training Scheme (YTS) 1982 to 1984 and Youth Opportunities Programme (YOP) for earlier years: 16 to 18 year olds only included here. [2]The following weights have been used in calculating full-time equivalents: Full-time (1.0); Sandwich (0.75); Day release (0.3). Other part-time day (0.125); Evening only (0.075).

23 The first initiatives in respect of NAFE by central government after 1979 were two joint reviews involving government and local authority representatives. The first, chaired by a junior education minister, produced *Education for 16–19 year olds* (Macfarlane Report) in December 1980. This considered the various organisational arrangements for 16–19 education evolved by local education authorities. The Macfarlane Report did not offer a recommendation for or against a tertiary model (i.e. institutions for 16–19 year olds including all school and FE elements) and the Government did not produce an overall policy. The other joint review of the law relating to FE led to the publication of *The Legal Basis of Further Education* (1981a) in June 1981 (See **1.2** 16), which, though it showed much of FE was *ultra vires*, had produced no substantial changes though the Government indicated its intention to tidy up the position.

24 The MSC made its first major impact on the Further Education service with the Youth Opportunities Programme (YOP) and in its association with the

Table 4
Enrolments on Non-advanced Courses by Mode of Attendance, Age and Qualification Aim: November 1984

England	*Full-time and sandwich*				*Part-time*			*Percentages*
Qualification aims of students	*16–18*	*19–20*	*21 and over*	*All ages*	*16–18*	*19–20*	*21 and over*	*All ages*
ONC/OND	1	4	1	1	0	0	0	0
BTEC (Technological)	9	13	9	9	9	11	3	6
BTEC (Other)[1]	16	18	8	15	7	7	1	4
City & Guilds	20	10	10	18	34	28	9	18
Royal Society of Arts	3	4	9	4	5	6	4	5
College Diplomas	3	8	6	4	0	0	0	0
GCE A level	19	18	8	17	6	12	6	7
GCE O level	10	4	4	8	11	13	9	10
Other specified qualifications	10	11	12	10	2	5	5	4
Unspecified examinable courses	5	5	11	5	7	7	7	7
All qualifications	94	93	79	92	83	89	44	60
Non-Examinable Courses								
Sciences	3	3	9	4	7	4	11	9
Social Studies	1	1	4	1	4	2	4	4
Arts (including leisure)	3	4	7	3	7	6	41	27
All Non-advanced	100	100	100	100	100	100	100	100
Numbers (000s)	(271)	(27)	(39)	(337)	(381)	(136)	(765)	(1,282)

Source: DES Statistical Bulletin 5/86. Enrolments on Non-Advanced courses of further education – November 1984 (March 1986).

NB: [1]Including courses in business studies, administration, hotel and catering trades and the arts.

DES on Unified Vocational Preparation (UVP). The YOP was developed following the Government's adoption of the principles of the Holland Report, *Young People and Work*, in 1977. The scheme, aimed at providing a year of integrated employment experience and vocational education, was only fully operational from 1979 to 1982 and subject to large scale criticism. Critics pointed in particular to the problems of job substitution by employers and the poor level of training offered by employer-based schemes. (See **1.7**).

25 In May 1981, the MSC published a Consultative document, *A New Training Initiative*, which set out three new objectives: training/employment experience for all young people up to age 18 (not just the unemployed); skills training; and adult training. The Government's response in the White Paper *A New Training Initiative: A Programme for Action* in December 1981 seriously

restricted the ambitious nature of the three objectives, particularly for training of young people. Following almost universal opposition on this issue, the Government conceded that the MSC should be allowed to develop an alternative approach to meet its original objective. The resulting MSC Youth Task Group Report (May 1982) made recommendations which, accepted by the Government, led to the Youth Training Scheme (YTS) – intended as 'a permanent bridge between school and work'. The YTS began operation in April 1983 and faced similar criticisms which had faced YOP, including underfunding of the scheme. However, Government and MSC commitment to YTS has continued, leading to the relaunching of the scheme in 1986 on a two-year basis (See **1.7**).

26 In 1981, the Employment and Training Act gave effect to a major revision of the industrial training boards, sharply reducing their numbers, encouraging the establishment of alternative non-statutory training organisations (NSTOs) and granting more exemptions from financial commitments to employers, while at the same time expecting industry to meet more of its own training needs.

27 In November 1982, the Prime Minister announced the launch of the Technical and Vocational Education Initiative (TVEI) to provide a four-year programme of full-time general, technical and vocational education for 14–18 year olds in schools and colleges. The scheme, set up under the aegis of the MSC, began with pilot schemes in 14 LEAs and expanded until most LEAs were involved. While LEAs have had varied experience of the degree to which TVEI met its objectives, and in terms of numbers staying-on roles after 16, the MSC have claimed that TVEI has succeeded in providing a significant steer to the curriculum in favour of technical and vocational education (see **1.7** 61–63 and **3.1** 4–9).

28 The next major Government initiative in respect of non-advanced further education was the White Paper *Training for Jobs* published in January 1984. This reflected a growing Government belief that LEAs and colleges were not sufficiently sensitive to central government priorities and employers' needs, and was set against the background of sustained Government legislative and administrative activity aimed at restricting the financial powers of local authorities generally. The most controversial feature of *Training for Jobs* was the decision, announced without prior consultation or warning, to shift a proportion of rate support grant funding in respect of work-related non-advanced further education (WRNAFE) from LEAs to MSC. This was to enable the MSC to purchase provision in colleges or elsewhere, amounting to 25 per cent of WRNAFE. This proposal provoked widespread concern and opposition concerning the principle, the premises on which it was based and the way in which it was announced. A further difficulty, a generally acceptable definition of WRNAFE, was not satisfactorily resolved. There followed lengthy discussions between Government and interested parties, during which ministers recognised many of the arguments put to them but refused to be deflected from the principle. In autumn 1984 the architect of the proposal, David Young, shifted from the Chair of the MSC to the Cabinet, subsequently becoming Secretary of State for Employment. His successor at MSC, Sir Bryan Nicholson, presided over an agreement between the MSC and the local authority associations, in which the local authorities agreed to cooperate but did not renounce their opposition. In the first financial year of operation of the new financial arrangements, 1985–86, the MSC agreed that resources should

be distributed broadly in line with the previous RSG distribution (See **1.3** 44–45).

29 The joint review group set up as a result of the agreement reported in May 1985[4] provided a basis for the distribution of the money transferred from the LEAs to the MSC. The report called for LEAs to prepare development plans for their WRNAFE provision, which would form the basis for future MSC allocation of resources. Development plans were prepared by almost all LEAs during early 1986: the plans are for a three-year period, and include annual programmes which are to be the subject of formal agreement with the MSC. The MSC has retained some of the resources allocated to it in a central reserve fund, which will be used to meet nationally agreed strategic objectives, although LEAs can make 'bids' to the fund. At the time of writing, a national joint consultative group, reflecting the interests represented on the MSC, set up to provide national guidance on the implementation of planning for WRNAFE, has recently started work in 1985.

30 In March/April 1985, the Government issued three further White Papers with a bearing on further education and training, in the preparation of which the Department of Employment played a central role as far as FE is concerned. These were *Better schools, Employment – the challenge for the nation*, and *Education and training for young people*. The three White Papers contained overlapping proposals for further education and training, carrying the concepts of *Training for Jobs* further. The key proposal, outlined in *Education and Training for Young People*, was the extension of YTS to a two-year scheme. The proposal was only sketchily put forward, and again set the MSC a very short timescale within which to implement the proposal, while making it clear that the central problem of the inadequacy of resources would not be addressed and that reliance on employers to deliver the scheme would be increased. The two-year YTS was started in April 1986. The key qualitative change was the intention that trainees successfully completing a two-year scheme would gain a recognised qualification (See **1.7** 3–11).

31 The other major outcome of *Education and Training for Young People* was the establishment of a Review of Vocational Qualifications under the aegis of the DES and MSC. The Review Body produced an interim report concerned mainly with vocational qualifications with respect to YTS in September 1985, and a final report in April 1986. The final report recommended a new National Council for Vocational Qualifications (NCVQ) to bring vocational qualifications within a single framework. The Government moved swiftly to implement the RVQ proposals. In July 1986, the Government issued a further White Paper, entitled *Working Together – Education and Training*, which gave effect to the RVQ recommendations, as well as announcing an extension of TVEI to form a national scheme from autumn 1987. The NCVQ held its first meeting in October 1986, under the Chair of Oscar de Ville, who chaired the RVQ itself. The Council moved quickly to establish a framework for the new National Vocational Qualification (NVQ), and issued an outline of the framework in March 1986. The framework comprises four levels: Basic; Standard; Advanced; Higher. At time of writing it is still to be determined how professional qualifications above the fourth level are fitted into the framework.

32 Other developments impinged on FE. In October 1986, the Secretary of State for Education and Science announced proposals for City Technology Colleges

(CTCs). These would be state funded and would operate in inner city areas, alongside LEA provision. Each CTC would provide for about 1,000 11–18 year olds. The Government sought industrial sponsorship and funding for each CTC proposal have come forward by the time of writing. The CTC policy has been presented as a direct challenge to the LEAs in the inner cities. In the general election of June 1987 the Conservative Government announced it would legislate for a national curriculum and for schools to be enabled to opt out of the LEA system.

33 The debates on vocational education and training following the White Paper *Training for Jobs* were fuelled by a growing body of data on the performance of the post-school education and training system in terms of relevance to industrial need; international comparisons; and 'value for money'. The MSC/NEDO publication *Competence and competition* (1984) drew attention to perceived shortcomings in British vocational education and training compared with West Germany, the USA and Japan. The Audit Commission report *Obtaining better value from further education* (1985) argued that further education could greatly increase efficiency by the application of a number of more strict management controls on a nationwide basis (See **1.3** 113–114). A wide range of official and semiofficial publications, including HMI Reports, suggest, however, that the sometimes simplistic prescriptions of these two influential documents should be seen in the context of the wide spectrum of practice which actually exists at local level.

34 **Adult education**

Although in some senses a great part of further education is the education of adults, 'adult education' is usually identified as non-vocational, that is, not leading towards a job or career but rather helping people fulfil themselves in their non-working time, whether leisure, unemployment or retirement. 'Adult education' in this sense does not lead to qualifications or, at least, does not regard qualifications as the main purpose of a course. However, whilst these characteristics have sometimes led to sarcastic references to ballroom dancing and flower arranging classes, 'adult education' has grown beyond limited definitions and could be seen as offering a tentative mapping of what a service of 'continuing education' or 'recurrent education' or even a 'learning society' might look like. Out of 'adult education' there developed during the 1960s and 1970s theory and practice for 'outreach' of educational services into the community, for 'community education' and for learning programmes for disadvantaged adults. This has produced a great diversity of courses and educational services, a diversity which is rarely present in any one locality but which suggests a broad potential for further development if resources were available. Thus, associated with 'adult education' provision in the 1980s are courses (sometimes referred to as Fresh Start or Return to Study) which provide access to higher education and vocational FE, often through non-standard admissions requirements (See **3.2** 7–10 and 19–21), courses responding to the needs and demands of ethnic groups, of women and of other oppressed sections of society, basic literacy and numeracy programmes, courses run in settings other than educational premises, daytime as well as evening classes, in some cases supported by creches and other social provision. Some adult education provision is conceived to play a part in wider community development, not only in reaching out to prospective students but also in cooperating with other activities in the community.

35 Adult education has strictly speaking the same statutory basis as the rest of further education, depending on Section 41 of the 1944 Act (See **1.2** 14). It is also in many localities organised within colleges of FE, although in others it is provided through separate institutions. However, in practice there are two substantial differences in its administration. First, the services are run in partnership with the 'responsible bodies' (Workers' Educational Association, extramural departments of universities and, in Wales, the Welsh National Council of the Young Men's Christian Association), 'residential colleges' and some voluntary organisations. Second, the adult education service has been perceived usually in political and administration terms as a lower priority and less important call on an LEA's resources than other parts of the education service; it has been seen as less of a duty to secure the provision of adult education than of other further education. Thus, provision of adult education has generally been among the first items of cuts in LEA budgets, and in many LEAs it has had to rely much more on fee income. Student numbers fell in the late 1970s but steadied at around 1,400,000 (England) in the first half of the 1980s (DES Statistical Bulletin 15/86). The administration of adult education has, then, produced a fragmented and under-resourced service, commonly referred to as a 'Cinderella', and the Russell Report (1973) (See the 1980 edition of *College Administration*) did not produce changes of substance.

36 Adult education services have been encouraged to look towards a number of different central funding agencies, such as the Adult Literacy and Basic Skills Unit (ALBSU), the Urban Programme, the Home Office for financing schemes for immigrants from the Commonwealth under Section 11 of the Local Government Act 1966, the DES for its PICKUP and REPLAN programmes, and most of all towards the Manpower Services Commission (MSC). The concerns and expertise of adult education in basic skills and in helping adults who had not succeeded in the school system suggested it could make an effective contribution to solving the pressing problems of retraining adult workers and rehabilitating – or least occupying – unemployed people. The MSC's influence increased after the publication of the *New Training Initiative* in 1981, the third objective of which was to open up access to training for adults (see **1.7** 31). However, the variety of funding programmes, though providing a lifeline for some activities, has not helped build up a system of education and training for adults, and sudden measures, such as the launch of the new Job Training Scheme in 1986–87 (See **1.7** 33–35) have wrong-footed some colleges and threatened to leave some initiatives under existing schemes without funding. The Advisory Council for Adult Education was wound up and replaced by a smaller Unit for the Development of Adult Continuing Education, suggesting that no coherent strategy was imminent and that the MSC could be seen as the predominant force for change.

37 **Commentary**

There can be little doubt that the period following the Conservative Party's victory in the 1979 election marked a new direction in Government policies towards post-school education. James Callaghan's launching of the 'Great Debate' in 1976 had already put the issue of education's relevance to industry and employment on the political agenda, and Governments throughout the 1970s had pursued policies of increasing stringency towards educational expenditure. However, from 1979 the Government of Margaret Thatcher presented policies which suggested quick solutions to perceived problems and sought to direct policy firmly towards education and training from the national perspective. National direction has not led to a concentration of power in the DES.

On the contrary, major responsibilities for education came to reside in the Department of Employment and its agency the Manpower Services Commission. This shift in power is not yet complete.

38 The education service has been traditionally characterised as 'a national service locally administered', and this remains a fair description (though see **1.2** 2). The local education authorities have not yet been effectively bypassed in the pursuit of national control of post-school education and training. Both the National Advisory Body (NAB) and the MSC through the NAFE development plans have worked through the LEAs. The reelection of the Conservative Government in June 1987 promised to press further with changes in this relationship, however. The 1987 White Paper planned to remove higher education from LEAs (see below Appendix 1). In the school sector its proposals for a national curriculum, for City Technology Colleges, and for provision to enable schools to opt out of LEAs also reduced the role of LEAs.

39 LEAs have also come under new pressures: they face closer scrutiny from the Audit Commission, tighter financial controls from central government and a variety of pressures for a more effectively 'managed' system. Public sector further and higher education is under pressure to be 'cost-led' rather than 'demand-led'. How this will fit with the Government's strictures on marketing and meeting the needs of industry remains to be seen. The Government is anxious for industry to take more responsibility for its own training needs, but so far this concern has met with a patchy response. However, it could in the longer term lead to an increasing diversion of resources from the public sector to private industry.

40 The Government is concerned to use the demographic downturn into the 1990s to remodel and reduce the size of the higher education system. On the basis of the lack of a nationally directed response to the demographic downturn in the 16–18 age group, it remains to be seen whether this can be achieved. The pattern of 16–18 provision continues to develop, but a question mark remains over the ability of the Youth Training Scheme (YTS) to meet the aspirations of young people and the needs of employers. However, the 16–18 age group will continue to be largely excluded from the mainstream labour market by Government pressures and market forces; the nature and quality of the education and training opportunities available to them remain to be seen. Education and training throughout adult life seem certain to become of increasing importance in further and higher education, and this is likely to be in response to demand rather than clear cut national directives. In public sector further and higher education as a whole, a new balance is evolving between local authority and central government control and policy making.

NOTES

1 Advanced courses are defined by the DES are courses followed by students undertaking postgraduate, post-diploma, or research work; courses in preparation for university first and higher degrees; CNAA first and higher degrees (including the former Diploma in Art and Design and the Higher Diploma in Art and Design); Higher Diplomas and Certificates of BTEC, the Higher National Diploma or Certificate; the Diploma or Certificate; the Diploma in Management Studies; or a final professional examination or college Diploma or Associateship if above the standard of instruction required for the

Ordinary National Certificate, or General Certificate of Education (advanced level), or any course of study of an equivalent standard. In the case of certain courses, the later year or years are treated as advanced and the earlier year(s) as non-advanced.

2 Tables and statistics quoted in this section are drawn from: *The Management of Non-University Higher Education*, DES Report on Education No. 90 May 1977; Report of the Working Group on the Management of Higher Education in the Maintained Sector, Cmnd. 7130, HMSO: Further Education, DES Statistics of Education 1976 Vol. 3, HMSO; Teachers, DES Statistics of Education 1976 Vol. 4, HMSO; Non-advanced Further Education DES Report on Education Number 94, December 1978; *Future Trends in Higher Education*, DES March 1979; DES Statistical Bulleting 9/85, *Student Numbers in Higher Education – Great Britain 1970 to 1983;* DES Statistical Bulletin 11/85: *Statistics of Further Education students in England – 1985* and DES Statistical Bulletin 7/86, *Enrolments in Public Sector Higher Education 1970–1985–1986.*

3 See for example DES Report on Education 99, *Future demand for higher education in Great Britain* (1983) and DES Report on Education 100, *Demand for higher education in Great Britain 1984–2000*, and *Projections of demand for higher education in Great Britain 1986–2000 (1986).*

4 MSC/Local Authority Associations Group on work related Non-Advanced Further Education. Report of Policy Group, May 1985.

APPENDIX 1

THE WHITE PAPER 1987

1 Secretary of State Kenneth Baker produced in April 1987 a White Paper *Higher Education: Meeting the Challenge* which introduced a fundamental reorganisation of public sector higher education in England. It proposed that the polytechnics and the colleges offering predominantly higher education would be taken away from the local education authorities and established as corporate bodies, funded through a new national Polytechnics and Colleges Funding Council (PCFC).

2 The new institutions would be freestanding corporate bodies, employing their own staff, owning and leasing buildings in their own name – instead of being maintained by their local authorities and hence dependent on the LAs for their legal standing. The White Paper left open the possibilities that the corporate status could be achieved either through setting up the institutions as companies limited by guarantee (as polytechnics in the Inner London Education Authority are) or by incorporating them through an Act of Parliament (as some universities and Scottish central institutions are). The Government did not think it essential that the institutions should be established as charities. (See **1.2** Appendix 1.)

3 The institutions involved in this reorganisation would, as listed in the White Paper, be the twenty-nine polytechnics (and Garnett College shortly to merge with Thames Polytechnic), twenty-four colleges maintained by LEAs, and three 'hybrid' institutions (colleges established jointly by LEAs and voluntary bodies). The criteria for being on the list were: 350 or more full-time equivalent (FTE) higher education students; and more than 55% of the institution's activity in HE (measured in FTEs). The White Paper also gave the option for eleven maintained colleges to be included which had more than 55% HE but fewer than 350 HE students. The calculations were based on numbers of home (and European Community) students on the 1985 Further Education Statistical Record. It proposed that seventeen voluntary colleges (See below paragraph 13) and eight other grant-aided colleges should also come within the ambit of the PCFC.

4 Many of these colleges offered non-advanced as well as advanced (HE) courses. The White. Paper's proposal was that LEAs should contract with the polytechnics and col-

leges to provide this. Conversely, many colleges not included among the transferred institutions provided some HE, and this would be contracted by the PCFC with those colleges.

5 The funding system proposed in the White Paper would be one of 'contracting' rather than making grants. The PCFC would make contracts with institutions to provide courses. The intentions of a contracting system were:
(i) To encourage institutions 'to be enterprising in attracting contracts from other sources, particularly the private sector, and thereby to lessen their present degree of dependence on public funding';
(ii) To 'sharpen accountability' for use of public funds; and
(iii) To 'strengthen the commitment of institutions to the delivery of the educational services which it is agreed . . . they should provide' (paragraph 4.17).

6 It was doubtful whether the contracting system would be introduced in an absolute form. The White Paper itself included a caveat: 'The Government recognises that a system of contracting must be so designed as to avoid damage to aspects of the work of institutions, such as the advancement of learning, which cannot readily be embraced by specific contractual commitments'. Subsequent discussions suggested the system would at least use elements of the methodologies used by NAB (See **1.3** 48). The Government's consultative paper *Changes in Structure and National Planning for Higher Education* (April 1987) spoke of financial memoranda which would underpin the contracts between PCFC and institutions. The White Paper was unclear whether PCFC would advise the Secretary of State about decisions on courses and intakes of initial teacher training.

7 It was basic that institutions should look for sources of money other than public funding, and the White Paper planned for an increase in student numbers without matching public finance. The White Paper also discussed how to improve 'quality' and 'efficiency' in higher education (See **2.8** 39–40). The White Paper said the Government would prefer 'to move away from use of (the) term "public sector higher education"': 'The Government finds the term "public sector" . . . unhelpful and, moreover, inconsistent with its desire to see all higher education institutions do more to attract private funding'. The White Paper spoke of the 'polytechnics and colleges sector'. (See **1.1** 2.)

8 The buildings used by polytechnics and colleges and other assets would, according to the White Paper, be taken away from the local authorities and given first to a Polytechnics and Colleges Assets Board (PCAB) before being transferred to the institutions. It saw no need for compensation: 'The assets now used in local authority higher education were acquired in most cases under arrangements which shared the cost between ratepayers and taxpayers on a national basis, to form part of the national provision of higher education. They will continue to serve that purpose. Accordingly, the local education authorities will not be compensated for the transfer of assets now in their ownership.' On 22 July 1987 the Secretary of State announced that he would be seeking in Parliament powers to prevent local authorities disposing of land or buildings 'used or held or obtained for or in connection with the purpose of' the polytechnics or colleges and that these powers would be made effective from midnight.

9 Staff in the polytechnics and colleges, the Government planned, would be transferred from the employment of the local authorities to the new corporate institutions. The Government's consultative paper (See above paragraph 6) said that teaching staff 'will continue on their prevailing rates of pay and conditions of service, as determined by the NJC (See **2.1** 15–16), until superseded by terms determined within new arrangement for the polytechnics and colleges sector'. It said that teachers should be able to continue to participate in teachers' superannuation arrangements and that those entering the sector should also be able to participate. Non-academic staff would also continue on prevailing pay and conditions until any new arrangements are set up. The paper said 'The Government does not intend that the proposed administrative changes should lead to any detriment to the pension arrangements for non-academic staff currently employed

in the colleges. It therefore proposes to make regulations under Section 7 of the Superannuation Act 1972 designating the new institutions as Part I Scheduled Bodies. The effect of this will be to keep those non-academic staff of the institutions who wish it within the Local Government Superannuation scheme and preserve in full pension rights already acquired'. Relevant to both teaching and non-teaching staff, the paper stated that the institutions would be free to reach local agreements with staff within national agreements but added 'However, the Government considers that it would be inappropriate for institutions to assume any no-redundancy agreements which had previously been entered into by certain individual local authorities'.

10 The White Paper proposed that governing bodies for the institutions should be 20–25 people, about half of whom would be local and regional employers or representatives of the professions – the initial composition of which group would be approved by the Secretary of State. The consultative paper (See above paragraph 6) envisaged: 11 representatives of industry, commerce and professional bodies; 3 nominated by LEAs; 3 teaching staff, 1 non-teaching staff; 2 from other educational institutions; up to 2 coopted members from, e.g., local community, trade unions or individuals; the principal/director. (See **2.8** 5.)

11 The PCFC, suggested the consultative paper, would have about fifteen members, including a leading industrialist as chair and perhaps six from industry, commerce and professions, four senior academics and others from the universities, from the voluntary colleges or church bodies and people with relevant expertise. By contrast NAB had substantial local authority participation (See **1.1** 13).

12 The implementation of the White Paper's proposals required the Government to introduce legislation in the 1987–88 session of Parliament so as, according to the consultative paper, to establish the PCFC and PCAB, incorporate institutions then maintained by LEAs (other than those becoming limited companies) and change the constitutions of assisted colleges, make arrangements for determining the pay and conditions of teaching and non-teaching staff and make financial arrangements. The Government would also establish a 'vesting day' for the transfer of the institutions.

13 The White Paper proposed that the PCFC should also cover seventeen voluntary colleges on the same criteria as the maintained institutions, which had all been colleges of education (or mergers of colleges) until the mid-1970s (See **1.1** 9–10) and eight other institutions grant-aided by central government. These institutions were already free-standing bodies and so would not need to be reconstituted, but the consultative paper thought the Secretary of State might take the opportunity to consider whether changes in their instruments and articles were desirable.

14 In Wales the Welsh Advisory Body for Local Authority Higher Education (WAB) would continue to plan and develop the public sector. The White Paper indicated that the Government would watch WAB, particularly for its ability to review course provision on national consideration. It would include the statutory basis for a PCFC in Wales but not to establish it – unless the Government later considered it necessary.

15 In Northern Ireland, also, no reorganisation was proposed for the public sector.

16 *Consultative paper on FE*

In summer 1987 the DES issued a consultative paper on *Maintained Further Education: Financing, Governance and Law* (DES 1987b) which sought to create more independence from LEAs for colleges not drawn into the new corporate status. Its proposals reduced LEAs' powers in finance and staffing, though LEAs retained ultimate legal responsibility, and reduced LEA representation on governing bodies.

1.2 THE LEGAL STRUCTURE OF FURTHER AND HIGHER EDUCATION

1 Education has traditionally been described as 'a national service locally administered'. The 1980 edition of *College Administration* took this formulation as fundamental and described a partnership between central and local government, '. . . whereby the (local) authorities do not enjoy total freedom of action but are more than the agents of the Secretary of State'. (Waitt 1980, p. 33)[1]. Each partner was held in the traditional model to recognise and acknowledge the legitimate concerns of the other in policy, organisation and delivery of the service. It assumed a broad consensus between central and local government which encouraged local differences of emphasis and priority and accommodated experimentation.

2 While this model of partnership may have been of value in the past, it has become of increasingly dubious validity. In F/HE a number of policy developments have shifted the balance of power: the transfer of funding for up to 25% of work related non-advanced FE (WRNAFE) from local authorities to the Manpower Services Commission (MSC) (See **1.1** 28); the development of specific grants including the introduction of education support grants (See **1.3** 28–31); the plan of the White Paper 1987 to transfer polytechnics and colleges of higher education from local authorities to the domain of central government (See **1.1** Appendix 1). These developments have had parallels in the school sector in proposals for City Technology Colleges, a national curriculum, and the temporary suspension of collective bargaining after the abolition of the Burnham pay negotiating machinery. The shift over recent years has appeared inexorable (See **1.1** and **1.4**). This section describes the legislative framework within which further and higher education is provided and then goes on to describe briefly how this has contributed to the process of centralisation.

3 A number of features of the legislative framework require attention to establish a context for later discussion. The UK, unlike most developed countries, does not have a written constitution. There is thus no formal codification of the relationships which exist between government and the individual, or between tiers of government. For the individual this is conventionally seen as implying freedom to engage in any activity unless that activity is proscribed by law. For local authorities the reverse situation applies: no action may be undertaken unless specific legislative sanction has been provided by Parliament; other activities are *ultra vires*; though LAs may spend a 2p rate on their own decision. Hence, local authorities are dependent on Parliament to set the powers and duties which enable them to act. Within these powers and duties lies a considerable 'grey area' of discretion and, moreover, of interpretation of the wording of the legislation, and views about the legitimate discretion and proper interpretation evolve over time. Thus, aspects of the law are not fixed or certain, as this section will discuss.

4 The 'grey area' is complicated by secondary legislation. Statutory instruments (SIs) are a device which permits general powers conferred by statute on the Secretary of State to be implemented and detailed. They add flesh to the bones of primary legislation (Acts of Parliament) and take the form of regulations which are binding on LEAs in the same way as those contained in primary legislation.

5 More ambiguous is the status of circulars, circular letters, and administrative memoranda. Circulars are issued by the DES to provide advice, guidance or interpretation on aspects of policy or legislation and to invite discussion or request information. Circular letters and administrative memoranda (AMs) deal with detailed, bureaucratic matters. Whilst local education authorities (LEAs), and where appropriate voluntary bodies also, are not legally bound by the advice or guidance of these documents neither are they free to ignore them. These documents carry the authority of the Secretary of State and the Department of Education and Science (DES), and it is of the nature of the constitutional partnership between central and local government that local authorities would follow or, at least, seriously consider – the guidance. Moreover, circulars have commonly been circulated in draft form to the local authority associations and authorities themselves for comment before being formally issued.

6 There can also be more crucial pressures on LEAs to comply with circulars, circular letters, and administrative memoranda. First, while LEAs are free to exercise discretion and to differ with the DES in interpretation of statutory requirements, instances may arise where protection under the law can be lost through failing to accept advice or guidance. The 1980 edition of *College Administration* showed that LEAs may leave themselves open to legal proceedings under Health and Safety and Race Relations Acts and under building regulations despite specific exemptions having been provided in all three areas to educational establishments (Waitt 1980; and see **4** below). Since specific exemptions and the circumstances in which they arise are often only defined in circulars or memoranda, courts may regard these as admissible evidence in cases brought before them. Second, LEAs may feel at risk from the sanctions available to central government. They are subject to a system of capital expenditure control, (See **1.3** 33–41) backed up by a system of project approvals; failure to conform with the Government's wishes can lead to delay or cancellation of building schemes either through the rejection of project proposals or through insufficient borrowing approval being made available. The Secretary of State also has powers of intervention in a wide range of areas under statutory powers, and rejection of DES guidance in circulars and memoranda may raise the threat of intervention.

7 Resistance by LEAs to Government policies is possible. Where a change of Government is anticipated, then delaying may be all that is required. An instance of this was provided by the requirement of the Education Act 1976 for secondary education to be provided in comprehensive schools. A number of LEAs had not moved through the process of planning and implementing comprehensive education provision when the requirement was repealed by the Education Act 1979, following the election of the Conservative government.

8 A clear trend in the framing of legislation and regulations was under way in the 1980s. The powers of intervention of the Secretary of State have been expanded while the duties placed on LEAs have become increasingly specific. More consideration is given to the form of these changes later in this section (See below paragraphs 46–51). The operation of a 'national service locally administered' produces some confusion between the powers and duties exercised by Ministers and LEAs respectively. The increase in centralisation has simplified this, but whether or not this is to be applauded must remain a matter for political analysis which goes beyond the scope of this book.

9 Whilst there exists a discrete and extensive body of law relating to education, various provisions of legislation drawn from other areas are important, particularly Health and Safety, and Employment Law. These are, however, dealt with elsewhere (See **2.4** and **2.7**) and are therefore, only touched on here where they interact with education law. In addition the structure, finance and powers and duties of LEAs are determined by an extensive range of Local Government legislation (See **1.6**), and some aspects of local government are within the remit of the ombudsman (See **1.6** 62).

10 **The 1944 Act**

The Education Act 1944 established the basis for the education system as a whole in England and Wales including the provision of further education. It established the initial basis from which the relationship between the Minister (latterly the Secretary of State) and the LEAs has evolved. It is sometimes referred to as the 'Butler Act' after R. A. Butler who, as President of the Board of Education (the then equivalent to Secretary of State) introduced the Bill, following the White Paper 1943.

11 Section 1 (1) placed a duty on the Secretary of State, '. . . to promote the education of the people of England and Wales and the progressive development of institutions devoted to that purpose, and to secure the effective execution by local authorities, under his control and direction, of the national policy for providing a varied and comprehensive education service in every area'. This statement was reinforced by powers of intervention in a range of circumstances.

12 Section 68 allowed the Secretary of State to intervene when satisfied that a local authority or governing body of a school, '. . . have acted or are proposing to act unreasonably with respect to the exercise of any power conferred or the performance of any duty imposed'. Intervention could be prompted either '. . . on complaint by any person or otherwise'. This power of intervention was extended by Section 99 which allowed the Secretary of State to issue an order declaring an LEA or governing body to be in default of a statutory duty and, subject to the issue of an order of mandamus (a judicial writ issued by the Queen's Bench division as a command to a lower court) requiring the duty to be performed. Section 93 gave the Secretary of State power to institute local enquiries relating to the exercise of any function under the Act. Finally, Section 77 required inspections of premises to be undertaken by Her Majesty's Inspectorate acting on instructions issued by the Secretary of State.

13 Alongside this framework of strategic powers vested in the Secretary of State, the 1944 Act set the powers and duties for LEAs to make provision for the education service. Thus, the 1944 Act was based on a 'partnership' between central and local government in which both parties depended on each other and could check or balance the other's powers and cooperated with each other on the basis of an agreed, if not explicit, view of each other's role.

14 The formal duties of local authorities, particularly in respect of further and higher education, were not closely defined. Section 41 of the 1944 Act placed a general duty on LEAs, '. . . to secure the provision for their area of adequate facilities for further education'. Further education was defined as:

(i) Full-time and part-time education for persons over compulsory school age; and

(ii) Leisure-time occupation, in such organised training and recreative activities as are suited to their requirements for any persons over compulsory school age who are able and willing to profit by the facilities provided for that purpose'.

15 Section 42 required the preparation and submission to the Secretary of State of schemes of further education; approval of these schemes by the Secretary of State being then required. In preparing these plans, authorities were required to have regard to provision made by universities, educational associations and other bodies. The creation and maintenance of county colleges was required by Section 43, as a mainstay of the provision planned in the Section 42 schemes, though none was established.

16 The enactment of these provisions is marked by enormous variation. The 'adequate facilities' referred to in Section 41 are not defined and very considerable differences are to be found between LEAs in the extent and form of provision established. As to the schemes of further education, all LEAs had prepared and received approval for schemes by the mid-1950s. However, these schemes have not generally been maintained or updated and consequently most further education provision in England and Wales is ultra vires (Liell and Saunders 1987) (See **1.6** 14). A joint working party of DES and local authority representatives which considered the issues arising from this fact in 1981 recommended that the duty to maintain these schemes should be repealed (DES 1981a). Although this has not been done, the proposal has been likened to burglars proposing the abolition of laws relating to theft in order that they might better go about their business (Burgess 1981). While the duty remains unrepealed, the prospect of the present or some future Secretary of State requiring that new plans be drawn up cannot be entirely discounted[2].

17 The drafting of these provisions in the Act was intended to permit LEAs the optimum freedom in the planning, organisation and delivery of further education consistent with national policies and with the approval of the Secretary of State. In this way the concept of partnership operated. While this partnership worked smoothly, the lack of precision in such wording as 'adequate facilities', 'effective execution', 'unreasonable behaviour' and 'able and willing to profit' did not present problems of real substance. Indeed, supporters of this arrangement argue that the vagueness had intrinsic value in permitting flexibility and responsiveness to the changing needs of a client group which is static in neither its composition nor its expectations.

18 **The Education (No. 2) Act 1968**

The government and conduct of colleges of further education is determined by provisions of the Education (No. 2) Act 1968. Derived largely from principles articulated in the Weaver Report (1966) on colleges of education, this Act attempted to reconcile the conflicting demands of institutional autonomy and public accountability. Guidance on the implementation of the Act was issued in Circular 7/70, though the DES had previously issued Administrative Memorandum 8/67 for the designation of polytechnics.

19 The Act required colleges of FE (and colleges of education since assimilated into the FE system) (See **1.1** 9–10), to be governed by instruments and articles of government. Circular 7/70 included model instruments and articles. The instrument of government provides for the establishment of a governing body and describes its composition; the articles of government determine the func-

tions to be exercised by the LEA (or voluntary body), the governing body, the principal, and the academic board respectively, and thereby the overall conduct of the institution. Articles of government have to be approved by the Secretary of State. According to the Act, for colleges of education instruments of government drawn up by an LEA require approval of the Secretary of State. For other colleges the instrument of government does not require approval by the Secretary of State. A single governing body may be constituted by an LEA for two or more maintained institutions, subject to the approval of the Secretary of State. Any such arrangement may be terminated at any time by the LEA by which it was made. Cases of dispute between governing bodies and LEAs, whether in respect of default of duties or unreasonable exercise of functions by either party may be referred to the Secretary of State for determination (See **2.8**).

20 **The Further Education Regulations**

The Education (Schools and Further Education) Regulations 1981 (SI 1981/1086) as amended (SI 1983/262) define limits on certain areas of LEA discretion, while further clarifying the respective roles of the Secretary of State and the local authorities. These and subsequent regulations supersede the Further Education Regulations 1975 (which integrated the teacher training sector into FE). The new regulations were also designed not to impede the introduction of an integrated tertiary system.

21 In planning further education courses LEAs are required by the 1981 regulations to consult with Regional Advisory Councils (RACs) (See **1.6** 65–66) to ensure, as far as possible, that courses do not duplicate provision at other establishments in neighbouring authorities. Provision of advanced courses also requires the approval of the Secretary of State; course approval may be granted subject to conditions and may be withdrawn. The Secretary of State may also issue directions under the 1981 regulations as to the number and categories of students which may by admitted to any course of teacher training. The regulations concerning course approvals and the categories of courses to which they apply can be found in Annex 1.

22 In addition to the formal course approval procedures outline above, other factors need to be considered. Articles of government normally confer duties of planning and coordination of academic matters on an academic board. This frequently extends into detailed scrutiny of the content of courses. In carrying out these duties, however, the requirements of validating and examining bodies need to be incorporated in order that course approval be obtained. The planning of advanced courses became, in the mid-1980s, increasingly subject to the scrutiny of the National Advisory Body (See paragraph **3.3** 54–65 below).

23 The 1981 regulations contain provisions on premises. Approval is required from the Secretary of State for the construction of new buildings, or the carrying out of alterations to existing premises, or premises to be acquired. This approval system interacts with the system of capital expenditure controls contained in the Local Government, Planning and Land Act 1980 to give the DES and the Department of the Environment (DoE) together effective control of building programmes (See **1.3**). Further controls are exercised through the operation of constructional standards as laid down by the DES. Current standards are described in AM 2/85 (See **4**) which in turn are derived from building regulations. Current regulations do not touch on Health and Safety aspects

of buildings although these are clearly of some importance (See **2.7** and **4**).

24 **Teaching staff**
The size and composition of the teaching body is in part determined by the Education (Teachers) Regulations 1982. These place a duty on LEAs and other employing bodies to employ a staff, '. . . suitable and sufficient in number for the purposes of securing the provision of education appropriate to the ages, abilities, aptitudes and needs' of students. Teachers in further education are also required by these regulations to hold 'qualifications appropriate to the giving of adequate instruction in the subjects in which courses are provided'. LEAs may not appoint staff unless satisfied as to the applicant's health and physical capacity for the post. (See **2.4**, Appendix 4).

25 **Student fees**
Student fees are not subject to statutory determination. Nevertheless because student awards include a fee element, each year the DES issues the fee levels for designated courses which the Secretary of State is prepared to take into account when fixing awards. Hence the determination of award levels and eligibility to awards is inextricably bound up with student fees. Recommendations on fee levels for non-designated courses are made annually to LEAs by the Council of Local Education Authorities (CLEA). In arriving at its recommendations CLEA fixes fee levels by reference to comparability or equivalence; clearly NAFE courses will not generally command fees at the same level as AFE and consequently tend to be set at somewhat lower levels. (See **1.3** 42).

26 Provision for overseas students has raised legal issues. Section 19 of the Education Act 1980 which limited the duty of the LEA to provide mandatory awards only to those 'ordinarily resident' in their area. This decision caused considerable controversy as a result of the exclusion of numbers of overseas students from both advanced and non-advanced courses to which it led. A number of court actions were instigated to challenge aspects of this decision and in Shah v. London Borough of Barnet (1983) (1All ER226) it was determined that 'ordinarily resident' should be taken to mean residence from choice and for a settled purpose. It was further determined that settled purpose could encompass education. As a result of this judgement and the apparent anomaly to which it led the law was amended by the Education (Fees and Awards) Act 1983 to permit the Secretary of State to make regulations authorising or requiring the charging of higher fees to overseas students than those charged to UK or EEC students. Regulations of the Education (Fees and Awards) Regulations 1983; (SI 1983/973), then empowered the charging of higher fees to students lacking a 'relevant connection' with the UK, i.e. to overseas students. (See **3.6**).

27 **Education Support Grants**
The framework of local authority financial control of further and higher education has traditionally allowed LEAs considerable discretion over the areas of work to be provided and for the establishment of local priorities. This local discretion was, to some extent, undermined by the Education (Grants and Awards) Act 1984. This Act provided for the introduction of Education Support Grants (ESG) to support expenditure on a range of centrally determined initiatives. (See **1.3** 28–31).

28 **Trading companies**
The Further Education Act 1985 empowered LEAs to establish machinery

for the commercial exploitation of the education activities and facilities of maintained institutions, as well as the expertise and innovations of both staff and students. In marketing goods and services in this way LEAs may establish trading companies in which they hold a minimum of 20 per cent of the vote-carrying share capital. They may also make loans to these companies at a rate of interest determined by the Secretary of State with the consent of the Treasury. Goods and services may normally only be supplied at 'open market value', that is to say on a commercial basis[3]. Wherever possible trading must be at a profit although where a deficit arises this may be charged by the LEA to a special fund or to the general rate fund.

29 **The 1986 Act**

Further changes in the statutory basis of education provision were introduced by the Education (No. 2) Act 1986, which received the Royal Assent on 7 November 1986. In the main the Act deals with the government of schools although provisions relating to four disparate areas of further and higher education are included. Section 50 provides for the introduction of specific grants, '. . . for more effective in-service training of teachers' (See **2.9**). Section 49 enables the Secretary of State to introduce regulations covering compulsory appraisal of teachers and lecturers. Section 51 covers recoupment of costs between LEAs and empowers the Secretary of State to give directions on rates. (See **1.3** 42).

30 A contentious provision of the 1986 Act, as it relates to further education, is contained within Section 43. This requires all those concerned in the government of institutions to secure, as far as is reasonably practicable 'freedom of speech within the law for members, students and employees of the establishment, and for visiting speakers'. When originally presented as a Bill this provision was rejected by the House of Lords as unenforcable, divisive and providing a platform of respectability to those holding provocative, inflammatory and possibly illegal views. The clause was subsequently re-introduced, albeit in an amended form, and forced through against heavy opposition both within and outside Parliament.

31 **Other legislation**

Other than the general body of education law (and health and safety, and employment legislation which were mentioned earlier), further and higher education is subject to provisions arising in a number of other areas. Discrimination, whether on grounds of sex or race is generally prohibited by the Sex Discrimination Act 1975 and the Race Relations Act 1976 (See below Appendices 2 and 3). Industrial and other training provided in colleges is covered by the Industrial Training Act 1964 and the Employment and Training Act 1973. The former provided for the establishment of industrial training boards while the latter established the Manpower Services Commission (See **1.7**). The Industrial Training Act 1964 was repealed almost entirely by the Industrial Training Act 1982. This consolidated the 1964 Act and subsequent amendments relating to industrial training boards and reduced the number of industrial training boards.

32 **Case law**

Difficulties are commonly encountered in the case law of education. One consequence of the widespread discretion conferred by the 1944 Act on Ministers and LEAs has been the considerable difficulty for parents or aggrieved parties who wish to challenge or overturn decisions. The courts have shown reluctance to become involved in educational disputes and then usually confined themselves to matters of procedure or legal technicality. Despite these difficulties some general principles have been articulated and although they derive mainly from the compulsory sector of education are nevertheless of general application. Their application is therefore of relevance to further education also, especially with reference to Sections 68 and 99 of the 1944 Act.

33 **Adequate facilities**

Section 41 of the 1944 Act required the provision of 'adequate facilities' for further education. Yet 'adequate' may mean different things to different people at different times. In common sense an attempt by an LEA to close down an adult education service would seem on the face of it to contravene this duty. Yet when Humberside CC did this as an economy measure in 1979, declaring twelve members of staff redundant, the decision was contested by NATFHE under the consultation requirement of the Employment Protection Act 1975 rather than the Section 41 provisions. This action followed the rejection by the Secretary of State of a Section 99 appeal. The reason for the approach adopted by NATFHE probably lies in the further duty placed on LEAs by Section 76 of the 1944 Act which requires '. . . the avoidance of unreasonable public expenditure'. A balance is therefore required between reasonableness and adequacy. Thus the provision of adequate facilities would appear to be not so much an independent criterion for the assessment of provision, but rather interdependent with the exigencies of financial management. In this case judgement was entered in favour of the LEA and the closure of the adult education service proceeded.

34 A different light was put on a broadly analagous issue in 1985 in a case involving Liverpool City Council (R. v. Liverpool City Council ex p Ferguson, *The Times* 20 November 1985). The authority attempted to dismiss its entire teaching force. This was presented by the LEA as an interim measure to avoid insolvency. Here, the judgement found that the proposed action was ultra vires as it was motivated by a desire '. . . to bring about a collision between the Council and the Government', and involved an attempt '. . . to cause the Council to take action which they (the councillors) knew, since they were so advised, was illegal'. The basis of the illegality was held to be a breach of Section 8 of the 1944 Act and regulation 7 of the Education (Teachers) Regulations 1982. The Act placed a duty on LEAs ' to secure . . . sufficient schools' (primary and secondary), 'sufficient in number, character and equipment' to afford opportunities for pupils 'in view of their different ages, abilities and aptitudes'. The Regulations required that staff, suitable and sufficient in number are employed to secure provision. Taking these two cases together, it would appear that the notion of 'adequate' provision, encompassing buildings, equipment and staffing, is as much a function of the policies being pursued as the financial and other circumstances which prevail in any given situation. In the school sector during the post-1979 Conservative Government there were attempts by parents' groups to get Secretaries of State to rule that certain LEAs were failing in their statutory duties because they had reduced provision to such an extent (responding to national policies of expenditure restraint) but these attempts were rejected.

35 During the same period, however, Secretaries of State called LEAs to account, following HMI reports on their schools. In 1982 Sir Keith Joseph asked Liverpool for plans to rationalise school provision to reduce expenditure and give prospects for improving qualities and opportunities. In 1987

Kenneth Baker asked Brent to take 'urgent and immediate action' and produce a programme for dealing with problems in the management of its education service.

36 **Reasonableness**

A crucial question in case law has been what constitutes acting 'unreasonably' in the terms of Section 68 of the 1944 Act. In May 1976 in the Metropolitan Borough of Tameside the newly elected Conservative council reversed the plans of its Labour predecessors to introduce comprehensive provision in the following September. The Labour Secretary of State, Fred Mulley, in June directed the new Council to proceed with the comprehensive scheme under Section 68 which was backed up by an order of mandamus under Section 99 by the Divisional Court (12 July 1976). Tameside challenged the decision and the Appeal Court decided in favour of Tameside. Lord Denning held that the test of reasonableness should be applied and that: 'No one can be labelled as being unreasonable unless he is not only wrong but unreasonably wrong, so wrong that no reasonable person could sensibly take that view'. Thus differences of opinion were held to be irrelevant where such opinions were in some acceptable sense defensible. The House of Lords dismissed the Secretary of State's appeal (*The Times Educational Supplement*, 20 October 1976). Lord Wilberforce judged that the framing of Section 68 did not exclude judicial review of the Secretary of State's view of what constituted unreasonable action. He also considered that, though Section 68 gave the Secretary of State discretion, the Secretary of State had to take account of the discretion which the local authority was entitled to exercise within its powers and duties; reversals of policy might take place within the democratic process. Within this context of law, the Secretary of State was operating under a misconception on what, given the facts, it was reasonable for the local authority to do.

37 In December 1986 the Secretary of State, Kenneth Baker, used his powers under Section 68 of the 1944 Act to direct Brent not to proceed with its disciplinary procedure against a primary headteacher, Maureen McGoldrick, on the grounds that 'no reasonable authority, having regard to all the circumstances of the case, would decide to impose any further disciplinary penalty . . . even if the allegation . . . were to be substantiated'. Brent did not contest this. It followed an Appeal Court ruling that the LEA could proceed with the disciplinary procedure (See **2.8**).

38 **Judicial review**

An important aspect of the Tameside case was that it went some way to define the relationship between and functions of LEAs and the Secretary of State in allowing for judicial review. A similar process was involved in the case of Meade v. London Borough of Haringey in 1979. This case arose following school closures in the borough as a result of an industrial action by school caretakers and ancillary staff; the LEA closed the schools, asserting that to reopen the schools would worsen an existing situation of industrial conflict. A group of parents made a complaint to the Labour Secretary of State, Shirley Williams, asking her under Section 99 of the 1944 Act to declare that the LEA had failed to discharge its statutory duty under Section 8 of the Act and to direct the LEA to fulfil its duty. The Secretary of State took the view that no breach of duty had arisen and rejected the application. A subsequent application for judicial review of this decision established in the judgment of Lord Denning in the Appeal Court (14 March 1979) that the existence of the complaints procedure to the Secretary of State did not preclude the right to seek a remedy in the courts. In the event the industrial action was called off before the judgment was entered. However, the case established a number of important principles: first, the right of parents or other aggrieved parties to go to court to establish whether the exercise of functions by an LEA is in accordance with the law; secondly, the right of the court to adjudicate on a matter which had previously been considered by the Secretary of State; thirdly, the right of a court under certain circumstances to overturn a decision of the Secretary of State taken under Section 99 where it could be shown that the Secretary of State had misdirected him or herself as to a point of law.

39 Probably the major implication of these cases is that despite the apparent statutory status of the Secretary of State as final arbiter in matters of education, decisions of the Secretary of State may be challenged through the courts. Similarly LEAs in making decisions are not immune from the possibility of legal challenge.

40 In the case of Herring v. Templeman (1973) (2 all ER 581) an action was brought which was firmly located within the HE sector albeit outside of the LEA maintained sector. A student at a grant-aided teacher training college was required by the governing body to withdraw from a course following the receipt of an adverse academic report. The notice was issued by the governing body following the receipt of a report from the academic board. However, the student had not been accorded a hearing by the academic board before its recommendation was made although he was present when the matter came before the governing body and had been furnished with a copy of the academic board report prior to this meeting. An action was brought by the student against three members of the governing body. It was claimed that the action of the college was ultra vires in that the procedure employed was a breach of natural justice and in injunction was sought ordering readmission. The college countered that Section 68 of the 1944 Act placed the matter beyond the jurisdiction of the court and that remedy was only available on appeal to the Secretary of State. The judgment referred to the earlier case of Cumings v. Birkenhead Corporation (1972) (2 All ER 881). This had established that appeal to the courts was available only in cases involving some fundamental breach of the law rather than a faulty exercise of discretion. Since the action of the college was held to be in breach of natural justice and therefore ultra vires, the Section 68 defence of the college was rejected. Nevertheless, it was also held that the regulations of the college which governed the management and administration of the institution were such as to place all such matters within the province of the college visitor[4]. Since the question of natural justice only arose in relation to the administration and procedures of the college, jurisdiction in the case was held to rest with the visitor and not with the courts. For these reasons the claim was rejected.

41 In that case there was reluctance on the part of the court to become involved in the general questions of professional competence and, more specifically, in the questioning of academic judgements. The case, however, showed an expectation that institutions would conform with the principles of natural justice when conducting their affairs. The judgment also appears to establish the principle of a separation of jurisdiction between the courts and the Secretary of State: jurisdiction of the courts involves fundamental aspects of law; that of the Secretary of State the administration of educational law

42 A general statement of principle on the grounds for judicial review was given

by Lord Diplock in the House of Lords in Council of Civil Unions v. Minister for the Civil Service (1984) (3 All ER 935) when the unions challenged a Government decision that the civil servants employed at the Government Communications Headquarters (GCHQ) should no longer be permitted to be members of a trade union (other than an approved departmental staff association). Lord Diplock categorised the grounds under three heads: illegality; irrationality; and procedural impropriety (See Grant 1986).

43 **Fiduciary duty**

The principles of law under which the education system and local government are expected to operate are not always readily apparent. In 1982 the House of Lords supported Bromley's case against the Greater London Council's Fares Fair policy by recourse to the principle of the fiduciary duty owed by local government to its ratepayers and by finding that the GLC's cheaper public transport did not conform with this concept (Bromley London Borough Council v. Greater London Council) (1982) (1 All ER 129).

44 **Commentary**

Neither statute law nor case law has provided firm guidance on a range of issues in the law of further and higher education. This situation would appear to derive from the basic formulation produced more than four decades ago. Reviewing the situation in 1980, Farley and Clayton (1980) contrasted the judgments entered in the Humberside, Haringey and other cases. They argued that following the Humberside case: 'It was thought that the power of enforcement of statutory duties . . . lies solely in the hands of the Secretary of State and, of course, the decision of the Secretary of State as to whether or not to take action is often influenced by political and other considerations and also perhaps by the fact that the exercise of powers of enforcement vested in the Secretary of State are subjected to the jurisdiction of the court'. However, following the Haringey case they felt a reformulation was necessary. They argued that a distinction needed to be drawn between a breach of statutory duty resulting from a positive decision of an LEA (as in the Haringey case) rather than an act of omission (as in Humberside). In the former case jurisdiction lay with the courts but in the latter with the Secretary of State. However, since both cases involved non-fulfilment of a statutory duty the question was put of '. . . whether a Secretary of State . . . who omits to act in relation to breachs of statutory duty solely on grounds of economic exigency is fulfilling his duty under Section 1 of the 1944 Act'.

45 Loughlin (1986) has argued that the '. . . duty of the Secretary of State under S.1 is a uniquely strong expression of the principle of central control and direction. . . . However . . . there is a mismatch between the duty of the Secretary of State and the powers available to secure it' (p. 120). This mismatch, he argues, has been recognised in recent years and provides the rationale for the increasingly dirigiste, centralist approach which has characterised policy and legislative developments.

46 The principles and framework which governed the education service since the 1944 Act became, as has been indicated in this section, increasingly problematic. On the one hand, the strength of the model of the 'national service locally administered' is testified by its durability and the flexibility to meet and respond to changing circumstances and needs which it has provided. On the other hand, the model need not be seen as immutable. The 1944 Education Act was drafted during a period of uncertainty on the potential for future edu-

cational development, the concept of partnership which it embodies can be viewed not only as a matter of principle but also of expediency. The sharing of responsibilities was to provide a framework for experimentation as well as growth and was to build on existing provision. If a similar balance of local authority initiative and national direction is required today, it is at least arguable that a reformulation or restatement would be helpful. Developments in the legal domain during the 1970s and 1980s tended to complicate, rather than clarify, the situation.

47 The legal changes were accompanied by a centralising tendency by both Labour and Conservative governments. The pressures to restrain local authority expenditure took central government into more detailed controls. The reorganisation of teacher training during the 1970s was undertaken through increasingly centralised measures (Locke, Pratt and Burgess 1985).

48 The Conservative government after its re-election in June 1987 planned legislative changes which will provide a foundation for a system of different principles from those of the 1944 Act. Secretary of State Kenneth Baker introduced a new Bill to enforce the introduction of a national core curriculum and the devolution of responsibility for the financial management of schools from LEAs to headteachers and to enable schools to opt out of LEAs. In F/HE, following the White Paper 1987, the Bill is to remove the fifty-seven largest public sector providers of higher education, including all twenty-nine polytechnics, from local authority control in England. (A further eleven smaller institutions were to be given the choice of opting to joint the new independent corporate sector). Twenty-five existing voluntary and grant-aided colleges were also to be transferred to the new system of funding and control (See **1.1** Appendix 1). The Bill is to take buildings and assets from LEAs and give them to an interim body, the Polytechnics and Colleges Assets Board (PCAB).

49 These changes are consistent with actions by the post-1979 Conservative government. The Secretary of State has accrued powers which were previously considered unnecessary, and duties have been placed on institutions and LEAs which reduce local discretion. These moves towards increased central control and direction on the one hand and reduced local authority discretion and control on the other hand already undermined the traditional model of partnership of DES and LEAs. Yet for the government this was consistent with its development of a framework in which institutions were more directly responsive to consumers and the market.

50 The law, in education as elsewhere, provides one method by which policy and change may be implemented. Two aspects of Conservative government policy towards further and higher education have been prominent: increasing central financial control in the pursuit of goals of 'efficiency, economy, and effectiveness'; and the promotion of income generation and entrepreneurial activities. The first is evidenced by the cuts in student fees, the introduction of education support grants, the new grant arrangements for INSET and the more general reductions in institutions' income introduced via reductions in the Rate Support Grant and the AFE pool (See **1.3**); the latter by the introduction of full cost fees for overseas students (See **1.3**) and by the provisions of the 1985 Act dealing with the sale of goods and services (See paragraph 28 above and **1.3**). The Conservative government sought to remodel the public sector of further and higher education on principles quite different from those employed in 1944.

51 This section has shown that the legal basis of further and higher education is complex. Only the barest outline of the legal structure has been provided here; a full description of education and related areas of law would require a major volume of closely annotated reference material (See Liell and Saunders 1987). Many areas of legal importance are dealt with elsewhere in this book. It must be also borne in mind throughout that educational institutions along with those that work in them, those that manage and administer them, and those that govern them are subject to the general laws of the land. Moreover, the law does not operate independently of political and informal pressures; it cannot be viewed in isolation.

NOTES

1 For more detailed discussion see Layfield 1976. The phrase is attributed to Sir William (later Lord) Alexander by Peter Newsam *The Times Educational Supplement* 26 September 1986.

2 It is doubtful if the submission of development plans for work-related non-advanced further education (NAFE) following the White Paper, *Training for Jobs*, would be judged to satisfy the requirements of Section 42. Such development plans are submitted to the Manpower Services Commission. The Secretary of State for Education and Science does not approve them individually, although current policy requires the MSC to satisfy the Education Secretary as well as the Secretary of State for Employment about the general arrangements (See **1.7**).

3 There are some exceptions to this (See Fletcher 1986).

4 The jurisdiction of a 'visitor' was upheld in Thomas v. University of Bradford (1 All ER).

ANNEX 1

SCHEDULE 2 REGULATIONS 14 AND 15

(SI 1981 1086 as amended by SI 1983 262)

Advanced further education courses to which regulations 14 and 15 apply

1 For the purposes of Regulations 14 and 15, the following courses are hereby designated as courses of advanced further education –

(a) any course for the further training of teachers, being a full-time course of 4 or more weeks' duration or a part-time course involving more than 60 hours of instruction; and

(b) any such course as is mentioned in paragraph 2, being a full-time course of 4 or more weeks' duration or a part-time course involving more than 60 hours of instruction.

2 (1) The courses referred to in paragraph 1 (b) are –

(a) a post-graduate course or a course comparable to such a course;

(b) a first degree course or a course comparable to such a course;

(c) a course for the Diploma of Higher Education;

(d) a course for the Higher National Diploma or Certificate (including certificate of supplementary study), the Higher Diploma or Certificate of the Technician Education Council, the Higher Diploma or Certificate of the Business Education Council or the Diploma in Management Studies;

(e) a course in preparation for a professional examination of a standard above that of the examinations for the Ordinary National Certificate or the examinations at advanced level for the General Certificate of Education;

(f) any other course in preparation for an examination of a standard above that of the examinations for the Ordinary National Certificate or the examinations at advanced level for the General Certificate of Education, being a course which, disregarding exceptions made in individual cases or classes of case, may be taken only by students who have attained the age of 18 years and (subject to sub-paragraph (2)) hold –

(i) an Ordinary National Certificate, or

(ii) a General Certificate of Education recording that the student attained grade 'C' or above in at least five subjects in the examinations at ordinary level, or

(iii) a General Certificate of Education recording that the student passed in at least two subjects in the examinations at advanced level or so passed in one subject and attained grade 'C' in at least one other subject in the examinations at ordinary level, or

(iv) a certificate or other qualification indicative of a comparable or higher level of attainment.

(2) For the purposes of sub-paragraph (1) any reference to a General Certificate of Education recording that a student attained Grade 'C' or above in a subject in the examinations at ordinary level shall be construed as including a reference –

(a) to such a certificate recording that he attained at least grade 'C' at ordinary level in the examinations in that subject at advanced level; and

(b) to a Certificate of Secondary Education recording that he attained grade 1 in the examinations in that subject for that certificate.

APPENDIX 1

CHARITY AND COMPANY LAW

1 The public system of further and higher education is made up largely of colleges which are maintained by local authorities. These colleges do not have legal personality of their own and are dependent on local authorities for their ability to act in law. They are in law part of their local authorities, and it is the local authorities which employ staff, own or lease buildings, who are legally responsible for financial affairs and can act in law. Thus, the colleges operate in the context of local government law (See **1.2** and **1.7**), and this has shaped the government of colleges (See **2.8**).

2 However, the public sector includes colleges with autonomous legal identities which enable them to employ staff, own or lease buildings in their own name, and take responsibility for their own financial and other actions. Voluntary colleges of higher education – which were colleges of education (teacher training institutions) until the reorganisation in the mid-1970s (See **1.1** 9–10) – are legally established by a deed of trust (See paragraphs 10–13 below) or are companies limited by guarantee. (See paragraphs 4–9 below). These colleges are funded directly by central government. The five polytechnics within the Inner London Education Authority (ILEA) are established as companies limited by guarantee, though funded by ILEA. There are also a few, though varied, other colleges which have their own legal identities, some funded by central government and some voluntary-aided by local authorities.

3 Such non-maintained status has attracted greater attention through the discussion on how to give polytechnics and colleges of higher education more independence from local authorities (See **2.8**). The White Paper 1987 proposed that the polytechnics and major colleges of higher education in England should be removed from local authorities and brought into the national domain (with voluntary colleges and others grant-aided by central government) under a Polytechnics and Colleges Funding Council (PCFC) (See **1.1** Appendix 1). So that they could employ staff, own or lease buildings and take financial responsibility, these polytechnics and colleges would be established with their own legal identities are corporate bodies either as companies limited by guarantee or as

corporations through act of parliament (See 19–20 below). The phrase most used in this debate in the mid-1980s was that the institutions would have 'corporate status', in other words that they would have legal existence in their own right rather than being dependent on local authorities.

4 *Companies limited by guarantee*
Colleges can be set up as a company under the Companies Acts with members whose liability is limited by guarantee. This liability is limited to a stated figure, such as £1 in the ILEA polytechnics. Companies can apply to the Secretary of State for Trade and Industry for authorisation not to use the word 'Limited' in their titles.

5 The foundation of a company is in the memorandum and articles of association, which have to be approved by the Registrar of Companies. The memorandum sets out the objects of the company, its powers to pursue those objects, the liability of its members, and the provision for winding up the company. The articles set out the membership of the company and its governing body, the membership of the governing body, terms of office and eligibility for being a governor, the rules for general meetings and meetings of the governing body, the powers and duties of the governing body, and the main provisions for running the company. The articles also provide for the common seal of the polytechnic. Thus, the governing body has the powers of and responsibility for controlling and managing the company, like a board of directors.

6 Articles of association do not usually carry as much detail as articles of government and are therefore accompanied by a set of bye-laws and perhaps a schedule attached to the articles. The bye-laws may contain such matters as: membership and functions of the academic board; appointment and promotion of staff; discipline of staff; discipline of students; arrangements for consultation with staff and students; provision for the students' union; establishment of committees and boards. The bye-laws are drawn up by the governing body, according to the wording of the articles.

7 A company is initially formed by seven or more subscribers whose names are in the memorandum of association; they become members once the company is incorporated. The articles state the number of members and say who are qualified to be members.

8 The liability of governors for the debts of the company is limited to the amount they guarantee as members under the memorandum of association. However, they are individually responsible for conforming to company law and are not protected against their own negligence or illegal actions. The position thus carries some personal risk and liability.

9 Company law requires certain reporting and record-keeping. The company has to hold an annual general meeting of members and submit an annual report in a specified form and audited annual accounts. Names of governors, as directors, have to be recorded with Companies House. Companies legislation makes provision for conduct of general meetings and meetings of the directors. Company law has tended in practice to be fairly permissive but presents some problems unfamiliar in maintained institutions, e.g. on insolvency. There is also a body of case-law relating to the operation of companies.

10 *Trusts*
Many colleges own their legal existence to a deed of trust. A trust deed sets out the purposes of the trust and sets up two or more people to take responsibility for the property and money of the trust. The trustees are legally obliged to ensure that these are devoted to the purposes described in the deed. In some colleges the trustees are named (with provision for their successors) or are postholders (usually in a church); they are then separate from the governing body and reserve some powers over property and finance. In others the trustees and governors are the same body. In the former case, the trustees are likely to be termed 'foundation governors'.

11 Colleges are founded as charitable trusts: a trust is not necessarily charitable; a charit-

able trust is registered as such by the Charity Commissioners, providing its trust deed meets their requirements, and then subject to charity law (See below paragraphs 14–18).

12 When the colleges of education were reorganised in the 1970s (See **1.1**), three new institutions were created from mergers of maintained and voluntary colleges. Because the trustees of the voluntary colleges could not hand over their assets to the local authorities, new trust deeds were created with trustees drawn from church and local authority. These colleges were thus 'hybrids' of maintained and voluntary systems but legally had the identity of a voluntary college.

13 Trustees have individual, personal liability for the assets of the trust and for seeing that they are properly applied. Beneficiaries and potential beneficiaries could take legal action against them if they misapplied funds. So, they could be subject to scrutiny from this quarter as well as, for a charitable trust, from the Charity Commissioners. The law of trusts is a particularly tricky area of law which has accumulated over the centuries, and expert opinion would be necessary on specific cases.

14 *Charitable status*

The questions of corporate status and charitable status are separate, though the debate of the mid-1980s often ran them together; either status is possible without the other. The White Paper 1987 did not consider charitable status was essential for the polytechnics and colleges in their new autonomous status.

15 To be registered as a charity the objects of the body, whether company or trust or other legal status, have to be charitable; the advancement of education for the public benefit is one of the basic criteria of charitable activity. The Charity Commission registers the body as a charity, having approved its constitution or memorandum and articles of association, and gives the charity a number. Some of the benefits of charitable status (See paragraph 16 below) also requires Inland Revenue to recognise the body as charitable, though this is not a formal procedure. Inland Revenue do not necessarily recognise all activities of a registered charity as charitable and might regard, say, profitable trading in courses as uncharitable.

16 Charities mandatorily receive a 50% reduction in rates from their local authorities, which the latter recoups from central government along with its rate support grant. The local authority has discretion to grant an additional 50% rate relief, but does not recover this from central government. It should be noted that universities, though charitable, are specifically exempted from mandatory rate relief, and it is conceivable the regulations could be changed to exempt also polytechnics and other colleges when they acquire corporate status. Charities have other tax advantages: exemption from capital gains tax, corporation tax, and capital transfer tax; a preferential position in terms of Stamp Duty and Development Land Tax.

17 Charity law is enforced by the Charity Commission. It has quasi-judicial functions and can replace trustees of charities. It acts with much discretion in a 'grey area' of law. Status as a charity is incompatible with trading (except as an incidental way of achieving objects) and with political campaigning.

18 Charitable trustees have individual responsibility and liability for the charitable funds. Where the charity is incorporated as a company limited by guarantee, this probably overrides the limited liability under the incorporation as a company, and their responsibility as individuals could in some respects be unlimited. Where colleges are founded on a trust deed, the trustees are undoubtedly liable, but where the trustees are named (i.e. not identical with the governing body) governors who are not specified as trustees may nonetheless be expected to carry a trusteeship and hence to carry a similar personal responsibility and liability. This is an uncertain area of law, but there does appear to be some need for caution. It is clear, however, that the responsibility of trustees is to the charity and not to the body which nominated or elected them. Under charity law be-

neficiaries are not meant to be members of the managing body, though a minority of staff and students has proved permissible on the same basis as in the governing bodies of maintained institutions.

19 *Corporations*
Universities are established as corporations under either a royal charter or an act of parliament. Central institutions in Scotland (the equivalent of polytechnics) are currently established as corporations under the Education (Scotland) Act 1980; statutory instruments under this act enabled the transfer of two colleges from local authority status to autonomy in law with central government funding. The White Paper 1987 left open the possibility of implementing its proposals through an act of parliament to confer corporate status on some or all of the named institutions, rather than create memoranda and articles of association for each as a company limited by guarantee.

20 It is generally thought that corporations have more freedom of action than limited companies. It seems that they can be whatever you want them to be, and there is not a specific body of law.

21 *Composite organisations*
A complicating factor in the legal status of colleges is how they have increasingly come to deploy bodies with different forms of status within the overall institutions. Colleges have established trading companies, stimulated in some cases by the Further Education Act 1985 (See **1.2** paragraph 28), to undertake more clearly commercial activities. This can give some freedom of manoeuvre outside local authority law. Similarly, a college established as a limited company and registered as a charity could create a separate non-charitable company for trading or income-generating activities. The different bodies are legally separate, though they can be linked through statements in the memorandum and articles. Trading companies can covenant money to charitable bodies.

22 *VAT*
Maintained institutions, as part of local authorities, do not pay VAT. Colleges with their own legal identities, as the voluntary colleges of higher education, are required to pay, although the ILEA polytechnics are treated on a par with maintained polytechnics. Colleges running commercial activities may be required to charge VAT on these services, though there does not seem to be consistent practice.

Notes

1 The feasibility of 'corporate status' and transition to 'corporate status' are discussed in Locke with Pratt, Silverman and Travers (1987).

APPENDIX 2

RACE RELATIONS

1 The Race Relations Act 1976 defined two kinds of racial discrimination which it is convenient to describe as 'direct' and 'indirect' racial discrimination. Section 1 (1) (a) of the Act dealt with the former and specified that if a person is treated less favourably by reason of his/her race, that person suffers discrimination.

2 Section 1 (1) (b) dealt with indirect discrimination which consists of treatment which, whilst equal between different racial groups in a formal sense, is in its effect discriminatory against a racial group. This can arise where a person seeking a job or promotion has applied to them a condition or requirements with which he or she must comply to qualify

for or benefit from the job or promotion and that condition or requirement is discriminatory. Discrimination occurs when all the following criteria hold:

(i) It is a condition or qualification that the 'discriminator' applies equally to persons of the 'victims' racial group who can successfully comply with it is considerably smaller than the proportion of persons not of that group who can comply with it;

(ii) Is to the detriment of the victim because she or he cannot comply with it; and

(iii) Cannot be shown by the discriminator to be justifiable irrespective of the colour, race, nationality or ethnic or national origins of the person to whom it is applied.

3 This definition of indirect discrimination is complex and allows for the possibility that a person may discriminate without intending to do so. In such cases an industrial tribunal can recommend that a respondent removes the discriminatory condition or requirement within a specified time but the tribunal cannot award compensation. Thus the applicant may not directly benefit from a finding in their favour. Compensation may be awarded if the respondent ignores the recommendation.

4 *Racial and ethnic groups*

The Act (Section 3) defined actions based on 'racial grounds' as grounds based on colour, race, nationality or ethnic or national origins, and 'racial groups' by reference to these categories. The definitions are somewhat limited and arguably tautologous. The House of Lords has defined ethnic by providing a checklist which establishes if a particular group is racial group. Its essential features are a long, shared history which sets it apart from other groups and its own cultural tradition. Additionally, it is likely to have a common language, literature and religion, be either from a particular geographical region or descended from a small number of common ancestors, and be either a minority or majority within a community. The House of Lords stated that a person was a member of such a group if they considered themselves to be members of it and were accepted by others as members.

5 *Employers*

In Section 4, the Act set out the ways in which employers must not discriminate on racial grounds. Section 4 (1) described three ways in which recruitment may be discriminatory. First, an employer may discriminate in the arrangements made for deciding who should be offered a job by, for example, the instructions given to a personnel officer. The person discriminated against need not have applied for the job in order to make a complaint about such arrangements. Second, discriminatory terms offered in relation to pay, holidays and conditions are unlawful. Third, an employer who refuses a person employment on grounds of race, etc. for example, by rejecting an application or by deliberately avoiding consideration of an application, is guilty of discrimination (See **2.4** 2–8).

6 *Promotion and training*

Where an employee has been engaged, it is unlawful for the employer to discriminate in the way he or she affords the employee access to opportunities for promotion, transfer or training or to other benefits, service or services, by refusing or deliberately omitting to afford the employee such access. This covers the arrangements made for selection for promotion, transfer or training as well as the actual selection itself.

7 These provisions in Section 4 (2) were supplemented in respect of training in Sections 13–15 of the Act. It is unlawful for bodies such as the Manpower Services Commission to discriminate in the terms on which they offer (or refuse) training. Nor may jobcentres, private agencies, or careers guidance services discriminate in provision of services. Any of them may be taken before an industrial tribunal by a complainant. If an employer under a training scheme discriminates against a complainant, or a firm refuses to take him or her on its training scheme because of the complainant's race, the employer can be taken to a tribunal if the scheme was arranged through the Manpower Services Commission.

8 *Statutory duties of local authorities*
Local authorities have a duty (Section 71) to make proper arrangements to secure that their functions are carried out with due regard to the need to eliminate unlawful discrimination and to promote equality of opportunity and good relations between persons of different races. It is difficult to see how Section 71 could be enforced but it has become the focus of policy development in a number of authorities and has become a major campaigning instrument for the promotion of multi-racial and anti-racist education in that it places race relations objectives within the duties of local education authorities (LEAs). This campaigning work has involved a number of organisations from ethnic communities including the All London Teachers Against Racism and Fascism, the Afro-Caribbean Teachers Association, the National Anti-Racist Movement in Education, and the Board of Deputies of British Jews. It has engaged NATFHE and the National Union of Teachers (NUT) on the employees' side and the Education Committee of the Association of Metropolitan Authorities (AMA) on the employers' side. Many of these organisations have received systematic advice from the Commission for Racial Equality (CRE), the Joint Council for the Welfare of Immigrants, the Runnymede Trust, and the United Kingdom Council for Overseas Affairs.

9 *Education*
Aside from Section 71, Sections 17–19 of the Act related to discrimination by providers of education. Section 17 made it unlawful for the responsible body for an educational establishment to discriminate

(i) in admission to the establishment;
(ii) by refusing or deliberately omitting to accept an application for admission;
(iii) in the way it affords a pupil whom it has admitted to the establishment access to any benefits, facilities and services, or by refusing or deliberately omitting to afford such access;
(iv) by excluding such a pupil or treating her or him in an unfavourable way. Aside from these provisions, LEAs must not discriminate in other functions like the award of Discretionary Grants (Section 2 of the Education Act 1962) or provision of facilities for social and physical recreation (Section 53 of the Education Act 1944). These provisions were covered in Section 18 of 1976 Race Relations Act. The legislation was further bolstered by Section 8 of the Employment and Training Act 1973 and Section 14 of the Race Relations Act, both of which required LEAs not to discriminate in the performance of their functions.

10 *Special educational needs*
Section 35 of the Race Relations Act made a general exception for acts done to enable the special needs of particular racial groups to be met as regards education, training, welfare and ancillary benefits. It permitted local authorities and their institutions to restrict access to facilities, services or benefits, or allow them to be allocated first to particular racial groups. However, they must be able to show that members of that racial group have a special need in regard to their education, training, welfare or ancillary benefits which can be met by a restrictive or preferential allocation.

11 *Victimisation*
Section 2 of the Act set out the circumstances which amount to victimisation. It occurs where a 'discriminator' treats another person less favourably than he or she treats other persons on the ground that the 'victim' has done (or intends to do, or is suspected of having done or intending to do) any of the following :
(i) Brought proceedings against the discriminator or anyone else under the Act;
(ii) Given evidence or information in connection with proceedings brought under the Act;
(iii) Otherwise done anything under or by reference to the Act in relation to the discriminator or anyone else (for example, by assistant the Commission for Racial Equality in the course of a formal investigation); and
(iv) Alleged that the discriminator or anyone else has committed an action which would constitute a contravention of the Act.

12 *Remedies*
Standard industrial tribunal forms are available to assist complainants to institute proceedings under Section 65 of the Act. They enable the aggrieved person to put questions to the person or organisation she or he considers responsible (the 'respondent') to ascertain reasons for the treatment or other relevant matters. They provide a basis for replies by respondents. These forms are available, free of charge, from jobcentres, Community Relations Councils, the Commission for Racial Equality, local Employment Offices or unemployment benefit offices of the Department of Employment.

13 The questions and answers draw attention to what must be shown to prove unlawful discrimination and to establish, where possible, the facts as well as the reasons for the respondent's actions. On occasions this process may show a complaint is groundless or based on a misunderstanding. It may lead to a settlement in advance of the tribunal and where proceedings are instituted it may identify what is agreed or in dispute between the parties, simplifying the hearing. There is a time limit of 21 days from receipt of a complaint, unless the tribunal consents to a longer period, for responses to questions.

14 If it appears to the court or tribunal that the respondent deliberately omitted to reply in the appropriate period without a reasonable excuse, or was evasive or equivocal in the reply, the court or tribunal will be entitled to draw the inference, if it seems just and equitable to do so, that the respondent committed an unlawful act. Failures or refusals to reply or attempts to subvert the process are, then, potential evidence of the illegality in question. If the respondent does not use the form but writes a letter, that is acceptable although it may be somewhat impractical.

15 The use of industrial tribunals to complain of racial discrimination has to be viewed against the record of proceeding by this route. In 1983 there were 310 applications on grounds of racial discrimination nearly all relating to employment and half relating to dismissal. 11% of complaints were upheld, compared with 7% of 273 cases in 1982. These percentages were low in comparison with successful sex discrimination and equal pay complaints, respectively 23% and 25% in 1983. In Race Relations cases, compensation was obtained in just 42 cases. Compensation was higher when agreed at conciliation rather than at a full tribunal hearing, the levels being marginally higher than for sex discrimination cases.

16 *Conditions of service*
The Scheme of Conditions of Service for Further Education Teachers in England and Wales (See **2.4** 3–8, 42–46) deals explicitly with equal opportunities. The employers' and lecturers' organisations are committed by Section 2 to providing equality of opportunity in selection, recruitment, training, and promotion and so opposing discriminatory practice in respect of all conditions of service. The Scheme prohibits such discrimination on the basis of colour, race, nationality or ethnic or national origins, as well as on the basis of creed, sex or marital status. All parties are enjoined to meet the requirements of the Sex Discrimination Act 1975 and the Race Relations Act 1976. The National Joint Council commends the spirit of the legislation and not just its specific provisions. It regards it as an 'educational principle' that education promotes equal opportunity and the avoidance of unfair and unlawful discrimination, noting that Section 30 of the Education Act 1944 forbids religious discrimination in schools. This principle should, in an extended form, apply to further education. In part, it would be expressed by a positive attitude to discrimination of a lawful kind, as when, for example, education and training are intended to meet the needs of a particular racial group.

17 *Incitement to racial hatred*
In recent years there has been an increase in the number of plays or performances of original materials authored by students. This usually occurs under the auspices of student unions but sometimes in association with staff who have responsibility for student resources and liaison. In any such play performed in public contains insulting, threatening or abusive words intended to foment hatred against any section of the public in Great Britain, that may be distinguished by race, colour, ethnic or national origin, this is an

offence. Equally, if the production as a whole has a tendency to foment such hatred, this is an offence. In the first kind of case, intention must be proved but in the latter the likelihood is in itself sufficient. The person who presents or directs the play is responsible whether the performance is for gain or not, or those involved are amateurs or professional and the possibility plainly exists that the presenter is the member of staff within the institution responsible for the performance space or student resources. Summary conviction may lead to a fine or imprisonment; conviction on indictment to a fine of up to £1000, or a maximum of two years imprisonment, or both (Section 5, Theatres Act 1968).

13 *Further information*
NATFHE, in January 1986, published *NATFHE Against Racism* (1986a), a policy and action pack which condemns the expression and dissemination of racist beliefs, attitudes and ideas in society and especially among its own members. The pack identifies objectives: in curriculum development; the scope of the curriculum offer; in employment practice and the elimination of harassment. It proposes a programme capable of monitoring and sets out objectives as a basis for negotiation between employers and staff. The Association is producing a procedure for handling allegations of harassment among its own members, between different grades and groups of staff, and in relations with the student body. Routine training of local Association Officers is undertaken to improve effectiveness in dealing with racism. NATFHE has working relationships with bodies like the CRE, National Anti-Racist Movement in Education (NAME) and National Association for the Care and Resettlement of Offenders (NACRO) and there is joint development of policy with the NUT.

APPENDIX 3

SEX DISCRIMINATION LEGISLATION

1 A number of recent enactments are referred to collectively as sex discrimination legislation. There are two enactments under that title, the Sex Discrimination Act 1975, and the Sex Discrimination Act 1986. However, there is supporting legislation in a number of the employment protection enactments of the last twenty years. Most importantly the Sex Discrimination Acts are supported by the Equal Pay Act 1970, and the more recent amendments to that Act as well as the Equal Pay (Amendments) Regulations 1983. This appendix deals only with sex discrimination; equal pay and value legislation are discussed in **2.4**.

2 *The 1975 Act*
The Sex Discrimination Act 1975 (as amended by the 1986 Act) made sex discrimination unlawful in
(i) Employment
(ii) Training and education
(iii) The provision of goods, facilities and services
(iv) The disposal and management of premises.
The Act dealt with discrimination on grounds of sex in all these areas and on grounds of marital status in respect of employment only. Direct discrimination exists against a woman where a person treats her less favourably than a man is or would be treated on grounds of her sex. Men are similarly protected in comparison to the treatment given to women. The treatment has to be less favourable, not just different. Indirect discrimination occurs where a person applies to a woman a condition or requirement with which she has to comply and where the condition
(i) Is or would be applied equally to men and to women, but
(ii) Is such that a smaller proportion of women can comply with it than men, and
(iii) Is to the woman's detriment, and
(iv) Cannot be shown to be justifiable irrespective of the sex of the person to whom it is applied.

3 Similarly, in relation to employment only, direct and indirect discrimination can operate against a married person if less favourable treatment is given on grounds of marital

status or a condition or requirement is applied which has the same effect. Finally, the Act defines victimisation. This arises, for example, where a discriminator treats another person of either sex (the victim) less favourably than he treats or would treat others because the victim has exercised his or her rights under the Sex Discrimination or Equal Pay Acts.

4 *Discrimination in employment*

Whilst a number of related bodies such as partnerships, trade unions, qualifying bodies, and vocational training bodies come under the scope of the employment provisions, it is for employers that Part II of the Act (dealing with discrimination in the employment field) is particularly onerous. It is worth noting that employers may be liable for the acts of their employees whether or not they are aware of their discriminatory character. The primary areas of employment dealt with are recruitment, terms of employment, fringe benefits, facilities and services, training, promotion and transfer, dismissal and selection for redundancy. In respect of recruitment three unlawful discriminatory acts can occur:

(i) In the arrangements made for deciding who should be offered the job;
(ii) In the terms offered;
(iii) In refusing to offer a person, or consider him or her for, employment.

Again, it is worth noting that a complainant concerned with (i) above need not have been an applicant for the post. Discriminatory practices in relation to advertisements (including job advertisements) are dealt with separately (See below paragraph 11).

5 There were three main exceptions to the requirement that employers must not discriminate in respect of employment. Private households and small firms were exempted by the 1975 Act – an exemption removed by the 1986 Act. The other two exceptions continue to apply. The first of these refers to pregnancy, childbirth, death, and retirement. Hence it is not discriminatory for an employer to afford women special treatment in connection with pregnancy or childbirth. Nor is it discriminatory for an employer to treat a woman less favourably in respect of pension or death benefits. The second remaining exception is in relation to genuine occupational qualifications (GOQs). These can apply only in relation to recruitment arrangements and the provisions relating to a refusal to offer a job in relation to access to promotion, transfer, or training. GOQs do not apply to marital status discrimination. The Act listed eight GOQs of which the main ones are physiology, decency, single sex accommodation, single sex establishment, and personal services (See **2.4** 2).

6 It is unlawful to discriminate in respect of dismissals (See above paragraph 2–4). The Act actually referred to dismissals and 'other detriment'. This can cover disciplinary procedures and is also one route for dealing with sexual harassment cases since harassment can create working conditions which subjects the woman to detriment.

7 Three other bodies and activities are covered by the employment provisions of the Act. First, qualifications awarding bodies must not discriminate in the terms on which they confer, renew, or extend a qualification or authorisation. Second, certain vocational training bodies must not discriminate in respect of employment related training in the matters of access to or termination of training. Third, the Manpower Services Commission must not discriminate in training or any other services it provides.

8 *Discrimination in education*

The Act imposed a general duty on responsible bodies for educational establishments in the public sector to ensure that their services are provided without sex discrimination. In addition, specific duties are imposed on bodies such as colleges and polytechnics[1]. Finally, LEAs are required not to discriminate in relation to their functions under the Education Acts which are not caught by the foregoing provisions.

9 The specific areas in which it is unlawful for a body responsible for an establishment to discriminate are in the terms of admission, refusal to accept an application, access to benefits, facilities or services, and by excluding a student or treating her unfavourably in any other way. The Act made a number of exceptions dealing with single sex establish-

ments (in respect of admission only), boarding accommodation, educational charities, and physical education.

10 *Other forms of discrimination*
Whether free or charged-for the provision of goods, facilities and services to the public must be free of discrimination in respect of their provision, quality and terms of provision. This section would make discriminatory practices in relation to banking, for example, unlawful, but it does not apply, to take another case, to private clubs. There are, again, a number of exceptions even in relation to services provided for the public e.g. on grounds of privacy and propriety. Discrimination in the disposal of premises and in subletting is rendered unlawful by the Act.

11 The Act dealt with a number of other unlawful discriminatory acts. The most important of these are the provisions relating to discriminatory practices, and those relating to discriminatory advertisements. The former made it unlawful to apply, or to operate a practice which would call for the application of, a condition or requirement which causes, or might cause, an act which is indirectly discriminatory. The latter provision made it unlawful to publish an intention to discriminate unlawfully. This provision also catches advertisements which might reasonably be taken to indicate an intention of this sort. It is the intention which is important hence it is sensible to record, in respect of any job advertisement, that it is open to both men and women (See **2.4** 2).

12 *General exceptions*
A number of the Act's specific provisions – on employment, education, goods and services – carry certain exceptions. In addition the Act provided some general exceptions. These relate to charities, sport, insurance, acts done under a statutory authority, communal accommodation, and positive action. The most important of these for those managing and administering colleges, are dealt with below.

13 Sports in which physical strength, stamina and physique are important and which would put the average woman at a disadvantage with the average man are excepted.

14 Communal accommodation is defined as residential accommodation which includes dormitories or shared sleeping accommodation, or accommodation which should be used by one sex only because of the nature of the sanitary facilities. Provision of such accommodation is excepted from the Act's scope. However, the accommodation has to be managed in such a way that men and women are treated as equitably as circumstances permit.

15 Positive action by those providing training, employers, and bodies such as trade unions is permitted under the Act. In respect of training the provider can arrange training for, or encourage applications from, a single sex if no, or few members of that sex are engaged in work in Great Britain to which the training relates. Equally, such a provision can be made if there is a shortfall in a particular geographical area. The same provision makes single sex courses for women returners legitimate. Again, employers can arrange single sex training, and trade unions and similar organisations can create reserved places for women on committees.

16 *The enforcement machinery*
Individuals can complain of defaults relating to employment to industrial tribunals; complaints in other fields are referred to the county or sheriff courts. Complaints of discrimination by bodies responsible for education in the public sector have to be referred in the first instance to the appropriate Education Minister. In advance of complaint, a prospective complainant may use forms provided by the Equal Opportunities Commission to question a respondent.

17 The Act established an Equal Opportunities Commission. Briefly, the Commission is charged to try to eliminate discrimination, promote equality of opportunity, and keep legislation under review. It may conduct formal investigations, require the production of information, make reports and recommendations, issue non-discriminatory notices,

keep a register of such notices, and deal with persistent discrimination. It can also assist complainants and issue codes of practice. These codes are admissible in evidence in tribunal proceedings.

18 *Further information*
The Equal Opportunities Commission is a source of advice about non-discriminatory practices. The Commission publishes a number of leaflets and codes dealing with subjects such as non-discriminatory recruitment procedures. NATFHE's Women's Rights Standing Panel has published a number of analyses of discrimination and guides on its avoidance. The Home Office's *Sex Discrimination: A Guide to the Sex Discrimination Act 1975* has stood the test of time as a lay person's guide to the Act. For those wishing to study the employment implications in depth Income Data Services provides a handbook on sex discrimination and equal pay. *The Encyclopaedia of Employment Law and Practice* (Walton, annual) provides a regularly updated account of the decisions made by the Tribunals and the Courts based on the Act.

NOTE

1 Colleges which have their own legal identity (see above Appendix 1) are included within the scope of the Act by order of the Secretary of State for Education and Science.

APPENDIX 4

COPYRIGHT

1 This Appendix considers two issues concerning copyright. Much recent attention has been focused on the use of copyright materials in education and the development of licensing agreements and is considered in the first part of the Appendix. Although it has received less attention, there is likely to be a growth in interest in the copyright ownership of materials produced for 'distance learning'. The concept of distance learning is far from new; there is a substantial tradition of correspondence courses in the United Kingdom, and there is a successful higher education institution configured around distance learning, namely the Open University. With the introduction of the Open Tech and rapid growth in providing curriculum packages away from colleges, the matter of ownership of rights in the materials used will become increasingly important. The second part of the Appendix notes the main issues.

2 Most materials used in education are covered by copyright and whilst this has always been the case, the legislation has only been a significant problem in the last 15 years. Traditionally, students used textbooks purchased by or for them and in as much as copying took place it was restricted to handwritten notes. Thus, there were few significant breaches of the restrictions in The Copyright Act 1956 which was itself built on Acts in 1709 (The Statute of Anne) which introduced copyright; The Dramatic Copyright Act 1833, which introduced the concept of performing rights; and The Copyright Act 1911, which introduced recording rights. The 1956 Act is the key statute at present although there are new proposals considered below. The issue has become sharper since the passage of the 1956 Act for two principal reasons. First, the development of new reprographic and transmission technologies have demonstrated major gaps in the 1956 Act. Enforcement and regulation now lie beyond most legal agencies, and the protection of owners of copyright is now extremely difficult. Second, current copyright law cannot solve problems of fair dealing arising from reprographic reproduction of facsimile copyright material because equipment for making high quality facsimile copies at low cost is widespread throughout educational institutions. These problems were not foreseen in the period covering hand and typewriter copying, and even where they are now understood, there is widespread indifference to the consequences in institutions.

3 Copyright materials can be used under specific conditions set out in the 1956 Act. The Act covers research, private study, libraries and educational instruction *inter alia*. In the case of research and private study it is 'fair dealing' (i.e. no infringement of copyright) if the literary, musical, dramatic or artistic work is used specifically for private study. A *single* copy may be taken for the purpose of research or private study and 'fair' to do so, but illegal for multiples to be taken (Sillitoe v. McGraw-Hill Book Co (UK) Ltd, 1983).

Use in libraries is related to these provisions provided they are not established or conducted for profit. Thus a library can take one copy of an article in any one periodical, or one copy of a reasonable part of one published work for a single individual to use for the purpose of research or private study (Regulation 4, The Copyright (Libraries) Regulations 1957, this flowing from Section 7(1) of the 1956 Act). Further, the researcher must pay for the copy an amount not less than the cost of making the copy (Section 7(2), 1956) and furthermore, the librarian must only supply the copy to a person who satisfies the librarian that the copy is for private study or research and will not be used for another purpose (Section 7(2)(b), 1956, and Regulation 4(a), 1957). A Form of Declaration and Undertaking is prescribed in the Third Schedule of the Copyright (Libraries) Regulations. Finally, libraries may take a copy of one article or part of a whole work for another library provided both have no commercial activity, again so long as the full cost of doing so is paid, and provided that the librarian making the copy does not know the name and address of any person entitled to authorise the copy or could not reasonably find such information.

4 No one in education is excepted from copyright liability where copying would constitute an infringement of the Act. Thus, a lecturer or student can make a copy for instruction, private study, or research provided it is not made on a multiple copying machine (Section 41(1)(a)(7), 1956). This restriction is true even for copyright materials that are to be used in examination papers. It will be seen that institutions and lecturers have minimal rights to reproduce copyright materials and this sits somewhat at odds with new technologies in reprographics and transmission particularly of specialist texts since the specialist texts have an increasingly high unit cost whereas copies are coming at an increasingly low unit cost.

5 The same kinds of restriction apply to broadcast copyright materials (and that is all broadcast materials). Students, lecturers, and institutions may not record wireless or television programmes off the air for subsequent replay even if this were to happen in private. Such recordings cannot be used for classes, even where the recording is of material which is itself out of copyright like a Shakespeare play. Although texts fall out of copyright fifty years after the end of the calendar year in which the author died (Sections 2(3) and 3(4), 1956), the specific production remains in copyright.

6 The aim of the legislation is to protect valuable commercial properties vested in literary, musical, artistic, sound recorded, televised, and filmed works. It is directed at ensuring a fair return for the 'authors' of such works and protects the commercial interests of those who produce the texts, etc. The legislation affords no protection for ideas or themes which only achieve protection in material form, although ideas for materials can be protected under the laws of confidentiality.

7 *Public Lending Right*

In March 1980, the Public Lending Right Act 1979, came into force. It establishes a central fund from which authors receive payments based on the numbers of times that their works are drawn from certain libraries. Authors cannot influence the amounts due to them by negotiation of fees but do have rights to receive the amounts determined by the Registrar of Public Lending Rights. Whilst this issue is tangential to copyright, it recognises an entitlement to income from multiple uses of a work which would otherwise have been rewarded only in the royalty paid to the author for the sale of individual copies. Income from this source is estimated to average about £300 per annum.

8 *Open and distance learning materials*

The main characteristic of these materials is that they are by their very nature the kinds of materials described in the first section of the Appendix. Students requiring materials in remote places will receive them in the form of text, pictures, musical scores, tapes, equipment, and computer software, etc. In many cases the materials will already exist having been published and manufactured as discussed above, and are subject to the same copyright legislation. In such cases either the institution or student buy copies of the original or authorised copies of originals. Some materials may not be available because consent to reproduce them may have been withheld. Important questions arise about the ownership of copyright when lecturers produce the materials for an open or distance learning package run by a college. Who should be entitled to profit from the commercial value of the materials when they are sold to, say, students or to another college desirous of running the same course? This is not a new issue and has been contentious since the initiation of the Open University.

9 The answers to these kinds of question will hinge on the character of the lecturer's contract which establishes the employment relationship and on the character of the exploitation of the commercial products. These questions will sharpen as open learning grows. At first sight there appears to be a direct analogy with the work undertaken by a lecturer who publishes a text on any subject. Although the text may have been developed within working time to which the employer is entitled and, indeed, it may be the subject of a lecture series largely produced during 'preparation time' as set out in the Silver Book (See **2.5**), there is never contention that the copyright or any other rights in the text should be the property of the employer. In the case of open or distance learning, it may be argued that there is a difference in that materials which are the property of the employer are used in the preparation of the materials. In that respect, the employer may have a position analogous to a commercial publisher where the costs involved are recovered (if the operation is commercially viable) in the commercial sale or hire of the materials. This does not, and should not, have any impact on the ownership of copyright. Broadly the same consideration applies to the involvement of, say, technicians in the process.

10 *Possible changes in copyright*

It has been widely recognised that the present copyright arrangements are inadequate for the new technical circumstances and for the needs of education. In 1986 the Government published a White Paper *Intellectual Property and Innovation* upon which legislation was to be based. The dissolution of Parliament in May 1987 has delayed the process but the Government intends to introduce legislation. Whilst it appears likely that there will be important revision to the law as it concerns education, the proposals do not change the basic structure of ownership of copyright.

11 The Council for Educational Technology has been developing a potential Private Members' Bill in this general area. Essentially, it would provide that the restrictions in education be significantly loosened. Where a voluntary licensing scheme for copying printed matter is in operation there would be a statutory obligation on the licensor to make a provision in the scheme which indemnifies the licensee against infringement actions in relation to copying works in any category covered by the licence but whose copyright owners are not members of the scheme. Where owners of rights do not offer a licensing scheme to education and training establishments, these establishments would have a right to copy up to ten per cent of a work per year. Off-air recording of all broadcast material would be permitted where recordings are for further copying and playback for educational purposes, and direct copying of audio material will be permitted for educational and training purposes. There would, of necessity, be a system for resolving disputes (a Copyright Tribunal) – for whilst such proposals will commend themselves to educational establishments who find the present system too restrictive, they would represent a most serious threat to the owners of rights. It is probable that there would be significant conflict with organisations like the Writers' Guild of Great Britain. Additionally, Council for Educational Technology proposals for a negotiated fee or lump sum payment for the production of open or distance learning materials, with the LEA or college owning copyright, would be likely to constitute a considerable infringement of the commercial rights of authors of such materials.

APPENDIX 5

THE DATA PROTECTION ACT

1 The Data Protection Act 1984 was intended to regulate the use of personal information held on computers in England (including the Channel Islands), Wales, and Northern Ireland. It provided that personal data held on computers has to be registered, to be accurate and relevant. This reflects a growing concern for privacy and a growing anxiety about the data handling capacity of new technologies. 'Personal data' is information relating to a living individual who can be identified from it or a combination of such data and other information held by the person using the data, the 'data user'. The Act also provided that data cannot be disclosed other than in specified circumstances either wholly or in extracts without the consent of the person to whom it relates. That person may check it on request. Further and higher education institutions typically hold a considerable amount of personal data and although the Act was not written with such institutions in mind, it has important ramifications for them.

2 The Act established the office of the Data Protection Registrar whose responsibilities and powers are central to its operation. The Registrar's duties include promoting the observance of eight data protection principles set out in Schedule 1 of the legislation. These are:

(i) The information to be lodged in personal data files must be obtained and processed fairly and lawfully.
(ii) Personal data should be held for one or more specified, lawful purposes.
(iii) Personal data held for any purposes shall not be used or disclosed in any manner incompatible with such purposes.
(iv) Personal data held for any purpose shall be adequate, relevant, and not excessive in relation to the specific purpose.
(v) Personal data must be accurate and, where necessary, kept up to date.
(vi) Personal data held for any purpose shall not be kept for any longer than is needed for such purposes.
(vii) An individual is entitled at reasonable intervals and without the imposition of unreasonable barriers to be informed of what personal data is held by data users of which the individual is subject, and to have access to the data. The individual can, where appropriate, have the data corrected or erased. To understand this principle, it is necessary to note that data users are those who hold and control data which is in a form suitable for processing or reprocessing.
(viii) Appropriate security measures shall be taken to prevent unauthorised access to, alteration of, disclosure or destruction of personal data, and the measures should take account of the accidental possibilities of such occurrences.

The Registrar's function includes consideration of complaints in respect of these matters made by data subjects, making random checks on data users and bureaux (persons or organisations providing computing services for others, for example, processing data), disseminating information about the Act to the public, encouraging the development of codes of practice, and providing an annual report and financial statement.

3 The Registrar also has important powers including the issuing of enforcement notices to secure compliance with the data protection principles, issuing transfer prohibition notices to prevent data users moving data to locations outside the UK, and powers of entry and inspection if a warrant has been obtained from a circuit judge.

4 The most potent power is to set aside registration of a person or corporate body as a 'data user' because the process of registration is central to the operation of the Act and central to users if they wish to continue to use data. Organisations or individuals holding computerised data were given six months from 11 November 1985 in which to register as data users. Thereafter it became a criminal offence to hold unregistered data or to use registered data for purposes other than those set out in the register. As new users and uses of data appear, there are new registrations. Thus registration is a major issue and deregistration a major power of intervention. Data users can face penalties short of deregistration including the enforcement of modifications to the kinds of data held. The

Act establishes a Tribunal appeal procedure against the decisions of the Registrar either in respect of deregistration or any other notices served. The Home Secretary has issued Rules for appeals, *The Data Protection Tribunal Rules, 1985*. There are further (Home Office 1985) rights to appeal from Tribunal decisions to the Higher Court. Data subjects have no rights of appeal to the Tribunal or beyond.

5 The registration must include:

(i) The name and address of the data user.
(ii) A description of the personal data held and a statement of the purposes for which it is held.
(iii) A description of the sources from which it was obtained and the persons to whom it may be disclosed.
(iv) The name of any country to which it might be transferred.
(v) The name and address of the person responsible for handling requests for access from individuals who are data subjects.

Once registration has been made it is an offence for a data user to act outside the terms of the registration and these terms must be sufficiently specific in the application for the Registrar to feel confident of the purposes of the data and that there is adherence to the principles. Thus it is important to make satisfactory registrations. The forms used for registration applications are Forms DPR1, Parts A and B. The first Part has to be completed by anyone registering and submitted with a fee of £22. In completing the detailed Part B, applicants are advised to use the standard 'purposes' descriptions provided as a template by the Registrar. Once the forms have been received, the Registrar has up to six months to announce acceptance or refusal. In reality it should take a far shorter time. Registration is initially for three years and renewal applications will only be made within the last six months of the initial registration period.

6 Some matters are exempt from registration provided that exempted materials are not later used for another purpose or disclosed. With these caveats in mind, payrolls, pensions, and accounting data are exempt. But where other data like gross pay, tax data, personal tax codes, national insurance record numbers, sickness records, disciplinary information, or other matters are kept in the same file, it will be assumed that the general purpose of the file is wider than payroll or pensions and must therefore be registered. It is likely that LEAs and individual institutions have not, by and large, sought exemptions in respect of employee files.

7 *Criminal offences*

In the Committee Stage of the Bill, the Home Secretary stated that 'the Registrar is in effect the guardian of the data subject's rights or, perhaps, a data protection ombudsman. . . . [I]t would be for him to uphold their rights by taking whatever action is appropriate, bearing in mind always his duty to promote observance of the principles'. If promotion fails or powers are disregarded, the Act gives scope for criminal prosecution to secure the Home Secretary's purposes. The Registrar can proceed to criminal prosecution in the Crown or Magistrates' Courts. For example, holding personal data without registering is a criminal offence for which there is no defence. Failure to comply with a notice is also an offence although it may be defensible on grounds that the user claims to have exercised all due diligence to comply. Whichever offence, a conviction may give rise to an unlimited fine in a Crown Court (limited to £2,000 in a Magistrates' Court). The courts can order the forfeiture, destruction, or erasure of data files. It is important to note that all criminal offences of this kind render individuals as well as corporate bodies liable.

8 *Access to data*

Individuals have a right to access to data under the Act on the following bases:

(i) To access personal data about themselves.
(ii) To seek compensation for damage suffered as a result of inaccurate data.
(iii) To seek compensation where personal data are lost or there has been unauthorised access.
(iv) A limited right to have inaccurate data corrected or erased.

(v) A limited right to seek erasure of data where unauthorised access has occurred and where disclosure may be repeated.

However, these rights do not produce automatic obligations on data users who are entitled to:

(vi) Be satisfied that the person making the request is indeed the data subject.
(vii) See the request in writing.
(viii) Ensure that disclosing the information does not have the effect of disclosing information about other, identifiable individuals.
(ix) Receive an appropriate fee with the request.
(x) Resist unreasonably frequent requests.

When data users do comply, as they generally should and will in practice, they must do so within 40 days. In education, there is an extension to five months in the case of requests to see examination results made prior to their public announcement, or to the end of a 40 day period from the date of the announcement, whichever is the earlier.

9 *Exemptions from subject access*

There are a number of exemptions limiting access. Domestic users in respect of their family or household affairs, non-personal data users – typically, historical, statistical or research data, corporate information and manual data are all exempt. So is personal data held for the following purposes:

(i) Safeguarding national security.
(ii) Prevention and detection of crime.
(iii) Apprehension and prosecution of offenders.
(iv) Assessment and collection of any taxes and duties.
(v) Payroll, pensions and accounting data (see Paragraph 6, above).
(vi) Statutory regulation of financial services.
(vii) Judicial appointments.
(viii) Legal cases where a claim of professional, legal privilege would apply.
(ix) Certain kinds of health and safety work.
(x) Data held by an unincorporated organisation, like a membership club where the data related exclusively to the club members.
(xi) Distribution lists (e.g. magazines) where the data subjects have agreed to listing.
(xii) Data in relation to which there is a statutory requirement to make the data available to the public.

There is a modification in respect of sensitive data such as that relating to racial origins, political beliefs, health, and criminal convictions.

10 However, despite these exemptions it should be understood that the Act takes a broad view of data to which there should be access and it does not exclude non-factual data. Thus, personal data may include 'soft data' about opinions, assessments of personal creditworthiness, appearance, promotion prospects, references and other opinions of third parties. It should be noted that information about the data user's intentions in respect of a data subject are not covered by the access provisions of the Act. Consequently, for example, a statement that a person is a 'very bad lecturer' would be covered and subject to access, whereas a statement that the LEA intends to dismiss the lecturer at the first available opportunity would not be covered by rights of access.

11 *Non-disclosure of information to others*

Data users may not disclose personal information to others without the consent of the subject of the data although even this protection is seriously circumscribed. Obviously it is not a restriction if individuals agree to disclosure, but they cannot prevent disclosure to any employee or agent of their employer who needs access to the information in order to carry out contractual functions. Equally, disclosure can be made to assist the prevention or detection of crimes, the apprehension or prosecution of offenders, the assessment or collection of taxes or duties, and where the information is required under any enactment, court order, or in the course of seeking legal advice or during legal proceedings in which the person making the disclosure is a party or witness.

12 *Further and higher education*
The full scope of the Act has widespread implications for further and higher education and it is prudent to identify the main areas in which careful compliance is needed. First, the LEAs and colleges will need to take an inventory of what personal data is being kept and used by their employees. It may pose a considerable task to discover all such materials. Some data are obvious – staff and student records, and client records (marketing). But in an organisation as complex as a college, it is likely that some students will keep records in respect of student activities, as will individual clubs. Unofficial data records may abound. A careful survey is needed to establish what data are held, what its sources are, and to whom it may be disclosed. Model questionnaires have been developed to assist this exercise (See Howard 1985).

13 Second, LEAs and institutions need to agree who is to respond to the registration provisions. Practice varies at present, and research by one of the authors (Scribbins 1986) shows some highly centralised systems of response and information dissemination (e.g. Avon and Wakefield) and some where responses have been left to individual colleges whether by policy or neglect of a policy. In respect of personal records, the Institute of Personnel Management suggests that the following steps be taken:
(i) Appointment of a data protection coordinator.
(ii) Establishment of a data protection committee.
(iii) Conduct of a data audit.
(iv) Development of a data protection policy.

14 Third, the written policy statement needs to cover a number of items including what data will be collected and why, what measures exist to ensure privacy and security, who is to make use of the data within any organisation, what subject access there should be, how external access should be managed and, finally, what measures exist to enforce policy in these areas. Within these areas, policy formulators will need to judge the balance between open access areas, which tend to decrease security, and strictly controlled subject access requirements. It is prudent to insist on written applications for access. Any fee needs to be decided in the light of the work needed to afford access and determined by where the policy is pitched on the open–closed continuum: the need for strict identification procedures; protection of third parties; as well as reasonableness of the sum charged in all these circumstances.

15 It is important to recognise that the security issue has become increasingly complex as networking technology has improved. Not only do large (mainframe) computers have multiple access points (a number of work stations) but it is common for a number of smaller machines, either mini-mainframes or micros, to be linked with the mainframe and with each other in a 'ring'. Thus, micros can be used either as free-standing 'intelligent' machines holding data in their own memories or on floppy discs, or as 'dumb terminals' linked to the mainframe with the potential to access the files in its memory. Indeed, the progress of networking technology has made it possible and commonplace to connect remote micros along telephone lines and this will become still easier with the advent of optic fibre and satellite connection. A large number of people may be able to gain access to computers in LEAs or colleges by these means, particularly in institutions where these technologies are being developed for teaching and research purposes and where the data is stored on the same central computers. Ability to access a computer does not automatically mean that files held within it can be easily entered if they are sensibly protected by access codes. However, no protection is perfect including mainframes used in defence establishments or the Duke of Edinburgh's personal electronic mail box. Therefore effort will be needed to maximise security. For this reason, it would be important to ensure that any data protection committee had the advice of a competent systems analyst.

16 Fourth, the general policy issues surrounding disclosure also provide a continuum of choices. Between registering every disclosure and always seeking the data subject's permission there need to be found compromises of a practical kind. They may be pragmatically based on a classification of sensitivity of data. Thus, disclosure of less sensitive

data would be simply registered whilst disclosure of more sensitive data would require subject permission.

17 Fifth, on training, the LEAs and institutions show variations of approach. A summary of good practice is provided in Scribbins (1986). It involves

(i) Running an awareness campaign;
(ii) Using payslip or pay packet notices to state policy and employee obligations;
(iii) Having a data protection notice board;
(iv) Including references in the staff handbook;
(v) Producing data protection newsletters;
(vi) Operating cascade training, open learning and programmed learning in this area.

18 Sixth, those responsible for registration will need to decide the breadth of the specified purposes they need to register. The Institute of Personnel Management state 'on the one hand, a simple Part A [of the Registration Form] can be submitted with any number of Part Bs in order to describe all the purposes for which data are held throughout the organisation (simple registration). On the other hand, organisations may sub-divide their register entry for administrative convenience and submit a separate Part A, and for each division, function, or location attaching to each Part A particulars of the data processing in that division, function, or location on relevant Part Bs'. Some institutions in further and higher education including the voluntary colleges, the five Inner London Polytechnics, and private colleges would have to make their own submissions as distinct legal entities; in the event that other institutions become legally separate from LEAs, they also would have to make their own submissions (See above Appendix 1).

19 Finally, it should be noted that trade unions are equally within the scope of the Act. As organisations they typically maintain records and, by virtue of the ballot requirements in the Trade Union Act 1984, they must keep up-to-date membership records which the Trade Union Act recognises will usually be on computer. The general provisions of the legislation all apply. Because it has become commonplace for local organisation units, such as union branches, to own or have access to micros, it would be wise for unions to make a careful assessment of the personal data held locally as well as nationally to be entered on the Part B Forms. In any case, it is unlikely that any central disclaimer for responsibility under the Act in respect of local operations would be an adequate defence from either notices served by the Registrar or legal actions.

1.3 FINANCE

1 Total expenditure on education in England, Wales and Northern Ireland in 1986–87 was £17.39 bn (£1 bn = £1,000 m). This relates to both capital and current expenditure and includes all aspects of provision from nursery schools to polytechnics and universities, as well as voluntary and direct grant colleges and the research councils. Of this figure £15.95 bn came either directly or indirectly under the control of the Department of Education and Science (DES). Further disaggregation is problematic given the format of presentation of published figures. However, it appears that of the DES total some £4.6 bn or 29% is devoted to further and higher education provision.

2 In common with many other services relying on public finance, education has been subject to financial constraint in recent years and has had to compete with other services for resources. Real terms expenditure on education (i.e. after the effects of inflation have been removed) has fallen both absolutely and as a proportion of total public expenditure, although recent planning figures suggest this trend is to be reversed and limited growth to be permitted. However, the achievement of these plans is heavily dependent on a number of factors, not least of which is the success of the Government's privatisation programme. This is designed to achieve income of approximately £4.5 bn per year between 1986–87 and 1989–90 compared to £2.7 bn in 1985–86. Should this or other objectives not be achieved then the planned growth in education expenditure may not materialise. Table 1 describes the position.

Table 1
Cash and Real Terms Expenditure on Education 1981–82 to 1989–90 (£m)

	Total Public Expenditure		*Total Education Expenditure*		*Education Expenditure*
Year	*Cash*	*Real terms[1]*	*Cash*	*Real terms[1]*	*As % of total*
1981–82	120,131	148,787	11,841	14,666	9.9
1982–83	132,578	153,128	12,750	14,726	9.6
1983–84	140,248	155,022	13,433	14,848	9.6
1984–85	150,006	159,006	13,951	14,788	9.3
1985–86[2]	158,489	158,489	14,479	14,479	9.1
1986–87[3]	164,400	159,900	15,954	15,513	9.7
1987–88[4]	173,700	162,800	16,604	15,566	9.6
1988–89	179,600	162,700	17,350	15,720	9.7
1989–90	187,800	165,200	17,840	15,690	9.5

Source: The Government's Expenditure Plans 1987–88 to 1989–90, vol. II; Cm 56 – II; Treasury, 1987.

NB: [1]These figures have been adjusted to 1985–86 price levels. [2]Figures up to and including 1985–86 are actual expenditure. [3]Estimated expenditure. [4]For 1987–88 and subsequent years all figures represent planned expenditure only.

3 The planning and control of both the volume and distribution of educational expenditure occurs at four broad levels. Central government is responsible for

decisions on aggregate financial planning and, principally through the operation of the rate support grant (RSG), the distribution of financial resources to local authorities. The University Grants Committee (UGC) and the National Advisory Body for Public Sector Higher Education (NAB) determine the distribution of resources, respectively, to the universities and public sector institutions of higher education. Individual local authorities are then free, within prescribed limits, to allocate resources to educational institutions and providers of other services. Finally, individual institutions determine the detailed apportionment to faculties, departments and courses within the constraints laid down at previous levels. The following section outlines some of the major features of the processes involved particularly where they are of significance for the management of further and higher education.

4 Statutory responsibility for the provision and maintenance of the greater part of the further and higher education system rests under the 1944 Education Act with the local authorities, who also provide the greater part of the sector's resources. In addition there are a number of voluntary and grant-aided colleges which are financed directly by the DES. Local authorities are heavily dependent on central Government grants, principally the rate support grant which in 1986 provided 46% of aggregate local government income. The Department of Education and Science (DES) makes only a small direct contribution to non-advanced further education finance, although central government does provide resources via other routes, most notably through the Manpower Services Commission (MSC). Polytechnics and colleges providing advanced courses receive income from their maintaining local authorities which, in the main, derives from the advanced further education (AFE) pool. Responsibility for decisions on the allocation of the AFE pool rests ultimately with the Secretary of State, although decisions are taken after advice from NAB. A further significant proportion of institutional finance is obtained from student fees, although the relative importance of fee income varies considerably between different types of institutions. Table 2 summarises the main sources of finance available in 1986–87.

Table 2
Sources of Further and Higher Education Income (Current Account), England and Wales, 1986–87 (£m)

DES	1,526
Local Authorities	2,773
Short Courses	6
Full Cost Courses	16
Industrial Training	4
Youth Training Scheme	54
MSC/Industrial Training Boards	120
Other	46
Total	4,545

Source: The Government's Expenditure Plans 1987–88 to 1989–90, Cmnd 56 – II, Treasury, January 1987, table 3.12; and Education Statistics – Estimates, CIPFA, 1987

5 Central government

Table 2 does not indicate the full significance of the influence or control of central government over educational expenditure which operate through three departments: the Treasury; the DES; and the Department of Environment (DoE). The major mechanisms involved are the annual rate support grant, the capital expenditure control system, and the AFE pool. An additional mechanism which applies in the AFE sector only is the provision of target student enrolments which operate at an institutional level and are designed, among other things, to exert downward pressure on unit costs (i.e. expenditure per student). All of these operate within the overriding constraints of relevant legislation and supporting circulars, administrative memoranda and regulations enacted by statutory instruments.

6 Constitutional control over Government expenditure rests with the House of Commons. In practice, however, the activities of the whips within the majority party in the House of Commons ensure that the financial priorities if not the fine details of Government expenditure plans are almost always realised. The procedure involved is known as the 'supply' procedure. This involves each spending department including the DES in an annual exercise of producing expenditure estimates for the following financial year for which Treasury approval must be sought. Submission of these estimates to the House of Commons for approval is made via a Treasury minister. This convention, among other things, prevents the submission of resolutions involving expenditure from individual MPs and thereby underlines the dominant role of the Treasury in financial policy matters. This Treasury power has been reinforced by developments in the system of public expenditure planning which was introduced following the publication of the Plowden Report (1961).

7 The major recommendation of Plowden was that, 'regular surveys should be made of public expenditure as a whole, over a period of years, ahead, and in relation to prospective resources; decisions involving substantial future expenditure should be taken in the light of these surveys'. Responsibility for the conduct of these surveys fell to an interdepartmental committee of senior civil servants known as the Public Expenditure Survey Committee; the entire process of public expenditure planning has now, somewhat inaccurately come to be known as the PESC process. The essential features of PESC are that it provides a purely factual assessment of the costs of the full range of policies and proposals being pursued by Government and its agencies (e.g. the MSC), local authorities, and nationalised industries. The survey covers both capital and current expenditure. PESC does not of itself provide authorisation to incur expenditure; rather its purpose is to inform the decisions on expenditure levels which are taken by the Chancellor of the Exchequer and subsequently in Cabinet by representatives of the various spending departments. Originally conceived as providing a medium-term planning horizon covering a five-year period, the scope of the PESC process has been gradually curtailed: current practice is for planning to cover only the coming year and two further years.

8 After Cabinet discussion and approval of spending plans a White Paper is published annually, usually around November, which describes the Government's expenditure plans over the coming period. The emphasis and criteria employed in arriving at these planning totals have changed considerably over the years as different economic views have gained ascendancy. Henley (1986) has identified six major criteria which have been employed:

(i) The expected growth rate of the national output (gross domestic product) was compared with the estimated growth of public expenditure, generally with the object of avoiding the latter exceeding the former.
(ii) An assessment was made of the demands of 'prior claims' on the national output – the resources required for productive investment and the balance of payments – and a view was taken of the desirable division of the remainder, itself the bulk of the total, between public expenditure and private consumption. This work centred on the 'medium-term economic assessment' and was essentially related to the use of resources in the economy rather than to financial objectives.
(iii) Linked to (ii), attention was concentrated on the implications for personal and company taxation of public expenditure plans, to see if prospective tax levels appeared acceptable or not.
(iv) The proportion of the national output likely to be taken by public expenditure was estimated, to enable Ministers to judge whether its growth rate was acceptable or excessive.
(v) The present Government has, since 1979, planned public expenditure within the context of a medium-term financial strategy. This places the main emphasis on control of certain monetary aggregates, which imply in turn a certain level of Government borrowing and thus, given the objective of reducing taxation, a certain level of public expenditure.
(vi) More recently, in addition to continuing concern for levels of taxation the Government's policy has been dominated by the importance it has attached to controlling public expenditure in cash rather than in volume or resource terms; and cutting down the size of the public sector.

The application of these differing criteria has been used by Heald (1983) to identify three distinct stages in the development of public expenditure planning:

(i) Pure volume planning (from 1961–62 to 1975–76) whereby annual adjustments were made to planning totals to compensate for changes in pay and prices;
(ii) Volume planning with cash limits (from 1976–77 to 1981–82) whereby an assessed amount for inflation was included within the planning figures with an absolute upper limit placed on expenditure within any given year, but then revised annually to take full account of inflation; and
(iii) Cash planning (from 1982–83 onwards) whereby an aggregate cash planning figure including inflation assumptions is employed but no adjustment introduced should these assumptions subsequently prove not to be realised.

Under cash planning therefore the effects of any shortfall in the inflation assumptions employed in one year are carried forward to future years and a cumulative effect produced. As Government assumptions on inflation have frequently proved to underestimate the true position local authorities have been required to find these lost resources from existing financial provision or, alternatively, to reduce spending. As such, cash limits provide a stricter and, from local authorities' point of view, considerably harsher control mechanism than cash limits or volume planning. An explanation of the underlying rationale and consequences of these changes would be lengthy and complex and is beyond the scope of this work. Discussion of these procedures and some of the issues involved can be found in Heald (1983) and Henley et al (1986). For present purposes it is sufficient to note that each of the changes has, among other things, accompanied attempts to control and reduce public expenditure and therefore to limit the resources available to providers of services, including education. Finally it should be noted that the planning process outlined above is circular: each set of expenditure plans forms the starting point for the next round of PESC. Changes in policies and priorities, as well as planned reductions in overall expenditure form the basis on which each annual review is undertaken.

9 While the PESC process determines the input of resources it makes no attempt to evaluate the quality of the services provided. A first attempt was made to confront this in the early 1970 with the introduction of a system known as Programme Analysis and Review (PAR). This set out to incorporate various techniques developed in private industry to evaluate the activities, organisation, objectives, alternative approaches to, and resource requirements of various Government programmes. It was envisaged at the time that this operation would become synchronized with PESC, though in the event this never occurred. For a variety of reasons PAR was gradually run down and finally abandoned in 1979. Of more current importance are the 'value-for-money' studies undertaken periodically by the Audit Commission and its agents. The operation of the Audit Commission and its work in further and higher education is discussed further (See below paragraphs 111–116).

10 The presentation of Treasury approved departmental estimates to the House of Commons takes place on Budget day. Statutory authority to incur expenditure is then provided by the Commons in the Consolidated Fund (Appropriation) Act. The estimates of each department are sub-divided into a number of separate headings or 'Votes', each of which requires separate approval. Of the 180–200 votes approved by the Commons in recent years twelve related to expenditure on Education and Science. However, these covered only a small proportion of total education expenditure, the remainder being covered by local authority expenditure administered by the DoE and covered by separate votes, the most important of which relate to the Rate Support Grant (RSG). RSG, while contributing a declining though major proportion of local government income (See below paragraph 16), is paid in an unhypothecated form, (i.e. its payment is not related to the cost or level of provision of individual services by local authorities). Nevertheless the financial constraints which have been imposed in recent years through the RSG have had a marked impact on the ability of local authorities to finance educational expenditure. The operation of the RSG is explained further in paragraphs 17 to 25.

11 **Local authority revenue expenditure**

Educational institutions in the public sector are maintained by local authorities who are therefore responsible for ensuring financial viability, though, as discussed in this section, considerable proportions of the funding of FE at all levels comes from other sources than local authority income.

12 Local authorities have three primary sources of income: fees and charges, rate income, and RSG. Of the three fees and charges realised some 12% of the total in 1986–87. Fees and charges are linked to the provision of particular services and are frequently not intended to cover costs.

13 Rates, which are the only substantial independent source of income available to local authorities, are a tax on the benefit of occupation of land and fixed assets, i.e. almost always buildings. For administrative convenience rates are not levied by all tiers of local government but only those adjudged as being

best placed to do so. In England and Wales those authorities which are not themselves rating authorities levy a rate on those which are. This practice is known as precepting. Under present arrangements rating authorities are the London boroughs (including the City of London), and metropolitan and county districts. Until 1 April 1986 precepting authorities were the Greater London Council (GLC), metropolitan and non-metropolitan county councils, parish councils in England, and community councils in Wales. Two further non-elected authorities in London, the ILEA and the Metropolitan Police Authority, were also empowered to precept on lower-tier authorities. Following the abolition of the GLC and the metropolitan counties the latter list has been considerably extended by the addition of the joint boards, residual bodies, etc, established to perform the functions previously exercised by the now defunct authorities.

14 The ability of a local authority to raise rate income is determined, in the first instance, by the size of its rate base. This in turn is determined by the distribution of domestic and non-domestic properties and by the size, type, age, etc of properties within its boundaries. Effectively each property within an authority must be individually assessed and assigned a rateable value in order that the cumulative rate base of an authority may be determined. Once a budget has been fixed by a local authority and all decisions taken on the revenue requirements (including precepts and balances) for the following financial year then the rate, referred to as a rate poundage and expressed as so many pence in the pound, can be fixed. This is achieved by dividing the total rate call by the cumulative rateable value of each individual property in order to arrive at the bill to be presented to each ratepayer. Because of the operation of the rate support grant domestic ratepayers are subject to a rate poundage which is 18.5p lower than that charged to commercial or industrial ratepayers.

15 **Rate Support Grant**

The rate support grant comprised 46.4% of local authority 'relevant expenditure' in 1986–87. A similar proportion is planned for 1987–88. RSG comprises three major elements: specific and supplementary grants, domestic rate relief grant, and block grant. Table 3 below shows the grant sums which were made available in 1986–87 as well as the Government's assessment of the aggregate level of expenditure which would be taken into account when setting grant allocations to individual authorities.

Table 3
Calculation of the Total of RSG 1987–88 (£ms)

1. Estimated Relevant Expenditure	27,746
2. Aggregate Exchequer Grant	12,842
3. Total of Specific and Supplementary Grants	3,293
4. Rate Support Grant (2–3)	9,549
5. Domestic Rate Relief Grant	717
6. Block Grant (4–5)	8,832

Source: Local Government Finance: The Rate Support Grant Report (England) 1987–88. Annex C, HMSO, 1987.

16 Detailed negotiations leading to the production of these figures takes place within a body known as the Consultative Council on Local Government Finance (CCLGF). This body, which has existed since 1975, is chaired by the Secretary of State for the Environment, who is supported by various Ministers or their representatives and senior civil servants from the eight Departments of State concerned with local government (the Treasury, the Departments of Environment, Education and Science, Health and Social Security, Transport, Employment, Trade and Industry and the Home Office). Local government is represented by selected representatives of the various local authority associations. The Council is served by an Official Steering Group, as well as a further tier of advisory groups each of which holds a remit to deal with a specialised area. This tier includes five expenditure steering groups including one which deals solely with education – the Expenditure Steering Group (Education) (ESGE). These latter groups, which are made up from senior officers from central and local government, attempt to assess likely expenditure levels for the current and coming year, the likely impact of changes in expenditure levels and the effects of changes in the mechanisms employed for the calculation of grant entitlements. Once agreed, expenditure figures are aggregated to arrive at the Relevant Expenditure figure referred to in Table 3 above. This includes all expenditure relevant for grant aid but excludes a small number of items, most notably Housing Benefit costs and, more importantly in this context, mandatory student awards, for which specific grants are available. Once the estimated Relevant Expenditure is agreed, the proportion to be met by grant is negotiated. This figure has been set at 46.4% in 1986–87 and 1987–89 although as recently as 1980–81 it was 60%. Again, as in Table 3, specific and supplementary grants (for expenditure on national parks, national transport, local authority housing subsidy, housing benefit, mandatory student awards etc.) are deducted to arrive at the RSG.

17 RSG comprises two elements: Domestic Rate Relief Grant and Block Grant. DRRG is designed to reduce the rate poundage levied on domestic ratepayers relative to non-domestic rate-payers. Its main purpose is to mitigate the regressive nature of domestic rates. The rate at which this element is paid can be varied from year to year although it has remained unaltered at 18.5p in the £ since its introduction in 1975–76. It has therefore been of decreasing value to domestic ratepayers since that time as overall rate poundages have risen considerably while no general revaluation of rateable values has been undertaken (outside of Scotland). Because entitlement to this element of grant is directly related to the number of domestic rate-payers in an area its yield can be predicted with a high degree of accuracy.

18 The second element of RSG is block grant. The objectives of the block grant system are to compensate for differences in needs and rateable resources between authorities and so discourage high levels of spending. To achieve this the grant is calculated in such a way as to enable authorities to provide comparable standards of service by levying similar rates in the pound. A single grant is paid to every authority. This form of block grant was established by the Local Government, Planning and Land Act 1980, although the rate support grant dates from 1958.

19 The mechanisms employed for the calculation of block grant entitlements are extremely complex and are not widely understood. (An introductory guide is provided by the ACC, 1987). Indeed, the DoE found it necessary at the end of 1986 to legalise the block grant calculations of previous years. Published mate-

rial which attempts to explain the workings of the block grant system frequently requires the inclusion of one or more appendices which define the technical vocabulary which has developed around the subject. In part this complexity reflects the diversity of the objectives which the system attempts to meet, but it also reflects the problems inherent in distributing over £8bn a year to hundreds of local authorities exercising different functions in enormously different circumstances.

20 The grant entitlement of any authority is most simply expressed as the difference between actual (relevant) expenditure and the product of a Government specified rate poundage, known as the grant related poundage (GRP), and the authority's rateable value. In order to discourage what the Government classifies as 'overspending', the GRP varies in line with total expenditure. It should be understood that 'overspending' in this context relates only to expenditure in excess of a notional and theoretical assessment by Government of the cost of providing a standard level of services in a way which attempts to have regard to the differences in circumstances and needs of different areas. This assessment is known as the grant-related expenditure (GRE).

21 In order to provide a disincentive to 'overspending', the GRP of an authority rises according to a standard tariff as expenditure rises above GRE. It is, however, recognised that the central assessment of spending need which GRE represents inevitably involves a measure of approximation. This is acknowledged by the establishment of a 'threshold' figure for each authority which is 10% higher than national average GRE per head. Above the threshold GRP rises more sharply than below and has the effect of increasing the *assumed* local contribution towards the cost of local services as expenditure rises. This is known as the 'taper'. There are separate schedules of GRP tariffs for each class of authority (i.e. Inner London Borough, Outer London Borough, Metropolitan District Council, etc.) which take account of differences in the functions exercised by each.

22 A further element in the block grant calculation is known as the 'multiplier'. Multipliers are designed to alter grant entitlement and are employed for a number of purposes, e.g. to allow London authorities to maintain some of the advantage of higher than average rateable values; to limit grant losses resulting from year on year changes in GRE methodology, (See paragraphs 24 and 25 below); and to reduce grant gains. Where multipliers are employed for more than one purpose these are combined to form a composite figure for each authority. The effect of a multiplier lower than one is to reduce the assumed local contribution towards the cost of services; a multiplier greater than one increases the assumed local contribution. As the assumed local contribution changes, so too does block grant entitlement.

23 Finally, the unusual circumstances which apply in London are recognised, London enjoys higher rateable values but also higher costs than elsewhere. If the standard block grant mechanisms were to apply to London then a large part of the rateable value advantage enjoyed by the capital would be lost. Traditionally London has been permitted to retain part of this advantage and this practice has been continued under the block grant regime by the use of a multiplier. Higher multipliers are employed for Inner than Outer London Boroughs in recognition of the higher costs of inner city provision. Also, the City of London and the City of Westminster enjoy considerable rateable value advantages over other boroughs. The London Rate Equalisation Scheme

requires these two authorities to make payments to all other London boroughs and thereby reduces the impact of disparities in rateable resources within the capital.

24 A number of bases are used by the DoE in assessing the cost of providing a 'standard' level of services as expressed by the GRE assigned to each authority. The first stage involves the establishment of five groups of indicators of spending needs. These are: population of client group including number of children under 5, number of non-advanced further education (NAFE) students and number of people aged 65 and over; physical features of the area, including size of the area served, sparceness of school population and number of non-domestic and domestic properties in the area; social and environmental problems, including special educational needs, youth unemployment and total unemployment; costs of providing services, including higher than normal costs in the London area in respect of salaries and the provision of particular services; and finally, special requirements of particular services, including expenditure on mandatory student awards, number of children under 5 considered to be 'at risk' and the costs of meeting debt charges arising from earlier capital investment financed by borrowing. In 1986–87 a total of 68 main indicators were employed although many of these were subdivided to produce further groups of indicators.

25 These indicators are then applied, as appropriate, to the provision of individual services and the sums of money attached to each form the basis of GRE calculations for each authority. Hence, for example, the relevant figure for adult education would be built up from indicators of people aged 18 to 64, people aged 65 and over and, where appropriate, higher costs in and around London. In 1985–86 the total GRE for expenditure on education, arts and libraries, which is treated as a single block, was somewhat over £11bn or 52% of the total expenditure on all services by local authorities for which the Government had planned. At this expenditure level the education service was, and remains, far and away the largest of all services provided by local authorities. It should, nevertheless, be noted throughout that the great majority of local authorities are free to determine their own expenditure levels and, while they may choose to pay regard to Government expenditure guidance there is usually no compulsion for them to do so. Hence actual local authority expenditure, either on education or in total is not tied to Government planning targets. Unfortunately a number of definitional problems arise when trying to compare Government planning figures, as expressed in the aggregate education GRE, with published actual expenditure figures. In consequence it is not possible to say with any degree of certainty how these figures compare. It should be remembered, however, that block grant allocations, while paying regard to the notional costs of individual services, are paid in an unhypothecated form rather than towards the costs of specific services. Indeed it is only since 1981 that details of the education GREs have been publicly available, and since 1983 that information on all services GREs could be obtained. In a research report on LEA responses to block grant Crispin and Marslen-Wilson (1984) found that '. . . education service GREs were largely ignored by both officers and members', during the process of budget preparation.

26 Some local authorities are no longer free to determine their own overall expenditure figures: these authorities have been rate-capped. Rate-capping was introduced by the Rates Act 1984 and may operate in either of two ways: selectively or generally. Selective rate limitation means that individual

authorities are assigned an upper spending limit for a financial year by the Secretary of State for the Environment. As well as limiting total expenditure this translates into a maximum rate levy. The alternative general rate limitation scheme, which has not been invoked to date, permits a limit to be placed on the rates of every authority in England. In 1985–86 eighteen local authorities were rate-capped; in 1987–88 the figure is forty, although this includes the twenty authorities subject to automatic control as replacement bodies for the now abolished Greater London Council and the six Metropolitan County Councils.

27 Clearly this inability to determine local expenditure levels among rate-capped authorities is of major importance when decisions are being made on levels of service provision. As the major consumer of revenue the education service is particularly liable to the impact of reductions which can be manifested in such things as tightening of student–staff ratios, reductions in support staff levels, cuts in library expenditure and in a number of other ways.

28 **Education Support Grants**

An extension of the Government's power to control the extent and direction of educational expenditure was contained in the Education (Grants and Awards) Act 1984, which introduced Education Support Grants (ESGs). These grants are paid direct to local authorities at the discretion of the Secretary of State for Education and Science in respect of particular activities considered to be of strategic importance. Grant is payable at the rate of 70% of approved expenditure, though in May 1987 the Secretary of State proposed that some would be paid at 50%. As such they may be viewed as being analogous to the specific grants contained within RSG.

29 The first ESGs were paid in 1985–86 and amounted to some £21m; total ESG-aided expenditure for the year was £30m. In 1986–87 planned ESG had risen to £28m and total expenditure to £40m. Originally twelve activities were designated as eligible for ESG support although this was subsequently increased (in 1986) to sixteen. These activities were '. . . chosen to improve the efficiency and effectiveness of the education service in responding to changing needs' (Treasury 1986a). This increasing concern by Government with the coordination and deployment of education resources and corresponding lack of confidence in LEA ability or willingness to adapt to changing circumstances is reflected in the decision to increase the level of ESG payable. Thus, the change has the effect of diminishing the level of control of LEAs over resources while simultaneously increasing the direct influence of the Secretary of State over the deployment of resources and the priorities which this reflects. Under the original 1984 Act, aggregate expenditure on activities supported by ESG was limited to 0.5% of relevant expenditure on education (as defined for RSG purposes); the Education (Amendment) Act, 1986 increased this figure to 1.0%.

30 The sixteen areas designated as eligible for ESG support covered a broad range of educational activities and all stages of provision. Of these, six related to further education: the provision of retraining and updating courses directed towards the needs of industry and commerce (PICKUP) (See **3.1** 66); development of the use of information technology at FE colleges by the provision of computer hardware, programmes and staff training; educational provision and guidance for the unemployed; provision of management information systems for FE colleges including hardware, software and staff training; provi-

sion of computerised learning aids at FE colleges for students with special educational needs; and the employment of staff to strengthen links between FE colleges and employers in order to improve the quality and relevance of courses.

31 For 1988–89 five themes were planned for new starts which included three activities for FE: curriculum and support for unemployed people, 'learning by achievement' for youth, open learning and computer-aided learning; information technology; and management information.

32 **Specific grants**

Other than ESG, the major form of specific grant available to the education service is for mandatory student awards. For such awards payable to students on 'designated' courses 90% of the cost is recoverable by LEAs from the DES; the remainder must be found from local resources. In addition, further grants of relevance to the education service can be obtained via the Urban Programme and for Commonwealth immigrants. The Urban programme was established by the Local Government Grants (Social Need) Act 1969. For approved capital and current expenditure 75% of the cost is recoverable on such things as nursery provision, play and advice centres, youth and community facilities, and the costs of materials and equipment including educational supplies. Organised on an inter-departmental basis, the role of lead department originally fell to the Home Office but in 1977 was switched to the DoE. The DES has been a supporting department throughout. Limited financial support is available for educational provision for Commonwealth immigrants via Section 11 of the Local Government Act 1966. This provides grants of up to 75% of staff costs directly associated with educational provision in areas containing '. . . substantial numbers of immigrants from the Commonwealth whose language or customs differ from those of the community'. While the grant is payable in a wide range of circumstances, perhaps the most important in terms of F and HE is in respect of special access courses. These courses which are conducted in FE colleges are designed to facilitate direct entry to professional and other HE courses for men and women from ethnic minorities lacking the normal entry requirements of HE.

33 **Capital expenditure**

Money spent by local authorities is classified into two broad categories: capital and current expenditure. Current expenditure can be broadly defined as that which relates to day-to-day operating expenses, e.g. salaries and wages, heating, lighting and water, and repairs and maintenance, which provide benefits within a year. Capital expenditure, alternatively, relates to the creation of tangible assets such as houses, schools, and roads which provide services over an extended period. Current expenditure must normally be financed from current income. Borrowing to finance current expenditure is only permitted in very limited and legally prescribed circumstances. Capital expenditure is normally financed by borrowing although other forms of finance may also be employed: capital receipts from the sale of assets; trading profits and revenue income. Leasing arrangements as an alternative to the purchase of capital assets have also become increasingly common in recent years. A third category of expenditure known as revenue expenditure combines current expenditure with the financing costs of capital expenditure (i.e. interest charges and repayments of principal). Thus revenue expenditure relates to total outgoings. In practice the distinction between capital and current expenditure is often extremely blurred at the margin (e.g. on major repair projects).

34 The planning and control mechanisms employed for local authority capital expenditure are contained in Part VIII of the Local Government, Planning and Land Act 1980. The system has been in operation since 1981–82. Prior to this date control was exercised through a system of loan sanction, i.e. permission to borrow. The post-1980 system operates a national cash limit on capital investment. The major difference between the two systems is that previously capital investment financed from sources other than borrowing could be undertaken at the discretion of the local authorities, while since 1980 total investment falls within the ambit of the control system.

35 The basis of control is 'prescribed expenditure'. At the time the legislation was initially drafted it was intended that prescribed expenditure should encompass total local authority capital investment. In the event, and as a result of considerable pressure from a range of sources, a number of exclusions were introduced: leaseholds of under 20 years; expenditure on individual items costing less than £6,000; and expenditure on police services. Nevertheless while these items fall outside of the main stream of the control system, some are taken into account when the size of national cash limit is fixed.

36 Local authorities undertake capital investment on diverse services and it is these services which form the basis of the allocation process. Authorities bid for and receive capital spending allocations in respect of five service blocks: housing, education, transport, social services, and other services. Bids are submitted to the relevant departments of State although the DoE, as the major department in local government matters, adopts the role of coordinator and clearing house. The allocations when received are not cash payments but authorisations to spend. Nominally authorities are free to combine allocations from all five blocks to dispose of as they see fit. In practice, there are strong pressures for them not to do this, for, as Holtham (1986) put it, 'Though this flexibility (to transfer or "vire" allocations between blocks) works at the margin . . . each block falls under the purview of a different central government department and they can feel that it is necessary to "protect their block". It is certainly not unknown for representatives of one particular central government department to warn authorities that if they transfer allocations out of "their" block the authorities will lose allocations in the following year'.

37 Allocations may be supplemented in a number of ways by:-

(i) Application of a prescribed proportion of capital receipts arising from the disposal of assets ie. principally though not exclusively from the sale of council houses;
(ii) Carrying forward of underspend from previous years or by the anticipation of the following year's allocation, up to a limit of 10%;
(iii) Obtaining transfers from the allocation(s) of other authorities; and
(iv) Employing any profits arising from trading undertakings.

38 The actual operation of these controls is extremely complex and subject to change over time, e.g. in the proportion of capital receipts which may be employed. Substantial differences of opinion and interpretation have also been advanced concerning such things as the appropriate or permissible source of finance for spending in respect of the 10% tolerance. The greatest uncertainty, however, arises because of the volatility and hence unpredictability of capital receipts accruing mainly from council house sales. In 1982, for example, capital receipts from the disposal of council housing in the UK amounted to £2,035m; in 1985 this had fallen back to £1,245m (Treasury 1986b).

39 The confusion and uncertainty which this situation engendered among local authority financial managers resulted in considerable underspending of the national cash limit during the first two years of operation of the system. This in turn led to the curious situation of the Secretary of State issuing annual exhortation to the local authorities to increase their planned levels of capital investment while simultaneously attempting to reduce the cash limit. Since 1983–84, however, increasing experience of the scheme has led to a reversal of this trend and overspending of the cash limit has resulted each year. In 1986–87 overspend was approximately £500 m (Treasury 1987, paragraph 4.13).

40 The Government's intention in introducing this system was to reduce the level of detailed control over individual investment schemes while simultaneously increasing control over aggregate spending. Broadly these twin aims have been met although many in local government would argue that the present project control mechanisms remain unnecessarily restrictive. The emphasis on aggregate control, however, formed a major plank of the Conservative Government's policy to reduce public expenditure and capital expenditure has undoubtedly borne a large part of spending cuts in recent years. In 1980–81, the year prior to the introduction of the new system, total capital expenditure by local authorities in England was £3,515m; the planned figure for 1986–87 was £2,652m. The corresponding figures for capital expenditure on education are £472m and £308m a reduction of 35%. It should be borne in mind that these are cash figures and contain no allowance for the effects of inflation.

41 The inadequacies and uncertainties inherent in these arrangements have been acknowledged by Government and proposals have been put forward for change (DoE 1986). The preferred approach is to move from control of net expenditure (i.e. total expenditure minus the items listed in paragraph 36 above) to control of gross spending. This would create greater certainty for local authorities in planning investment programmes by removing doubts about the level of capital receipts and other income available for reinvestment. Nevertheless, it would mark a further centralisation of control of spending decisions and loss of local authority autonomy. The results of a review of the system of capital controls were expected to be published soon at time of writing.

42 **Recoupment**

Recoupment is a procedure whereby the costs of providing primary, secondary or further education for students normally resident outside of an LEA can be transferred to the students' home authorities. The statutory basis for recoupment is provided by Section 51 of the Education (No. 2) Act 1986. This requires that recoupment rates be established either by agreement between LEAs or, failing this, as directed by the Secretary of State. The purpose of this was to remove the discretion previously enjoyed by LEAs to reject standard rates as recommended by the Local Education Authorities' Inter Authorities Payments Committee (IAPC) and to set their own rates. The previous system had the effect of excluding some potential students from courses provided by LEAs charging above IAPC rates, where the maintaining authority was only prepared to pay at the standard rate. The reserve power given to the Secretary of State is designed to require enforcement of the standard. The rates as recommended by the IAPC for 1986–87 and 1987–88 are shown in Table 4. The 1986 Act thus extended the automatic recoupment of tuition costs and 'free trade' across England and Wales.

Table 4
Recoupment Rates 1986–87 and 1987–88 (£/hour)

Burnham Category	Inner London	Out London	London Fringe	Rest of England/Wales
		1986–87		
II/III	3.50	3.40	3.29	3.21
IV	2.14	2.07	2.00	1.95
V	1.83	1.76	1.69	1.64
		1987–88		
II/III	3.63	3.51	3.38	3.29
IV	2.34	2.26	2.16	2.10
V	1.96	1.87	1.78	1.72

Source: IAPC letter 1/1987

Note: These rates are payable on the basis of imputed course hours, calculated on a formula basis, irrespective of actual attendance.

43 **NAFE**
In the financing of further and higher education in the public sector, a distinction has been drawn between advanced (AFE) and non-advanced FE (NAFE). While both levels of work are provided by institutions maintained by local authorities different financial arrangements apply to each. Broadly speaking finance of NAFE is the responsibility of each local authority, whereas AFE or public section higher education (PSHE) is seen as having a regional and national role and therefore the financial responsibility has been shared among all LEAs collectively. AFE or PSHE relies primarily on a system of national pooling of costs, the operation of which is described below.

44 A major development in both the control and financing of NAFE was announced by the Government in the White Paper *Training for Jobs* (1984). This document laid out the Government's strategy for improving skills training among school-leavers and for easing the transition from full-time education to work. It was argued that the strategy demanded that '. . . public sector provision for training and vocational education must become more responsive to employment needs at national and local level'. In order to achieve this it was decided to increase and expand the role of the Manpower Services Commission (MSC) in the provision of work-related NAFE. In 1984 total expenditure on NAFE in England and Wales was approximately £1.2 bn of which some £800m was deemed work-related. At the same time MSC expenditure was £90m per annum. Between 1983–84 and 1986–87 MSC expenditure was to increase to £200m so as to account for 25% of work-related NAFE provision. Consequent reductions in LEA provision were introduced via the RSG. (See **1.7**).

45 This switch in the control of finance had a number of quite major implications. The earlier bipartite links between FE colleges and their maintaining authorities were, in many cases, effectively replaced by a tripartite arrange-

ment involving the college, the LEA, and the MSC. While colleges continued to be the major providers of FE, the emphasis of the MSC on serving the needs of the labour market required the introduction of planning and coordination of provision which had previously not been deemed necessary. Three year rolling development plans were drawn up by each LEA in consultation with the colleges, the MSC and other interested parties, supplemented by more detailed one year programmes of provision. Also the basis on which financial provision was made by the MSC introduced an element of commercialism which had previously been lacking. The White Paper referred to this as the 'purchase' of work-related NAFE provision by the Commission (White Paper 1984, paragraph 45). For many LEAs the increased role of the MSC coupled with corresponding reductions in their own resources led to the setting of targets for colleges for the achievement of MSC and other income.

46 **AFE**

The funding system for advanced further education (AFE) is distinct from that for NAFE. Since 1959 it has relied mainly on a system of national pooling of costs. A maintained college providing 100% advanced level work would have access to three main sources of revenue: the various national pools (principally the AFE pool), student fees and, possibly, a local authority contribution commonly referred to as 'topping-up'. A college providing both advanced and non-advanced work would have additional local authority funding for the latter. Although AFE has been funded largely from national pools, overall responsibility for the maintenance of institutions remained with the local authority. The AFE-NAFE split led to confusion for institutions and authorities in differentiating between the resources made available in respect of each. Problems were also faced by some polytechnics and other major institutions, principally or solely providing advanced courses, in that local authorities, themselves subject to tighter financial constraints, have reduced or removed the financial contribution on which many institutions have relied.

47 In April 1987 the Government announced in its White Paper *Higher Education: Meeting the Challenge* a new way of funding AFE or higher education in public sector institutions. It committed the Government to introducing legislation to remove from LEAs the polytechnics and other colleges with a majority of their work in HE and to establish them as freestanding corporate bodies funded through the Polytechnics and Colleges Funding Council (PCFC). The White Paper proposed that the funding system should be a process of contracting between the PCFC and the instructions. This process would, at first sight, have swept aside the problems and complexities of the AFE pool and National Advisory Body (NAB) (See below paragraphs 49–65). However, discussions about the implementation of these proposals suggested that 'contracting' pure and simple would not be adopted and that the new funding processes would need to develop from existing practices and adapt NAB's arrangements in some measure. There were hopes that the PCFC could learn from NAB's attempted solutions to the problems of funding HE in the public sector (See **1.1** Appendix 1).

48 At the time of writing both NAB and the DES have recently produced papers which provide clues to the way that contract funding may operate, although it must be acknowledged that these are tentative if not speculative. The approaches discussed in these papers are referred to as providing 'marginal funding' and are designed to permit institutions to attract additional resources for enrolling students above target, although the additional resources would

be pitched at a level considerably below the standard unit of resource. Two approaches appear possible: tenders or bids could be presented by institutions which include details of student numbers, disciplines or programme areas and the price at which provision can be made; alternatively bids could be submitted in which the price would be a predetermined fraction of the standard unit of resource as set by the PCFC. Both of these approaches would permit increased access to the HE system, one of the major priorities of the White Paper, while restraining the demand for new resources. They would also tend to increase the efficiency of the PSHE system as a whole, although the ability of individual institutions to respond to either approach would be constrained by the level of spare capacity in terms of staffing, buildings and other resources (NAB 1987a and 1987b).

49 **The AFE pool**

The 'AFE pool' has been the largest and most important of the pools. Established in 1959 by the General Grants (Pooling Arrangements) Regulations it recognised the geographic disparities in AFE provision and the consequent disparities in the distribution of expenditure for what was regarded as a regional and national, as well as local, service. It was also argued at the time that in the absence of some mechanism for the redistribution of costs, expansion of provision would be resisted by providing LEAs. In 1975 the AFE pool was merged with the teacher training pooling system.

50 Up to and including 1984–85 the formula for contributions to the AFE pool apportioned 69% of poolable expenditure in proportion to the school population of each LEA; the remaining 31% was based on the distribution of non-domestic rateable values. This approach was held to balance the potential (though not actual) demands made on AFE provision nationally be each LEA while having regard to the future benefits to be derived by employers from an educated labour force. Contributions to the AFE pool were then calculated net of allocations from them. However, the relatively high rateable values in Inner London had the effect of making the ILEA the biggest net contributor to the pools despite supporting five polytechnics and a number of other institutions providing AFE courses. This was felt by ILEA to be inequitable. In consequence court action was mounted by ILEA in which it was successfully argued that the relative rateable resources of LEAs are not a relevant consideration in deciding the appropriate contribution to the provision of AFE nationally. As a result the formula was changed in 1985–86 to being based exclusively on the AFE student population of each area.

51 During its early years of operation all contributions to the AFE pool were calculated retrospectively so as to equal the sum of the claims made. No limit was imposed on institutional expenditure financed from the pool, while LEAs were unaware of the contribution they were required to make until after the end of the financial year. This created serious problems for LEAs for fixing annual budgets.

52 A major change was introduced when Section 63 of the Local Government Planning and Land Act 1980 (and Schedule 10, paragraph 6) gave power to the Secretary of State to impose a limit on the size of the pool. This exercise subsequently came to be known as 'capping the pool'. The imagery of this expression is worth noting for it suggested an exercise like capping an oil-well gushing and out of control. The message implicit in the decision to introduce this measure was clear and unambiguous: the resources available to the AFE

system were to be cut and a period of financial constraint had been entered. The immediate consequence for institutions was that, whereas previously pool resources had been unlimited, henceforward they were to be fixed before the start of the financial year: resource planning and strict financial control became a necessity. For LEAs the open-ended commitment of the uncapped pool had been ended.

53 But for central government a new problem was created: placing an upper limit on the size of the pool inevitable required that some mechanism be developed for distributing the now-limited resources and for reconciling the competing institutional claims which were being made on them. Several solutions were attempted for this problem. Different methodologies were employed for distributing the capped pool in every year from 1980–81 to the time of writing, and each produced a different pattern of distribution. Detailed examination of each of these methodologies and their consequences is beyond the scope of this book, but for present purposes two developments need to be described. First, the period of financial constraint heralded by the capping of the pool was accompanied by increasing intakes of students to the AFE system. These two factors – reducing resources and increasing student numbers – have combined to produce major reductions in unit costs or spending per student. In 1984 a research study undertaken by the Chartered Institute of Public Finance and Accountancy (CIPFA) showed that net expenditure in twenty-three polytechnics between 1979–80 and 1983–84 fell from £411m to £404m in real terms (i.e. after allowance had been made for inflation) while average enrolments over the same period rose by 18%. The net effect was an average reduction in unit costs of 17.6% (CIPFA 1984). This emphasis on increased 'efficiency' has been a fundamental feature of Government higher education policy since 1979.

54 **National Advisory Body**

The second major development was the creation and operation of the National Advisory Body (NAB) (for further details of the creation of NAB See **1.1**). Formally NAB was made responsible for advising the Secretary of State in two principal areas: the apportionment of resources from the AFE pool; and the academic provision to be made by each institution. Additional areas of responsibility cover the allocation of resources for capital spending, the approval of advanced courses and coordination of higher education provision both within the public sector and between the public and university sectors. For Wales the Welsh Advisory Body was established with a corresponding role.

55 Responsibility for the distribution of the AFE pool rested with NAB from 1983–84. Its methodology represented a continuation of an historic unit-cost approach first employed in 1982–83, albeit with a number of refinements. In 1984–85, however, quite fundamental change was introduced. Prior to this year, the unifying feature of the various approaches employed in distributing the capped pool was the overriding dependence on historic cost and enrolment data. As part of a major planning exercise, the results of which were implemented in 1984–85, the emphasis of pool distribution was switched to producing a planned student output from the PSHE system. This required funding to be linked to predetermined student enrolments, distributed among fourteen subject groupings known as 'programme areas'. Cost relativities for teaching in each programme were calculated on the basis of advice offered by HMI on what were termed 'best practice' student : staff ratios and other cost

factors. When combined with target student enrolments these were subsequently translated into an implied minimum unit of resource, i.e. resources per student.

56 Different units of resource were employed for polytechnics, major colleges and other institutions both in recognition of historic disparities in costs and to damp down the effects of change. This sub-division of the pool quantum led to the distribution methodology being referred to as the 'sub-quantum' method. Initial institutional allocations were derived by multiplying target enrolments, enhanced by a London weighting factor where appropriate, by a programme-differentiated net unit of resource for the category of institution. Additional allowance was then made for catering and residence costs. No institution was to be subject to a cash cut in allocation greater than 5%. This was achieved by a process of scaling all allocations known as 'mitigation'. Finally, changes from the previous year's allocation adjusted to the 1984–85 basis, were halved to further limit the impact of the changed methodology. This process was termed 'moderation'. In some instances allocations so calculated had fallen below a floor unit of resource of £1,250 per Humanities student (the 'base' programme). A further scaling process was used to reestablish this figure. Allocations were then the highest of three alternative figures: the programme weighted target student enrolment multiplied by the £1,250 minimum unit of resource; the 1983–84 cash allocation minus 5%; or the moderated basic allocation.

57 Clearly this approach involved considerable complexity, yet its importance lies not so much in the degree of difficulty required to explain its workings, but in the ground-rules it established for later pool distribution. The essential features which it introduced were the switch to future as opposed to past enrolments as the basis for allocations; increased emphasis on the differences in the cost of educating students in different disciplines; higher prioritisation of the needs of industry and the professions (exercised through the system of target enrolments and by the use of control numbers for enrolments on part-time and sub-degree level courses); and finally, efficiency (by the employment of normative 'best practice' figures for student : staff ratios). Subsequent operation of the pool has not substantially altered these priorities although the mechanics have been adapted to reflect changes in emphasis or in attempts at increasing equitability between institutions. In 1985–86 the basic sub-quantum approach was retained. However, it was acknowledged that the calculation of pool allocations in respect of a financial year starting in April but based on student enrolments mainly in September produced serious anomalies for institutions subject to large year-on-year changes in intakes. Because September enrolments in 1984–85 would remain on-roll during the start of the 1985–86 financial year, it was decided that one third the basic financial allocation for 1984–85 should be carried forward and added to two thirds of the corresponding figure for 1985–86, calculated as per the previous year, in order to arrive at the basic allocation for the year. Scaling and mitigation then followed broadly as in the previous year. However, the process of moderation as operated in 1984–85 was abandoned. A further control device of limiting increases in allocations to 25% of the previous years' figure was then introduced. For the first time selective allocations in support of research activity were also included.

58 In 1986–87 the sub-quantum was abandoned as its continuation was held to

lock the system into a pattern of distribution between the different types of institution which no longer reflected enrolment patterns or changes in relative financing needs. The new guiding principle was 'similar funding for similar work'. In practice if this principle had been applied uniformly across the sector, the shift in resources would have been enormous and would have threatened the viability of a number of major institutions. The difficulty this presented was overcome by recourse to research undertaken for NAB during the 1984–85 planning exercise. This had shown that up to a point, a statistical relationship could be found between AFE as a proportion of total work (i.e. the AFE/NAFE split) and institutional costs.

59 These changes in approach led to a radically different methodology for distributing the pool. The new approach involved two distinct stages: the first was designed to give effect to the principle of similar funding for similar work; while the second was designed to compensate for observed differences in institutional costs. A floor unit of resource for a base (Humanities) student was established at £1,150. This was presented as being the minimum resourcing requirement below which it was held that quality of provision would suffer. The first stage of the allocation process was to multiply the floor unit of resource by the programme weighted target student enrolment (calculated, as in earlier years, by rolling forward the target enrolment figure for the previous year). This stage distributed £508m or 79% of the £646m available to LEA maintained institutions.

60 The remaining sum was then distributed by reference to AFE provision as a proportion of total provision. A lower cut-off point of 25% AFE provision was established with an upper cut-off of 90%. This AFE factor rose linearly between the two points. Thus, for example, two institutions of similar size and student composition, but with one providing 25% AFE and the other 50%. The former would receive no enhancement from this second tranche, while the latter would receive an enhancement for 25% of its weighted targeted enrolment. This use of an 'AFE factor' was justified within NAB as a means by which it was possible '. . . to take account of the additional costs which institutions incur as they become primarily or essentially "higher education" establishments, rather than primarily NAFE establishments with some advanced work. It represents the additional costs associated with the creation of a physical and academic environment conducive to the effective provision of higher education' (NAB 1986). Further allowances were then made for London weighting and catering and residence costs and in limits in year-on-year changes as previously in order to produce allocations.

61 The major issue which exercised NAB, the DES, the Secretary of State and all of the other concerned parties, not least the institutions themselves, during the planning exercise current at time of writing was fundamental, namely the trade-off between access and the unit of resource. Put simply, as resources fall either spending per student must fall also or access to the system must be restricted. This was acknowledged by NAB in 1984–85 when it determined that access was to be the overriding consideration and the unit of resource was therefore required to fall. An attempt to protect standards of provision was introduced by the imposition of a floor unit of resource of £1,250 per weighted FTE although this was permitted to fall to £1,150 (plus the AFE weighting) in 1986–87. The result of this process was ever increasing 'efficiency' gains within the PSHE system as manifested by rising student : staff ratios and falling unit costs.

62 The dichotomy presented by this trade-off was not then resolved. As early as March 1985, institutions were informed by NAB of the need to remove 6,800 FTEs or 5% of 1984–85 target enrolments from the system if the Government's expenditure plans were to be achieved and the unit of resource to be protected. It was pointed out that the whole of this reduction would need to fall on first year intakes in 1986–87 if spending per student was to be protected, a policy to which NAB had previously declared itself committed (NAB 1985). The other major changes announced in this letter were a reconstitution in the programme areas and an increase in number from fourteen to nineteen.

63 By January 1986 NAB's decision to protect the unit of resource had led to the grouping of programmes which were to be subject to differential rates of reduction in intakes of 6%, 11% and 17%. By this stage details of likely pool income had become available and, in the light of this, it was felt necessary to remove between 16,000 and 18,000 FTEs from the system depending on programme mix. The approach adopted by NAB was that it was only prudent to plan provision on the basis of the best information available: better to reinstate cuts at a later stage should resources permit than to remove them in a hurry at an advanced stage of the exercise as a result of making over optimistic assumptions.

64 These developments had the effect of undermining the figures submitted by the institutions to a degree which threatened their use as a basis for further planning. Moreover, they led to confusion, uncertainty and resentment within all parts of the PSHE system to an extent which challenged the credibility of NAB as a planning agency. In particular institutions had little idea of the overall level of enrolments which would be permitted or possible or which courses would be threatened as a result of cuts in target enrolments. Also, since financial allocation from the AFE pool were largely determined by target enrolments forward financial planning was widely deemed to be meaningless.

65 The situation was somewhat defused by an announcement in August 1986 by Kenneth Baker, the newly appointed Secretary of State, of the Government's intention to provide an additional £54m or 8% for 1987–88 over and above the provision planned in the Public Expenditure White Paper. This supplementation which included £15m under a Special Initiatives' scheme, raised the quantum of the AFE pool to £700m, although remaining some £7m short of the amount deemed necessary by NAB to maintain both access and the unit of resource. Nevertheless, speedy recalculation of student enrolment data was undertaken to reinstate most of the planned cuts.

66 **Other pools**

In addition to the capped AFE pool, a number of other open pools remained in operation in AFE and NAFE, although major changes were planned for some of these. Details of the operation of these pools are notified to LEAs each year as an accompanying document to form 510F which is issued by the DES under the Block Grant (Education Adjustments) (England) Regulations 1985. The information provided by LEAs in this form is subsequently employed in the calculation of pooling adjustments since all transfers are calculated on a net basis.

67 **The capital related pool**

Expenditure which could be charged to this pool is under four headings:

(i) Loan charges – including interest and principal;
(ii) Rent or other outgoings under leases on land or buildings but excluding rent on buildings wholly owned by the maintaining authority or on buildings and equipment on which all loan charges have been repaid;
(iii) Payment for leasing of equipment under contracts entered into prior to 1 April 1982; and
(iv) Capital expenditure from revenue on minor works and equipment not exceeding £100,000 in the case of polytechnics or £40,000 in the case of all other FE institutions.

Although this pool continues in operation in 1987–88, its further existence is uncertain; a decision was taken 'in principle' early in 1985 that it should be abolished. The intention was to integrate the operation of this pool with the block grant system, but an acceptable mechanism for achieving this objective had not been found at time of writing.

68 **Compensation and safeguarding payments (Crombie)**

This pool was made available to protect the salary level of former teacher trainers who were redeployed to serve in some other capacity. The LEA could claim the difference between the protected salary level and the salary level which would normally be payable in the post to which the individual has been redeployed. These payments would, however, be claimable only where the redeployment resulted from the discontinuation of a course as a result of a direction issued by the Secretary of State under Section 15 or 16 of the Education (Schools and Further Education) Regulations 1981 (See **2.3** 48–57 and Waitt 1980 Section 5).

69 **Redundancy and premature retirement compensation (PRC) payments**

Following the capping of the AFE pool in 1980 provision was made to underwrite the costs to LEAs associated with staff losses. For both academic and non-academic staff 90% of redundancy and premature retirement compensation (PRC) payments to those who were employed in the provision of AFE were claimable from this pool, provided that employment ceased on or after 1 April 1981. PRC is normally payable only to people above the age of fifty, under regulations issued under Section 24 of the Superannuation Act, 1972, although in certain exceptional circumstances FE teachers below this age may qualify. However, no applications to this pool made after 1 September 1985 would be considered. This pool is therefore closed, and all redundancy and PRC payments are not the responsibility of the maintaining authority (See **2.3**).

70 **The no-area pool**

Further education students (other than those on advanced courses) who are not the responsibility of any particular LEA are financed under the Education (Areas to Which Pupils Belong) Regulations 1980, issued under Section 32 (2) and 35 of the Education Act 1980. Students financed in this way include those whose parents are for the time being or ordinarily resident outside England or Wales; those ordinarily resident and receiving further education in hospital; those normally resident in a charitable institution; dependants of parent(s) or legal guardian(s) who are temporarily resident in England or Wales by virtue of being a member of, or being attached to, a visiting military force and those resident in a camp provided for refugees or other displaced persons. Dependants of travelling people are also covered by the no-area pool and are defined under separate regulations as those '. . . who have no fixed abode by reason of the nomadic way of life of their parents'. Recoupment is normally claimable from the pool at 45% of the relevant IAPC rates (See above paragraph 42). Students receiving mandatory awards are deemed to be taking advanced courses and the cost of such awards is not poolable. Similarly, the cost of discretionary awards to those on advanced courses are also excluded. Awards to students attending other courses are, however, poolable at 100%. Overseas students or, more accurately, those from outside the EEC, are deemed to pay full-cost fees and are excluded.

71 **In-service training pool**

The in-service training pool was abolished in 1987–88. Up to and including 1986–87, LEAs were able to pool the costs of secondment or in-service training and updating for teachers in further and higher education, youth and community workers, educational psychologists and education advisers and inspectors. From 1 April 1987 the in-service training pool was closed, and in its place was put a grants scheme known as the Local Education Authority Training Grants Scheme (See **2.9** 22–27). In effect, a range of specific grants directed towards centrally determined 'national priority areas of training for 1987–88' was to be made available. These would be supplemented by grant moneys in respect of locally determined priorities. Of the nineteen national priority areas notified to LEAs ten relate in whole or in part to further and higher education.

72 Training activities financed under this scheme would not normally require specific approval from the DES. Rather approval is to be taken as automatic provided that specified criteria have been satisfied. Virement between priority areas (i.e. transfer of allocations from one to another) would with one exception, be permitted up to 10% of each category of approved expenditure. This exception relates to expenditure on in-service training of AFE teachers where virement out of this category would require DES approval. Grant is to be paid at the rate of 70% of approved expenditure for national priority areas and 50% for other locally determined priorities. Virement of approved expenditure from local to national priority areas would be permitted but continue to attract support only at the lower rate.

73 This new arrangement effectively 'caps' the INSET pool as well as providing for increased central control of the overall deployment and use of resources. The decisions on deployment are to be based on a bidding system and allocations will constitute a cash limit. However, the pattern of allocations will also reflect Government priorities; this is implicit in the creation of national priority areas but explicit in respect of INSET provision for teachers on AFE courses.

74 **Student fees**

Two aspects of fee determination are of particular importance: first, was the decision by the DES to cut free levels by nearly 50% in 1982–83; and second, is the treatment of overseas students. In 1982–83 the standard tuition fee for home AFE students (including EEC nationals) was cut from £900 to £480; a counterbalancing increase of approximately £70m was then introduced to the pool quantum. No clear evidence is available to explain this decision although a move to target student enrolments as the basis for distributing the AFE pool was already planned. The 1982–83 reduction in fees therefore considerably reduced the financial advantage which would have otherwise resulted from recruitment above target and may have produced a brake on over-recruitment.

Table 5
Recommended Fee Levels 1986–87 and 1987–88 (£)

	1986–87	1987–88
Post graduate courses	1680	1730
First degree and diploma courses	536	556

	1986–87 AFE	1986–87 NAFE	1987–88 AFE	1987–88 NAFE
Full-time	536	342	556	360
Sandwich/block release (weekly rate)	14.90	9.50	15.50	10
Part time/course hour	0.50	0.32	0.52	0.34
Part time annual fee for one session/week	53.60	34.20	55.60	36.00

Source: DES press release 56/87 and CLEA circular 87/2.

Note: The figures above the broken line are those recommended by the Secretary of State; those below the line were issued by CLEA.

75 Since 1982–83 overseas students have been required to pay 'full-cost' fees, following the phased withdrawal of a specific subsidy previously available to allow these students to enrol at similar rates to those charged to home and EEC nationals (See **1.8** 6). Present practice in determining overseas student fees is for the University Grants Committee (UGC) and CLEA to issue annual recommendations on minimum fee levels which should be charged to this category of student. The DES, UGC and CLEA all emphasise that institutions and LEAs are free to charge above the minimum where it is estimated that this figure does not constitute full costs. Many have exploited this discretion to achieve, in some cases considerable, extra revenue. Table 6 provides details of the recommended minimum figures for 1986–87 and 1987–88.

Table 6
Universities

	1986–87	1987–88
Arts courses	3480	3690
Science courses	4570	4840
Clinical courses (medicine, dentistry, and veterinary science)	8450	8960

Public Sector Institutions

	1986–87	1987–88
Advanced courses	3540	3720
Non-Advances courses	1947	2055

Source: DES press release 56/87, and CLEA circular 87/2.

NB: No separate figures are specified for post-graduate courses and LEAs and institutions are therefore free to determine these subject only to the proviso that they are above the minimum.

76 **Local authority financial management**
Local education authorities derive their powers and duties from Parliament and their political legitimacy from periodic elections. Their actions and decision-making are circumscribed by Parliament through legislation, and the exercise of powers and duties is influenced, in large measure, by departments of state through the use of administrative memoranda, circulars, notes of guidance, etc., all of which may preempt the use of financial resources. Within this broad framework, however, authorities are free to organise their financial management and administration in a manner appropriate to local circumstances (but See **1.2** 32–43). Because of the enormous diversity to be found within local government no two authorities go about this in quite the same way. Within the confines described above and other than specific and supplementary grants, the financial resources available to local authorities can be disposed of in a manner which reflects local choice and decision. The most common mechanism for making these decisions in recent years has been through the operation of a committee structure which reflects the corporate planning of the authority as a whole. The primacy of corporate planning has developed over the last two decades, following the Bains Report (1967) and the Redcliffe–Maud Report (1969) (See **1.6** 9). This approach has at its centre the operation of a policy and resources committee (although different titles are employed) which is concerned with broad issues of policy, strategic planning, and the overall deployment of resources. All other committees, including the education committee, are subordinate to this overarching body. In effect, many of the decisions concerning relative financial and other priorities within education and between education and other services are taken outside of the education committee, although in law decisions about the education service require the consideration of a report from the education committee (See **1.6** 5). However, in addition to statutory requirements which preempt resources, a major element of local authority budgetary planning is concerned with meeting prior commitments. These prior commitments can range across such diverse areas as staffing, building, and debt redemption costs. While some of these areas of cost are amenable to change in the medium to longer term, in the short term they can be regarded for all practical purposes, as fixed. Two things follow from this: first, local discretion on the deployment of financial resources operates at the margin. This marginal discretion can vary considerably from one LEA to another, but in all cases the combination of statutory preemption of finances and prior commitments limits freedom of manoeuvre. Second, and as a consequence of this, significant shifts in the pattern of resource deployment can be achieved only with some difficulty and normally quite slowly. To varying degrees depending on local circumstances authorities can find themselves locked into existing patterns of resource usage.

77 During a period of expansion this situation need not be regarded as problematic: as new resources become available, new policies and initiative can be pursued and, where necessary, old activities can be wound down without undue disruption or loss of continuity. However, during a period of financial constraint or contraction, the reverse situation can hold. A financial imperative is created to cut budgets and reduce expenditure levels to match reductions in income. And, as much of the expenditure can be regarded as fixed, at least in the short term, a general tendency is for reductions to be found among those items of expenditure which can be varied. This can lead, for example, to a suspension of repairs and maintenance work, or sharp reductions in permitted expenditure on such things as book purchases, teaching equipment, furniture, or educational visits.

78 The financial duties of LEAs in respect of provision of further and higher education are not prescribed extensively. Section 41 of the Education Act 1944 required that each LEA must, '. . . secure the provision for their area of adequate facilities for further education', not stipulating the form or extent of such facilities (See **1.2** 14–17), nor that they should be established by the LEAs themselves. The Education Act 1962 required LEAs to provide grants to residents holding relevant academic qualifications admitted to first degree or comparable courses. This duty was extended by Section 1 of the Education Act 1975 to cover students admitted to courses of initial teacher training and to Diploma of Higher Education and Higher National Diploma courses. The list of qualifying courses was further extended by Section 19 and Schedule 5 of the Education Act 1980 to include Higher Diploma courses validated by the Business and Technician Education Council and certain courses provided in conjunction with overseas institutions. The list of designated courses (i.e. those courses which attract mandatory awards) may be varied by regulations issued by the Secretary of State. The current list of designated courses can be found in the Education (Mandatory Awards) Regulations 1985, 90% of the amount LEAs pay in mandatory awards can be reclaimed as a specific grant.

79 In contrast to this short list of specified financial duties, LEAs exercise extensive discretionary powers. Section 41 and 53 of the Education Act 1944 were deliberately vague in their wording to promote local discretion and experimentation in the provision of facilities of further, higher, and adult education as well as facilities for '. . . recreation and social and physical training'. In providing these facilities, LEAs have made extensive use of their power under Section 90 of the 1944 Act to purchase compulsorily land required to the exercise of these functions. However, the exercise of this power is constrained by the operation of the capital expenditure control system as well as the revenue consequences which flow from the provision of these facilities.

80 Further financial powers available to local authorities permit the undertaking or promotion of educational research and the organisation of conferences (Sections 82 and 83, 1944 Act); the provision of assistance to universities and university colleges (Section 84, 1944 Act); and the granting of discretionary awards to students enrolled on non-designated courses (Education Act 1962, Section 2 (as amended)). LEAs have exercised wide discretion in their application of the guidelines issued by the Burnham Committee on the grading and salaries of lecturers. Nevertheless, in recent years the general environment of financial constraint has promoted increasing questioning by some LEAs of the numbers of staff operating at the top of each grade and has prompted an increasing use of part-time staff and temporary staff especially for courses for which finance is guaranteed only for a fixed period. Finally, LEAs exercise considerable discretion in the degree of autonomy granted to institutional managers. This applies particularly to the employment and deployment of non-teaching staff, the provision of supplies and services, and the overall deployment of resources within institutions.

81 Because of this high degree of discretion exercised by LEAs, no generalised picture can be given. The number of institutions, the number, range and level of courses provided and the level of resources made available varies considerably from one authority to another. Nevertheless the financial constraints within which authorities have, of late, been required to operate has produced an ever increasing emphasis on measures designed to promote institutional efficiency (See below paragraphs 105–116). In addition a number of LEAs have

conducted reviews of staffing levels (both academic and non-academic), criteria for the payment of discretionary grants, fee levels and other aspects of institutions' net cost profiles, with a view to achieving savings. Few, if any, institutions have been immune from this process.

82 **Internal management**
Apart from contributions to the education pools and recoupment payments to other authorities, LEA expenditure on further and higher education takes three main forms. Maintenance awards, whether discretionary or mandatory, are paid to students on qualifying courses. Course fees are also paid on behalf of these students to the institutions at which they are enrolled. But the major element of recurrent expenditure takes the form of an annual settlement made on each institution in respect of general running costs. The size of this settlement is determined by the preparation and approval of annual estimates of revenue expenditure. The major areas of local authority recurrent expenditure on institutions of further and higher education are summarised in Table 7. They exclude debt charges and any revenue contributions to capital expenditure, which amount to about 10% of recurrent expenditure, and any boarding or catering costs.

Table 7
Estimated categories of gross expenditure 1983–84 (England and Wales)

	Polytechnics (%)	*Other FE (%)*
Teaching staff	51.2	62.2
Other employees	24.7	16.3
Premises	10.4	9.5
Supplies and Services	8.0	8.0
Transport	0.7	1.3
Establishment Expenses	3.0	1.8
Miscellaneous Expenses	2.0	0.9

Source: Education Statistics 1983–84 Estimates; CIPFA; August 1983.

NB: More recent figures are not available because of changes introduced by CIPFA in the format in which data is presented

83 The system of financial management for establishments of further and higher education is governed by the Education (No. 2) Act 1968 and the proposals in Circular 7/70 and for polytechnics Administrative Memorandum 8/67. The 1968 Act required that maintained colleges should be conducted according to articles of government made by the local education authority and approved by the Secretary of State. The articles specify the functions of the local education authority, the governing body, the principal, and the academic board, if any (See **2.8** 6–8).

84 Article 6 in the model appended to Circular 7/70 proposed a provision on the management of finance, premises and supplies, outlining a structure which is broadly operative for most maintained establishments, although the detailed procedures are varied. Institutions draw up estimates of expenditure annually in a manner prescribed by the authority. Responsibility for assembling the

estimates is formally that of the principal, although in practice it is commonly the task of the finance office, chief (or senior) administrative officer, or a designated vice-principal. The estimates are then submitted to the governing body, although commonly after prior scrutiny by a finance committee of the governors. Thereafter the governing body submits the estimates to the local education authority for approval by the Education Committee. After such approval the governors can then incur expenditure involving the ordering of supplies and equipment, undertaking minor repairs and maintenance, and exercising virement within (and in some cases between) approved headings. However, they are not permitted, without consent from the authority, to undertake expenditure with financial implications beyond the end of the financial year.

85 The preparation of the annual estimates brings together officers and members of the LEA, the principal and finance officer of the institution, the governing body and in some cases the academic board also. During the current period of financial constraint the process by which estimates are produced represents a reconciliation of estimates of required or desired expenditure on the one hand and limited financial resources on the other. This inevitably involves trade-offs. Implicit in every set of estimates is a statement of institutional priorities, whether financial or educational. Increasingly, purely financial considerations provide an imperative in the preparation of estimates, and educational considerations are relegated to a secondary position. This frequently leads to reductions in those variable heads of expenditure most amenable to immediate pruning (See above paragraph 76).

86 It is at the time of the preparation of estimates that the distinction between institutions principally engaged in AFE work and those principally concerned with NAFE courses is most pronounced. NAB allocations from the AFE pool prescribe specific amounts in respect only of those institutions where advanced level work constitutes a significant proportion of total provision; allocations to other institutions within the boundaries of an LEA are aggregated by NAB and are known as the 'LEA aggregates'. At those institutions providing solely or mainly advanced courses, the base line for the preparation of estimates is provided by the pool allocation plus anticipated fee income. Negotiations between the LEA and institutional management in such cases are normally confined to the level of 'topping-up' to be provided and, possibly, the extent of any external income generating activities. In other cases a mechanism must be found to disaggregate the LEA aggregate in order to apportion it between the various institutions making claims upon it. The way that this exercise is undertaken is a matter for the discretion of the LEA, tempered only by the negotiating ability of institutional managers. In those institutions providing only one or two advanced level courses this is a matter of little consequence; in those where advanced work constitutes, say 25% or 30% of total provision it can be of crucial importance.

87 Decisions on the local authority contribution to institutional budgets are invariably subject to considerable informal discussion, advice and negotiation, quite separate from the formal procedures. Indeed, the preparation of annual estimates provides the single most important opportunity for discussion and debate between LEAs and institutions on the academic priorities and developments for which resources are to be made available. LEAs use this opportunity to varying degrees, with some adopting a prescriptive approach while others grant considerable discretion to institutions. Many colleges are now

subject to LEA imposed income generation targets to be met from MSC income, full cost courses or other sources. Achievement of these targets is a precondition of producing a balanced budget while allowing LEAs to reduce their own contributions to institutional costs. However, differences of approach not withstanding, the preparation of annual estimates provides the major focus within Town and County Halls on inter and intra institutional planning and coordination of provision of further education. In higher education these planning and coordinating functions of the LEAs were increasingly taken over by NAB because of the system of allocating target student enrolments. As a result LEA influence on polytechnics and major colleges is being eroded.

88 Irrespective of the approach adopted to the preparation of institutional estimates, the timing must be coordinated with that of the maintaining authority. Typically, the preparation and planning involved in the production of local authority and institutional revenue estimates commences up to twelve months before the start of the financial year to which they relate. Publication of the final accounts takes place in the September following the end of the financial year; thus the whole budgetary cycle can take up to thirty months. Figure 1 outlines the different stages involved, as described by the Chartered Institute of Public Finance and Accountancy (CIPFA).

89 Figure 1 shows that detailed estimates are first produced around December, i.e. approximately three months prior to the start of the financial year. Because of movements in pay and prices over time a decision is necessary on the price base to be employed. Conventionally estimates are produced on the basis of 'November Prices', i.e. the price levels prevailing at the time the draft estimates are produced. Provision for inflation is then made in one of two ways. Either an allowance is made for inflation at the start of the year within each area of the budget or, alternatively, a central contingency is established. In the latter case supplementary estimates are required in which the contingency provision is transferred to the various expenditure heads after information about pay and price movements has become available. Revised estimates are normally produced in the November of the financial year to which they relate and are presented simultaneously with the draft estimates for the following financial year.

90 A number of advantages are held to follow from this approach. First, the presentation of revised estimates, whether to the full council of a local authority or the governing body of a college, permits the identification of areas where expenditure is out of line with planned provision so that corrective action may be taken. Second, the 'anticipated outturn expenditure' represented by the revised estimates presents a base line for the planning of expenditure in the following year. Simultaneous presentation also permits comparisons to be made from one year to another so that changes in the level of provision can be identified. Finally a measure of predictability and stability are held to be built into the system so as to avoid potentially disruptive or damaging year-on-year shifts in resource deployment.

91 Against these advantages this 'incrementalist' approach is sometimes argued to direct attention towards purely financial concerns rather than the underlying educational activities which the budget is supposed to facilitate. It is also sometimes held to be overly rigid rather than promoting flexible or more 'efficient' use of resources and to be unnecessarily short-term in its outlook. In the

Figure 1
A financial planning and control timetable

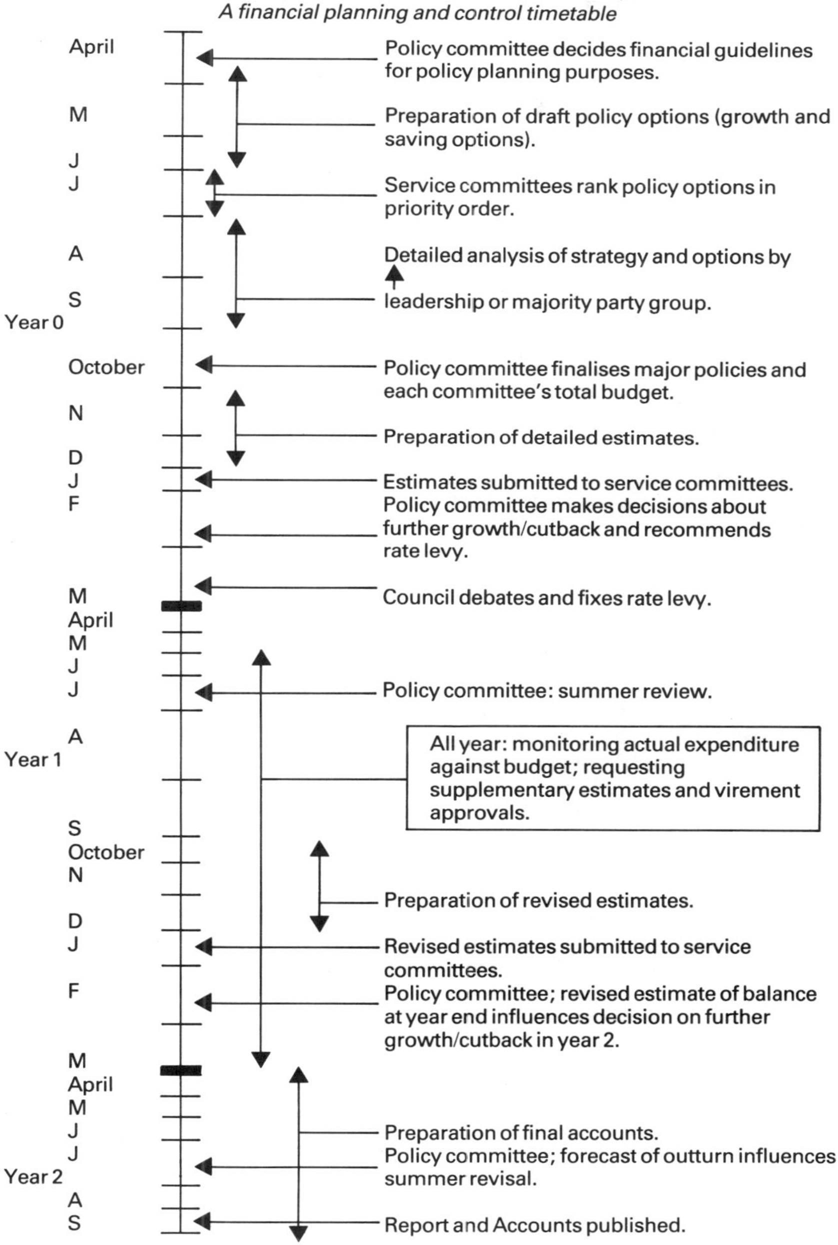

Source: Guide to Local Authority Finance; CIPFA; 1984; section G.

past attempts have been made to promote the idea of rolling budgets covering a period of three or more years which can be updated annually (See, e.g. Oakes 1978). Those are designed to direct attention towards the medium to longer term educational goals of authorities and institutions and thereafter for decisions to be taken on the most appropriate deployment of resources to achieve these plans. The limitations and restrictions operating on LEAs and colleges, principally through the RSG and the AFE pool, mean that such planning has seldom been undertaken in the past. However, the rolling planning of the MSC work-related NAFE exercise could lead to a more widespread revival of these ideas.

92 **College revenues**

College and polytechnics obtain income from a number of sources. The major source of income is the LEA although the LEA itself receives all or nearly all of the expenditure related to advanced work from the AFE and other pools, to which, of course, it contributes. Colleges have a number of other sources of income, the most important of which is general student fees (See above paragraphs 74–76). These amount, on average, to approximately 20% of total income to polytechnics but considerably less to other institutions. In addition many institutions, particularly at HE level, run a range of self-financing short courses which may be generally available or tailored towards the needs of specific groups. These courses may be financed by students themselves or, more usually, by employers. In 1985–86 full cost course income in fourteen polytechnics amounted to £7.3m while short courses mounted by thirteen polytechnics provided a further £2.1m. An important aspect of self-financing courses is the way in which charges are calculated. In order to be genuinely self-financing it is necessary for all relevant costs, and particularly staff time, normally the most expensive resource, to be accurately costed. Some discretion may, however, be available on the extent to which short course income should contribute to central institutional overheads.

93 Different arrangements apply for fees for different kinds of NAFE. Fees for courses chargeable in general to students and employers are normally set by reference to CLEA recommendations and are based on an annual survey of costs conducted by the DES. Payments to the MSC are normally the subject of negotiation between local authority associations and the MSC at national level.

94 A further form of fee income which has developed considerable importance in recent years is obtained from overseas students. Since 1980–81 institutions have been required to charge full cost fees to all overseas students other than European Community nationals (See above paragraphs **3.6** 76 and 1–5). LEAs and institutions enjoy considerable discretion subject only to market conditions and a prescribed set of minimum rates depending on level of work.

95 Other income is derived from sales, hiring of buildings and facilities, and from research and consultancy activities by staff. As with other forms of income generation these activities have grown in importance as general financial constraints have increased. The ability of institutions to retain some or all of this income is determined by the articles of government and the financial regulations (See **2.8** 6–10), although informal negotiations between institutions and their LEAs may extend the discretion granted by these formal mechanisms. In some cases the financial regulations themselves may be amended in order, for example, to permit a college to operate on the basis of an approved net

budget. Such a device removes the disincentive to staff engaged in income generation of seeing some or all of the product of their efforts being 'clawed-back' by their LEA. Arrangements of this type are by no means common but can now be found with growing frequency. Crucial to agreement being reached between LEAs and institutions on the introduction of this type of arrangement is the confidence of the LEA in the ability of the college to manage its own financial affairs.

96 Increased reliance in recent years on external income generation can create particular problems during the preparation of estimates. Legally, anticipated expenditure must balance with anticipated income as no deficit may be carried from one year to the next. Yet by its nature externally generated income can be volatile, being subject to factors outside the control of institutional managers: short courses may be cancelled by industrial sponsors who are themselves experiencing financial problems; or overseas fee income may collapse following a change in Government in another part of the world. In primarily NAFE institutions fee income can be particularly difficult to predict due to the fee waivers that are granted to many students, including most of those in receipt of DHSS benefits. Hence dependence on externally generated and fee income also requires contingency planning of finance. Since staffing costs frequently amount to 70% of gross institutional expenditure, reliance on such sources of income can directly result in greater emphasis being placed on the use of fixed term and part-time staff appointments.

97 The increasing drive towards entrepreneurialism in further and higher education was reinforced by the Further Education Act 1985. This empowered LEAs to establish trading companies to market the goods and service of further and higher education institutions on a commercial basis (See **1.2** 28).

98 **Internal resource allocation and control**

There is little body of research about the way that colleges and polytechnics allocate resources to faculties and departments. Indeed the diversity of institutional circumstances is such that there could be as many mechanisms in use as there are institutions. Articles of government and financial regulations set out the respective powers of the governing body, the principal and the LEA, but these vary from one institution to another and the implementation of the formal rules also varies.

99 A study of university resource allocation undertaken between 1979 and 1982 showed that 'Norms and formulae have been widely used . . . in academic resource allocation', although these were 'rarely the final determinant of a decision . . . resource allocation committees will generally balance statistical data . . . with their own academic judgements' (Shattock and Rigby 1983). However, the use of norms and formulae was first established during the 1970s when financial resources were growing, and it appears that a judgemental approach is increasingly employed in order to overcome the rigidities of fixed formulae. A later study of polytechnics and colleges identified a general, though not universal, trend towards centralisation of control of the resource allocation process as the pressures of financial constraint increased (Pratt and Gill 1987). Particular emphasis was directed towards the control process for the allocation and monitoring of staffing as this is the predominant influence on institutional costs (See **2.8** 69–78).

100 A traditional incrementalist approach to resource allocation is still employed

in many colleges whereby estimates of spending needs are drawn up by faculties of departments, sometimes based on centrally determined guidelines. These estimates are then centrally combined as a precursor to negotiations designed to reduce aggregated estimates to match anticipated income. Where a centralist approach is adopted such a bidding system may be dispensed with and allocations simply handed down having been based on criteria which are not available for scrutiny. In either case the operations of NAB are assuming increasing importance. In particular best practice student : staff ratios are being imported, whether in a pure or a locally modified form, in the determination of faculty or departmental staffing budgets. This importation acknowledges the increasing influence of NAB by institutional managers on intra-institutional decisions in AFE and the pressures exerted by the Audit Commission within NAFE.

101 An area of considerable diversity between LEAs is in the extent to which use of virement is permitted. The freedom to vire between headings is frequently not permitted. In some cases no virement whatever is permitted without a lengthy process of reference back to the relevant LEA Committee. This restricts institutions in their use of resources to that which was approved with the original estimates. A device which has been used in some instances to overcome this is to reduce the number of heads under which estimates are presented for approval, perhaps to as few as six, although this also reduces the degree of detailed information available to the governing body.

102 This diversity of approaches to financial management creates particular difficulties in drawing comparisons between resourcing levels across institutions for similar activities. In an effort to overcome this, as well as to provide an internal financial control system, CIPFA have advocated the introduction of cost-centres (CIPFA 1979). This approach to financial management is designed to promote the accountability of each area of an institution by identifying those accounting units which consume more than a predetermined share (however arrived at) of total resources. Under the CIPFA approach the basic accounting unit of operation was ideally held to be the award bearing course. Administrative practicality, however, dictates that cost-centres operate at a somewhat higher level; normal practice appears to be for cost-centres to be based on departments or groups of courses in matrix structures.

103 Despite the increasing use of a cost-centre approach general comparisons of the deployment and consumption of resources are not available due to differences in course design as well as in the range of courses offered by departments with similar specialisms. However, the Polytechnic Finance Officers Group (PFOG) do provide comparative data on expenditure classified by discipline (PFOG 1987). Similar data is not available outside of the polytechnic sector.

104 **Internal and external audit**

Polytechnics and colleges as publicly maintained institutions are subject to annual audit. The major legislation governing the audit of accounts is the Local Government Finance Act 1982, although this revises rather than redefines the earlier provisions of the Local Government Act 1972. These statutory provisions are further defined by the Accounts and Audit Regulations 1974 and 1980 issued by the Secretary of State for the Environment and by the Audit Code auditors undertake more detailed surveys of various areas of local authority activities, including colleges. Their major work is to ensure that systems are operating properly, in accordance with the relevant standing orders and financial regulations of the authority and with records and accounts kept up to date. In addition internal auditors may monitor activities for adherence to council policies. They also share some of the functions exercised by external auditors, particularly on the prevention or detection of fraud and the examination of procedures designed to minimise this risk. In relation to colleges and polytechnics internal auditors would be likely to pay particular attention to matching records of income and expenditure maintained internally with those of the authority. The internal auditor reports to the authority's chief finance officer but may also liaise with the external auditor. In smaller institutions internal audit may be undertaken by local authority finance staff while in larger colleges these duties are commonly assigned to the college finance officer.

105 **The efficiency option**

The financial constraints currently being experienced in further and higher education have served to direct attention to the efficiency with which institutions operate and in particular to their use of staffing. Indeed a wide and growing range of publications can now be found on different aspects of the subject. In the main these publications attempt to identify and develop quantitative techniques for measuring the efficiency of resource utilisation.

106 The oldest and best established measure of efficiency in further and higher education is the student : staff ratio (SSR). Bands of recommended SSRs were first put forward by the DES in 1972 following an initial cost study of advanced level work undertaken two years earlier. The ratios were based on '. . . target "norm" bands that, given certain conditions, such as increasing student numbers within main faculty groupings, were considered to be capable of achievement by 1976' (DES 1980). An annual monitoring exercise was established to measure progress towards the achievement of these bands. The formal title given to this exercise was the Annual Monitoring Survey (AMS) although as a result of popular usage it is now frequently referred to as the Delany exercise after the DES official largely responsible for its introduction. The target norm bands established in 1972 related to three groups of faculties: group 1 faculties were broadly laboratory and workshop based; group 2 were classroom based; and group 3 comprised art and design.

Table 8
Target norm bands established in 1972

Faculty	*Target SSR band*
Group 1	7.5– 8.5
Group 2	9.2–10.2
Group 3	7.5– 8.5

In the event the polytechnics achieved these figures for the first time in 1979 and other institutions some time later.

107 The importance of the SSR as measured by the AMS lies in the relationship which it establishes between teaching methods and staff use. While an SSR

can be calculated by dividing full-time equivalent student numbers by staffing, a more sophisticated arrangement is employed by the DES. On this basis an SSR can be calculated as:-

SSR	= ACS x ALH/ASH
where ACS	= average class size
ALH	= average lecturer hours, and
ASH	= average student hours.

Hence an increase in ACS or ALH or a reduction in ASH achieves an increased SSR. Thus the application of this formula encourages increased teaching group sizes and lecturer hours but less teaching to be received by each student.

108 By the time of the first NAB planning exercise the SSR had been adopted as a central feature of the national resource allocation process through the incorporation of best-practice SSRs (see above paragraph 100). These best practice figures were neither prescribed nor even recommended by NAB for adoption by institutions – rather NAB maintained that its sole objective was to see the system as a whole move to an SSR of 12:1. Nevertheless the importance and visibility of these best practice figures has placed considerable pressure on institutions to adopt them for internal purposes.

109 A measure of the extent to which this objective was achieved was provided by an exercise undertaken within NAB in May 1986. The SSRs of ninety-four institutions providing 92% of the AFE provision in England in 1984–85 were compared with recommended staff numbers for 1986–87, assuming the operation of best practice SSRs. The results of this exercise need to be treated with some caution as, for example, the 1984–85 data included staff financed through externally generated income but excluded members of directorates, while the NAB data excluded full cost overseas and short course students and associated staffing. Thus the results can be taken as indicative only. Table 9 shows the results of this exercise.

Table 9
Advanced Work

	Estimated staff			
	1986–87 HMI SSR	*1984–85 AMS SSR*	*reductions No.s*	*required %*
29 Polytechnics	11.6	11.5	35.9	0.2
35 Colleges › 750 AFE	11.9	10.5	447.1	9.9
30 Colleges ‹ 750 AFE	10.9	8.6	226.3	15.4
All 65 Colleges	11.7	10.1	673.4	11.3
All 94 institutions	11.6	11.1	709.3	3.4

Source: NAB, Technical and Data Group Paper 19/86.

Overall the exercise showed an 'excess' number of lecturing staff of some 709 or 3.4%. This compares to a national 'excess' of 2,396 lecturers or 11.0% when a similar exercise was conducted in 1984 (NAB 1984). Overall therefore the efficiency option appears to have been widely implemented throughout the PSHE system by 1984 with staff loses and increased productivity being used to reduce costs.

110 Outside NAB probably the single most important development in the promotion of institutional efficiency was the creation of the Audit Commission and its remit to promote the three Es: economy, efficiency and effectiveness. In addition to its regular audit function (See above paragraph 105) the Commission has undertaken a series of studies of various areas of public sector financial management. Two of these studies are of particular concern although only one relates directly and solely to further and higher education.

111 The first of these examined the effects of block grant operation on local authorities operational efficiency (Audit Commission 1984). Among other things the report highlighted the impact of contradictory policy guidance being offered by different central departments. For example, the GRE formula employed by the DoE assumes that falling secondary schools rolls will result in a corresponding reduction in the number of places provided, with a twenty-one month time lag. The DES, alternatively, have calculated that only 40% of excess secondary school places are capable of being removed by the end of the 1980s because of, among other things, the lengthy statutory consultations required. The Commission estimated that 'The difference could easily amount to £2–3m in GRE for every year of "slippage" in rationalising education provision in an authority with rapidly failing rolls'. Factors such as these tend to introduce major pressure on education budgets within authorities which are then passed on to the institutions.

112 The second Audit Commission report deals specifically with the management of further education (Audit Commission 1985). Auditors examined the way the resources are used in 165 out of 650 polytechnics and colleges of further education; the study was therefore the largest of its type ever undertaken. The study claims to have identified potential savings of £50m per year, or an average of over £300,000 per institution. Put another way this suggests that an additional 75,000 FTE students could be enrolled 'without overstraining existing teaching resources'. Proposals were advanced under four main headings.

(i) Improving marketing skills, both to increase the number of students (and thus capacity utilization) and also to forecast demand more accurately, and thus avoid non-viable courses.
(ii) Tailoring academic staffing levels more closely to local market needs. Since academic costs account for well over half of total expenditure, the way these resources are used is clearly critical to economy and to efficiency – not to mention effectiveness.
(iii) Recovering costs promptly, and to the extent permitted by law.
(iv) Reducing administration and other non-teaching costs without prejudicing teaching standards or management effectiveness.

113 While it is not possible here to deal in detail with the arguments deployed by the Commission, it is fair to say that the overall response to the report from within further and higher education was hostile, particularly in relation to the proposals on staffing. Much of the Commission's analysis concentrated on the annual monitoring survey ratios employed in the calculation of SSRs (See above paragraphs 106–109) and the interaction of these with Burnham maxima

for contact hours for different grades of lecturing staff. It was argued that by increasing control of remission allowances, teaching group sizes, lecturer contact hours for different grades of staff and promotions policy, considerable increases in efficiency and productivity could be obtained. Criticisms tended to concentrate on the over rigid application of performance ratios without adequate regard to the diversity of circumstances faced by institutions or the demands made on staff time by non-teaching activities (NATFHE 1985a). (See **2.8** 36–40).

114 The difficulties inherent in the production of useful performance indicators for further and higher education have been acknowledged by CIPFA as an area '. . . where genuine complexities make simple indicators seem impractical. Most significantly LEAs differ widely in the particular colleges, and range and level of courses, (CIPFA 1984). Despite these acknowledged complexities, crude performance indicators have increasingly come to be employed as a mainstay of efficiency measurement and resource allocation and reduction in further and higher education (See also **2.8** Appendix 1 on management information system).

115 What has received considerably less attention in the current debate on educational efficiency has been the distinction between measures of input, of process and of output. Most of the currently available indicators fall into one of the first two categories. Existing output measures tend to concentrate on course completion rates, examination passes and employment take up after completion. Yet these measures vary considerably between courses, levels and modes of study and local labour market conditions. These proxy measures of output, coupled with the variations in the results, produce a failure to direct attention towards the quality of education received by students: in the language of the Audit Commission little regard is being paid to the effectiveness of the service on offer. This may well be because educational effectiveness is not a quantifiable measure. Rather it requires the introduction of normative measures which are concerned with purpose and content as well as explicit evaluation of the value systems in which they are grounded. The quantitative assessment of inputs and the equation this presents between resource levels and value for money requires no such analysis.

116 **Voluntary institutions**

The financial arrangements for voluntary institutions differ in some significant ways from those for maintained establishments. They are funded for both capital and revenue expenditure for the most part by direct grant from the DES. Proposals for capital expenditure are submitted by the governing bodies to the DES, which approves, rejects or amends them in the light of its perceived needs and priorities. If the college's governing body has a majority appointed to represent the interests of a particular religious denomination the maximum grant towards such expenditure is 85% of the total, although a loan to cover the outstanding 15% is available from the DES (Regulation 19, Further Education Regulations 1975). Some colleges have established building funds, drawing upon private incomes, donations and fund-raising activities, to meet the difference between DES grants and total expenditure, or to provide facilities which have not been approved for expenditure by the DES. The voluntary colleges' case is represented nationally by the Voluntary Sector Consultative Council (VSCC), which has two principal tasks: to comment on course allocations by NAB, and on funding by the DES.

117 The current expenditure of voluntary colleges is obtained on submission of estimates from the governing body to the DES, in a form prescribed by the Department. Negotiations between college and DES officials result usually in revised, then approved, estimates. Staged payments are then made by the DES through the financial year, and the college must operate within the approved limits, although supplementary grant is normally available to cover unforeseen additional costs, such as salary increases. Voluntary colleges normally have greater freedom than maintained colleges in their acquisition and expenditure of supplementary income from sales, rents and hire charges, grants, donations and special course fees. Such activities are subject only to the approval of the governing body. Vacation lettings and conferences have become substantial sources of income for some establishments.

118 A distinctive form of institutional financial management has been that of the Inner London Education Authority's five polytechnics which are registered as limited companies and, therefore, subject to company law (See **1.2** Appendix 1).

1.4 THE DEPARTMENT OF EDUCATION AND SCIENCE, AND THE WELSH OFFICE EDUCATION DEPARTMENT

1 **Statutory background: the 1944 Education Act**

The Education Act 1944 provided for the replacement of the Board of Education (created in 1899) by a Ministry of Education. The function of the Minister was to 'promote the education of the people of England and Wales and the progressive development of institutions devoted to that purpose'. He or she also had a duty to 'secure the effective execution by local authorities under his control and direction, of the national policy for providing a varied and comprehensive education service in every area'. In 1964 the Ministry of Education and the office of the Minister of Science were amalgamated to form the Department of Education and Science, and the post of Minister became that of Secretary of State. The new Department took over responsibility for the universities from the Treasury.

2 The legal basis of further education links central and local government through sections of the 1944 Act quoted above together with section 41 which requires an LEA to secure the provision of 'adequate facilities' for FE for its area. Section 41 linked this duty formally to 'schemes of further education' which were to be approved by the Secretary of State though this process has lapsed (See **1.2** 12–14 and **1.6** 14–15).

3 **The Department of Education and Science**

The Department is almost wholly concerned with policy. It is responsible for the broad allocation of educational resources (including grants in support of spending on specific areas of the education service), for standards and guidelines for educational building, for the supply and training of teachers, and for the Teachers' Superannuation Scheme which covers England and Wales. In administering resources for education the Department acts within a framework of estimates approved by Parliament (as do other government departments). The money the Department spends directly is only a small part of the total public expenditure on education. The major part of capital and recurrent educational spending is local authority expenditure which is financed largely from rates and from rate support grant. The provision of publicly maintained schools and most further and higher education establishments is the responsibility of local education authorities, which also employ the teachers. The universities, though, are autonomous institutions. The Government discharges its responsibilities for all the maintained universities, other than the Open University, through the University Grants Committee.

4 Though the Department does not own educational premises, employ teachers or control the curriculum or teaching methods the Secretary of State is concerned with the quality and content of the education which is provided, with the calibre of teaching and management, and with the standards achieved by pupils and students. This concern has recently been expressed in a Government statement of objectives for the Department of Education and Science which appeared in the 1986 White Paper *Working Together – Education and Training*:

> The principal aim of the Department of Education and Science is to improve standards throughout the education service and to increase the value obtained for the substantial resources allocated to it by the taxpayer and the ratepayer.

In *schools*, the Department aims

to promote agreement on the curriculum and ensure that it is broad and balanced for all pupils
to foster the application of what is learned to real problems and situations
to stretch pupils of all abilities
to give parents more influence, and
to enhance the powers of governing bodies.

In *non-advanced further education*, the Department aims

to increase the responsiveness of the service to the needs of employers
to provide a sound education for young people and adults, and
to secure an improved use of resources – and in particular a significant tightening of student : staff ratios.

In *higher education*, the Department aims

to raise quality and standards while preserving the full breadth of education provision
to make the system more responsive to the needs of the economy
to improve management systems in universities, polytechnics and colleges, and generally to increase value for money by rationalisation

The Department is also responsible for

Adult and continuing education. The principal aim is to update the skills of the national workforce at all levels
The civil science base financed by the University Grants Committee and the Research Councils. The principal aims are to promote excellence by greater concentration and selectivity of research activities and to stimulate commercial applications of new ideas
Teachers. The aim is to secure the supply of sufficient teachers of the quality needed to teach the agreed curricula and to update the skills of the existing teacher force.

Throughout the education system – at all levels – output of citizens competent in mathematics, science and technology must be increased. The DES – in cooperation with the other government departments concerned – is developing a range of policies to that end.

The publication of these 'objectives' (which are translated into broader 'aims' in the opening sentence) has stimulated some comment on the Department's elevation of the economic function of education over the personal (e.g. intellectual and creative) and social functions. The non-vocational purposes of further and higher education as well as adult and continuing education are not mentioned; the youth service is completely forgotten.

5 **Ministers**

The Secretary of State for Education and Science is a member of the Government of the day, and has a place in the Cabinet. He or she is currently assisted in the execution of his or her duties by a Minister of State and two Parliamentary Under-Secretaries of State. Ministerial responsibility is at present distributed as follows, though subject to change:
The Secretary of State has overall responsibility for the work of the Department. He or she also retains specific responsibility for the Department's public expenditure programmes and teachers' pay.
The Minister of State has responsibility for the whole of the work of Schools 3 (curricular and examination reform; the Assessment of Performance Unit; health and sex education, except alcohol, smoking and drugs) plus the work of divisions A and C of Schools 2 (educational disadvantage, ethnic minorities, behaviour and discipline; school to work; educational technology). Teaching

quality: all school and FE teacher policy issues other than pay. Education of 16–19 year olds; and all of NAFE. Relations with the MSC including the Technical and Vocational Education Initiative (TVEI). Reform of Local Government Finance.

The Parliamentary Under-Secretary of State (1) deals with the whole of the work of Schools I other than TVEI (ie Section 12–16 proposals; relations with the voluntary sector; the ILEA; falling rolls; school government; independent schools etc). The work of Architects and Buildings and of Division B of Schools 2 (special education, Aids). Youth and community services. Education research. Drugs misuse. Health education aspects of alcohol and smoking.

The Parliamentary Under-Secretary of State (2) deals with Higher Eduction: the planning and provision of university and public sector higher education; higher education and business including technology transfer; tuition fees; student awards and student affairs. Civil science policy; the Research Councils and other bodies funded from the Science Vote. Adult and continuing education; the Open University.

Two Peers act as spokespersons on education matters in the House of Lords.

6 **The Office**

The Department of Education and Science is staffed by civil servants, whose appointments are not dependent upon political decisions or considerations. The Department is under the general direction of a Permanent Under-Secretary of State (known as the Permanent Secretary) who is assisted by three Deputy Secretaries. They deal respectively with schools and educational buildings; further and higher education, and science; and teachers, pensions, statistics and information technology. The Permanent Secretary is also assisted by the Department's Legal Adviser and the Senior Chief Inspector, both of whom have Deputy Secretary rank. In addition the Department's Accountant General (its Principal Finance Officer), the Director of Establishments (who is responsible for the management of the Department's manpower, staff inspection and common services) and the Head of Information Branch report directly to the Permanent Secretary.

7 Work is then further delegated into branches of the Department, headed by Under-Secretaries. An organisation chart of the Department appears in Table 1. DES branches are of two types: those which assist Ministers to develop and subsequently monitor the implementation of policy; and those which are concerned with providing services common to the Department as a whole.

8 **Policy Branches: Schools I, II and III**

The schools branches together deal with the entire range of schools provision. Schools I comprises teams which are organised on a territorial basis and maintain day-to-day contact with local education authorities on school matters. The teams advise Ministers on proposals made under Sections 12–16 of the Education Act 1980 for establishing, closing, significantly changing the character of, or significantly enlarging, schools. They give advice when cases concerning individual pupils are referred to the Secretary of State for Education and Science by parents who are not satisfied with decisions reached by LEAs or school governing bodies. The branch also deals with school capital expenditure, policy on falling school roles, voluntary schools, school government, school admission, attendance and leaving dates, under-fives and boarding education, independent schools, the assisted places scheme, the Technical and Vocational Education Initiative (TVEI), the European Schools, and the follow-up

Table 1
Department of Education and Science

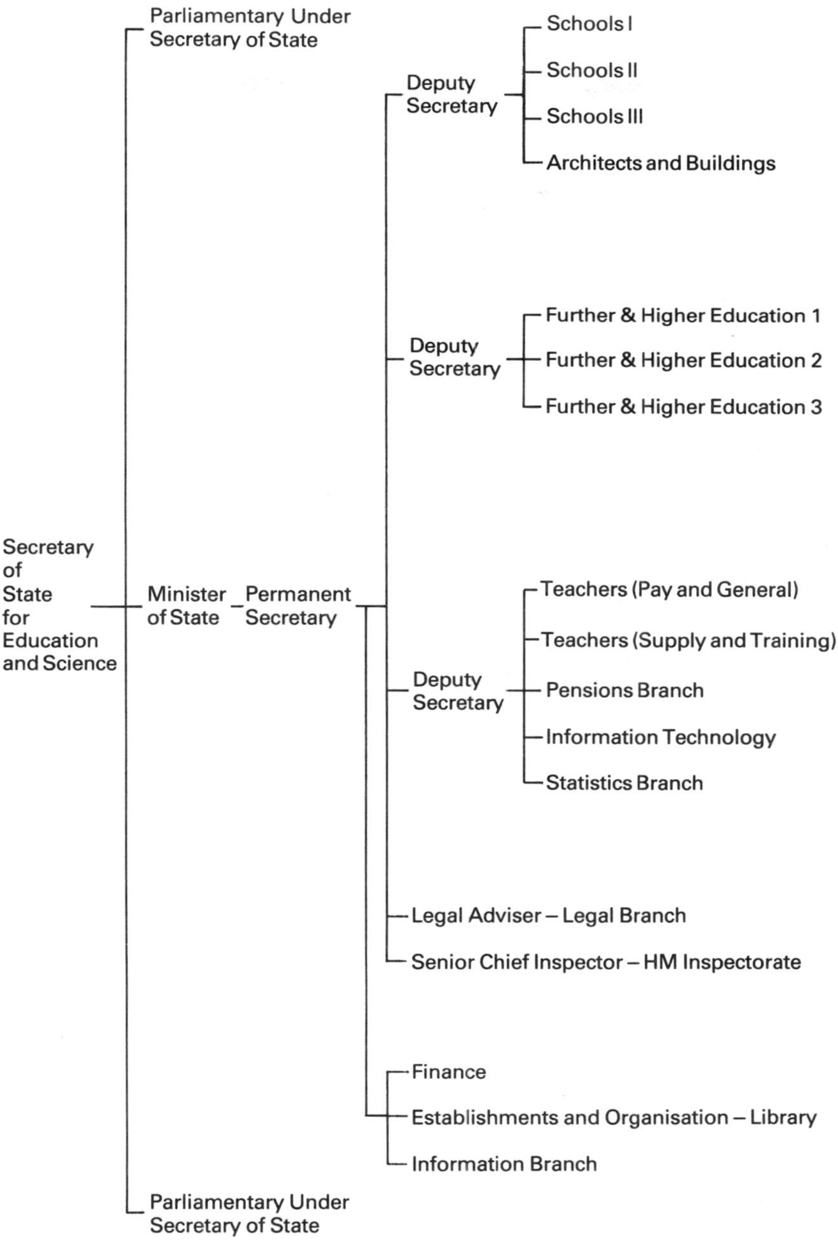

of HMI reports on schools. In addition it deals with issues relating to the school meals service, school transport, education maintenance allowances and school clothing, constitutional matters affecting LEAs, inter-authority recoupment and the part-time employment of children of school age.

9 Schools II has four divisions. One is responsible for policy on educational disadvantage and the education of ethnic minorities, truancy and behaviour in schools, and the Education Welfare Service. The second division deals with the education (in special schools or classes provided by local education authorities and voluntary bodies, and in other ways) of pupils with special educational needs. This division also liaises with the Department of Health and Social Security on the provision by district health authorities of health services to the local education authorities. The third division is responsible for the branch's functions in connection with the preparation of young people for adult and working life, including school/business liaison and careers education and guidance. It is responsible for the Lower Attaining Pupils Programme (LAPs), the Micro-Electronics Education Programme (MEP), other educational technology matters, broadcasting and copyright. The fourth division is responsible for coordinating the United Kingdom's interests in the educational cooperation programmes of the European Community (EC), the Organisation for Economic Cooperation and Development (OECD) and the Council of Europe. It also advises on questions of educational cooperation within the Commonwealth. In the bilateral field it is responsible for coordinating the UK's interests in cooperative programmes with a number of countries, as well as for policy (in England) on the exchange of teachers, modern language assistants and education administrators. It also supervises the Department's grants to the Central Bureau for Educational Visits and Exchanges (CBEVE), the League for the Exchange of Commonwealth Teachers (LECT), and the United States – United Kingdom Education Commission and other bodies working in the area of education for international understanding.

10 Schools III also has three divisions. One is concerned with school curriculum matters, including the coordination of policy initiatives directed at raising educational standards in schools. The second division deals with examinations during the years of compulsory schooling and at 18 plus, including the General Certificate of Secondary Education (GCSE), commenced September 1986, and the Advanced Supplementary (AS) level examination, commenced September 1987. This division is responsible for policy and records of achievement, and for the DES's relations with the Secondary Examinations Council (SEC). The third division contains the Assessment of Performance Unit (APU). It is also concerned with English, foreign language and health education in the curriculum, and is responsible for relations with the School Curriculum Development Committee (SCDC).

11 **Policy branches: Further and Higher Education 1, 2 and 3**

Three branches administer policy for post-16 education and training. FHE 1 has four divisions. One is responsible for academic and institutional development in the local authority sector of higher education. This includes the sector's future management, approval of advanced courses and liaison with the Council for National Academic Awards (CNAA) (See **3.1** 52–59). The division plays a large part in the formulation of policy for local authority current expenditure on higher education and in monitoring the effects of this policy. It is also concerned with the building provision for further and higher education in the local authority sector. The division is the first point of contact between the Department and the National Advisory Body for Public Sector Higher Education (NAB) (See **1.3** 54–65). The second division is concerned with academic and institutional development and overall recurrent and capital expenditure resources for higher education in the university sector, including universities in Scotland and Wales. Its other responsibilities include the policy for overseas students and a long term planning for higher education. The third division is responsible for around thirty voluntary and direct grant colleges, the Royal College of Art, and the Cranfield Institute of Technology, including payment of recurrent and capital grant. The fourth division comprises the secretariat to the Computer Board for University and Research Councils. The Board makes recommendations to the Secretary of State for Education and Science regarding the provision of university computing facilities and advises the research councils on their computer proposals. It also plans the scale and nature of such provision to ensure that users in all disciplines have access to a full range of computing facilities for research and teaching.

12 FHE2 has three divisions. Division A deals with links between education and industry in general, and more particularly with education for engineering and related industries, including electronic engineering and computing. It is also concerned with the general response of the education system to information technology. Its responsibilities are youth service development and policy, and it maintains close contracts with youth organisations. Grants are made to national voluntary youth organisations to meet part of their headquarters' expenditure and to aid development work. Matters concerning youth work and training are also considered by this division. Division B is concerned with general policy and training for the 16–19 age group, including expenditure planning for non-advanced FE. It is currently taking the lead in a joint study with the local authority associations on NAFE efficiency. It is also concerned with the use of management information systems in colleges, including the development of the Further Education Staff College's FEMIS system, and the publication and follow-up of HM Inspectorate's reports on further education, and education grants for trade unions. The division is also concerned with the educational element of special measures for the young employed. In this connection it maintains close links with the Manpower Services Commission (MSC), the industrial training boards and voluntary training organisations on such matters as industrial training policy and the Youth Training Scheme (See **1.7**). The division keeps in touch with the MSC about the implementation of the funding arrangements for work-related NAFE announced in the 1984 White Paper *Training for Jobs*, and is responsible for further education aspects of the Technical and Vocational Education Initiative (TVEI) administered by the MSC. Other responsibilities include the College–Employer Links Project (CELP) and dealing with education for particular industries including hotel and catering, distribution and printing, also with management and business studies, maritime studies, and modern languages. The third division deals with the examining and validating bodies active in further education at sub-degree levels, in particular the Business and Technician Education Council (BTEC) (See **3.1** 44–49). It has a general concern with further education curricular matters below degree level maintaining close links with the Further Education Unit (FEU) and the Further Education Staff College (FESC) (See **3.1** 83–84). Its responsibilities cover the new Certificate of Pre-Vocational Education (CPVE), in-service training for teachers in further education, and follow-up of the *Review of Vocational Qualifications in England and Wales* (1986). This division also deals with further education

for ethnic minorities, has responsibility for further education in a number of subject areas, such as agriculture, art and design, dance and drama, music, architecture, town planning and surveying, and looks after education for particular industries.

13 FHE 3 also has three divisions. The first is concerned with policy for adult and continuing education including the REPLAN and the Professional, Industrial and Commercial Updating Programme (PICKUP) programmes (See **1.7** 41–42 and **3.1** 66). REPLAN is aimed at encouraging the development of better educational opportunities for adults who are unemployed. PICKUP is designed to encourage universities, polytechnics, and further education colleges to provide more post-experience vocational education to meet the needs of adults in employment. This division also deals with grants to departments of extra-mural studies in certain universities, the long-term residential adult education colleges, the Workers' Educational Association and other national associations concerned with adult education. The second division has a general concern with student affairs such as careers advisory services and student union matters. It has a particular responsibility in connection with the provision of further and higher education for students with special needs. Its other responsibilities include liaison with the MSC on the Open Tech, and the development of credit transfer and of open and distance learning. It authorises direct grants to the Open University, the British Academy, and the European University Institute at Florence. Other responsibilities include college and university government, careers guidance in further and higher education, international liaison on matters concerned with higher education, and education within the non-university sector for nursing and social work, for the professions supplementary to medicine, and for legal studies and librarianship. The third division is responsible for policy relating to financial support for students in higher education in England and Wales (See **3.3**). It advises on the application of the regulations governing payments of grants to students for which local education authorities are responsible. The division also administers the centrally awarded post-graduate studentships and bursaries for certain professional and vocational courses. In addition, it consults with the research councils and the British Academy (which administers the state studentship scheme on behalf of the Department).

14 **Policy branch: Science**

Science branch has two divisions. The first maintains liaison with the research councils and is involved in the appointment of members of the councils and of the Trustees of the Natural History Museum. This division's responsibilities also include the approval of senior posts and of major capital and recurrent expenditure on civil science and the supervision of research council commitments to certain international scientific organisations. The second division deals with questions that relate to the size and distribution of the Science Budget, and with general issues concerning the research council system. It also supplies the secretariat for the Advisory Board for the Research Councils (ABRC), and deals with international civil science matters affecting the DES and the research councils.

15 **Policy branches: Teachers Supply and Training, Teachers Pay and General, and Pensions**

Teachers Supply and Training Branch (TST) has four divisions. The first is responsible for policy on school teacher numbers and deployment, including provision for shortage subjects and the supply of ethnic minority teachers. The second is responsible for the national planning of initial teacher training, including the control of numbers and the balance of training, and for liaison with the Council for Accreditation of Teacher Education (CATE) (See **3.1** Appendix 2). It also has the responsibility for policy on FE teacher training, on the induction of new teachers, and on education and training (INSET) for serving teachers, including the scheme of grants to local authorities for those purposes. The third division provides economic advice to the Department on relevant macro-economic issues and on educational issues varying from the economic aspects of higher education to the measurement of educational output in schools. The Branch also contains an operational research unit which, among other things, develops financial models for policy formulation and expenditure forecasting. The fourth division is an operational research unit which, among other things, develops financial models for policy formulation and expenditure forecasting.

16 Teachers Pay and General Branch (TPG) has two divisions. The first is concerned with school and FE teachers' pay and conditions of service. The second takes references on universities pay and conditions of service (including tenure) and handles non-financial local government, educational research and general questions.

17 Pensions Branch is responsible for the administration of the superannuation scheme for teachers in England and Wales in maintained and independent schools, for teachers in public sector further and higher education, and for certain other staff employed by local authorities and other bodies.

18 **Common services**

Finance Branch is responsible for the Department's financial and accounting policies and procedures. It deals with forward estimating, including the costing of functions and policy for the Public Expenditure Survey; the preparation of Parliamentary estimates and cash limits; and the regularity and propriety of expenditure including the work of internal audit. It advises other branches, local education authorities and grant-aided bodies on financial matters; and is involved in consultations with HM Treasury and the Department of the Environment. The branch liaises with other partners in the education service on statistical and financial matters and makes all payments for the Department (except teachers' pensions). It is also responsible for overseeing the education support grant (ESG) scheme, the aim of which is to encourage local education authorities to devote a certain amount of expenditure to activities which appear to the Secretary of State for Education and Science to be of particular national importance (See **1.3** 28–31).

19 Architects and Building Branch is responsible for education building policy. It deals with the approval of building projects and with questions of standards and costs. It maintains statistics on educational building and, working in conjunction with HM Inspectorate, other DES branches and local education authorities, investigates the architectural and technical implications of new educational trends. The branch also provides information and guidance on design techniques through it development projects and publications (See **4**).

20 Information Branch advises Ministers and officials on the presentation of policy. The Head of Information Branch deals directly with all parts of the Office – Ministers, senior officials, branches and HM Inspectorate – in the discharge of his/her duties. The Branch comprises two sections which work closely together:

The Press Office which is responsible for relations with the press, radio and TV. It advises the Department on media presentation, drafts press notices, briefs media representatives, and arranges interviews and press conferences; *The Publications and Paid Publicity Section* which produces free and priced publications, plans exhibitions and displays, makes films and video programmes, and mounts paid publicity campaigns. It has responsibility, too, for the DES's PRESTEL input. A team within the section deals with enquiries from members of the public. A graphic design studio is attached to this section and is responsible for the preparation of art work, publications design, exhibition and display, and the production of visual aids.

The Head and Deputy Head of Branch, the Chief Press Officer and the Head of Publications Section constitute an Information Policy Management Group (IPMG) which meets regularly under the chairmanship of the Head of Branch and occasionally under the chairpersonship of the Permanent Secretary.

21 The Department Library has several important collections of educational books, reports and other documents, and stocks a wide range of periodicals.

22 Information Technology Branch provides computing, advanced communications and office technology services for the Department, including HMI and the UGC. Facilities include a central computer installation at Darlington which serves the Department through a terminal network, a number of mini-computers, and a growing range of micro-computers. Technical staff within the branch provide consultancy and programming services.

23 Statistics Branch provides a service to the Department, to Government, to Parliament and to the general public on educational statistics. Some of the topics covered by professional statisticians in the branch include statistical advice covering further and higher education and related economic and social matters, educational expenditure data, and UK educational statistics and international statistical comparisons. The branch provides other statistical advice concerning schools, teachers, pupils, school leavers, curriculum, and examinations. It also has responsibility for publications policy and the development of performance initiatives for schools. Statistical bulletins are issued by Statistics Branch throughout the year to provide and interpret new data relating to educational matters. Augmenting this information is a priced annual volume of Education Statistics for the United Kingdom published through HMSO. A priced digest of statistics and various Education Statistics Volumes are also published and tabulations – mainly in the form of computer print-out – are available on request and repayment.

24 **HM Inspectorate (HMI)**

The 1944 Education Act required the Secretary of State to cause inspections to be made (Section 77). Although the Act does not define the purpose or the nature of such inspections they are clearly designed to assist the Secretary of State in the performance of his/her functions. Thus the primary responsibility of the Inspectorate (which was established in 1839) is to report to the Secretary of State for Education Science on the health of the education service. (Inspectors in Wales report to the Secretary of State for Wales.) They do this by using the evidence gained from visits of various kinds. All schools – publicly maintained, grant-aided and independent, colleges of further education, polytechnics and institutes of higher education are open to formal inspection by teams of Her Majesty's Inspectors, as are adult education classes (whether provided by local authorities or the universities) and youth groups. The Inspectorate has recently begun to report on aspects of education in LEAs as a whole, and is likely to continue inspecting LEA provision in whole or in part at the rate of two or three authorities a year. 'Inspection' also covers shorter, less formal visits by individual inspectors or by small teams. In addition HM Inspectors visit university departments of education by invitation.

25 Since January 1983 it has been the normal practice of the Secretary of State to authorise the publication of reports which follow full, formal inspections. However, HMI also discuss their observations with individual lecturers, and in less detail with the senior staff and head/principal, before they leave an institution no matter whether they are on formal or informal visit. Each year the Inspectorate produces a score or so of publications on general themes, in addition to inspection reports based on its work throughout the education system. These are sold through HMSO or are made available free from the Department. Like HMI's inspection reports such publications are published with the agreement of the Secretary of State, but they are published as written by the Inspectorate, in accordance with HMI's continuing professional independence.

26 Inspectors are also involved in the in-service education and training of teachers at national, regional and local levels. They mount the Department's annual programme of short courses for serving teachers, and help to plan and organise the regional programmes of courses set up jointly by the Department and regional committees established for this purpose. They contribute to courses and conferences organised by other bodies and also, from time to time, contribute articles to various educational journals.

27 The Government's policy statement *The Work of HM Inspectorate in England and Wales* published by DES and the Welsh Office in 1983, states that the Inspectorate:

(i) Assesses standards and trends and advises the Secretary of State on the performance of the system nationally;
(ii) Identifies and makes known more widely good practice and promising developments and draws attention to weaknesses requiring attention;
(iii) Provides advice and assistance to those in educational institutions through its day to day contacts, its contributions to training and its publications; and to other bodies, for example by serving as assessors on examining/validating bodies.

To do this the Inspectorate needs both a field force and a body of senior Inspectors at the Department's headquarters.

28 The Senior Chief Inspector (SCI), 7 Chief Inspectors (CIs) and over 30 other Inspectors (mainly Staff Inspectors who offer general duties' support to CIs) are based at the Department in London. They form the major link on matters of policy and planning between officers of the Department and the majority of Inspectors who are deployed throughout England. Those Inspectors working in the field who have a national responsibility for a subject or a special aspect of education, or are responsible for liaison with a particular local education authority, also have direct links with the Department. There is a small nucleus of Inspectors whose chief concern is with teacher training, but many others inspect in this field as well as in schools and further education.

29 The Senior Chief Inspector is the head of the Inspectorate and the senior educational adviser to the Secretary of State. His or her responsibilities include inspection policy, relations of the Inspectorate with Ministers and the Office, the deployment and personnel management of the Inspectorate, and the management of the HMI Cost Centre. The SCI is advised in these matters by the Chief Inspectors collectively and assisted in their execution by two civil service principals one of whom gives general administrative support while the other works mainly on HMI personnel matters. The SCI is also assisted by a Staff Inspector for personnel, on personal matters concerning Inspectors.

30 Each of the seven Chief Inspectors is responsible for inspection of, and policy matters related to, particular categories of institution and/or particular phases and aspects of education, including certain cross-phase and cross-curricular matters. CIs can draw on the whole of the staff and expertise of the Inspectorate to undertake work related to their responsibilities. The relative priorities of major inspection and other tasks are determined by the SCI and CIs collectively but final decisions about inspection priorities rest with the SCI. One Chief Inspector deals primarily with education in the nursery, infant, junior and middle years, also with home-school links, libraries, museums, relations with the assessment of performance unit, and policy for equal opportunities. Another has secondary schools (11–19) as a main responsibility together with examinations and assessment, and a number of other cross-phase issues. A third has independent, European and expatriate schools, and services education (in schools) as an institutional remit together with curriculum (5–19), reviews of LEA provision, and international relations. A fourth is concerned particularly with special educational needs in schools and further education, educational disadvantage, ethnic minorities and links with the Home Office, Department of the Environment, and Department of Health and Social Security.

31 Three Chief Inspectors are particularly concerned with further and higher education. Their responsibilities are:

(i) Non-advanced further education including pre-vocational and technical education, the Youth Training Scheme, services education (FE), and youth and community provision; links with MSC, FEU, and examining and validating bodies.
(ii) Advanced further education, adult and continuing education, education in prisons; links with NAB, CNAA, Architects and Building Branch.
(iii) Initial teacher training and voluntary colleges; in-service education and training (schools and FHE), education research TVEI, information technology, educational technology, broadcasting, school-industry links and other matters.

32 Inspectors in the field normally work both as specialists and as generalists, both individually and as members of either national or territorial teams. This pattern of operations applies throughout the organisation to the two main groups of Inspectors, those for schools and those for further and higher education. Field Inspectors are assigned to one of the Department's seven divisions, each headed by a Divisional Inspector – though the FHE team in each Division works under a Regional Staff Inspector for further and higher education.

33 **Commentary**

The role of the DES and its relationships with the rest of the education system have been changing since the mid-1970s. These changes were continuing at time of writing, and there was debate about more radical changes, including even the creation of a Department of Education and Training.

34 The 'Ruskin Speech' of Prime Minister James Callaghan in October 1976 – when he said he wanted to see education related 'as much as possible to improving industrial performance and thereby increasing national wealth' – can now be seen as a watershed in the activities of the Department of Education and Science. For the quarter century after World War II the Department, local government, and the teachers had worked within an interpretation of the 1944 Education Act which gave the Secretary of State general duties and powers but left the ownership and administration of the service to local education authorities, and the major professional decisions in the hands of teachers. The biggest external influence on the curriculum came from the examining, validating and professional bodies which devised or approved courses and syllabuses, and assessed and certificated the attainment of students. The Ruskin Speech came at a time of increasing adverse criticism, in some sections of the community, of the standards of education among school leavers and of the relevance of the curriculum to the needs of employment. Unemployment was rising, and young people were affected as hard as any other section of the community. These circumstances led to a reappraisal, at all levels of the education system, including a stronger inclination on the part of Government to influence the content, standards and output of the system and to a new relationship between the Department and its partners in the education service.

35 The Ruskin Speech was followed by the so-called 'Great Debate', a series of conferences around the country on four topics – the school curriculum, assessment and standards, the training of teachers, and the transition to working life – which are still major issues in the 1980s. A number of documents from the Government, HMI, the political parties, the (now defunct) Schools Council and the teachers' unions have been published on the nature and content of the curriculum in schools. There has been a steady movement towards the idea of a 'core curriculum' to which all school children should be entitled no matter what their social circumstances or place of study, though some, not least in the local authorities and teachers' unions, see the idea of a core curriculum as an undesirable interference in local and professional rights. On the second topic, both Labour and Conservative governments have been committed to improving standards in education (in order to meet the need of a complex technological society) and the Conservative government was instrumental in securing the introduction of the General Certificate of Secondary Education (GCSE) for which the first examinations will be held in 1988 (See **3.1** 16–20). This reform together with the proposed introduction of Advanced Supplementary (AS) level examinations and experimental work on Records of Achievement are designed to secure that the school curriculum should contain a stronger practical element and attend to the application of knowledge and understanding. This objective is seen as relevant to pupils of all abilities, not least those previously outside the ambit of public examinations (the so-called 'bottom 40%').

36 On the third topic there has been an increased emphasis on 'teaching quality', and a White Paper was published in 1983. In 1984 the Government established a new Council for the Accreditation of Teacher Education (CATE) to advise the Secretary of State on the approval of initial teacher training courses and issued in the same year criteria which deal with the selection of students for training, the academic and professional content of courses, and the practical element of training. The transition to working life, the fourth topic, continues to be a subject of debate, controversy and experiment and has strengthened the role of the MSC in the education system. It is the Government's view that

in the last two years of compulsory schooling the programme of all pupils should begin to have relevance to working life, perhaps through work experience. Two major curriculum developments have increased concerns for vocational relevance: the Technical and Vocational Education Initiative (TVEI) (launched as a pilot in 1983) was in 1986 extended to a national scheme to enrich the curriculum and encourage a close collaboration between education and industry (See **3.1** 4–9). The Certificate of Pre-Vocational Education (CPVE) began in 1985 (See **3.1** 10–15).

37 The steady advance of the Department of Employment and its agency, the MSC, into what were primarily education territories has caused more controversy about central government interference than any of the other issues mentioned above. The DES has been working closely with the DE and its agencies since the mid-1970s. In 1975 the Training Services Agency issued a document *The Vocational Preparation of Young People* which led to a joint initiative by DES and TSA to establish schemes of Unified Vocational Preparation and give further education and training to young people in jobs which traditionally did not offer a planned introduction to work. Similarly the DES and FE service were involved in the implementation of the Youth Opportunities Programme, which followed MSC's *Holland Report* (1977), and the YTS. However, the use of MSC as a direct funding agency (first to purchase courses in FE to implement aspects of the Government's New Training Initiative, and then to support TVEI in schools) led to charges of unwarranted central interference in the direction and content of education and criticism of a narrow vocational ethic. At time of writing there were still fourteen local authorities in England and Wales which have not adopted TVEI, but its becoming a permanent programme may lead them to a change of heart. One decision above all others gave particular offence to the local authorities – the Government giving 25% of work-related non-advanced further education monies to the MSC to improve the responsiveness of further education to the labour market. After extensive wrangling the local authorities agreed to produce three-year development plans, with one-year detailed programmes with MSC for their work-related FE services (See **1.7** 8). The Government's preference for using MSC to bring about the quick changes in education provision (which was always said to take a decade to change) led to rumours in the press about its desire to unite education and training, or perhaps post-compulsory education and training, in one government department. However, after the publication of the White Paper *Working Together* in summer 1986, it seemed more likely that the existing Employment and Education Departments would continue as they were for the foreseeable future, but with their objectives closely aligned (See above paragraph 4). (See **1.7**).

38 The Department of Education and Science, while coming in for considerable criticism for not 'standing up to MSC' from its partners in the local authorities and the teachers' bodies, pressed ahead, particularly under Sir Keith Joseph as Secretary of State, with initiatives of its own. Some of these are related to employment interests, such as the College Employer Links Project (CELP), the Professional, Industrial and Commercial Updating Programme (PICKUP) and REPLAN (See above paragraphs 13 and **1.7** 41–42 and **3.1** 66). The Department has also been carrying forward developments in special education after the 1981 Education Act; it initiated a lower attaining pupils programme (LAPS); and it introduced a major programme aimed at ensuring that children are properly prepared for life in a society in which devices and systems based on microelectronics are common-place. Through its Education Sup-

port Grants (ESG) scheme the Department encourages LEAs to re-allocate a limited amount of funding to activities which appear to the Secretary of State for Education and Science, of the Secretary of State for Wales, to be of particular importance. Through the in-service training grants scheme the Department encourages the release of teachers for in-service training in priority areas with direct financial assistance to LEAs (see **2.9**).

39 On the non-advanced further education front the Department worked with the local authority associations in a joint efficiency study to improve the cost-effectiveness of NAFE in the light of Audit Commission reports (See **2.8** 36–38), and in Circular 1/86 it promoted a new form of in-service training to improve the standard of management in the sector.

40 The part played by the Department in the management and funding of polytechnics and other provision of higher education enlarged steadily during the 1970s and 1980s (see **1.1**, **1.3** and **2.8** 29). The White Paper 1987 put forward the Government's plans for funding centrally higher education in the public sector (See **1.1** Appendix 1).

41 **The Welsh Office Education Department (WOED)**

In April 1978 responsibility in Wales for all non-university further and higher education, the youth and community services, and adult education was transferred to the Secretary of State for Wales. The Secretary of State for Education and Science continues to exercise responsibility in Wales, as in England, for the universities, the Research Councils, mandatory and post-graduate awards to students, and for the pay, superannuation, qualifications, probation the medical fitness of teachers and cases of teachers' misconduct. The WOED, which is headed by the Under Secretary, comprises three divisions: the first deals with schools; the second with further and higher education; and the third with general educational services such as building, research and finance (including the payment of grants to LEAs, and certain other bodies for the teaching of the Welsh language and the teaching of other subjects in Welsh). In discharging his educational responsibilities the Secretary of State for Wales is assisted by HM Inspectorate in Wales which numbers over 50 Inspectors and is on loan to the Welsh Office from the Department of Education and Science. It is led by a Chief Inspector, assisted by seven Staff Inspectors, and has the same functions as the Inspectorate in England but reports to the Secretary of State for Wales.

NOTE

This section has drawn for much of its factual material on *The Department of Education and Science – A brief guide* published by the DES in 1986.

1.5 NORTHERN IRELAND

1 **Central and local government**

The evolution of educational provision in Northern Ireland is complex. This complexity derives not only from the necessity to provide educational opportunity in keeping with technological and social change, but also from the political complexity of Northern Ireland's development.

2 Between 1801 and 1921 the Parliament of the United Kingdom was responsible for legislation in the whole of Ireland. The law was administered by an executive based in Dublin. The Government of Ireland Act 1920 resulted in the division of Ireland into two parts and the establishment of a Parliament in Northern Ireland. The Northern Ireland Parliament was enabled to make laws in accordance with the provision of the Government of Ireland Act 1920. Since the early 1970s, however, there have been a number of changes in the way in which Northern Ireland is governed. Since 1972 Northern Ireland has not had a separate legislative body (except for a period of four months in 1974), and the functions of government are carried out under the ministerial direction of the Secretary of State for Northern Ireland and other Ministers of the Northern Ireland Office. The Secretary of State and his/her Ministers are appointed by the Prime Minister.

3 The Northern Ireland Departments are separate from the Northern Ireland Office but are subject to the direction of the Secretary of State. The work of the Department is coordinated by the head of the Northern Ireland Civil Service. There are six Departments: Agriculture; Economic Development; Education; Environment; Finance and Personnel; Health and Social Services.

4 There are twenty-six district councils in Northern Ireland. They were established under the Local Government Act (N.I.) 1972. Their functions fall into three broad categories, namely: executive, representative, and consultative. Under representative functions councils nominate representatives to various statutory bodies such as the Education and Library Boards.

5 The Education and Library Boards (ELBs), of which there are five, were established in 1972 through the Education and Libraries (Northern Ireland) Order 1972. It is under this combination of central and local government, along with statutory body (in the case of education, Education and Library Boards), that the provision of education is administered and developed in Northern Ireland.

6 **Department of Education for Northern Ireland**

The Department of Education for Northern Ireland (DENI) is a department of government in Northern Ireland. It is separate from the Northern Ireland Office but carries out its duties under the direction and control of the Secretary of State for Northern Ireland. The Department is required to work closely with a number of other departments, particularly the Department of Economic Development (DED) which, among other things, coordinates the Youth Training Programme and the work of the Northern Ireland Training Authority. There is also close involvement with the Department of Agriculture which has among its responsibilities the provision of agricultural education and training.

7 DENI is responsible for policy, financial control, legislation standards, programmes and priorities. The Department is organised under nine divisions:

(i) Finance and Statistics
(ii) Higher Education, Teacher Training, Postgraduate Awards and Scholarships
(iii) Further Education, Youth Services, Youth Training Programme
(iv) Sport and Community, Arts and Museums
(v) Personnel, Area Boards, Libraries, HQ Co-ordination, Private Office, Legislation
(vi) Teachers' Salaries, Conditions of Service and Superannuation, Information Technology
(vii) Schools I (includes School Building, School Management, Policy, Residences, Independent Schools, Primary Schools Administration, Special Education, School Development and Nursery Education)
(viii) Schools II (includes Grammar and Secondary Schools' Administration, Grammar Schools' Finance, Secondary Schools' Development, Transfer Procedure and Examinations)
(ix) Professional Education Development

8 As can be seen from the organisational divisions, the Department's functions are wider than might be suggested by its title. the functions include responsibility for the development of primary, secondary and further education, including higher education. The two universities are grant-aided by DENI on the advice of the University Grants Committee[1]. The functions also include developments in community and adult education as well as special education. DENI also oversees the Education and Library Boards and controls the training and supply of teachers, as well as regulating the staff of schools and further education colleges. It further has oversight of teachers' salaries and superannuation, the arts and libraries, youth services, sport and recreation, community services and facilities, as well as examinations.

9 In relation to community development, DENI grant aids and funds a wide variety of community-related activities directly. For example, DENI gives funding to the Citizens' Advice Bureaux, the Workers' Educational Association, the N.I. Association of Youth Clubs, the Corrymeela Community and many other organisations as part of the contribution towards adult and continuing education. This system of direct central funding has implications for the development of community organisations since other funding from local councils also derives indirectly from DENI. In the case of Belfast City Council, for example, provision for community and leisure facilities are made by two Council committees dealing with these matters; all decisions, however, regarding the funding of such facilities, though initiated by the Council, would require approval by DENI. DENI is therefore more deeply involved in the provision of grassroots community services than the central government body in England. The history of DENI's involvement in these areas is complex but partly derives from the fact that DENI assumed responsibility for the functions of the Department of Community Relations after the collapse of the 1974 power-sharing government structure. All of these activities derive from DENI's responsibility for policies to improve community relations in Northern Ireland.

10 In the case of examinations for GCSE the conduct of the examinations is carried out by an independent body which is the Northern Ireland Schools Examination Council. Schools and colleges of FE in Northern Ireland may,

however, enter candidates for GCSE boards outside Northern Ireland (See **1.5** 15).

11 The Department is informed on professional matters by the Inspectorate who carry out inspection of schools, colleges, and youth clubs. The Inspectorate plays a leading role in the development of curriculum and in-service training and represents the Department on a wide variety of educational committees both inside and outside Northern Ireland.

12 DENI is advised by a number of committees representing areas of special interest and development in education:
(i) Northern Ireland Council for Educational Development
(ii) Northern Ireland Council for Educational Research
(iii) Council for Continuing Education
(iv) Advisory Committee for Teacher Education
(v) Northern Ireland BTEC Education Council
(vi Liaison Committee
(vii) Advisory Board for Postgraduate Awards
(viii) Advisory Body on Community Work
(ix) Centre for Learning Resources
(x) Committee for Centre for Education Management
(xi) Teachers' Negotiating Machinery
(xii) Northern Ireland UNESCO Committee
(xiii) Youth Committee for Northern Ireland

13 **Contextual issues**
The shape of contemporary educational provision in Northern Ireland was determined by the Education Act 1947. It made provision for a typical tripartite system of education. However, the Act had '. . . little direct effect on technical education apart from introducing the apparently innocuous term "technical intermediate school" ' (Gillies and White 1982). The provision of technical intermediate schooling disappeared and was replaced by pre-apprenticeship courses which recruited at fifteen years of age. This remained the case until 1983 when the full-time entry age to FE colleges became sixteen; there are two exceptions to the sixteen entry rule in the Southern Board (See below paragraph 29).

14 A major reorganisation of educational administration occurred in 1972. The Education and Libraries (Northern Ireland) Order 1972 established five Education and Library Boards (ELBs). Along with central government, the Education and Library Boards are responsible for the provision of primary, secondary, and further education in Northern Ireland. The 1972 Order has now been replaced by the Education and Libraries (Northern Ireland) Order 1986. However, the 1986 order retains the substantive regulations as set out in 1972. The 1947 Act, 1972 and 1986 Orders continue the trend towards centralisation; this point was made by both Sutherland (1983) and Marsh (1982) with respect to former legislation and development.

15 While there may be a high degree of centralised power in the hands of DENI and the Northern Ireland Schools' Examination Council which affects the nature of the curriculum experience by students in Northern Ireland, there is nonetheless considerable diversity in the types of schooling available. First, the school population is for the most part divided almost evenly along religious lines with separate schooling provision. Secondly, there is selective transfer to

second level education at 11+; approximately 30% of eleven year olds transfer to grammar schools and the remainder to secondary schools, formerly known as secondary intermediate schools.

16 Division along religious lines can be identified in two broad categories namely 'controlled schools' (for the most part attended by pupils with a Protestant background) and 'maintained' (for the most part attended by pupils with a Roman Catholic background). These divisions permeate both primary and secondary provision. Further education colleges do not retain this division but the degree of cultural integration has not been the subject of any major research report to date, so it is difficult to say at what level and in what ways integration occurs.

17 The separate school system along with selection at 11+ has created major problems for rationalisation policies in the 1980s and is a drain on already scarce resources. Wilson (1983) notes '. . . it is possible to have eight post-primary schools, four grammar and four secondary in a small Northern Ireland market town. The record is actually four plus three'. This has obvious consequences for FE development to meet new community needs; Marsh (1983) makes the point that, while DENI has the power, it is not always able to 'allocate its funds as rationally as it would wish'. DENI is able to encourage development through its approval for new courses while at the same time it may through withholding approval affect the pattern of provision available. Final approval for courses to operate rests with DENI except in the case of non-vocational courses, such as recreational courses, provided they do not require additional resources. Such requests for the operation of new courses are required to be forwarded to DENI through the appropriate ELB. This procedure is not always followed. It is difficult for ELB officers to plan support programmes when they are not always fully informed of local intentions. There is little room for negotiation between the Department and ELBs due to the severe restrictions on funding. Control of funding is firmly in the hands of the Department. The Department is able to earmark funding for special developments and this it does in the case of the Youth Training Programme (YTP) and the Adult Unemployment Initiative (AUI). In the first half of the 1980s these were the only areas of real expansion within the FE sector. Since 1980 DENI has only approved two additional full-time teaching appointments to the FE sector in areas other then YTP. However, there were signs of change in 1987–88, with DENI giving approval for thirty new posts in FE related to science and technology. ELBs are able to approve part-time teaching hours within their area but funding for this has to be found within allocated budgets.

18 In the further education sector DENI decided to follow the recommendations of the Review of Vocational Qualifications (RVQ) (See **3.1** 50):

> In the light of representations from Northern Ireland, and in view of our own commitment to improving opportunities for recognition and progression, we recommend that the National Council be responsible from the outset for the development of a coherent system of vocational qualifications in England, Wales and Northern Ireland (10.10).

This, together with the review of school curriculum undertaken by the Northern Ireland Council for Educational Development and a major research project on *Transition From School to Adult Working Life*, was intended to form the basis of a wide-ranging review of '. . . the present mix of educational training and employment opportunities for the 14–19 age group . . .' (DED/DENI Interdepartmental Executive 1986).

19 Such a policy points to closer collaboration between school and college provision, which would have to be achieved alongside the development of local and relevant curriculum capable of meeting the criteria of access and progression. Such a policy would test the effectiveness of local support structures and the willingness of providers to maximise opportunities in the interests of young people.

20 **Other departments: Education and Training**

Department of Economic Development

The Industrial Training Act (Northern Ireland) 1964 placed responsibility for developments in industrial training under the Department of Education. This responsibility was later transferred to the Ministry of Labour and has subsequently become the responsibility of the Department of Economic Development (DED).

21 The Industrial Training Order (Northern Ireland) 1984 established the Northern Ireland Training Authority (NITA) which assumed responsibility for direct training services and a training development unit, as well as administrative and financial services, for the industrial training boards, of which there are eight:

(i) Catering Industry Training Board (Northern Ireland)
(ii) Clothing Industry Training Board (Northern Ireland)
(iii) Distributive Industry Training Board (Northern Ireland)
(iv) Engineering Industry Training Board (Northern Ireland)
(v) Food and Drink Industry Training Board (Northern Ireland)
(vi) Textiles Industry Training Board (Northern Ireland)
(vii) Construction Industry Training Board (Northern Ireland)
(viii) Road Transport Industry Training Board (Northern Ireland)

NITA promotes research into future training needs and provides training services. It also houses the centre for the promotion of open learning in Northern Ireland.

22 The Department of Economic Development plays a major role in the coordination and provision of the Youth Training Programme for young unemployed. The three main categories of provision under the control of DED are: Community Workshops, of which there are forty-two, Employer-Led Schemes, and Youth and Community Projects.

23 **Department of Agriculture**

The Department of Agriculture is the body responsible for agricultural education and training. It provides courses at all levels from part-time and day release courses to post-graduate courses at agricultural colleges. There are three residential agricultural colleges in Northern Ireland. These are: Enniskillen Agricultural College in County Fermanagh; Greenmount Agricultural and Horticultural College, Co Antrim; and Loughry College of Agriculture and Food Technology, Co Tyrone. These, along with Queens' University in Belfast, provide for the needs of agricultural education and training in Northern Ireland.

24 **Education and Library Boards**

The five Education and Library Boards (ELBs) established by the Education and Libraries (Northern Ireland) Order 1972 are: Belfast, North-Eastern, South-Eastern, Southern, and Western. Since 1972 there have been a number of provisions amending the order of 1972. These are now consolidated in the Education and Libraries (Northern Ireland) Order 1986. Each ELB serves one or more of the local government districts established under the Local Government Act (NI) 1972.

25 The ELBs and the districts which they serve are listed in Schedule I of the 1986 Order

Table 1

Education and Library Board	*Name of Local Government District*
Belfast	Belfast
South-Eastern	Ards; Castlereagh; Down; Lisburn North Down
Southern	Armagh; Banbridge; Cookstown Craigavon; Dungannon; Newry and Mourne
Western	Fermanagh; Limavady; Derry; Omagh; Strabane
North-Eastern	Antrim; Ballymena; Ballymoney; Carrickfergus; Coleraine; Larne; Magherafelt; Moyle; Newtownabbey

26 The way in which the membership of ELBs is determined is complex and reflects the complexity of school provision in Northern Ireland. Members are not directly elected to the ELBs. All are ministerial appointments. However, 40% of Board membership consists of elected councillors who have been nominated to serve on the Board by their respective councils. The remaining 60% of membership is made up of appointees reflecting the interests of three broad categories as follows: (1) persons who appear to represent the interests of transferors[2] of schools in the area of the ELB; (2) persons who appear to represent the interests of trustees of maintained schools in the area of the ELB; (3) persons who appear to have an interest in the services for which the ELB is responsible. (The Order makes provision for the appointment of three serving teachers.) Each ELB is required to have a Teaching Appointment Committee and a Library Committee and may appoint other committees as considered necessary. ELBs have established a range of committees dealing with Education, Finance, General Purposes, and Youth.

27 The responsibilities of Education and Library Boards fall into five broad categories identified as follows in *Ulster Year Book 1985*:

(i) To ensure that there are sufficient schools of all kinds to meet the needs of their area;

(ii) To manage controlled schools and educational institutions (including technical colleges) and to be responsible for the day-to-day maintenance of most voluntary schools other than voluntary grammar schools;

(iii) To make awards for certain school, higher and continuing education courses;

(iv) To make arrangements for the provision of meals and milk, for the operation of the free books scheme, and transport services for pupils; to enforce attendance; to regulate the employment of children and young people, assist education research, and provide recreational and youth service facilities;

(v) To develop a comprehensive and efficient library service for their areas and to make library services available to grant-aided schools and other grant-aided educational establishments.

28 Each ELB is headed by a chief officer who is supported by a full-time staff of board officers and educational advisers. At any given time there are a number of seconded teachers working alongside education officers in support of various priority areas of curriculum and staff development. ELBs are more concerned with the administration of educational provision in their area than with policy-making. They are not empowered to raise funds locally. Policy and priority areas are established by central government. ELBs tend to deal with resource allocation under broad guidelines established centrally for the region.

29 The 1986 Order identified three stages of educational provision which it is the responsibility of ELBs to provide. The stages are: primary, secondary, and further education. Further education provision is described as, 'full-time and part-time education other than secondary education provided for persons over compulsory school age' (Part III, 5(c)). Prior to 1983 pupils could transfer to a further education college at 15 years of age. Since 1983 transfer is not permitted until 16 years of age, with the exception of the colleges in the Southern Board Area where Lurgan and Portadown colleges are allowed to take pupils at 14 years of age. There is provision for linked courses involving schools and colleges in programmes whereby students can attend their local FE college for part of their studies prior to 16 years of age. The new Certificate of Pre-Vocational Education (CPVE) qualification allows for and encourages joint curriculum provision between schools and further education colleges at 16+ (See **3.1** 10–15).

30 The 1986 Order makes provision for cooperation between ELBs in the provision of further education, and between ELBs and other bodies for the provision of vocational and industrial training. With regard to the former, some specialist vocational courses are undertaken within certain designated colleges, while the latter refers to vocational and industrial training carried out by the Department of Economic Development and the Department of Agriculture.

31 The Education and Library Boards face many problems in reorganising educational provision for the latter part of the twentieth century. The amount of financial support which they can devote to developments in further education is restricted by a number of features peculiar to Northern Ireland. On the one hand, dispersed population in rural areas makes school rationalisation difficult. At a time of falling roles it is difficult to maintain and develop curriculum provision. On the other hand, the divided school system (See paragraphs 15–17 above) makes rationalisation in the interests of expanded curriculum opportunity difficult. ELBs have to maintain school units because of factors which are built into the history of schooling in Northern Ireland. The cost of these divisions is a loss of curriculum opportunity. While schools and colleges of further education are encouraged to seek ways of cooperating in

the interests of curriculum opportunity, the full potential of the education system has not yet been realised.

32 ELBs are at time of writing considering the introduction of new procedures for governing Institutes of Further Education. DENI has issued guidelines known as the *Model Scheme*, and Boards have been asked to adopt the model with minimum of amendment. The governing body is to be responsible for the management of the college other than:

'(i) The general educational character of the college and its place in the educational system which shall be determined by the Board; and

(ii) The internal organisation, management and discipline of the college which shall be the responsibility of the Principal.'

33 The governors are to make arrangements for the establishment of a student union or other body representing students. Also they are to arrange for student representation through student representatives to the governors or the principals on matters of proper concern to the students. The membership of the governing body is to include: members appointed by the Board from among its members; the principal; elected teachers of the college; Board appointees representative of industrial, commercial and other appropriate interests; student representation. The governing body is to meet at least four times in each academic year. They may appoint appropriate committees and carry out the following tasks:

(i) Prepare annual financial statements

(ii) Inspect premises and make recommendations to the Board

(iii) Ensure efficient use of premises

(iv) Deal with appointments, promotions and suspension of staff in accordance with the regulations set out in the model scheme

34 **Colleges of Further Education**

Harbinson (1985) identifies four features of the further education system in Northern Ireland which makes it different in some ways from FE provision in other parts of the United Kingdom. First, the facility existed up until 1982 for students to undertake their final year of compulsory schooling in FE colleges. As a result many colleges tended to have a secondary school ethos. Secondly, for a variety of reasons Northern Ireland FE colleges have fewer full-time students over 18 years of age than is the case elsewhere. Thirdly, as Northern Ireland's FE colleges are one of the key providers of the Youth Training Programme (YTP) (the equivalent to the Youth Training Scheme – See **1.7**) there has been a significant emphasis on curriculum and staff development needs in the context of radically new approaches to education and training. Fourthly, the merger of Ulster Polytechnic with the New University of Ulster in 1984 to form the University of Ulster has effects on an area of potential collaboration between colleges and polytechnic. The results of the merger have implications for the provision of advanced FE courses within the region.

35 To the above may also be added the developments which have placed agricultural education and training under the Department of Agriculture; also, and more significantly, the transfer from the Department of Education of responsibility for the implementation of the Industrial Training Act for (Northern Ireland) 1964 to the Ministry of Labour, now the Department of Economic Development. While the provisions of the Act did in fact result in wide college participation with increased numbers of apprentices undertaking day-release

classes at local colleges, Gillies and White (1982) state that an opportunity was missed.

> . . . an opportunity was lost of involving the technical colleges directly in the overall training of the young people entering industry and commerce in their neighbourhoods instead of acting as assistants when required by the new training centres.

36 There are twenty-six institutions of further education in Northern Ireland. They are spread throughout the region. Two are specialist colleges: Northern Ireland Hotel and Catering College located in Portrush, Co Antrim, and the College of Business Studies located in Belfast. The colleges range in size from grade 2 to grade 6.

37 The Department of Education, in its directory of courses for further education published jointly with the Department of Agriculture under the title *Directory of Courses In Colleges of Further Education and Agricultural Colleges in Northern Ireland in 1986/87* lists seven categories of courses:

(i) General education: usually consists of GCE O and A level subjects taken on either a full-time or part-time basis.

(ii) Pre-vocational: the Certificate in Pre-Vocational Education (CPVE) (See **3.1** 10–15); Foundation Courses of the City and Guilds of London Institute (CGLI) (See **3.1** 33–39). In this area courses are available in Community Care, Construction, Engineering, Food Industries, Science Industries, Agricultural Studies, Commercial Studies, Garment Manufacturing and Distribution; college-devised pre-vocational courses which provide students with opportunities for work experience in agriculture, catering, engineering, construction, hairdressing and nursing. Youth Training Programme for young unemployed, both full-time and part-time, in collaboration with other YTP providers.

(iii) Vocational: leading to awards of national examining or validating bodies, City and Guilds of London Institute (CGLI), Royal Society of Arts (RSA) (See **3.1** 40–43), Business and Technician Education Council (BTEC) (See **3.1** 44–49), Central Council of Education and Training in Social Work (CCETW), National Nursery Examination Board (NNEB).

(iv) Commercial courses: full-time and part-time courses leading to certificate of RSA or to certificates and diplomas of BTEC.

(v) Craft courses: full-time and part-time courses leading to certificates of CGLI.

(vi) Technician courses: full-time and part-time courses leading to BTEC awards for certificate and diploma.

(vii) Courses for professional bodies: these courses are provided in a limited number of colleges and lead to awards of professional bodies such as: Institute of Housing, Institute of Chartered Secretaries and Administrators, Chartered Insurance Institute, Institute of Statisticians, Society of Chiropodists, Hotel Catering and Institutional Management Association, Institute of Banking in Ireland, Institute of Building Societies and Institute of Marketing.

38 The major recent development for further education colleges in Northern Ireland has been the introduction of the Youth Training Programme (YTP) which began in 1982. YTP is coordinated by the Department of Economic Development (DED) in close cooperation with the Department of Education

(DENI). This cooperation is accomplished through the DED/DENI Interdepartmental Executive. As well as being responsible for the overall coordination of YTP, the Interdepartmental Executive commissions programme evaluations and promulgates agreed policy statements on the purposes, aims, and operation of the programmes.

39 Further education colleges currently provide approximately 3,000 full-time places and about 10,000 part-time places. the part-time places are taken up by young unemployed persons released from YTP provided by Government Training Centres, Community Workshops, and Employer-based schemes. YTP – with its emphases on an integrated programme of training, education and work experience – required colleges and college staff to adopt new practices in planning and delivery of curriculum. For the most part the traditional organisation of colleges along rigid departmental lines was not conducive to the development of new integrated programmes of study. Since the introduction of YTP in 1982 colleges have been developing new approaches to college management and strategies of staff development. This task has been supported by Education and Library Boards through the establishment of ELB staff development committees and college staff development committees. Each FE college within Northern Ireland has appointed a staff development tutor responsible for implementing college staff development policy and for coordinating the college's own efforts with ELB programmes of staff development. These new directions in curriculum/staff development are supported by the Regional Curriculum Base located at the University of Ulster in Jordanstown. These efforts reflect the concerns of DENI expressed in its survey *The Youth Training Programme and Further Education Colleges: The First Year 1982–83.* The survey noted that 'The Traditional FE approach is strongly represented on many college courses . . . There is urgent need for the development of more college-based in-service training programmes on informal teaching methods which are relevant to the learning needs of young adults'. NATFHE (1981) expressed similar concerns in its policy statement, *Further Education in Northern Ireland.* There is strong evidence that many colleges within the region are in the process of developing approaches to these new demands.

40 While the internal management of colleges still reflects traditional patterns which are hierarchical and department-based, experiences gained through coping with new directions have enabled many within the system to reflect on alternative structures of management. These experiences have, to date, promoted such approaches as management through course teams, interdepartmental committees, college staff development committees, and attempts at curriculum-led institutional development. Experience gained in response to new directions brought on by the introduction of YTP will be helpful in meeting the challenges to emerge from RVQ (See **3.1** 50).

41 Through analysis of student population in the FE sector for the year 1984–85, some of the key features of provision can be identified. Analysis also reveals some of the relationships with other providers of education and training such as DED-funded YTP, agriculture, and industry/commerce.

42 There was a total student population of 54,235 of whom 40,004 were registered as part-time students. Of the total enrolled 1,924 (3.5%) were undertaking advanced vocational courses; 54% of these were on a part-time day-release mode. Non-advanced vocational courses were being followed by

52,311 full-time and part-time students; of these 13,756 (26%) were registered as full-time students.

43 Of the total part-time and full-time students 276 were undertaking courses identified as agriculture, forestry, and veterinary science, while 7,439 or (14%) were engaged in part-time day-release courses, and 288 were engaged in part-time block release courses. Of the day release and block release courses 68% of the students were engaged in courses identified as engineering and technology. There seems to be no significant carry-through to advanced vocational courses in this category.

44 Of part-time and full-time students registered under non-advanced vocational courses 16,210 students (31%) were undertaking O level and A level courses. The next largest single group of students, both part-time and full-time, were registered on courses identified as social, administrative, and business studies. The total here was 14,834, 4,313 registered as full-time. The third largest group was 13,790, full-time and part-time, undertaking courses identified as engineering and technology. In the non-advanced category 5,641 students were students under compulsory school-leaving age who are registered as part-time students on link courses.

45 **Staff Development**

The report of the Sub-committee of the Advisory Committee on the Supply and Training of Teachers (ACSTT) (1980) made a number of recommendations regarding FE staff development. A major initiative on FE staff development was announced by DENI in 1983 in Circular No. 1983/24. Under the sub-heading 'Requirements for Post-Entry Training: New Entrants', the circular states:

> In accordance with the recommendations of ACSTT, all new entrants to full-time teaching in further education who take up a permanent post on or after 1 September 1983 and who have not obtained a teacher qualification listed in the Departments' Circular No. 1972/55 should undertake the first year of the course comprising both training and induction components in the first year of service.

46 The course referred to was the Certificate in Education (Further Education) provided by the Ulster Polytechnic and validated by the Council for National Academic Awards (CNAA) (See **3.1** 53–59). The induction component was a college-based programme. The circular further required that all trained new entrants should undertake the college-based induction component. The circular further encouraged colleges and ELBs to make plans which would enable candidates who had successfully completed the first year of the Certificate to undertake the second year of the course.

47 All colleges appointed teacher tutors to plan and implement the college-based component of the programme. These tutors also worked closely with the Ulster Polytechnic in supporting the college-based component of the first year of the Certificate. This resulted in a much closer relationship developing between colleges and the higher education provider of professional development.

48 Prior to 1983 the average annual intake to FE teacher training in Northern Ireland was fifteen. Since 1983 the average intake to the first year of the Certificate was fifty-five. Most first-year candidates proceed to year two of the course. The programme is provided by the University of Ulster and is offered

at two locations, Magee and Jordanstown. Following a recent re-validation the course has been re-named: Advanced Diploma in Education (FE).

49 Experienced teachers may avail of the range of in-service courses offered by the universities and colleges, as well as ELB and college-based programmes of study. In the case of award-bearing in-service programmes, DENI pays fees, travel and subsistence costs to teachers on courses which meet DENI criteria for awards.

50 In 1984 DENI funded the establishment of a Regional Curriculum Base (RCB) at the University of Ulster, part of the network of RCBs of the Further Education Unit (FEU). The RCB is designed to support staff development initiatives undertaken by ELBs and colleges of further education in Northern Ireland. Project officers are seconded from the further education sector to work in priority areas of staff and curriculum development, usually for a period of three years. Their tasks include providing assistance to ELB advisers in the design and delivery of Board-based programmes of staff development and working with college staff development tutors on in-house staff development initiatives. In 1985 the Department of Economic Development funded two posts within the RCB to support staff development for DED-funded YTP. This development seeks to promote greater cooperation between YTP agencies within the region. The RCB is advised by a number of committees which draw their membership from DENI, ELBs, colleges, DED-funded YTP schemes, employers, local broadcast services, and the trades unions.

51 Through the FEU link, Northern Ireland is able to benefit from experience, expertise and materials development elsewhere. The RCB also works in cooperation with the Further Education Staff College (See **3.1** 83–84) in providing a range of FE Management Development programmes for Northern Ireland colleges of further education.

NOTES

1 The White Paper 1987 proposed that the Universities Funding Council (UFC) should replace the University Grants Committee (UGC) and continue to advise DENI (See **1.1** Appendix 1).

2 'Transferors' means:

(i) Any trustees or other persons by whom a school has been transferred to a former education authority under the Education Act (Northern Ireland) 1923, to a former local education authority under the Education Act (Northern Ireland) 1947 or to the Department under the 1972 Order or this Order and includes trustees appointed in place of such trustees and the representatives or successors of such persons; or

(ii) The Department, where a school is placed under the management of a board under Article 17 (6) (The Education and Libraries (Northern Ireland) Order 1986: Part I Interpretation 2.2).

1.6 LOCAL AUTHORITIES

1 This Section examines the local government service which has conditioned the administration of further and higher education. The focus is largely upon the work of the local education authority, but the development of more complex and more integrated structures of local administration requires that some consideration be given to the broader aspects of local government.

2 The present structure of local government in England and Wales has been shaped by the Local Government Acts 1972 and 1985. The first of these established, from 1 April 1974, 53 counties, 47 of them non-metropolitan counties, and 6 metropolitan counties, for the major conurbations of Greater Manchester, West Yorkshire, South Yorkshire, Merseyside, West Midlands and Tyne and Wear. The metropolitan counties survived for barely a decade, being abolished in turn by the 1985 Act. The 1972 Act subdivided all counties into a number of districts, and 333 district councils were established. A third tier of parish councils (community councils in Wales) was maintained in non-metropolitan counties, and in some metropolitan areas, with mainly advisory responsibilities. The division of responsibilities between county and district councils has been modified on several occasions since 1974. At the time of writing, education, libraries, personal social services, housing, and some youth employment (careers) services are the responsibility of the non-metropolitan county councils and of metropolitan district councils. Police, fire and transport services are commonly administered through joint boards or committees of the county and district councils. Most aspects of environmental health are district council responsibilities, but the major health and medical concerns of the National Health Service were separated from the local government system and under the National Health Service Reorganisation Act 1973 were administered by Area Health Authorities until these were again reorganised as 201 District Health Authorities in 1982. The delineation of responsibilities is further complicated by the increasing use of joint or shared responsibilities, including the establishment of various forms of joint boards and the delegation of agency powers by one authority to another. The delegation of educational responsibilities in this way is, however, specifically prohibited.

3 In London the 20 Outer London borough councils have powers which resemble those of the metropolitan district councils, but the education services for the 12 Inner London boroughs are undertaken by the Inner London Education Authority (ILEA). The Local Government Act 1985 abolished the Greater London Council (GLC), devolving most of its responsibilities to the 32 London boroughs which had been established by the London Government Act 1963. The 1985 Act also abolished ILEA but it was reconstituted as a unique directly elected body, with responsibilities only for education. The Isles of Scilly also have special local government arrangements, with a council which undertakes both county and district functions.

4 Thus responsibilities for the education service are discharged by, in total, some 105 local education authorities, comprising 47 counties, 36 metropolitan districts, 20 Outer London boroughs, ILEA and the Isles of Scilly. Technically the full councils are, under the Education Act 1944, the local education authorities, comprising all the elected council members. However, the Education Act 1944 required such councils to appoint education committees, whose composition had to be approved by the Secretary of State and had to

'include persons of experience in education and persons acquainted with the educational conditions prevailing in the area for which the committee acts'. Although this does not specifically demand co-option of members to the education committee, DES Circular 8/73 made it clear that the Secretary of State would only approve the composition of committees which included at least two-thirds elected members but between one quarter and one third co-opted members.

5 The Local Government Act 1972 confirmed the special status of education committees endowed by the 1944 Act, which laid down that councils had to consider reports from their education committee before exercising their education powers[1]. Only the police and social services similarly have to be governed by specified committees. DES Circular 8/73 went further and pointed out that, under the Local Government Act, a council could 'not arrange for the discharge of any of its functions in respect to education by any committee or sub-committee other than its education committee or a sub-committee of its education committee'. Hence considerable disquiet has been expressed when some authorities have, on occasions, permitted committees other than their education committee to undertake certain educational responsibilities. These have occurred most commonly when corporate planning structures (described below) have been adopted.

6 Most authorities delegate some of their educational powers and duties to their education committee, as they were encouraged to do by the Department of Education and Science (DES), thus further increasing the significance of what is normally the largest council committee. However, a minority of education committees have no delegated powers, and some others have very few such powers. The chair of the education committee must be an elected member of the council, and is usually a senior member of the ruling political group.

7 A distinctive feature of education committees is that most contain co-opted employees of the council in the form of teacher representatives. The Local Government Act 1972 permitted teachers and others employed in an authority's schools, colleges and higher educational institutions to be appointed – though not elected – members of education committees. DES Circular 8/73 encouraged the co-option of teachers from primary, secondary and further education, and recommended the co-option of teachers in colleges of education. Representatives of industry, commerce, religious denominations, and even parents are also co-opted by the elected members of the education committee, who must comprise at least two-thirds of the committee. In practice only one authority (Croydon), whose committee structure was established before 1973, has no co-opted members. The impact of co-opted members has been criticised in recent years. The Widdicombe Committee of Inquiry into the Conduct of Local Government Business (1986), reviewed the system of co-option, and recommended that decision-making committees should not contain co-opted members.

8 The tasks of the education committee are in turn deputed to a number of sub-committees. There is no central control over the number, type or composition of the sub-committees that an education committee may establish. A common pattern is for some sub-committees to undertake sectoral responsibilities, including schools, further education and the youth service, while other sub-committees discharge resource responsibilities for buildings, finance, etc. Sub-committees tend to be the arenas for the detailed discussion of policies and

problems, whose resolution at sub-committee level tends then to go to the full education committee for formal ratification. In turn, education committee decisions go to the full council which, acting in its capacity as local education authority, ratifies the education committee's decisions. Clearly the extent to which such ratification is a mere formality depends largely upon the extent of powers delegated to the education committee. In the shire counties fairly extensive delegated powers often mean that full council meetings are quite infrequent, in some cases not more than quarterly. In the urban authorities, delegation tends to be less extensive, with the consequent need for more frequent council meetings. One result of this can be a heavy programme of sub-committee, education committee, and council meetings for many councillors. These commitments can be compounded by service as school and college governors, working party membership, and, increasingly in recent years as local government has become politicised on national party political lines, attendance at party meetings. Indeed, a major part of some education authorities' decision-making tends to take place in private meetings of the ruling political party group rather than in formal committee or council meetings. This trend has probably increased since the Public Bodies (Admission to Meetings) Act 1960 compelled authorities to open council and education committee meetings to the public, except where this would be prejudicial to the public interest. In recognition of the demands made upon elected councillors, sections 173–178 of the Local Government Act 1972 established the entitlement of councillors (except parish councillors) to attendance allowances in respect of any loss of earnings, and travelling and subsistence allowances. Such allowances are available for attendance not only at council, committee and sub-committee meetings, but at all other relevant meetings and conferences, including those of governing bodies and their various committees, except meetings which are convened by 'a body the objects of which are wholly or partly political'. The Education Act 1986 permits local authorities to make travel and subsistence payments to all college governors. The Local Government, Planning and Land Act 1980 allows local authorities to pay special responsibility allowances to certain councillors such as committee chairs, and enables councillors to claim a financial loss allowance (currently £24 per day) in place of the attendance allowance. One result has been the emergence of full-time local councillors, a phenomenon examined by the Widdicombe Committee (1986), whose Report recommended that the attendance and financial loss allowances should be replaced by a basic flat rate allowance of £1,500–£4,000 according to the size and responsibilities of the local authority.

9 Corporate management

Since the early 1970s a large number of local authorities have developed systems of management rather different from the traditional pattern of separate committees dealing with the major areas of local administrative responsibility. These have become known as 'corporate planning' or 'corporate management'. Although it had evolved in some authorities before local government reorganisation in 1974, its adoption was hastened by the resultant changes, and particularly by its advocacy in the Bains Report (1972), the recommendations of a study group set up to examine appropriate management structures for the new local authorities. The traditional committee system had been extensively criticised for its inefficiency, with poorly coordinated services, wasted resources – financial, human and material – and its ineffective personnel management procedures, with no consideration of relative priorities. Bains recommended that authorities should establish a Policy and Resources Committee which would function as a management board consisting of senior elected members, including the major committee chair. The committee's task would be to establish priorities, to set objectives for the authority, coordinate policies, manage the authority's resources and review its performance. In such a system, the service committees, including the Education Committee, are required to serve the objectives fixed by the Policy and Resources Committee. Such objectives would take account of concerns broader than just the needs of the education service, or any other sectoral interest. Similarly, the resources available to the service committees, including education, would be determined by the priorities set by the Policy and Resources Committee, and not just the perceived needs of the education service.

10 The integration of services and other activities has been taken further by some authorities with the adoption of complex organisational or financial management planning systems. These include Management by Objectives (MbO) and Planning Programming Budgeting Systems (PPBS), and a variety of performance review systems. The distinctions between these are technical and there are many forms of each. They share in common the definition of specified objectives and their refinement into sub-objectives, which in turn are related to specified activities. The evaluation of the extent to which objectives have been achieved leads to their reconsideration and to the examination of possible alternative strategies, and can include various forms of personnel appraisal. The thorough implementation of such systems could well result in the establishment of sub-objectives for individual components of the local authority, including its colleges, and in the subsequent assessment of the extent to which they have been achieved.

11 Most local authorities have adopted some features of corporate management, commonly in co-existence with the traditional committee structure. A few have rejected the innovations, and returned to the traditional pattern, after a change in political control. The extent to which corporate management impinges – if at all – upon the authority of the Education Committee and the Chief Education Officer (CEO) (See below paragraph 24) varies from authority to authority. Disquiet has been expressed by some chief officers that the effectiveness of the Committee's work had been reduced by some forms of corporate planning. Significant areas of decision-making which rest with the Policy and Resources Committee might include the establishment of new policy, the priority to be given to the development of educational services, financial control over capital programmes, and the appointment of the Chief Education Officer. Furthermore, in some authorities Personnel Committees, or Manpower Sub-committees of the Policy and Resources Committee, undertake some staffing functions traditionally undertaken by the Education Committee, including the appointment of non-teaching staff and, in a few authorities, consideration of the appointment and conditions of service of teachers and lecturers. In other authorities responsibilities related to the education service, and traditionally undertaken by the Education Committee, have been taken over by the Leisure and Recreation Committees, most contentiously in the case of community education and the youth services. In these respects a number of authorities might seem to be acting in breach of the Education Act 1944 by exercising educational duties and powers without first considering a report from the Education Committee. In some cases this has been pointed out to the local authority by the DES. Some of the implications of corporate management structures are explored below for local authority departments (paragraphs 28–34) and for establishments of further and higher education (paragraphs 58–59).

12 In spite of some criticism of corporate management, it seems likely that forms of it will increasingly characterise local government in England and Wales, particularly in large authorities, and it is desired by many elected members. As authorities find it more difficult to obtain desired resources, and as pressures increase for the more integrated use of local authority services and facilities, there are heightened demands for management systems which emphasise the implications for all local authority departments of decisions made in any one sector. Similarly, approaches are sought which improve communication and understanding between local authority departments. However, as the education service is by far the largest consumer of local authority resources, such approaches are likely to seek means for controlling and examining the effective deployment of those resources – and this seems likely to reduce the autonomy of the Education Committee. Furthermore, corporate management approaches are attractive for political reasons to some councillors, especially where the 'cabinet' of the ruling political party can form itself into the Policy and Resources Committee.

13 **Local authorities' educational responsibilities**

Whatever the system of management, local authorities are required by statute to undertake a number of specified duties, and have the discretion to discharge a further large number of powers, as specified by Parliament. Should any local authority attempt to undertake any activity or responsibility not so specified by legislation, it would be acting *ultra vires* (beyond its powers) and may be restrained by the courts. An authority's educational responsibilities arise from the Education Act 1944 and its subsequent amendments and additions. Apart from the duty to establish an education committee, authorities are required to appoint a suitable person to be Chief Education Officer – one of only three such specified appointments.

14 Most of the educational duties demanded of a local authority refer to the provision and maintenance of schools. Sections 41 and 42 of the Education Act 1944 required merely that 'it shall be the duty of every local education authority to secure the provision for their area of adequate facilities for further education', and that authorities should prepare schemes of further education and present them for the approval of the Minister of Education. In practice such schemes were not updated, and have not been required since (except when the London Government Act 1963 required their restatement by the newly established London boroughs and ILEA), although this does not mean that a Secretary of State who so chooses might not again require their presentation. Nor has any definition of just what would be considered to be 'adequate facilities' been anywhere defined (See **1.2** 12–14 and 31). The whole legal basis of further education provision is sufficiently ambiguous to have been examined by a working group of civil servants and local government officers in 1981 (DES 1981a).

15 The 1944 Act imposed very few other duties upon local authorities with respect to further education. Section 43 required every authority to provide adequate facilities for recreation and social and physical training, as part of primary, secondary and further education provision. Section 48 obliged authorities to encourage and assist pupils to take advantage of any medical provision, and to provide facilities for the medical and dental inspection of students by what is now the Department of Health and Social Security. Section 55 made it the duty of every authority to provide either free transport where it considers it necessary (or as the Secretary of State might direct), or reasonable

travelling expenses of students attending establishments of further education as well as schools.

16 Legislation following the 1944 Act further controlled and directed the local authorities. The Education Act 1962 required them to make awards to students accepted for certain courses of higher education who have the requisite educational qualifications. Although initially this applied almost entirely to the university sector, the subsequent development of higher education in the maintained sector has greatly extended its applicability. Furthermore, the courses for which grants are mandatory were extended by the Education Act 1975 to include courses leading to the Diploma in Higher Education, the Higher National Diploma and courses of initial teacher training (See **3.3** 2–4). The Education Act 1981 required local authorities to make provision for young people with 'special needs' as defined by the Act up to the age of 19 (See **3.7**).

17 The Education (No.2) Act 1968 established the present system of college government, requiring authorities to prepare instruments of government for each college, constituting the institution's governing body (See **2.8**). Articles of government which determined the functions of LEA, governing body, principal and academic board (if any) were to be prepared and presented for the Secretary of State's approval. Such approval was also required for the instruments of government of colleges of education. Apart from the above, other significant duties demanded of local authorities by the law include those of the Health and Safety at Work etc. Act 1974 (See **2.7**), and the other extensive labour legislation of the last decade (See **2.4**).

18 The local authorities are expected to develop and maintain their further education service with a considerable degree of discretion. Under the 1944 Act the Secretary of State can intervene in the prescribed circumstances, should the local authority, or college governors, exercise its powers 'unreasonably' (Section 68) (See **1.2** 36–37). Section 99 allows the Secretary of State to intervene when an authority has failed to discharge a duty (See **1.2** 12). In practice these powers have been rarely used since 1944, and the occasions they have been called upon have involved schools rather than further education establishments (See **1.2** 38–40).

19 Reference should be made to the requirements of the Town and Country Planning Act 1971. County councils were required to produce a structure plan, outlining the social and economic development planned for the area. Such plans naturally incorporated suggested educational developments, including proposals for further education. Draft plans were to be made available to the public and were expected to stimulate a participatory planning debate before finalisation. Economic difficulties have since hindered their implementation, while the regional economic planning network which had been expected to coordinate neighbouring counties' proposals has now largely been dismantled.

20 In contrast to the rather limited range of duties demanded of local authorities, they have considerable discretionary powers in further education. The differential exercise of these powers by authorities since 1944 has resulted in the remarkable diversity of provision from authority to authority, in scale of provision, type of establishments, and range of available courses therein. Authorities have interpreted their duties under Section 41 of the 1944 Act very

differently. Some have built upon substantial pre-1944 provision to provide a wide range of institutions of further, higher and adult education which serve not just the authority's own population but a regional or even national demand. Other authorities seem to have made only minimal provision, or to have depended upon facilities provided either by local voluntary establishments or neighbouring authorities.

21 Other powers especially relevant to further education which have been, and are still, very differently exercised between authorities are those obtained through the Education Act 1962, allowing authorities to bestow discretionary awards on persons over compulsory school age attending full or part-time courses of further education. The diversity both in the range and type of courses qualifying for such awards, and in the levels of financial support provided by different authorities, has often been commented upon critically (See below paragraph 52 and **3.3**).

22 Local authorities also have powers to inspect any educational establishment maintained by them, to accept gifts for educational purposes, to purchase land compulsorily where required for educational purposes, and to make provision for educational research and conferences where they might lead to the improvement of the area's educational facilities. Authorities also might make grants to universities for the purpose of improving facilities for further education in their area.

23 Although non-metropolitan district councils have no educational responsibilities they are empowered by Section 137 of the Local Government Act 1972, to spend up to the product of a 2p rate on 'expenditure which in their opinion is in the interests of their area or any part of it or all or some of the inhabitants'. This can include contributions to the funds of any non-profit-making public body. A 1980 Appeal Court judgment has confirmed that this can include educational expenditure, even where this might be counter to the policies of the local education authority. It seems possible, therefore, that further education establishments might be influenced by the educational policies of local authorities other than LEAs, who already have some influence through joint provision and dual-use schemes. These have been encouraged in recent years to maximise utilization of facilities and provide as wide a community service as possible.

24 **The Chief Education Officer**

In order that the local authority can exercise its statutory powers and duties, it is authorised to 'appoint such officers as they think necessary for the proper discharge by the authority of such of their or another authority's functions as fall to be discharged by them'. It has already been noted that one such officer which every local education authority must appoint is the Chief or Country Education Officer (CEO), entitled in some authorities (although fewer than previously) the Director of Education. The requirement of the Education Act 1944 that the Secretary of State examine an authority's short-list when appointing a CEO and eliminate any applicants considered not fit persons to be the chief education officer has been repealed, although the final appointment can still be vetoed. Although no formal professional training or qualifications are required, virtually all CEOs have similar backgrounds, with an honours degree from a British university, a period of teaching experience, followed by experience in educational administration, usually in a local authority's education department, although a few have come straight from senior posts in educational institutions, such as principal of a college of further education.

25 In spite of the requirement that a local authority appoint a CEO, there are no regulations or guidelines as to what he or she (although at time of writing only one of the 104 CEOs is female) should do once appointed. In consequence the role differs from authority to authority. In part this depends upon the relationship between the CEO and the Education Committee, and in particular with its chair. This relationship is complicated still further where authorities have employed systems of corporate management – and in at least two cases the resultant tensions have led to the resignation of the CEO. Resignations have also arisen from tensions between the CEO and the ruling political group on the Council. The traditional distinction between elected members as policy-makers and officials as executives of that policy does not hold today in many authorities. Distinctions between policy formulation and implementation are blurred, and most CEOs – as research in the last decade has amply demonstrated – take an active part in the determination of the authority's educational policies. However, the CEOs are not the administrators and providers of professional services in quite the same ways that the chief officials of the other local authority departments operate, as responsibilities for educational institutions are diffused through governing bodies. Their control of institutions of further and higher education is more indirect since the changes instituted by the Education (No. 2) Act 1968. On the other hand legislation such as the Health and Safety at Work etc. Act 1974 and the Employment Protection Acts have laid considerable duties upon the employer, and, where this is specified as the CEO, have emphasised his or her controlling role. The result is a complex and dynamic system of local authority management which differs in every authority, and within authorities over time. It owes a great deal to the personality, the vision and the interpersonal and political skills of the CEO and the other chief officers, and their relationships with the leading elected members, particularly the Council Leader and the Chair of the Education Committee. The party political structure and the attitudes and priorities of the major political groupings and their leading members will also shape strongly the authority's education management processes.

26 **The Education Department**

The one management role clearly specified for the CEO is that of managing the Education Department. In common with the other local government departments, this has grown substantially in recent years. However, it differs form the other departments in that most of its professional administrators tend to specialise only in educational work, and move between the education departments of different authorities, rather than between education and other local government departments. The administrative structure varies from authority to authority, but is normally hierarchical, compromising one or two Deputy Chief Education Officers, then Senior Assistant Education Officers, one of whom is commonly responsible for FE, one tier below, then Assistant Education Officers, with Professional Assistants at the junior professional level. Normally – and this is a further area of difference between education and other departments – some teaching experience is a necessary prerequisite for appointment, and officers are usually graduates of British universities. Nowadays departments are usually augmented by professional administrators without previous teaching experience, and by specialist officers with professional qualifications such as accountants, statisticians, and architects. Furthermore, as part of the rationalisation of local government services following reorganisation, the education department increasingly is likely to make use of the services of other specialist local government departments. In the larger authorities area administrative structures have been established, for education and other local government services. Each area has its separate administrative department, headed by an Area Education Officer, but the autonomy of such areas is normally considerably less than that of the Divisional Executive and Excepted Districts which were abolished in 1974.

27 In addition to the administrative officers of the Education Department, local education authorities also employ a number of advisers and/or inspectors. Their tasks are to give advice to both schools and administrators, to inspect schools and colleges, to monitor standards, to advise upon appointments and to stimulate and review innovations. There are very considerable differences between the sizes and composition of advisory teams between authorities. Few authorities meet the recommendations of the 1977 Taylor Report that they should appoint one adviser for every 20,000 people in the authority. Inspectors and advisers are, like most administrators, drawn from the teaching profession, although the point of transfer is usually somewhat later in their career. Unlike administrators, whose salaries like those of other local government officers are related to size of authority, the salary scale for advisers and inspectors, the Soulbury Scale, has until recently been linked to the Burnham Committee Scale for head teachers. Advisory services are usually organised under a Chief or Principal Adviser. Senior Advisers can hold sectoral responsibilities, including further and/or community education, area responsibilities, where the authority is organised in areas, or subject responsibilities. Advisers normally are concerned either with a sector or a curricular area. Bolam, Smith and Cantor (1976) found that only 5% of their sample of advisers held responsibilities for further and adult education, but the sphere of responsibility of many, if not most of the curriculum subject area advisers (70% of Bolam, Smith and Cantor's sample), and of the advisers with district responsibilities would include further – and possibly also adult and community – education. Bolam, Smith and Cantor also found that about a quarter of the sample had previous teaching experience in colleges of education, and half had previous experience in colleges of further education. In recent years the number of LEAs which have appointed advisers with specified responsibilities for further education seems to have increased, possibly because of the increased interaction between local authorities and the Manpower Services Commission over the management of the further education sector (See **1.7**).

28 **The other local authority departments**

It has already been noted that the local education service increasingly utilises the services of other local government departments. The integration of educational and other services is normally greatest where a system of corporate management is employed. The corporate structure described above (paragraphs 9–11) is served by a team of chief officers acting as a Management Team in accordance with the recommendations of the Mallaby (1967) and Redcliffe-Maud (1969) Management Reports. The Team, headed by the Chief Executive, is expected to ensure the integrated pursuit of the authority's objectives by each of its departments, whose chief officers should operate as a unified group of managers. The relative importance of the Education Department in both financial and employment terms argues for the inclusion of the Chief Education Officer in the Management Team as is usually the case. In a few authorities, however, an 'inner cabinet' of some chief officers has excluded the CEO, and has led to some conflict between educational and other local authority objectives. However, in most cases the Management Team and Education Department's closer liaison can be seen to have contributed to the greater effectiveness of local authority services, and has enabled authorities to cope with the stringent resource constraints imposed upon them in recent years.

29 One effect of the adoption of corporate planning systems by local authorities has been that tasks traditionally undertaken by the Education Department are now undertaken by or in consultation with other departments. Certain broadly educational responsibilities are thus partly or wholly under the control of committees other than the Education Committee, and undertaken by officials other than the CEO and Education Department staff. The key committee in a corporate management system is the Policy and Resources Committee (or its equivalent). Commonly it has not only taken over the traditional tasks of the Finance Committee, but has impinged on areas previously those of the Education Committee by exercising control over education's capital programmes, including the acquisition of sites; by deciding the scale, priority and nature of educational building programmes; by fixing fees and charges; and by negotiating with employees' associations and unions over conditions of service as well as influencing or controlling the appointment of the Chief Education Officer. In consequence, tasks formerly undertaken by the Education Department have fallen to the Treasurer's (or Finance) Department, or to the Legal and Administrative Department, including the clerking of Education Committee and sub-committee meetings, the production of reports and the preparation of budgets. Additional professional expertise is thus made available for educational purposes, but this has on occasions led to criticism of some resultant duplication of effort, lack of knowhow and time-wasting (source).

30 The Establishment Committee and its Personnel Department have also taken over a number of activities and responsibilities from the Education Committee/Department in some authorities. These include the consideration of institutional establishments, the monitoring of all appointments, the review of non-teaching staff establishments, the administrative work involved in staff appointments, and the appointment, secondment and approval for conference attendance of Education Department staff. While in almost all authorities attempts to transfer the responsibility for the appointment of teaching staff from the Education to the Personnel Department have been strenuously resisted, so that the Education Committee retains responsibility for appointing teaching staff, the Personnel Department has been criticised for delays in decisions concerning the appointment of temporary staff, the approval of secondments and leave of absence and the payment of expenses to teaching and other staff (e.g. in Locke with Pratt, Silverman and Travers 1987). Delays are compounded in some authorities where appointments have to be approved not only by Education and Establishment Committees but also by the Management Team. Recent financial restrictions on local government have led to an increase in the development of such complex controls on staffing procedures, in order to avoid the severe penalties incurred by over-spending, with consequential delays in appointments procedures. However, many local education authorities have benefited considerably from Personnel Department expertise in the sphere of labour relations.

31 In many authorities the development of Recreation and Leisure (or Amenities) Departments has led to encroachments upon traditional Education Department territories. This has led to the rationalisation of recreational facilities in educational and other establishments, and to standardised

maintenance procedures for playing fields and other open spaces. Problems have arisen where the Recreation Committee has taken on responsibility for the community uses of educational premises, for the provision and administration of community centres, and the allocation of grants to village halls and other centres providing adult education. However, the Recreation Department can be better placed than the Education Department to negotiate with district councils over joint use projects, in that the Education Department otherwise has no district council responsibilities.

32 A number of committees and departments liaise with the Education Department in the spheres of land and buildings. In some authorities the Land and Buildings Committee undertakes the sale and acquisition of sites, the rental of premises, including school houses, and the control of non-operational property. In Walsall the Land and Property Committee took over responsibility for all educational buildings. The Surveyor's/Engineer's/Buildings/Architect's Department might control the maintenance of playing fields and buildings, the acquisition of sites, the submission of planning applications, the application for and consideration of tenders, and the supply and maintenance of educational transport. While this has made possible the integration of acquisition, disposal and maintenance policies for educational services with other local government services, it has led to complaints about delays and lack of consideration of and consultation concerning educational needs and priorities.

33 The establishment of a local authority Purchasing Department usually has implications for education. In some authorities this department has organised a central purchasing system, and has placed contracts for supplies, including those for schools and colleges (see below paragraph 49). Other responsibilities might include the purchasing, storage and disposal of equipment, goods and vehicles.

34 Other committees and departments which in some authorities undertake responsibilities exercised in other authorities by the Education Committee and Department include the Road Safety Committee, the Library Committee, and the General Purposes Committee (which in some authorities elects members to governing bodies of schools and colleges and to other educational bodies). The Social Services Department might undertake responsibilities for educational welfare officers and for some aspects of the Educational Psychology service. An authority's Central Research Unit might produce formulae for staffing levels in, and for the allocation of resources to, educational establishments. The Computer Unit in some authorities handles salaries and the processing of invoices to and from schools and colleges. Committees with responsibilities for developing policies for ethnic minorities and equal opportunities have also made significant contributions to the work of the education service in some authorities.

35 **Local government staff: numbers, training and organisation**

The local government service employs about 2 million workers (full-time and full-time equivalent). The education service accounts for nearly half of this total, and for over half of the total local government salary bill, as the educational labour force includes a higher proportion of professional employees than the other major departments.

36 The training of some groups of employees, including teachers, educational psychologists, police and firemen, is organised nationally, with arrangements

for pooling the costs of such training, although from April 1987 the national pooling of in-service training costs of teachers, lecturers and others has been replaced by a system of specific grants to each local authority. Most other local government employees, including Education Department officials, have since 1967 come under the auspices of the Local Government Training Board for their training needs. The Board is financed by deductions from the rate support grant, and it aims to increase local government efficiency by providing appropriate in-service training to all levels of staff. Thus, in recognising the particular needs of education officers, the Board has published detailed recommendations for a suitable four-stage training programme. The Board, however, stresses that the prime responsibility for training its employees rests with the local authority, and some authorities have established comprehensive internal training programmes for both officers and manual workers. Colleges of further education and polytechnics are substantial providers of training programmes at all levels, including ONC and HNC courses in public administration, Certificate in Municipal Administration programmes, and courses leading to the Certificate and Diploma in Management Studies, as well as those for over a hundred different professional examinations. Non-teaching staff in schools and colleges are eligible as local government employees for appropriate training programmes. The Further Education Staff Colleges (See **3.1** 83–84), the Institute of Local Government Studies and a number of polytechnics and colleges are amongst the providers of such programmes and courses.

37 The staff associations of local government employees have been prominent in the organization of training programmes for their members. Education officers are represented by the Society of Education Officers (SEO), founded in 1970. It has over 1,100 members, drawn from all local authorities, and has an active regional structure. It maintains a small salaried secretariat and promotes the interests of its members and the local education service by seeking representation on outside bodies, promoting training, research and publications, meeting regularly with appropriate civil servants and politicians and with other groups with related concerns, drawn from local authorities and national bodies. The Society has also intervened when local authority policies have appeared to threaten its members' interests, by investigating problems and, on occasions, warning members not to apply for specified posts. Advisers, inspectors and organisers have their own association, the National Association for Inspectors and Educational Advisers, with about 1,300 members and concerns similar to those of the Society of Education Officers. It publishes a journal and undertakes a variety of training and other development activities.

38 Local government employees are represented by a large number of other professional and staff associations, indicative of the fact that over 500 different occupations are found in local government. Professional groups tend to be represented by specialist organisations such as the Association of Educational Psychologists and the Institute of Careers Officers. A recent development has been the establishment of white-collar trade union organisations which have grown out of and are related to some of these professional associations. The Association of Education Officers (AEO) has grown from the Society of Education Officers as a trade union with membership restricted to SEO members, and is represented on the negotiating body for chief officers' conditions of service, where it forms part of the Federated Union of Managerial and Professional Officers (FUMPO). Chief executives are represented professionally by the Society of Local Authority Chief Executives (with appropriate acronym)

and in conditions of service negotiations by the twin Association of Local Authority Chief Executives.

39 In contrast to these diverse and frequently highly specialist staff and professional associations, local government is unusual in that the great majority of employees are represented by one major trade union, whose membership extends broadly across occupational and hierarchical categories of employment. The union is the National and Local Government Officers Association (NALGO). It represents administrative, professional, technical, and clerical staff in all sections of local government, including Education Departments and schools and colleges. Its membership is now over 700,000, the fourth largest trade union in Britain. NALGO's major activity remains the consideration and negotiation of its members' salaries and conditions of service. It is the major union represented on the National Joint Council for Administrative, Professional, Technical and Clerical Services (APT&C), and its Provincial Councils (on which each local authority is represented), whereby local government salaries and conditions of service (the 'Purple Book') are negotiated. NALGO has a substantial national secretariat, employing over 300, a district structure allied to the 13 APT & C Provincial Council Areas, and a branch organisation based on individual local authorities. It maintains an active educational and training programme, including correspondence courses and residential courses. Other activities include the provision of legal services, insurance and holiday facilities, and welfare services including convalescent homes for its members. A number of other trade unions operate within local government. Many local government workers are represented by their craft unions. Manual workers tend to be members of the National Union of Public Employees, the Transport and General Workers' Union, and the General and Municipal Workers' Union. Establishments of further and higher education could well, therefore, include amongst their staff, members of a score or more different associations and unions.

40 **The college and the local authority**

The considerable diversity of the local government system means that relationships between maintained establishments of further and higher education and their local authority are both complex and vary greatly between – and even within – authorities. In general terms the LEA, according to articles of government, is responsible for the general educational character of the college and for its place in the local education system (See **2.8**). The authority is legally responsible both as LEA and as employer, and cannot avoid its responsibilities by delegation to the establishment's governing body. The major variations in both formal and actual structures of control and communication preclude any confident generalizations about resultant relationships. In consequence, all that can be offered here is an outline of the most usual manifestations of local authority control, and of the most common points of contact between colleges and authority. These differ according to a number of variables, including the instruments and articles of government, the nature of the authority's political structure, its management system, and the proportion of advanced work in the college. However, consideration of some significant differences of practice is intended to illustrate the extent of local authority discretion.

41 Local authority control has become more indirect as a result of the changes in college government instituted by the Education (No. 2) Act 1968, placing powers on governing bodies, principals and directors, and academic boards. The

Department of Education and Science's pressure for the adoption of its model articles of government polytechnics, colleges of education and the major institutions of further education has resulted in substantial autonomy in some areas for these institutions. Smaller establishments, undertaking a lower proportion of advanced work, were given less autonomy by many authorities – a cause of complaint within some of those colleges. These complaints are echoed in some major establishments, where the actual degree of local authority control is stated to be considerably greater than is laid down formally, and had been intended in the model articles of government. Conversely, complaints have been heard from local authorities that, with the pooling of all expenditure on advanced work and the growing influence of the Manpower Services Commission, they have had difficulties in exercising their legal and political responsibilities[2]. Such concerns have contributed to a number of proposals for changes in the existing system, whereby the AFE institutions would be removed from local government control, as recommended in the 1987 White Paper *Higher Education: Meeting the Challenge* (See **1.1** Appendix 1 and **2.8** 39).

42 The major direct influence of the local authority upon any of its colleges is financial. The articles of government normally specify that a college's financial estimates should be submitted by the governing body to the Education Committee, which either approves or amends those estimates, and hence sets the college's budget for the coming year – though the funding of advanced level work is substantially set by the allocation from the AFE pool (See **1.3** 49–53). The LEA can apply for Education Support Grants, which might contribute to the college's income (See **1.3** 28–31).

43 Local authority control of revenue expenditure varies considerably between institutions. To some degree such variations arise from differences in virement practices, for the greater the latitude for virement the greater the institution's financial autonomy. Major differences also arise from local authority practice and policies with regard to staffing establishments for both teaching and non-teaching staff, purchasing and supplies, and the extent to which institutions might retain income from student fees, letting and other college services including catering, and grants. Financial regulations set out procedures which govern such functions as making orders, considering tenders, paying invoices, book-keeping, accountancy and audit (See **2.8**).

44 The Education Committee authorises capital expenditure. Capital programmes, when financed by borrowing, have significant long-term revenue consequences not only for loan charges and repayments but also for staffing and other expenses arising from the new development. It is the local authority's decision whether to apply to the DES for the inclusion of a further education capital project in the authority's bid for the education capital spending allocation (See **1.3** 33–41). It is further an authority decision whether or not minor capital works should be financed out of revenue, or from the sale of capital assets, or whether educational capital expenditure should be 'vired' from one of the other service block allocations. Authorities are expected to liaise with neighbouring authorities when planning capital expenditure on the provision of further education. In making any of these decisions the authority can influence fundamentally the size and nature of its further education establishments.

45 Staffing costs usually amount to over two-thirds of total expenditure on further

education, and many local authorities keep a particularly close control over staffing policies and practices. The formal control is normally stated in terms of approving the college's establishment of teaching and non-teaching staff[2]. However, in practice more detailed interventions have become common. Institutions are in many authorities required to conform with authority-wide appointment procedures, which may well involve not only the Education Department, but also the Personnel Department and possibly the Establishment or Policy and Resources Committees, with reference to the Management Team. Thus the initial request for new staff by a college might have to proceed through an elaborate process of examination and discussion in departments and committees before permission is received to advertise the post. The advertisement procedures might then be the responsibility of a local authority department (not necessarily the Education Department) rather than of the college. Selection procedures thereafter might well be subject to local authority influences, through the presence of an adviser or education officer, or through the presence of councillors as members of the governing body's (or principal's) Selection Committee.

46 The Burnham FE Committee's annual salary agreements have permitted quite substantial areas of discretion for local authorities in fixing the proportions of staff and the salary grades. Some authorities implemented the agreement more generously than others in permitting appointments at the more senior grades. For example, the proportions of senior lecturer posts created in respect of non-advanced work could vary between 0% and 5%. Some LEAs adopted the minimum, others adopted the mid-point, while a few permitted the maximum. Another area of discretion has been the amount of enhancement to be given under premature retirement schemes. Again, while local authorities are no longer free to establish the rates paid to part-time teachers, previous discretion has led to considerable variations between the regional rates set by the Burnham salaries document. Similarly the variations in locally negotiated conditions of service agreements for teaching staff, which supplement the model agreement between the Council of Local Education Authorities (CLEA) and the recognised unions, result in variations between establishments' student : staff ratios, etc., which are not accounted for only by differences in levels and types of work.

47 Many differences occur between authority policies with regard to permitted levels of secondment and study leave. It is very largely the authority's decision as to what priority should be given to full-time one-year secondment, in relation both to other forms of in-service activities and other educational expenditure. Other variations occur in the estimated secondments for less than one year. It is too early to identify the impact of the in-service training funding mechanisms established by the Education Act 1986 (sometimes known as 'GRIST'), but it seems likely that the development of more formal LEA inservice education and training (INSET) policies will provide new constraints on college secondment and study leave practices (See **2.9** 22–27).

48 There are major variations in staffing levels for non-teaching staff in different authorities. The constraints on staffing levels arising out of the model conditions of service agreements for teaching staff have as yet no equivalent for non-teaching staff. In consequence authorities have allowed colleges to establish very different patterns and proportions of non-teaching staff, which are by no means wholly explained by differences in types of courses and levels of work between colleges. Furthermore, the control and deployment of non-teaching

staff varies considerably between colleges and authorities. In some authorities, whereas teaching staff are the responsibility of the Education Department, non-teaching staff come under the Personnel Department, which may well seek to establish and maintain staffing establishments applicable throughout the authority's services.

49 The extent to which colleges are required to make use of specified local authority services varies considerably between authorities. Some establishments are required to employ the authority's direct labour system for all or a specified part of its repairs and maintenance programme. Others, within the overall budget heading approval, can seek tenders for such work within only the constraints of Section 135 of the Local Government Act 1972, which governs contracts for the supply of goods and materials and the execution of work for local authorities.

50 Similar variations occur with respect to a college's supplies and purchasing system. A number of authorities operate centralised purchasing schemes, organized through a Supplies or Purchasing Department. Colleges, like other educational establishments, can then be required to purchase all, or a specified proportion of certain items of expenditure through that department, thereby benefiting from the discount arrangements negotiated by the authority, which can involve very substantial savings. Centralised purchasing arrangements have been criticised not only for the limited choices available, but also for long delays in the supply of items from the Supplies Department. More commonly, most authorities arrange contracts with some suppliers for certain items of educational equipment and materials, including books. Colleges then must order those materials from the specified suppliers, in some cases being restricted to a limited range of possible choices. Again this has been the subject of some criticism from colleges.

51 There is also concern in many colleges at the diversity of budgetary control for supplies, including books, equipment, stationery, and other educational materials. Single items of equipment which cost more than £10,000 have needed to obtain the approval of the Secretary of State, but otherwise local authorities can decide themselves what levels of expenditure within these headings are permissible, with the proviso only that the articles of government permit widely different degrees of virement within and sometimes between budget headings for different colleges. In practice, authorities have in response to increasingly stringent central government restrictions established a variety of internal checks and controls, involving, for example, the need for Education Committee or Council Leader approval for single items of expenditure over specified limits, even where such expenditure remains within the overall college budget head.

52 Similarly, the priority given to further education expenditure in relation to the other sectors of education varies very considerably between authorities. Comparisons of unit costs are particularly difficult in further education because of the problems of defining full-time equivalent students, a problem compounded by the inability of authorities to agree as yet upon a standardised method of calculation. There is no nationally agreed definition of a full-time equivalent (FTE) student. The Pooling Committee has recommended a formula for advanced further education, whereby the total number of class-contact hours of students per course or department in the spring term is divided by the number of class contact hours that a typical full-time student on a normal

equivalent full-time course would undertake during that term, to obtain the number of full-time equivalent students. NAB operates on the basis of conversion factors for students studying by different modes, with full-time students as 1 FTE, sandwich 0.9, part-time day 0.4, and part-time evening 0.2 FTE. However, some authorities use a weighting system which takes account of type and level of course as well as mode of attendance. This can and does result in differences between LEAs in their calculation of FTEs. For non-advanced further education, a method has been devised by education officers of the Outer London boroughs which weights students according to mode of attendance, with part-time day students amounting to 0.25 FTE, part-time day and evening students 0.33, and evening students 0.08. A different set of weighting factors is used by the DES when calculating FTE students for building purposes.

53 One further sphere of financial decision-making by the local authority which has considerable import for its further education colleges concerns discretionary student grants. Sections 1(4) and 2 of the Education Act 1962 empower local authorities to make awards for both 'designated' courses to students not eligible for mandatory awards, and non-designated courses. The latter include most courses below first degree of HND levels (except DipHE), a variety of vocational postgraduate courses, courses of professional training for youth leaders, social workers and other groups, and courses undertaken outside the UK and in private institutions. They also include part-time degree courses such as those of the Open University, and those leading to external degrees of London University. Although the Secretary of State has drawn local authorities' attention to the undesirability of wide variations of practice both in policy in making discretionary awards and in the rates and conditions applicable to them, wide variations between authorities' policies and rates of grant do occur. Concern has been expressed that, even where demand for such awards is increasing, many local authorities have reduced both the numbers and the size of their discretionary grants. The local authority associations have advised their members that rates and conditions for grants for students over 19 should not differ from those currently applicable to mandatory awards, and that students under 19 should receive assistance equivalent to that available had they stayed at school (i.e. free tuition, books and equipment allowance, subsidised meals, and where appropriate travel and hardship maintenance allowances). In spite of this, differences between local authority practices remain considerable, while financial difficulties have caused more and more authorities to cut back on the levels and availability of their discretionary grants (See **3.3**).

54 **Secondary and further education**

Other major areas of local authority decision-making which affect the nature of its further education service are those involving educational provision for 16–19 year old students, and for community and adult education. The development of GCE and now GCSE courses in many colleges of further education has brought them into direct competition for students with the secondary schools, at a time when the establishment of 11–18 and 13–18 comprehensive schools has commonly had the effect of encouraging a larger proportion of the 16–18 age group to remain at school. Resultant problems are now being intensified by demographic change, with the decline in size of the 16–19 age cohort. Where 11–16 comprehensive schools have been established, the choice is often clearer for 16 year olds between sixth-form colleges and colleges of further education, but the sixth form colleges are particularly vulnerable as school populations contract, and class sizes dwindle. Some authorities are attempting to rationalise 16–19 education, and nearly half the LEAs have established policies for 16–19 provision. These include the encouragement of cooperation between further education colleges, schools and sixth-form colleges, in order to minimise uneconomically small classes, in some cases by the establishment of consortia, and restrictions on competitive course developments in further education colleges. In implementing such policies the authority, stressing its right to control the college's system, can come into conflict with the college's principal and governing body. Arguably the absence as yet of any policy for 16–19 year olds from central government has not helped[3]. A growing number of authorities have attempted to rationalise further, by establishing tertiary colleges, incorporating the functions of both sixth-forms and further education colleges. To date, however, only a small minority of local authorities in England and Wales has adopted this solution (See **3.1** 28–31).

55 **Adult and community education**
Local authority systems for community and adult education vary. Further education colleges are normally the major providers of adult education, but in some authorities such provision may be made within secondary schools and community colleges or in separate centres for adult and community education. Some authorities have clearly defined policies maintained by a distinctive community and adult education service, including specialist advisers and administrators. Parts of the service in a few authorities have been made the responsibility of a department and committee other than the Education Department/Committee, usually the Recreation and Leisure Department. In ensuring provision for adult education LEAs work in partnership with the 'responsible bodies' – the Workers' Educational Association and university extra-mural departments.

56 The duty of LEAs under Section 41 of the 1944 Act is interpreted as leaving LEAs with discretion about the level, as well as the nature, of provision, and adult education services have been subject to heavy cuts under pressures of financial restraint on local authorities. Many authorities have attempted to make adult education classes more self-financing by drastically increasing fees and by increasing the minimum viable class size. Colleges which have developed a substantial commitment to community education may find themselves affected adversely by cutbacks in financial provision and by attempts to rationalise provision. In a period of declining secondary school rolls, pressures to utilise spare school resources for adult education have been significant.

57 **Contact and communication between college and local authority**
The forms of communication differ between authorities, and the following paragraphs are no more than a checklist of common contacts. The Education Department personnel most likely to come into direct contact with the college are the Senior Education Officer and/or Assistant Education Officer for further, adult and community education, and the adviser (or inspector) for further and/or adult and community education. As explained earlier, some authorities have established structures without specialist advisory responsibilities for further education, but where there are advisers (or inspectors) their roles are likely to overlap with the education officers. Education officers with resource responsibilities are likely to influence strongly local authority decisions concerning college developments which demand extra resources, such

as building programmes. In many authorities the advisory service also holds resources which are released to stimulate curricular developments and to stem deficiencies. These extra resources, over and above the college's capitation allowances, can sometimes make significant differences in specific departments and curricular fields.

58 Contacts with departments other than the Education Department vary according to the authority's management system. Winter (1977) found that chief officers other than the CEO communicated directly with colleges and schools without reference to the CEO, in about three-fifths of the authorities in his sample. The main contacts are with the Treasurer's Department, concerning salaries and wages, invoicing and the collection of money, accounting and auditing arrangements, and enquiries about superannuation.

59 Where centralised supply schemes operate, contacts between the college and the Purchasing Department are inevitably frequent. Similarly repair and maintenance queries are dealt with in some authorities by a separate department. Problems can occur for colleges where a Recreation and Leisure (or Amenities) Department has been established with areas of interest which overlap with those of the Education Department. Activities within further and adult education can become matters of conflict between the two departments or, at the very least, responsibilities and lines of communication can become blurred, particularly in areas involving the community use of college premises, community activities and youth services.

60 Officials of the Personnel Department are likely to come into contact with colleges where systems of corporate management are employed which delegate substantial staffing responsibilities to that department. In some authorities it is the Personnel Department which handles negotiations concerning conditions of service for both teaching and non-teaching staff, and union negotiators have found an advantage in dealing with employers' representatives with substantial experience of such negotiations in varied occupational spheres. In spite of the formal responsibilities of the governing body for non-teaching staff, the Personnel Department is likely to be interested in staffing levels and grades, particularly if attempting to implement a common staffing policy throughout the authority. It is thus possible that it might attempt to influence the procedure for selecting, deploying, and training all local authority staff, including those in colleges. The Department may well thus seek to influence, if not control, policies for the secondment and staff development of teaching and non-teaching staff. Such policies might come into conflict with the policies of the institution and the Education Committee.

61 **The elected members**

The most likely contact between a college and local authority councillors is with those appointed as members of the institution's governing body. As establishments of further and higher education are often the largest establishments controlled by the authority, their governors usually include senior councillors from the ruling political party, including commonly the Education Committee Chair[2]. The involvement of such members can extend far beyond attendance at quarterly governors' meetings and meetings of the governing body's various committees and sub-committees. It has been on occasions extended to the acceptance of individual students by institutions, and the nature and existence of courses and departments. In consequence the distinction between politicians and officials has sometimes become blurred, a matter of some concern to at least one CEO who has warned that 'politicians will take care to tell the truth and nothing but the truth. It may sometimes fall to officers to see that the whole truth is also told'.

62 **The local ombudsman**
As the above paragraphs indicate, a substantial area of further education administration is controlled externally to the college, and there is a means of possible redress where this is considered to have led to injustice or maladministration. The Local Government Act 1974 established Commissions for Local Administration for England and for Wales, which comprise the Local Commissioners, often known (along with the Parliamentary Commissioner) as 'ombudsmen'. Their tasks are to investigate complaints of 'injustice in consequence of maladministration in connection with action taken by or on behalf of an authority'. Complaints can be made by an individual or a body of persons but not by an institution such as a college. They must concern an individual member of the public, but the ombudsman cannot investigate matters affecting all or most of the authority's inhabitants. Nor can he or she investigate matters where alternative remedies, such as legal action, appeal to a tribunal or to the Secretary of State (as under Sections 68 and 99 of the Education Act 1944) are possible. Furthermore, Schedule 5 of the Act precludes investigation of secular and religious instruction, or the conduct, curriculum, internal organisation, management or discipline in colleges of education and further education. The Commissioner's reports are made public, and he or she must be told by the authority the action it proposes to take, or has taken, in response to the report. If not satisfied the Commission can then issue a second report, but has no powers to enforce the implementation of any recommendations. Most of the complaints concerning further and higher education which have been investigated by the ombudsman have concerned student grants (See **3.3**).

63 **Local authority associations**
Local authorities are represented nationally in consultation and negotiation with central government and with other national organisations by a number of powerful associations, two of which represent those authorities with educational responsibilities. These are the Association of County Councils (ACC), representing the non-metropolitan counties, and the Association of Metropolitan Authorities (AMA), representing the metropolitan districts and the London Boroughs. They exist to safeguard their members' interests; to provide a forum for discussion of matters of common concern to their members and others; and to provide appropriate central services. The latter includes a secretariat for each association, each run by an education officer, answerable to the association's Education Committee. Their Education Committees are increasingly active, and their officers send out circulars to constituent members as well as advising individual authorities. Furthermore, the committees are represented on a wide variety of national and international bodies, including the Expenditure Steering Group for Education which forecasts educational expenditure for the Consultative Council on Local Government Finance, in the annual rate support grant negotiations (See **1.3** 16).

64 Although the interests of AMA and ACC commonly differ, they have established a joint body for education, the Council of Local Education Authorities (CLEA). This comprises 12 AMA and 12 ACC members, and has a small secretariat. CLEA undertakes a wide variety of negotiating tasks on behalf of all local authorities. Thus it has established in negotiation with NATFHE and the other recognised unions model conditions of service for lecturers in further

and higher education; has advised on the clearing houses for polytechnic and teacher training applicants; issued circulars on pooling arrangements and awards; and it has been given responsibility for negotiating with the Manpower Services Commission the arrangements for work-related non-advanced further education, after the White Paper *Training for Jobs* (1984) transferred responsibility for this area to the MSC. CLEA's Further Education Advisory Team – comprising an education officer and a finance officer – has been established to investigate the uses of resources in advanced further education. It has examined, first in polytechnics, then in other establishments providing advanced further education, unit cost variations and problems arising from the open-ended nature of the pooling system. It has sought standardised means of measuring unit costs, and has looked at the information needs of any organisation which might be established to ensure the equitable distribution of pooled resources. CLEA's size and range of activities is restricted, partly by the limitations of being able to operate only in those areas where AMA and ACC interests and policies coincide, but largely because of both Association's distrust of any powerful organisation which might represent local education authorities nationally, and thus perpetuate the education service's distinctiveness from the rest of local government. One of CLEA's major initial functions, that of negotiating conditions of service for teachers in further and higher education was transferred to the National Joint Council for Further Education Lecturers in England and Wales (See **2.1**) under an independent chairman, wherein LACSAB (see below, paragraph 69) and the Education Officers of ACC and AMA form the secretariat for the employers' side.

65 **The Regional Advisory Councils**

A system of nine Regional Advisory Councils for Further Education (RACs) in England was established in 1946. It was intended to coordinate the provision of further education within regions and thus between LEAs, and to ensure that further education responded to the needs of industry. The nine English regions are territorially anomalous, neither coinciding with the boundaries of existing LEAs and other regional planning structures, nor indeed, in some cases even having clearly defined boundaries at all, so that institutions have been able to transfer from one region to another. Furthermore, the Councils differ in the extent to which they concern themselves with non-advanced further education, as they have been allowed to develop separately in response to local circumstances. The full Councils are large, with up to 100 members, but meet infrequently. They are financed by constituent local authorities and include representatives of the LEAs – both elected members and officials – principals and teachers from further education and, anomalously, university representation, for while the latter might comment upon the provision of education in the maintained sector, the RACs do not effectively influence university provision. Most Council activities are delegated to their Standing Committees and Regional Academic Boards, which, along with associated sub-committees, are serviced by small secretariats. A number of proposals for the reform or abolition of the RACs have been made in recent years, but they continue to survive.

66 The RACs' major function is the scrutiny of proposals for advanced courses of further education, before their submission to the Secretary of State for approval as required by the Further Education Regulations (See **1.2** 17–19). The RACs have been required to approve proposals for Diploma in Higher Education and initial teacher training courses, part-time non-degree courses and courses leading to a postgraduate award without further reference to the

Secretary of State. For other courses the RACs (or rather their executive standing committees) forward recommendations to a committee of the Inspectorate, after discussion with the Regional Staff Inspector (RSI). The committee's decisions are then normally endorsed by the Secretary of State. RACs are expected to bear in mind the criteria by which RSIs are to assess advanced course proposals (established by FECL 1/80 under Regulation 8 of the Further Education Regulations 1975). RACs are further required to ensure that not only are courses not duplicated unnecessarily in neighbouring authorities, but that fees charged do not vary substantially between authorities. Thus the RACs have attempted to cope with the rapid expansion of advanced further education provision since the 1960s and to rationalise it, against pressures from local authorities and colleges for course approval. The result has been some 'horse-trading', which has intensified pressures for the replacement or abolition of the RACs. Their reputations further suffered when the DES did not consult them concerning the location of the polytechnics, the closure or merger of colleges of education and the establishment of the National Advisory Body for Local Authority Higher Education (NAB), which overlaps with several RAC functions.

67 **Joint education committees**

The RAC function in Wales is undertaken by the Welsh Joint Education Committee (WJEC). Unlike the RACs this is a statutory body under Part II of Schedule 1, Education Act 1944, which permitted joint committees of local education authorities with executive responsibilities. The WJEC comprises representatives of all eight Welsh LEAs, and coopted members representing other interests, including teachers, industry and the University of Wales. It undertakes a heterogeneous collection of functions, as well as those of an RAC. It coordinates activities in special education and in-service education. It act as the only examining body with responsibilities for GCSE examinations, and is responsible for technical examinations. More generally, it facilitates the regulation of Welsh LEAs' interests, and acts to express Welsh educational concerns, including the promotion of Welsh language teaching, and the administration of the Welsh National Youth Orchestra.

68 Other joint education committees have been established with more specific tasks. Two polytechnics are responsible to a joint education committee of two or more local authorities. Less formal organisations of local education authorities occur in several parts of England, including the London boroughs, and Yorkshire and Humberside. They serve to make recommendations on a host of administrative matters, to reconcile differences and to act, when necessary, as a regional pressure group. In some areas an RAC sub-committee provides a structure for discussion and coordinated action by CEOs.

69 A host of other local authority organisations undertake activities with educational implications. Some, such as the Local Government Training Board (See above paragraph 36) have already been mentioned. Reference to just a few of the others is possible here. The Local Authorities' Conditions of Service Advisory Board (LACSAB) is of major and increasing significance in further education. Established in 1948, it exists to coordinate the activities of local authorities as employers, in their negotiations on wages, salaries, and conditions of service. As such it provides the employers' secretariat for most of the national negotiating organisations such as the National Joint Council. It collects and disseminates information, and advises individual authorities

on their role as employers, and represents local government in discussions with central government concerning employment and staffing. The Board comprises 19 members, appointed by the local authority associations, and the employers' side of the major national negotiating bodies. A secretariat of about 70 has grown rapidly in recent years, in response to the massive labour legislative activity of the last decade. It is financed by the local authorities, and the provincial councils which deal with local authorities' collective bargaining on pay and conditions of service. It is important to stress that LACSAB is an advisory body, and its advice is not always taken. Advice is in the form of commentaries and interpretations in individual cases, and through handbooks such as the *LACSAB Employee Relations Handbook*. LACSAB's involvement in further and higher education is extensive, having provided the secretariat not only for the employers' side of the Burnham Further Education Committee, but also for the negotiating bodies dealing with wages and conditions of service for non-teaching staff. Furthermore, it is the focal point of the management secretariat in the reorganised negotiating machinery for conditions of service of teachers in further education, thus aligning salary and conditions of service negotiations more closely together.

70 The Local Authorities' Management Services and Computer Committee (LAMSAC) was established in 1969 to assist local authorities with the introduction and use of computers and management sciences in local government. It is funded principally through Section 2(7) of the Local Government Act 1974. It comprises four advisory panels for Computers, Organisations & Methods and Productivity, General Management, and Purchasing. LAMSAC collects and disseminates information, offers advice and proposes guidelines, and operates a more detailed consultancy service. It also provides training in management techniques, and undertakes research into new systems of computing and management. It has undertaken comparative studies of non-teaching aspects of the education service with planning and the social services. A more specialist service is provided by the Local Government Operational Research Unit of the Royal Institute of Public Administration, which seeks rational systematic approaches to decision-making which can be expressed and evaluated quantitatively. Its studies have included school transport, and the development of more effective decision-making approaches to educational administration. Reference also should be made to a number of local authority consortia. Six building consortia were established between 1957 and 1966 to apply industrialised building methods and standardised designs to school buildings, initially, but the expertise thus acquired has since been applied to college building. Consortia have also been formed to plan and advise upon the design and purchase of furniture, science equipment and kitchens.

71 **Commentary**

The establishment and development of the local authority associations and organisations described above are indicative both of the changing needs of local authorities and the increasing pressures upon them. Authorities face an unprecedented series of complex problems, many of which they are no longer capable of dealing with individually, and substantial powers have, therefore, been passed to powerful local authority associations. Some of these pressures have been created by central government encroachment upon traditional local responsibilities. The Manpower Services Commission has taken over responsibility for a quarter of work-related non-advanced further education (See **1.7**), and central government has removed many local authority discretionary powers by the use of specific grants to ensure that government-favoured initiatives are funded despite local priorities (See **1.3**). Requirements that many local government services be privatised have further reduced local influence. The power to negotiate teachers' (though not, at the time of writing, FE lecturers') salaries and conditions of service has been removed from local authority control (See **2**). Central government seeks increasingly to occupy areas traditionally held by local government, in its demands for firmer direction of the education service and for reductions in rate-borne spending levels. This not only challenges the autonomy of local authorities, making it difficult for some authorities to carry out their statutory responsibilities, but raises questions as to whether education should be provided through the local government system at all. The provision of public sector higher education through the local government system has been challenged for a decade or more, and the 1987 White Paper proposed that polytechnics and major colleges of higher education be removed from local authority control (See **1.1**). In the meanwhile, the challenge has been extended to the rest of the education service. The long-held concept of a national service locally administered is increasingly unrealistic (See **1.2**).

72 Within many local authorities, intensified political conflict and growing demands for more effective management systems have disturbed traditional patterns of authority, and are shifting remaining responsibilities for educational provision away from the local education committee and department. The broader and increasingly clearly articulated priorities of a corporately managed local authority inhibit the development of effective planning or accepted sense of direction within the local education service. The requirements that educational institutions pursue explicitly the often conflicting political objectives of local and central government controllers are at the expense of the LEA's influence. Moves towards greater institutional autonomy further weaken the patterns of LEA control over the further education service. The diversity which long has characterised the British further education system is still being promoted at institutional level, at the expense of traditional local government control mechanisms. Current central government policies seem certain to bring about more changes, which will reduce still further local authority control over the further education service. Colleges will need to look forward to the opportunities and problems presented in delivering further and higher education services when local authorities will have a smaller role than in the past in the management of those services.

NOTES

1 For example in Regina v. Liverpool City Council, Ex parte Professional Association of Teachers (QBD) (*The Times* 22 March 1984) it was held, in a case when the Education Committee had not made a report but authorised its chair to make a recommendation to the local authority, that the LA was required to consider a report from the Education Committee under the Education Act 1944 Part II schedule 1, paragraph 7.

2 The Government's consultative paper on FE (DES 1987b) proposed inter alia, substantial reductions in LEA influence on college financial management; transfer of responsibility for selecting, appointing and dismissing staff from LEA to college governing body; fewer LEA members on governing bodies.

3 However, the consultative paper (DES 1987b) suggested LEAs should plan on an annual basis for post-16 provision.

1.7 THE MANPOWER SERVICES COMMISSION[1]

1 **Introduction**

The Manpower Services Commission (MSC) was established on 1 January 1974 under the Employment and Training Act 1973 to run the public employment and training service. In the corporate plan 1987–91, the Commission defines its role as: fostering the creation of a better trained, more adaptable workforce; supporting employment growth and its job creation; continuing to encourage the development of enterprise; improving the functioning of the labour market; assisting back into employment those people who have been out of work for a long time or who because of their sex, ethnic origin or disability have difficulty in obtaining suitable work or training. By 1986–87 the Commission's expenditure totalled some £3,000m, and, as well as the development of its own services, it was financing 25% of work-related non-advanced FE (WRNAFE) (See below paragraphs 68–71 and **1.3** 44–45) and making a substantial contribution to colleges and schools through its Technical and Vocational Education Initiative (TVEI) (See below paragraphs 61–63 and **3.1** 4–9).

2 **Organisation of the MSC**

The Manpower Services Commission is separate from the Government but accountable to the Secretary of State for Employment and to the Secretaries of State for Wales and Scotland in respect of its operations in those countries. The Secretary of State for Education and Science is involved in the consideration of the Commission's plans and in proposals substantially affecting non-advanced further education provision in England, and is also consulted about matters which affect his or her responsibilities. The Commission has a chair and nine members who are appointed by the Secretary of State after consultation so as to provide representation of the Trades Union Congress (TUC) (three), Confederation of British Industry (CBI) (three), local authority associations (two) and professional education interests (one). There is a separate Manpower Services Committee for Wales which advises the Commission on its plans and operations in Wales; it comprises a chair and nine members appointed by the Commission with the approval of the Secretary of State for Wales and, as with the Commission, members are appointed after consultation with the four interested parties.

3 MSC was, at time of writing, organised in two groups, Vocational Education and Training Group, and Employment and Enterprise Group. The operating divisions delivered their programmes through their own structure of headquarters, regional and area offices. The Vocational Education and Training Group covered: the Training Division, which administered the Youth Training Scheme (YTS) and adult training programmes; the Skills Training Agency which provided training both in skillcentres and on employers' own premises; and branches coordinating the Technical and Vocational Education Initiative (TVEI). The Employment and Enterprise Group included the Employment Division, which ran the jobcentre network and special programmes to help disabled people with additional employment problems, and the Special Measures Directorate, which ran the Community Programme and other special measures for unemployed people. However, in June 1987 Secretary of State for Employment Norman Fowler indicated in a letter to the

Chair of the MSC that he would take jobcentres back under the responsibility of his Department.

4 **Area Manpower Boards**

Area offices are linked with the Area Manpower Boards (AMBs) whose role is to provide the Commission with advice and assistance in the delivery of its employment and training initiatives. On YTS, the Community Programme and the Voluntary Projects Programme, the AMBs examine proposals for individual schemes or projects and advise area offices whether to approve them. The boards' priority tasks are to:

(i) Develop local labour market plans and to assist MSC management to develop a strategic approach in fitting its programmes to local needs;
(ii) Promote and improve the quality of YTS schemes;
(iii) Assure the quality of Community Programme projects;
(iv) Contribute to the implementation of MSC's Adult Training Strategy by stimulating greater awareness amongst employers of the need for adult training, and to evaluate the impact of the Strategy in their areas and suggest improvements;
(v) Monitor the operation of MSC's equal opportunities policy.

5 The geographical boundaries of AMBs coincide approximately with those of the 55 Training Division Area Offices; in July 1986 the number of AMBs was increased to 58. The Boards broadly mirror the tripartite composition of the Commission. They have an independent chair and 16 or 17 members, five each representing employers and employees (nominated by the CBI and TUC respectively), two or three local authority representatives and one each representing the education service, professional education interest, voluntary organisations and the chair of a local Committee for the Employment of Disabled People. In addition, the AMBs may coopt up to four non-voting members to represent other important views. They may also invite representation of specific interests, for example, managing agents or young people to attend their meetings on appropriate occasions.

6 Area offices are also advised by the 87 Committees for the Employment of Disabled People.

7 **Youth Training Scheme**

The Youth Training Scheme (YTS) is now a permanent and integral part of vocational education and training provision for the 16–18 year old age group. It aims to provide a foundation of broad-based vocational education and training, and planned work experience, which gives all trainees the opportunity to obtain a vocational qualification related to competence in the work-place or to obtain a credit towards such a qualification. YTS is primarily employer based involving partnership between employers, training providers, and the Government, with employers bearing their share of the costs.

8 YTS has evolved from the Youth Opportunities Programme (YOP) which the Government established in 1977 to cater for the growing numbers of unemployed 16–18 year olds. (See 1980 edition of *College Administration.*) YTS was initiated in 1983 as a one-year programme (See **1.1** 25). From April 1986 it was transformed into a two-year programme, the first year of which gives a broad base of training and the second more specialised skills training.

9 Key features of the two-year YTS are:

(i) Increased emphasis on quality of schemes, with a new Training Standards Advisory Service to carry out in-depth inspections of individual schemes;
(ii) A new status of Approved Training Organisation, which all managing agents must secure;
(iii) Rolling contracts for managing agents;
(iv) Increased opportunities for obtaining a relevant vocational qualification;
(v) Illustrative model schemes produced by MSC in conjunction with industry training organisations.

10 YTS provides:

(i) A two-year training programme for 16 year olds with at least 20 weeks off-the-job training over two years;
(ii) A one-year training programme for 17 year olds with at least seven weeks off-the-job training;
(iii) The opportunity for all young people to obtain or work towards recognised qualifications which indicate competence in the workplace;
(iv) An emphasis on the outcomes of training;
(v) A Training Agreement for each young person which describes their training programme and the arrangements under which they take part in it;
(vi) Nationally agreed standards of training.

11 The chart (Fig. 1) outlines the main principles which are required to underlie the design of YTS programmes. It stresses four 'outcomes' (competences and abilities that trainees should acquire) which, taken together, make up occupational competence, and these competences are intended to be recognised through certification involving vocational qualifications.

12 **The Inputs**

Properly planned and organised work experience and on-the-job training enables trainees to acquire and practise skills by providing a realistic work setting in which competences achieved can be demonstrated and assessed. Off-the-job training is a planned and directed programme of learning which takes place outside the day-to-day pressures of the workplace and allows trainees to prepare for, reinforce and develop what they learn during work experience. A training plan with competence objectives is necessary to show the main stages and content of training programmes, and to provide clear targets for the trainees on it. Induction is essential to brief trainees and to give them information at the beginning of their training programme (and at other key transitional stages). Initial and then continuous assessments are necessary in order to provide a basic record of a trainee's level of attainment and a progressive record of achievements leading to certification. Participative learning involves trainees and should be a first priority at every stage. Guidance and reviewing involve giving practical advice and counselling to trainees on all matters affecting their training and ensuring they are fully aware of their progress.

13 **The Outcomes**

At the end of their training, trainees should have acquired a range of basic skills which could lead to a variety of jobs and provide a base for further training. Competence in a job means having basic technical knowledge, skills and

1.7

Figure 1

Design Framework for YTS: Training content to be delivered through integrated inputs

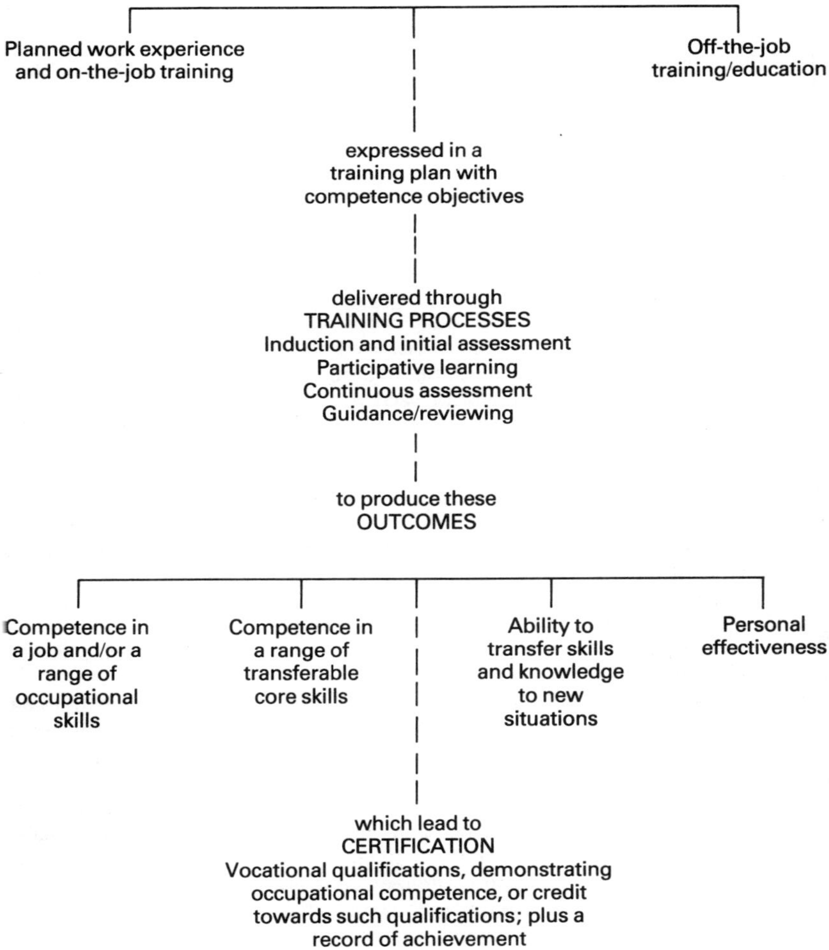

understanding. Core skills are those associated with numbers and their application, communication, problem solving and planning, practical skills and computer and information technology. Trainees should develop and demonstrate their ability to transfer occupational and core skills and knowledge to new tasks, jobs and situations. To develop this ability trainees need to grasp the underlying principles of tasks and be exposed to unfamiliar situations. Personal effectiveness involves the development of initiative, the ability to handle interpersonal relationships, the acceptance of responsibility and the development of self-sufficiency.

14 **Certification and Vocational Qualifications**
Managing agents issue a standard YTS certificate to all trainees who leave their programmes. The certificate includes information about the training completed, a statement about competences in the four outcomes and a summary about competence objectives achieved, including any qualifications obtained.

15 **Minimum periods of off-the-job training**
All two-year training programmes have to include a minimum of 20 weeks off-the-job training. MSC normally require there to be at least 13 weeks in the first year of training and 7 weeks in the second year. Managing agents can apply to alter this balance if they have good training grounds for wanting more off-the-job in the second year, but there must be at least 7 weeks of training in each year.

16 All one-year programmes have to include at least seven weeks off-the-job training. Some of the young people entitled to only one-year on YTS (normally those who leave full-time education at the age of 17) will have pursued academic subjects in the further year at school or college, while others will have undertaken vocational courses. They can enter either the first or second year of a two-year programme. Managing agents should take account of vocational studies already undertaken and the extent to which work experience was part of the pre-entry studies.

17 **Eligibility and Entry**
Young people may participate in YTS either as employed or non-employed trainees. The wage paid to any employed trainee should not be less than the minimum rate of training allowance which is to be paid to a non-employed trainee.

18 Young people's entitlement to YTS training depends on when they leave full-time education:

(i) *Two years' training:* young people leaving full-time education on or after the date they are first eligible to leave school but before the beginning of the third term of the next academic year will be entitled to two years' YTS;

(ii) *One year's training:* those who stay on at school or college into the third term of the academic year following that in which they are first eligible to leave but leave before the beginning of the third term of the following academic year will be entitled to one year's YTS;

(iii) *No entitlement;* those who stay on into the third term of this second academic year will have no YTS entitlement.

19 Disabled young people leaving full-time education up to and including the age of 21 are entitled to two years' training with the opportunity of an additional six months at the beginning or end of YTS if this enhances their training and employment prospects. Some young people's entry to YTS is delayed by pregnancy, custodial sentence, care order, sickness or by staying on at school after 16 to improve their English.

20 All young people eligible for YTS have one year from the date they leave full-time education in which to enter. So those young people entitled to two years' training must complete their time on YTS within three years of leaving full-time education, and those entitled to one year's training must complete within two

years. This means that it is possible for young people to delay entering YTS for up to a year after leaving full-time education, without reducing their normal entitlement. Any subsequent interruptions reduce their entitlement.

21 **Recruitment**

Careers services are responsible for giving guidance and advice to school-leavers about their choice of career and appropriate training and further education. Managing agents are free to recruit young people directly to their programmes, but potential entrants to premium places must be endorsed by the careers office/jobcentre before entry to such places. For additional funding or assistance for young disabled people with special training needs, the support of a Specialist Careers Officer or the Disablement Resettlement Officer at one of MSC's jobcentres has to be secured before the additional funds can be made available.

22 **Funding**

Managing agents are paid on the following basis:

(i) Management fee payable for each contracted place, for each of the two years;
(ii) Basic grant, payable for each filled place for each of 24 months of the two-year programme; and in certain cases
(iii) Premium grant payable for a limited number of training places for young people with special training needs, or where there are insufficient employer-based places; and
(iv) Additional payment will be made available for disabled people with particular training needs.

23 **Employer Contributions**

The MSC expects managing agents to seek contributions from work experience providers and/or other sources where they are needed. Levels of contributions are decided through negotiations between individual managing agents and work experience and training providers; the MSC does not set levels.

24 **Approved Training Organisations**

Managing agents are contractually required to apply to become an Approved Training Organisation. There are 10 main criteria:

(i) Arranging a two-year training programme;
(ii) Previous record in training;
(iii) Resources;
(iv) Competence of staff;
(v) Premises and equipment;
(vi) Assessment of trainees;
(vii) Effective programme review;
(viii) Positive commitment to equal opportunities;
(ix) Positive commitment to health and safety;
(x) Financial viability.

25 When an application to become an Approved Training Organisation has been received, Training Division Area Office staff draws up a report on the organisation which together with any comments by the managing agent will be considered by the Area Manpower Board. The final decision on Approved Training Organisation status is taken by MSC's Regional Directors, on the recommendation and advice of Area Manpower Boards.

26 YTS is open to all young people who are eligible and can benefit from training, regardless of race, religion, sex or disability. Managing agents must not discriminate on these grounds, either directly or indirectly in the recruitment, dismissal of young people, or in the management of their training. Managing agents must also offer all young people who join the programme a full range of training and work experience so that each may have equal opportunity to benefit from YTS.

27 The MSC is committed to ensuring that YTS takes place in environments where potential hazards are properly managed and that safe working practices are properly integrated into training programmes. As well as having a legal duty to satisfy relevant health and safety legislation, managing agents are required to give safety induction training to all young people on YTS, and all necessary information, training and instruction on health, safety and welfare arrangements, and on safe working practices.

28 **Information Technology Centres (ITeCs)**

ITeCs are to help young people obtain employment in the area of new technology by providing training and work experience in micro-computing, electronics and computer applications, in particular for the electronic office. Initial training is undertaken within the ITeC and normally lasts for up to 12 months. Under two-year YTS, most ITeC trainees spend the whole of their second year on work placement. Trainees can be from varying backgrounds; most ITeCs recruit a mix of abilities, though some prefer to recruit trainees with academic qualifications and others cater for those with few or no qualifications.

29 ITeCs are run by sponsors, who may be any organisation with the ability to run a high quality training programme. Sponsors include high technology companies as well as local authorities – and in many cases, from consortia of the two. There are 175 ITeCs covering most parts of the country.

30 ITeCs are funded from three sources; the MSC, the sponsors themselves and a pump-priming contribution from the Department of Trade and Industry of £75,000 over three years. Under the funding rules the MSC contracts with each ITeC for a specified number of training places. The approach to funding under two-year YTS is intended to be more flexible and responsive to the needs of trainees, ITeCs themselves and employers. ITeCs are also being encouraged to generate a greater amount of their own funding and so to become IT training resources for their locality, and many ITeCs have developed training courses for local companies and employers. Special arrangements are necessary for ITeCs because of their relatively high cost in relation to other modes of provision and transitional funding arrangements were designed to support them in the change to the two-year YTS. ITeCs are also offered:

(i) Additional premium places if they manage to reduce the minimum period of training in the ITeC to six months;

(ii) A subsidy for each unit of additional adult training for the next two years.

31 **Adult training**

One of MSC's major objectives is the opening up of widespread opportunities for adults to acquire, increase or update their skills and knowledge during the course of their working lives. MSC is therefore conducting an Adult Training

Campaign which aims to raise awareness of the need for adult training and to promote changes in the education and training systems generally. MSC's own programmes have been restructured to focus them more clearly on skills needed in the future, and to make them more flexible, relevant and responsive to changing labour market needs. Its adult training programmes consist of two broad categories: the Job Training Programme (which subsumes elements of the previously known TOPS in occupational and enterprise training) and the Wider Opportunities Training Programme (which replaces the work preparation element previously a part of TOPS). Trainees on these programmes receive an allowance from MSC.

32 **Job Training Programme**

This is designed to meet the known needs of employers and employees and to create new businesses. Its main components are:

(i) A Job Training Scheme, which aims to meet known employment needs, mainly local, by offering intensive occupational training to update, upgrade, extend or convert the skills of unemployed individuals (See below paragraphs 33–35);

(ii) A National Priority Skills Scheme, which helps employers to train employees in priority skills identified by their industrial training organisations;

(iii) Training for Enterprise, for people aiming to become self-employed or to start businesses. Provision includes one-day Small Business Workshops, which spell out to participants the implications of self-employment; Start Up Courses, providing specific training in management skills; training modules for owners and managers of existing businesses; and projects through which unemployed managers and graduates can be seconded to help growing firms;

(iv) Access to Information Technology, which aims to promote awareness of information technology, and to provide training outside normal working hours;

(v) Local Training Grants to help employers provide better training for their existing employees and to train recruits for hard-to-fill vacancies;

(vi) Local Consultancy Grants, which help firms obtain professional advice about their training needs;

(vii) Local Collaborative Projects, whereby employers and providers of vocational education and training establish a joint approach towards analysing and meeting training needs. This scheme is run jointly by MSC and DES;

(viii) A Management Development Initiative to promote new ways of meeting the development needs of managers.

33 **Job Training Scheme**

In autumn 1986 the MSC introduced a new Job Training Scheme (JTS) in ten pilot areas. Priority for these schemes was given to the under-25s – which distinguishes it from the previous Job Training Scheme. The aim of JTS is to offer everyone under 25 who has been out of work for six months or more either a job club (See below paragraph 43), or a place on the Enterprise Allowance Scheme, or a place on the JTS.

34 In January 1987 the Government announced a major extension of the JTS. The plan was to increase to 110,000 places nation-wide by September and 250,000 in a full year. The speed of the extension – and particularly its announcement before the monitoring of the pilots was complete – created considerable concern among unions and local authorities. The TUC and the

National Association of Local Government Officers (NALGO) decided in 1987 not to cooperate with the JTS, having reservations also about the level of payments and about the quality of the programmes.

35 JTS programmes last between two and twelve months and aim to increase and update people's skills for employment within their existing occupations or to provide foundation skills for new occupations. This involves work experience and training courses, programmed through individual Training Action Plans. Participation in the scheme is voluntary, and participants receive an allowance equal to their benefit entitlement prior to entry (plus cost of travel). The scheme is run by managing agents, following the pattern set by YTS. Managing agents are expected to seek a contribution of around £20 per week on average from employers offering work experience placements.

36 **Wider Opportunities Training Programme**

This programme aims to help unemployed people improve their work-related skills, retain employability and cope with the changing contents of jobs and patterns of work. It includes:

(i) Work-related skills and assessment courses for people whose occupational skills need broadening or updating;
(ii) Preparatory courses focusing on work-related literacy and numeracy;
(iii) Work-related language training, linked to occupational skills training, for speakers of English as a second language;
(iv) Courses for women wishing to return to work;
(v) Work preparation programmes for unemployed managers and professionals;
(vi) Work preparation and basic skills training for Community Programme participants.

37 **Open Tech Programme**

This programme is intended to stimulate the use of 'open learning' as an approach to training – that is, learning outside a classroom at a time, place and pace which suit the needs of the individual. It is primarily focused on the training and retraining of adults in technician and supervisory level skills. It operates through collaborative, locally delivered projects with colleges, employers, industry training organisations, local authorities and others, for which MSC provides pump-priming finance. Most projects are concerned with producing open learning materials and setting up open learning systems. Responsibility for the programme including its evaluation, has now passed to the Open Learning branch which is in a position to effect links with the Open College. The Further Education Unit has published a report on *Implementing Open Learning in Local Authority Institutions* which the Department of Education and Science and MSC have endorsed.

38 **Skills Training Agency**

The Skills Training Agency (STA) is a separate organisation within MSC which provides training services on a cost-recovery basis to clients (including the other parts of MSC). In the past STA training has concentrated on manual craft skills covering the construction, engineering, plant and automotive, electrical and general servicing trades, but the agency is seeking new markets and is extending its range of services, particularly in new technology. STA's main customer is Training Division. In addition, governments and employers, both in Great Britain and overseas, take advantage of the agency's facilities and training expertise to increase the knowledge and skills of their workforces. There are three broad types of training available:

(i) *Sponsored training* Individual training packages are tailored to meet the particular requirements of customers. The training is delivered in a national network of Skillcentres.
(ii) *Mobile Training Service* Where it is more beneficial for training to use a customer's own equipment and machinery, a mobile trainer can conduct a course on the customer's premises, producing a customised training package.
(iii) *Instructor Training* STA training facilities are available to customers who want their experienced workers to be trained to undertake instructional duties.

39 **Jobcentre services**

The original function of jobcentres is the filling of employer vacancies and placing of individuals in jobs, but jobcentres in addition offer a gateway to the range of MSC schemes and to some non-MSC programmes. They offer information and advice on employment, enterprise, training, adult education and voluntary work. Jobcentres provide special help to disabled people, and intensive counselling, Jobclubs and Restart schemes for long-term unemployed people.

40 **Professional and Executive Recruitment**

Professional and Executive Recruitment (PER) is a specialist branch of the public employment service and the largest executive recruitment consultancy in the UK. PER offers a complete range of recruitment services on a competitive commercial basis, from advertising in its own weekly jobs newspaper, *Executive Post*, to a consultancy service including interviewing. All managerial, technical and professional occupations are handled through this service, including those related to the Community Programme and other special measures.

41 **Restart**

Restart is a programme of counselling interviews for people who have been out of work for a long time. The purpose of the interviews is to help people review their employment prospects, inform them about the range of assistance available and explore their chances of applying for a job, training or some other suitable opportunity. The programme was launched nationally on 1 July 1986, with the aim of inviting all people claiming unemployment benefit for more than a year to an interview before 1 April 1987. It was planned to be extended in 1987/88 to all people who have been out of work for more than six months. In addition further interviews will be provided at regular intervals for those remaining out of work.

42 At the Restart counselling interview a number of possibilities are explored. They include:

(i) Submission to a job, possibly with a Jobstart allowance;
(ii) A place in a Jobclub (See below paragraph 43);
(iii) Participation in the Enterprise Allowance Scheme;
(iv) A place on the new Job Training Scheme (See above paragraph 33–35);
(v) A place on one of the MSC's other training courses;
(vi) A place on the Community Programme (See below paragraph 46);
(vii) The Voluntary Projects Programme;
(viii) A Restart course.

43 **Jobclubs**
Jobclubs encourage and enable people to engage in intensive and effective jobsearch. They do this by providing: training in jobsearch techniques: resources such as stamps, stationery, free access to telephone and photocopiers; and motivation and support (from the jobclub leader and, most importantly, other jobclub members). Their aim is to help members find the best possible job for themselves in the shortest possible time. They have been successful in this throughout the country, with over 60% of members finding a job and a further 13% a place on a training course or the Community Programme. Within three years of the first jobclub opening 1,000 are in operation. Restart has clearly identified a strong demand for jobclubs among long term unemployed people. Accordingly the number of jobclubs will if necessary be increased early in the Plan period by up to a further 1,000. Most of the expansion will be achieved through the use of external agents who will operate jobclubs on MSC's behalf.

44 **Assistance for disabled people**
The majority of disabled jobseekers, whose needs are broadly similar to those of other jobseekers, are catered for by the mainstream jobcentre services, but for those with special needs, specialist counselling is available from Disablement Resettlement Officers. A comprehensive range of special schemes is provided, including:

(i) Grants to employers (up to £6,000 per employee in 1987) to facilitate adaptations to premises or equipment to permit the recruitment or retention of a specific disabled worker;
(ii) The loan of special tools or equipment to registered disabled people for use at work;
(iii) Assistance with fares to work to people who cannot use public transport;
(iv) A grant to employers who employ disabled people for a trial period (Job Introduction Scheme);
(v) For blind and partially-sighted people, a contribution towards the cost of engaging a part-time reader at work.

45 The Disablement Advisory Service, comprising small specialist teams at local level, aims to help individual disabled people at work; to encourage and advise employers about adopting progressive practices towards disabled people; and to promote facilities for disabled people on other MSC programmes. Employment Rehabilitation Centres and Asset Centres assist people who are handicapped, or have been ill, to return to work. There are 27 ERCs, three of which have residential facilities, and three Asset Centres. Courses provide assessment, work experience and jobsearch training. MSC also gives financial assistance to local authorities and voluntary bodies who run rehabilitation courses. Sheltered employment is provided for severely disabled people who are unlikely to be able to work except under special sheltered conditions. Such conditions are provided in Remploy factories and sheltered workshops, and in Sheltered Placement Schemes where individuals or small groups of severely disabled people work within a company alongside the rest of the workforce. All employees in sheltered employment work a normal week, receive wages and pay tax and national insurance contributions in the normal way. Local authorities and voluntary bodies who provide sheltered employment receive a contribution from MSC towards the capital and revenue costs. MSC also contributes to the costs incurred by local authorities on home-working schemes for severely disabled people.

46 **Community Programme**
The Community Programme (CP) is the Government's principal programme for long-term unemployed people. It provides full-time and part-time temporary work of up to a year's duration, on projects of benefit to the community. Participants must:
(i) Have been unemployed continuously for the last twelve months;
(ii) Also have been unemployed for at least six of the last nine months if aged 18 to 24, or for 12 of the last 15 months if aged over 25;
(iii) Be in direct or indirect receipt of an appropriate state benefit.
Projects are managed by sponsors, who are reimbursed by MSC for the wages of participants provided these do not exceed £67 per week (1987) on average. The programme is administered locally through the MSC's Employment Division area offices.

47 **Criteria for projects**
(i) All Community Programme Projects should produce something of practical benefit to the community, e.g. environmental improvement projects; the provision of social and personal services for disadvantaged members of the community; the conservation of energy.
(ii) Projects should be designed to provide jobs which can be done by people who have been out of work for several months. Wherever possible CP jobs should aim to meet the skill requirements of the local labour market so as to provide employment and training which will improve the employment prospects of participants.
(iii) Projects must involve work which would not otherwise be done. Existing businesses or jobs in normal employment must not be put at risk as a result of a project.
(iv) The appropriate local hourly or equivalent 'rate for the job' should be paid to workers on projects.
(v) If projects are likely to involve the interests of unions – in either the public or private sector – or existing employers, they should have the written support of the relevant trade unions' and employers' organisations, e.g. building and construction projects must have the support of the Building Employers Confederation.
(vi) Projects must be financially viable as regards any costs not met by MSC funds. Sponsors of CP projects must have the staffing and expertise to take on the full responsibilities of an employer and to run their projects efficiently.
(vii) The Community Programme must not be used to override limitations on public expenditure.

48 Any organisation or group of individuals, except political parties, may sponsor a project – local authorities, private firms, trade unions, voluntary bodies, charities or community groups. There are a variety of ways they can become involved in the Community Programme: as independent sponsors, where they are responsible for the whole project; as associate sponsors under a CP agent; as a CP agent where they administer a number of projects sponsored by themselves or by associate sponsors; or as a task patron when the work is carried out by a sponsor on their behalf.

49 **Agents**
A CP agent is an organisation which contracts with the Commission to provide a specified number of filled places on a number of CP projects. The projects

must number five or more and offer a total of 50 or more filled places, or at least two projects offering a total of 100 or more filled places. There can be three types of agents:

(i) Bodies which administer projects sponsored by their own organisation only, i.e. the agent is also the sponsor;

(ii) Bodies which administer projects sponsored by other organisations only;

(iii) Bodies which administer projects sponsored both by their own organisations and by other organisations.

CP Agents are paid an additional £100 per year per filled place. They can spread average wage costs over all the projects and can pool operating costs. An agent may develop expertise in areas of management support, accounting and training, e.g. it might employ a specialist training officer to give training to people across a number of projects.

50 CP agents are responsible for the following, in addition to the general responsibilities of all CP sponsors for management and supervision:

(i) Delivering a specified number of filled places on projects within an agreed timescale;

(ii) Undertaking tasks for sponsors, such as centralised administration, professional support services, bulk-buying of materials, central recruitment, assistance with finding appropriate projects;

(iii) Vetting and monitoring projects to ensure that sponsors conform to CP rules;

(iv) Operating their own financial systems and ensuring that financial systems operated by sponsors within the agency conform to MSC's requirements.

51 **Employees**

Sponsors can recruit CP employees through jobcentres, careers offices or Professional Executive Recruitment (PER), or using whatever method they wish; the eligibility of all those recruited to CP jobs must be checked with the jobcentre. Young people under the age of 18, students seeking vocational work, men aged 65 or over and women aged 60 or over are not eligible for employment on the Community Programme. (People employed on CP projects should not be less than a year from normal retirement age.) Where it proves impossible to recruit managers, supervisors or skilled manual workers who are essential to the project, the CP area office may waive the recruitment criteria for that post.

52 Sponsors are the employers of all people recruited to projects and responsible for the payment of salaries/wages and other payroll matters (i.e. income tax, National Insurance and, where appropriate, redundancy payments) arising out of such employment. Additionally, sponsors are responsible for hours of work and matters of sick pay, holiday pay, superannuation, absence, discipline etc. Within an agency it is possible to pool the combined total approved operating costs of all projects. Thus, high cost projects e.g. construction projects can be funded above the MSC maximum level but be counterbalanced by low cost projects within the agency. However, no project, except for a central administration project within the agency, may have operating costs funded above a level of £660 per approved place for 52 weeks. An agent's fee is paid to agents for the work and responsibility, e.g. assembly and submission of monthly accounts, planning and budgeting, allocation of resources, market-

ing and training. The fee is £100 (1987) (plus VAT if appropriate) for each filled place (including managers and supervisors) of 52 weeks and pro rata for lesser periods. In addition to receiving the fee a CP agent may either: set up a project under CP rules to handle the administration of the agency centrally; or use up to 20% of the total operating costs made available by the Commission to fund central services. A sponsor with other permanent employees should offer employees under the Community Programme the terms and conditions of employment under which other workers in similar jobs are employed. Where employers offer different terms and conditions to temporary workers these terms should be offered to their CP workers.

53 Participants can be employed on projects for any length of time between two days (or 16 hours spread over more than two days) and five days per week. Because of the requirement that workers should be paid at the local rate for the job within the average weekly amount, most sponsors manage a mix of part and full-time jobs.

54 Individual employees may not be employed on the CP for more than 52 weeks. However, with the prior approval of the CP area office, supervisors and others with skills essential to the continued successful operation of the scheme, and for whom no suitable qualified replacement is available, may be retained for additional periods not exceeding 52 weeks.

55 **Funding**

The MSC reimburses full-time wages of supervisors and managers, which reflect the local rate for the job up to agreed limits, employer's National Insurance contributions and employer's superannuation contributions where applicable. It reimburses the costs of wages for workers up to a maximum of £67 per week (1987) for each full or part-time worker on a project, plus employer's National Insurance contributions and employer's superannuation contributions where applicable. Individual workers may receive more than £67 in wages provided it does not exceed the local rate for the job and the average wage across a project or agency does not exceed £67 over the lifetime of the project (up to 52 weeks).

57 The MSC refunds operating costs for essential overheads, materials and equipment up to a maximum of £440 per year (1987) for each full or part-time approved place over 52 weeks with the exception that manager and supervisor places do not attract operating costs.

58 **Enterprise allowance scheme**

This scheme is intended to help unemployed people who want to start their own business but who may be deterred by the fact that they would lose their entitlement to unemployment or supplementary benefit. Applicants must be at least 18 years old and under retirement age, have been unemployed for at least eight weeks and be receiving unemployment or supplementary benefit. They must be prepared to work full-time and to invest at least £1,000 of their own money in the business. The business must be new, independent, suitable for public support, and must not employ more than 20 people in the first three months. The allowance is a flat-rate taxable £40 per week paid for a maximum of 52 weeks. Business advice and counselling are also available to all scheme participants.

59 **Voluntary projects programme**

The main purpose of this programme is to help improve the employment prospects of unemployed people by providing a constructive activity which will enable them to develop existing skills or learn new skills. Involvement in the programme is voluntary and does not affect entitlement to statutory benefits. The range of projects funded are education, training and community work-related projects. The programme operates through sponsors who can reclaim their costs from MSC.

60 **Community industry**

This scheme aims to improve the job prospects of young people who are personally or socially disadvantaged, by providing temporary work of benefit to the community. The sole provider of places is Community Industry Limited, a company with charitable status. The young people on the scheme are employees of the company and work in teams, supervised by adults. The range of work undertaken includes construction, landscaping, carpentry, dress-making and social care.

61 **TVEI**

The Technical and Vocational Initiative (TVEI) was created with MSC funding and administered through the MSC's TVEI Branches, liaising with DES, HMI and the Welsh Office. LEAs submitted schemes for approval by the MSC. Despite some misgivings, LEAs were involved from the launch and were represented on the national Steering Group which considered LEA schemes submitted for approval.

62 In a framework for extension agreed by the National Steering Group, the MSC invited LEAs in England and Wales (and education authorities in Scotland), once they have operated a pilot scheme for a minimum of three years, to submit proposals to give all 14–18 year olds in maintained and voluntary-aided schools and colleges access to curricular programmes of the type being piloted. Authorities which started pilot projects in 1983 and 1984 were previously invited to submit proposals to begin their extension in 1987, and some started then. To allow time and flexibility to prepare and implement proposals for the introduction of TVEI developments in all secondary schools and colleges, the extension of TVEI was to be phased over a period of years. The Government wanted every education authority to take part. The MSC invited those authorities which had not operated pilot programmes to submit proposals in 1987 or 1988 for a three year preparatory stage leading to full involvement. The involvement of LEAs and individual schools and colleges remained voluntary but the MSC hopes to see the majority of eligible institutions participating by the end of the Plan period. It did, however, insist that proposals from LEAs are of a quality and advanced state of readiness to merit support.

63 Criteria on which the MSC judged TVEI submissions from LEAs were:

(i) Draw up specific objectives for, and expected outcomes to be achieved from, the curriculum development plan, relating to the authority's curricular policy as a whole;

(ii) Provide wider opportunities for young people, through a more relevant and practical curriculum, leading to the achievement of recognised standards of competence, and the qualifications;

(iii) Provide a broad and balanced curriculum, as indicated by the White Paper 1985 *Better Schools* and the Consultative Committee on the Cur-

riculum's *Curriculum Design at 53 and 54: Guidelines for Headteachers*;
(iv) To improve access of students to technology;
(v) To share expertise and experience from a number of institutions;
(vi) To improve collaboration with further education;
(vii) To develop collaboration with higher education;
(viii) To strengthen structures for effective management of curriculum development;
(ix) To develop a more effective partnership between industry and education;
(x) To establish local support arrangements;
(xi) To establish mechanisms for continuing assessment and review.

64 **TRIST**

In March 1985 the MSC was invited by the Government to run the TVEI Related In-Service Training Scheme (TRIST) for two years prior to the introduction by the Secretary of State for Education and Science of a wider scheme to grant-aid in-service training generally. The MSC established detailed arrangements for the scheme through its TVEI National Steering Group. Proposals from LEAs had to be based on a systematic assessment of in-service training needs against the authority's relevant curriculum development plan. They had to assist and promote developments across the curriculum of the kind envisaged in particular by TVEI, for example practical, non-didactic, non-directive pupil-centred learning, relevant to working and adult life. In April 1987 TRIST was superseded by the LEA Training Grants Scheme under Section 50 of the Education (No.2) Act 1986, sometimes called GRIST (Grant Related In-Service Training). (See **2.9** 22–27).

65 **Work-Related Non-Advanced Further Education**

In the 1984 White Paper *Training for Jobs* the MSC was given new responsibilities in the field of vocational education. The Commission was asked to purchase a higher proportion of work-related non-advanced further education (WRNAFE) provided by LEAs in England and Wales. The intention was that these arrangements would enable provision to become more responsive to employment needs and to give a greater incentive to efficiency. Priority was to be given to provision for newly emerging skills, and to occupations where traditional programmes no longer matched modern industrial need. There were concerns and difficulties raised about these proposals.

66 A joint MSC – Local Authority Associations group was set up to look at arrangements for involving MSC in the provision of WRNAFE in 1986–87 and beyond. The policy group on WRNAFE reported in May 1985. The report proposed that planning for all WRNAFE in any area should be based on a three-year rolling development plan, to be drawn up by each LEA in discussion with MSC and in consultation with all interested parties of the local labour market. The plans should contain a detailed programme of provision planned by the local authority for the first of the three years. MSC support is made available to local education authorities in response to an acceptable plan and programme (See **1.3** 43–45).

67 The report was accepted by the parties represented on the group, though there were strong objections, particularly from the Association of Metropolitan Authorities, to the reduction of the LEAs' role in NAFE. Discussions about implementation took place with the local authority associations and others and guidance on the new arrangements was issued in October 1985 in the

shape of a guidance handbook. The first three year plan covered the period September 1986–August 1989.

68 **The impact of MSC**

The MSC has, over the last few years, faced sustained and increasing criticisms of its programmes and mode of operation. While it would not be appropriate or indeed feasible to enter into a comprehensive critique of the Commission here, there are issues of general concern which are recognised by a broad band of opinion in further education. This will have to be taken into account whenever discussions about new MSC schemes or initiatives are being considered.

69 The MSC's funding regime, short-term and often pump-priming, has presented colleges and local authorities with a number of difficulties. Notably, these have included an increased reliance on the issue of part-time and temporary contracts. Furthermore, the method of funding college programmes often by-passes the local Education Committee altogether a matter which, when viewed in the context of the Government's current and projected policies, places a question mark over LEAs' future role in providing further and higher education. Essentially, it is a debate around the issue of central versus local control and involves, among other things, issues discussed in other sections: the national extension of TVEI; the possible transfer of more RSG money to the MSC for work-related NAFE; Government proposals for a national curriculum, for City Technology Colleges and for schools to be allowed to 'opt out' of local authority control; the use of grant-related in-service training; the effect of the 1987 White Paper *Higher Education: meeting the Challenge* (See **1.1** Appendix 1); any national performance indicators from recommendations of the DES/LAA Joint Efficiency Study in NAFE; a national framework of vocational qualifications (See **1.1** 32 and **3.1** 50–51). The MSC, as an agent of Government, is very much involved in a significant number of these initiatives, and will, therefore, play a crucial role in any moves towards greater central control.

70 The other major concern which has frequently been expressed about MSC schemes is that of the quality of delivery and outcomes. Few doubt the ability of the MSC to provide for quantity but there has been a constant flow of criticism about quality; typified by the apparent failure to publish an adequate evaluation of the Open Tech programme or to evaluate the Job Training Scheme pilots before the national extension was agreed. It should be noted that the MSC has to some extent acknowledged this problem by establishing the procedure by which 'approved training organisation' status can be gained and by introducing the Training Standards Advisory Service which will also look at JTS schemes.

71 The catalogue of concerns about YTS is not restricted to any one quarter. The first six mentioned below arose from an employers' survey, as described by Chapman and Tooze (1987):

(i) Level of trainees allowances are too low.
(ii) The removal of Mode B type funding is taking us in the direction of what Disraeli called 'two nations'.
(iii) The scheme is underfunded.
(iv) The occupational distribution of places is grossly skewed.
(v) The voluntary nature of employers' involvement is helping to stabilise those who do not take part.

(vi) There is evidence of job substitution.
(vii) Poor record of health and safety.
(viii) Race discrimination and a sex stereotyping are evident.
(ix) There is a threat of withdrawal of state benefits to young people in the event of a refusal to join the Scheme.

72 Such concerns could return the debate to 1981 and the MSC consultative document *A New Training Initiative* before it was reworked and partially undermined by the Government's White Paper *A New Training Initiative: A Programme for Action*. The consultative document identified three key objectives:

(i) 'We must develop skill training including apprenticeship in such a way as to enable young people entering at different ages and with different educational attainments to acquire agreed standards of skill appropriate to the jobs available and to provide them with a basis for progression through further learning'.
(ii) 'We must move towards a position where all young people must, under the age of 18, have the opportunity either of continuing in full-time education or of entering training of a period of planned work experience combining work-related training and education'.
(iii) 'We must open up widespread opportunities for adults, whether employed, unemployed or returning to work to acquire, increase or update their skills and knowledge during the course of their working lives'.

73 NATFHE (1986b) commented that it was 'a matter for great regret and a major lost opportunity that Government and the MSC have failed to put NTI Objective One into effect. It is all the more tragic since the economic recession and Government policy have resulted in the continued decline of traditional apprenticeships'. It is a matter for some debate as to whether the two-year YTS programme, combined with other forms of education and training, represents adequate provision which satisfies Objectives (i) and (ii). However, the National Council for Vocational Qualifications (NCVQ) (See **3.1** 50–51) could encourage the development of a comprehensive curriculum for this age-group which ensured an appropriate balance of education and training based on individual need. Will the NCVQ, by the end of its developmental period in 1991, have devised a pattern of vocational qualifications which will facilitate the operation of the system of training envisaged by Objective One – a decade before? The NTI consultative document's objectives remain an agenda for action. Can the NCVQ help provide a framework in which progress could take place and build a bridge between 'academic' and 'vocational' routes? The questions of how to deliver quality are still current.

NOTES

1 As this book was going to press the Government published The Employment Bill 1987 which includes the proposal to replace the Manpower Service Commission with the Training Commission.

1.8 THE EUROPEAN COMMUNITY

1 **The European Community: Structure and Legislation**

The European Community (EC) comprises three distinct Communities with separate legal bases but common membership and institutions. These are the European Economic Community (EEC), which is the most important in education and training terms; the European Coal and Steel Community (ECSC); and the European Atomic Energy Community (EURATOM). The six founding members of the EEC (and the ECSC and EURATOM) were Belgium, the Federal Republic of Germany, France, Holland, Italy and Luxembourg. The United Kingdom, together with Denmark and Ireland, joined in 1973. Greece joined in 1981, Spain and Portugal joined at the start of 1986.

2 The primary purpose of the EEC, as set out in the Treaty of Rome, is 'to promote throughout the Community a harmonious development of economic activities, a continuous and balanced expansion, an increase in stability, an accelerated raising of the standard of living and closer relations between the States belonging to it' (Article 2).

3 The Community's main institutions are the Commission, the Council, the Parliament, and the Court of Justice. The Commission is the Community's executive. It is responsible for developing policy, for implementing the Treaties and the decisions of the Council, and for the day-to-day administration of the Community. It is independent of national governments. It is organised into Directorates-General (DGs), which are similar to government departments. DG V is responsible for education and training, amongst other matters. The Council is the highest political authority in the Community. It consists of ministers representing the individual member states. It is responsible for enacting major legislation and for other key decisions, and has the primary responsibility for the Community budget. The chair of the Council rotates between the member states on a six-monthly basis: the United Kingdom had the chair in the second half of 1986. The Parliament has limited formal powers but, especially now that it is directly elected, has considerable influence. In recent years it has on occasion used its leverage over the budget to encourage the development of the Community's education policy. The Court of Justice has jurisdiction over the application and interpretation of Community law.

4 Though the Commission itself has some legislative powers, major legislation is enacted by the Council of Ministers on the basis of Commission proposals. The European Parliament is consulted, as is in specified areas the Economic and Social Committee, on which employers and workers are represented. The legislation can take many forms. Regulations are directly binding throughout the Community. They do not require any national legislation in order to take effect. Directives bind the member states to achieve a specified result by an agreed date, but it is for member states to decide on the means of implementation. Decisions have similar force to regulations, but are addressed to specified individuals or member states. There are also various non-binding Community instruments, used for example to record a shared policy objective. These include recommendations, resolutions, and opinions. Such instruments have been used frequently in the field of education and training, on which the Treaties have little to say.

5 **Education and the European Community**
Education policy is not directly mentioned in the EEC Treaty, though it does provide both for the development of a common policy on vocational training (Article 128) and for the financing of training programmes through the European Social Fund (Articles 123–127). The relatively weak legal basis for Community action on education seems to have become less significant in recent years. Three factors lie behind this.

6 First, the nature of Community education and training activities has been changing. In this and other fields, progress through debate and consensus has become more important than the simple exploitation of the formal powers provided under the Treaties. Second, the relationship between education and other areas of common interest – such as the Community's need for technological development – has been more widely appreciated. Thirdly, a judgment by the Court of Justice has suggested that the position of education within the EEC Treaty is not as weak as had been thought: in its 13 February 1985 judgment (Gravier v. the City of Liège), the Court seemed to give a wide definition to 'vocational training' which does clearly lie within the scope of the EEC Treaty. Indeed, the Commission's view is that the Court's judgment shows that all education and training, except general education at the primary and secondary level, falls within scope of the Treaty. This view is not universally accepted, but the Gravier judgment has already led to changes in the way in which Community students studying in Britain are treated by the Government. On 1 July 1986, the Secretary of State for Education and Science announced in Parliament that, from 1 September 1986, students who were nationals of Community member states and studying in the UK on courses designated for mandatory award purposes would have their fees paid on the same basis as UK students (See **3.6**).

7 **Related Community legislation**
The relative absence of education legislation does not mean that there is no Community legislation of interest to educationalists. In addition to the education and training policies discussed below in paragraphs 13–22, there are important and binding provisions in the areas of equality of opportunity and employment law. These were discussed in detail in the 1980 edition of *College Administration* (Waitt 1980, **6.1** 14–33). The following paragraphs summarise and update this.

8 The Directive is the main legal instrument used by the Community in these areas, where the member states have varying collective and legal traditions. This is because it combines precise legal obligations on member states with a large measure of freedom in how to achieve those obligations. As a result, each member state has its own particular set of legislative provisions, which may in some cases be out of line with the Directive. Because of this, national law has been (and will continue to be) frequently tested, both directly by the Commission, and by individuals who have requested national courts to refer their cases to the Court of Justice. This potential for individual enforcement is particularly important in the education sphere following the Marshall case. This established that, where national law is inconsistent with the obligations of a Directive, public employees may ask a national court to apply Community law directly in their favour, in place of the inconsistent national provision.

9 Equality between men and women has been characterised by the Court as a

fundamental right, protected by Community law. The right of equal pay for equal work or work of equal value is guaranteed by Article 119 of the EEC Treaty, as amplified by the Equal Pay Directive 1975. It has been exemplified in British law by the Equal Pay Act 1970. There have been significant decisions made in favour of individuals by the Court taking a broad approach to what is regarded as 'pay' for the purposes of the Directive (including pensions, supplementary payments and non-contractual perks). The concept of 'equal value' was introduced into British law as a result of a Court of Justice decision against the UK in an action brought by the Commission. The Act was amended to give employees the right to bring equal value claims. This is an important change to British legislation, both with regard to the creation of a powerful new legal right, and for trade unions carrying on collective bargaining on behalf of women members.

10 The right to equal treatment with regard to employment and vocational training, working conditions other than pay, and dismissal, is guaranteed by the Equal Treatment Directive 1976. This is represented in British law by the relevant provisions of the Sex Discrimination Act 1976. The Act has been the subject of considerable litigation. As a result it has been amended to include partnerships, private households and small businesses, to nullify discriminatory clauses of collective agreements and to require a common age of compulsory retirement from employment. On this last point, provisions of the Employment Protection (Consolidation) Act 1978 also had to be altered. It is likely that there will be further changes to the 1976 Act to bring it into line with the Directive.

11 Pensions and pensionable age are the subject, amongst other provisions, of two Social Security Directives. These seek to guarantee that state and occupational social security schemes do not discriminate between men and women. A British allowance which was available only to men who gave up their jobs was extended to married women as a result of a Court of Justice decision. A third Social Security Directive is expected. This will move further towards the goal of complete individualisation of rights.

12 Account should also be taken of the two less widely-known general labour law Directives on collective redundancies (1975) and transfers of businesses (1977). These are represented in British law respectively by Part IV of the Employment Protection Act 1975 and the Transfer of Undertakings (Protection of Employment) Regulations 1981. Both provide for the compulsory consultation of recognised independent trade unions. The latter seeks to ensure that individual and collective rights accrued or agreed with an employer are automatically transferred to the new employer on the sale of a business. The Regulations are expressed in a somewhat tortuous manner, and are likely both to be revised by the Government and to be tested in the Courts.

13 **The European Community: education and training policies and programmes**

The first formal meeting of Education Ministers within the framework of the Community was held in 1974. An Education Committee, comprising national and Commission officials, was also set up in 1974. In February 1976 the Council adopted the first Community education action programme, which covered the education of migrant workers and their families; cooperation in higher education; the improvement of foreign language teaching; equal opportunity in education; and the exchange of ideas and information within the Community. In

December 1976 the programme was extended to cover the transition of young people from education to adult and working life. The December 1976 Council Decision also stressed the close relationship between education policy and Community action in the fields of vocational training and employment, and this has been a consistent theme of subsequent Community activities.

14 Though some member states remain less enthusiastic about the growth of the Community's education activities than others, these have continued to develop. From the late 1970s, the main political pressures derived from the rising level of youth unemployment, which led to a massive expansion of education and training programmes for young people in the Community. In the last two–three years, renewed impetus has come from the growing concern about the Community's industrial performance, especially in high technology sectors, and the consequent demand for action to improve the technical and vocational skills of the workforce. Measures to improve the mobility of students, teachers, and workers within the Community are also attracting increasing interest, as an essential complement to the renewed efforts to secure free movement of goods, services, and capital.

15 The following paragraphs look first at the current state of the education action programme and related activities, and then at the operation of the European Social Fund.

16 **Major Community education activities**

With the major exception of the European Social Fund, the main characteristics of Community activities in the field of education and training are that:

(i) They involve only modest expenditure, though this has been increasing in recent years.

(ii) They usually involve the exchange of information and experience between the member states, whose primary responsibility in this area of policy is accepted. The Commission plays a predominantly service role, though it frequently takes the initiative;

(iii) Because Community projects tend to focus on educational innovation, and are managed in cooperation with the national authorities – at a high level – their importance is greater than their scale and budgets might suggest;

(iv) There is almost no binding Community legislation in this area. There are, however, a number of joint policy declarations which commit the member states to work with each other and with the Commission to achieve agreed objectives;

(v) The range of small-scale programmes managed by the Commission is very wide. It includes research, study visits, and the support of innovatory education and training programmes. These activities may well expand rapidly in the next few years.

17 The main areas of current interest remain those set out in the 1976 action programme, with the important addition of a new programme of work concerning education, training, and the new technologies.

18 The major activities are in the following areas:

(i) Action to encourage mobility within the community, including: mutual recognition of qualifications; student and teacher mobility; youth exchanges; foreign language teaching.

(ii) Action to promote equal opportunities, including: women and girls; the disabled; migrants and their children; the illiterate.

(iii) Measures relating to young people and work, including: the transition from school to adult and working life; youth training; vocational guidance.

(iv) The action programme on the new information technologies and education and training.

19 Education and training measures designed to encourage mobility within the Community are one of the oldest aspects of Community policy, because the free movement of labour is a key principle of the EEC Treaty (Articles 48–51). That said, progress in the field of vocational qualifications has been difficult, because of the complexities of the various member states' training arrangements. A Council Decision on the mutual recognition of vocational qualifications was finally achieved in July 1985 and a network of information centres is now being established throughout the Community. There is already a network of such centres dealing with problems of academic recognition, although – unlike the training information centres – these are purely advisory. The Commission also seeks to encourage student and teacher mobility by funding 'Joint Study Programmes' involving higher education institutions from different member states. There is also a scheme of grants for short study visits by higher education teaching and academic staff. In 1986, 1800 applications were received and about 750 grants awarded. Finally, the Commission has long promoted foreign language teaching, and in June 1984 Education Ministers committed themselves to encouraging the acquisition of a working knowledge of two foreign languages before young people leave school.

20 Equality of opportunity is another key principle of the EEC Treaty. This has led to Community legislation in the fields of employment and training (See above paragraphs 9–11). The Commission has also taken complementary action in education, on the basis that inequality begins with unhelpful sexual preconceptions acquired before young people enter the labour market. Both the 1982–85 and the 1986–90 action programmes on equal opportunities for women stress the importance of education and of vocational guidance, for example in encouraging girls to move into careers in which they are currently under-represented in 1984 the Commission set up a network of national correspondents responsible for encouraging the diversification of women's vocational choices. With respect to the disabled, the Community's activities include a network of experimental projects on the integration of the disabled in schools, exchanges between young people, and the transition to working life. A major aspect of the Commission's work to assist migrant workers and their children is monitoring the implementation of the 1977 Directive on the education of such children. The required member states to set up reception classes for new arrivals and special training for their teachers. Though primarily concerning migrants from other Community countries, member states were asked to extend its provisions to all migrants. The Commission also funds pilot projects exploring improved reception and teaching methods.

21 With respect to young people, the December 1976 Resolution on education established a network of Community pilot projects to explore problems and share good practice concerning the role of schools in preparing young people for the transition to adult and working life. A second programme began in 1983 and runs until 1987. The outcomes of these projects have been exten-

sively documented. A Council Resolution of July 1983 set a broad framework for the development of youth training programmes in the Community. In it member states committed themselves to the target that all young people leaving school should have the opportunity of at least six months of training and/or work experience. The Commission published a report on the implementation of this in May 1986.

22 Action on education and training in relation to the new information technologies is one of the most recent areas of Community activity, but it is already one of the largest. The policy framework was established by two Council Resolutions agreed in June 1983, which covered education and vocational training respectively, and strengthened by the joint Education and Social Council of June 1984, which discussed a broad ranging Commission paper on technological developments and social change. Activities have included a series of Community seminars, all documented, which have examined themes such as teaching software (the Newcastle upon Tyne seminar in 1984) and teacher training (considered at the 1985 Bologna seminar).

23 **The European Social Fund**

The relationship between the Community's policy work, as described above, and the management of the European Social Fund is subtle and complicated. The Fund – for which the 1987 new allocation exceeded £2,300 m – is a Community instrument. However, in practice – to simplify – there is a tension between those in the Commission who wish to see the Fund disbursed to support explicitly Community policies, and those in the member states who see it as a source of financial aid for their national policies. The Commission guidelines for the management of the Fund, the complex annual negotiations between the Commission and the member states about the allocation of money, and the procedure for applying for Fund support, all reflect the ambiguities inherent in the current arrangements.

24 The tasks of the European Social Fund are clearly set out in Articles 123–127 of the EEC Treaty. It is an employment and training fund, charged with 'rendering the employment of workers easier and of increasing their geographical and occupational mobility within the Community' (Article 123). It finances projects jointly with public authorities (national, local, and some others). Its aid does not normally exceed 50% of the eligible costs, and is never more than that provided by the public authorities within the member state concerned. Applications for aid cannot be made directly to the EEC: in the UK, they must be channelled through the Department of Employment's Social Fund Unit.

25 In 1986 United Kingdom receipts from the Fund totalled £279 m, 16.4% of the total. This compares with the £306 m received in 1985, which was 23.9% of the total. The main reasons for this drop were the accession of Spain and Portugal to the Community; fluctuations in the exchange rate of sterling against the European Currency Unit (ECU); and changes to the Fund's guidelines, which meant that some Manpower Services Commission schemes (including the Community Programme and the Job Training Scheme) became ineligible for aid.

26 The Fund has been heavily oversubscribed for a number of years. In 1987 the total amount requested far exceeded the funds available. To meet this prob-

lem, the EC Commission has developed a set of guidelines with criteria. According to how far they fulfil these criteria, projects may receive all or part of the aid for which they have applied, or none at all. The following paragraphs discuss the guidelines in force for 1988. The guidelines are examined by the EC annually, and at present the Fund is under review.

27 Forty-five per cent of the Fund's resources are devoted to what are known as the 'absolute priority regions'. In the case of the United Kingdom, the only such area is Northern Ireland. In these areas, Fund assistance can be as much as 55% of eligible costs, rather than the 50% which is the ceiling elsewhere. Second priority in the allocation of funds goes to 'other areas of high and long-term unemployment and/or industrial and sectoral restructuring'. At present, the following areas of England and Wales fall within this category:

(i) Counties/local authority areas: Cleveland, Clwyd, Cornwall, Durham, Gwent, Gwynedd, Humberside, Isle of Wight, Merseyside, Mid Glamorgan, Northumberland, Nottinghamshire, South Glamorgan, South Yorkshire, Staffordshire, Tyne and Wear, West Glamorgan, and West Midlands.

(ii) Travel-to-work areas: parts of Cheshire, Cumbria, Derbyshire, Dyfed, Greater Manchester, Lancashire, Leicestershire, Lincolnshire, Northamptonshire and W. Yorkshire.

In addition to the overall priority which the above areas receive in the allocation of money, much of the Fund operates exclusively in these areas.

28 Most of the Fund's resources are spent on vocational training projects, although the Fund can also finance recruitment and wage subsidies, for example. Priority is given to training schemes which: last at least 200 hours; include at least 40 hours of training related to the new technologies; equip trainees with job skills.

29 Within the geographical framework set out above, the Fund is split into four sections.

30 Seventy-five per cent of its resources are devoted to young people under 25. For young people under 18, the Fund guidelines provide that courses should last at least 800 hours, and include work experience of between 200 and 400 hours. Most of the categories of projects eligible for funding are restricted to the various priority areas listed above, but there are two important exceptions. Schemes of training in new technology skills, and employment and training schemes linked with local employment initiatives, can be financed in any part of the Community.

31 The second section of the Fund covers employment and training schemes for people over 25. No projects outside the areas listed above are financed. The main categories are employment and training schemes for the long-term unemployed; training for small firms; and local employment initiatives.

32 Thirdly, the Fund can finance some projects without age requirements. These include projects designed to assist firms to cope with technological change or major restructuring, schemes for women, for disabled people, and for migrant workers, and schemes involving more than one member state. Most of this type of aid has no regional restriction.

33 Fourthly, within the Fund up to 5% of resources can be spent on innovatory projects designed, for example, to test out new training approaches which might be adopted more widely. Such projects can be financed in any region.

34 **Other sources of Community finance**

Though the European Social Fund and the other, smaller, education schemes described above are the most obvious potential sources of Community finance for British educational institutions, there are many others. Some examples are the following:

(i) Many of the Commission's Directorates-General finance research studies. Usually these are of short duration (under 12 months) and linked to a specific Community interest;

(ii) The Community funds demonstration projects which examine how new or improved techniques can be used to reduce dependence on external energy supplies;

(iii) There are specific programmes for financing technical, economic, social and medical research linked with the coal and steel industries, and for the retraining and resettlement of workers affected by job losses in those industries;

(iv) The Commission has a continuing programme of scientific and technological research in a wide range of fields, such as energy, nuclear power, the environment, information technology, and biomolecular engineering. Grants of around 50% of costs may be available.

35 **Future prospects for education in the Community**

The future of education policy in the Community looks secure. The continuing high level of unemployment, the growing concern about the Community's technological weakness in relation to the United States and Japan, and the recent Court judgment in the Gravier case (See above paragraph 6), are among the factors working in this direction. The Commission has recently produced a wide range of proposals for the further development of the Community's education policy which, as they are implemented, will lead to a period of major expansion in the impact of the Community – in both financial and other terms – upon education and training within the member states. These Commission initiatives include the following:

(i) COMETT: the action programme of the Community in Education and Training for Technology. Put forward by the EC Commission in August 1985, this programme is scheduled to run from 1986 to 1992. Its essential purpose is to improve the Community's technological base by building up closer links between industry, and universities and other institutions of post-secondary education. A programme of activities for the first phase (1986–89) was agreed by the Council in June 1986;

(ii) ERASMUS: the European Community Action Scheme for the Mobility of University Students. Proposed by the Commission in December 1985, this is intended to massively increase the geographical mobility of students within the Community, and thus to promote the Community's economic and social development. The Commission's target is that, from 1992, 10% of the Community's student population – i.e. 150,000 students – should undertake some study abroad during their course. A more modest programme on these lines was agreed in June 1987;

(iii) YES for Europe: an action programme for the promotion of youth exchanges in the Community. Put forward in March 1986, this Commission proposal is designed to given new impetus to exchanges of young people between member states, usually involving short visits during which the young people stay with local residents. A particular aim is to secure participation from those who would not otherwise be able to travel abroad. It is currently under discussion.

36 It is also worth noting that, although historically the focus of Community action has been young people, there are already some programmes to support adult education and training, and these are likely to be developed further in future.

37 **Conclusion**

This chapter has sought to give a brief overview of current Community activities and likely future developments. The opportunities for colleges and for their staff and students, individually and collectively, to participate in Community programmes are wide ranging and seem set to expand. However, the multinational nature of the Community means that the administration of these schemes is necessarily more complex than that of national or local programmes. It is important that steps are taken to obtain up-to-date details of the financial and other assistance available before commitments are made. Some useful sources of information and advice are given below.

FURTHER READING

Legislation

Treaties Establishing the European Communities, Office for Official Publications of the European Communities, Luxembourg, 1978.

Emile Noel 1985 *Working Together: The institutions of the European Community*, Office for Official Publications of the European Communities, Luxembourg.

The EEC in Transition, The Economist Newspaper Ltd., 1983.

The EC Commission's Directorate-General for Information, Communication and Culture (DG X) produces a series of booklets called *European File* on various topics of Community interest, including education (no 3/85, February 1985) and general information on the Community of Twelve (nos 5–6/86, March 1986), all published by the Office for Official Publications of the European Communities, Luxembourg.

FINANCE

Finance from Europe: a guide to grants and loans from the European Community, Commission of the European Communities, June 1983.

Report on the Activities of the European Social Fund, Commission of the European Communities, Brussels, annual.

Key current texts on the European Social Fund are the Council Decision of 17 October 1983 'on the tasks of the European Social Fund' (reference 83/516/EEC); the Council Regulation of the same date 'on the implementation of Decision 83/516/EEC on the tasks of the European Social Fund' (reference 2950/83); the Commission Decision of 22 December 1983 'on the management of the European Social Fund' (reference 83/673/EEC); and the Commission Decision of 29 April 1987 'on the guidelines for the management of the European Social Fund in the financial years 1988 to 1990' (reference c(87) 814 final). Advice and help on all aspects of the Fund are obtainable from the Department of Employment, to whom all applications should also be sent is:

Department of Employment, European Social Fund Unit, St Vincent House, 30 Orange Street, London WC2 7HT.

1.8

OTHER ASPECTS OF EDUCATIONAL COOPERATION

The European Community and education, European File no 3/85, Office for Official Publications of the European Communities, Luxembourg, February 1985
European Cooperation on Education:Activities of UNESCO,OECD, the Council of Europe, the European Community, and the Nordic Council of Ministers Report to the Standing Conference of European Ministers of Education held in Brussels on 7–9 May 1985. Available from participating organisations.
Social Europe (the DG V journal), Office for Official Publications of the European Communities, Luxembourg. Three times a year plus supplements.

SOURCES OF INFORMATION

General advice and information is available from the London office of the Commission of the European Communities, which is at: 8 Storey's Gate, London SW1P 3AT.
The Commission is at: 200 Rue de la Loi, B-1049 Brussels.
The Commission finances a European network for the exchange of information on education, known as EURYDICE. The first edition of their journal, *EURYDICE News*, was published in June 1986. Information on this and on other aspects of Community educational cooperation is obtainable from: EURYDICE European Unit, Rue Archimede 17/Bte 17, B-1040 Brussels.

Section 2

THE INSTITUTIONS AND THE STAFF

2.1 NATIONAL NEGOTIATING MACHINERY

1 **The Teachers' Pay and Conditions Act 1987**

In March 1987 the Teachers' Pay and Conditions Act received the Royal assent. It repealed the Remuneration of Teachers Act 1965 and, *inter alia*, removed the familiar Burnham Committee structure as a means of determining the salary scales and allowances of all teachers in primary and secondary schools, and public sector further and higher education institutions. The Act applies to England and Wales but not to Northern Ireland and Scotland. It has two principal effects. First, it abolishes all bargaining arrangements for school teachers. It provides that for the schools there will be, for the time being, an advisory committee appointed by the Secretary of State for Education and Science to examine and report to him or her on all matters concerning school teachers' pay and conditions. He or she may take that advice or vary it, but retains the absolute right to impose salary and conditions arrangements. The only remaining role for school teachers' unions and the employers of school teachers is that they must be consulted during the process by the Secretary of State. These arrangements have been condemned by the teachers and their employers and have given rise to criticism from the Trades Union Congress (TUC) and international teachers' organisations. A complaint has been lodged with the International Labour Organisation. Second, the Act enabled the employers of further education lecturers and the lecturers' trade unions which had been members of the Burnham Further Education Committee prior to its abolition to establish machinery on a free, collective bargaining basis. That is to say, the machinery would stand outside any statutory mechanism and replaced the mechanism which had been introduced by the 1965 Act. The only specific intervention by the Secretary of State allowed is the specification of the bargaining parties.

2 In order to understand the machinery which has been developed by the local education authorities and the lecturers' unions since February 1987, it is essential to understand the history of the National Joint Council (NJC) for Further Education Teachers in England and Wales. It is this body which has inherited the rights and responsibilities for all bargaining including that formerly conducted under the auspices of the Burnham FE Committee. The National Joint Council came into existence in 1979 as a result of a joint agreement between the Association of County Councils (ACC), the Association of Metropolitan Authorities (AMA), and the Welsh Joint Education Committee (WJEC), on one side, and the National Association of Teachers in Further and Higher Education (NATFHE), the Association of Agricultural Education Staffs (AAES), the Association of Principals of Colleges (APC) and the National Society for Art Education (as it then was, now the National Society for Education in Art and Design (NSEAD), on the other. The Department of Education and Science (DES) had a tangential role in the negotiations and had a seat as an observer on the employers' side. The purpose of this new bargaining forum, for which there was no statutory provision, was to deal with conditions of service matters.

3 This development was itself the result of an important process. Before 1974 representatives of the local education authorities and teachers' associations met, discussed and issued model recommendations on conditions of service to the local education authorities (LEAs). Before and for a period after that date, there was no national or regional machinery to secure joint enforcement of

any such recommendation except in as much as Schedule 11 of the Employment Protection Act provided that a report could be made to the Advisory, Conciliation and Arbitration Service (ACAS) that an employer was failing to observe recognised terms and conditions of employment. That was, however, a poor substitute for reliable bargaining arrangements. The Council of Local Education Authorities (CLEA) was formed in 1974 by the ACC and AMA following local government reorganisation (See **1.6** 64). It was intended to provide a forum for educational discussion on matters of common interest, stimulated by the Education Committees of the two local authority associations. CLEA rapidly assumed the role of negotiating conditions of service with the representatives of the lecturers' associations that were represented on the Burnham FE Committee.

4 Negotiations between CLEA and the lecturers generated national collective agreements of a serious kind whether described, as they variously were, as agreements or recommendations. These were the arrangements which were further developed by the formation of the NJC which adopted as its first task a rigorous exercise to codify the plethora of agreements and arrangements reached up to that point. This codified document, *The Scheme of Conditions of Service,* is popularly known as the Silver Book and was published in 1981. The initial Constitution of the NJC provided that it would be a forum for the negotiation of all conditions of service for lecturers in all establishments of further education within the meaning of the Further Education Regulations 1975, and other full-time teachers employed in FE by the LEAs. It included adult education lecturers but excluded lecturers assigned to work in prison education departments. It is important to note that the Constitution explicitly prevented the determination of salaries and allowances in the NJC (with the exception of those for Research Staff) because the determination of these matters was covered by the statutory requirement that the Burnham Committee should undertake it as set out in the Remuneration of Teachers Act 1965. In 1982 the scope of those covered by the NJC was enlarged to include Associate Lecturers as a result of a collective agreement to provide for the employment of lecturers on fractional appointments (that is, with salaries and conditions set on a scale proportionate to those of full-time lecturers) where these lecturers had previously been paid on part-time hourly rates but had sufficient service under the terms of the agreement to be 'converted' to Associate status.

5 Thus, it will be seen that a tradition of bargaining in separate bodies on pay and conditions existed. For at least five years before the formation of the NJC, the lecturers' unions and the local authority associations had publicly expressed the view that separate arrangements for bargaining on pay and conditions were unsatisfactory and that this separation was an unfortunate consequence of the 1965 Act. Indeed, such a separation was almost unknown in bargaining outside education where mature machinery existed. Repeal of the 1965 Act would enable the two sides to enter into collective bargaining on any matter they chose, and upon an operational basis determined by the two sides themselves. By 1985, although the 1965 Act had not been repealed, the first steps were taken in this unifying direction when both sides agreed to amend the NJC Constitution to allow the body to consider matters of remuneration. The Act still prevented the NJC from determining such matters. The amendment reflected the growing maturity of the NJC and meant that it became the principal focus for discussion on all issues of remuneration and conditions during the three bargaining rounds in 1985, 1986 and 1987.

6 Consequently, when the 1987 Act expressed the intention that employers and lecturers in further education should form non-statutory bargaining machinery after abolition of the Burnham structure, the scene was largely set for doing so. The Sides of the NJC concluded that, with suitable constitutional amendments, this was the body that best fitted the legislative prescription and met, substantially, their own long-term aspirations.

7 It is easiest to understand the present constitution by comparing it with the constitution up to March 1987. The pre-March NJC Constitution had the following key features:

(i) The existence of two Sides whose constituent organisations were present by mutual consent and without Government interference (unlike Burnham where the participating organisations and their numbers of seats were determined by the Secretary of State).

(ii) The presence of a group of observers representing the Department of Education and Science (2), the Catholic Education Council (1), the Church of England Board of Education (1), the Methodist Church Division of Education and Youth (1) and the Boards of Governors of the Inner London polytechnics (1)[1]. These bodies were regarded as bound by the agreements reached in the Council by virtue of their presence and ability to take part, on a non-voting basis, in the employers' Side.

(iii) Encouragement of regular negotiation on conditions of service but a restriction, as stated, on determination of remuneration.

(iv) A means of securing adherence to agreements on both Sides.

(v) Methods of clarifying agreements by those required to operate them.

(vi) Means of resolving disputes.

(vii) Provision for data collection and information sharing on relevant matters.

(viii) A channel for cooperation with other bargaining bodies including the two Burnham Committees.

(ix) Consideration of pay and conditions for research staff.

(x) Servicing by Joint Secretaries who are the Secretaries of the Local Authorities Conditions of Service Advisory Board (LACSAB), the AMA and the ACC, and the General Secretary of NATFHE (in recent years, the Negotiating Secretary of NATFHE has been specified as a Deputy Secretary).

8 Following Royal Assent to the 1987 Act, the major changes that have been made to the Constitution of the NJC provide that:

(i) It negotiates on all terms and conditions of employment without statutory restraint.

(ii) The concept of 'Sides' is abolished and that whilst the AMA, ACC and Welsh Joint Education Committee (WJEC) representatives meet as a group together with one group of observers – those listed in paragraph 7 (ii) above – the lecturers' associations meet as an informal group comprising NATFHE, APC, AAES and NSEAD, those being the associations present by common consent.

(iii) A further organisation is in membership of the NJC, namely the Association of Polytechnic Teachers (APT), by virtue of Government imposition[2], this occurring without the willing agreement of the other organisations in membership of the Council.

(iv) Because of the close relationship between bargaining in Northern Ireland and the England and Wales arrangement, two observers have been added in respect of the Province, one representing the employing Education and Library Boards, and one representing the lecturers (this being the Northern Ireland Official of NATFHE). (See below Appendix 2.)

(v) It brought into scope lecturers assigned to work in prison education departments who had formerly been covered by their own Joint Bargaining Committee and whose negotiations will be undertaken, henceforth, in a sub-committee of the NJC; an observer from the Home Office Prison Education Department has been added to the employers.

(vi) All references to 'management' have been changed to 'employers' and 'teachers' to lecturers[3], this change having been made for purposes of clarity so as to distinguish between school teachers and lecturers and between managers, who are represented among the lecturers' associations, and employers who do strictly fulfil the employer role.

The Constitution of the NJC as presently composed is set out below in Appendix 1, showing the numbers of members of all associations represented, and the detail of the arrangements.

9 The NJC retains its capacity to form Subcommittees and will have, aside from the Subcommittee on Prison Lecturers, Subcommittees on Grading of Courses and Agricultural Education. It is possible that a new Subcommittee will be introduced within a short time of writing to cover staff in institutions largely concerned with higher education which the Government announced in the 1987 White Paper would be removed from local authority control (See **1.1** Appendix 1).

10 For the foreseeable future, negotiations will take place in this body. The staff now in scope may be summarised as follows:

(i) *Full-time lecturers* This category includes all those paid on Lecturer scales as Lecturers and those in substantial administrative posts in lecturing such as Heads of Department, Vice-Principals and Principals. Where posts involve divided service, as when lecturers are employed in two discrete areas of education, the lecturers shall be paid on the salary appropriate to the post in which the majority of time is spent. If split equally, payment is on the higher of the possible rates. Thus, Lecturers paid on these scales come into scope of the NJC and Silver Book arrangements.

(ii) *Associate Lecturers* As noted above, those part-time staff employed by LEAs on terms proportional to those applying to full-time staff, not centred in the full-time lecturer establishment of any institution, 'at the discretion of the authority', and those who became entitled to this status by virtue of the 1980 salary settlement which provided that all hourly-paid staff who, at that time or subsequently, taught 13 or more hours per week in a single institution for the normal college teaching year and who have consequently come to be Associate Lecturers. (It should be noted that the same settlement provided that those with 20 or more hours per week over the normal teaching year were converted to full-time lectureships.)

(iii) *Hourly-paid part-time staff* Other part-time lecturers paid on hourly rates computed from the full-time salary ranges in a formula based on notional hours of work. (See **2.2** 47–49.)

(iv) *Research staff* Those staff, other than Readers for whom the normal full-time lecturer arrangements pertain, who are either staff required to undertake assigned research (Researchers A); or are required either to supervise other research whilst undertaking more demanding research themselves, or to undertake postdoctoral research (Researchers B). This definition of those in scope explicitly excludes students receiving grants or individuals whose pay is determined by government departments, research councils or others as a direct result of the terms of a research grant. This group was always covered by the NJC and not by the Burnham Committee Report prior to March 1987, and it remains in scope of the NJC.

11 **Chair**

The NJC has had an independent, non-voting Chair who has, since its inception, been Sir John Wordie, recently reappointed for three years. The Chair holds office for three year periods but may be reappointed. In the absence of the Chair, the Council appoints a chair at the meeting. In Subcommittees and Working Parties, the chair alternates between the employers and lecturers.

12 **Arbitration**

There has been and continues to be provision for arbitration in the event of a dispute over pay and conditions of service in respect of any group in scope of the Council. Arbitration requires the agreement of the employers' and lecturers' associations and is conducted by the Advisory, Conciliation and Arbitration Service. Traditionally, further education negotiators have bargained to conclusion and incidences of arbitration have occurred on a fraction of the occasions they have occurred in schools.

13 **Local negotiation**

Whilst the general description of local negotiating practice is to be found in **2.10**, it should be noted that the national arrangements of the NJC play an important role in guiding local negotiations. For example, many employing authorities make parallel arrangements for negotiation of local agreements within the NJC system through bargaining committees which replicate the NJC itself. Obviously, not all authorities have, say, agricultural lecturers, but in general NATFHE, APC, AAES and NSEAD are recognised and cooperate in local negotiating sides. The presence of the APT has not been presumed by the employers, nationally, to convey any obligation on individual authorities to recognise. In the discussion of conditions of service, it will be noted that national arrangements exist to assist in the resolution of local disputes (See **2.5**). This channel for disputes presumes the relationship between the NJC mechanism and local mechanism to which this paragraph refers.

14 **The late Burnham machinery**

In repealing the Remuneration of Teachers Act 1965, the Government made a number of criticisms of the Burnham Primary and Secondary Committee, focusing on the lengthy dispute from 1984 and the alleged inability of the various school teacher unions to agree among themselves, thus immobilising the Burnham P & S machinery. No specific criticisms were made of the Further Education Committee although that may have been by default. For a full description of the Burnham Committees, their Subcommittees and pattern of work, readers are advised to consult the 1980 edition of *College Administration* (Waitt 1980, **11.1**).

15 **Repeal of the Remuneration Act: Legal consequences**
The repeal of the Remuneration of Teachers Act 1965 left the status of the Burnham Further Education Document in some doubt. The Document was last published in full in 1983 although there have been a number of statutory instruments updating its provisions for full- and part-time salaries, allowances, London area weightings, and to encompass the change in progression between scales (Lecturer Grade 1 to Lecturer Grade 2) that became an entitlement in 1985 (See **2.2** 50), all of these statutory instruments having been promulgated since 1983. As regards the legal status, there has been detailed consideration between the bargaining sides and the Department of Education and Science prior to March 1987. This confirmed that the document continued and continues to have statutory force because it results from statutory instruments laid before and confirmed by Parliament. The Act that generated these Instruments was repealed, but the Instruments the last of which was laid in 1985 continue to have force. However, as new agreements are made in the NJC which will change salaries, allowances, London area allowances and, potentially, structures of scales and arrangements, the text of the Document will gradually change to incorporate agreements which were struck outside the framework of statute. Each modification will modify the Document to the extent of the agreement out of the statutory form. Indeed, it is the intention of the bargaining machinery of the NJC to incorporate the Burnham document and Silver Book into a single document for ease of use. This exercise will not change the legal status of the Burnham provisions until and unless they are changed by new agreements rather than by a process of codification.

16 It is worth noting that among the elements that remain in force are the grading of courses document (See **2.2**), the arrangements for scale placements on initial appointment and promotion (See **2.2** 60–62), and the evaluation of qualifications from a wide variety of educational establishments around the world. These detailed Appendices to the Burnham Document may continue to guide a number of technical and evaluative decisions for a number of years to come. They are unlikely to change or be changed to any extent, and certainly will not change unless the systems for which they were introduced are replaced. Thus, so long as there is a remuneration system based on academic standards of courses taught by lecturers, there will be use of the Report of the Burnham Grading of Courses Committee (new work being graded in an NJC Grading of Courses Subcommittee). Provided that concepts like 'a good Honours degree' have meaning in determining incremental credit on appointment as a Lecturer, the listing of academic institutions providing such qualifications will be required. In respect of this latter listing, it will be noted that the bulk of the technical work required to keep the work up-to-date was undertaken in the Burnham Primary and Secondary Committee by its Secretariat. Since there are no bargaining rights persisting in the schools sector, any further modifications will necessarily take place in the NJC as far as further education is concerned.

17 **Joint Secretaries' 'Commentary'**
From time to time the Joint Secretaries have published a *Commentary* on the Burnham FE Document. The last was published in 1985. It provides detail on the meanings given to clauses of the Report as well as understandings of the interplay between the Report and the Scheme of Conditions of Service. This is needed for several reasons. Whilst every effort is made to draft the documents with clarity and in everyday English, the density and legalism of the language in the Burnham Report, the unintended gaps that occurred because the

salaries and conditions bargaining on the same issues were done separately, and the emergence of marginal cases which require interpretation, has meant that the documents require practical interpretation by practitioners. The Joint Secretaries, who fulfil a role akin to mandarins in this respect, are generally asked to make interpretations on a joint, agreed basis, by LEAs, institutions and the lecturers' trade unions. The interpretations give rise to a considerable body of case precedent which guides future operation of the agreements. These form the basis of the *Commentary*. On occasion, gaps appear in understanding the documents without cases having arisen, and the Joint Secretaries meet, discuss and conclude on interpretations which are also written into the *Commentary*. Needless to say, these detailed recommendations on understanding and operating the documents do not give the *Commentary* the status of a statutory document or a collective agreement. The NJC would be entitled to tell its Joint Secretaries that they are wrong. However, the *Commentary* has considerable status in the management of the further education system and is generally to be preferred to guesswork about the meaning of documents.

NOTES

1 The observer status given to the five Inner London polytechnics is in recognition of the fact that they are corporate bodies limited by guarantee, that is, they have corporate status and are employers in their own right. As independent companies, they employ their own staff and these staff are not employees of local education authorities (See **1.2** Appendix 1). At the time of writing, Government proposals to remove a number of institutions of local authorities, including all the polytechnics, would increase the number of such institutions for which special arrangements will be needed very considerably (See **1.1** Appendix 1).

2 The organisation was first imposed on the Burnham Further Education Committee by the Secretary of State despite very small numbers of members in the sector and in the face of opposition from all the employer and trade union organisations represented on the Committee. Membership of the Burnham Committee provided a channel to the reformed NJC, although the Government initially omitted them from the NJC in the 1987 Act. They were re-inserted by means of an amendment in the House of Lords, moved by Baroness Cox, an APT member declaring her interest when moving the amendment.

3 These terms are, therefore, used in this book in **2.2** on salaries and **2.5** on conditions of service.

APPENDIX 1

CONSTITUTION OF THE NATIONAL JOINT COUNCIL FOR LECTURERS IN FURTHER EDUCATION IN ENGLAND AND WALES (as amended 27th March 1987)

1 *Title*
The Council shall be known as 'The National Joint Council for Lecturers in Further Education' (hereinafter referred to as the Council).

2 *Area*
The area of operation of the Council shall be England and Wales.

3 *Scope*

The functions of the Council as specified in Clause 7 shall relate to:

(a) Lecturers in all establishments of further education and other lecturers employed by local education authorities in the provision of further education including adult education and lecturers assigned to work in prison department establishments; and

(b) Research staff, who are defined as those staff other than Readers, employed by LEAs to work in establishments of further education in posts which have been established by the employing authority and which are remunerated by either the LEA or the establishment concerned under a contract of employment primarily to undertake research.

Without prejudice to the generality of this definition, the following two groups are expressly excluded from the definition of research staff:

(i) individuals in receipt of a student grant from a government department, research council or any other body.

(ii) individuals paid on other rates of pay determined by government departments, research councils or any other body as a direct result of the conditions of a research grant.

4 *Membership*

(i) The Council shall consist of 32 members of whom 15 shall be appointed to represent the local education authorities and 17 to represent the lecturers' associations.

(ii) The composition of the local education authority representation shall (by agreement with the lecturers' associations listed in sub paragraph (c) below) be as follows:

Association of County Council	8
Association of Metropolitan Authorities	6
Welsh Joint Education Committee	1

(iii) Representatives of lecturers' associations shall be appointed as follows (this composition being with the agreement of the local authority associations as listed in sub paragraphs (b) above):-

NATFHE	12
Association of Principals of Colleges	2
National Society for Art and Design Education	1
Association of Agricultural Educational Staffs	1

(iv) The following lecturers' association has been placed on the National Joint Council by virtue of section 4 of the Teachers' Pay and Conditions Act, 1987.

Association of Polytechnic Teachers	1

(v) If any organisation referred to in paragraphs (b), (c) or (d) above fails to appoint the number of representatives provided for by the constitution, such failure to appoint shall not vitiate the decisions of the Council.

(vi) In the event of any member of the Council or of any committee or subcommittee thereof being unable to attend any meeting of the Council, whether ordinary or special, or of any committee or subcommittee as the case may be, the organisation appointing such member shall be entitled to appoint another representative to attend in his or her place.

5 *Retirement of Members*

The members of the Council shall continue in that capacity for so long as their appointing organisation may determine.

6 *Observers*

(i) Observers from the bodies listed below shall have the right to sit with the representatives of the local education authorities in the numbers shown, but shall not have the right to vote on any matter:

Department of Education and Science	2
Catholic Education Council	1
Church of England Board of Education	1

The Methodist Church Division of Education and Youth	1
Courts of Governors of the five ILEA Polytechnics	1
The Home Office	1
The Management Side of the Further Education Negotiating Committee, Northern Ireland	1

(ii) The National Association of Teachers in Further and Higher Education Regional official for Northern Ireland shall have the right to accompany the representatives of that Association on the Council, but shall not have the right to vote on any matter.

II *FUNCTIONS*

7 The Council will engage in collective bargaining on pay and other conditions of service for lecturers and research staff as defined in Clause 3 and it may take any action that falls within the scope of this general definition. Among the specific functions of the Council are:

(i) Provision for the regular negotiation of pay and other conditions of service;
(ii) Securing adherence by all employers and lecturers and research staff to collective agreements relating to pay and other conditions of service;
(iii) Clarification and interpretation of such of the Council's agreements as may be referred by employers and/or their lecturers and/or their research staff;
(iv) Securing the provision, both locally, in all matters affecting relations between the employer and their lecturers and research staff, and nationally on pay and other conditions of service matters, of appropriate procedures for the resolution of collective differences and disputes;
(v) The collection of statistics and information on matters appertaining to the pay and other conditions of service of lecturers and research staff;
(vi) Cooperation with other joint negotiating committees on matters of common interest.

III *PROCEDURE*

8 *Committee and Subcommittees*
The Council may appoint such committees, subcommittees and working parties as may be considered necessary. The Council shall determine the composition, the terms of reference of any such committees, subcommittees and working parties and the reports of all committees, subcommittees and working parties shall be submitted to the Council for approval. Such approval may be given with or without modification.

9 *Co-opted Members*
The Council may co-opt, or allow any committee, subcommittee or working party to co-opt, such persons of special knowledge, not being members of the Council, committee, subcommittee or working party, provided that persons so co-opted shall serve only in a consultative and non voting capacity. The Council may also invite, or allow any committee, subcommittee or working party to invite the attendance of any person whose special knowledge would be of assistance, but such a person shall not have the power to vote.

10 *Chair*
The Council shall appoint an independent non voting Chair to be selected by agreement between the local education authority representatives and the lecturers' representatives. He shall hold office for a term of three years, and be eligible for re-appointment. The Chair shall preside at all meetings of the Council, but in his absence from any meeting, a Chair shall be appointed from amongst the members of the Council. A committee, subcommittee or working party shall appoint from its members at each meeting a Chair drawn alternately from the local education authority representatives and the lecturers' representatives.

11 *Officers*

The Council may appoint joint secretaries, a treasurer, an auditor and such other staff, if any, as it may think fit, and any such officers and staff may be either honorary or paid as the Council shall determine.

12 *Ordinary Meetings*

Ordinary meetings of the Council shall be held as often as may be necessary, but at least once in each year.

13 *Special Meetings*

The Chair shall call a special meeting of the Council if so requested in writing by a majority of the local education authority representatives or a majority of the lecturers' representatives. The requisition and also the notice summoning the meeting shall state the nature of the business proposed to be transacted thereat, and no other matters shall be discussed. The meeting shall take place within 21 days of the receipt of the requisition by the Chair.

14 *Voting*

No resolution shall be regarded as carried unless it has been approved by a majority of the members present and representing the local education authorities and a majority of the members representing the lecturers on the Council, committee, subcommittee or working party, as the case may be. Where, in the absence of the independent Chair, an alternative Chair has been appointed from among the members of the Council, that person shall retain his or her vote.

15 *Notice of Meetings*

All notices of meetings of the Council and of any committees, subcommittees or working parties thereof shall be sent to the respective members at least seven days before the date of the meeting.

16 *Finance*

The expenses of the Council including those of persons attending by joint agreement under Clause 9 shall be borne in equal proportions by the local education authority and the lecturers' associations in the Council. Expenses of members appointed to the Council, committees, subcommittees or working parties under Clauses 4 and 8 shall be met by the respective local education authority and lecturers' associations. The accounts of the Council shall be presented at the first meeting of the Council after the 30th day of June in each year.

17 *Reports and Minutes*

The Council shall send to each of the constituent associations referred to in Clause 4 a copy of the minutes of the proceedings for all its meetings. The minutes as agreed between the joint secretaries shall be forwarded to the secretaries of such organisations within 21 days after each meeting; such minutes shall be subject to approval by the Council at its next meeting.

18 *Amendment*

The Constitution shall be amended only with the assent of all the constituent organisations referred to in Clause 4 (ii) and Clause 4 (iii).

19 *Interpretation*

The Interpretation Act 1978, shall apply to the foregoing provisions.

20 *Arbitration*

In the event of a dispute over terms and conditions of service as defined in Clause 7 arising between the local education authority representatives and the lecturers' representatives on the Council on any matter of general application to lecturers or research staff or of application to particular classes of lecturers or research staff, the dispute shall, if the local education authority and lecturers' representatives agree, be reported to the Advisory Conciliation and Arbitration Service for settlement by arbitration.

APPENDIX 2

NEGOTIATING AND CONSULTATION MACHINERY IN NORTHERN IRELAND

1 *Salaries and Conditions of Service*
In Northern Ireland salaries and conditions of service for further education lecturers are negotiated in the same forum: the Further Education Negotiating Committee (FENC). Established by agreement between the employers (the Education and Library Boards – See **1.5** 24–31), the Department of Education Northern Ireland (DENI) (See **1.5** 6–19) and the recognised lecturer unions, its current constitution dates from 1984. The employers' side is represented by five members from the education and Library Boards and two members from the Department of Education. On the lecturers' side there are five members appointed by NATFHE, one by the APC and one by the National Association of Schoolmasters/Union of Women Teachers (NAS/UWT).

2 Although salaries for lecturers in Northern Ireland are negotiated at the FENC there has for some time been a policy of parity with salaries negotiated in England and Wales. With some minor exceptions, this policy is adhered to.

3 *Colleges of Education Negotiating Committee*
A separate Negotiating Committee exists for the two colleges of education (Stranmillis and St Marys). This body is responsible for agreeing the salaries and conditions of service for lecturers employed at these establishments. As in the further education sector, a policy of parity with England and Wales exists. The composition of the Committee is currently two members representing the management of colleges; two members representing the Department of Education and four members representing NATFHE. A Colleges of Education Consultative Committee which dealt with matters other than salaries and conditions of service has been absorbed into the Negotiating Committee.

4 *The Conditions of Service Negotiating Committee for Primary and Secondary Schools (Northern Ireland)*
This committee deals with superannuation matters for all teachers, including further education lecturers and lecturers at the colleges of education. Therefore NATFHE has two representatives on this Committee who attend when matters relating to superannuation are discussed. For the primary and secondary sectors, this is the Committee that deals with all matters relating to salaries and conditions of service.

5 *Standing Conference for Further Education*
The Standing Conference exists to consult on trends and developments in further education in Northern Ireland. Representatives are drawn from the DENI, the Education and Library Boards, NATFHE and the APC.

6 *Education and Library Boards Further Education Consultative Committees*
Under the Education and Libraries (NI) Order 1986 Boards have powers to establish committees. In practice each Board has established a Consultative Committee for Further Education, as well as a separate committee for the primary and secondary sector. The composition and constitution of these committees varies, but the recognised FE lecturers are represented. The consultative committees deal with matters requiring consultation between a Board and the lecturers' unions, but do not negotiate on salaries or conditions of service, which is the preserve of the FENC.

7 *Agricultural colleges and prison education*
The Department of Agriculture in Northern Ireland is responsible for the provision of agricultural education and training, including the three colleges of agriculture. The Department also provides staff and facilities for the Faculty of Agriculture and Food Science at Queens University Belfast. The teaching staff are employees of the Department of Agriculture on salary scales negotiated for Civil Servants in Northern Ireland. The Education service in Northern Ireland's prisons operates under the auspices of the Northern Ireland Office. Teaching staff are employees of the Northern Ireland Office.

2.2 SALARIES, STAFFING ESTABLISHMENTS AND GRADING OF COURSES

1 The system for determining the staffing establishment, which is not just a reference to the number of staff but also to the grading of posts which they occupy, provides a basis for determining the salaries of the principal, vice-principal and head of department, and apportions the grades of staff within any college. It is widely regarded as barely intelligible throughout the public sector further and higher education system although it has such important functions. This account starts with the underpinning methods for determining staffing establishments and provides a description and critique of their consequences. It is an important matter because the total number of teaching and non-teaching staff to which a college or polytechnic is entitled influences many aspects of college life. It affects the efficiency of the institution and provides its system of management and organisational structure. It is a major determinant of the institutional budget. It provides a basis for staff relations including promotion opportunities and career development. When the wrong balance between all these effects of the staffing establishment calculation occurs, staff are less likely to identify with the aims of the institution or work in a coherent way within it. In view of the importance of the determination of staffing establishments and the inordinate complexity of the mechanism described in this chapter, it is hardly surprising that the formulae used to determine numbers of staff and their gradings generates a good deal of debate. Recently, many of these debates have focused on the fundamental matter of the grading of courses system itself, which encourages some types of work as against other types by offering greater rewards in respect of advanced further education as against non-advanced work. Thus, it is not merely a technical matter but rather a fundamental issue of educational philosophy reflected in a technical method.

2 **The grading of courses**

The grading of courses system has attracted a great deal of criticism from employers, unions and educational pressure groups[1]. Yet it was introduced with the intention of providing an objective way of relating lecturers' salaries and promotion opportunities to the perceived status of the work they undertook. In essence, lecturers' and employers' associations grade a wide variety of courses, and years within courses, into categories so that a formula can combine numbers of students and the category to which a course has been assigned and in which the students are enrolled. This determines many of the arrangements for paying the lecturers under the Burnham FE Report (Salaries document). When the system was introduced, it established the proportions of staff on different grades in colleges and it generated a large number of promotions. It replaced the exercise of local discretion by local education authorities (LEAs) on promotion opportunities and the grading of principals, vice-principals and head of department posts with a national system which generated comparable practice throughout the country. Whatever these gains, however, critics have argued that the system is intrinsically élitist and favours academic over non-academic and vocational work, or that the gradings of some courses are unfavourably low in terms of the responsibilities associated with such courses. The origins and details of the grading of courses system require explanation.

3 The national grading of courses system was introduced in 1967 and a fourfold

classification of courses was subsequently developed by the Burnham Further Education Committee. A committee known as the Grading of Courses Committee was established. It in turn established a working group to carry out the monumental task of placing all courses into four categories ranging, broadly, from work which had degree or degree equivalents to non-advanced courses which gave rise to no qualification. The Committee and Working Group comprised representatives of local education authorities and recognised further education teachers' unions, and the secretariat work was undertaken by the Department of Education and Science (DES). The department also provided specialist advisors, in the form of HM Inspectors, to assist the Committee and Working Group. The first graded course list[2] was published in 1968 and attached to it was a statement setting out the considerations that had been taken into account when the Committee reached its conclusions.

4 These considerations have shaped the work of the Grading of Courses Committee from that time and despite the variations that have occurred it is important to understand the original methodology which has persisted. The 1968 statement referred to the following principles.

(i) It was necessary to break up courses so that, in many cases, parts of them fell into different categories.

(ii) Account was taken of more than purely academic factors. For example, the age of the students and the need to recruit specialist and experienced staff was considered[3].

(iii) The Committee thought it impractical to grade college courses. In the main, only courses leading to external examinations and recognised qualifications could be classified. It was believed that LEAs could grade individual courses following the principles established by the Committee.

(iv) Normally, it was not practical to grade non-vocational courses. However, the Committee felt it important that such courses should be graded (presumably by the LEA) according to the principles adopted for vocational courses. These principles, for example, involved grading of courses in parts where it involved progression by parts; to have regard to the character and standard of the course and the calibre and expertise of the teacher required.

(v) It was felt right to classify the final examinations of professional bodies (for example Associateships and Licentiateships) as equivalent to degree standard but not necessarily leading to the qualification of a degree or equivalent graduate status where such studies were beyond the OND/ONC or GCE A level standard. However, the early years of these courses were plainly not of an advanced nature and were graded below this level.

(vi) Courses accepted as poolable (See **1.3** 49–50) under the Rate Support Grant 'Pooling Arrangements' Regulations 1967, were also classified as equivalent to the standard of a degree without necessarily involving the qualification or, where they led to a qualification entitling a lecturer holding such a qualification to receive a graduate equivalent incremental allowance, they were classified in the highest possible category.

(vii) Postgraduate courses in the same field or technology as first degree courses were also classified at the highest possible grade. However, where this was not so the particular course should be considered from the point of view of the content and the previous education of the students taking it.

(viii) The main purpose of the grading exercise was to ensure that an adequate level of staffing was provided in all further education colleges.

5 The continued development of new courses, curricular changes affecting all courses and requests for guidance from local authorities, lecturers and administrators, has meant that the work of the Committee and the Working Group has continued. In 1975 the Committee was reconstituted following changes in the composition of the Management and Teachers' Panel of the Burnham FE Committee, and the secretariat work passed from the DES to the Local Authorities' Conditions of Service Advisory Board (LACSAB).

6 A far more fundamental change occurred in 1975 following the recommendations of the Houghton Committee. Houghton (1974) recommended that a new fivefold classification of courses should be used, subsequently known as Categories I to V. Later in 1975, a further revised Edition of the Grading of Courses List was published; this replaced the categories which had existed from the beginning of the system with Categories I, II, III, IV and V and dealt with many new courses. Discontinued courses were deleted. The recommendations of the Houghton Committee also meant that teacher education courses (See below paragraph 18) had to be graded for the first time and decisions of the Grading of Courses Committee on this area of work were set out in the new 1975 listing. Following previous practice, purely individual college courses were not graded and those which had been included, for guidance, in previous editions were deleted.

7 The final major change which has occurred in the grading of courses system took place in 1979 when the Burnham FE Committee agreed to merge two of Houghton's work categories. The new fourfold classification is now defined as follows:

I(i) Taught courses or research programmes, or combinations of the two, leading to a higher degree.

(ii) Courses leading to qualifications agreed to be of postgraduate standard, where a first degree or equivalent qualification in an appropriate discipline would normally be a prerequisite for a student taking the course. Where an extra period of time is required to bring the student up to the entry requirements of a postgraduate course, such as a 'bridging course' will normally be graded Category (II).

II/III Courses above Ordinary National Certificate standard and leading directly to degrees of universities of the United Kingdom or degrees of the Council for National Academic Awards (CNAA See **3.1** 53–59); and courses with entry standards equivalent to one or two A levels and which lead directly to qualifications which satisfy the academic criteria accepted for graduate status for salary purposes or study of an equivalent standard but not necessarily leading to the qualifications mentioned.

IV Study or courses above the Ordinary Level of the General Certificate of Education or comparable level leading directly to the Ordinary National Certificate or courses or parts of courses of a comparable standard.

V Courses other than those described above.

8 These changes simplify the grading of advanced level work by dispensing with the distinction between degree courses and courses giving graduate status, on the one hand, and courses of the same academic standard, but not leading to

such qualifications, on the other hand. Accordingly a new edition of the Grading of Courses List was published in 1980.

9 **The present grading of courses committee and reference to it**

The composition of the present Committee is:

(i) *Management Side* Association of County Councils (2); Association of Metropolitan Authorities (2); Welsh Joint Education Committee (1);

(ii) *Teachers' Side* Association of Principals of Colleges 1; NATFHE 4; National Society for Education in Art and Design 1;

However, the Committee is no longer a Committee of the Burnham FE Committee given the abolition of the Burnham Committee system under the Teachers' Pay and Conditions Act 1987. It will be a subcommittee of the National Joint Council (NJC) for Lecturers in Further and Higher Education (See **2.1** 9) but will retain the same basic structure. There will be two joint chairs of the subcommittee, one from the Employers' and one from the Lecturers' Associations. It will be noted that the word 'Employers' has replaced the term 'Management' and the term 'Lecturers' has replaced the term 'Teachers' and the concept of sides as formally used has now gone. By custom and practice one of the Association of Metropolitan Authorities (AMA) representatives is a member of Her Majesty's Inspectorate. In addition an assessor from the DES attends meetings.

10 References to the subcommittee can be made only by local education authorities via the Employers' Associations, and by lecturers via the Lecturers' Associations. Correspondence should be addressed, as appropriate, to the Secretary of the Employers' or the Lecturers' Associations. There is one exception to this requirement. The subcommittee's work obviously depends on the receipt of current information concerning examining regulations and curriculum changes from the examining bodies and professional institutes (See **3.1**). These bodies may make reference to the subcommittee about relevant changes where a course has already been graded.

11 Whilst the subcommittee does not publish decisions about individual college courses, it does give advice to local authorities or lecturers about their grading. Local authorities in grading college courses, or in grading other courses not so far graded by the subcommittee, are under an obligation which remains, until new agreements replace it, statutory. They must grade courses 'in accordance with the . . . criteria' for the classification of courses[4]. It is likely that some form of obligation to proceed in this way will continue so long as the grading of courses system is in existence, but all new determinations made by the subcommittee of the NJC will have no statutory impact. They will be agreements binding in honour. Obviously a teacher who feels that a particular course has been wrongly graded by the LEA can refer this matter for determination by the Grading of Courses Subcommittee of the NJC via the Lecturers' Associations assuming that they support the case. Once the course has been considered by the subcommittee, the local authority is obliged to grade it in the way advised by the subcommittee.

12 **Using the Graded Courses List**

Since 1968 the Graded Courses List has been arranged in two parts. Part I deals with General Courses, such as the General Certificate of Secondary

Education, and National Certificate and Diploma Courses. It also deals with the industrial parts of integrated training courses. Part II is split into two schedules. Schedule A deals with City and Guilds courses (See **3.1**); Schedule B with Professional and Vocational Subjects. City and Guilds Courses are listed under their DES and City and Guilds numbers and are arranged under subject areas. The courses in Schedule B are listed under their DES number where they have one, and again, are arranged according to subject or, under the Council, Union of Institutes or Committee offering the examination. The course as a whole is classified under its category or, where it has been considered in parts, the various parts are listed under the appropriate categories. On occasion, a particular year of a course (for example the final year) will be listed under the appropriate category and the remainder of the course listed under a lower category.

13 Amendment sheets are routinely published to the 1980 edition of the List and it is important to consult these sheets as well as the List itself.

14 **Decisions made by the committee**

The methodology described above is guided by three considerations. First, the academic standard of the course has, in the vast majority of cases, determined its grading. Second, consideration has been given to the age of the students taking the course. Where the students are mature this may lead to a higher grading. Thirdly, the need to recruit specialist staff, or staff in short supply, has had an influence on the grading of courses.

15 The Committee has taken the view that the academic standard of a course is determined primarily by the entry requirements laid down for intending students. Thus, however high the level of qualifications of students, unless those qualifications are required for entry to the course they would be regarded as irrelevant for the purpose of grading courses. Further, the fact that a course may be mounted with the intention that it should recruit students of a particular calibre is also irrelevant unless the course qualifications require the inclusion only of students possessing such qualifications. Again, it is not sufficient for grading purposes if colleges are only advised to accept students with certain qualifications, if the advice can be disregarded. Often, courses will 'lay down' certain intended entry qualifications that allow students not possessing these qualifications to enter the course at the discretion of the principal of the college or its academic board. Such an arrangement may incline the Committee to give less weight to the envisaged entry requirements attached to the course[5]. This is not to say that the Committee ignores curriculum matters in deciding the academic nature of a course. Indeed, it considers not just the academic complexity of the syllabus but also features such as the number of hours of teaching laid down in the course details and, on occasion, examination papers. In general, however, the Committee does expect that there will be a correlation between these features and entry requirements.

16 The 'Specialist Staff' criterion has had some interesting consequences. It was certainly a criterion readily relied upon in the past when there was a chronic difficulty in recruiting staff from certain backgrounds, for example, accountants, and it appears likely that it could be relied upon extensively again given the new shortages in subjects like electronic engineering and computing. The maturity of students criterion is also interesting. The Committee will not be impressed by the fact that all students following a particular course are over a

certain age. The maturity of students criterion is relevant only where the course *requires* the recruitment of older people. Clearly, the operation of these two 'minor' criteria can lead to anomalies if courses are compared purely at the academic level. However, it should be noted that the Committee said in its 1968 statement that the point of the grading exercise was to ensure an adequate level of college staffing, the issue to which this chapter is principally addressed.

17 Although no complete summary of decisions reached can be presented the following comments may assist in understanding the pattern of decisions made:

(i) *National Certificate courses*
The GCSE O level and the ONC/OND are the foundations of the system. Courses at O level and below are graded in Category V. Courses at ONC/OND are graded at Category IV. Hence, a day release ONC course is graded the same as a full-time ONC course even though the latter has required many more hours of teaching. GCE A level courses are graded at Category IV.

(ii) *Craft and technician courses*
Generally, years one and two of the craft courses are graded at Category V, years three and four in Category IV and the remaining years in the new Category II/III (formerly in Category III). Again, in a very general sense, year one of a technicians' course is graded in Category V, years two and three in Category IV and the remaining years in Category II/III. In grading the ultimate stages of certain craft courses as Category II/III the Committee has been anxious to ensure that this Category is awarded only where there is an extension to the depth of work. Part II subjects studied subsequent to the Part II stage should not, for example, be graded in Category II/III. Where the Part III stage of a craft studies course involves specialised craft subjects, the study of which is based upon the knowledge gained in the earlier stages of the course, or, where the Part III stage involves the treatment in greater depth of the subject studied at an earlier stage, the grading should be Category II/III providing there is an extension of work undertaken at Part II or there is a basis in Part II studies as a prerequisite. However, where the Part III stage involves only a sideway step, such as an appreciation study of another craft, or an optional study from an earlier stage of the same course, but not previously taken up by the student, the grading will normally be at Category IV.

(iii) The Committee devised a generic grading for TEC courses and subsequently devised a generic grading for BEC courses. BTEC courses leading to ordinary certificates and diplomas are graded Category IV. Those leading to higher certificates and diplomas are graded II/III. Supplementary studies to ordinary level courses are graded II/III provided that there is an extension in the depth of work.

(iv) *TUC and NEBSS courses* In recent years the most controversial decisions of the Committee concerned Trades Union Congress (TUC) training courses on the other hand and National Examinations Board for Supervisory Studies (NEBSS) courses on the other. At the same time the Committee decided to grade all 'shop stewards' courses in Category II/III and to downgrade NEBSS courses to Category IV. A political outcry ensued, whatever the intended academic character of the debate, and whilst the TUC course grading was maintained the parent Burnham Committee has deferred action on the NEBSS grading which remains at II/III category.

18 **Teacher education courses**

When the Committee came to classify teacher education courses under the fivefold classification system it made some very interesting decisions – decisions which subsequently had a considerable influence on the agreement to merge Categories II and III. A course with O level entry requirement such as the Three Year Certificate of Education, would normally have its first year graded in Category IV. Yet the Committee graded the whole of this certificate in Category III. Similarly, a Post-Graduate Certificate in Education (PGCE) was graded in Category II even though it was evidently not a degree course, nor a course giving graduate status for salary purposes. Other teacher education 'post experience' courses were also graded in Category II and the Committee made a general decision that post experience courses were not to be graded less than Category III. Decisions of this sort made the distinction between courses in Category II and III less and less reliable and the distinction was abandoned. In the later description of the impact of the grading of courses on measures of institutional size, it will be seen that these steps protected teacher education establishments which were often very small but undertaking advanced level work.

19 **CNAA diploma courses**

The introduction of Category I has caused the Committee to look in some depth at CNAA and other diploma courses which are aimed at postgraduate students. It was decided that CNAA postgraduate diploma courses which form an integral part of a Master's taught degree course should be graded Category I. So should other CNAA diploma courses for which the normal entry requirement is a first degree, or its equivalent in a subject of direct relevance to the subject matter of the diploma and in which the content was such as to involve study *beyong the level associated with a first degree*. Where this is not so because the course involves a broadening rather than a deepening of knowledge the diploma is graded as Category II/III.

20 It should be noted that there are now three new and significant pressures on the grading of courses system.

(i) Competitive methods for categorising courses have emerged under the auspices of the National Council for Vocational Qualifications (NCVQ) (See **3.1** 50–51). This categorisation has been directed to the new kinds of courses sometimes described as the 'new FE'. Suffice it to say in this context, the propositions subdivide the Burnham Categories IV and V and have impact on the category above. Many of the new FE courses have arisen because of local development of curricula in conjunction with the Manpower Services Commission (MSC) (See **1.7**). As a result of these initiatives, a major extension is likely during 1987–88 of the local negotiations of categories for these courses. This will impose an entirely new pressure on local negotiation which has not, in general, had to take initiatives in an area dominated by the National Grading of Courses Committee discussions.

(ii) A series of propositions have been made in the context of the 1986–87 national salary and structure negotiations, not complete as at the time of writing, and these include propositions from the Employers to merge Categories IV and V and to separate out the merged Category II/III for class contact purposes and return it to its state before the categories were joined. The first proposition in respect of Categories IV and V has been motivated by the effects of joining for salaries purposes the two basic salary scales in FE, namely the Lecturer Grade I and Lecturer

Grade II scales. Second, the proposal to disaggregate Category II/III is motivated by the desire to identify advanced further education in a more traditional sense so that if as a result of negotiations lecturers teaching advanced further education have different entitlements in respect of conditions of service, these entitlements should only apply to those lecturers whose higher education work is directly comparable to the work of the universities. Whilst both of these proposals are intended to be short term, they would make a significant difference to the current provisions.

(iii) There have also been proposals which have commanded support on both sides of negotiations during 1986–87 that for the first of April 1988 a new system should be devised to replace the grading of courses system. Employers' and Lecturers' Associations have both made statements which indicate their desire to eliminate élitism. The Lecturers' Associations have insisted on a need for a new national system because they do not wish to see a return to the system of local discretion that predates the grading of courses system. NATFHE has been considering a model originally elaborated by the present authors in 1983 which: recognises the rate of change in FE and the desirability of modifying the grading of courses system; takes account of the major differences between traditional and new FE and training; recognises the differences between the education and training balance in the offer of further education colleges and the more limited vocational training offered outside of the FE colleges; simplifies the salary system; has a capacity to be changed by negotiations whether national or local; utilises staff : student ratios as a means of determining staffing levels and other aspects of institutional resourcing; and provides a method for the unambiguous determination of the size of the workload in each college. The model generates formulae which provide new measures of institutional size and reflect the important differences between different kinds of institution[6]. This alternative is mentioned briefly because it is the only model currently under discussion as a permanent replacement for the grading of courses system and it is likely to form a significant component of discussions during the year 1987–88.

21 **The purposes of grading courses**

It was noted above that the Committee saw the main purpose of the grading of courses exercise as to ensure an adequate level of staffing exists in all further education institutions. It provides a means of measuring the size of an establishment in terms of the number of students and the level of work which they undertake, with additional formulae covering the work of part-time students. When this formula is applied in conjunction with the Burnham Further Education Committee Report (Appendix IIA) it is possible to determine the proportion of posts ranges laid down in that Report. Thus the grading of courses determines the grading of posts of Lecturer I, Lecturer II, Senior Lecturer and Principal Lecturer level. Hence, the grading of courses system has a direct bearing on all key measures which give rise to salary grades, promotion opportunities and the staffing structure of colleges and for this reason it is described in advance of describing those arrangements.

22 However, there are a number of other purposes to which grading of courses decisions are put either (in the past) by intention of the Burnham Further Education Committee, or by other bodies. An explanation is given of the unit total system and its relationship to the measurement of departmental and college

size in paragraph 33 and Table 2. Clearly the grading of the courses offered in colleges directly determines the college's and its departments' unit totals and hence, the salaries of the Principal, Vice-Principal and Heads of Department.

23 Another major purpose of the grading of courses is outlined in paragraphs 51 and 52 which deal with the arrangements for transfer for the Lecturer II to the Senior Lecturer scale and with passage through the bars on the Senior and Principal Lecturer scales. Here again the grading of the courses taught by staff directly determine whether or not they will proceed past certain points in their salary scales.

24 The grade of a course also determines the hourly rate paid to part-time staff teaching on it (See below Table 6). However, some LEAs still make payments at a rate below that applicable to Category V work for some non-vocational studies.

25 Finally, the grading of courses has been used to determine the student fee structure of courses, inter-authority payments for courses, but does not determine whether or not expenditure for a course is poolable.

26 Given the ramifications of decisions reached in the Grading of Courses Committee, the work of the Committee is clearly crucial to the further education salaries system as present operated. Whatever the character of the academic judgements made in grading courses the exercise gives rise to the entire pay system of the further education system. The following paragraphs deal with the relationship of the grading of courses to academic staffing establishments.

27 **Academic staffing establishments**

The Burnham Salaries documents lays down a scheme for determining the proportion of Lecturer Grade I, Lecturer Grade II, Senior Lecturer and Principal Lecturer posts in a college. This scheme does not itself determine the total number of posts. However, in one method of its application, in fact the most popular one, it can be used to determine the size as well as the structure of the academic staff establishment.

28 There are three basic methods, not necessarily mutually exclusive, for determining the size of the establishment of a college, First, as indicated above, the Burnham proportions of posts can be applied to the volume of work in the college, measured in staff or student hours, so as to produce an overall figure for the number as well as the grades of staff. Second, a staff : student ratio can be used to determine the number of staff required. Thirdly, the number of posts can be determined by the political decision of the LEA based on budgetary considerations (See **1.6** 46). These three methods have been elaborated by the introduction of a number of performance indicators for the sector. Not only are staff : student ratios used but computer based measurement systems have been introduced in the FEMIS programme (See **2.8** Appendix 1 2–3). Briefly, it should be noted that performance indicators now involve measurement of unit costs and of various performance criteria including student retention rates and measurements and outcome for students after completion of courses.

29 The Burnham Salaries document and the successor documents which will be produced by the National Joint Council do not lay down a method for determining the size of the establishment or its structure. Rather the Burnham document has laid down certain perimeters within which the structure of the

establishment must be determined. It is this latter consideration, the proportion of posts at various levels, which concerns the NJC and formerly concerned the Burnham FE Committee. The NJC will negotiate a range of proportions of posts by category of work from which LEAs have to adopt particular proportions for determining the balance between grades. LEAs can be 'generous' in this matter by adopting the maximum proportion of senior posts for each category of work, or 'ungenerous' by choosing the minimum proportion. Most LEAs choose the mid-point of the range of proportions laid down in the national agreements. The current range of proportions in respect of each category of work is shown in Table 1.

Table 1
Proportion of posts

Category of Work	*Grade of Lecturer*	*Proportion of Posts* — *Establishments of FE*	*Colleges of Education (Technical)*
I	Principal	20–30%	35–40%
	Senior		
	Grade II	70–80%	60–65%
II/III	Principal	10–25%	25–35%
	Senior		
	Grade II	75–90%	65–75%
IV	Senior	0–5%	
	Grade II	40–65%	
	Grade I	30–60%	
V	Senior	0–5%	
	Grade II	15–25%	
	Grade I	70–85%	

30 A popular method of using these proportions in fact gives rise not just to the particular ratio of posts in any college but also to the overall number of posts. This method can be illustrated by the formula, which is based on the mid-point within the range of proportions (See above paragraph 29):

Method for using the proportions calculation

Number of Lecturer Grade I Posts (77.5% × D/LI) + (45% × C/LI)
Number of Lecturer Grade II Posts (20% × D/LII) + (52.5% × C/LII)
Number of Senior Lecturer Posts (2.5% × D/S) + (2.5% × C/S)
Number of Principal Lecturer Posts (17.5% × B/P) + (25% × A/P)
Number of Lecturer II and Senior Lecturer Posts (82.5% × B/S) + (75% × A/S)*

Where:

A = volume of category I work
B = volume of category II/III work
C = volume of category IV work
D = volume of category V work
LI = class contact level for Lecturers Grade I
LII = class contact level for Lecturers Grade II
S = class contact level for Senior Lecturers
P = class contact level for Principal Lecturers
* As indicated, the actual number of Lecturer Grade II posts derived

from this part of the formula must not exceed 50% of the total. In this example, the Senior Lecturer class contact level is used as the denominator but in some cases the average of the Lecturer Grade II and Senior Lecturer levels is used.

31 The application of the range of proportions of posts give rise to important features in the system:

(i) The establishment of a college is determined college by college. This apparent truism is important – the Burnham FE Committee did not lay down the internal departmental allocation of the establishment. At its most basic, the provisions of the salaries document were satisfied if the minimum points in the range of proportions of posts existed in each college. To take an extreme example, all the senior posts could be allocated to one department and all the junior posts to the other departments, irrespective of the balance of advanced and non-advanced work between departments. In fact, of course, most colleges work on a principle of equity in distributing the posts in the establishment but this is not always automatically the case and where it is not it sometimes generates conflict.

(ii) The fact that work in Categories I and II/III generate only posts at a Lecturer Grade II and above, does not mean that Lecturers Grade I (if they exist in the college) cannot be called upon to teach work in these categories. Further, there is no compulsion on LEAs or college administrators to promote staff teaching advanced work to the senior posts which this work generates. Again, in equity, many colleges do have regard to the level of work attached to a post in deciding its grading or regrading but, again, there is no automatic connection between these two considerations.

(iii) The general principle that college establishments are college based admit some exceptions. The Burnham FE Salaries Report lays down that in respect of departments in Grade III or above there must be a minimum number of Senior Lecturer posts. These minima are:
Grade III Department – 1 Senior Lecturer
Grade IV Department – 2 Senior Lecturers
Grade V Department – 2 Senior Lecturers
Grade VI Department – 3 Senior Lecturers

(iv) The FE Salaries Report does not put any limit, apparently, on the number of Head of Department or Vice-Principal posts in a college. Again, it does not lay down a basis for determining the number or proportion of Reader Posts or Academic Posts above Reader. However, it does express certain conditions under which Reader and academic posts above Reader can be established (Appendix II A Part II). Clearly, these posts are intended for use in colleges with major commitments to advanced work and research. In recent years there has been greater development of such posts but there are still not sufficient of these posts to close the significant differences between such institutions and universities. This is due to the continuing financial restraints imposed by LEAs and upon LEAs.

(v) It is worth noting that it is not possible to create, on a mandatory basis, Principal Lecturer posts in respect of work in Categories IV and V. This can cause administrative difficulties in further education colleges with little advanced work. It imposes, in effect, a restriction on the middle management options in large departments. Equally those in colleges with a mixture of Category V, IV and II/III work but with a majority of the work at the lower level may find other establishment problems. Typically, Senior Lecturers may be regarded as deputy Heads of Department with specific functions within a department but may not themselves have sufficient Category II/III work to enable them to pass through the bar in the Senior Lecturer Scale whereas those whose work they administer may have sufficient work at this level to pass through the bar and be paid on points above those of the staff responsible. The Burnham Proportions of Posts Table and the provisions regarding scale transfer and bar passage have been amended in ad hoc ways over recent years resulting in significant anomalies within and between institutions.

(vi) It will be noted that in respect of work in Categories I and II/III there is no separate range of proportions for Senior Lecturer and Lecturer Grade II posts. This is necessary because of the transfer arrangements between Lecturer Grade II and Senior Lecturer Grades in respect of those undertaking 50% or more lecturing in these Categories (see paragraphs 51 and 52). This arrangement makes it impossible in practice to distinguish these posts for establishment calculation purposes. In the extreme case, a college doing only work in these Categories which experienced no mobility of staff out of the institution, would have eventually all lecturers at Senior and Principal Lecturer level. The Burnham FE Committee has made provision to avoid the reverse situation of all posts being graded at the Lecturer Grade II and Principal Lecturer levels. It has been agreed that, at any point in time, no more than 50% of the posts created in the Senior Lecturer and Lecturer Grade II grades in respect of advanced work should be at the Lecturer Grade II level.

(vii) Following the agreement in 1978 to transfer lecturers on the top point of the Lecturer Grade I Scale to the seventh point of the Lecturer Grade II Scale there are established LI posts and established LII posts in accordance with explicit proportions of posts formula. Progressed LIIs are replaced by LIs, established LIIs by LIIs.

32 It has been noted that the grading of courses system is central to the determination of many of the arrangements in the sphere of further and higher education. The measurement of the scale of work depends on this mechanism and the payments of senior staff and the proportions of posts for more junior staff are determined by it.

33 **Unit total**

The unit total for a college or department (the measure of size of these entities in further and higher education) is the device by which colleges are grouped by size and departments graded by size. The college unit total determines the salaries of the principal and vice-principal. The unit total varies between years and the operative unit total is calculated retrospectively for the immediate past academic year. To calculate the unit total the LEA calculates student hours and then applies divisors to the student hours totals based on the grading of the courses undertaken by the students, as shown in Table 2.

34 **Student hours**

Student hours are calculated by four methods:

(i) The actual registered hours spent in a college by part-time and block release students are counted except where students attend courses for less than one term's duration. In this case the actual registered hours are increased by 10%.

(ii) Where full-time students are following courses of a duration of more

Table 2
Calculation of unit totals

Category of Work (Grading of courses)	*Divisors*
I	for each 100 student hours count 1 unit
II and III	for each 300 student hours count 1 unit
IV and V	for each 600 student hours count 1 unit

than one term but less than one year then the numbers of students enrolled on the various courses is counted and credit given for 95% of the student hours for the particular course as defined in paragraph 35 below. Where the course is for less than one term's duration, credit is given for 110% of the actual full-time student hours.

(iii) In respect of other full-time students, those enrolled on 1 November are counted according to the year of the course being taken and credit is then given for 95% of the student hours for the year as determined in paragraph 35 below.

(iv) For each sandwich course, credit is given for 100% of the student hours spent in the college or department during the year as determined under paragraph 35 below, together with an addition determined by the authority according to the duties and responsibilities of the college staff for students during the period of the year spent in industry or commerce, if any. The Burnham Committee has recommended that the addition be 10% of the student hours for the year of the course.

35 The student hours for a particular course is the time spent in the college or department as determined by the LEA in consultation with the principal of the college. The Burnham Committee has specified that what should be taken into account is the maximum time spent in the college or department during normal hours, whether in lectures, practical work, tutorials or individual work (for example in the library).

36 Two features of this pattern should be noted. First, the adjustment of the percentages is intended to reflect the character of the burden placed upon colleges and departments by organising work of particular kinds. The distinctive vocational characteristic of further and higher education in the public sector often means that students have different and unconventional patterns of attendance. These impose a greater burden on college staff and administrators. Such work would be less attractive than conventional modes of attendance unless a premium attached to the hours calculation. Second, there has been a debate in recent years about the possibility that some students are 'overtaught', that the hours allotted to a course may be artificially high so as to gain advantage from the hours calculations and the consequential salary arrangements. The debate has heightened as demographic change has reduced the numbers of students in the 16–19 age-group, a decline which is not always compensated by a rise in the participation rate among people of this age. It is

sometimes argued that colleges seek to compensate by increasing the numbers of hours spent on courses by students. No specific evidence has been provided for these conclusions although they form a significant element in debate.

37 **The grouping of a college**

When the unit total for a college has been calculated, it is placed into bandings or groups as shown in Table 3. The authority can determine the group of a college on the basis of an estimate of its work for the third complete academic year after its opening or reorganisation.

Table 3
Grouping of Colleges

Unit total	*Group*
Up to 250	1
251–500	2
501–1000	3
1001–1750	4
1751–2750	5
2751–3750	6
3751–5000	7
5001–6500	8
6501–8500	9
8501–11000	10
11001–13500	11
Over 13500	12

38 **Grading of departments**

When the unit total for a department has been calculated, it is graded as in Table 4. In the grading of a department the following provisions also apply:

Table 4
Grading of Departments

Unit total	*Grade*
76–140	I
141–250	II
251–400	III
401–600	IV
601–900	V
over 900	VI

(i) If the staffing of a department includes the post of Senior Lecturer, it cannot be graded less than II. If the staffing includes a Principal Lecturer or reader, the grade shall not be less than III. If the Principal Lecturer is entitled to pass through the bar on the Principal Lecturer scale in a department graded lower than IV, the LEA is empowered, at its discretion, to grade the department to IV.

(ii) Where a department of grade III or higher normally undertakes work of category I or II/III standard and the LEA considers its grading to be inadequate, then the LEA may place the department into such higher grade as it considers appropriate. This decision should be guided by the volume and standard of research or academic development work undertaken.

(iii) Pending the reorganisation of a department the LEA can establish a temporary grade for it or make other arrangements for the direction of the work without establishing a departmental post. However, this should not continue for more than two years. It will be seen that there are no specific rules about how courses or students should be grouped, and it is possible for an LEA to organise colleges broadly as they judge fit. LEAs are usually commended not to establish over large departments (which can pose administrative problems or cause an imbalance with other organisational units in a college). In some LEAs there is a routine consideration of breaking over large departments into smaller units. These remain, however, matters of educational and administrative judgment. The same mechanism for estimating the size of departments in their first three years as applies to colleges obtains.

39 Because college groupings and departmental gradings depend on a variable – student hours – the unit totals may decline. This affects the salaries of principals, vice-principals and heads of department. Where there is a decline, the group of a college or grade of a department is considered to be one above that calculated from the actual figures. Where the group or grade falls by one, the *status quo* obtains. Where the fall is greater than one, the salary is determined within the group which is one above the actual group or grade that results after the decline. In such circumstances, a personal allowance would be paid to the member of staff involved, the allowance being the sum necessary to bring the salary back to the level being received within the group of the college or grade of the department before the decline. The allowance is subject to reduction. As the new salary scale move upwards, the amount of the allowance declines.

40 The arrangements in adult education vary somewhat from those set out above (See paragraphs 65 and 66).

41 **Staff in penal establishments**

In 1978 new arrangements were agreed in the Joint National Council for Prison Education Staff to deal with the grading of education officers and lecturing posts in prisons. These arrangements relate to the grade of the education officers' posts to the unit, total calculations for which are shown earlier in this chapter and which are generated by the student hours. There is one exceptional arrangement which has been added to this pattern. The Education Officer is also awarded an additional thirty units for each civilian instructor employed in his or her establishment. The unit total range, grade of education officer and his or her deputy is in Appendix 2 of Chapter 2.5.

42 The rule which makes a Senior Lecturer mandatory in a Grade III and Grade IV Department applies that in practice the deputy grade is always likely to be a Senior Lecturer. For other posts a global approach is taken with all the work

in the prison being aggregated and used as the base to calculate the Lecturer Grade II pool of posts. These are then allocated to the education establishment. It is frequently the case in practice that these arrangements are made in association with either an adult education institute in the locality or with an adult education department of a further education college in the locality.

43 Following Royal Assent to the Teachers' Pay and Conditions Act 1987, the Joint Negotiating Committee for Further Education Teachers in Prison Service Establishments has ceased to exist; this was not a requirement of the legislation which simply dismantled the Burnham Committee structure. However, in revising the constitution of the National Joint Council for Lecturers in Further Education in England and Wales (See above paragraphs 9–11) consideration was given to incorporation of groups whose work was sufficiently analogous to further education lecturers as to make it impractical to retain separate bargaining systems. In consequence a subcommittee of the National Joint Council will deal with prison education establishments in future. The Home Office has an observer sitting with the Employers' Associations on the main committee.

44 **Grading of posts in agricultural and horticultural establishments**

The grading of Lecturer IA, Lecturer IB and Lecturer II in agricultural and horticultural establishments is a matter which is determined by the local education authority although they are guided by provisions in the Burnham FE Report. Lecturers IA are the basic grade for full-time lecturers in such establishments whilst Lecturers IB are considered to be the grade normally appropriate for lecturers who, as a core element of their duties, have responsibilities for administrative or practical tasks. Such tasks are of widespread importance in agricultural and horticultural establishments because they invariably run farming and horticultural marketing activities in order to provide the basis for the practical education in the industry. Aside from running these activities there are additional responsibilities for the organisation, care and maintenance of equipment and stores and demonstration facilities required. Additionally since some of the establishments are relatively small responsibilities are taken for the organisation of the establishment library where no separate librarian is employed. The managerial systems in agricultural and horticultural establishments have given rise to a number of questions as to their suitability to the task and discussions in the course of 1986–88 may give rise to new arrangements for middle management jobs. This process may be accentuated by the fact that there are no normal head of department arrangements in much of agricultural and horticultural education despite the grouping of responsibilities and disciplinary areas.

45 **Salary scales**

There are nine salary scales: Principal, Vice-Principal, Head of Department, Academic Post above Reader, Reader, Principal Lecturer, Senior Lecturer, Lecturer Grade II, Lecturer Grade I. The ranges of salaries applying to Principals, Vice-Principals and Heads of Departments depend upon the unit totals attached to the college or to the department as a result of the calculations made on the basis of the grading of courses system. There are twelve groups of colleges each reflecting a range of unit totals (See above paragraph 37). The salaries of Principals and Vice-Principals are on fixed points determined by the LEAs from the range of salaries that attaches to each group of colleges. There are six grades of department, each with an appropriate salary scale upon which the Departmental Head is paid (See above paragraphs 38–39). All these arrangements are among the complex outcomes of the grading of courses system. Where there are exceptional circumstances in the cases of Principals, Vice-Principals and Heads of Department Grade VI which justify a salary higher than that permissible within the appropriate salary range or scale, then application must be made to the Secretary of State for approval of a payment of a higher salary. Following the annual settlement in 1985, lecturers who had completed a year or more on the top point of the Lecturer Grade I Scale were transferred to point seven on the Lecturer Grade II Scale, or point eight of the Lecturer Grade II Scale where the lecturer had enjoyed a special responsibility allowance as a Lecturer Grade I (See below paragraphs 50–52). Although lecturers transferred to the Lecturer Grade II Scale retained the conditions of service that they had as Lecturers Grade I, the effect of this agreement was that for salary purposes the two basic grades have become a single grade of lecturer. From a legal point of view transferred Lecturers Grade II, although counted as Lecturers Grade I for establishment figure purposes, are Lecturers Grade II and not Lecturers Grade I with additional payment.

46 **Salary scales and points ranges: 1 April 1986**

The salary scales set out in Table 5 for further education and agricultural education will inevitably be out of date by the time of publication of this book, but they illustrate the ranges of salaries paid at the 1 April 1985.

47 **Part-time hourly rates**

The part-time hourly rates are based upon the grading of courses system. Part-time hourly paid lecturers are paid for each hour depending on the category of the course taught during that hour. The categories of work give rise to three different hourly rates which, as at 1 April 1986, are shown in Table 6.

48 Some part-time staff qualify to be treated as Lecturers Grade I where they teach more than twenty hours per week for a full academic year in an institution. Also, staff teaching more than thirteen hours for a full year in an institution qualify to be paid a proportionate fraction of a full-time lecturer's rate of pay. The concept of a full academic year is understood to be a year equivalent to that taught by a full-time lecturer taking account of the usual pattern of work within the college and this means that it does not necessarily mean thirty-six teaching weeks. Part-time hourly rates are supplemented in London by London Allowances expressed at hourly rates.

49 Prior to 1980 part-time hourly rates varied across the regions of the country as well as by categories of work. Thus the figures shown in the 1980 edition of *College Administration* and in some other documents which show these regional variations, often expressed authority by authority, are of no applicability now.

50 **The scales, bars, and transfer arrangements for FE lecturers**

In has been noted in paragraph 45 above that new arrangements came into existence on 1 September 1985 under which lecturers on the maximum of the Lecturer Grade I Scale are permitted progress automatically to point seven on the Lecturer Grade II Scale, this arrangement being set out in the 1986 Amendment Order to the Burnham Report. The condition for automatic progression was that the lecturer on point fifteen of the Lecturer Grade I Scale prior to that date would have had sufficient service in the previous year as to qualify them to progress on that date to point seven of the Lecturer II Scale

Table 5
Salary scales (from 1 April 1986)

Lecturer I & IA

Point	£
0	6843
1	7104
2	7371
3	7641
4	7908
5	8196
6	8472
7	8793
8	9120
9	9435
10	9756
11	10074
12	10401
13	10722
14	11037
15	11865

Lecturer IB

Point	£
0	7620
1	7890
2	8160
3	8421
4	8700
5	8985
6	9261
7	9582
8	9894
9	10239
10	10575
11	10899
12	11229
13	11598
14	11916
15	12381
16	12768
17	13152
18	13536

Lecturer II

Point	£
0	8595
1	9090
2	9573
3	10059
4	10551
5	11031
6	11571
7	12063
8	12615
9	13131
10	13656

Senior Lecturer

Point	£
0	12615
1	13131
2	13656
3	14232
4	14820
5	15351
6	15873

Principal Lecturer

Point	£
0	14784
1	15318
2	15852
3	16458
4	16986
5	17526
6	18060
7	18588

Heads of Department (£)

Grade I

Point	£
0	12306
1	12732
2	13161
3	13587
4	14016

Grade II

Point	£
0	14136
1	14580
2	15036
3	15480
4	15933

Grade III

Point	£
0	15456
1	15909
2	16347
3	16806
4	17253

Grade IV

Point	£
0	16704
1	17202
2	17712
3	18207
4	18714

Grade V

Point	£
0	18174
1	18663
2	19176
3	19674
4	20181

Grade VI

Point	£
0	19638
1	20142
2	20643
3	21135
4	21639

Lecturer II Agriculture

Point	£
0	12381
1	12768
2	13152
3	13536
4	13929
5	14430
6	14820
7	15210
8	15609
9	16002
10	16398

Vice Principals Agriculture

Point	£
0	12768
1	13152
2	13536
3	14046
4	14430
5	14820
6	15210
7	15609
8	16002
9	16398
10	16785
11	17184
12	17640
13	18162
14	18621
15	19062
16	19524
17	19971

Principals Agriculture

Point	£
0	16398
1	16785
2	17184
3	17640
4	18162
5	18621
6	19062
7	19524
8	19971
9	20424
10	20874
11	21507
12	21960
13	22422
14	22884
15	23346

Table 5 – continued
Principals and Vice-Principals

Group	Vice-Principals Min	Vice-Principals Max	Principals Min	Principals Max
1	13785	14892	16158	17478
2	15096	16203	17796	19119
3	16515	17625	19491	20841
4	18024	19125	21420	22749
5	19413	20532	23082	24258
6	20694	21801	24633	25818
7	22029	23142	25863	27045
8	23241	24225	27174	28353
9	24441	25431	28359	29547
10	25455	26445	29580	30753
11	26472	27462	31044	32238
12	27486	28479	32517	33726

Table 6
Part-time hourly rates (from 1 April 1986)

Category

I and II/III	IV	V
£14.36	£12.57	£9.05

and thereafter by annual increments to the scale maximum. Under Section 13 of the Burnham document some Lecturers Grade I had been in receipt of a responsibility allowance and were also on the maximum of the Lecturers I Scale. They moved by automatic progression to point eight of the Lecturer Grade II Scale so as to take account of the responsibility allowance and thereafter also moved by annual increments to the maximum of the Lecturer Grade II Scale unless they are eligible for transfer to the Senior Lecturer Scale on the basis set out in paragraph 51. From 1 September 1985 the responsibility allowance ceased to be payable to any Lecturer Grade I who transferred to the Lecturer Grade II Scale. Provisions for incremental assessment on the Lecturer Grade I and Lecturer Grade II Scales were not changed by the agreement so that lecturers appointed to the Lecturer Grade I Scale continued to receive incremental credit up to the point at which they are at the maximum of the Lecturer Grade I Scale. They are then entitled to progress to the Lecturer Grade II Scale after spending six months or more on the maximum of the Lecturer Grade I Scale, the condition which qualified them for an increment under Appendix 3 of the Burnham Report. Some lecturers will have qualified on the necessary six months stipulation at some stage in the past rather than in the year in which they were on the fifteenth point of the Lecturer Grade I

Scale, typically following a break in service or a temporary promotion to another post. In these circumstances the lecturer will progress immediately to point seven on the Lecturer Grade II Scale. These arrangements have not ended the capacity of lecturers to be promoted rather than transferred between the two scales and a promotion from the maximum of the Lecturer I Scale takes precedence over an entitlement to transfer to the Lecturer II Scale. Two key differences exist between promotion and transfer. First, lecturers who are promoted to a substantive Lecturers II post are entitled to a sum equal to one and a half increments on the higher scale, this usually producing a figure lying between two incremental points from which the salary is calculated by 'rounding up'. Second the promoted lecturer will enjoy LII class contact hours whilst the transferred lecturer will continue to work LI class contact hours.

51 In certain circumstances Lecturers Grade II can transfer to the Senior Lecturer Scale, and this provision encompasses those who have been either promoted or transferred from the Lecturer Grade I to the Lecturer Grade II Scale. The final three points of the Lecturer Grade II Scale are identical to the first three points of the Senior Lecturer Scale. Unlike the Lecturer Grade I/ Lecturer Grade II progression, this transfer is not 'automatic' but depends upon satisfying specific criteria. The key criteria were introduced by the Houghton Committee of Enquiry in 1975 and demand that a lecturer must have 'satisfied the efficiency requirements' and be responsible for a significant amount of work in Categories I and/or II/III of the grading of courses system. If the criteria are satisfied when a lecturer completes work at point eight of the Lecturer Grade II scale she or he may move to point one of the Senior Lecturer Scale rather then progressing to point nine on the Lecturer Grade II Scale. Although the points carry the same monetary value the individual who has transferred to the Senior Lecturer Scale may proceed up the Senior Lecturer Scale as if appointed to that scale. If the work and efficiency requirements are not satisfied on the first possible occasion of eligibility there is an opportunity at subsequent later points to transfer when the conditions are satisfied. Transfer will then take place at points nine or ten of the Lecturer II Scale to the equivalent next point on the Senior Lecturer Scale.

52 It will be appreciated that the terms 'efficiency' and 'significant' in respect of the work being undertaken require some interpretation and this interpretation does not occur in the formal documents. The Joint Secretaries of the Burnham FE Committee have built a body of interpretation around the advanced work criterion for scale transfer and this body of interpretation also applies to progression through bars within the Senior Lecturer and Principal Lecturer Scales.

(i) Local authorities have been advised that the case of the person who becomes eligible for transfer should be reviewed in good time by the Principal and Governors as it is necessary to enable a decision to be made. The Principal ought to submit the name of the lecturer concerned to the Governors, or to the local education authority, as appropriate, and to specify in each case whether the individual has satisfied the requirements. This is done without a specific definition of 'efficiency'.

(ii) Scale transfer only takes place on the date that an increment is due – 1 September. This applies to full-time lecturers and associate lecturers although it should be noted that associate lecturers cannot transfer in a year in which they do not satisfy the Burnham FE provisions for award of an increment, namely that they have completed six months work at the relevant level.

(iii) To qualify for transfer a lecturer must be responsible for 'a significant amount' of work classified as Category I or II/III during the year he or she is on the relevant scale point. Alternatively the three years immediately prior to the date on which transfer is to be considered may be used for the calculation if that is more favourable to the teacher. A 'significant amount of work' is defined as at least 50% of a lecturer's 'work time'. This latter expression also required definition and the Joint Secretaries have advised that for full-time and associate lecturers the hours to be taken into account are the annual class contact hours which are appropriate to the post. These are the class contact hours plus remitted hours as defined in paragraphs 8.2 and 8.3 of the Silver Book (See **2.5** 20(i)–(vii). There are two exceptions to this rule. The LEA should completely discount any hours for which a lecturer cannot be timetabled and which the LEA has not specifically defined as 'remitted time' and also any hours which a lecturer is entitled to have as time-off for trade union duties or as a safety representative. This latter provision should avoid the possibility that a person undertaking such duties will lose their entitlements to career progression.

(iv) The academic level of the class contact is determined by reference to the Burnham Grading of Courses Book (See above paragraph 8). Some classes contain students who are being taught at different academic levels but in the same class which is an integral part of a number of different courses or years within courses. In that case the class should be calculated as being of the grading as applicable irrespective of the proportions of students in that class. Class contact itself is defined in the Silver Book as teaching, invigilating and supervising examinations and test and timetabled tutorial and supervision work with individual students or groups both inside and outside the college.

(v) When considering whether remitted work can be counted as being equivalent to 'advanced' courses, it is necessary to consider carefully whether it is a legitimate equivalent to academic work in Categories I or II/III. If it is not a lecturer will not be entitled to count it in the calculation and it is recognised that much work done in remitted hours is not related to specific courses. It will then be counted as equivalent to Categories IV or V. For example, if a teacher had an allocation of eighteen class contact hours, three of which were remitted, then unless those hours were legitimately spent on advanced level work, at least nine hours of advanced teaching would be required within the eighteen hours in order to qualify for transfer between scale.

(vi) If a lecturer approaching a possible point of transfer to the Senior Lecturer Scale is released on secondment it should be made clear to the lecturer prior to the secondment that if the work or study undertaken whilst on secondment away from the institution is not within scope of the Burnham Report or of subsequent documents to be drawn up under the auspices of the National Joint Council it will not be taken into account for transfer purposes.

(vii) The Silver Book has incorporated the following statement of agreement which deals with possible abuses within this system: 'Once teachers are passed through the bar they will continue to progress up the Senior Lecturer Scale; in view of this the balance of their timetables (as between advanced and non-advanced work) ought as a matter of policy to be broadly maintained in future years, unless there are compelling educational reasons to the contrary. Similarly, the timetables of those approaching the bar should be planned so that there is not a sudden increase in advanced work, without good reason, during the years spent on the eighth increment point'.

(viii) Where a decision against transfer is taken the lecturer should be advised of a right to appeal, and where a decision to appeal is taken the Principal ought to prepare a report on the matter and issue copies of that report and such documents as are relevant to the appellant. The appeal should be heard within the process of the agreed grievance procedure (See **2.5** 26 and 27). The description of these arrangements has been couched in terms of transfer between one scale and another. It should be noted that the same criteria apply for transfer through bars within the Senior Lecturer and Principal Lecturer Scales, save for the provision concerning appeal set out above.

53 **Scale arrangements in agricultural and horticultural establishments**

The 1986 Amendment Order to the Burnham FE Report also incorporated arrangements for the automatic transfer of Lecturers Grade IA on the maximum of the scale to point fourteen of the Lecturer Grade IB Scale on 1 September 1985 and thereafter to the maximum of the revised Lecturer IB Scale. The arrangements shown in the paragraphs for mainstream further education apply to this transfer arrangement. However, the Lecturer IB Scale was extended by three incremental points with effect from 1 September 1985 and lecturers who from that date were on the top of the Lecturer IB Scale became eligible to progress through the new points to the maximum of the scale. The Amendment Order also revised arrangements for the Lecturer II Scale removing the bottom two points and renumbering the remaining points 0–10. Lecturers Grade II in agriculture and horticulture are paid on five point ranges within this scale. The consequence of the change was that those with individual scales running from points 0–4 or points 1–5 on the old Lecturer II Scale are placed on points 0–4 of the new Lecturer II Scale. Lecturers on points 0 and 1 of the old Lecturer II Scale progressed to point 0 on the new Lecturer II Scale from 1 September 1985.

54 **Allowances**

All allowances are subject to review and alteration and the figures given are those applying at 1 July 1986.

(i) *London Area Allowances* Lecturers serving in the London area receive payments according to the area in which they serve. These are: Inner area – £1215; Outer area – £795; Fringe area – £309. These allowances are renegotiated annually. The Inner London area is the Inner London Education Authority (ILEA) area and the boroughs of Barking, Brent, Ealing, Haringey, Merton and Newham. The Outer London area is Greater London excluding the inner area. The fringe area comprises Surrey and certain districts in Berkshire, Buckinghamshire, Essex, Hertfordshire, Kent and West Sussex. Where a lecturer works in a split site institution with premises in more than one designated area, an allowance appropriate to the location at which more than half the time is spent will be the one that applies. Temporary employment away from one of these areas does not change the entitlement to receive the appropriate London Allowance. Negotiations of London area payments are made in the National Joint Council.

(ii) A lecturer who takes charge of a department or undertakes the duties of a Vice-Principal or a Principal in the absence of those appointed to such posts, or pending their appointment to those posts, may be eligible to receive an acting allowance. The payment of such an allowance and its amount is at the discretion of the employing authority. National agreements do not specify time limits over which acting allowances may be paid and Joint Secretaries have advised that there would be cause to question the basis for an acting allowance paid for a period in excess of two years. After receipt of an acting allowance for a period of excess of two years and circumstances where the lecturer's salary was to be reduced as a result of closure or reorganisation, a safeguarding arrangement would protect and include the acting allowance. There are no acting allowances payable under the Burnham Document to staff acting up in posts below Head of Department. Where there is a need for staff to act up in lecturing grades temporary promotion is regarded as more appropriate and at the end of such a period the lecturer promoted on temporary basis is reassimilated on his or her original scale by reference to the salary in the acting post.

(iii) At the discretion of the LEA, a temporary allowance can be paid to a lecturer who returns from a period of seconded overseas service. While payment is discretionary the amount of the allowance is mandatory. The allowance cannot be paid for more than two years and consists of an amount which brings the lecturer's remuneration to the level of salary earned in the post held immediately before the secondment. The allowable circumstances for the payment of the temporary allowance are that the secondment was under arrangements approved by the Ministry of Overseas Development, to Ministry of Defence schools which provided for the education of the children of members of HM Forces, or any such other service as might be approved by the Burnham FE Committee for this purpose or which may be approved by the National Joint Council.

(iv) It is mandatory to establish a full-time Vice-Principal post in establishments over Group 4 or above, except where a Head of Department was appointed before 25 February 1972 to undertake the duties of Vice-Principal in addition to his or her Head of Department duties, and continues to be so employed. Most colleges, even those below group 4 where it is not mandatory, have established Vice-Principal posts. However, where this has not occurred in establishments below group 4, a Head of Department has often been appointed to undertake the duties and responsibilities of a Vice-Principal in addition to the responsibilities as Head of Department and where this is so it is mandatory to pay an allowance to the Head of Department in question. Further it has not always been mandatory to create Vice-Principal posts in colleges above group 4. Hence in a few cases, heads of Department still hold 'Vice-Principal' allowances to which they became entitled several years ago in establishments above group 4. The allowances to both groups of staff are as follows. The normal *maximum* allowance for a Head of Department appointed to undertake, in addition, the duties of Vice-Principal in establishments below group 4 is £1,494. The allowance for a Head of Department appointed before 25 February 1972 to undertake, in addition, the duties of Vice-Principal in an establishment of group 4 or higher is between £1,590 and £2,307. The actual amount between these limits is at the local education authority's discretion.

(v) The Burnham Report permits the payment of allowances to Heads of Department or other appropriate staff exercising coordinating responsibilities within faculties. In some institutions faculty allowances are paid for a fixed term at the end of which they are transferred to another appropriate member of staff for another fixed term. Where departments in a group 5 or larger establishment are grouped into faculties and a Head of Department exercises coordinating responsibilities within the faculty, the local education authority may pay an allowance not exceeding £1,326. An allowance not exceeding £1,056 will be paid to the Head of Department exercising faculty duties in an establishment below group 5 where he or she received an allowance under the corresponding provisions of the 1974 Further Education Salaries Document. These kinds of arrangement have become far more commonplace in recent years as colleges have introduced matrix structures. There is no provision for such structures in the Burnham Further Education Report which makes reference only to departments. Nonetheless there are now so many such arrangements across the country that it is unlikely that further development will be restrained by any legal impediment. Not all matrix arrangements depend on the formation of faculties and there are a number of alternative organisational formats. The staff who might in a normal departmental structure have held the posts as Heads of Department based upon the grading of their departments in terms of unit totals may now find themselves paid upon a different basis since there are no departments within which unit totals may be calculated. This gives rise to interesting problems when some groupings are responsible for an overwhelming proportion of the student units numbers created and other members of staff are responsible for activities like marketing and administration. The latter posts enjoy Head of Department salaries whilst generating no student unit numbers and the former group of posts command Head of Department salaries though often at a sum less than would be achieved on the basis of the student numbers had the institution been organised in conventional departmental format.

55 **Safeguarding**

Both the Burnham Further Education and Primary and Secondary documents make provision for the safeguarding of a person's salary in certain circumstances where his or her post formerly held is lost. In such circumstances lecturers continue to be paid on the salary scale applying to the post that has been lost for as long as this is beneficial. The most common form of safeguarding arises as a result of an LEA's decision to close or to reorganise 'an educational establishment'. A loss of post which can also give rise to safeguarding, although it is now less common, may arise from the closure or reorganisation of a college of education or the issue of a direction by the Secretary of State (See **2.3** 48–55). A lecturer who loses a post in a teacher education establishment due to a direction of the Secretary of State to close or reorganise the establishment is entitled to receive a safeguarded salary if he or she moves to a new teaching post in England and Wales, provided that the post falls within the scope of the Burnham Reports. If the closure or reorganisation is not related to teacher training, the safeguarding entitlement only occurs when the lecturer moves to a new teaching job with the same local education authority. In both cases, the teacher must remain in continuous service, there being no gap between the date of termination of the lost employment and the commencement of the new employment. Lecturers may be entitled to safeguarding in new posts within the scope of the Burnham FE Salaries Report even where the previous post was in an educational establishment within the same local education authority but outside the scope of the Burnham Document. A teacher displaced from an unattached unit, the peripatetic service or home tuition service is entitled to safeguarded salary. Tutor wardens and other 'teaching' staff in teacher's centres are also entitled to safeguarded salaries if they return to a teaching post in a college following the closure or reorganisation of their centre.

56 The Burnham Committees have expressed their intentions in regard to safeguarding provisions by telling LEAs that lecturers who lose their posts or whose salaries are diminished or who would be placed on a salary scale with a lower maximum as a result of the closure or reorganisation of an educational establishment, or in any other circumstance approved by the local education authority, should be deemed for all salaries purposes to continue to hold the post which they held immediately before the closure or reorganisation etc. Section 14 of the Burnham FE Report is intended to show that a lecturer who might receive an immediate increase by virtue of the assimilation procedure on to a new salary scale with a lower maximum should *not* receive the immediate increase but should remain on the former scale and enjoy the long-term benefits of the higher salary maximum by virtue of this arrangement. The salary to be compared in order to determine whether the safeguarding should apply is the salary at the maximum of the substantive grade plus any acting allowance paid for a period in excess of two years and any other allowance paid under the Burnham Documents except an allowance for service at a Social Priority School or a School of Exceptional Difficulty. However, a lecturer in receipt of a safeguarded salary is not entitled to any new additional allowances which did not form part of the previous salary – the lecturer is entitled either to salary scale and allowances applicable to the former post or to salary scale and allowances in the new post whichever is the greater but to a mixture of both.

57 Whilst the foregoing provisions are mandatory local education authorities also have discretion to safeguard the salary of lecturers who lose their posts or whose salary would be diminished or who would be placed on a salary scale with a lower maximum in circumstances other than the closure or reorganisation of a college. This arrangement also appears in the Primary and Secondary Salaries document. Its purpose is to facilitate the redeployment of teachers from schools affected by falling pupil numbers. In the cases of further education lecturers it is intended that the provision should be of assistance to those displaced as a result of demographic changes.

58 Lecturers who would have passed through the bar point on their salary scale are in a complicated position which has required the interpretation of the Joint Secretaries of the Burnham FE Committee.

(i) *Senior Lecturers and Principal Lecturers* A former Senior Lecturer whose salary and present post is safeguarded on one or other of those scales should be allowed to pass on to the extended part of his or her safeguarded scale if during the last complete academic year before the date of the loss of post he or she satisfied the provisions concerned with responsibility for advanced work discussed in paragraph 52 above.

(ii) *Lecturer II/Senior Lecturer Transfer* Lecturers Grade II who, were it not for the loss of their post, would have been considered for progression to the Senior Lecturer Scale are assessed on their balance of advanced work and their efficiency as a Lecturer Grade II. This is complicated if it coincides with a loss of post. The local education authority may therefore apply the balance of work and efficiency criteria to the Lecturer Grade II who loses a post and becomes eligible for a safeguarded salary as though the last year of service in the lost post was the year before his or her eligibility to progress to the Senior Lecturer Scale. Alternatively, the period of three years preceding that date may be used for assessing the lecturer's levels of responsibility for advanced work if this is more favourable. In such circumstances the safeguarded salary scale will be the maximum of the Senior Lecturer Scale since the criterion for passing through the Senior Lecturer bar will already have been satisfied.

59 Certain conditions apply to the receipt and continued receipt of a safeguarded salary. These are:

(i) The lecturer must not unreasonably refuse to accept an alternative post with the employer.

(ii) Safeguarding may only be carried by a lecturer from one LEA to another where entitlement arises from the closure or reorganisation of a college of education or a direction of the Secretary of State.

(iii) The employer must approve any subsequent move to other employment but must not unreasonably withhold such approval.

(iv) The lecturer holding a post which is a fixed-term appointment and, at the time of closure, reorganisation or direction, has held that post for less than two years will not be entitled to safeguarding.

It is important to note that the safeguarding arrangement does not apply to non-teaching staff.

60 **Individual salaries: salary on first appointment**

On first appointment to the education service as a Lecturer Grade I, salary is the total of:

(i) The minimum of the scale.

(ii) Three increments if the lecturer possesses a degree or a qualification approved as a degree equivalent.

(iii) One additional increment, where the qualification in (ii) above is a first or second class Honours Degree, or a higher degree, or a qualification equivalent to such degrees.

(iv) One increment if certain teacher education qualifications such as the Standard Certificate or the Certificate in Education (Technical) are held.

(v) One increment for each year of full-time study, training or research in excess of three after the age of 18 (normally up to a maximum of three).

(vi) Increments for previous educational, industrial or professional experience after the age of 18 which, in the authority's opinion, is relevant to service as a Lecturer Grade I.

Incremental credits given for the reasons shown may not give rise to circumstances where the maximum of the scale is exceeded. The Burnham FE Committee has expressed its intention that any period of work or experience which is regarded by the LEA as relevant or equivalent (as the case may be) to teaching service should on appointment be taken *fully* into account in reckoning the incremental credit. In other words each year of such work or experience merits *one* increment. Thus, for example, a lecturer with three years two months relevant/equivalent full-time experience on appointment on 1 September is entitled to four increments on the scale on appointment. A lecturer with four years six months half-time experience on appointment on 1 September is entitled to three increments on the scale, since the half-time work is equivalent to two years three months full-time and this would give rise to a three increment entitlement.

61 Salary scales from Lecturer Grade II upwards are treated in a different way. The scales are consolidated and have no allowance for qualifications. A new appointee receives:

(i) The minimum of the scale;

(ii) Increments for previous educational, industrial or professional experience which, in the opinion of the authority, is equivalent to service as a lecturer at the appropriate level. It will be noted that in connection with Lecturers Grade I the word 'relevant' is used whilst in respect of Lecturers Grade II the word 'equivalent' is used. What is relevant is generally more easy to determine since most experience is relevant teaching in further education. Equivalent means generally that the experience was in a post which commanded the same or a higher salary than that which the lecturer would have received if he or she had been a Lecturer Grade II or higher at the time. The authority may determine a higher salary on the scale if it considers the award of extra increments appropriate. Reference is made usually to the salary of the individual before appointment.

62 **Salary on promotion**

Two methods are provided by the Burnham Salaries Document for calculating salary on promotion. The first method is that outlined in the paragraphs on the salary on first appointment. This calculation usually produces a lower figure than the second method which is to take the previous salary and add to it one and a half increments on the higher scale. Such a calculation often produces a figure between two incremental points and when this occurs the salary is rounded up. In some cases the addition of one and a half increments does not bring the total to the minimum of the new scale. Where this is so, the teacher enters the new scale at point zero. On 1 September following promotion the lecturer will receive a full increment on the new scale. However, local education authorities are entitled to place lecturers promoted from Lecturer Grade I to Lecturer Grade II on any point up to and including the sixth point of the higher scale. These provisions also apply to the appointment of former schoolteachers to the further education service.

63 **Increments**

There is a standard incremental date of 1 September. Since 1 September 1975 all teaching staff have received whole incremental points for each year of service provided they have served at least six months full-time or equivalent service in the previous year.

64 **Non-teaching staff paid on Burnham rates**

The Joint Secretaries of the Burnham FE Committee have advised that librarians, research staff and other staff who are paid on Burnham Scales 'as a matter of convenience' should be paid the appropriate increases which accrue to lecturers under the provisions of the Burnham Documents. There is considerable variation in the payment of research staff, although they are now paid on ranges within the scales negotiated in the National Joint Council. At present (1 April 1986) the scales for researchers are as follows:
Reseacher: £6060; £6321; £6582; £6843; £7104; £7371; £7641; £7908; £8196; or on a seven-point scale selected from the Lecturer II Scale.

55 **Adult education**
Lecturers in adult education establishments are included in the provisions of the Burnham Reports and will be in the provisions of the National Joint Council. A lecturer in adult education is defined as one employed as a lecturer in adult education for 50% or more of the working time, except that in the case of a Principal or Vice-Principal, as one whose responsibilities are concerned directly with adult teaching for 50% or more of the working time. An adult education establishment is that part of the adult education service of a local education authority recognised by the authority as a separate unit, irrespective of the number of centres it comprises. In the recent past some local education authorities have attempted to alter these definitions and to move certain aspects of adult education into other local authority departments. Whilst this may have the effect of reducing the part-time hourly paid rates, if those engaged are not regarded as lecturers covered by the Burnham Reports and NJC, the Burnham FE Committee consciously undertook to make arrangements for adult education of all kinds whether vocational or non-vocational and in all disciplines.

56 There are specific arrangements to deal with the unit totals in adult education since the patterns of work in adult education reflect the high proportion of part-time students and part-time lecturers. Where the unit total exceeds 250, the local authority *may* appoint staff at Senior Lecturer or Head of Department level regardless of the proportions of posts formula which is set out in paragraph 29, above. This provides for a proper management structure and for promotion prospects for adult education staff. A unit total of 250 is the level that marks off a Group II Principal from a Group I Principal. In the case of a single establishment the provision will secure at least one Senior Lecturer and may encourage local education authorities to consider instituting a departmental structure in their adult education institutions. Some institutions are spread among a number of local centres and it is normal to establish posts at 'head of centre' level and to ensure that the grading of this post takes account of the unit totals for students in the centre. Thus, if there is a unit total of more than 250 in a centre it is appropriate to ensure that there is at least one senior lecturer in the centre who may be the 'head of centre'. Where the unit total for the centre is over 400 it is appropriate to seek the establishment of at least one principal lecturer. It may be appropriate where unit totals exceed 250 for a head of department on an appropriate Head of Department Scale to be appointed instead. Vice-principals must be appointed if the unit total is over 1000 in an adult education institution. If they are appointed where the unit total is less than 160 they have a scale between 80–85% of the Principal's Scale but otherwise the normal further education scales apply.

NOTES

1 NATFHE has expressed opposition through Conference resolutions for a decade. The employers' side leader of the NJC, Mr John Pearman, made a major criticism in November 1984 in that Council. Groups like the National Bureau for Handicapped Students have argued that the system is a barrier to recognition for major work (See **3.7** 13 and 20).

2 The list is updated regularly and amendment sheets issued.

3 These factors were particularly important given the vocational character of FE and the need for staff with vocational experience.

4 It is not impossible that more local machinery will be needed. The proliferation of the MSC sponsored courses with some strong local characteristics may require

more local determination of grading. It is a process likely to become more complex as a result of the NCVQ development (see paragraph 20).

5 The development of access courses has accelerated this process.

6 The model recognises a range of protections for small HE institutions like art colleges and small teacher education institutions.

2.3 SUPERANNUATION AND PREMATURE RETIREMENT

1 The regulations for the administering of the Teachers' Superannuation Scheme are made by the Secretary of State under Section 9 of the Superannuation Act 1972. These regulations, The Teachers' Superannuation Regulations 1976 (Statutory Instrument 1976 No. 1987), therefore have the force of law. Comment on the regulations is available in leaflet form from the Department of Education and Science (DES) Pensions Branch, the address of which is given at the end of this section.

2 **Eligibility**

The scheme is compulsory for full-time teachers under the age of 55 in schools, colleges and other educational establishments maintained by local authorities or, in some cases, in receipt of government grants. Voluntary colleges within the purview of The Further Education Regulations 1975 participate in the scheme. Youth leaders, youth employment officers and educational organisers are among those in educational employment who can participate in the scheme. Many independent schools participate; they are given the status of 'accepted' schools, provided that the terms of their employment so allow.

3 Not all educational service qualifies for benefit under the scheme:

(i) A modified version of the scheme was operated in some independent schools until 30 April 1975. Service in such an 'admitted' school affects pension. Details of the effect are available in the DES leaflet, 430 Pen.

(ii) Part-time teachers who receive a proportional Burnham salary and who work regularly for a regular proportion of the week may choose whether or not to participate in the scheme. Part-time teachers paid on hourly rates are not eligible for participation.

(iii) Teachers who enter the service after the age of 55 may choose not to participate if they wish.

(iv) Contributions to the scheme cease when a teacher has completed 45 years of service; a serving teacher over 70 pays no contributions. Any service after such time does not count for pension purposes.

4 **Contributions**

Employment pensionable under the teachers' scheme is called reckonable service. 'Reckonable service' is defined in a number of ways in the regulations. It includes full-time employment as a teacher, certain kinds of part-time employment as a teacher, war service, in certain cases, and purchased added years. It also includes leave on full pay. Sick leave is included unless either the teacher has been continuously absent for more than 12 months (18 months in the case of pulmonary tuberculosis) or, he or she is not entitled to at least half pay, disregarding any reduction or refund provided for by the terms of his or her employment. Teachers in reckonable service pay contributions of 6% of this salary. Salary is the amount appropriate under the Burnham salary document and includes London and other relevant allowances. The larger part of the cost of the scheme is financed[1] by contributions made by employers. Contributions to the additional component of the state pension scheme have been lowered by the Secretary of State's decision to 'opt-out' of that arrangement. Pensioned teachers will still receive the basic pension benefit but the bulk of their income after retirement will come from the teachers' scheme. Contributions to the teachers' scheme are allowed as a deduction from income in the assessment of income tax liability. This is normally done by the employer.

5 **Repayment of contributions**

Except as indicated below, there is no automatic right to repayment. Although a teacher may leave reckonable service the entitlement to pension remains; hence, should the teacher re-enter reckonable service, pension is based on the whole period of participation in the scheme. Service does not have to be continuous. Repayment is made when a teacher reaches the age of 70 without having qualified for benefits; and to a teacher who has been out of reckonable service for three months who so elects, unless since 31 March 1972 the teacher has completed five years' reckonable service or is entitled to retirement benefits immediately on leaving reckonable service.

6 Where repayment operates it includes compound interest of 3% per year on the teachers' contributions reduced by payment in lieu of national insurance contributions which the DES has had to make to secure for the teacher a national insurance pension as if all contributions at the full rate had been paid during the relevant service period. A standard tax charge of 10% is then made.

7 **Return of contributions previously repaid**

Eligibility for this provision is limited to teachers who:

(i) Withdrew their contributions before 1 June 1973 and,

(ii) Have returned to reckonable service or external service (external service is that under relevant schemes in Scotland, Northern Ireland, Guernsey, Jersey and the Isle of Man).

The contributions, together with compound interest at 3% per annum, may be repaid by a lump sum payment; or by regular and equal instalments where the total sum, including interest, amounts to £500 or more.

Tax relief on repayment applies only where repayment is made by regular and equal instalments. Further details can be found in DES leaflet 240 Pen.

8 **Benefits: eligibility and amounts**

Application for benefit is made to the Department on Form 14 Pen; part of this form has to be completed by the employer. In order to receive benefits promptly, application should be made at least four months before they become due. Benefits consist of an annual allowance (pension) and an additional allowance (lump sum) and are paid to:

(i) A teacher aged 60 or over who has retired;

(ii) A teacher aged under 60 who, because of infirmity, has become permanently incapable of serving efficiently;

(iii) A teacher who is entitled to claim superannuation benefit under a scheme of premature retirement. These conditions are subject to a minimum service provision: the teacher must have rendered at least five years' reckonable service. The only exception is a teacher who has rendered service before and after 1 April 1972 or 6 April 1975 but was not actually in service on that date: such an individual must serve either five years from 1 April 1982 onwards, or a total of ten years.

9 Where a person possessing at least five years of reckonable service leaves the teaching service before benefits are due to be paid, the right to a pension based on the length of actual teaching service has nonetheless been established. Pension benefits will be received, on application, from the age of 60; the size of the pension will have increased under the terms of the pension increase provisions during the period between leaving service and the receipt of the pension. All periods of service are aggregated: a gap in service has no significance apart from the reduction in the length of possible reckonable service. The pension increase provisions allow for pension increases according to inflation rates, and are applicable from the age of 55.

10 Both pension and lump sum are based on the 'average salary'. The average salary is the highest for the best consecutive 365 day period of salary in the last 1095 days of reckonable service. In most cases this will mean the last year of service. Pension is calculated at 1/80 of the average salary for each year of service , A teacher with 30 years of reckonable service would receive a pension of 30/80 of the average salary. This pension is subject to income tax, and may be reduced on account of national insurance.

11 The lump sum is calculated at two rates. For each year of reckonable service from 1 October 1956, the rate is 3/80 of the average salary; the rate for each year's reckonable service before 1 October 1956 is 1/30 of the average salary. Odd days count at 1/365 of the appropriate rate for a year.

12 The maximum amount of reckonable service which can count for lump sum is 45 years but, if total service is in excess of this amount, deduction is made from the beginning of the service so that as much of the lump sum calculation can be made at the rate of 3/80 as possible.

13 **Infirmity benefits**

A teacher aged under 60 who has become permanently incapable of fulfilling duties while in reckonable service, or in the circumstances which are directly linked to ill-health which began during reckonable service, becomes eligible to pension and lump sum as indicated above. Such calculations are subject to the following forms of enhancement:

(i) Service of the last five years but less than ten years counts as double, subject to what could have been completed by age 65;

(ii) Ten to 13⅓ years reckonable service counts as 20 years, subject to what could have been completed by age 65;

(iii) More that 13⅓ years reckonable service qualifies for an addition of six and two-thirds years, subject to what could have been completed by age 60 (up to a maximum of 40 years), or, if more favourable, counts as 20 years limited by what could have been completed by the age of 65.

14 Where a teacher has served for at least one year and suffers a breakdown in health but who has not served the five year qualifying period, there is an entitlement to a short service gratuity. This gratuity, which is a single payment, is calculated as 1/12 of the average salary for each year of reckonable service. As for a normal pension, days of service are included pro rata in the calculation.

15 **Death gratuities**

Without being subject to the five year qualifying period, where a teacher dies in reckonable service, or within 12 months of leaving reckonable service because of ill-health but without having received an ill-health retirement pension, a death gratuity is paid to the teacher's estate. The gratuity is whichever is the greatest of:

(i) The salary in the best 365 day period in the final 1095 days of reckonable service;

(ii) The lump sum which would have been paid if the teacher had retired because of ill-health, including the enhancement provisions;

(iii) Repayment of the teacher's accumulated contributions with compound interest at 3% per annum.

The gratuity payment will be reduced by the sum of any benefits previously paid.

16 Where a teacher with preserved entitlement dies after having left reckonable service at some previous date, the estate receives whichever is the greater of:

(i) A lump sum without enhancement calculated by the normal method on the amount of actual service completed or

(ii) Repayment of contributions with compound interest at 3% per annum less any benefits previously paid and less half of any payment-in-lieu of national insurance contributions. This form of benefit is subject to the five year qualifying period.

17 **Dependants' benefits**

Benefits are paid to persons dependent on a teacher. The main beneficiaries are the widows and children of male teachers, but a female teacher or an unmarried male teacher may make application to the DES to nominate a financially dependent close relative to receive benefits. The conditions for nomination are:

(i) That the Department is notified of nominations while the teacher is in reckonable service;

(ii) The nominee is wholly or mainly dependent on the nominator and is: the teacher's parent; or an unmarried descendant of either of the teacher's parents; or the teacher's widowed stepmother or stepfather; or any unmarried descendant of the deceased wife of a man teacher; or the husband of a woman teacher.

Nomination becomes void when the Department receives written notice of revocation, when the nominee dies or marries, when the nominee is a child and become of age, and, where the teacher is a man, on his marriage.

18 Automatic provision for dependants' benefits was made only on 1 April 1972. Before this date there was a voluntary scheme and both when that scheme and the 1972 improvements were instituted it was possible for a teacher to submit an earlier superannuation record by undertaking to pay additional contributions for dependants' benefit purposes. The main provision of the dependants' scheme may be summarised as follows for someone who has all years of reckonable service covered for dependants' benefit purposes:

(i) Where a male teacher dies after retirement, the widow is entitled to one half of his pension;

(ii) Where a male teacher dies in service, the widow is entitled to one-half of the ill-health retirement pension he would have received had his health broken down (enhancement therefore is included);

(iii) Where there is one dependent child, the fractions referred to above become three-quarters; the whole pension is awarded where there are two or more dependent children;

(iv) Where there is no spouse, the pension for one child is one-third and the pension for two or more children is two-thirds of the teacher's pension.

A child is defined as: a child of the teacher, legitimate or illegitimate, or is an adopted or accepted member of the family, wholly or mainly dependent, either under 17 or if over receiving full-time education or a specified two year training course, and who is not married or receiving a disqualifying income.

19 Where a part of the teacher's reckonable service is not applicable for dependants' purposes the benefits under (i), (ii) and (iii) above are calculated according to the proportion of service which has been covered for these purposes. Calculation of reckonable service depends for the purpose upon whether voluntary contributions were made to the widows and orphans scheme before April 1972 and/or the number of years bought into that scheme.

20 **Short-term pensions**

Where a male teacher who has qualified for the above benefit dies, the widow will receive, for the first three months after his death, the salary or pension he was receiving rather than the lower pension which she will ultimately receive.

21 If there is no entitlement to dependants' benefits, the period over which the salary is paid to the widow is increased to four and one half months if there is one dependent child, and to six months if there are two or more dependent children. If there is no widow, the period is two months for one dependent child and four months for two or more dependent children. No subsequent benefits are payable in these cases. Similar payments are made in respect of dependants nominated under paragraph 19 above, where the teacher dies without sufficient qualifying service for a dependant's pension.

22 **Modification**

Teachers who entered service from 1 July 1948 onwards, together with those in service on that date who opted accordingly, paid contributions very slightly less than 6% up until 31 March 1980 and consequently have their pension reduced. The reduction is never greater than £67.75 per year. The technicality, known as 'modification', derives from previous national insurance arrangements.

23 **Absence from service**

A teacher who leaves reckonable service for a period may be allowed to continue to pay employer's and employee's contributions for up to three years, and up to six years in respect of certain educational employment outside the United Kingdom. Application must be made within three months of leaving service, or six months in the case of employment outside the UK.

24 **Pensioners returning to service**

If a retired teacher in receipt of a pension decides to return to full-time reckonable service the pension will be either reduced or suspended according to the amount of the new salary received. A comparison is made of the earnings from the re-employment with the salary of reference[2]. If the new earnings exceed the salary of reference, the pension is suspended. If this is not so, the pension is abated so that it does not exceed the difference between the salary of reference and the new earnings. If the new earnings and the pension are together less than the salary of reference, payment of the pension is not affected.

25 If the re-employment is as a part-time teacher (i.e. an engagement to teach regularly for part only of each day or week or as a relief teacher) the pension

may be affected if the new earnings are paid out of public funds. If, in any pension quarter, the earnings are less than the difference between one quarter of the teacher's annual pension (as increased by the pension increase provisions) and one quarter of the salary of reference (similarly increased), the payment of his or her pension will be unaffected. However, if in any pension quarter, the earnings are more than the difference between one quarter of the annual pension and one quarter of the salary of reference, the quarter's pensions is reduced by the amount of the excess. The phrase 'pension quarter' means either each quarter commencing from the teacher's birthday or the conventional quarter the first day of which starts on 1 January of any year.

26 The arrangements described in paragraph 25 above, apply also to other types of re-employment, the earnings from which are paid out of public funds, if the employment could be pensionable (if it were full-time) under the teachers' superannuation scheme. This means that most non-teaching re-employment does not affect the payment of pension. Also, some types of teaching are exempted, for example, part-time teaching in an independent school (since, even though such teaching if done full-time could be reckonable, the earnings do not come from public funds).

27 Paragraphs 24–26 above deal with the abatement of pension when a teacher takes up a full-time re-employment after he or she has commenced the receipt of a pension. We now turn to look at a different pension effect of re-employment: the further pension benefit which might be obtained from that employment.

28 Re-employment in teaching is pensionable and involves the deduction of contributions in most cases. The exceptions are:

(i) Where the teacher is over 70 or reaches this age during the re-employment, in which case the time spent over 70 is not pensionable;

(ii) Where the teacher has 45 years' reckonable service or achieves this during the re-employment, in which case the time in excess of 45 years' total service is not pensionable.

In other cases, the pension position of someone ceasing re-employment is as follows. If the average salary is equal to or higher than that on which the benefits were originally calculated, pension and lump sum will be calculated on the new total of service. If the new average salary is less than that on which the original benefits were calculated, the original pension is resumed and a separate pension and lump sum is awarded in respect of the re-employment. None of the provisions described in this paragraph apply to re-employment in part-time teaching, except in the case where re-employment is of an individual who is in receipt of an infirmity pension.

29 **War service**

The war service of those who served in the Armed Forces of the Crown may be reckonable for pension purposes under certain conditions. Briefly, these are:

(i) The teacher must have been engaged in contributory teaching service which he or she left to join the Forces; or

(ii) The teacher must have completed a teacher training college course (but not taken up his or her teaching post) prior to joining the Forces; or

(iii) The teacher must have left such a course to join the Forces; or

(iv) The teacher must have been registered for such a course but could not take up his or her place due to joining the Forces.

(v) Unless the teacher earned more by way of Forces pay than he or she would have done as a teacher, the service is counted free.

(vi) The period eligible for consideration as 'war service' is that between September 1939 and the end of March 1949. There is another scheme for the part coverage of war service which provides for those who after war service entered reckonable service for the first time before July 1950. This scheme also applies to those entering reckonable service later than this on completion of an emergency training course, a course in respect of which grants were paid to him or her under the Ministry of Education (Further Education and Training) Grant Regulations 1946 (or the equivalent Scottish Scheme), or any other approved course of training providing it was begun before July 1950. Those who began the final year of a four year combined degree/teacher training course before November 1950 are also covered. Male teachers who satisfy these qualifications and who served in the Armed Forces, the Merchant Navy, the Mercantile Marine or specific parts of the Palestine Police Force at any time during World War Two (3 September 1939–1 April 1949) are able to reckon one half of their service for pension purposes. Similarly, women who satisfy the qualifications and who served at any one time in the same period in one of a large variety of women's services (e.g. the Queen Alexandra's Royal Naval Nursing Service) are also able to reckon one half of the service for pension purposes.

30 **Past added years**

The purchase of past added years ('buying-in') is the arrangement by which a teacher may fill a gap in a superannuation record by purchasing the required number of years service at full cost. The main restrictions on the scheme are that the period in question must be when the teacher was over the age of 20, that it was not superannuable in any other scheme and that it relates only to gaps in the service before age 60. Employers make no contributions to the purchase of the added years; the intent of the buying-in tables is that they should provide 'value for money'. However, as the 'value for money' consideration does not take into account the operation of the pension increase provisions election to purchase added years may be found by some generally to be beneficial. The four methods of buying-in are:

(i) The payment of between 1% and 9% of salary until the payment period has been completed. These periodic payments will attract tax relief.

(ii) The payment of a lump sum, but this payment does not attract tax relief. Associate Lecturers may only use this method.

(iii) The payment of fixed instalment over a period of between five and ten years. This method avoids the linking of payments to a progressively higher salary as in the first method, and the whole of the payments attract tax relief. However, an election under this method would not take effect until 1 October following acceptance of the election.

(iv) A lump sum payment deducted from the retirement lump sum. This method may only be used by some people also using method (i), above.

Contributions for all superannuation purposes, including the purchase of added years, must be kept within the Inland Revenue limits concerning levels of pension contributions. This limits pension contributions to 15% of salary. Elections can be made using form 375 Pen. NATFHE advises that teachers who elect to purchase added years by method A in that leaflet declare an intent to use method (iv) when they make their election.

31 **Allocation of pensions**

Allocation of pensions may be made only by a retiring teacher, or a teacher over the age of 60 whose length of service qualifies for retirement benefits but who does not wish to retire immediately. Allocation may be made in addition to the normal family benefit provision. Before any allocation is allowed the applicant must satisfy the Department's conditions regarding good health. There are two forms of allocation:

(i) An allocation which would ensure to the beneficiary a pension payable from the date of death of the allocator;

(ii) An allocation made in favour of the spouse only which provides:
An annuity payable from the date of commencement of the pension (this annuity is payable only during the lifetime of the beneficiary and the allocator and ceases on his or her death) together with:
A pension of double the amount of this annuity, payable to the beneficiary after the death of the allocator.

Allocation in favour of a spouse may be made under either option, but provision for another person may only be made under the first option. In making any decision to allocate, it is highly important to note that under either option, if the beneficiary dies first, the pension of the allocator will continue to be reduced by the amount allocated (or will be reduced by the amount allocated when the pension is eventually put into payment).

32 It is not possible to allocate more than one third of the gross pension or make an allocation of a size which would exceed the balance of the beneficiary's pension against that of the allocator. Both the pensions of allocator and beneficiary remain subject to income tax, but only to such proportions as they receive. The pension increase provisions apply similarly here. As this is a somewhat complex matter, a person considering the allocation of pension should consult DES advisory leaflet 207 Pen.

33 **Transferability**

Provision for transferability should, in time, reduce substantially the need for purchase for added years. Where a person enters teaching service from another superannuation scheme, the teachers' scheme is prepared to accept from the administrators of that scheme a transfer value; similarly, the teachers' scheme is usually prepared to offer reciprocal arrangements. It must not be assumed that such a transfer will be on a year for year basis, since the transfer will be governed by the benefits and rules of the respective schemes. However, transfers between public sector schemes will normally be on a broadly comparable basis.

34 **Premature retirement**

Two circumstances can stimulate a teacher's right to gain pension and lump sum benefit before reaching normal retirement age or retiring through incapacity. Where a teacher ceases to be employed in reckonable service having attained the age of 50 provided that the service was not terminated by incapacity, then that individual is eligible to receive the normal superannuation allowances if the employer gives written notice to the Secretary of State that the employment was terminated by:

(i) The reason of redundancy, or

(ii) In the interests of the efficient discharge of the employer's functions.

35 A person at the time of redundancy aged under 50 does not qualify for the scheme, even if on attaining the age of 50 that person has not been employed

since their loss of employment. A teacher aged, for example, 49 at the time of her or his loss of employment would not qualify for the payment of superannuation allowances until the minimum retirement age of 60. If benefits are not claimed by an eligible individual, then other forms of public pension compensation received (for example, under the Colleges of Education (Compensation) Regulations) could be reduced by the sums to which the individual is eligible, whether they have been claimed or not.

36 Application for superannuation allowances is made in the usual way on Form 14 Pen at least four months before the allowances are due to be paid. In this instance, however, the employer must certify on the form that the reason for the termination of reckonable service was either because of redundancy or in the efficient exercise of the employer's functions.

37 **Compensation for premature retirement**

In parallel to the regulations allowing premature retirement are regulations which allow compensation to be paid at the time of the early retirement. These regulations apply to full-time teachers of at least five years' reckonable service, subject to the conditions set out below. Part-time teachers qualify only if their posts are superannuable under the Teachers' Superannuation Scheme and they have elected that they be so. Teaching posts are specified as:

(i) In a school; or
(ii) A maintained or voluntary establishment of further education; or
(iii) A polytechnic wholly assisted by a local education authority; or
(iv) An opting direct grant school.

Employment by a local education authority, or by a local authority otherwise than in one of the above capacities, are also eligible but the person must nonetheless be subject to the Teachers' Superannuation Regulations. Further conditions are:

(v) That on or after 1 April 1976 the individual suffered a loss of employment certified to the Secretary of State by the employer to be due to redundancy or the efficient discharge of the employer's functions.
(vi) At the date of the termination of employment, the age of 50 but not the age of 65 had been attained; and
(vii) The teacher is not eligible for compensation under local government schemes or schemes made under Sections 1 or 24 of the Superannuation Act 1972.

38 Condition (vi) means that whereas the Teachers' Superannuation (Amendment) Regulations lower the age at which retirement is possible to between age 50 and 60, the compensation regulations allow for the consideration for compensation of a teacher aged in excess of the normal minimum retiring age. Thus a teacher aged, for example, 63 could qualify for a compensation payment.

39 **Enhancement**

The compensating authority has the discretionary power to credit the eligible teacher with an additional period of service. The amount of such service awarded is again discretionary, subject to a maximum limit. The limit of such service will be the shortest of:

(i) A period of ten years;
(ii) A period equivalent to the teacher's reckonable service;
(iii) A period which, when added to reckonable service, does not in aggregate exceed 40 years;

(iv) A period equal to the time between ceasing to hold the terminal employment and reaching the age of 65.

The amount of compensation when aggregated with accrued pension together with any other occupational pension payment must not exceed 50% of the teacher's average salary at retirement. Where the aggregate does exceed this figure, the authority must reduce the enhancement accordingly. Payments generated by enhancement, including increases in those payments under the pension increase provisions, will be borne directly by the compensating authority (see above paragraph 19) and not the superannuation fund. However these payments are 90% poolable under regulations made in 1985 (Statutory Instrument No. 1985 2030).

40 **Annual allowance and lump sum: compensation**

While the compensation lump sum and pension received are enhanced forms of the benefits usual under the teachers' scheme, because of the years of service which an authority can add they are described as compensation. Annual compensation is calculated in the same way as the annual allowance (pension) in respect of accrued service. The annual compensation (pension) will be 1/180th of the average salary in respect of each year of compensation. As usual, this sum is subject to taxation. Lump sum compensation (additional allowance) will be 3/80ths of the average salary in respect of each year of compensation.

41 If an employing authority is prepared to award a teacher, retiring on grounds of redundancy, enhancement in excess of $6\frac{2}{3}$, there is a reduction in the compensation lump sum amounting to 30% of the redundancy payment for each year of enhancement in excess of $6\frac{2}{3}$ years. Accordingly, if a teacher receives the maximum ten years' enhancement, the compensation lump sum would be reduced by the whole of the redundancy payment. In a few cases, the compensation lump sum may not be sufficient to meet that deduction. In such circumstances the compensation pension would suffer an actuarial reduction to cover the excess. This is dealt with in more detail in paragraph 46 below.

42 **Short term compensation**

Where a teacher's widow or widower is entitled to a short term pension under the Teachers' Superannuation Regulations, then under the Teachers' (Compensation for Premature Retirement) Regulations that person receives for three months following the day of the death of the teacher a short term compensation payment. This payment will be an annual rate equal to the annual compensation payable to the teacher before his or her death.

43 **Dependant's benefits**

Where a teacher dies leaving a widow or widower entitled to a pension under the Superannuation Regulations, then that beneficiary will be entitled to receive long term compensation of one half of the annual compensation paid to the teacher before death. No account is taken here of any reduction in, or suspension of compensation which may have occurred. If, prior to death, the teacher had been re-employed to such an extent that the compensation pension ceased to be payable, then the payment to the widow will be without compensation enhancement: the pension received will be calculated solely in accordance with the Superannuation Regulations. The beneficiary is entitled to one half of the ill-health retirement pension the teacher would have received had a breakdown in health been suffered (including therefore the enhancement benefit of the ill-health scheme).

44 Where there is one dependent child, three quarters of the annual compensation of the deceased is awarded. The whole of the annual compensation is awarded where there are two or more dependent children. Where there is no surviving widow or widower, the benefits are: one-third of the annual compensation for one child and two-thirds for two or more children. Where the deceased teacher had been re-employed, these benefits are calculated on the basis of compensation received during re-employment.

45 These benefits are payable until the death of the beneficiary or, in the case of a child, on ceasing to be a child within the meaning of the Superannuation Regulations. Eligibility for payment commences at the time of the cessation of short term compensation, if applicable or on the day after the date of death. Where the widow or widower remarries then unless the compensatory authority directs otherwise, the whole compensation shall cease to be payable, except that: if the remarried widow has reached pensionable age, her annual compensation will be restored but reduced where, when added to the pension payable under the Superannuation Regulations, it exceeds her guaranteed minimum pension. The compensatory authority also has the discretion to reinstate the compensation pension upon the termination of the recipient's marriage. These conditions relating to remarriage apply similarly to cohabitation. If cohabitation ceases or the remarriage is terminated, compensation becomes payable again should the Secretary of State so direct.

46 **Adjustment and reduction of compensation**

The regulations governing compensation for redundancy and premature retirement provide that adjustments may be made to certain payment under the TSS on account of other compensation payments. The main provisions are:

(i) If a teacher is credited with an additional period of service of more than $6\frac{2}{3}$ years and he or she is also entitled to a redundancy payment in respect of the loss of a former employment the compensation will be reduced to offset the amount of the redundancy payment.

(ii) Similarly, the lump sum compensation may be reduced if the teacher has received other lump sum payments by way of compensation for the loss of a former employment.

(iii) If a teacher is receiving relevant periodic payments by way of compensation for loss of a former employment, the annual compensation payable under the TSS provision will be reduced or suspended.

47 If as a result of re-employment in reckonable service, the aggregate of the teacher's reckonable service used initially in calculating the accrued pension and the compensation, together with the number of years spent in re-employment, exceeds the number of years the teacher would have been able to reckon if he or she had remained in reckonable service up to age 65, there will be a reduction in the compensation pension to offset the additional service used in recalculating the accrued pension. If there is no excess, the accrued pension would be recalculated in the same way as described for teachers who retire in the ordinary way, and the compensation pension would not be reduced.

48 **Other Schemes of Compensation**

From time to time the Government has introduced other schemes of compensation for the loss of office caused by particular factors. A short lived scheme enabling staff between 40 and 49 who lost their posts due to a reduction in higher education directed by the Secretary of State, existed for the years between 25 July 1983 and 1 September 1985. It was used hardly at all because, most commentators believe, the levels of compensation were unattractive. The scheme allowed compensating authorities to enhance the redundancy payment up to maximum limits of (a) four weeks pay for each year of employment which consisted wholly of weeks in which the employee was not below the age of 41, and (b) two weeks pay for each year of employment not covered by (a). A related set of provisions (which continue) enable teachers of any age who are made redundant and who are not offered suitable alternative employment to have continuous service with public sector bodies counted for redundancy payment calculations up to a maximum of 25 years. Normally redundancy payments are calculated on the basis of years of employment with the employer making the redundancy.

49 Another shortlived scheme of compensation but one which was more widely used was the College of Education (Compensation) Regulations, popularly known as 'Crombie'. This scheme is dealt with in detail in the 1980 edition of *College Administration* (Waitt 1980, **11.5**, and See **1.3** 68). This scheme applied to staff who lost their employment or suffered a loss or diminution of emoluments due to a direction of the Secretary of State concerning intakes to initial teacher training courses. Three types of compensation – resettlement, long-term and retirement – were provided by the scheme. Resettlement compensation was, in fact, an enhanced lump sum payment; long-term compensation sought to compensate for loss or reduction in income, and retirement compensation in pension benefit. To achieve any of these a number of qualifying conditions had to be satisfied. For example, the offer of a 'reasonable comparable' job would rule an individual out of benefit in the case of long-term or retirement compensation. This was also so for resettlement compensation and, in addition, in this case the offer of suitable employment involving substantially the same duties and in the same locality, would also disqualify the teacher from benefit. Since no interpretation of these terms appeared in the regulations they became a source of much litigation with industrial tribunals, and on occasion the High Court, being asked to interpret 'reasonably comparability' between jobs and whether or not one involved 'substantially the same duties' as another.

50 Similarly, many cases arose in which tribunals were asked to decide whether or not a loss of employment was 'attributable' to a direction made some years previously by the Secretary of State. The cases of those on temporary contracts were particularly fraught since they raised the question, when their period ran out, of whether or not a loss of employment had occurred at all. Similarly, staff who had residential emoluments found that it was often necessary to go to industrial tribunals to have their value determined. Again, compensated staff who took on other work found the regulations far from clear about the effect of this on their compensation payments.

51 The Secretary of State amended the regulations, effectively limiting their life. The amendment provided that only those whose employments were lost or emoluments reduced due to directions (on teacher training intakes) made between 1 August 1975 and 1 September 1981 would qualify to be considered for Crombie compensation. In spite of this three issues have continued to haunt the compensation authorities and tribunals. These are dealt with below.

52 In the 1980s some teachers working in colleges of education and other institutions performing teacher training have lost their employment often because of

a reduction in the size of the higher education workforce in their areas. If the immediate cause of the loss was not a direction (on teacher training intakes) made by the Secretary of State, could the loss nevertheless be said to be attributable to a direction made between the key years of 1975 and 1981? Some early Crombie cases and cases under similar regulations had wrestled with the meaning of 'attributable'. In Tuck and Others v National Freight Corporation[3], Lord Wilberforce had said: 'There remains the question of proper attributability which, as in all questions relating to causation and similar concepts, is one of considerable difficulty. I think that two things can be said. First, the expression is not identical with 'caused by'. Secondly, it is not identical with having (the relevant event as) a sine qua non. There must be a nexus or linkage less exclusive than the one but stronger than the other. If there is no causal link whatever between the event and the worsening, if the latter is caused exclusively by something else, the claimant does not succeed.' In a case brought under the Crombie regulations, Pearson v Kent (QBD, 12 February 1979), Mr Justice Forbes had followed suit saying 'it must be a cause: there must, in other words, be no break in the chain of causation. It need not be the proximate cause or the only cause. As long as it can be said to be one of the causes, then whatever follows can be said to be 'attributable'.

53 These definitions of attributable set a number of hares running. For example, could a person claim compensation for a redundancy from non-teacher education employment if the reason for seeking and acquiring such employment was the actual or envisaged loss of employment that an original direction might cause? The information booklet *Redundancies of Teaching and Non Teaching Staff in Colleges and Departments of Education* (LACSAB 1978) comments on this point in some detail: 'It can be concluded that a claimant who seeks to discharge the burden on him to show that his loss of employment, or diminution of emoluments, occurring sometime after the material date . . . was attributable . . . to the original direction of the Secretary of State can be required to produce evidence to prove that the direction contributed to the existence of the situation which resulted that, for example, in the case of a member of staff redeployed from teacher training to another department of a polytechnic, a reduction in student numbers which later brought about his redundancy in his new department would not have occurred but for the direction . . . As the years pass, any chances of such a member of staff successfully establishing that his dismissal on grounds of redundancy from the post in which he was redeployed was attributable to the original direction of the Secretary of State becomes even more remote.'

54 In reality the limits on the meaning of attributability have been faced by a number of tribunals. Perhaps the most significant is the case of Collinge and Allen v DES (1986 London 2902/86). They were both employed at Goldsmiths' College and lost their posts in 1985. It was argued successfully for the applicants that the cumulative effect of directions made in 1979 and 1980 was that the college restructured its courses on a temporary basis and that whilst the immediate loss of employment was due to the cessation of these temporary arrangements the root cause was the directions that had led to the arrangements being made in the first place. Similarly, in Breach v DES (1986, London, 29618/85) a redundancy made on 31 August 1985 was found to be attributable to a direction.

55 A second ghost of the Crombie regulations has been the requirement on those receiving long-term compensation to seek suitable employment. In their

advice on this subject the Local Authorities Conditions of Service Advisory Board (LACSAB) advised LEAs on the policy they might adopt in relation to this requirement. LACSAB quotes one compensating authority as accepting evidence of applications for three posts as acceptable for the purposes of review. This, LACSAB states, 'is not unreasonable, bearing in mind the state of the labour market and that reviews occur every six months in the first two years, but it cannot be recommended as a policy to be adopted generally by compensating authorities' LACSAB suggests that the following factors are also relevant:

(i) The age of claimant (those below 50 are expected to make strenuous efforts to obtain suitable employment, and it is acknowledged that for those over 60 the chances of such efforts being successful are remote);
(ii) The health of the individual, and
(iii) The evidence provided by the claimant of effort to find suitable employment.

56 LACSAB puts some store by an industrial tribunal decision on the Local Government Compensation Regulations, in which there is a similar power vested in compensating authorities to reduce long term compensation on account of the failure of the claimant to seek suitable employment. In this case Maude v East Devon County Council (1976 Exeter, 24223/76), Mr Maude, a 49 year old claimant, was appealing against a decision to reduce long term compensation from £1,355 to £678 per annum on account of the fact that he had applied for only seven posts between 1974 and 1976. There was a ten month period during this time when no application had been made. However, Mr Maude had been ill from April until November 1974 and he also showed that he would be penalised if he sold his house to facilitate a move since he had undertaken not to sell it for five years as part of a discount purchase arrangement he had made in 1973. The tribunal reached a compromise decision, reducing the long term compensation to £1,221 and not to the £678 the Council had intended. It is hard to say, as LACSAB recognises, what inferences can be drawn from this case in respect of college staff. The more recent cases of Weaver v Kent County Council (1985 Ashford, 30780/84) shows the need for compensating authorities to apply the two year limit on the review period precisely. The decision to withdraw Mr Weaver's long-term compensation was overruled by the tribunal because the review was not made by the county council within two years of the decision to award compensation.

57 Finally, the Leeds County Council v Pomfret (QBD, 21 October 1982 (1983) p 674) case heard in July 1982 in the High Court gives directions to compensating authorities in one aspect of the treatment of residential enrolments. Ms Pomfret had persuaded a tribunal that the money value of the flat and other allowances with which she had been provided should be increased to take into account basic rate taxation. The county council appealed unsuccessfully to the High Court.

58 **Personal Pension Plans**

As a result of provisions in the Social Security Act 1986 from January 1988 employees will be able to opt out of the Teachers' Superannuation Scheme, or out of the State Earnings Related Pensions Scheme (SERPS) if they take out an approved Personal Pension Plan. These are sometimes known as 'portable pensions' and a variety of financial institutions are preparing to sell them. The minimum contribution which must be paid to a Personal Pension Plan is 5.75% of salary falling within national insurance contribution limits and a

2.15% share falls to the employee, the balance to the employers. 5.75% is about one third of the total contribution invested in a good 'company' pension scheme. The figure is equivalent to the contracting out rebates on national insurance.

59 Personal Pensions Plans are tax-free savings accounts which offer a restricted set of pensions benefits available on retirement. These are restricted by the IR Regulations to prevent tax avoidance. As noted above, they are restricted compared with good 'company' schemes and the TSS. Nonetheless, they are likely to be marketed on the basis of lower contributions. Some marketing finance companies are planning telephone sales campaigns where a 'quotation' will be given on benefits but will not be guaranteed - they are no more than a guess about levels of inflation and performance in the securities markets are periods of up to three decades. United States experience suggests that these guesses are based on the assumption that every aspect of finance can do no other than prosper.

60 Naturally, such quotations reflect a high level of risk. If a lecturer dies before retirement (actuarially, 25% of people now under 30 in employment will), the benefits will be poor, based on accumulated investment at the time of death. If inflation is high, and particularly if lecturers' salaries do not keep pace, the out-turn value of the pension could be disastrously low. Thus, despite some criticisms of the TSS, there appears to be little doubt that it is a great deal better than proposed personal pension plans. The greatest threat to the TSS would be if significant numbers of younger teachers (primary, secondary, further and higher) opted out as this would lead to a decline and make it significantly more difficult to negotiate or discuss increases in benefit.

61 Individuals, then, will need to take account of the following factors. First, the TSS pension is index linked and the replacement schemes cannot be so linked. Second, the personal pension plans cannot be guaranteed and nobody will be able to tell in advance what levels of benefits will actually mature. Third, for these reasons, it is not possible to plan income on retirement with a personal pension plan, though such planning is entirely practicable in respect of the TSS. That is not to say that some personal pension plan schemes may not do very well and exceed the estimates of performance, but this will be a matter of chance and incalculable in advance.

NOTES

1 The scheme operates on the basis of a notional fund and money, as such, is not collected into a real fund. There has for long been a good deal of controversy about the funding of the scheme: see, for example, Peter Knight, 'Pay Now – Live Later'. *The Technical Journal*, December 1975. pp 6–7.

2 The basic salary of reference is the highest annual rate of salary received during the last three years of pensionable service prior to retirement. In most cases it will be the rate in payment at retirement.

3 The full judgment can be found in Tuck, Moody and Wray v National Freight Corporation, House of Lords, 23rd November 1978, ICR (1979), p 123.

FURTHER READING

Teachers Superannuation (War Service) Act 1939 HMSO
Pensions (Increase) Act 1974 HMSO
The Pensions Increase (Teachers) Regulations 1974. Statutory Instrument No. 1974 831. HMSO
Colleges of Education (Compensation) Regulations 1975 Statutory Instrument No. 1975 1092. HMSO
The Further Education Regulations 1975 Statutory Instrument No. 1975 1074, HMSO
The Teachers' Superannuation Regulations 1976, Statutory Instruments No. 1976 1987, HMSO
The Teachers' Superannuation (Amendment) Regulations 1978, Statutory Instrument No. 1978 422. HMSO
Colleges of Education (Compensation) (Amendment) Regulations 1981, Statutory Instrument No. 1981 1088. HMSO
Teachers' Compensation for Redundancy and Premature Retirement) Regulations 1985, Statutory Instruments No. 1985 1181. HMSO
DES publications
Teachers' Superannuation – England and Wales – Age and Early Retirements Benefit – A Guide. DES Leaflet
Teachers' Superannuation – England and Wales – Infirmity Pensions – A Guide. DES Leaflet
Teachers' Superannuation Scheme – A Guide to Presentation and Transfer. DES Leaflet

These and other useful leaflets can be obtained from DES Pensions Branch, Mowden Hall, Staindrop Road, Darlington, Co Durham
Re-employment of Retired Teachers – Effect on Age Pensions, DES Leaflet 192 Pen
A Guide to Teachers' Superannuation, DES Leaflet 199 Pen
Allocation of Pension, DES Leaflet 207 Pen
Teachers' Superannuation: Return of contributions previously repaid. DES Leaflet 240 Pen
The Teachers' Superannuation Scheme – Past Added Years, DES Leaflet 374 Pen
Teachers' Superannuation Regulations: Repayment of Contributions, DES Leaflet 381 Pen
Teachers' Superannuation Regulations: Teachers from Overseas, DES Leaflet 425 Pen
Service in Independent Schools Admitted to the Special Superannuation Arrangements of the Teachers' Superannuation Regulations, DES Leaflet 430 Pen
Teachers' Superannuation Regulations (Death: General Information), DES Leaflet 450A Pen
Redundancies of Teaching and Non-Teaching Staff in Colleges and Departments of Education, A LACSAB Information Booklet, 1978

2.4 EMPLOYMENT LAW

1 This chapter does not intend to provide an exhaustive guide to employment law. Detailed comment on the law in practice and its significance for management is provided in the *Encyclopaedia of Employment Law and Practice* Walton, Annual. Helpful information is also to be found in the guides published by the Department of Employment, the Equal Opportunities Commission, and the Commission for Racial Equality. This section is intended to outline those provisions of the employment protection and related legislation relevant to college administrators.

2 **Advertisement of posts**

The advertisement will usually include a summary job description and the salary range, with a more detailed job description being sent later to prospective applicants. It is important to ensure that nothing in the advertisement or the job description can be construed as implying an intention to discriminate on grounds of sex, marital status, or race. Under the relevant Acts: the Sex Discrimination Acts 1975 and 1986 and the Race Relations Act 1976, it is unlawful to publish or cause to be published an advertisement which indicates an intention to discriminate on grounds of sex, marital status, or race, except where one or other of the *genuine occupational qualifications* specified in the Acts applies to the post. Examples of genuine occupational qualifications are:

(i) Where a person of a particular sex should hold the post because of considerations of decency or privacy; or

(ii) Where the holder of the job will provide individuals with personal services promoting their welfare and those services can most effectively be provided by a man (or by a woman, as the case may be) or by a person of a particular racial group.

Advertisements and job descriptions frequently contain statements that the employer is an equal opportunity employer.

3 **Unlawful discrimination in selection for employment, promotion, etc.**

The Sex Discrimination Acts (see **1.2** Appendix 3) and the Race Relations Act (see **1.2** Appendix 2) make it unlawful at any stage of the selection process to discriminate on grounds of sex, marital status, or race:

(i) In the arrangements made for determining who should be offered a post;

(ii) In the terms offered; or

(iii) By refusing or deliberately omitting, on one or other of those grounds, to offer the person the post.

Thus the design of application forms, the process of short-listing, the conduct of the interview, and the method of selection must all be free of bias relating to sex, marital status, and race.

4 An unsuccessful job applicant may complain that he or she has been unlawfully discriminated against, either directly or indirectly. Direct discrimination means treating a person less favourably because of their sex, marital status, or race. Indirect discrimination means applying a requirement or condition which may exclude a person on one or other of those grounds. The only defence to a complaint of indirect discrimination is for management to show that the requirement or condition (e.g. experience of a certain type) was justi-

fiable irrespective of the sex, marital status, or race of the individual. In practice this can be a difficult justification to prove.

5 It is unlawful to discriminate, directly or indirectly, on grounds of sex, marital status, or race against persons already in post:

(i) In the way access to opportunities for promotion, transfer or training, or to any other benefits, facilities or services, is provided, or by a refusal or deliberate omission to afford access to them; or

(ii) by dismissing the person, or subjecting him or her to any other detriment.

6 Unlawful discrimination under the Acts may also occur if a person is victimised for taking proceedings, giving evidence or information, or alleging that discrimination has occurred, provided that the person has not made a false allegation not in good faith.

7 The Acts provide an aggrieved person seeking to complain of unlawful discrimination with a right to question the employer or manager. Statutory questionnaire forms are available for this purpose. The questions and answers are admissible in evidence before an industrial tribunal if the complainant pursues the matter that far. In such a case the tribunal is entitled to draw an inference from an unsatisfactory reply by management, or from a failure to reply, that unlawful discrimination has occurred.

8 When an allegation of unlawful discrimination on grounds of sex, marital status or race is heard by an industrial tribunal, management, if contesting the case, is expected to show by persuasive evidence that discrimination on the ground alleged has not occurred.

9 **Contracts of employment**

A contract of employment (other than a contract of apprenticeship) does not have to be in writing, and rarely is. The contract is formed by the original words of the engagement – the offer and acceptance of the post. Its *performance* begins when the employee starts work.

10 Part I of the Employment Protection (Consolidation) Act 1978 required the employer to provide the employee with a written statement of the main terms and conditions of employment within 13 weeks of starting work. Often referred to as 'the contract', this document is not a contract of employment, but only confirmation of the main terms of the contract. In some cases it may not even be conclusive evidence of the terms of the contract. It is therefore important that the offer of the job should be expressed in sufficient detail for the person receiving the offer to be clear at that stage about the main terms and conditions relating to it. If, however, a conditional offer of an appointment is made and accepted (e.g. a verbal offer explained as being subject to the issue of a formal offer in writing and its written acceptance by the applicant), the contract may not be held to have been entered into.

11 Much, if not all, of the information to be included in the written statement can be provided in the job offer. If this is done, the document in which it is set out becomes a contractual document once the terms are accepted by the individual. The law requires the written statement to include the following information, or to refer the employee to a document which he or she has reasonable

opportunities of reading in the course of employment or which is made reasonably accessible in some other way:

(i) The names of the employer and the employee, the date of commencement of the employment and, if any employment with a previous employer counts towards the period of continuous employment under the current contract, the date on which the employee's period of continuous employment began;

(ii) The scale or rate of remuneration, or the method of calculating it, and the intervals at which it is paid;

(iii) *Any* terms and conditions relating to hours of work; holiday entitlement (including public holidays); holiday pay; entitlement to accrued holiday pay on the termination of employment; incapacity for work due to sickness or injury; sick pay; and pensions and pension schemes (except where employees are covered by statutory schemes and where employers are already obliged by law to provide information), and whether a contracting-out certificate is in force for the employment;

(iv) The length of notice which the employee is obliged to give and entitled to receive, or, in the case of a fixed term contract, the date of expiry of the contract;

(v) The tile of the job which the employee is employed to do;

(vi) A note specifying any disciplinary rules applicable to the employee, and – by description or otherwise – a person to whom the employee can apply if he or she is dissatisfied with any disciplinary decision relating to him or her, and explaining any further steps available to the employee;

(vii) A note specifying, by description or otherwise, a person to whom the employee can apply for the purpose of seeking redress of any grievance relating to his or her employment, and the further steps consequent upon any such application.

12 The information to be given under (iii) above must relate to the terms of employment applying at a date not more than one week before the statement is given. Where the information has been provided as part of a job offer, it is suggested that, to comply with the law, a brief statement should be given to the employee within 13 weeks of starting work referring the employee to the document already provided. Any changes to the information provided, or confirmation of it, can be included in this document.

13 Where a change in the terms of employment occurs after the issue of the written statement, the employer must notify the employee of this in writing within one month, or refer the employee to an accessible document where he or she can see details of the change.

14 There is no requirement for an employee to sign a written statement, although in practice employees are often asked to sign to say that they have received a copy of it. A signature to a written statement does not necessarily convey that it has contractual effect. An established term of a contract of employment cannot be changed merely by putting a new written statement in front of an employee and asking him or her to sign it. More is needed, namely the employee's knowingly given consent to the change.

15 Once formed, if one party or the other unilaterally varies a term of the contract, this will be a breach of it, although tacit acceptance of the breach may be enough to amount to an implied consent to the variation. However, if a contract of employment allows for the employer to vary its terms and the

employer does so, this is unlikely to be a breach, but it could still be an unreasonable act on management's part, having regard to the circumstances of the individual. For example, if a contract were to provide for a member of staff or a local education authority college to be liable to serve at any college within the authority's area, the employer's contractual right to move that person from one end of the county to the other could still be unenforceable if it were unreasonable in the individual's personal circumstances.

16 Another example might involve the teaching duties of a member of staff. If appointed to teach a particular subject without any flexibility clause in the contract enabling management to switch the person to other teaching duties, the individual's consent will be necessary if the need for the teaching he or she was appointed to do declines and a proposal for the person to undertake other duties is formulated. the proposal must be a reasonable one. The Employment Appeal Tribunal found it 'a startling proposition' that all teachers could be asked to teach any subject at any time. Further, the tribunal found that 'no doubt there is a need for flexibility and for teachers normally engaged in one type of teaching at a particular level to be ready to undertake teaching at different levels . . . provided that the request is reasonable . . . [which] . . . will depend on circumstances . . . and it would be relevant to take into account the custom and practice of the profession' (London Borough of Redbridge v. Fishman [1978]IRLR 69). In this case a teacher who had refused to teach a timetable because the duties of the post to which she had been appointed had been 'eroded to the point of destruction' was found to have been unfairly dismissed for maintaining her refusal. However, she received minimal compensation from the industrial tribunal because, with the diminution in the need for the duties for which she had been specifically appointed, it was held that in law she had become redundant and, if management had realised this, her employment would have been reasonably terminated for redundancy at about the same time that she was dismissed for failing to comply with the instruction which management had no contractual right to give, not having offered a valid flexibility clause in her job offer.

17 Although an employee has an implied duty to work within the scope of the contract and cannot refuse to comply with a reasonable instruction within the terms of it without incurring liability to disciplinary action, the employer does not have the right to make unrestricted and unreasonable demands on the employee. The overriding consideration is that terms enabling management to impose changes may be unenforceable if they are too widely drawn.

18 Nowadays it is customary for job offers and written statements of particulars to refer to collective agreements and state that these form part of the person's terms and conditions of service. Collective agreements between unions and employers, whether national or local, are only legally binding between the parties to them if they contain a written statement that they are intended to be; but their terms and collectively agreed changes to them, when clearly expressed as terms and conditions of employment, become binding by being incorporated into the individual employee's contracts of employment if the contract documents make this clear.

19 Disputes concerning an employer's failure to issue a written statement, or to clarify in a statement the required particulars (see above paragraph 11), can be referred to industrial tribunals. However, allegations of breaches of the terms of contracts of employment are not within the jurisdiction of industrial

tribunals, although they are often relevant in unfair dismissal cases, and particularly where constructive dismissal is alleged.

20 **Confidential information**

In the absence of an express term in a contract of employment restraining an employee from disclosing confidential information about his or her employer's business, an implied duty not to do so will be held to exist. While the employee remains in the employment the implied term imposes a duty of good faith or fidelity on the employee. The extent of the duty of fidelity varies according to the nature of the contract. Once an employee has left an employment, the implied duty is less onerous, so that the obligation not to use or disclose information will only apply in relation to secret processes or other information of a sufficiently high degree of confidentiality as to amount to a trade secret. For employees who have left, the continuing obligation does not extend to information which is only 'confidential' in that any unauthorised disclosure will be a clear breach of the duty of fidelity during the employment.

21 To decide whether a particular piece of information falls within the implied term so as to prevent its use or disclosure after an employee has left his or her employment, the matters to consider may include:

(i) The nature of the employment, and whether the employee habitually handled confidential material;

(ii) The nature of the information, because information will only be protected if it can be classified as a trade secret or as material of such a highly confidential nature as to require the same protection as a trade secret;

(iii) Whether management impressed on the employee the confidentiality of the information; and

(iv) Whether the information can be easily isolated from other information which the employee is free to use or disclose.

22 **Fixed term contracts**

A fixed term contract is a contract of a specific stated term fixed in advance or which can be ascertained in advance by reference to some relevant circumstances identified with a precise date in the future (e.g. the end of an academic session). However, 'a fixed term contract is a contract for a specified term even though it contains a provision allowing for it to be terminated by notice during that term' (Dixon v. BBC [1979] IRLR 114) (see below paragraph 28).

23 A person engaged under a fixed term contract will be held as having been dismissed at the expiry of the contract. Provided that the necessary qualifications are satisfied and the individual has not agreed to waive his or her right to complain of unfair dismissal (see below paragraph 105) or to claim a redundancy payment (see below paragraph 118), he or she can petition an industrial tribunal with an unfair dismissal and/or a redundancy payment claim if the contract is not renewed. The possible consequences for the management of colleges, where fixed term contracts are common, should be examined in the context of the legal provisions relating to dismissal, redundancy and redundancy consultation later in this section.

24 **Right to notice**

The Employment Protection (Consolidation) Act 1978 specifies *minimum* periods of notice which must be given to terminate a contract of employment, unless:

(i) Either party waives his or her right to notice; or
(ii) Pay in lieu of notice is accepted; or
(iii) The employee commits an act of serious misconduct entitling the employer to treat the contract as summarily terminated; or
(iv) The employee is entitled to leave without notice by reason of the employer's conduct; or
(v) The employee works under a fixed term contract and the contract ends on the expiry of the period specified in it.

25 Other than where those exceptions apply, the employer is required to give notice of:
(i) One week if the employee has been continuously employed by the employer for one month;
(ii) One week for each year of continuous employment with the employer if the employee's period of continuous employment is two years or more but less than 12 years;
(iii) 12 weeks if continuously employed by the employer for 12 years or more.

An employee who has been continuously employed by the employer for one month or more is required to give minimum notice of one week to terminate his or her contract.

26 Where an employee is contractually entitled to a longer period of notice, the contractual provision overrides the statutory minimum.

27 Employees whose periods of employment are not expected to last for more than three months and who are not employed for longer than this period have no statutory right to a minimum period of notice.

28 A fixed term contract in effect contains a notice period expiring on the date when the contract is due to end, thereby complying with the statutory minimum notice provisions. However, it is normal for fixed term contracts to contain provisions for the giving of notice during their currency so that, if a decision is taken to terminate the contract before its full period is completed, appropriate notice can be given.

29 **Continuous employment**

In order to qualify for most of the individual employee rights under the employment protection legislation, the person must have been continuously employed for the period stipulated for the right. Where a dispute about continuity of service arises, it is presumed that the service is continuous unless the employer proves otherwise. The application of the statutory provisions relating to the calculation of the continuous employment of college staff, particularly part-time staff, can be complex. The main principals are explained in paragraphs 30–38 below.

30 Statutory continuous employment is calculated in weeks, with a week ending on a Saturday. The effect of this is that, if the employment is terminated other than on a Saturday, it is treated as continuing until the next following Saturday. Weeks of continuous employment are:
(i) Any week in which the employee is employed under a contract of employment for 16 hours or more, or which normally involves employment for 16 hours or more weekly;
(ii) Any week during which the employee's relations with his or her

employer temporarily cease to be governed by a contract of employment which normally involves work for 16 hours or more weekly and become governed by a contract which normally involves employment for eight hours or more weekly, up to a maximum of 26 weeks between any two periods (BUT note that the 26 weeks are in addition to any weeks which although involving employment for less than 16 hours, do not break continuity of employment because of some other statutory provision – see paragraph 31 below for the main examples);

(iii) For an employee whose relations with his or her employer are, or have been, governed by a contract of employment which normally involves employment for eight hours or more, but less than 16 hours weekly, those weeks and all subsequent weeks of continuous employment after the employee has been continuously employed by the employer for five years or more.

For these purposes an employee, such as a part-time lecturer, working simultaneously under different contracts for the same employer can aggregate the hours of each contract to show that he or she has been employed for 16 or more hours a week, or eight or more as the case may be, if the contracts are terminated at the same time (*Lewis v. Surrey County Council* [1986] IRLR 461).

31 The week counts as a period of employment if in any week an employee is, for the whole or part of the week –

(i) Incapable of work because of sickness or injury; or
(ii) Absent from work because of a temporary cessation of work; or
(iii) Absent from work in circumstances such that, by arrangement or custom, he or she is regarded as continuing in the employment of the employer for all or any purposes;
(iv) Absent from work wholly or partly because of pregnancy or confinement,

The 'temporary cessation of work' mentioned in (ii) has given rise to problems of interpretation. In Ford v. Warwickshire County Council [1983] IRLR 126, a case involving a part-time lecturer employed on a series of sessional contracts, the House of Lords held that the gaps between one contract and another, occurring as they did when the college courses ceased in the summer and were resumed in the autumn, amounted to a temporary cessation of work. Thus continuity of employment was established.

32 This judgment was subsequently expanded upon by the Court of Appeal in Flack v. Kodak Ltd [1986] IRLR 255, when it was explained that:

(i) A temporary cessation of work applies to the work of the employee, not necessarily to that of the employer: hence a temporary cessation can count towards continuity if during it there is work for other employees, although not for the particular employee;
(ii) When deciding whether continuity has been broken by a cessation of work, the right approach is to look back at the length of the gap between one temporary contract and its immediate predecessor, the expectations of both employer and employee that the cessations would be for a relatively short time, and the whole period during which the employee was intermittently employed by the same employer;
(iii) A much longer gap in the course of a long period of work extending over many years might well be considered temporary, whereas, if the same gap occurred in the course of a shorter period, it would not.

33 Faced with the difficulty of applying this approach to particular cases, it is recommended that the presumption of continuity of employment should be applied by management unless it can confidently be shown that a particular cessation of work cannot reasonably be characterised as temporary.

34 When an employee has qualified for statutory rights by the completion of the necessary period of continuous employment, these rights are retained until such time as the contract is varied to provide for less than eight hours a week.

35 No week in which an employee is on strike counts towards a period of continuous employment, but continuity is not broken by the participation in the strike, nor is it broken by a lock-out.

36 If, having complied with the statutory provisions relating to the right to return to work after absence for pregnancy and confinement, an employee exercises her right to return to work, every week between the date of her first absence from work and her date of return counts towards her period of continuous employment as though she had been working for the employer for that time.

37 If a complaint of unfair dismissal is upheld by an industrial tribunal and an order for the employee's reinstatement is made and complied with by the employer, all the weeks falling between the date when the dismissal took effect and the resumption of work count towards the employee's period of continuous employment as though the dismissal had never occurred. A similar effect applies if a re-engagement order is made by a tribunal and complied with.

38 The rules for calculating a period of continuous employment apply only to statutory rights accruing from employment with the same employer (or, in the case of companies, with an associated company). It therefore follows that, for example, the right not to be unfairly dismissed does not exist until a member of staff has completed two years' continuous service with the same college authority. However, an important exception to this applies to redundancy payments, when all *continuous* (i.e. successive) employment by local authority and related employers counts as years of service.

39 **Calculation of a week's pay and normal working hours**

Once continuity of employment for the relevant statutory rights has been established, certain payments arising from those rights are calculated on the basis of a *week's pay* as defined in the legislation. The calculation of a week's pay is dependent upon whether the employee's pay in normal working hours is subject to variation. Where employees are paid entirely by an hourly time rate or by a fixed wage or salary and the pay for work done in normal working hours does not vary, a week's pay is the pay obtaining for normal weekly hours as at the date of calculation. All non-variable bonuses and allowances (except expenses and subsistence allowances) are included.

40 Where an employee's pay varies with the amount of work done, a week's pay means pay for the normal weekly hours worked calculated over the preceding 12 weeks. The hours to be taken into account are only those, including overtime hours, when the employee was working. Any week in which the employee did not work should be replaced by the last previous week in which work was done. This process is continued until the 12 week period is established. The pay to be taken into account is the pay for all the hours when the

employee was working (including overtime, but subject to the adjustment of overtime pay), but excluding any pay for hours not worked. The hourly rate is obtained by dividing the pay to be taken into account by the hours to be taken into account. Apart from special cases such as output bonuses, it is generally the case that, where pay for overtime is greater than the pay for the same work at the normal rate, the reckonable amount will be the lower sum which would have been payable had the work been done in normal working hours.

41 The interpretation of a part-time teacher's hours of work, when having to decide whether he or she normally works for 16 hours or more a week (or eight or more hours after five years), was clarified in *Lake v. Essex County Council* [1979] IRLR 241. There, when deciding whether time spent in the preparation of teaching work counted as hours of work for employment protection purposes, the Court of Appeal decided that, unless there is an *obligation* or *requirement* in an employee's contract for him or her to perform work for the employer outside the hours of attendance at the place of work, any time spent on such duties does not count. The key word is *obligation*. If there is an obligation to do certain hours which are not specified or implied in the contract, it may be necessary to see what the employer has *required* the employee to do, or what hours are actually done under that obligation, in order to decide whether the contract has normally involved employment which includes those hours weekly.

42 **Equal treatment in employment**

Legislation relating to discrimination in employment has been outlined in paragraphs 3–8. This is supplemented by the Equal Pay Act 1970 which, like the other legislation against discrimination, applies equally to men and women, and references to women in the ensuing paragraphs should be read as applying equally to men.

43 The Equal Pay Act says that, if the terms of a woman's contract or employment do not include (directly or by reference to a collective agreement, or otherwise) an *equality clause*, 'they shall be deemed to include one.' An equality clause relates to pay and other terms of employment under which a woman is employed, and means that:

(i) Where the woman is employed on *like work* with a man in the same employment, if any term of her contract is less favourable than a similar term in his, her term must be treated as so modified as not to be less favourable; and, if at any time her contract does not include a term corresponding to a term which benefits him under his contract, her contract must be treated as including such a term;

(ii) Where a woman is employed on work *rated as equivalent* (i.e. by job evaluation) with that of a man in the same employment, if any term of her contract as determined by the rating of the work is less favourable than a similar term in his contract, her term must be treated as so modified as not to be less favourable; and, if at any time her contract does not include a term corresponding to the term which benefits him under his contract and determined by the rating of the work, her contract must be treated as including such a term;

(iii) Where a woman is employed on work which, not being work in relation to which (i) or (ii) above applies, is, in terms of the demands made on her (e.g. effort, skill, decision taking), of *equal value* to that of a man in the same employment, if any term of her contract is or becomes less favourable to her than a term of a similar kind in the contract under which he is employed, that term of her contract must be treated as so modified as not to be less favourable; and, if at any time her contract does not include a term corresponding to a term benefiting him in his contract, her contract must be treated as including such a term.

44 *Term* in these provisions has been interpreted by the Court of Appeal in *Hayward v. Cammell Laird Shipbuilders Ltd* 5 March 1987 as applying to all pay related terms in the contract of employment. Therefore, when deciding whether the term in a woman's contract concerning pay is less favourable than the corresponding term in the man's contract, adjustments must be made to take into account differences in hours of work, the comparative value of all pay related terms, and the value of any benefits in kind. In other works, anything which forms part of the employees' respective remuneration packages are to be looked at as a term relating to pay when deciding an equal pay claim.

45 As with allegations of unlawful discrimination in employment, a person can make an equal pay claim to an industrial tribunal. Comparisons for the purposes of establishing the claim may be drawn with individuals in establishments of the employer other than the place of work if the terms and conditions of employment are common between them. For a *like work* claim to succeed, the work of the applicant and her comparator must be of the same or a broadly similar nature, with the difference (if any) between what they do not being of practical importance in relation to terms and conditions of employment.

46 A defence open to an employer in an equal pay case is to prove that the variation between the woman's contract and the man's is genuinely due to a material factor which is not the difference of sex, and that the factor:

(i) In respect of a *like work* or a *work rated as equivalent* claim, *must* be a material difference between her case and his; and

(ii) In respect of an *equal value* claim, *may* be such a material difference.

47 **Guarantee payments**

The Employment Protection (Consolidation) Act provides that, when an employee is not provided with work which under his or her contract would normally be required to be done, because of either a reduction in the employer's requirements, or any other occurrence affecting the natural workings of the undertaking, the employee is entitled to a statutory minimum guarantee payment. These payments can only be made in respect of complete working days lost. In colleges guarantee payments will not be made if any of the following conditions apply:

(i) The employee is employed under a fixed term contract of three months or less;

(ii) The employee works under a contract of employment which normally involves employment for less than 16 hours weekly (or less than eight hours weekly if the employee has been continuously employed for five years or more);

(iii) The employee has no normal working hours;

(iv) The employee has not been continuously employed for one month;

(v) The employee has unreasonably refused an offer from the employer of suitable alternative work;

(vi) The lay-off or short-time working results from a trade dispute involving any employee of *the employer*.

48 The amount of a statutory guarantee payment is calculated by the multiplica-

tion of the number of normal working hours for the day in question by the guaranteed hourly rate, subject to an upper limit which is normally varied annually by a government order. Payments are limited to any five days within any period of three months. Any payments made by the employer under a contract of employment (e.g. contractual lay-off pay) are offset against the employer's liability under the Act. Unemployment benefit is not paid for a day in respect of which a guarantee payment is payable.

49 An employee who does not receive a guarantee payment but who considers that he or she is entitled to it can complain to an industrial tribunal.

50 The Secretary of State for Employment may grant an exemption from the Act when an employer and a union have a collective agreement covering guarantee pay not less favourable than the statutory minimum.

51 **Itemised pay statement**

Under the Employment Protection (Consolidation) Act every employee, other than those who work under contracts normally involving employment for less than 16 hours weekly (or less than eight hours weekly if they have been continuously employed by the employer for five years or more), is entitled at or before any pay day to receive from the employer a written pay statement containing details of:

(i) The gross amount of the wages or salary;
(ii) The amounts of any variable and fixed deductions and the purposes for which they are made;
(iii) The net amount of wages or salary payable;
(iv) Where different parts of the net amount are paid in different ways, the amount and method of each part payment.

52 The employer may issue either a pay statement which specifies the amounts and purposes of every fixed deduction separately, or a pay statement specifying only the aggregate amount of all fixed deductions. In the latter case, the employee must be provided with a standing statement of fixed deductions at or before the time this latter form of pay advice is adopted. The employer is required to notify the employee in writing of any change in the amount, purpose or number of fixed deductions. Amendments to statements of fixed deductions should be made by notice in writing to the employee giving particulars of the amendment, and before any increase in fixed deductions is implemented.

53 Standing statements are valid for 12 months. At the end of this period, and before a further deduction is made, the employer must reissue to each employee a standing statement incorporating any amendments which have occurred during the preceding 12 months. If this is not done, the employer must henceforth provide in each pay statement the full particulars (see above paragraph 51). Standing statements must not include variable deductions. These must continue to be specified in pay statements.

54 Under the Wages Act 1986, subject to certain exceptions (see below paragraph 55), no employer is allowed to make any deduction from the wages or salary of, nor receive any payment from, any employee unless the deduction or payment:

(i) Is required or authorised to be made by virtue of any statutory provision or any *relevant provision* of the employee's contract; or

(ii) The employee has previously signified in writing his or her agreement or consent to the deduction or payment.

A *relevant provision* is a written term of the contract issued to the worker on any occasion prior to the deduction or payment, or is a provision to be found in one or more terms of the contract, whether express or implied, or in writing or not, whose existence and effect has been notified to the worker in writing prior to the deduction or payment.

55 Exclusions from the general principle that unauthorised deductions must not be made, or payments received, include payments:

(i) To reimburse the employer in respect of overpayments of wages, salary, or expenses (although under different legislation an employee may be able to contest an employer's attempt to recover an overpayment);
(ii) Made by the employer in compliance with a statutory provision to deduct and pay over to a public authority amounts determined by that authority as being due to it from the employee;
(iii) Made to a third party, provided that these have been authorised by the employee, either under a contractual provision or specifically, and are in accordance with the notification by the third party of the amounts due;
(iv) Made by the employer because the employee took part in a strike or other industrial action; or
(v) Made in compliance wholly or partly with a court or tribunal order requiring the payment of any amount by the employee to the employer, subject in this case to the employee's prior written agreement or consent.

56 Disputes relating to pay statements or allegedly unauthorised deductions from wages or salary can be referred to industrial tribunals to decide. However, tribunals are not empowered to consider arguments about the accuracy of amounts paid or deducted.

57 **Maternity**

The Employment Protection (Consolidation) Act contains three important provisions concerning maternity: the right not to be dismissed for a pregnancy-related reason; the right to return to work after the birth of the child; and the right not to be unreasonably refused paid time off for antenatal care. The normal employment protection qualifying conditions apply to the first two of these, namely that the employee must have been continuously employed by the employer under a contract which normally involves 16 or more hours work a week for two years or more (or eight or more hours after five years continuous service). There are no qualifying requirements for the right to paid time off for antenatal care.

58 Where an employee's contractual rights provide better benefits, the Act does not affect these. However, if the employer's package is less favourable than the statutory rights in any respect, the employee is entitled to the statutory right even if, under the employer's scheme, this means giving up one or more of the preferential rights otherwise available under the scheme. (See **2.5** 22.)

59 Dismissal of a pregnant employee for a reason related to her pregnancy is unfair if she meets the qualifying conditions mentioned in paragraph 57, unless:

(i) At the effective date of termination of her employment she had become incapable of adequately doing the work which she was employed to do; or

(ii) Because of her pregnancy she would not be able to continue to do her work without contravening a duty or restriction imposed by an enactment,

– AND there is no available vacancy for her which is both suitable and appropriate for her in the circumstances of her pregnancy. If such a vacancy exists and is not offered to her, the dismissal will be unfair even if the reason otherwise comes within (i) or (ii). In colleges and large organisations it is unlikely that a pregnancy-related dismissal will be regarded as fair.

60 An employee who is dismissed for a pregnancy-related reason, whether or not she qualifies for the right to complain of unfair dismissal, can nevertheless complain to an industrial tribunal that she has been unlawfully discriminated against on grounds of sex. She will have to show that 'her pregnancy (with its associated consequences) is capable of being matched by analogous circumstances (such as sickness) applying to a man and, if so, whether they are closely enough matched to enable a fair comparison to be made between the favourableness of treatment accorded to a woman in the one situation and to a man in the other' (*Hayes v. Malleable Working Men's Club and Institute* [1985] IRLR 367). If, therefore, a man with comparable service in the same employment would be allowed to take sick leave equivalent to the length of time a pregnant woman would be absent because of her pregnancy and confinement, it could be unlawful discrimination to sack her in anticipation of her absence for that length of time.

61 The right to return after absence for pregnancy and confinement is established by meeting the qualifying conditions mentioned in paragraph 57 and by:

(i) The employee continuing to be employed by her employer (whether or not she is at work) until immediately before the 11th week before the expected week of confinement;

(ii) The employee informing her employer in writing at least 21 days before her absence begins or, if that is not reasonably practicable, as soon as is reasonably practicable, that she will be (or is) absent from work wholly or partly because of pregnancy or confinement and intends to return to work with her employer, and supporting this statement with a medical or midwife's certificate stating the expected week of confinement if required to do this by the employer.

62 At their discretion, the employer has the right, not before 49 days counting from the beginning of the employee's expected week of confinement, to write to the employee asking her to confirm in writing that she still intends to return to work with them. If she fails to confirm this within 14 days of receiving the request, or as soon as reasonably practicable thereafter, her right to return lapses.

63 The employee must notify the employer at least 21 days before the date of her intended return, provided that the date notified for her return is within a period of 29 weeks beginning with the week in which the date of confinement fell. The employer may delay the employee's return for up to four weeks from the notified date, provided that reasons are given and she is told when she may resume work. If she is ill and produces a medical certificate, the employee may

similarly delay her return for up to four weeks from the notified date (or for four weeks from the end of the 29 weeks if no notified date has been given), but no further statutory right of postponement exists and, if the employee has not by then returned, she loses her right to do so. If the return to work is prevented by an interruption of work, such as an industrial dispute, the employee should return as soon as practicable, but not later than 14 days after the end of the interruption.

64 The right to return is a right:

(i) To return to the job in which the employee was employed under her original contract of employment on terms and conditions not less favourable than those which would have been applicable to her if she had not been absent, and for her absence to count as a period of employment for statutory employment protection purposes; or

(ii) If it is not practicable by reason of redundancy for her to return to work, to be offered alternative employment with the employer where there is a suitable available vacancy on terms and conditions not substantially less favourable.

65 Where an employer does not allow an employee to return to work after she has established her right to do so, the employee can complain to an industrial tribunal that she has been unfairly dismissed.

66 Entitlement to statutory maternity pay (SMP) is provided in regulations made under the Social Security Act 1986. Employers are liable to pay SMP to employees who:

(i) Have been continuously employed by the employer for at least 26 week continuing into the 15th week before the baby is due (the *qualifying week*); and

(ii) Have average weekly earnings of not less than the lower earnings limit for the payment of national insurance contributions; and

(iii) Are still pregnant at the 11th week before the expected week of confinement, or who have been confined by that time; and

(iv) Have stopped working for the employer.

67 For her part, the employee must:

(i) At least 21 days before her absence from work is due to begin, or as soon as is reasonably practicable thereafter, give notice to the employer, in writing if required, stating when she intends to stop work because of pregnancy; and

(ii) Provide evidence of her expected week of confinement.

68 SMP is paid for up to 18 weeks. For the first six week there is an earnings related payment at 90% of average earnings if the woman has been continuously employed by the employer normally for at least 16 hours weekly for two years or more, or normally for at least eight but less that 16 hours weekly for five years or more, up to and including at least one day in the qualifying week. Circumstances in which SMP may be paid by an employer for less than 18 weeks include:

(i) If the employee does not give up work prior to the sixth week before her expected week of confinement: each week or part thereof worked subsequent to this reduces the SMP entitlement by one week at the lower rate, but not the 90% of earnings rate if she is entitled to this;

(ii) If the employee dies, then the employer's liability will cease at the end of the week in which the death occurs;
(iii) If the employee is taken into legal custody;
(iv) If the employee goes abroad to a country outside the European Community.

69 An employee will not be entitled to SMP if she has not been employed by her employer at any time during the *qualifying week*, or if she is outside the European Community at any time in the first week of the 18-week period for which SMP is payable.

70 An employee who is employed by more than one employer and who satisfies the qualifying rules with each can receive SMP from each of them. If an employee is working under two separate contracts with the same employer at the same time and the employer's national insurance contributions are being paid separately for each contract, she will be entitled to two payments of SMP, provided that she qualifies under each contract.

71 Employers are entitled to recover all SMP they have been liable to pay and have paid, including tax and usual deductions, plus an extra amount to compensate for the employers' national insurance contributions paid on that SMP. Recovery is made by deducting from the monthly payments of national insurance contributions sent to the Collector of Taxes.

72 **Time off for public duties**

Employers are required under the Employment Protection (Consolidation) Act to permit employees holding public positions to have time off in which to perform their public duties. To be eligible employees must have been continuously employed for 16 or more hours weekly for five years or more. The relevant public positions include:
(i) Justices of the Peace;
(ii) Members of a local authority;
(iii) Members of any statutory tribunal;
(iv) In England and Wales, members of a regional or area health authority, a water authority, the managing or governing body of a maintained educational establishment.

73 The duties for which time off must be allowed are those which arise from the office or membership held and are defined as attendance at meetings of the body or any of its committees or sub-committees, and the performance of duties approved by the body concerned which are required to fulfil its functions. The amount of time off permissible under the Act is that which is 'reasonable in all the circumstances', having regard to:
(i) The amount of time off required in general to perform the particular public duty, and the amount required on the particular occasion in question;
(ii) The amount of time off the employee has had already for this purpose, as well as time off for trade union duties, if any; and
(iii) The circumstances of the employer's undertaking and the effect thereon of the employee's absence.

74 An employer is not obliged to pay an employee for time off for public duties, although this may be done as a result of an individual or collective agreement. An aggrieved employee has the right to complain to an industrial tribunal that

the employer has unreasonably refused to allow him or her time off for public duties.

75 **Trade union membership and activities**

Every employee has the right not to have action taken by the employer against him or her as an individual for any of the purposes of:

(i) Preventing or deterring him or her from being, or seeking to become, a member of an *independent trade union*, or penalising him or her for doing so;
(ii) Preventing or deterring him or her from taking part in the activities of an independent trade union at any appropriate time, or penalising him or her from doing so;
(iii) Compelling him or her to be or become a member of a trade union;
(iv) Enforcing a requirement (whether or not imposed by his or her contract of employment or in writing) that, in the event of his or her failure to become or cease to remain a member of a trade union, he or she must make one or more payments.

An *independent trade union* is a union which is not under the domination or control of, or liable to interference by, an employer or group of employers or an employers' association. Proof of a union's independence is the holding of a certificate of independence issued by the Certification Officer.

76 The activities in which a union member is entitled to take part are not defined in the legislation, although the Employment Protection (Consolidation) Act establishes rights to time off for members of unions to participate in the affairs of the union (with or without pay, at the employer's discretion), and to representatives of the union (e.g. shop stewards, branch officers) to time off with pay to execute the duties of their office. The entitlement to time off for union members to participate in the activities of their union is for reasonable time off during working hours. Examples of these activities are likely to include:

(i) Discussing trade union matters;
(ii) Attending union meetings;
(iii) Recruiting new members;
(iv) Distributing union literature;
(v) Collecting union subscriptions;
(vi) Placing notices on notice boards.

77 The general principle is that the statutory right to take part in union activities was introduced to 'discourage employers from penalising participation in activities of a fairly varied kind . . . It should be reasonably, and not too restrictively, interpreted' (Dixon v. Hest Ella Developments Ltd [1978] IRLR 151). An ACAS code of practice *Time Off for Trade Union Duties and Activities*, approved by Parliament, offers some guidance on the provision by employers of reasonable time off. These recommendations are likely to be considered by industrial tribunals when having to decide complaints of refusals by employers to provide reasonable time off.

78 When receiving a request for paid time off, before agreeing to it management is entitled to know whether:

(i) The employee is an official of an independent trade union recognised by the employer for collective bargaining purposes;
(ii) The duties which are to be undertaken during the employee's working hours are part of his or her duties as a union official; and
(iii) The duties are concerned with industrial relations between the

employer and his employees, or whether the time off is for training in aspects of industrial relations relevant to the carrying out of those duties and is training approved by the TUC or the union.

79 In Sood v. GEC Elliott Process Automation Ltd [1980] ICR 1 the Employment Appeal Tribunal said that, although the provision allowing paid time off should not be 'narrowly construed', nevertheless the Act makes it clear that 'the duties must concern industrial relations between the official's employer and its employees . . . The test is whether the time off is required to enable the official to carry out his duties in relation to a matter which arises in relations between employees and management.' The right to paid time off for union duties is not therefore confined to meetings with management, as long as the reason for the time off meets the test suggested.

80 The dismissal of an employee will be unfair if the reason, or principal reason, for it was that the employee:

(i) Was, or proposed to become, a member of an independent trade union; or

(ii) Had taken part, or proposed to take part, in the activities of a trade union at an *appropriate time*; or

(iii) Was not a member of any trade union, or of a particular trade union, or of one of a number of particular trade unions, or had refused, or proposed to refuse, to become or remain a member.

An *appropriate time* means a time which is either outside the employee's working hours or, if by arrangements agreed by the employer, within his or her working hours at a time when it is permissible for him or her to take part in the union activities. For this purpose, the activities of an independent trade union exclude activities which consist of industrial action.

81 Where an *approved* union membership agreement (i.e. approved in a secret ballot by 80% of those entitled to vote and 85% of those who voted) for a closed shop applies, dismissal for non-membership of an appropriate union in the closed shop will be fair unless:

(i) The employee genuinely objects on grounds of conscience or other deeply held personal conviction to membership of any union or of a particular union; or

(ii) The employee belonged to the employment group before the closed shop took effect, but has not subsequently been a member of a union in accordance with the agreement; or

(iii) The employee is bound because of his or her qualifications to observe a written code of conduct and has left, or been expelled from the union, or has refused to join a union, because of a conflict between that code of conduct and a requirement to take industrial action; or

(iv) The employee has obtained, or is seeking, a declaration from an industrial tribunal that he or she has been unreasonably excluded or expelled from the union.

A code of practice *Closed Shop Agreements and Arrangements* issued by the Department of Employment after approval by Parliament and aimed at providing practical guidance on questions which arise out of the formulation and operation of closed shop agreements is available.[1]

82 **Trade union immunities**

Subject to the provisions described in paragraph 78, an act done by a trade union if authorised or endorsed by a *responsible person* in contemplation or furtherance of a *trade dispute* is not actionable in tort (i.e. for a civil wrong) on the grounds that:

(i) It induces another person to break a contract or induces any other person to interfere with its performance; or

(ii) It consists in threatening that a contract will be broken or its performance interfered with, or that another person will be induced to break a contract or interfere with its performance.

83 For this purpose a *responsible person* means:

(i) The principal executive committee of the union; or

(ii) Any other person empowered by the union's rules to authorise or endorse acts of the kind in question; or

(iii) The union's president or general secretary; or

(iv) Any other employed official of the union; or

(v) Any committee of the union to which an employed official regularly reports.

A union will not be held liable if an unlawful act has not been authorised or endorsed by a responsible person, although whoever was responsible for it may himself or herself be proceeded against.

84 The definition of a *trade dispute* is limited in its scope. It means a dispute between workers and their employer which relates wholly, or mainly, to such things as terms and conditions of employment, working conditions and the allocation of work.

85 The immunity described in paragraph 82 does not apply if, without the support of a ballot, an act is done by a union which induces a person:

(i) To break his or her contract of employment or to interfere with its performance; or

(ii) To break a commercial contract or to interfere with its performance and one of the facts relied upon to establish the union's liability is that a breach of, or interference with, a contract of employment was induced by the union; or

(iii) The breach or inducement to breach, or threats to do so, involves secondary industrial action which is not intended directly to prevent or disrupt the supply during the dispute of goods and services to or by the employer who is a party to the dispute.

Organising unlawful picketing is also not covered by the immunities of trade unions. Picketing is lawful if a person in contemplation or furtherance of a trade dispute attends at or near his own place of work or, if he is a union official, at or near the place of work of a member of his union whom he is accompanying and whom he represents. Guidance on picketing is contained in a Department of Employment code of practice, *Picketing*, approved by Parliament.

86 Thus a union which expresses an intention to call upon its members to go on strike or take other industrial action leaves itself open to an application for an injunction to restrain it from doing so, and to proceedings for damages if going ahead with the action, if it has not already obtained support for its decision through a properly conducted ballot. The law provides an upper limit for the amount of damages which can be awarded against a union in actions for tort. For example, for a union with between 25,000 and 99,999 members the maximum liability under any one action is £125,000.

87 **Rehabilitation of offenders**

Under the Rehabilitation of Offenders Act 1974 persons convicted of offences for which sentences, suspended or otherwise, of up to two and a half years were imposed, after completing a prescribed rehabilitation period have the right to have the conviction regarded as 'spent'. In many instances this means that the offence is treated as if it had never occurred: a spent conviction may not be used as a proper ground for dismissing or excluding a person from any office, profession, occupation or employment, or for prejudicing him or her in any way in any occupation or employment.

88 However, some types of employment are exempted from the Act. Employment in colleges may come within the general exclusion reading:

> Any office or employment concerned with the provision to persons aged under 18 of accommodation, care, leisure and recreational facilities, schooling, social services, supervision or training, being an office or employment of such a kind as to enable the holder to have access in the course of his [or her] normal duties to such persons, and any other office or employment the normal duties of which are carried out wholly or partly on the premises where such provision takes place.

89 The restriction on questions about spent convictions does not apply to any question asked by or on behalf of any person in the course of the duties of his or her office or employment which is intended to assess the suitability of another person for any post coming within the exclusion in paragraph 88 if:

(i) The post would normally enable the person to have access to people referred to in the exclusion; or

(ii) The question relates to a person who lives in the same household, and the provision mentioned in the exclusion would normally take place in that household.

90 No penalty attaches to a failure to disclose a spent conviction in connection with a job excluded from the scope of the Act, but the application can be rejected, or the person subsequently dismissed, if management learns that the individual has a spent conviction.

91 **Suspension on medical grounds**

An employee suspended on medical grounds under any of the regulations listed below is entitled to receive a week's pay for each week up to a minimum of 26 weeks. The intention is to protect employees who, although not incapable of work because of a physical condition, cannot be employed in their jobs if the condition from which they are suffering is specified statutorily as prohibiting this. The employer does not have to pay suspension pay in addition to the contractual pay he may be obliged to pay to the employee, although if the contractual pay is less than the statutory entitlement the employer will have to make up the difference. The specified regulations are:

(i) The India Rubber Regulations 1922;

(ii) The Chemical Works Regulations 1922;

(iii) The Ionising Radiations Regulations 1985;

(iv) The Control of Lead at Work Regulations 1980.

92 Employees are not entitled to medical suspension pay:

(i) If they have not been in continuous employment with the employer for four weeks before suspension begins; or

(ii) If they normally work for less than 16 hours a week, or for less than eight hours after five years continuous service;
(iii) For any time when unable to work because of illness or physical or mental disability; or
(iv) So long as suitable alternative work offered by the employer is unreasonably refused; or
(v) If any reasonable requirements imposed by the employer to ensure availability for work when necessary are refused.

93 An employee who considers that suspension pay is not being paid in full may complain to an industrial tribunal. A complaint of unfair dismissal can also be entered if an employee is dismissed when he or she would otherwise have been suspended for medical reasons. In such a case the length of continuous employment necessary to establish the right is one month.

94 **Disabled persons**

The Disabled Persons (Employment) Act 1944 and its subordinate legislation imposes a duty on every employer of not less than 20 employees to give employment to a quota of registered disabled people. The standard quota is 3% of an employer's total workforce. A failure to employ the quota does not of itself constitute an offence, but it remains the duty of employers to allocate to suitable registered disabled persons vacancies as they occur on the staff until the quota is reached. The employer is subject to two restrictions:
(i) In all engagements of staff (except when complying with a reinstatement or re-engagement order made by an industrial tribunal) the employer must not engage a person who is not a registered disabled person if the employer is below quota, unless a permit is obtained from the Department of Employment to allow this;
(ii) An employer must not discharge a registered disabled person without reasonable cause if he or she is below quota, or if the discharge would result in the quota being breached.

The 1944 Act does not provide a remedy where the registered disabled person is dismissed without reasonable cause. If qualified by length of service and the hours worked per week, the employee would be able to complain of unfair dismissal under the employment protection legislation.

95 An employer's quota is determined by applying the appropriate percentage to the numbers of employees employed for more than ten hours a week. A person normally employed from ten to 30 hours a week is counted as a half unit, and a person normally employed for more than 30 hours a week as a full unit. Where no special percentage has been fixed after consultation between an employers' association and representatives of the employees in a particular employment, the standard percentage of 3% applies. An employer may apply for a reduction in quota, but cause for the reduction has to be shown.

96 Every employer subject to quota obligation is required to record information necessary to demonstrate compliance with the law, and to produce those records for inspection. The records should show the total number and names of all employees as well as the dates of engagement or termination of employment. The record must also give such information as is necessary to identify the following individual employees:
(i) A registered disabled person, including a person whose registration has lapsed during employment with the employer;

(ii) A person in an employment to which a special percentage applies, and the figure of that percentage;
(iii) A person who has been engaged by virtue of reinstatement or re-engagement rights;
(iv) A person employed under a permit;
(v) A person whose employment ordinarily involves less than ten hours work per week; and
(vi) A person whose employment ordinarily involves not less than ten but not more than 30 hours work per week.

97 The 1944 Act was originally intended to assist persons disabled during the war. Nowadays the register contains relatively few disabled persons, and accordingly it is not the policy of the Department of Employment to insist on the law being observed, although it still wishes to emphasise to employers their statutory obligations. These are supported by sanctions under the Act. For example, if an employer dismisses a registered disabled person without reasonable cause, an offence has been committed for which the employer may be liable to a fine or imprisonment, or both.

98 Of perhaps more relevance than the legislation itself, the Manpower Services Commission has published a non-statutory code of practice on *The Employment of Disabled People*. It contains a comprehensive summary of the relevant law and identifies good practices and 'realistic objectives for which employers, employees and their representatives can aim'. An *Appendix* to the code lists the assistance, financial and otherwise, for which application can be made by those who recruit and employ disabled persons and who want to achieve the code's objectives.

99 **Dismissal: definition**

The Employment Protection (Consolidation) Act states that an employee is treated as dismissed by his or her employer if, but only if:
(i) The contract under which he or she is employed is terminated by the employer, whether or not with notice;
(ii) The employee is employed for a fixed term and the term expires without being renewed under the same contract; or
(iii) The employee terminates the contract, with or without notice, in circumstances such that he or she is entitled to terminate it without notice because of the employer's conduct (i.e. the employee is constructively dismissed).

100 Associated with this definition is the date when the contract of employment ends. Some important employment protection rights depend on claims being made to industrial tribunals within specified time limits counting from this date. In law the effective date of termination means:
(i) Where the contract of employment is terminated by notice given either by the employer or the employee, the date on which the notice expires;
(ii) Where the contract is terminated without notice, the date on which the termination takes effect;
(iii) The date on which the term of a fixed term contract expires without being renewed under the same contract.

101 When pay in lieu of notice is paid to a dismissed employee as compensation for the pay due for the notice period to which the employee is entitled under his or her contract, with the employment to end immediately, the effective

date of termination will be the date of that payment for most employment protection purposes. However, for the right to complain of unfair dismissal if the employee qualifies for that right, the effective date of termination will be when the statutory notice period to which the employee is entitled would otherwise expire. If notice is given with pay in lieu, but with the employment notionally to continue until the notice period would otherwise end, the effective date of termination will be the expiry of the notice period. An important exception to these variations on the effective date of termination applies to summary dismissal for gross misconduct, when the right to a minimum period of notice is lost and the effective date of termination is the actual date of dismissal.

102 If after being dismissed with notice an employee gives notice to terminate the contract of employment at an earlier date than the date for the expiry of the employer's notice, the employee will still be regarded as having been dismissed by the employer. In this case the effective date of termination will be the date when the employee's notice takes effect.

103 **Dismissal: written statement of reasons for**

Employees who have completed six months continuous service with their employers and whose employment is terminated with or without notice, or whose fixed term contracts expire without being renewed, have the right to ask their employers for a written statement of the reasons for their dismissal. This right applies to employees who normally work for 16 hours or more a week, but it will also apply to employees who work for 8–15 hours a week after they have completed five years continuous service.

104 The employer must comply with the request within 14 days. The employee may complain to an industrial tribunal if the employer unreasonably fails to provide the statement, or if the employee considers that it is inadequate or untrue. If finding in the employee's favour, the tribunal will award him or her two weeks pay.

105 **Unfair dismissal**

Apart from employees who are specifically excluded, the Employment Protection (Consolidation) Act gives every employee the right not to be unfairly dismissed and to complain to an industrial tribunal within three months counting from the effective date of termination if he or she considers that his or her dismissal was unfair. Employees in colleges who do not have this right are:

(i) Those who are not employees (e.g. self-employed visiting lecturers);
(ii) Those who have not completed two years continuous employment with the same employer at the effective date of termination;
(iii) Those who work for less than 16 hours a week, unless they have been continuously employed by the same employer for eight or more hours a week for five years or more;
(iv) Those who before their effective date of termination have reached the normal retiring age for their employment or, where there is no normal retiring age, have reached the age of 65;
(v) Those employed under fixed term contracts for one year or more where the dismissal consists only of the expiry of the contract without renewal who have previously agreed in writing to forgo the right of complaint in that circumstance.

106 The exclusion of employees without sufficient qualifying service does not

apply to any dismissal if the reason, or principal reason, for it was that the employee:

(i) Was, or proposed to become, a member of an independent trade union; or

(ii) Had taken part, or proposed to take part, in the activities of an independent trade union at an appropriate time; or

(iii) Was not a member of any trade union, or of a particular trade union, or of one of a number of particular trade unions, or had refused or proposed to refuse to become or remain a member.

However, if at the date of dismissal the employee is taking part in industrial action, a tribunal will not decide the fairness or otherwise of the dismissal unless it is shown that one or more of the employees taking part on that day were not dismissed, or that any employee taking part has, before the period of three months beginning with that employee's date of dismissal, been offered re-engagement and the complainant has not. Complaints of this sort must be presented within six months counting from the effective date of termination.

107 It should be noted that dismissals for reasons related to sex, marital status, or race are unfair. If a complainant has not completed the necessary qualifying period of service to complain of unfair dismissal, he or she may nevertheless proceed with an allegation of unlawful discrimination in respect of his or her dismissal.

108 **Fair dismissal**

The employer has the burden of showing the reason, or the principal reason, for dismissal. It must be a reason which:

(i) Related to the *capability* or *qualifications* of the employee for performing work of the kind which he was employed by the employer to do; or

(ii) Related to the employee's conduct; or

(iii) Was that the employee was redundant; or

(iv) Was that the employee could not continue to work in the position which he or she held without contravention of a duty or restriction imposed by an enactment (e.g. a work permit was required which the employee did not possess); or

(v) Was some other substantial reason of a kind such as to justify the dismissal of an employee holding the position which this employee held.

Capability is defined as meaning capability assessed by reference to skill, aptitude, health or any other physical or mental quality. *Qualifications* are any degree, diploma or other academic, technical or professional qualification relevant to the position which the employee held.

109 A failure to establish a reason falling within one or other of the reasons listed in paragraph 108 is enough to make the dismissal unfair. However, to show the reason for dismissal is not an onerous burden: management will know why the dismissal decision was taken and should have no difficulty in explaining this to an industrial tribunal.

110 In an unfair dismissal case the industrial tribunal has to decide whether, having regard to the reason shown by the employer, in the circumstances the employer acted reasonably or unreasonably in treating it as a sufficient reason for dismissing the employee. The tribunal is required to have regard to the size and administrative resources of the employer's undertaking (and for this purpose most tribunals can be expected to assume that a local authority has substantial administrative resources in comparison with most other employers).

The tribunal will also decide the question of the employer's reasonableness in accordance with equity (meaning fair play) and the substantial merits of the case.

111 The reasonableness test described in paragraph 110 means that management's handling of a dismissal will be scrutinised. Evidence will have to be given to show not only that the reason for the dismissal was sufficient, but that management acted reasonably throughout. In practice this means demonstrating that a fair procedure has been followed by management. A key question will be whether management's decision to dismiss fell within the band of reasonable responses of a reasonable employer in the circumstances.

112 Of less importance is whether or not the employee, for example, committed the alleged act of misconduct, or was lacking in capability within the meaning of capability explained in paragraph 108. It has been held that it is not necessary for the employer to *prove* that an employee committed a particular act of misconduct or was incapable or incompetent. The test is whether management honestly and reasonably held the belief that the employee had committed the act of misconduct, or was incompetent, and whether on the balance of probabilities there were reasonable grounds for that belief. Those are the questions on which management's attention should be focused when dealing with a problem employee. For its part, fair play (or equity) means that management should have investigated the matter, provided the employee with an opportunity to explain and considered the explanation before coming to a decision. In addition, where relatively minor misconduct has occurred, or inadequate performance has been manifested, warnings about the consequences of a failure to improve are regarded as the actions of a reasonable employer.

113 **Dismissal: remedies**

Where a complaint of unfair dismissal is successful, three remedies are available to the industrial tribunal: reinstatement, re-engagement or compensation. Re-engagement accompanied by some compensation is sometimes ordered. Where an employee is ordered to be reinstated, the intention is that he or she will be treated in all respects as though the dismissal had not occurred. If re-engagement is ordered, it is unlikely to be into the same job or on the same terms and conditions of employment, nor will it necessarily date back to the effective date of termination. In deciding whether to make an order for reinstatement or re-engagement, the tribunal will consider the employee's wishes, evidence from management about the practicability of him or her returning to work for the employer, and whether it would be just to make such an order if the employee was partly to blame for the dismissal. If a reinstatement or re-engagement order is made and the employer declines to comply with it, the effect will be that the employee will be awarded the compensation which would otherwise have been assessed for the unfair dismissal, plus an additional award of compensation for the employer's failure to comply with the order.

114 Awards of compensation are made in three forms: a basic award equivalent to the employee's statutory redundancy payment entitlement (if this has not already been paid by the employer), a compensatory award to reflect the employee's loss, and in cases where an employee has been dismissed for belonging, or not belonging, to a trade union, a special award in addition. The upper limits for these awards are reviewed annually by the government.

115 **Redundancy: general principles**

The law relating to redundancy is contained in the Employment Protection (Consolidation) Act. This provides that an employee who is dismissed will have been dismissed for redundancy if the dismissal is attributable wholly or mainly to the fact that:

(i) The employer has ceased, or intends to cease, to carry on the business for the purpose of which the employee was employed by him, or to carry on the business in the place where the employee was so employed; or

(ii) The requirements of the business for employees to carry out work of a particular kind, or to carry out work of a particular kind in the place where the employee was employed, have ceased or diminished, or are expected to cease or diminish.

116 The repeated mention of *dismissal* in this definition is important: termination by mutual consent is not normally a dismissal, and without a dismissal the employer is not liable in law to pay a redundancy payment. From this it follows that, if volunteers for redundancy are sought, it should be made clear to them that they are volunteering for dismissal for redundancy. This will require the issue of dismissal letters giving redundancy as the reason for dismissal and specifying the date when the contract of employment will end.

117 In the circumstances of colleges, persons not eligible for a redundancy payment are:

(i) Someone performing services under a contract of service (i.e. a self-employed person or a contractor) as distinct from a contract of employment;

(ii) Anyone who has not completed at least two years continuous employment and normally works for 16 hours or more a week, or five years continuous employment for 8–15 hours a week, with the same employer *or* with another local government or related employer (see paragraph 118);

(iii) A woman whose reckonable service ends on or after her 60th birthday and a man whose reckonable service ends on or after his 65th birthday;

(iv) An employee engaged under a fixed term contract for two years or more if he or she has made a written agreement with the employer to forgo any right to a redundancy payment in the event of there being no re-engagement when the term of the contract expires.

118 Under the Redundancy Payments (Local Government) (Modification) Order 1983 a redundant employee in local government and related employment can have his or her redundancy payment calculated on the basis of continuous employment with two or more of these employers, provided that the employment has been successive. Included in the list of related employers are all local authorities; the governing bodies of further education establishments mainly dependent for their maintenance on assistance from local education authorities, or grants under the Education Act 1944, or on a combination of these; colleges of education; and central institutions in Scotland. Similar provisions apply to the schools sector.

119 In the case of (iv) in paragraph 117, if the person is dismissed for redundancy before the expiry of the contract but the two-year qualifying period of continuous employment has been completed, the person will be entitled to a redundancy payment. The waiver clause can only relate to the expiry of the contract on completion of its fixed term. Where a contract is renewed for a further

term, a fresh waiver clause will need to be agreed in writing if it is the intention of the parties to continue with the waiver clause.

120 When an employee under notice of dismissal for redundancy accepts an offer of alternative employment with the same employer or, if in local government or related service, another employer in that category and continues in the new employment beyond the end of a *trial period* (see below paragraph 121) in the new job, no entitlement to a redundancy payment arises if the new job starts not later than four weeks after the end of the current contract. If the offer is for *suitable* alternative employment and is unreasonably refused by the employee, no entitlement to a redundancy payment will exist.

121 The trial period is of four weeks duration, starting from when the employee begins work in the new job. During the trial period the employee may terminate or give notice of termination of the new contract, in which case the employee will be treated as though he or she had been dismissed on the day the old job ended and be entitled to a redundancy payment calculated as at that date, provided the qualifying conditions are met. Similarly, if during the trial period the employer, for a reason connected with the change to the new job, terminates the contract or gives notice to terminate it, the employee's entitlement to a redundancy payment at the end of the previous contract will not be lost. Trial periods can be extended for the purpose of retraining the employee for employment under the new contract, provided that a written agreement is entered into specifying the date of the end of the trial period.

122 Where an employee is under notice of dismissal for redundancy but wishes to leave before the expiry of the employer's notice and the employer does not object, entitlement to a redundancy payment is not lost. It will be calculated as at the date of the end of the employee's notice. When an employer objects and informs the employee in writing that, if the employee leaves early, the employer will contest liability to pay a redundancy payment, the employee can apply to an industrial tribunal for a decision.

123 If a dismissal is wholly or mainly due to a cause other than redundancy, there is no entitlement to a redundancy payment. If, however, the employee argues that he or she was in fact redundant, a claim for a redundancy payment, and perhaps also for unfair dismissal, can be made to an industrial tribunal. The employer will have to satisfy the tribunal about the reason for the dismissal. In law, when the right to a redundancy payment for a dismissed employee is disputed, there is a presumption that the employee was dismissed for redundancy unless the employer proves the contrary.

124 The law on redundancy is complex. When, for example, an employer wishes to reduce the numbers of employees for economic reasons even though the quantity of work to be done remains constant, the dismissed employees will be entitled to redundancy payments. The words quoted in (ii) or paragraph 115 would be read as meaning that 'the requirements of the business for employees' was diminishing, regardless of whether the work they were doing was increasing, remaining static or declining. In any situation where redundancies are contemplated, management would be well advised as an initial step to seek advice on whether what is being proposed would come within the statutory definition of redundancy.

125 **Redundancy: unfair selection for**

Dismissal for redundancy will be unfair if:

(i) The employee was selected because of trade union membership (or non-membership) or activities; or

(ii) The employer contravened a customary arrangement or agreed procedure for redundancy selection and there were no special reasons justifying a departure from that arrangement or procedure in the employee's case; or

(iii) The selection was made on grounds of sex, marital status, or race.

126 Dismissal for redundancy may be unfair if:

(i) Management failed to consult the recognised union representatives about the proposed redundancy and/or failed to consult the employee individually;

(ii) Management failed to consider alternative employment for the employee;

(iii) Management acted otherwise unreasonably in selecting the particular employee (e.g. by not deciding appropriate criteria for selection and applying them equitably between employees in the redundancy field).

127 **Redundancy: time off for job finding**

An employee under notice of dismissal because of redundancy who has been continuously employed by the same employer for two years or more for 16 or more hours a week (or eight hours or more after five year continuous employment) is entitled to reasonable time off with pay to look for other employment or to arrange for training for future employment. Complaints of refusals by employers of reasonable time off in these circumstances, or of failure to pay for such time off, can be made to industrial tribunals. If finding in the employee's favour, the tribunal's award will be limited to two-fifths of a week's pay.

128 **Redundancy: consultation with recognised unions**

The Employment Protection Act 1975 requires every employer to consult the appropriate trade union recognised by him for collective bargaining purposes whenever a redundancy is proposed, and to notify the Secretary of State for Employment if it is planned to make ten or more employees redundant at one establishment within a specified period. This requirement applies regardless of how long an employee has worked for the employer, whether the employee is part-time or full-time, and whether a particular employee is a member of a union. Only employees engaged under fixed term contracts of 12 weeks or less are excluded. The intention of the legislation is for the consultation to take place before the identities of those to be made redundant are decided.

129 The statutory consultation procedure should be commenced by management at the earliest opportunity once redundancies are proposed and in any event must begin:

(i) Where the employer is proposing to dismiss as redundant 100 or more employees at one establishment within a period of 90 days or less, at least 90 days before the first of the dismissals takes effect; or

(ii) Where the employer is proposing to dismiss as redundant ten or more employees at one establishment within a period of 30 days or less, at least 30 days before the first of those dismissals takes effect.

The consultation periods can, at least in part, be concurrent with the individual notices issued to the redundant employees, but the object of the consultation requirements will be lost if the notices are issued at the same time as the consultation procedure commences. In practice it is wise not to issue redundancy dismissal notices until some 14 days after the consultations were initiated.

130 The consultation procedure requires the employer to disclose to the recognised union in writing:

(i) Reasons for the proposals;
(ii) Numbers and descriptions of employees whom it is proposed to dismiss as redundant;
(iii) Total number of employees of any such description employed by the employer at the establishments in question;
(iv) Proposed method of selection; and
(v) Proposed method of carrying out the dismissals, with due regard to any procedure, including the period over which the dismissals are to take effect.

The employer must consider the comments, if any, of the union and reply to them, giving reasons if any of them are rejected.

131 If a union complains that an employer has not fulfilled the consultative obligations, the employer must show that the requirements were fully complied with, or that there were special circumstances which prevented full compliance and that all possible action which was reasonably practicable had been taken to secure compliance.

132 A union can complain to an industrial tribunal that an employer has not complied with the consultation requirements. If deciding that the complaint is justified, the tribunal will make a declaration to that effect. If the complaint was that the employer had not consulted the union in sufficient time, the declaration will require the employer to postpone the dismissal notices so that the consultations can take place. In some cases, whether or not the employees are still employed, the tribunal may make a protective award requiring the employer to pay each employee covered by the award his or her normal week's pay for a specified period ('the protected period').

133 The duty to notify the Secretary of State when it is proposed to make ten or more employees redundant is similar to that for consultation with the recognised union. Notification forms are obtainable from any office of the Department of Employment.

134 **Redundancy payments**

There is no need for an employee to submit a formal claim if the employer accepts liability for a redundancy payment and makes a satisfactory payment at or soon after the date of dismissal. If the payment is not satisfactory or is nor made, the employee should take up the matter with the employer (where appropriate, through the union representative) and then make a written claim. If neither a written claim to the employer nor a reference to an industrial tribunal is made within six months of the effective date of termination, the employee is likely to be time-barred, and the employer will no longer have a statutory obligation to make the payment.

135 The amount of a redundancy payment depends on how long the employee has been continuously employed by the employer and, in the case of colleges, successive local authority or related employers. The number of completed years of continuous employment, up to a maximum of 20, is reckoned backwards

from the effective date of termination. The scale of payments for each year of employment is:

(i) At age 41 and over but under 65 (60 for a woman), one and a half week's pay;

(ii) At age 22 or over but under 41, one week's pay;

(iii) At age 18 and over but under 22, half a week's pay.

No payment is due for a fraction of a year. An employer must give a redundant employee a written statement indicating how the redundancy payment has been calculated.

136 Employees aged 60 (female) or 65 (male) at the effective date of termination of employment are not entitled to redundancy payments. Employees aged over 59 (female) or 64 (male) at the effective date of termination receive payments reduced by one-twelfth for each complete month after attaining these ages.

137 Redundancy payments do not affect entitlement to unemployment benefit, nor are redundancy payments subject to income tax. However, in cases where a severance payment is also made, it is possible that part of the total sum may incur liability to tax if it exceeds the tax-free limit for the time being in force. Advice on liability in this respect can be obtained from Inland Revenue enquiry offices.

138 **Codes of practice**

A failure to observe a recommendation of a Parliament-approved code of practice does not of itself render an employer, a manager, or an employee liable to proceedings, but the codes themselves are admissible in evidence in tribunal cases. Breaches of them will be taken into account by tribunals, but they do not necessarily have to follow them.

139 Codes of practice relating to employment legislation have been prepared and issued, after approval by Parliament, by ACAS (the Advisory, Conciliation and Arbitration Service), the Department of Employment, the Commission for Racial Equality, and the Equal Opportunities Commission. The titles of these codes are:

Disciplinary practice and procedures in employment ACAS code no. 1
Disclosure of information to trade unions for collective bargaining purposes ACAS code no. 2
Time off for trade union duties and activities ACAS code no. 3
Closed shop agreements and arrangements Department of Employment
Picketing Department of Employment
Code of practice for the elimination of racial discrimination and the promotion of equality of opportunity in employment Commission for Racial Equality
Code of practice for the elimination of discrimination on the grounds of sex and marriage and the promotion of equality of opportunity in employment Equal Opportunities Commission

140 Following an amendment to the law relating to unfair dismissal in 1980, it became widely accepted that the ACAS code no. 1 was no longer as relevant as when it had been issued in 1977. A revised and significantly up-dated code was submitted to the Secretary of State by ACAS in 1986, but was not approved.

141 The codes issued by the Commission for Racial Equality and the Equal

Opportunities Commission contain highly relevant recommendations for all employees. It is strongly recommended that these should be made known to all staff, and particularly to those with responsibility for short-listing and interviewing both external and internal applicants for posts.

NOTE

1 The Employment Bill which was introduced in autumn 1987 was intended to restrict trade unions' actions in these areas.

APPENDIX 1

THE CERTIFICATION OFFICER (AND INDEPENDENT UNIONS)

1 The Certification Officer is responsible under the Employment Protection Act 1975 and the Trade Union Act 1984 (and related legislation) for:
(i) Maintaining lists of trade unions and employers' associations;
(ii) Determining the independence of trade unions;
(iii) Seeing that trade unions and employers' associations keep accounting records, have their accounts properly audited, and submit annual returns;
(iv) Ensuring the periodical examination of members' superannuation schemes;
(v) Securing observance of the statutory procedures for transfers of engagements, amalgamations and changes of name of trade unions and employers' associations;
(vi) Supervising the statutory requirements as to the setting up and operation of trade union political funds, dealing with complaints by members about breaches of political fund rules, and ensuring that political fund ballots are lawfully conducted if they are to qualify for support from public funds;
(vii) Administering the provision of public funds for trade union secret ballots, including those for elections to unions' principal executive committees, and pre-strike and pre-industrial action ballots;
(viii) Receiving applications from any person who claims that a trade union has failed to comply with its statutory duty – (a) to compile and maintain a register of its members, and/or (b) to hold elections for membership of its principal executive committee, and/or (c) to conduct secret ballots for those elections, – and to hear and decide such applications and, where appropriate, to make a declaration about an application.

2 For trade unions entry in the Certification Officer's list is an essential preliminary to applying for a certificate of independence. Listing also entitles unions to tax relief for expenditure on provident benefits. Employers' associations do not have corresponding advantages.

3 The Certification Officer is required to keep a public record of all applications for certificates of independence and of all decisions reached. In making a decision he or she must take into account any relevant information submitted by third parties. Reasons for refusal must be given. In such cases the union concerned has a right of appeal to the Employment Appeal Tribunal. A certificate may be withdrawn if the Certification Officer is of the opinion that the union is no longer independent. Where a question concerning the independence of a particular union arises in proceedings, the question can be referred to the Certification Officer for a ruling.

4 The *Annual Report of the Certification Officer* gives a detailed account of activities.

5 The Certification Officer's address is: 15–17 Ormond Yard, Duke of York Street, London SW1Y 6JT.

APPENDIX 2

ACAS

1 The Advisory, Conciliation and Arbitration Service (ACAS) is an independent statutory body operating under the direction of a Council appointed by the Secretary of State

for Employment. The Council consists of a chair and nine other members, including three appointed after consultation with the Confederation of British Industry, three after consultation with the Trades Union Congress (TUC), and three independent members. ACAS is not subject to direction from any member of the government as to how it should carry out its functions, the principal of which include:

(i) Promoting the improvement of industrial relations;
(ii) Providing on request conciliation or other assistance in collective disputes;
(iii) Referring a dispute to arbitration, with the consent of the parties to it, normally after the procedures agreed between the parties have been exhausted;
(iv) Providing the services of conciliation officers for the settlement by conciliation of matters which could be the subject of proceedings before industrial tribunals;
(v) Provision of industrial relations advice;
(vi) Enquiring into any general industrial relations question or into industrial relations in an industry or a part of it at its own discretion;
(vii) Issuing codes of practice;
(viii) Publishing annual reports of its activities.

2 When an originating application is received at the Central Office of Industrial Tribunals (COIT) (see below Appendix 3), a copy of it is sent to the local ACAS conciliation officer. It is his or her duty to try to promote a settlement if asked to do so by the employer and the employee concerned, or on the conciliations officer's own initiative if believing that there is a reasonable prospect of success. In matters involving individual employees, there is provision for a conciliation officer to attempt conciliation before an application has been sent to the COIT.

3 If a conciliation officer succeeds in promoting a settlement, the complainant is normally barred from pursuing his or her complaint to or in a tribunal. This consequence of successful conciliation can be particularly useful if management is aiming to agree severance terms with an employee: in such a case the conciliation officer will explain to the employee that, if agreeing to the terms, the matter will end there, with no residual right existing to accept the settlement and embark upon, or continue, tribunal proceedings in respect of the termination of the employment. The agreement means that the employee contracts out his or her right to go to a tribunal. It should be noted, however, that any clause in a severance agreement purporting to contract out an employee's statutory rights is void unless the agreement has been promoted by a conciliation officer.

4 *ACAS Regional Addresses*

Northern Region, Westgate House, Westgate Road, Newcastle-upon-Tyne NE1 1TJ; Tel: 091-261 2191

Yorkshire and Humberside Region, Commerce House, St Albans Place, Leeds LS2 8HH; Tel: 0532 431371

London Region, Clifton House, 83–117 Euston Road, London NW1 2RB; Tel: 01–388 5100

South East Region, Clifton House, 83–117 Euston Road, London NW1 2RB; Tel: 01–388 5100

South West Region, Regent House, 27a Regent Street, Clifton, Bristol BS8 4HR; Tel: 0272 744066

Midlands Region, Alpha Tower, Suffolk Street, Queensway, Birmingham B1 1TZ; Tel: 021–631 3434

Nottingham Office, 66–72 Houndsgate, Nottingham NG1 6BA; Tel: 0602 415450

North West Region, Boulton House, 17–21 Chorlton Street, Manchester M1 3HY; Tel: 061–228 3222

Merseyside, Cressington House, 249 St Mary's Road, Garston, Liverpool L19 0NF; Tel: 051–427 8881

Wales, Phase 1, Ty Glas Road, Llanishen, Cardiff CF4 5PH; Tel: 0222 762636

APPENDIX 3

INDUSTRIAL TRIBUNALS

1 Industrial tribunals are a type of court hearing matters arising out of the employment protection and related legislation, the Sex Discrimination Act 1975 and the Race Relations Act 1976. They sit in all the major cities, as well as in other centres. Each tribunal consists of a legally qualified chair and two lay members, one with experience of management and the other with trade union experience. Although intended to be informal, tribunal hearings of necessity involve a fair degree of formality, not least because their duty is to apply the law to the evidence they hear and the facts they find established. Evidence is given on oath or by affirmation, cross-examination is allowed, and submissions on relevant law and case law are often presented by the representatives of the parties. Tribual proceedings come within the civil law, with decisions reached on the balance of probabilities and not on the criminal law burden of proof beyond reasonable doubt.

2 Appeals against industrial tribunal decisions can be made to the Employment Appeals Tribunal (EAT), but only on points of law (with the exception of a small number of provisions of limited effect, where the right of appeal can be on fact or on law). For example, a person dissatisfied with a finding by an industrial tribunal in an unfair dismissal case will not get a full appeal hearing unless a clear point of law can be identified. Briefly, points of law of this type include a misdirection by the tribunal as to the law or a misapplication of the law, or that the tribunal came to a decision which no reasonable tribunal, properly addressing itself to the facts as found and to the law, could have reached. Appeals against EAT judgments can be made to the court of appeal, but again only on a point of law, and after leave to appeal has been granted. In cases involving points of law of significant public interest, leave to appeal to the House of Lords may be granted by the court of appeal or by the House of Lords. Some important cases originating in industrial tribunals have also been referred to the European Court of Justice.

3 Forms on which to make originating applications to industrial tribunals are available from local unemployment benefit offices, jobcentres and offices of the Department of Employment. When completed, the forms must be sent to the Central Office of Industrial Tribunals at 93 Ebury Bridge Road, London SW1W 8RE to reach there within the time limit for the particular right of complaint.

APPENDIX 4

MEDICAL FITNESS OF TEACHERS

DES Circular 7/82 provides a commentary on certain sections of the Education Act 1980 which deal with medical fitness of teachers.

1 There is no requirement in regulations for persons appointed to teaching posts in establishments of further education to satisfy the Secretary of State of their medical fitness for teaching. However, the Secretary of State expects employers to make arrangements for checking the medical fitness of all teachers appointed to teach young persons in further education; and states that it is for employing authorities to satisfy themselves of the medical fitness of such persons before offering them employment.

2 There is provision in regulations under which the Secretary of State for Education and Science or the Secretary of State for Wales may require that on medical grounds a teacher shall not be employed in a maintained or grant aided establishment of further

education, or that the employment shall be restricted. These are reserve powers, however, and are not intended to remove from the employing authorities the responsibility for taking under their own procedures whatever action may be necessary when teachers become medically unfit. Particularly where there may be risk to students, employing authorities are advised to ensure that a teacher does not continue to perform teaching duties.

3 Where a teacher is either unable to continue duties or has no intention of resuming them until declared fit to do so, suspension will amount to no more than a formality; but in a few cases it may be needed in order to ensure that the teacher does not stay at work or resume duties when his or her presence entails a risk to students or other staff members, or the teacher concerned is unable to give efficient service. Authorities are requested to inform the DES or Welsh Office Education Department whenever suspension or prolonged absence occurs. Whilst it is the responsibility of the employing authority to decide whether a teacher is fit, the DES advises that greater consistency in dealing with cases will be achieved if the department's medical adviser is consulted whenever there is doubt in the matter. The medical adviser will also offer advice on the action to be taken in the case of any disorders other than those instanced in paragraph 4.

4 While the medical conditions which may lead to the suspension of a teacher from duty are wide ranging, specific recommendations have been made relating to:

(i) *Psychiatric disorder*

Ignoring short breaks, a teacher absent from duty for more than three months because of psychiatric disorder (a term which includes conditions described as nervous illness and depression) should be advised that, when he or she feels fit to resume duties, arrangements should be made for a consultant psychiatrist, preferably one familiar with the case, or else the family doctor where referral to a psychiatrist has not been considered necessary, to submit a report to the authority indicating whether the teacher is sufficiently fit and recovered to teach young people and be a member of the college community. The teacher should not be permitted to return unless satisfactory evidence of fitness has been provided.

(ii) *Epilepsy*

It is usual for there to be available complete, or almost complete control of this ailment. However, should a teacher suffer severe or recurrent attacks, the Specialist in Community Medicine (Child Health) should be informed and his or her advice sought on the need for temporary suspension while investigations occur and treatment is established. Where a teacher suffers occasional attacks and his or her condition was known at the time of appointment, suspension should not be necessary. Seizures occurring in a teacher not previously known to be subject to them should be fully investigated. Physical education teachers suffering epileptic attacks should always be suspended from specialist duties pending further investigation. Before allowing any suspended teacher to return to service, the authority should normally require a report detailing the circumstances of the case, including treatment and prognosis. It will also be necessary to consider the age ranges of the students in the teacher's charge and the circumstances of his or her employment; whether, for example, the teacher is engaged in work involving particular physical risks in instances such as physical education, home economics, laboratory, and craft work. When seeking the advice of the DES medical officers it will be helpful if the fullest information is made available about the nature, frequency, location and duration of the attacks.

5 A decision to terminate a teacher's employment on medical grounds is one for the employing authority to take unless the Secretary of State has prohibited the teacher's continued employment. It will be sensible to seek the advice of the DES medical officers. It would also be advisable to contact the DES to enquire as to its view if the teacher were to apply for an infirmity pension. Teachers whose employment may be terminated on medical grounds should seek also the advice of their relevant professional association.

APPENDIX 5

TEACHERS FROM OVERSEAS

1 Teachers from overseas, other than those who are nationals of full European Community (EC) states and Gibraltar, who wish to work in the United Kingdom need to hold work permits issued by the Department of Employment (DE) in respect of a specific post with a specific employer before they can enter the country. This requirement will continue to apply to the nationals of Greece, Spain, and Portugal until those countries have attained full membership of the EC.

2 However, certain nationals of non-EC countries may be admitted for employment without work permits, provided that they hold a current entry clearance or other satisfactory documentary evidence. These categories include:
(i) Ministers of religion and members of religious orders;
(ii) Commonwealth citizens who can prove that one of their grandparents was born in the UK;
(iii) Commonwealth citizens seeking teaching posts which are incidental to a holiday in this country and who do not intend to remain indefinitely;
(iv) Teaching and language assistants under exchange schemes approved by the Education Departments or administered by the Central Bureau for Educational Visits and Exchanges or the League for the Exchange of Commonwealth Teachers.

3 For prospective members of staff in colleges, work permits may only be issued in respect of such categories as:
(i) Those holding recognised professional qualifications;
(ii) Highly qualified technicians having specialised experience;
(iii) Other key workers with high or scarce qualifications in occupations requiring specific expert knowledge or skills;
(iv) People coming for a limited period of training on the job, or work experience approved by the DE;
(v) People whose employment, in the opinion of the DE, is in the national interest.
Persons in these categories will be expected to have an adequate command of the English language and, except for trainees, be in the 23–54 age band. However, in general work permits are only granted where a genuine vacancy exists which necessarily requires someone meeting the above requirements, where no suitable resident person is available, and where the application is for a named worker for a specific job with a specific employer. Management is expected to have tried to recruit a suitable employee from within the country and the EC, and to offer a salary and other terms and conditions of employment not less favourable than those obtaining for similar work.

4 Applications for work permits to employ overseas workers must be made at least eight weeks before the permit is required. These should be sent to the nearest Personnel and Executive Recruitment office, jobcentre, or employment office, unless the person is already in the UK, when the application must go to the Home Office Immigration and Nationality Department, Lunar House, Wellesley Road, Croydon CR9 2BY. Work permits, if granted, are normally valid for up to 12 months in the first instance.

APPENDIX 6

RESTRICTION ON EMPLOYMENT OF TEACHERS ON GROUNDS OF MISCONDUCT

1 Regulation 14 of the Further Education Regulations 1975 (S.I. 1975 No. 1054) provides that:
'A person who is on grounds of misconduct or conviction of a criminal offence determined by the Secretary of State to be unsuitable for employment as a teacher, or suitable for employment as such only to a limited extent, shall not be employed as a teacher or, as the case may be, shall be employed as such only to the extent determined by the Secretary of State.' Paragraph 10 of the Education (Teachers) Regulations 1982 (SI 1982/106) continues this provision and the 'List 99' procedure. DES Circular 4/86 provides a commentary on these regulations.

2 If a teacher is convicted of a criminal offence, the DES may refuse to allow her or him to continue in teaching employment. In making its decision, the department may require medical reports. The teacher has a right to receive a written statement detailing the reasons for the department's action. If the teacher is not satisfied with these reasons, an appeal can be made to a senior official of the department, where the appellant will have the right to be accompanied and represented by a friend.

FURTHER READING

Walton, F. (ed) *Encyclopaedia of Employment Law and Practice* Professional Publishing Ltd, London W1R 8AB. Loose-leaf publication updated four times a year to subscribers and widely available in colleges
Manpower Services Commission *The Employment of Disabled People* Code of Practice, HMSO
Department of Employment *Closed Shop Agreements and Arrangements* Code of Practice, HMSO
Department of Employment *Picketing* Code of Practice, HMSO
ACAS, *Codes of Practice*
ACAS *Disciplinary Practice and Procedures in Employment* Code of Practice 1, HMSO
ACAS *Disclosure of Information to Trade Unions for Collective Bargaining Purposes* Code of Practice 2, HMSO
ACAS *Time Off for Trade Union Duties and Activities* Code of Practice 3, HMSO

A range of leaflets and booklets explaining aspects of employment law is available from offices of the Department of Employment. Guidance booklets on the prevention of discrimination on grounds of sex, marital status and race, supplementing the relevant codes of practice, are available from HM Stationery Office or from the appropriate Commission at the following addresses:
Equal Opportunities Commission, Overseas House, Quay Street, Manchester M3 3HN; Tel: 061–833 9244
Commission for Racial Equality, Elliott House, 10–12 Allington Street, London SW1E 5EH; Tel: 01–828 7022

2.5 CONDITIONS OF SERVICE: TEACHING STAFF

1 The arrangements for conditions of service are made within a national framework by the National Joint Council for Further Education Lecturers in England and Wales (NJC) (see 2.1). Before 1980 agreements were made quite separately from agreements on salaries and allowances and this occurred in negotiation between the recognised further education lecturers' associations and the Council of Local Education Authorities (CLEA). In that period and at present the recognised lecturers' associations were the National Association of Teachers in Further and Higher Education (NATFHE), the Association of Principals of Colleges (APC), the Associations of Agricultural Education Staff (AAES) and the National Society for Education in Art and Design (NSEAD) (formerly the National Society for Art Education). The contemporary version of the conditions of service agreements reached are set out in the *Scheme for Conditions of Service for Further Education Teachers in England and Wales,* a document widely known as the 'Silver Book'. The Silver Book contains binding collective agreements in most areas of conditions of service; nationally agreed frameworks designed to guide or be incorporated into local agreements in some areas of conditions; and recommendations and model procedures in the remainder. It is important to identify the status of the various sections although, it should be added, even where sections provide frameworks or recommendations this does not mean that they can be lightly disregarded. All local authorities, the five Inner London Polytechnics, the voluntary colleges and all lecturing staff are bound in honour by the collective agreements by virtue of their position on the NJC.

2 Aside from setting down the conditions of service agreements, the Silver Book contains the salaries of Research Staff, the only group for whom salaries are not promulgated in the Burnham Further Education Report. It contains scales of compensation for staff in the event of death or permanent injury arising from assault. Further, it shows in summary the legislation which bears upon lecturers' conditions of service.

3 A number of local education authorities (LEAs) and individual institutions have elaborated the sections of the Silver Book where it provides frameworks or discretions to do so. Some of the larger LEAs publish insert sheets containing local variations and it is important to ascertain whether such local variations exist in order to operate the agreements properly. Equally, local practice is enshrined in other documents which should be consulted where relevant. For example, reference to procedures for appointment and dismissal of staff are usually described in the articles of government of individual institutions. Thus, those wishing to operate a system of conditions need to be aware of all these sources of information.

4 The necessity to specify some conditions of service arises from employment rights established by statute. These are dealt with extensively in **2.4**, and some of these rights are also itemised in Appendix I of the Silver Book. That appendix makes particular reference to rights concerning the issue of particulars of employment, trade union membership and activities, time off from work, maternity notice periods, dismissal and redundancy. The appendix also comments on the statutory position regarding sex and race discrimination and health and safety at work. (See **1.2** Appendices 2 and 3, **2.4** and **2.7**.)

5 These legislative requirements to establish a wide spectrum of conditions went hand-in-hand with the other impetus, a long-standing process of collective bargaining on these issues. Indeed, many of the conditions agreements predate the legislative requirement to have such agreements although some of them had to be rewritten to take account of the new laws. The two processes generated a number of distinctive agreements which were codified by negotiation into the Silver Book as a single authoritative document in 1980–81. The process was unique in education since the arrangements for primary and secondary schools were not set out in any detail until the winter of 1986–87 when a basic contract was negotiated under the auspices of the Advisory Conciliation and Arbitration Service (ACAS) between the local authority associations and the six primary and secondary teachers' unions.[1] Despite the fact that these negotiations reached an agreement between the local education authorities and a majority of school teachers, not all the school teachers' unions were parties to the agreement. In April 1987 a package of conditions of service arrangements and salaries was imposed upon the school teachers by the Secretary of State under the terms of the Teachers' Pay and Conditions Act 1987, brought on to the statute books for this purpose.

6 **Tenure**

Section 3 of the Silver Book, 'Contract of Employment', shows the link between the collective agreement on the character of the contract and the relevant statutes. Section 4 sets out the specific arrangements for tenure together with some of the arrangements for remuneration. The main arrangements for remuneration are not found in the Silver Book but in the Burnham Further Education Report (See **2.2**). It is intended that within the next year the two documents, the Silver Book and the Burnham Report, should be drawn together into a single authoritative document (See **2.1** 15).

7 Lecturers may only be required to undertake duties connected with the institution in which they are employed, and they may undertake other occupations provided that these do not interfere with the performance of their duties in the institution. Some authorities impose tighter definitions of these matters, especially where research, consultancy or other activities connected with private undertakings make any use of institutional premises or equipment. Such additional restrictions, whilst inhibiting some activities, benefit employers and staff by providing clear guidance which, if observed, limits the probability of misunderstandings about the use of resources. This provides legal as well as employment safeguards. In any case, the Silver Book specifies that equipment and stores may be used only with the approval of the principal (who may delegate the responsibility, of course), and only for the purpose of teaching, approved research or approved consultancy. It is acceptable that such work although relevant to the institution need not be performed on its premises.

8 The calendar year comprises three notional terms – that is 'terms' which do not necessarily have any relation to the actual term dates in an institution. The spring term runs from 1 January to 30 April, the summer term from 1 May to 31 August, and the autumn term from 1 September to 31 December. This continuous format, when associated with arrangements for pay and periods of notice, provides for continuity of employment irrespective of the timing and duration of holidays. The provision was thought prudent because the relatively longer holidays in education might give rise to a supposition of involuntary breaks in service for full-time staff. The length of the holidays are now

seen as no reason for supposing discontinuity in most circumstances even in the case of hourly paid part-time staff who are not paid during holiday periods. The case of *Ford v Warwickshire* (1983) (IRLR 26) clarifies the fact that even the break for the long summer vacation has the effect of making work 'seasonal' without necessarily having the effect of discontinuity for certain employment rights specified in legislation (see **2.4** 31–38).

9 Salary payments start from the first day of each of the notional terms irrespective of whether the actual term starts on the same day or some days later. On many occasions, generally because of the vagaries of when Easter falls, the actual summer term starts before 1 May (the notional term commencement date), and payment must then start from the actual date rather than the notional date. This can also happen in the autumn term. If employment as a lecturer follows immediately upon a period in employment outside education, salary payments must start from the date set out in the letter of appointment. Thus, any lecturer commencing employment during a term will be paid from the first day of duty. This pattern is related, in part, to the arrangements under which lecturers may give or be given notice of termination of contract. When an appointment is coming to an end, the salary shall be paid up to the last day of the notional term as set out in paragraph 13 above. An exception occurs when a lecturer is taking up a new appointment in an establishment in another authority at the beginning of a summer term or autumn term which actually starts before 1 May or 1 September respectively. The final salary from the old authority should date from the day preceding the date of commencement in the new authority.

10 Salaries have to be paid in monthly instalments, with one third of the annual salary paid for each term of service. Some local arrangements have been negotiated to permit the July and August salaries to be paid in July. In other local agreements there is accord about the day of the month (usually earlier than the last day) upon which the instalment should be paid.

11 The bulk of the national agreement on these matters was made in 1973. The agreement also sets out a lecturer's rights in the event of disciplinary action including termination, suspension and dismissal but it should be noted that these issues were renegotiated in 1985–86, and the 1986 agreement (Amendment 6 to the Silver Book) makes up Section 5 of that document. Dates for termination of contract, other than in cases of dismissal for misconduct or other urgent cause, or because of retirement, must accord with the provisions above unless the authority and lecturer come to a specific arrangement to vary this. The LEA or lecturer (other than heads of department, vice-principal or principal) must give written notice of not less than two calendar months before the end of the summer term. In cases of principals, vice-principals and heads of department each of these periods is extended by a calendar month.

12 **Retirement**

Whilst lecturers have rights to retire early under the terms of the Teachers' Superannuation Regulations, or the Local Government Superannuation Regulations, they automatically retire at the end of the term during which they attain their sixty-fifth birthday. Extensions or terminations of service can occur beyond the end of that term if mutually agreed. It will be noted that this provision pays no regard to gender. These provisions are always capable of change by virtue of changes in the law covering retirement.

13 **Discipline, suspension and dismissal**

The elements of the national procedures for discipline, suspension and dismissal, which appear as Section 5 of the Silver Book have to be incorporated into local procedures agreed between LEAs and recognised lecturers associations. They are primarily for use in cases of alleged misconduct. The elements of the procedure must have the following characteristics:

(i) The lecturer who is alleged to have committed misconduct should normally be interviewed by the principal or an appropriate officer of the LEA. The latter would certainly be involved if the allegation is against the principal.

(ii) The lecturer will be told in writing that the interview is to be held under the provisions of the disciplinary procedure. Full details of the complaint must be made available to the lecturer prior to the interview.

(iii) As a result of the interview, the principal or other LEA officer can decide to take no further action, reprimand the lecturer, or issue an oral, written or final warning that it may be necessary to refer the matter to the governing body. Whatever the result, the lecturer should be informed in writing.

(iv) At the interview the lecturer is entitled to be accompanied by a representative or friend. This is usually understood to be a union representative.

14 Alleged offences of a particularly serious character may justify the principal or LEA in suspending the lecturer rather than permitting continued attendance at the college, although it remains the normal procedure for full salary to be paid unless there is a compelling reason for not doing so. There have been cases where LEAs have decided to pay a proportion of the salary rather than the full salary but it is emphasised that there is no provision in the Burnham FE Report for this variation, and it is of doubtful legal propriety whatever local practice. In cases of suspension, the decision must be reported to the governing body and the LEA. It will be appreciated that such a step requires judgement to be exercised as to the seriousness of the allegation. The Silver Book provides no specific guidance but a prudent approach would potentially involve consideration of the precedents in the institution and authority, and the question of whether the allegation involves unlawful behaviour of a kind that would, on conviction, attract a serious sentence.

15 The procedures outlined thus far relate to misconduct. The possibility of suspension or dismissal can arise in cases of professional incompetence. In cases of alleged incompetence, before any procedures are inaugurated, representatives of the employer (who may be local college managers) should discuss with the lecturer the forms of supportive action capable of improving the lecturer's performance. If this is impossible or unsuccessful, the procedures set out in the remainder of this paragraph apply. These are also the procedures which apply to misconduct after the steps shown in paragraph 19 have been exhausted. In other words, the remainder of this paragraph shows the steps appropriate to either misconduct or professional incompetence.

(a) Where a complaint of misconduct or professional incompetence is reported to the governing body, the precise form of procedure will be that established in the instruments and articles of government of the institution. But in all cases the lecturer must receive full information on the arrangements, allegations and entitlement to representation in writing.

(b) Following a hearing undertaken in accordance with the appropriate arrangements, the governing body may dismiss the allegation or, if it finds against the lecturer, may impose one or more of the following sanctions:

(i) A reprimand
(ii) A written warning of the probable consequences if there is further recourse to the procedures.
(iii) Transfer to another post, although regard must be had to the lecturer's contract.
(iv) Recommendation to the LEA that they should withhold a salary increment (as provided by Paragraph 2, Appendix III of the Burnham FE Report which states that 'No increment shall be withheld in respect of any year unless the service in that year has been declared unsatisfactory by the local education authority. In such a case, payment of the increment in respect of that year shall be withheld only during the following year unless the local education authority otherwise expressly determines'). This sanction is intended to penalise the lecturer for one year and not to introduce a financial sanction which would persist in every year in which the lecturer is below the top point of the scale on which she or he is serving.
(v) Recommendation to the LEA to dismiss. In (iv) and (v) above, the extent of the governing body's powers only go beyond 'recommendation' in rare cases. It is also possible for the LEA to transfer the lecturer to another establishment.

16 The agreement also provides for appeals. Appeals against the procedures or decisions taken under procedures as shown in paragraph 13 above, will be heard under the Grievance Procedure, the general terms of which are described below (paragraphs 26 and 27), whilst appeals against the decisions or recommendations of the Governors taken under the terms of the college instruments and articles and in conformity with paragraph 15 above, will be heard by the LEA. These latter appeals will be held concurrently with any LEA hearing relating to such a recommendation so as to avoid any duplication of procedures. With written or oral warnings, a lecturer may indicate a dissenting view or explanation on the file, this statement being an alternative to appeal. The appeal body will confirm, vary or dismiss the decision or recommendation placed before it. Section 5.9 of the Silver Book states that warnings or reprimands should remain on the file normally for no longer than 12 months depending on the nature of the offence and the type of disciplinary action. It further requires that all steps of the procedure specify notice periods in terms of working days other than for the interview at the very beginning of the process. Confidentiality must be observed throughout. If records of proceedings are kept on computer files, it is recommended that **1.2** Appendix 5 concerning data protection should be consulted.

17 Two further and important provisions concern the people who may be involved in disciplinary procedures. First, in the case of procedures against a trade union representative, the ACAS Code must be followed and the relevant full-time official of the trade union involved must be notified. The trade union representative against whom allegations are made has particular rights to representation. Second, in the determination of the composition of disciplinary and appeals bodies established under these procedures for any lecturer they must include either a lecturer member of the LEA's Education Committee or a lecturer specially selected for the purpose by the FE lecturers in the authority, save that no individual directly involved may serve.

18 **Probation**

LEAs or governing bodies can require that the first year of teaching may be regarded as probationary for a lecturer in his or her first teaching appointment. If an LEA decides to terminate the contract at the end of the year, the arrangements set out for termination, above, apply. There are differing local agreements on whether probation is used and it is essential to check both whether and how the local scheme is operated.

19 **Day-to-day conditions of service**

In 1975 a far-reaching agreement was reached which deals with the day-to-day working practices of the further and higher education system. It covers daily, weekly and annual working arrangements for all lecturers. The agreement remains unique in education although it was subjected to disparagement and misrepresentation from the outset as either 'a Skiver's Charter' (*Daily Mail*) or a straitjacket on the working arrangements of lecturing staff. In reality it is neither, and the fact that either is believed is probably due to the lack of detailed attention given to this aspect of conditions of service. It does *not* set a maximum professional workload or provide a set of restrictions on what a lecturer should do. On the contrary, it says what it is reasonable for the employer to require. By reflecting a variety of possible ways of organising college days and weeks, and providing for the extension of college years beyond the normally published term times, it engenders considerable flexibility both in theory and in practice. It also ensures that there are reasonably comparable arrangements with other sectors of education. The flexibility of its provisions has been such that within its framework and without further modification to it, between 1982 and 1986, some 25% more full-time equivalent students were admitted to public sector higher education, and the LEA/MSC Joint Efficiency Study (see **2.8** 38) shows significant increases in non-advanced further education student numbers, without appreciable increases in staffing levels giving rise to productivity gains of six per cent in 1985–87. Some of these gains have been due to bigger classes. As many of these students are part-time adult students, considerable varieties of working practice have evolved to achieve these levels of provision at times suited to the students, something which would be unlikely to occur in an inflexible system.

20 The 1975 Agreement is found in codified form in Sections 6 to 9 of the Silver Book. The main elements are:

(i) Section 6 sets out the length and distribution of the lecturer's working year as being, at maximum, 38 weeks of which no more than 36 should be teaching weeks. This does not imply that the college should be open for no more than 38 weeks in each calendar year but deals exclusively with the maximum requirement on individual lecturers to attend. Thus different patterns of attendance among lecturers could secure almost continuous college opening. Lecturers may not be required to teach for continuous periods exceeding 14 weeks. Between the beginning of June and end of September arrangements should be made for at least six and preferably seven weeks' continuous holiday for the lecturer. Special regard should be paid when scheduling holiday periods to the position of lecturers with children at school or who wish to attend courses during vacation times. The schedules for the academic year should be made available by the end of October at the latest. Colleges should not run classes during periods of seven consecutive days at Christmas or Easter. Union representatives are entitled to have access to detailed information about timetables to verify compliance with the provisions of the agreement.

(ii) Section 7 deals with teaching load which is constrained in two ways. First, no lecturer can be required to attend for more than ten sessions in a week. By custom and practice a week runs from Monday to Friday. A session is a morning, afternoon or evening, and should not normally exceed three hours duration and never exceed four hours. An evening session is one which lasts at least half an hour but not more than three hours starting after 5.30pm. Taken together, the ten sessions of a normal duration of three hours provide a weekly contractual maximum requirement of 30 hours attendance time. Secondly, the class contact hours of a lecturer (the time spent in actual teaching, invigilating, supervising individual students or groups, and supervising examinations or tests), are laid down according to the grade of lectureship held by an individual. The contact hours for each grade are expressed as bands and local negotiation between LEAs and recognised lecturers' associations has determined the maxima to be worked in each authority within these bands. It is worth noting that the bands adopted reflected the spread of local arrangements prior to the 1975 agreement and an inability to agree single figures for each lecturing grade through national negotiation. No such agreement has proved possible since. The national bands are:
Lecturer I 20–22 hours
Lecturer II 17–20 hours
Senior Lecturer 15–18 hours
Principal Lecturer 13–16 hours
There are no specified class contact hours for grades above Principal Lecturer although a number of Heads of Department teach, and, on occasions, other college managers who prefer to maintain some contact with the classroom, laboratory or workshop. As a result of a salary settlement in 1985, Lecturers Grade I became eligible for transfer to the Lecturer Grade II scale on completion of the appropriate proportion of a year at Point 15 of the Lecturer Grade I scale (See **2.2** 50). Although for Burnham FE document and remunerative purposes, those transferring became Lecturers Grade II, the 1985 agreement specified that they should retain the class contact hours appropriate to Lecturers Grade I in their authority. In this way they differ from lecturers promoted to the Lecturer Grade II scale who have an entitlement to move to the appropriate contact hour for Lecturers Grade II in their authority.

(iii) Lecturers cannot be required to teach for more than three hours in an evening session nor to undertake more than two evening sessions per week. The caveat to this provision (Section 7.5 of the Silver Book) says that in some cases appointments will be made with special responsibilities for evening work. In practice, this happens most frequently in adult education where there is a variety of practice across the country. There are a number of local agreements restricting evening sessions to three, but the limit in practice appears, most widely, to be four sessions.

(iv) The definition of class contact given in the paragraph above does not encompass all the work of a lecturer, and it is expressed in the Silver Book as the maximum that can be required in terms of class contact. Lecturers have many other responsibilities. Section 8 of the Silver Book identifies a far wider range of tasks and professional duties and provides that LEAs shall negotiate in appropriate cases a scheme of abatement from class contact duties to enable lecturers to perform these other duties. Historically this abatement has been known as 'class contact remission', a term which has fallen out of favour in further education because of the negative connotations of the word 'remission'. The Section gives examples of these professional duties which are not exhaustive. The agreement notes that some responsibilities are necessarily identified and defined by LEAs and may, of course, be institution-specific. Among the examples given for general understanding of the purpose of Section 8.3 of the Silver Book are: research undertakings, setting and marking examinations, a wide range of kinds of supervision of activities, duties connected with student welfare, and liaison with student unions[2]. Thus, abatement can be seen to have taken two forms. First, there is a built-in abatement associated with the grade of Lecturer ('grade-related remission') which works on the assumption that as a lecturer moves from one grade to a higher grade, she or he will, in all likelihood, assume greater responsibilities in the areas set out in Section 8.3. Second, there are the abatements specifically given in appropriate cases for tasks of the kind set out in Section 8.3. In respect of this latter kind of abatement, it reduces class contact availability for individual lecturers and in aggregate for the institution. It is therefore necessary that a proportion of the college's potential class contact should be set aside for these purposes, and this is necessarily part of the regular consultation between the LEA and recognised lecturers' associations on the college establishment. Whilst the responsibility for securing smooth, high quality academic performance is essential to college managers, and they look in part to the abatement system to meet these objectives, in reality there is very little by way of remission hours in further education. A broad estimate in October 1986, based on the Audit Commission Report on FE[3], suggests that the percentage of the establishment set aside for abatement is under four per cent. The Audit Commission themselves, whilst commending that colleges should undertake more tasks that would require abatement, perversely recommended that colleges should aim down to three per cent of establishment, a figure which led to widespread criticism among LEAs, educationalists and the staff unions (See **1.3** 112–113, **2.8** 37).

(v) Whilst the maximum figures set for hours is intended to cover every working week, Section 8.5 recognises that in some colleges and departments, the programme of work is unbalanced by sandwich, block release and short courses. Other than in sudden or short-term emergencies, it is unreasonable to expect lecturers to undertake excessive class contact in any week. Only in cases where lecturers supervise students in placements as a practical element in their course (particularly in teacher education in respect of teaching practice), can a lecturer be required to work above the negotiated contact maximum. In these cases, subsequent weeks should be averaged downward so that the overall balance created by the negotiated maximum is not distorted. In many LEAs there is a local restriction on the ceiling for hours even within an averaged arrangement and on the number of weeks for which it can operate. Other than in the circumstances set out in Section 8.5, averaging is not permitted in the national agreement.

(vi) Some unforeseen circumstances do produce sudden and/or short-term variations which breach the otherwise clear provision that systematic additional duties should not exist, a provision in Section 9 of the Silver Book. If late decisions to mount a course or cope with temporary staff shortages are taken, lecturers who undertake the resulting work may receive an extra 'overtime' payment at the appropriate hourly rate for the course on which they undertake the work. Overtime should not be used to deal with systematic teaching duties and should be avoided. Systematic overtime is usually the result of failure to recruit appropriate staff and forms something of a 'slush fund' in the system. If possible, the additional contracts (for that is what overtime contracts are) should be awarded to part-time hourly paid staff of whom there are over 100,000. College managers should also give careful attention to ascertain whether existing, appropriate full-time lecturers have space within their timetables such that the timetabled classes and abatements add up to less than their agreed local maximum for their grades. It has been noted above that in certain circumstances lecturers will be paid on additional contracts at the appropriate hourly rate. The exceptions are when (i) the lecturer substitutes for a colleague who is absent for three consecutive days or less in the event of a sudden emergency, although when the absence stretches beyond three days payment must be made for the whole period of cover starting at day one; and (ii) where the lecturer elects to take paid leave of absence (time in lieu) instead of the overtime payment.[4]

(vii) When the agreement was made, it was known that working arrangements varied between colleges in the same LEA. For this reason a safeguarding clause was agreed (Section 22 of the Silver Book). Safeguarding takes two forms. First, where existing conditions in force prior to the introduction of local agreements introduced in 1975–76 are better than those in the agreement, or local variations of it, the better conditions shall apply to lecturers who were in post at the time of the introduction of the 1975–76 agreement so long as they remain in their existing posts. Second, in respect only of the provisions for lecturers' contact hours and length of year, the existing arrangements in the college should be retained. Two examples may illustrate the character of safeguarding. If lecturers in a college traditionally had a 35 week teaching year, then that 'year' would apply to existing and new staff. Where a college had an arrangement to pay all lecturers substituting for absent colleagues without applying the 'three day' qualification, then lecturers in post in 1975 would enjoy this advantage whilst they remain in their post, as the condition would be protected.

21 **Sick leave and sick pay**

The basic arrangements for all LEA colleges and schools are provided in the Teachers' Sick Pay Regulations and are codified in Section 11 of the Silver Book as a result of an amendment in 1983. This amendment incorporates legislation on Statutory Sick Pay (The Social Security Act 1982):

(i) The amount of sick leave entitlement depends on length of service, as Table 1 shows. LEAs have discretion to improve on the minima shown in the table. Working days are any days on which the establishment is open for teaching but is not part of the lecturer's personal holiday entitlement. Saturdays and Sundays are excluded.

(ii) Sick pay includes Statutory Sick Pay where there is appropriate, the total of sick pay not exceeding the total of normal full pay. This gives rise to the calculations shown in the following sub-paragraphs (iii), (iv) and (v).

(iii) The sick pay year runs from 1 April to 31 March. Lecturers on sick leave

Table 1
Sick leave entitlement

Length of Service	*Full pay (working days)*	*Half pay (working days)*
Under one year	25	50 after four months' service
Two years	50	50
Three years	75	75
Four or more years	100	100

on 31 March are not entitled to fresh allowances until they have resumed teaching duties.

(iv) Because sick pay may not exceed normal full pay, deductions are made from sick pay when it is equal to full pay. The amount receivable under the Social Security Acts 1975–82 in respect of the first three days of illness will be deducted if the benefit has in fact been received. There will be deduction of compensatory payments under the Workmen's Compensation Acts in respect of accidents sustained before 5 July 1948. Finally, the dependency (but not the disability) element of any treatment allowance received from the Department of Health and Social Security (DHSS) is deducted.

(v) If sick pay results from an accident occurring in the course of college duties, lecturers are entitled to six months' full pay and, at the discretion of the LEA, six months' half pay. If any damages are recoverable from a third party in respect of any injury, the LEA can reclaim some of the allowances paid. The allowances are not paid in any case when accidents occur due to active, professional engagement in a sport other than when the LEA has resolved to do so. There are other variations in arrangements where absence arises from pulmonary tuberculosis or a lecturer resides in a house in which another occupant is suffering from an infectious disease.

(vi) A lecturer absent for more than three college working days owing to illness is required to provide a 'self certificate' to the employer, that being an explicit account of the nature of the illness or incapacity. Since most doctors do not provide certificates for periods of a week or less under current legislation, self certification has been introduced. Certificates are required for longer periods and a lecturer can be required to submit certificates at the end of each month of absence or upon return to duty. If hospitalised, certificates on entry and discharge are substituted for periodic certificates.

(vii) Sickness during periods of college closure or during the lecturer's personal holiday entitlement do not affect entitlements to sick leave but do affect deductions of benefit. Lecturers on full or half pay do not have the closure or holiday periods counted against entitlement in the respective levels of pay and, equally, if sick pay entitlement has been exhausted, no payment will be made in such a period of closure or holiday.

22 Maternity

The scheme in further education, somewhat modified by the Employment Protection (Consolidation) Act 1978, is found in Section 12 of the Silver Book. It makes provision for the following arrangements:

(i) The basic provisions apply to women lecturers who have one year's full time service with one or more LEAs, or equivalent part-time service immediately before the start of maternity absence. In addition, lecturers with two or more years of continuous service have the rights set out in sub-paragraphs (vi) and (vii) below.

(ii) The lecturer must notify the LEA of her intention to take leave as soon as practicable and, unless she can show good cause, must do so not less than 14 weeks prior to the expected date of confinement. If she wishes to return to work in the job in which she is employed, she should so inform her employer in the same notification.

(iii) She may absent herself from work at the beginning of the eleventh week before the expected date of confinement or at a later date unless she has been certified as unfit to work.

(iv) She may remain absent for 18 weeks from the commencement of leave, this being limited to a period up to six weeks from the confinement in the case of stillbirth.

(v) From 6 April 1987, provisions for Statutory Maternity Pay came into operation. This replaces the provisions of Section 12.7 of the Silver Book as currently printed. Lecturers eligible for Statutory Maternity Pay (SMP) will have payments made in the first six weeks of absence at the appropriate SMP rate offset against payments made under the general terms of the Scheme. For the first four weeks the lecturer not eligible for SMP receives 100 per cent and the full rate maternity allowance is deducted. Where the lecturer is entitled to additional benefits there is also deduction of the earnings-related supplement and/or the increased maternity allowance attributable to dependants. The total of these sums shall not be less than 9/10 of a week's salary reduced only by the flat rate maternity allowance. The next two weeks of absence attracts 9/10 of a week's salary reduced by the flat rate maternity allowance when the lecturer is not eligible for SMP. During the remainder of the 18 week's absence, half pay is made from which there are no deductions except where the pay and SMP (or maternity allowance and any dependants' allowances if the lecturer is ineligible for SMP) when combined exceed full pay. This is not detrimental when compared with the past arrangements except that the whole amount is not taxable. The tax arrangement is not, of course, subject to any element of negotiation but results from free-standing arrangements.

(vi) These payments are made on the condition that the lecturer returns to work for at least 13 weeks full time (or the equivalent part-time, if agreed with the LEA). The LEA may reclaim payment if the condition is breached, except from lecturers with two years or more of continuous service for whom rights to the first six weeks' pay is absolute. The 13 week period for this calculation runs from the date on which the lecturer returns to duty or the date in any college holiday on which she is deemed to be available for duty.

(vii) Absence due to illness attributable to pregnancy occurring outside the maternity leave period is subject to the arrangements for sick leave provided it is covered by self certification or a doctor's certificate as appropriate.

(ix) Employing authorities may, and a number do, extend the relevant post-

natal provisions of maternity leave to adoptive mothers.
(See **2.4** 57–71).

23 **Redundancy Procedures**

In 1975 a revised redundancy procedural agreement was made establishing procedures to be adopted in instances of anticipated redundancy. It appears as Appendix III of the Silver Book. The wording of the agreement contains the formulation 'The recommendations on which agreement has been reached are as follows . . .', and in respect of the period of notice in circumstances of redundancy, the word 'recommended' appears once again. The formulation has led to disagreement between the employers' and lecturers' associations in the National Joint Council, the former contending that the agreement bound only those LEAs which explicitly adopted the 'recommendation' or who had done so in practice whether having passed a resolution to do so or not. The lecturers have argued that the style of wording chosen in the old bargaining machinery, where such terminology was more common, did not alter the fact that the agreement was binding and had been intended as a contractual provision. The issue has been tested in Cains vs London Borough of Ealing where the Industrial Tribunal held that the period of notice specified, namely 12 months, was a collective agreement and binding on the parties because Caines' contract confirmed his entitlement to benefits of national 'collective' agreements.

24 The agreement in Appendix III should be read alongside other provisions. First, Appendix III has, by way of a preamble, a statement guiding use of the agreement and cross-referencing to the relevant legislation. Second, there is considerable case precedent that has emerged in respect of redundancies in teacher training and in the operation of the Crombie Compensation Regulations (See **2.3** 49–57). Third, in Appendix IV of the Silver Book, there is an agreed procedure covering the use of premature retirement compensation arrangements under the Teachers' Superannuation Scheme (See **2.3**). Finally, the provisions of the Employment Protection (Consolidation) Act 1978 must be considered. With these additional factors in mind, the main provisions of Appendix III of the Silver Book are:

(i) It is intended to cover redundancies arising in further education from periodic contraction or changes in work patterns. It was not designed to cope with the large scale redundancies caused by the reorganisation of teacher education although many LEAs and institutions have found it useful to apply the procedures to such redundancies. In essence, such redundancies should be subject to distinctive local procedures designed to deal with the specific circumstances prevailing.

(ii) The procedures envisage the earliest possible discussion between employers and recognised further education lecturers' unions whenever redundancies are thought likely by either side. Both have obligations to draw the attention of the other to possible problems. Every effort should be made to find alternative employment and this should include consultations with neighbouring authorities.

(iii) Notice of at least one year should be given to the lecturer(s) concerned and individuals should have a right to appeal against redundancy.

(iv) Secondment to facilitate retraining should be given to redundant lecturers. The period may overlap or run consecutively with the period of notice.

(See **2.3** and **2.4** 115–137.)

25 In recent years there has been a considerable growth in the use of fixed term contracts by local authorities. Whilst these contracts do not necessarily overcome the rights under legislation, they do provide specific points at which termination is relatively quicker than the provisions of Appendix III. The most common form of these contracts still requires the normal process of dismissal at the appropriate point set out in the contract, for period of notice. The contracts, if they run consecutively, will provide employment protection on the basis of their aggregate length. However, some contracts are issued containing 'waiver' clauses whereby the person working under the terms of the contract, whether they have signed it or not, is taken to have given up or waived the statutory rights specified in the waiver clause. A more recent innovation reflects the fact that many fixed term contracts have emerged as a response to short-term funding of courses or posts by the Manpower Services Commission or other external funding bodies. In a few cases, the contract specifies that it is for the performance of a specific task rather than for a specific period, the task being defined in terms of the purpose for which the external funding was given. These forms of contract are sometimes said to be an employers' response to the 12 month notice period in the Redundancy Procedures agreement in the Silver Book. Such innovations are, for obvious reasons, disliked by the lecturers' associations and by individual lecturers thus employed. They are regarded as methods for securing more casual forms of employment, the insecurity giving rise to industrial relations tensions.

26 **Grievance procedures**

Appendix II of the Silver Book provides a Model Grievance Procedure in accordance with the Contracts of Employment Act, 1972. The Appendix derives from an agreement struck in 1973. As will be seen, whilst the procedure is intended to suit the needs of all lecturing staff, it requires slight modification to apply to heads of department, vice-principals and principals in part because it is reasonably common that these staff, as the institutional line managers, are the subjects of the grievances of more junior staff. The main provisions are:

(i) An informal procedure which is intended to resolve problems by encouraging lecturers to approach the other member of staff against whom they feel they have a grievance and, if the matter remains unresolved, to take it to the head of department. At this, or later stages, the lecturer expressing the grievance can be accompanied by a friend who may be a trade union representative. The interview with the head of department should take place within five working days of the request for it. Finally, in the informal phase of the procedure, an interview can be held with the principal, to be arranged within ten working days of the request, this latter interview being intended to resolve anything not earlier resolved

(ii) A formal procedure in two stages, at the first of which the aggrieved party has to submit a written notice of grievance to the Chair of Governors of the institution. The aggrieving party and principal should receive copies. Unless the principal is the aggrieving party, she or he should make a written report to the Governors. Between five and ten working days after the submission of this report, a hearing should be convened to which both parties should be invited. The hearing should make whatever finding it regards as appropriate given the facts and circumstances. Secondly, there should be a right of appeal against the findings of the hearing open to either of the parties involved. The constitution of the Appeal Committee should be agreed between the LEA and the recognised further education lecturers' unions. Documents should be submitted within ten working days of the notice of appeal and the appeal heard not more than 21 working days after receipt of the notice.

27 It should be noted that many industrial relations professionals find the grievance procedure (and grievance procedures in general) unsatisfactory. In part that is because it is cumbersome and seldom resolves the issues at the informal level. In part it is because the aggrieving person may and often does issue counter-grievances and this produces unduly complex procedural problems. Generally, the reservations focus on the fact that it is difficult to restrict issues to strictly interpersonal grievances rather than to deal with them as by-products of structural stresses or matters affecting larger number of people. When the issues have these latter characteristics, they are better resolved by local collective bargaining than by use of the grievance procedures.

28 **Facilities for representatives of recognised lecturers' associations**

In 1976, the employers' and recognised lecturers' associations made an agreement on time off for trade union activities designed to enhance the conduct of industrial relations. The union representatives covered in Appendix V of the Silver Book are the elected, accredited lecturers' representatives and not the paid officials of the unions. The recommendations commend local negotiation on the amount of time off and there is a suggestion that disagreements should be clarified by reference to the national negotiators. It is the responsibility of the unions to notify local employers of their accredited representatives, who will be likely to have an involvement in:

(i) Grievance and disputes procedures,
(ii) Organisational responsibilities,
(iii) Negotiating responsibilities at local level,
(iv) Functions connected with training of lecturers' representatives and attendance at local, regional and national union schools, and
(v) Responsibilities at regional and/or national level if elected to these levels.

29 It is recommended that the facilities provided include:

(i) Arrangements and leave of absence to undertake the duties set out above.
(ii) Provision of lists of new members of staff and arrangements for direct communication with them.
(iii) Provision by the LEA of complete staffing lists each year.
(iv) Provision of rooms for meetings in institutions and in other employers' premises.
(v) Facilities to circulate materials through the employers' distribution system.
(vi) Arrangements for deduction of subscriptions at source ('check off') where requested by the local organisation of any nationally recognised lecturers' union. The deducted subscriptions are typically paid to the recognised unions on a monthly or quarterly basis and, in a small number of cases, have a small administrative, handling charge deducted by the LEA.

30 Time off for trade union Health and Safety representatives together with the provision of other facilities is a matter which has been introduced by legislation since the codification of the conditions of service agreements into the Silver Book. In general, the distribution of Health and Safety functions among mem-

bers of the staff of an institution are such that whilst all unions in the institution are entitled to and will have Health and Safety representatives, the specific distribution of tasks and areas of responsibility among the trade union representatives as a whole, and the consequential division of time allocated among them, will vary considerably from place to place. The legal provisions for both staff and managers is set out in **2.7**.

31 **Facilities for training and education**

In 1985 the National Joint Council concluded a new agreement on the responsibilities of LEAs to advise their lecturing staff on courses of study and training, the provision for which lies in their discretion bearing in mind the needs of the service and the lecturer concerned. When an authority encourages a lecturer or gives consent to the lecturers to attend a course of study, different provisions should be made depending on whether the course is full or part-time.

(i) With full-time, block release, sandwich or short courses of more than 23 hours duration (i.e. more than one day), the LEA should pay full salary, course fees and other approved educational expenses arising from attendance, any reasonable sums resulting from attendance as are approved by the LEA, and an out of pocket expense allowance currently of £2.20 per night with a normal weekly maximum of £8.80 if it is a residential course. This is to take account of the fact that one of the major benefits of residential courses may involve additional expenditure. This curious form of words and parsimonious allowance is designed to cover the fact that members of residential courses may derive benefit from having a chat over a drink.

(ii) Where the course is a part-time, approved day time course, the same provisions for salary, fees, expenses and allowances apply, and where the course is undertaken by distance learning, the LEA should consider the kinds of facilities that would assist. If the course falls within college hours, the LEA can grant remission from class contact time and the 30 hour contractual obligations.

32 The conditions attached to these study opportunities are that where a lecturer fails to sit an appropriate examination without good reason or fails to show satisfactory progress, facilities can be withdrawn. A second attempt at an examination or continuance to further stages of study are at the discretion of the LEA. If the course leads to a qualification, the LEA may stipulate that on gaining the qualification the lecturer must undertake to remain in the authority's employ for a further two years. Failure to honour such an undertaking entitles the authority to seek repayment in full of financial assistance. A lecturer leaving the employ of the authority before the course is completed may also be asked to repay the financial assistance. These repayments exclude salary.

33 **Indemnification of lecturers**

Section 14 of the Silver Book sets out the entitlements to payment for lecturers in the event of disablement or to their dependants in the event of death arising from a violent or criminal assault suffered by the employee in the course of, or as a consequence of his or her employment. In the event of death within 12 months of the date of the assault and as a result of the assault (in the opinion of the authority), where one or more dependants have been left, the authority shall pay them five times the gross remuneration at the rate applying at the time of the assault (or £15,000, whichever the greater). Where there are no dependants, a sum of £400 shall be paid. In the event of permanent total or partial disablement resulting from the assault, a proportional payment based on the figures shown above shall be made depending on the character of the injury. The percentages for each kind of injury are shown in Section 14 of the Silver Book and this should be consulted. The payments, at the employer's discretion, may be reduced by the amount of any damages or compensation recoverable in respect of the injury. Dependants include spouses domiciled with or supported by the employee, and children under the age of 16 or who have not attained the age of 19 and are pursuing a course of full-time education or are undergoing an apprenticeship. The recommendations do not prevent an authority paying amounts exceeding those set out.

34 **Collective disputes procedure**

Almost any of the matters discussed in this chapter can give rise to a disagreement on the interpretation and operation of the agreements. In order to establish methods for resolving disputes in the sphere of conditions of service, the National Joint Council reached a procedural agreement in 1985 directed to minimising the possibility of disputes and providing effective means of resolving them if they nonetheless occurred.

(i) LEAs are enjoined to make proper bargaining arrangements which, inter alia, enable the discharge of negotiation on matters which are purely further educational in character. This provision should discourage the merging of such negotiations into local bargaining machinery established for schools, administrative or manual staffs in any authority. Such negotiations can take place at the request of either party.

(ii) To define matters that are appropriate to negotiation rather than consultation since some matters cannot be expected to be resolved by bargaining, including the level of the rate call or the share of income allocated to further education or any other service. Attention is drawn to the fact that certain of the decisions which remain the prerogative of the LEA give rise to issues which are proper matters for local bargaining like work load, security or staff transfers.

(iii) Provision of time limits for holding meetings is commended.

(iv) It is commended that disputes at establishment level be resolved if possible between the principal and recognised lecturers' association(s), and, if necessary, between these associations and the governing body of the establishment. For this to succeed, both parties will need to understand that it is an issue capable of resolution at establishment level rather than, say, an issue of applicability throughout the LEA. In any case, if there are unreasonable delays in dealing with the matters in contention, it must be open to either party to take the matter to the LEA. The same procedures for resolving disputes as appear in sub-paragraph (v) are recommended.

(v) Where the dispute is at local authority level, affecting more than one establishment of further education, every effort should be made to achieve a resolution by discussion between authorised representatives of the recognised lecturers' associations and the chief education officer and/or his or her nominees. It is commended that the two parties agree a timescale for the discussion and that if the dispute is not resolved at the end of this period, the discussion should be moved to the level of LEA members and the representatives of the recognised lecturers' associations. There should be an agreed period of time which should not be exceeded between the failure to agree at officer level and the involvement of the members.

(vi) If the matter is not resolved in the mechanisms shown, the national representative of both sides may be asked to assist in dealing with the dispute provided both sides locally agree to this procedure. If this does not succeed, reference to the Advisory, Conciliation and Arbitration Service should be considered.

(vii) Where a reference is agreed to the national disputes procedure, the services of the Joint Secretaries of the NJC are available in the first instance at the request of either party to advise on the interpretation of agreements or to assist the parties on an informal basis by advising and conciliating if asked to do so. This will normally precede any other step. If this does not assist, a formal reference to the NJC may be made provided both parties do so. A Disputes Committee will be established comprising equal representatives of employers' and lecturers' associations with a Chair being nominated within the Disputes Committee. Both sides to the dispute will submit written cases, to be exchanged seven days before the hearing. At the hearing, oral statements may be made and witnesses called if appropriate. The decision of the Disputes Committee will take the form of a recommendation to the disputing parties and the NJC will seek to ensure compliance with the recommendation. The parties may ask the Disputes Committee to determine the issue, in which case the decision will be binding. The decisions of the Disputes Committee will be made available within seven days of the hearing.

(viii) In dealing with a particular dispute, the recognised unions and authorities may agree to vary the procedures but they can only be varied by agreement.

(ix) Where a dispute has arisen because of attempts to change existing procedures, it is recommended that the status quo ante be maintained until the procedures have been exhausted.

(x) Variations in time limits for discussions should only occur by agreement and, in general, parties should adhere to time limits. The appropriate timescale is best determined locally by those familiar with the circumstances. (See **2.10**.)

NOTES

1 The agreement reached was not ratified by all six primary and secondary teachers' unions but by a narrow majority largely comprising members of the National Union of Teachers, and Assistant Masters and Mistresses Association. The agreement was set aside by the Secretary of State for Education who imposed salaries and specified conditions under the terms of the Teachers' Pay and Conditions Act, 1987. Both the incomplete agreement and imposed arrangements imported detailed conditions of service for school teachers. In addition, the High Court has decided (Sira and others v Rotherham Metropolitan Borough Council and others, 23 May 1986) that in certain matters in regard to which there are or were no written contractual specification (of which cover for absent colleagues is the principal example), there is a contractual obligation to comply with the request of a Head Teacher to undertake the activity. This obligation rests upon what has been accepted as a normal part of professional obligations in the past. Thus, the case shows that a contract can extend well beyond written contract. The case has ramifications for all professional staff including lecturers.

2 Attempts by the LEAs and lecturers' unions to renegotiate the conditions of service during 1986–87 here produced a new definition of the professional duties of lecturers about which there appears to be a degree of consensus.

3 The estimates, by D. Triesman and D. Betts, were prepared for the National Joint Council negotiations held in Nottingham in October 1986. Details are available from NATFHE.

4 A different arrangement exists by virtue of local negotiation in the Inner London Education Authority where substitution is a term of contract and may be required but where payment is assumed from the outset.

APPENDIX 1

AGRICULTURAL AND HORTICULTURAL ESTABLISHMENT LECTURERS

1 The matters set out in **2.5** 20 are varied for lecturers in agricultural and horticultural establishments to take account, as Section 10 of the Silver Book has it, of the continuous processes of production in the industry necessitating longer working periods. It has always been maintained that the inexorable progress of the seasons pays small regard to the normal provisions of the Silver Book. The longer periods are specified as:
(i) A maximum working year of 42 weeks (although the evidence suggests that in practice there is a movement toward the same college year as in mainstream FE in an increasing number of agricultural education institutions).
(ii) A leave entitlement to not less than four weeks' continuous holiday between the beginning of June and the end of September.
(iii) A normal maximum requirement of between 20 and 22 hours class contact each week, except in cases of sudden and/or short term emergencies when contact can go up to but not exceed 24 hours.

2 In other major respects the conditions of service are as provided for lecturers in further education in general. It should be noted that the union representing this group of lecturers, the Association of Agricultural Education Staff (AAES), has been seeking, with the support of all the recognised unions, harmonisation of arrangements with further education in respect of the matters set out above, and that at the time of writing this is under negotiation.

APPENDIX 2

PRISON EDUCATION STAFF

1 Prior to March 1986, the Joint Negotiating Committee for Further Education Teachers employed by Local Education Authorities in England and Wales and assigned to Prison Service Establishments, negotiated the terms and conditions of service of such staff. This body had existed since 28 March 1977 and considered 'salary scales and other provisions', taking account of the Burnham Further Education Document, and agreements reached in the NJC for Further Education. Those represented on the JNC included the AMA, ACC and Welsh Joint Education Committee on the Employers' Side, together with a non-voting representative of the Secretary of State for the Home Department, and NATFHE and the APC on the Staff Side. By tradition, a proportion of the NATFHE seats were held by former members of the Association of Teachers in Penal. Establishments (ATPE), the ATPE having merged with NATFHE. Most of the JNC procedures mirrored the NJC except that either side could seek conciliation or arbitration of unresolved disputes without the consent of the other in the pre-1981 position in the Burnham Committees.

2 The need for distinctive arrangements flowed from the facts that
(i) The place in which education occurred was almost always an institution managed under secure arrangements by the Home Office, rather than by an LEA, and therefore with a Governor in final authority, and
(ii) The pattern of courses had to suit establishments where, potentially, new students might start courses on any day. Nonetheless, the education staff are employed by LEAs. Thus the arrangements reflect the NJC where practical, but are distinctive in some keys respect for the reasons given.

3 The distinctive arrangements are:

(i) The first year of assignment is always probationary because of the adjustment required to teaching in prisons and similar institutions.

(ii) The work relationships are necessarily different from say a college. First, the Governor (by virtue of Prison Rule 86(2) and Youth Custody Centre Rules 70(2) and Detention Centre Rules 69(2)) may exclude anyone including a lecturer from the establishment. In addition, Governors may, if dissatisfied with a lecturer's professional performance, refer the fact to the LEA, and the LEA will need to consider the position of the lecturer. In general, however, before Governors take the extreme step of excluding a lecturer – in short, where there is no question of emergency or serious breach of discipline – an attempt should be made to resolve problems amicably by informal discussion between the Governor, lecturer, representatives of the Prison Department Chief Education Officer's Branch, the LEA and any other appropriate body. Where this does not work or where the case is sufficiently serious and the Governor decides to exclude the lecturer, the decision must be reported immediately to the lecturer, the LEA and appropriate Prison Department Regional Director and the Prison Department Assistant Chief Education Officer. The only reason for not providing a full written statement would be risk to security. Within seven days the lecturer must be afforded a formal opportunity to respond, call witnesses and be accompanied by a friend. If the Governor will not re-admit the lecturer to the prison, there is a right of appeal to the Regional Director who will personally hear the matter. Notification of appeal must be lodged within seven days and a detailed statement provided within 14. If the appeal is unsuccessful, or no appeal is made, the LEA must be notified immediately so as to consider whether it has suitable alternative employment to offer.

(iii) If the LEA decides to terminate the lecturer's contract, it was the case that local arrangements based on the 1973 disciplinary arrangements were enacted. However, it was recognised that new arrangements would replace these and, indeed, they did in 1986. Although not formally adopted for the Prison Service, there is agreement that they should be and it can be anticipated that Section 5 of the Silver Book now applies.

(iv) Prison education generally entails an extended college year and this shall be negotiated with the recognised lecturers' unions. With this proviso, the bulk of the NJC arrangements apply.

(v) The general provisions for teaching load and class contact apply. Special remission arrangements may be appropriate in Prison Service Establishments. The Education Officer should undertake teaching on the same or a similar basis to heads of department in colleges, whilst their deputies should undertake the class contact appropriate to their grade. The same arrangements as are in the Silver Book apply to additional teaching duties.

4 *Grading of posts*

(i) Education Officers

A variation of the standard grading of departments is made for Prison Education Officers, each 1 September.

Table 2

Standard Grading of Departments for Prison Education Officers

Department with Unit totals of	*Grade of Education Officer*
51–100	HOD I
Over 100–210	HOD II
Over 210–350	HOD III
Over 350	HOD IV

These unit totals are calculated as in paragraph 1 of Part III; Appendix IIa of the Burnham FE Report. The student hours calculated are those for the immediately proceeding academic year. The variation is that for each vocational training instructor (the instructors are not counted as lecturers and are, in general, members of the Civil Service) who has been in post for a minimum of nine months in the establishment by the end of the academic year concerned , a further 30 units is added to the annual total. The totals are confirmed with the Home Office Prison Department each year and gradings are revised with effect from 1 September.

(ii) Deputy Education Officers
All Grade III and IV Departments must have Deputy Education Officers graded at Lecturer II/Senior Lecturer (but excluded from the pool of promotion posts calculation). Deputies graded at Senior Lecturers are not additional to mandatory Senior Lecturers as shown in sub-paragraph (iii), below.

(iii) Mandatory Senior Lecturers
In Grade III Departments there must be one Senior Lecturer, and in Grade IV Departments there must be two.

(iv) Lecturers Grade II
The number of Lecturers Grade II will be 20% of the pool of Lecturers Grade I calculated on the proportion of Category V work, but calculated without reference to the number of Deputy Education Officer posts, whether at Lecturer Grade II or Senior Lecturer. LEAs should notify the Prison Department of the names of full-time Lecturers Grade I they propose to promote to Lecturer Grade II as soon as practicable prior to 1 September. This machinery reflects a clear management prerogative, subject to discussion with the unions before decisions are taken and to any representatives to the Joint Secretaries of the JNC. If more individuals are nominated than there are posts to be filled the Home Office will allocate vacancies having regard to the unit totals, special characteristics of the institution's work and existing ratios of staff grades.

5 Whilst it will be noted that the description of the bargaining forum of the JNC is in the past tense, the agreements are extant and the arrangements for bargaining are now transferred to a Sub-Committee of the NJC for FE Teachers in England and Wales.

APPENDIX 3

RESEARCH STAFF

1 After a number of years of negotiation, agreement was reached in February 1985 on a package of conditions of service for research staff. These staff are largely concentrated in institutions with high proportions of advanced further education (Grading of Courses Categories I and II/III) although not exclusively so. The staff within scope of the agreement, and of the Silver Book are defined in Section 16 of the Silver Book as:

(i) Researchers A – research staff who are required to undertake assigned research; and

(ii) Researchers B – research staff who either supervise other research, and/or who undertake more demanding research, and/or who are engaged in postdoctoral research.

The definition does not include Readers who have the same conditions and salaries as Principal Lecturers, or those in posts of responsibility above Reader whose major contribution to academic leadership may involve research leadership. Section 16 sets out the annually negotiated salary scales and is, for this reason, amended each year. The Silver Book provides the only explicit statement to the effect that these kinds of researchers are in scope although disagreements arise from time to time with employing authorities who seek to use the terms of the APT&C 'Purple Book' for such staff (See **2.6**). The Purple Book makes no claim to have research staff in colleges in scope and use of its terms are inappropriate.

2 Appendix VII of the Silver Book details the conditions of service. The Appendix does not confer any rights which override the individual's contract in respect of termination dates nor does it convey continuity of service. It does commend the use of the Silver Book redundancy procedures wherever reasonable. It does import a number of provisions directly from the lecturers' conditions including:

(i) Rights in respect of equal opportunities (Section 2 of the Silver Book);
(ii) Advice to have regard to all relevant statutes;
(iii) Use of the discipline, suspension and dismissal procedures in Section 5 of the Silver Book;
(iv) Sick leave and sick pay arrangements (Section 11);
(v) Maternity entitlements as in Section 12;
(vi) Rights to indemnification as enjoyed by lecturers and the scale of compensations specified for injury in Section 14.

3 The general rights to a specific contract apply subject to the salaries specified in Section 16 and there are rights to early retirement arrangements except that the scale of compensation in the superannuation scheme is determined separately from the Silver Book. Salaries must be paid in monthly instalments (1/12 per calendar month) and each odd day is paid on the basis of division by the number of days in that month.

4 The LEA or governing body of an institution may decide to impose a probationary period on a researcher but this should not exceed six months given the relatively short periods of contract for such staff. If probation is failed, the normal methods for dismissal as set out in Section 5 of the Silver Book shall be used. In general, periods of notice should be clearly defined in the contract and the normal period of notice to terminate the contract should be the period between one salary payment and the next subject to the statutory minimum embodied in the Employment Protection (Consolidation) Act 1978.

5 Researchers cannot be required to undertake duties beyond 37 hours per week (36 in the area covered by the Metropolitan Police District as defined in the London Government Act 1963), and systematic additional teaching duties should never normally be required. Some overtime may be unavoidable and, where authorised by the LEA, will attract time off in lieu for Researchers A, at a later and mutually convenient time. If Researchers A are paid overtime, it is calculated on the basis of the basic weekly salary (7/365ths of annual salary) divided by 37 or 36 as appropriate given location, the formula providing the hourly rate. Periods under half an hour do not count and all such periods are aggregated for each calendar month and only complete hours are paid for. Overtime is paid at time and a half, and on Sundays is paid at double time, and on general or public holidays is paid on the basis of normal salary plus payment at plain time for all hours worked in what would have been normal working hours. If time off in lieu is used, overtime of less than four hours gives rise to half a day off, and of four or more hours gives rise to a full day off. Researchers B, whilst they should not be asked to undertake overtime in any normal circumstances, are entitled to time off in lieu when it occurs, or to payment of an honorarium the amount of which is determined by the LEA.

6 Researchers may not be required to teach more than six hours per week, nor on more than one evening, or for more than 36 hours in any period between 1 September and the following 31 August. In practice, many do so on a voluntary basis. Time for marking and preparation should be allocated within the normal working week. When researchers are asked to teach, they should not be expected to do so outside the areas of knowledge, qualification or experience associated with the research. Not only would a request to do so be poor pedagogy, but places an unreasonable burden on the researcher.

7 At least seven consecutive days of holiday at Christmas and at Easter, and not less than five continuous weeks between the beginning of June and end of September are entitlements.

8 In a number of authorities, better arrangements than those specified are in existence. These better provisions should prevail under the Safeguarding clause of Appendix VII.

APPENDIX 4

LABOUR LAW IN NORTHERN IRELAND

1 Labour law in Northern Ireland is broadly the same as that in Great Britain although the title of a particular piece of legislation is sometimes very different. Laws passed at Westminster do not normally cover Northern Ireland (except where that law is to apply specifically to Northern Ireland, e.g. The Fair Employment Act 1976), further legislation is required to extend Great Britain's legal provision to Northern Ireland.

2 The main pieces of labour law in Northern Ireland are set against their Great Britain equivalent below.

Great Britain	*Northern Ireland*
Contracts of Employment Act 1965.	Contracts of Employment and Redundancy Payments Act 1965.
Equal Pay Act 1970.	Equal Pay (N.I.) Act 1970.
Sex Discrimination Act 1975	Sex Discrimination (N.I.) Order 1976.
Race Relations Act	Fair Employment (N.I.) Act 1976.
Trade Union and Labour Relations Act 1974.	Industrial Relations (N.I.) Order 1976.
Employment Protection Act 1975.	Industrial Relations No 2 (N.I.) Order 1976
Health and Safety at Work Act 1974.	Health and Safety at Work Order 1978.
Employment Act 1980.	Industrial Relations (N.I.) Order 1982.
Employment Act 1982.	Industrial Relations (N.I.) Order 1987.
Trade Union Act 1984.	(No Northern Ireland equivalent as yet.)

3 *The legal framework*

Three types of judicial bodies may be involved, Industrial Tribunals, Industrial Courts and the ordinary courts.

(i) Industrial Tribunals

These are constituted similar to those in Great Britain and have broadly the same jurisdiction. Unlike Britain however, Northern Ireland's industrial tribunals cannot deal with cases of religious or political discrimination outlawed by the Fair Employment Act (N.I.) 1976. Such cases are taken by the Fair Employment Agency if necessary to the ordinary courts of law.

(ii) The Industrial Court

Established by the Industrial Courts Act 1919, this body is similar to Great Britain's Central Arbitration Committee. Unlike the C.A.C. however the Industrial Court can still hear cases relating to trade union recognition. The provision abolishing recognition machinery in the 1980 Employment Act was not introduced in its Northern Ireland equivalent.

(iii) Courts of Law

Their jurisdiction is the same as that in Great Britain. However they have a more central role in employment law than is the case in Great Britain. Northern Ireland does not have an Employment Appeals Tribunal, instead appeals from an industrial tribunal go straight to the Court of Appeal, Civil Division.

4 *Third Party Machinery*

The Department of Economic Development has responsibility for legislation and manpower policies (See **1.5** 20). It provides for the Wages Council machinery and the Health and Safety Inspectorate. Four statutory bodies have been established by the D.E.D. and given duties and responsibilities. These are the Labour Relations Agency, Equal Opportunities Commission, Fair Employment Agency and Health and Safety Agency. Like similar agencies in Britain these bodes are led by a Board composed of a Chair, and representatives of employers, trade unions and independent members.

(i) The Labour Relations Agency
This body has a similar function to the Advisory, Conciliation and Arbitration Services in Great Britain.

(ii) The Equal Opportunities Commission
Similar in function to the body of the same title in Great Britain

(iii) The Fair Employment Agency
This body has no direct equivalent in Great Britain. Established by the Fair Employment Act 1976, its function is to promote equality of opportunity and to work for the elimination of discrimination on the grounds of religious belief or political opinion. The FEA has the legal right to intitate legal proceedings on behalf of an individual, to investigate employment practices and patterns of employment and to give advice and training to promote equality of opportunity.

(iv) The Health and Safety Agency
Great Britain's Health and Safety Commission has a subordinate Executive with enforcement powers. The Northern Ireland Health and Safety Agency has no enforcement powers, this remains with the Department of Economic Development. The HSA can review health safety and welfare in connection with work and make recommendations to government, it can provide information and advice, conduct research and training and issue codes of practice.

5 Northern Ireland's Health and Safety Inspectors and Employment Medical Advisory Service are directly under the control of the government department.

2.6 SALARIES AND CONDITIONS OF SERVICE: NON-TEACHING STAFF

1 Pay and conditions of the majority of non-teaching staff are determined by the appropriate national joint council (NJC): the National Joint Council for Local Authorities' Administrative, Professional, Technical and Clerical Services (APT&C) or the National Joint Council for Local Authorities' services (manual workers). There are also separate national bodies for craftsmen.[1] The National Joint Councils are bodies comprised of representatives of employers, i.e. local authority councillors, and employees, i.e. recognised trade unions. A majority of each side of an NJC is required before agreement can be reached. The National Joint Councils lay down terms and conditions that may be supplemented on at provincial council or local level.

2 There are 26 provincial councils (13 for manual and 13 for white collar workers) whose principal functions include: the implementation, interpretation and augmenting of national agreements, the provision of conciliation and the control of entry into and training for local authorities' services. The NJC for APT&C Staff provides a national framework for pay and conditions of service. Actual grades of individual jobs are determined at local authority level. Laboratory and workshop technicians are one of the few groups where grades are laid down at national level. The use and application of these grades may be subject to local agreement. Non-teaching staff who are dissatisfied with their gradings can appeal to provincial council and if appropriate national level. APT&C staff employed by the Inner London Education Authority are covered by separate negotiating arrangements.

3 Gradings of manual workers have been revised following a major job evaluation exercise. Ninety per cent of jobs have their grades determined at national level, but the remainder may be determined at either provincial council level or local authority level, by joint agreement. Hours of work may also be revised by local agreement.

4 Details of the nationally negotiated terms and conditions are contained in the handbooks of the National Joint Council for Local Authorities Services (Manual Workers) (the 'Green Book') and the National Joint Council for Local Authorities' APT and C Services (the 'Purple Book'). Local authority colleges can acquire copies of these handbooks from their authorities; voluntary colleges can obtain copies from the Local Authorities' Conditions of Service Advisory Board (LACSAB). In addition to the national handbooks there are provincial handbooks detailing constitutions, wage rates, occupational classifications, conditions of service, NJC decisions, ratings and amendments which are particularly useful for manual workers. These may be obtained from local authorities or, in the case of voluntary colleges, from the relevant provincial employers' secretariat. (Details from LACSAB, 41 Belgrave Square, London SW1X 8NP, Tel: 01–235 6081.)

5 As agreements continue to be made and modified, it is essential to have access to the up-dating services. The volume of information, however, is detailed and formidable and for this reason precise details of current provisions are not given here. It would be a considerable task for college administrators to become entirely familiar and expert in all areas affecting non-teaching staff. They need, therefore, to liaise closely with the local authority educational and personnel departments. Maintained colleges must adopt any local agreements reached by the authority with the unions, unless otherwise agreed by all parties concerned. Voluntary colleges may adopt such agreements where circumstances are similar, and this would obviate the need for a separate agreement and forestall difficulties between colleges and unions. Nonetheless, college administrators need to become familiar with the general pattern of agreements, and they may need to impress upon their local education authorities that they ought to be consulted when changes in grades or conditions for non-teaching staff are proposed. Changes in grades or conditions recommended by institutions will usually have to be approved by the LEA. Procedures for ratification vary and may in some instances be devolved to the institution itself. Some institutions have established arrangements for consulting with trade unions, and joint negotiating bodies exist in local authorities.

6 There are two issues to which it is necessary to draw attention: the interpretation of agreements; and procedures. Regional differences in the interpretation of agreements, particularly for manual workers, have caused difficulties in colleges. In these circumstances reference should be made to the authority. The largest difficulty in colleges has been caused by procedures. The procedures agreed by unions and local authority have to be followed, though these may need to be reconciled with powers allocated in articles of government. (Voluntary colleges may have agreed to follow the procedures of the authority in which they are situated.) The provisions of the articles of government concerning where powers and responsibilities lie in dealing with non-teaching staff have to be understood, and thereafter for the agreed procedures to be followed. Procedures must be observed but ought not, unless warranted by the occasion, to become too formal. Employer liability remains with the local authority except where the college is the employer (as in voluntary and corporate institution), and the college is obliged to ensure that the LEA's conditions and procedures are followed exactly. However, the proposals of the White Paper 1987 to establish polytechnics and colleges of HE as corporate bodies are intended to make them, not the local authority, the employer (See **1.1** Appendix 1).

7 Negotiations for all staff are becoming more complex, and as agreements for non-teaching staff have a wider employment application than those for teaching staff, difficulties can be compounded. An obvious example is the hours of employment: irregular college hours may involve locally negotiated arrangements within the framework of national and regional agreements for non-teaching staff. Another difficulty is the practice for some posts of using a mixture of pay determined by one negotiating body and conditions determined by another, i.e. 'hybrid posts'. This can cause industrial relations problems, and all unions are agreed that the pay and conditions for any one post should fall within purview of only one negotiating body.

NOTE

1 JNC for Local Authorities' Services (Building and Civil Engineering; JNC for Local Authorities' Services (Engineering Craftsmen); Standing Conference for Electricians; and Standing Conference for Heating, Ventilating and Domestic Engineers.

2.7 HEALTH AND SAFETY AT WORK

1 The main enactment governing health and safety at work is the Health and Safety at Work etc Act 1974 (hereafter referred to as the 1974 Act). Originally introduced with the aims of simplifying the vast range of legislation dealing with aspects of health and safety and promoting self-regulation by employers, in practice the Act has given birth to hundreds of new and revised regulations, codes of practice, and guidance notes with which employers are expected to comply. For organisations with a wide range of operations and functions, such as colleges, the implications are substantial. One solution is to observe the self-regulatory provisions of the legislation, particularly through an effective safety policy known to all in the establishment, with the intention of making sure that in this way the relevant provisions of the legislation and regulations will be complied with. The appointment of safety officers (see below paragraph 38) can also contribute to this.

2 This section of the book therefore concentrates mainly on the self-regulatory requirements. Space does not provide room for lists of safety regulations and other material, and in any event lists of this sort are soon out-of-date as existing regulations become superseded and new regulations are made. The focus is therefore on the 1974 Act and its implications for college management, although information about three specific areas of employer responsibility deriving from regulations (reporting of injuries, diseases, and dangerous occurrences; first aid; and radiological protection) is given (see below paragraphs 43–51).

3 **Summary of the 1974 Act**

The principles of the Act can be summarised under five headings:

(i) *Action rather than reaction* Management should plan safety policies (see paragraphs 39–40) and anticipate incidents, rather than follow events, and regularly monitor the effectiveness of their policies;

(ii) *Cooperation* In its safety planning, management should attempt to gain the cooperation of the employees through trade union nominated safety representatives with the right to consult and to inspect;

(iii) *Clarity* The interpretation of safety law should be easily understandable and capable of quick modification as and when the need arises;

(iv) *Incentives for enforcement* Enforcement procedures are flexible, but also carry criminal law penalties sufficient to be an incentive to observe the law;

(v) *Unrestricted protection* Employers should protect not only their own employees from danger, but also all members of the public who are affected by their undertakings.

4 The 1974 Act is an enabling device. It establishes principles and general statutory duties; but, unlike the Factories Act 1961 or the Offices, Shops and Railway Premises Act 1963 (only to parts of which the education service was previously subject), it contains no detailed provisions on the standards to maintain in respect of specific risks. Detailed safety measures are required of employers through regulations and codes of practice made under the Act. Regulations, being statutory instruments, have the force of law. They are normally made by the Secretary of State after proposals by the Health and Safety Commission (HSC) following consultation with relevant bodies. Codes of practice may be approved and issued by the HSC, again after a consultative process. They

stand in the same relation to the 1974 Act as does the Highway Code to the road traffic laws: contravention of a code is not necessarily an offence given all the circumstances of the event, but the code is admissible in evidence, and the onus of proof will rest on the contravenor of the code to prove that the actions were justifiable. Official notes of guidance on the regulations have no legal stature and are intended to provide guidance on compliance with the Act and not as authoritative statements of the law; but they can be used in argument at law. (See **4.2** 2.)

5 Sections 1–12 of the 1974 Act are summarised as follows, with other sections mentioned only for the purposes of this book:

Section 1 lays down the purposes of the first part of the Act: the maintenance and improvement of health, safety, and welfare standards of people at work; the protection of others against risk arising from work activities; the control of the use and storage of dangerous substances; and the control of the emissions into the atmosphere from certain premises.

Section 2 imposes a general duty on employers (see below paragraph 17) to ensure, so far as is *reasonably practicable* (see below paragraph 6), the health, safety, and welfare of their employees. The employer is required to consult the employees on matters concerning joint action on health and safety affairs. At the request of trade union representatives, the employer is required to establish safety committees (see below paragraphs 35–37). A written statement of safety policy and arrangements is required of the employer, as is its publication (see below paragraphs 39–40).

Section 3 places on employers and the self-employed a general duty to ensure that the prosecution of their business does not endanger employees or the public and, where applicable, to provide information to the public about any potential dangers which their activities involve.

Section 4 requires those responsible for places and premises of work to ascertain that those places, as well as their contents, do not endanger the people using them. Reference is made to 'risks to health arising from plant or substances in any such premises'. *Plant* has a wide legal definition: it is a term which includes any machinery, equipment or appliance. This duty does no more than expressly state a contractually implied obligation on principals, vice-principals and all members of staff of a college in control of premises or workplaces.

Section 5 refers to the general duty of persons in control of certain premises in relation to harmful emissions into the atmosphere: the best practicable means have to be applied to render harmless and inoffensive such noxious substances as may be emitted.

Section 6 requires that anyone who designs, manufactures or supplies an article or substance for use at work should ensure, so far as is reasonably practicable, that such items are safe when used according to that person's instructions. Necessary testing, research and inspection must be carried out, and necessary information supplied. Installers of plant are required to ensure that it is safely installed.

Section 7 (see below paragraphs 14–16) states that all employees while at work have a duty to take reasonable care to ensure that they neither endanger themselves nor others by their work activities. This is, like Section 4, an express statement of a contractually implied obligation, this time applying to all members of staff. It is therefore important to impress upon all employees in a college that a failure to comply with this statutory duty will render the individual liable to disciplinary action. The employee must also cooperate with the employer so far as is necessary for the employer to fulfil his or her statutory duties and refrain from recklessly or intentionally interfering with anything provided in the interests of their health, safety and welfare.

Section 8 forbids the misuse of, or interference with, anything provided for health and safety purposes under a statutory requirement.

Section 9 prevents employers from charging employees for any equipment provided for health and safety purposes or for anything done in compliance with statute.

Sections 10–12 relate to the establishment, functions and powers of the HSC and the Health and Safety Executive (HSE). The HSC is given a general duty 'to do such things and make such arrangements as it considers appropriate for the purposes of', *inter alia,* securing the health, safety and welfare of persons at work; protecting persons other than persons at work against risks to health or safety arising out of or in connection with the activities of persons at work; and arranging that employees are provided with an information and advisory service on health and safety at work. The HSC has a standing education service advisory committee (ESAC), which provides it with relevant information and advice about the service. The HSE is the HSC's executive arm and is primarily engaged on securing compliance with the statutory requirements for health and safety at work, mainly through advice, recommending appropriate procedures and, in extreme cases, enforcement. Its other functions include providing the HSC with information and advice, and developing research into health and safety at work. The HSE has a network of area offices which can be contacted by employers for advice. A list of these is given at the end of this chapter.

Sections 18–26 cover the enforcement powers of inspectors, including improvement and prohibition notices (see below paragraphs 7–10).

Sections 27–28 refer to the obtaining and disclosure of information. HSE inspectors are required to supply certain information to employers or their safety representatives. However, Section 28 provides for a restriction on the information which an employer can be required to supply.

Sections 29–32 apply to agriculture.

Sections 33–42 refer to offences.

Section 47 refers to civil liability. Proceedings in respect of an infringement of the Act may be brought only by the inspectorate, except by permission of the Director of Public Prosecutions. The common law route through the civil courts remains open to employees seeking redress for injuries caused in the course of their employment.

Sections 55–60 refer to the Employment Medical Advisory Service (see below paragraph 11).

Sections 61–76 refer to building regulations.

6 The test of whether something is *reasonably practicable* involves weighing the risk against the measures necessary to eliminate it (*Edwards v. National Coal Board* [1949] 1 All ER 743). In practice this involves assessing in advance the risk and the cost of safeguarding against it. If, for example, preventive measures can be taken without significant cost or inconvenience, it would be reasonably practicable to take them. If, however, a risk is slight and the cost of safeguarding against it is likely to be disproportionate, the employer may be able to prove that it was not reasonably practicable to have taken the measures

necessary to protect against it, but in order to prove it the employer must be able to show that he or she had assessed the risk and the cost, and how this had been done (see below paragraphs 12–14).

7 **Improvement and prohibition notices**

When an inspector discovers what he or she considers to be a breach of health and safety law, or that a breach has occurred in circumstances which make it likely that such a breach will continue, he or she is empowered to serve a notice on the person or organisation concerned. This notice will state the alleged breach of statute and the reasons why it is considered that an offence has been committed. It may go on to require that the breach be remedied within a specified period of not less than 21 days from the date of the notice. This is an *improvement notice.*

8 Improvement notices apply only to breaches of statute. There is no power to issue such a notice where a code of practice has been contravened. Improvement notices will usually contain advice on remedies. They may be withdrawn by the inspector before expiry after the defect has been remedied and checked. The recipient of an improvement notice may appeal to an industrial tribunal if he or she considers the notice unjustified, or that more time is needed to comply with its requirements. The tribunal may cancel, affirm or modify the notice, which in the case of claims that a notice is unjustified will be suspended until the tribunal hearing has been concluded. Unless an appeal is pending or has been upheld, once its time limit has expired without the improvement taking place, an offence will have been committed, and prosecution may follow.

9 When an inspector believes that work activities are causing a risk of serious personal injury, he or she may serve a *prohibition notice.* This must state which statute, in the inspector's opinion, is being breached, and the circumstances creating the risk. The prohibition can become operative at once. If a time limit is stipulated, the notice is described as a *deferred prohibition notice.* Appeal machinery similar to that against improvement notices is available, except that the prohibition will not be suspended during the appeal unless the employer successfully makes a separate application to continue the practice against which the prohibition is aimed. Tribunals will arrange for the urgent hearing of appeals against prohibition notices.

10 It is not the policy of the HSE to issue notices whenever a contravention of statute is discovered. The usual procedure is for the inspector to allow the employer an opportunity to remedy matters (unless the risks are grave, or the employer is a persistent offender). A quick response is important when an improvement notice is under consideration, and essential when the issue is one of prohibition.

11 **Employment Medical Advisory Service (EMAS)**

The Employment Medical Advisory Service (EMAS) consists of a medical staff in the employment of the HSC. The tasks of the service are the identification of health hazards; to function as a central information bank; to advise on the environmental control necessary as a result of work activities and to monitor such action as is taken; to advise employers and employees of any risks to health to which they may be exposed; to advise on the medical aspects of any employment problems, particularly the employment of the handicapped, and rehabilitation for employment; and to act as a focus for the development of occupational medicine in Britain. The service advises on the effects of a particular job on health, undertakes medical examinations and studies the medical requirements for various types of work, taking special cognisance of the handicapped. It is recommended that, wherever problems arise relating to occupational health, early recourse by employers or safety representatives should be made to the local EMAS area office.

12 **Liability of individual members of staff**

Section 37(1) of the Act states that 'where an offence . . . committed by a body corporate is proved to have been committed with the consent or connivance of, or to have been attributable to any neglect on the part of, any director, manager, secretary or other similar officer of the body corporate or a person who was purporting to act in any such capacity, he as well as the body corporate shall be guilty of that offence and shall be liable to be proceeded against accordingly'. Therefore an individual can be prosecuted as well as the corporate body of which he or she is an employee. For the purposes of s.37(1), *Consent* means conscious acquiescence; *Connivance* means active participation in bringing about the contravention of the Act; *Neglect* could include a failure to fulfil duties imposed by an employer's publicised safety policy.

13 However, it is the HSE's advice that for senior college staff to have a criminal liability under the Act, one or all of the following conditions would need to be satisfied:

(i) The senior member of staff would have to have fulfilled a policy making role within the body corporate (i.e. to have had a position of consultation within the local education authority or, in a voluntary college, the governing body, analogous to that of a member of the board of directors of a company); or

(ii) The senior member of staff had a responsibility for the implementation of the safety policy; or

(iii) He or she had been given designated safety responsibilities by the employer.

An instance of employee liability under Section 37(1) is discussed in paragraph 16 below.

14 While this advice offers some clarification, further qualifications are necessary. If the contract of employment or the instrument and articles of government lay any such responsibilities as enumerated in paragraph 13 upon a senior staff member, then a liability is incurred. It is the general view of the HSE that most principals of colleges, as at present structured within a local education authority, are too far down the chain of responsibility to incur liability under s.37(1). To quote the HSE, 'a teacher is paid to exercise control, but the principal responsibility for carrying out the provisions of the 1974 Act lies with local education authorities (or governing bodies in the case of independent and voluntary colleges) because they are the employers'. This confirms the HSE's general policy of placing responsibility on employers: employees should not therefore be required to undertake duties, responsibilities and liabilities which were not intended under the Act to apply to them. It must, however, be emphasised that the courts alone can decide the ultimate interpretation.

15 In relation to teachers, the HSE (1978) has confirmed this advice by saying:

'There has been considerable misunderstanding about the extent of the teacher's duty under S.7 and there has been a tendency to assign to teachers duties which they do not have. The argument has been that the 1974 Act requires local education authorities to provide safe conditions, including safe apparatus, fittings and laboratory space, etc. This having been done, the teacher, it is said, is responsible if unsafe procedures or inadequate apparatus are used.

'This widely held view is misleading in two respects. First because it lays upon teachers duties far beyond those set out in the Act and directs it towards the protection of students and pupils, whereas it is, in fact, the teacher as an employee who is equally entitled to this protection. Only by due process of delegation could an LEA shift the substantial part of its responsibility to teachers. Delegation is an individual overt act, precisely defined in the authorities.

'A teacher is paid to exercise control, but the principal responsibility for carrying out the provisions of the 1974 Act lies with LEAs because they are the employers. Their main duty is towards their employees, the teachers, lecturers, technicians, and multifarious non-teaching staff. These duties extend beyond the provision of safe conditions (apparatus, premises) to include safe systems of work and the maintenance of such systems and such apparatus and premises, and the like. The teacher is often the instrument whereby these duties are carried out, but does not himself thereby necessarily assume the LEA's responsibility.'

16 Blatant failure by an employee to take reasonable care could result in prosecution, even if the culpable individual had suffered personal injury as a result of his or her behaviour, but in most cases it would be more likely to provide grounds for disciplinary action under the employer's procedure. It is the HSE's policy in most instances to prosecute only where the law is being deliberately and persistently flouted. However, prosecution of an individual can occur, as in the case of the Director of Roads for the Strathclyde Regional Council, who was found guilty of five charges concerning the accidental death of a council employee. The charges related to neglect. In the appeal judgment it was stated that Section 37(1) refers to 'any neglect, which means neglect in duty, however constituted'. The judgment continued, 'The Council's statement of safety policy . . . imposed on the appellant the duty to prepare . . . a written general safety policy in relation to the work of his department. His failure to do so thus constituted neglect'. The director was fined. ([1977] IRLR 310.)

17 **Duties under the 1974 Act**

The majority of duties imposed by the Act fall upon employers. These general duties differ little from obligations under common law (see below paragraphs 52–58). The basic difference is that, whereas the common law duty of care provides for civil liability and civil damages, the 1974 Act imposes criminal sanctions for disregard of statutory duties. Under Section 2 the employer's duties are, so far as is reasonably practicable (see above paragraph 6):

(i) To provide and maintain safe plant and systems of work;
(ii) To ensure the safe using, handling, storing and transporting of articles and substances;
(iii) To provide instruction, information, training and supervision;
(iv) To provide a working environment which is safe and without risk to health;
(v) To provide adequate welfare facilities;
(vi) To ensure that the employer's activities do not expose the public to risk;
(vii) To make no charge for any equipment or materials (such as goggles) required by statute for the safety of employees;

(viii) To provide a safety policy and to ensure that the policy is brought to the notice of employees;
(ix) To consult safety representatives and, when requested, to establish safety committees;
(x) To prevent offensive or noxious fumes from entering the atmosphere.

18 **Prosecution**
It is for the enforcing authority – in the case of colleges, the HSE – to decide whether to institute proceedings and, where there is a choice, whether they are to occur in a crown court or a court of summary jurisdiction (i.e. a magistrates' court). The maximum penalty at a magistrates' court is £2,000. If the HSE elects for indictment in the crown court, fines are without limit and an offender is liable for up to two years imprisonment. A continuing fine of £100 per day is incurred for non-compliance with improvement or prohibition notices.

19 On conviction, a court may issue an order which will compel specified remedial action within a given time. Orders may also be issued for purposes such as the destruction or removal of dangerous substances.

20 **Safety representatives**
The Safety Representatives and Safety Committee Regulations made under Section 2(4) of the 1974 Act provide for a wide trade union function in the implementation of the Act. Only recognised trade unions are allowed to appoint safety representatives (i.e. an independent trade union recognised by the employer for collective bargaining purposes – See **2.4** Appendix 1).

21 Selection of safety representatives should occur via the procedures issued by the unions involved, and once they have been appointed the employer should be notified in writing. As the employer is the local education authority (except in certain polytechnics and in voluntary establishments – See **1.2** Appendix 1), safety representatives should make their representations to the authority and not to principals and senior academic staff unless those persons have been so designated by the authority. The representatives must be employed in the workplace where they carry out their functions and, where reasonably practicable, should have had at least two years' employment with their present employer or two years' experience in similar employment. Where, as in colleges, there are situations in which several unions have representation, the HSC has advised that a safety representative can represent more than one group of workers where there is 'mutual agreement between the appropriate unions'.

22 The numbers of safety representatives to be appointed are not specified. Some colleges will have diverse functions resembling those of industry, some will have several sites, and some will be relatively easily inspected monotechnic institutions. Any decision on the numbers and location of representatives rests with the relevant unions. In practical terms small establishments (e.g. small annexes) should be grouped with others and served by one representative, whereas in large colleges separate representation for teaching and non-teaching staff may be appropriate. All colleges should have their own safety representatives.

23 An employee ceases to be a safety representative when the union which appointed him or her has notified the employer in writing that the appoint-

ment has been terminated. The appointment would also be terminated by the resignation of the representative or where the employer dismissed, or transferred, him or her.

24 The statutory functions of safety representatives are:

(i) To investigate hazards, dangerous occurrences, the causes of accidents, and complaints by employees;

(ii) Arising from the investigations made, to make representations to the employer on general matters affecting health, safety or welfare;

(iii) To consult with inspectors and receive information from them;

(iv) To attend meetings of safety committees in connection with his or her functions;

(v) To make formal inspections at three monthly intervals or where there has been a substantial change in the conditions of work, and to make formal inspections following reportable accidents, occurrences and diseases; and

(vi) To inspect and take copies of any relevant information which the employer is required to keep by virtue of statute.

25 The regulations state that, without prejudice to the duty of care on an employee and the requirement not to misuse or interfere with anything provided for health and safety purposes, 'no function given to a safety representative shall be construed as imposing any duty on him [or her]'. Thus the risk of criminal liability is removed from the representative's functions, although no protection is afforded to provide for a wide trade union function in the implementation of the Act any duty on him [or her].' Rather than react to events, the representative is expected to perform his or her functions on a day to day basis, attempting to prevent accidents before they can occur – an expectation which requires ease of access by the representative to the college premises and to senior staff, as well as the need to keep proper records and to liaise with inspectors.

27 Inspection is a vital part of a representative's duty. It is therefore important in a safety policy document, or in some other suitable form, to set out the scope of a representative's powers. College managements are required to place no unnecessary barriers in the way of a representative's inspection.

28 The forms of inspection which are permissible under the regulations are:

(i) Regular inspections of the place of work, these to be carried out at least once a quarter;

(ii) Inspections following a reportable accident, a dangerous occurrence or the identification of a notifiable disease within the workplace;

(iii) Inspections where there has been a substantial change in the conditions of work (e.g. the introduction of new machinery);

(iv) Inspections consequent upon the publication by the HSC or the HSE of information relevant to the hazards of the workplace;

(v) The investigation of complaints by employees relating to their health, safety or welfare at work;

(vi) The inspection and the taking of copies of any document relevant to the workplace or the employee which the employer is required to keep by virtue of any relevant statutory provision (excluding the health records of an identifiable individual).

29 While formal inspections are no substitute for regular informal monitoring,

they nevertheless provide opportunities for a full examination of the premises, consultations between representatives, and discussion with management concerning remedial action. It is necessary for the arrangements for formal inspections to be agreed with management (and, in multi-union concerns like colleges, for all the relevant unions to be consulted). During joint inspections representatives are allowed private discussions with their members, but have no right to exclude members of management during inspections.

30 Representatives should complete a report form after an inspection has been carried out. This will record the date, time and details of the inspection. One copy should be sent to the employer and the other retained by the representative. Where the inspection has been the result of a serious occurrence, the representative should complete a hazard report form. Once management has filled in the 'remedial action or explanation' part of the form, it should be returned to the representative. Books of inspection and hazard report forms are available from HMSO.

31 HSE inspectors have a duty to disclose to representatives certain kinds of information following a visit to college premises. This includes the result of monitoring or sampling, testing, measurements and any action which the inspector proposes to take. A representative should be informed by management of the time of any intended visit by an inspector, and when an inspector is on the premises. The representative should also have the opportunity of private consultation with the inspector and be permitted to accompany him or her during the inspection.

32 Employers are required to furnish such facilities and assistance to representatives as they may reasonably require to assist them in their inspectoral duties. For the purpose of analysis, representatives are allowed to take samples of any substance used at work. *Facilities* are not defined in the 1974 Act, but the facilities recommended by the Trades Union Congress (TUC) are:

(i) A room and a desk;
(ii) Storage for correspondence, papers and inspection reports;
(iii) Access to telephones;
(iv) Access to typing and duplicating facilities;
(v) A notice board;
(vi) Use of the internal mailing system;
(vii) Noise meters, dust level samplers, and detector tubes; and
(viii) Copies of all relevant statutes, regulations, codes, guidance notes and all legal and international standards relevant to the workplace.

If an employer refuses to make arrangements, or provide facilities, which are adequate, resort may be made to an industrial tribunal (a provision which extends to time off for training – see below paragraphs 33–35).

33 **Time off and training**

Under the Safety Representatives and Safety Committee Regulations, safety representatives have the right to take time off work in order to carry out their safety functions and to be paid for time taken off work in order to undergo union training courses for safety representatives in accordance with an HSC code of practice on time off. There is no right for a representative to demand time off with pay. It must be negotiated and agreed with the employer. Under the 1974 Act employers have a duty to train all employees in basic job safety, but the initial training of safety representatives is generally a matter for unions alone.

34 As soon as possible after appointment, a safety representative should be allowed paid time off to attend a course of basic training approved by the TUC or by the independent union or unions responsible for his or her appointment. Further time off for training should be allowed as and when a need arises. When a trade union wishes its safety representatives to receive training, the employer should receive details of the particular approved course, a copy of the syllabus and contents (if required) and a satisfactory notice of absence from work. The numbers of representatives attending a course at any one time should be reasonable and not disrupt the operation of the college. Consultation about this is both advisable and necessary.

35 **Safety committees**

Employers are required to establish a safety committee when at least two safety representatives have requested it in writing, and after consultation with representatives of the recognised trade unions. A notice stating the composition of the committee must be posted and the committee established within three months of receipt of the written request.

36 HSC notes of guidance on the Safety Representatives and Safety Committee regulations emphasise that arrangements for committees should result from negotiations between employer and safety representatives and that the areas of reference should include health and welfare as well as safety. Functions of the committees are specified thus:

(i) To study trends and statistics concerning accidents and reportable diseases and make recommendations for corrective action;
(ii) To examine safety audit reports, and to consider reports and information provided by the inspectorate and by safety representatives;
(iii) To assist in the development of safety rules and safe systems of work;
(iv) To maintain a watch on the effectiveness of the safety content of employee training;
(v) To monitor the adequacy of safety and health communications and publicity in the workplace;
(vi) To provide a link with the appropriate inspectorates of the enforcing authority; and
(vii) Possibly to carry out inspections additional to those done by management and safety representatives.

37 The HSC emphasises that the number of management representatives should not exceed the number of employee representatives, and that management representatives should possess knowledge, expertise and adequate authority. Safety representatives are not responsible to the committee, nor are they bound by its findings. Representatives of employees other than safety representatives should have seats on the committee. The guidance notes stress the need for regular meetings and quick decisions by management on committee recommendations. Also recommended is the presence of *ex officio* members, such as doctors or professional workers in the field of health and safety, and the stricture that a committee should not be unwieldy in size.

38 **Safety officers**

Safety officers are regarded at law as the representatives of the employer on health and safety. They fall into the managerial category and have no protection against criminal liability should they fail in their duties. Where a college has a full-time safety officer, or where an authority safety officer has specific duties regarding a college, employees have a statutory duty not to obstruct him or her and to cooperate in the pursuit of the employer's safety provisions. In view of the fact that unions have rights to determine safety representatives, they have developed policies which caution their members about taking on titles and duties which may imply delegation of employers' duties to employees which go past the delegation implied in their normal contracts of employment. Hence staff who are asked by their LEAs or governing bodies to take on specific titles and roles in relation to health and safety are advised to take advice from their professional association.

39 **Safety policies**

Under the 1974 Act all employers have a duty to draw up and bring to the attention of their employees a written statement of their safety policy. This statement must be revised whenever necessary. The HSE advises that the safety policy document should be in three parts: a general statement; the organisation for implementation; and the arrangements for ensuring health and safety. The general declaration should indicate the intention to provide a healthy and safe working environment. The organisation for the implementation of the policy should detail the allocation of responsibility within the institution. The third part of the policy should cover the full extent of the employer's enterprise and itemise detailed safety procedures or else, where appropriate, refer to other printed information on safety available to the employees.

40 Unless the safety policy contains analyses of precautions, possible hazards and relevant legal standards, it is unlikely to have great value and may constitute a failure to fulfil the duties imposed by the 1974 Act. Policies can be supplemented by the inclusion of HSE material: the HSE has waived copyright to allow for such eventualities.

41 **Students**

Sections 3 and 4 of the Act cover all students attending a college (i.e. the right, as far as is reasonably practicable, not to be exposed to risks to their health and safety). For their part students should receive information on hazards and should not be left unsupervised without the employer's consent in potentially dangerous situations. General protection of students, and of all other lawful visitors, is given by the Occupier's Liability Act 1957, breach of which can give rise to civil actions for compensation.

42 Further protection is afforded to day release, sandwich and other part-time students, and Youth Training Scheme (YTS) trainees through the general duty on employers not to endanger their employees or the public.

43 **Reporting of injuries, diseases and dangerous occurrences**

Under the Reporting of Injuries, Diseases and Dangerous Occurrences Regulations 1985 employers must notify the enforcing authority (for colleges it is the Factory Inspectorate; for farms and horticultural premises the Agricultural Inspectorate) by the quickest practicable means (e.g. by telephone) if any person, as a result of an accident arising out of or in connection with work, dies, or suffers a serious injury, or is acutely ill through absorbing a substance or exposure to a pathogen or infected material. The list of specified dangerous occurrences is lengthy and includes the collapse of lifting machinery; explosion, collapse or bursting of a pressure vessel; fire or explosion caused by electrical short circuits resulting in the closure of the plant for more than 24 hours; explosion or fire due to the ignition of process materials which causes the suspension of normal work for more than 24 hours; the sudden uncontrolled release of one tonne or more of highly flammable liquid; collapse of scaffolding; collapse of a building or structure; the accidental release of dangerous substances. In addition, an immediate report is required if a person suffers from one of over 40 conditions listed in a schedule to the regulations and his or her work involves one of the activities specified in the schedule.

44 If because of injury a person is incapacitated at work for more than three consecutive days and the cause is not one which has to be reported immediately, the matter must be reported to the enforcing authority on an approved HSE form within seven days. Records containing details of all matters reported must be kept at the place of work for at least three years.

45 The regulations require that a *responsible person* should be given the duty of receiving immediate reports of injuries, diseases and dangerous occurrences at work and, where appropriate, notifying the enforcing authority. It is an offence to fail to comply with the regulations. An employer has a statutory defence to such accusations if he or she can prove that he or she was not aware of the accident, occurrence or disease leading to the commission of the alleged offence *and* had taken *all* reasonable steps to have all reportable matters brought to his or her notice. This underlines the importance of ensuring that within a college there is a designated person responsible for receiving information as soon as an incident occurs, and that all members of staff know who he or she is and how to make contact.

46 The common law duty of care on employers (see below paragraphs 52–58) extends to industrial disease. Employees must be warned about the risks which exist for them in their working environments when handling, or otherwise working with, hazardous materials. The issue of protective clothing and equipment suitable for the purpose without explaining how and why it should be used does not discharge the duty of care satisfactorily.

47 **First aid**

Advice on the implications for the education service of the Health and Safety (First Aid) Regulations 1981 was issued by the HSC's Education Service Advisory Committee (ESAC) and is reproduced at Appendix 2. The regulations themselves impose a statutory duty on employers to provide, or ensure that there is provided:

(i) Such equipment and facilitates as are adequate and appropriate in the circumstances for enabling first aid to be rendered to their employees if they are injured or become ill at work;

(ii) Such number of suitable persons (i.e. first aiders) as are adequate and appropriate in the circumstances for rendering first aid to their employees.

48 Employers must inform their employees of the arrangements made for first aid provision, including the location of equipment, facilities, and personnel. These should be located where every employee can have reasonably rapid access to them. The HSC has issued an approved code of practice on the first aid regulations, and reference to this is made in Appendix 1.

49 **Radiological protection**

The Ionising Radiations Regulations 1985 impose statutory controls on all workplaces where ionising radiations are used. They apply to employees as well as non-employees who may be affected by the activities. Further and higher education establishments are covered by the regulations. The controls required include, for each organisation where an employee is at any time exposed to more than a specified limit of radiation, or when a person enters a designated controlled area, the need to appoint a radiation protection adviser, not necessarily as an employee. Contractors can be engaged for this purpose. Details of the adviser's qualifications and experience must be notified to the HSE not later than 28 days before the appointment is made.

50 Employers are advised to ascertain (by enquiring of the HSE in the first instance) whether or not any of their establishments where ionising radiations occur is, or may be, within the scope of the regulations. An approved HSC code of practice, *The Protection of Persons against Ionising Radiations Arising from Any Work Activity* states:

> 'Those whose undertakings cause people to be exposed to ionising radiation have a duty to weigh the costs of the possible health detriment from exposure against the costs of reducing or eliminating that exposure (taking into account possible risks to health and safety arising from alternative methods of carrying out the work), to the extent of questioning whether a particular use of ionising radiation can be justified at all.'

51 The regulations impose other duties on employers, including drawing up and making known to employees local rules for safe working, nominating and training employees as radiological protection supervisors, and providing and maintaining equipment for monitoring radiation levels and contamination.

52 **Duties at common law**

Every employer has a duty of care for the safety of those employed by him or her. This is an obligation on an employer to take the steps which are reasonably necessary to ensure the safety of his or her employees. The common law duty of care does not mean that an employer is automatically liable in law to pay damages for an injury resulting from any accident which occurs. The test is whether the accident happened because the employer had failed to act reasonably with regard to the steps he or she had taken, or not taken. The burden of proof is on the injured plaintiff to establish negligence on the part of the employer or someone acting on his or her behalf. Thus an injury allegedly caused by a failure to take reasonable care and/or to take action to counter a reasonably foreseeable risk of injury may more readily be established if the employer can be shown to have failed to comply with a statutory duty.

53 The standard of care is 'the care which an ordinary prudent employer would take in all the circumstances' (*Paris v. Stepney Borough Council* [1951] 1 All ER 42). The common law test of the reasonableness of an employer's provision may be decided by asking:

(i) Was a safe place of work provided?
(ii) Was a safe working system provided?
(iii) Was a safe means of access provided to the workplace?
(iv) Were the materials provided adequate?
(v) Were the others with whom the employee was required to work competent?

54 Breach of the duty of care, if damage results, constitutes the tort of *negligence*, meaning something more than mere carelessness or inadvertence. Negligence, as a legal wrong, was defined by Lord Wright as 'more than heedless or

careless conduct – whether in omission or commission – it properly connotes the complex concept of duty, breach and damage thereby suffered by the person to whom the duty was owing (*Lochgelly v. M'Mullen* [1934]).

55 In *Donoghue v. Stevenson* (1932) Lord Atkin laid the foundation for the modern view as to the general extent of the duty, saying:

> 'You must take reasonable care to avoid acts or omissions which you reasonably foresee would be likely to injure your neighbour. Who, then, in law is my neighbour? The answer seems to be persons who are so closely and directly affected by my act that I ought reasonably to have them in contemplation, when I am directing my mind to the acts or omissions which are called in question.'

Translated into the sphere of employment, this doctrine means not only that the employer must eliminate every possible, foreseeable danger, but that he or she must take such precautions as experience has shown to be necessary.

56 The test of whether something was reasonably foreseeable is generally applied in civil actions relating to injuries, etc allegedly suffered at work. Thus an employer will not be liable in negligence except where the damage is the reasonably foreseeable consequence of his or her act or omission. There is no liability without fault, and even then only for the foreseeable result of the fault. However, the principle is that 'forseeability does not of itself, and automatically, lead to a duty of care. Foreseeability of harm is a necessary ingredient of a relationship apt to give rise to a duty of care, but it is not the only one' (*Yuen Kun Yeu and others v. Attorney General of Hong Kong*, TLR 11.6.87). There must also exist a clear relationship between the parties, such as between an employer and one of his or her employees, or between the employer and persons in respect of whom the 1974 Act imposes a statutory duty.

57 Employees are also under a common law duty to take reasonable care for their own safety and the safety of others. They must use the skill and care which the work demands and, as was said in one case where the act of a crane driver was under scrutiny, 'use that degree of care which an ordinary, prudent crane driver would have used' (*Staveley Iron Company v Jones* [1956]). If the employee's negligence contributes to the damage sustained, then the employer's liability will be diminished in proportion to the degree of fault, but here the court will 'give due regard to the actual conditions under which men work in a factory or mine, to the long hours and the fatigue, to the slackening of attention which naturally comes from constant repetition of the same operation, to the noise and confusion in which a man works, to his preoccupation with what he is doing at the cost perhaps of inattention to his own safety' (per Lord Wright in *Caswell v. Powell Duffryn* [1940]).

58 If the employee's negligence is the *sole* cause of the harm, then the employer will not be liable at all. So it was in *O'Reilly v. National Rail Appliances* (1966), where two men working in a scrapyard found what appeared to be a live shell. They tested it by striking it with a 14lb hammer. The result was not the fault of the employer, for the men had voluntarily accepted the risk (and it would not have been a reasonably foreseeable risk on the employer's part).

59 **Statutory duties**

In addition to the common law duties outlined briefly above, certain legislation imposes a code of statutory duties, some of which have been referred to in the preceding paragraphs of this section. The general rule of English law is that, if a statute provides that breach of its provisions is punishable by the inflicting of a fine or other criminal punishment, then a person injured by such breach has no right to sue for damages. However, the courts have held that, where a statute is passed for the protection of a class of persons (e.g. persons at work), then a member of that class may sue, whether or not the breach also incurs a penal sanction. A claim in negligence and a claim for breach of statute must be separately pleaded. If one claim fails, then it is not permissible to fall back on the other, unless both were pleaded together or in the alternative. The standard of duty in negligence is that of reasonable care: in breach of statutory duty the standard is strictly fixed by the actual words of the statute itself. Further, in negligence the resulting harm must be foreseeable. In breach of statutory duty it need not. It must be shown that the breach was a cause of the damage, but where harm occurs which the statute was intended to prevent, and it is shown that there was a breach of the statute, then the court will need little persuasion to find that the breach was in fact the cause. As in common law negligence, contributory negligence on the part of the person harmed will reduce the liability for the breach of statute, and the damages will be diminished proportionately. If the statutory duty breached is one imposed upon the employer, or upon both employer and employee, the defence that the risk was voluntarily undertaken will not be accepted.

60 **College management and the 1974 Act**

All those employed in education come within the jurisdiction of the Act. It is therefore important that procedures exist for ensuring that the Act's requirements are continuously met. Key elements for doing this include:

(i) Having a well constructed safety policy statement which includes details of the arrangements necessary to implement it; the objectives of the policy; and the managerial responsibilities identified in it and to whom these have been allocated;

(ii) Provision for reviewing health and safety arrangements and procedures; the person responsible for doing so; and how it will be done;

(iii) Making newly appointed members of staff, both teaching and non-teaching, aware of the policy, and giving them guidance on their health and safety responsibilities as employees;

(iv) Ensuring that all who work in the college know what to do if they come across something hazardous;

(v) Systematic inspection of work areas;

(vi) Designation of a responsible person to receive information about accidents, dangerous occurrences and reportable diseases, and ensuring that all employees know how to contact the responsible person in emergency;

(vii) Ensuring that there are adequate ambulance and fire drills which will work in case of emergency (liaison with the local ambulance control and with the fire service will help to achieve this);

(viii) Ensuring adequate first-aid provision (see Appendix 1).

Of relevance to item (v), guidelines have been issued by the HSE relating to the inspection of educational establishments, and these are reproduced as Appendix 2.

61 The HSE has a list of statutory instruments and regulations which relate to compliance with the 1974 Act, and a list of its advisory publications applicable to colleges. Copies of these lists are available from the HSE. Observance of

advisory publications and guidance notes is not a statutory duty, but will support a contention that all reasonably practicable steps have been taken to avoid hazards.

ADDRESSES

HEALTH AND SAFETY EXECUTIVE

Head Offices
Baynards House, 1 Chepstow Place, Westbourne Grove, London W2 4TF. Telephone: 01-229 3456; and
Magdalen House, Stanley Precinct, Bootle, Liverpool L20 3QY. Telephone: 051-951 4000.

Public enquiry points
Library and Information Services, Broad Lane, Sheffield S3 7HQ. Telephone: 0742 752539.
Library and Information Services, Baynards House, 1 Chepstow Place, Westbourne Grove, London W2 4TF. Telephone 01-221 0870.
Library and Information Services, Magdalen House, Stanley Precinct, Trinity Road, Bootle, Merseyside L20 3QY. Telephone: 051-951 4381.

Area Offices
South West (Avon, Cornwall, Devon, Gloucestershire, Somerset, Isles of Scilly) Inter City House, Mitchell Lane, Victoria Street, Bristol BS1 6AN. Telephone: 0272-290681.

South (Berkshire, Dorset, Hampshire, Isle of Wight, Wiltshire) Priestley House, Priestley Road, Basingstoke RG24 9NW. Telephone: 0256-473181.

South East (Kent, Surrey, East Sussex, West Sussex) 3 East Grinstead House, London Road, East Grinstead, RH19 1RR. Telephone: 0342-26922.

London NW (Barnet, Brent, Camden, City of London, Ealing, Enfield, Hammersmith, Harrow, Hillingdon, Hounslow, Kensington & Chelsea, City of Westminster) Chancel House, Neasden Lane, London NW10 2UD. Telephone: 01-459 8855.

London NE (Barking, Hackney, Haringey, Havering, Islington, Newham, Redbridge, Tower Hamlets, Waltham Forest) Maritime House, 1 Linton Road, Barking, IG11 8HF. Telephone: 01-594 5522.

London S (Bexley, Bromley, Croydon, Greenwich, Kingston, Lambeth, Lewisham, Merton, Richmond, Southwark, Sutton, Wandsworth) 1 Long Lane, London SE1 4PG. Telephone: 01-407 8911.

East Anglia (Essex, Norfolk, Suffolk) 39 Baddow Road, Chelmsford, Essex CM2 0HL. Telephone: 0245-84661.

Northern Home Counties (Bedfordshire, Buckinghamshire, Cambridgeshire, Hertfordshire) 14 Cardiff Road, Luton LU1 1PP. Telephone: 0582-34121.

East Midlands (Leicestershire, Northamptonshire, Oxfordshire, Warwickshire) Belgrave House, 1 Greyfriars, Northampton NN1 2LQ. Telephone: 0604-21233.

West Midlands (West Midlands) McLaren Bldg. 2 Masshouse Circus, Queensway, Birmingham B4 7NP. Telephone: 021-236 5080

Wales (Clwyd, Dyfed, Gwent, Gwynedd, Mid-Glamorgan, Powys, South Glamorgan, West Glamorgan) Brunel House, 2 Fitzalan Road, Cardiff CF2 1SH. Telephone: 0222-497777.

The Marches (Hereford and Worcester, Shropshire, Staffordshire) The Marches House, Midway, Newcastle-under-Lyme ST5 1DT. Telephone: 0782-610181

North Midlands (Derbyshire, Lincolnshire, Nottinghamshire) Birbeck House, Trinity Square, Nottingham NG1 4AU. Telephone: 0602-470712.

South Yorkshire (Humberside, South Yorkshire) Sovereign House, 40 Silver Street, Sheffield S1 2ES. Telephone: 0742-739081.

N & W Yorks (North Yorkshire, West Yorkshire) 8 St Pauls Street, Leeds LS1 2LE. Telephone: 0532-446191.

Greater Manchester (Greater Manchester) Quay House, Quay Street, Manchester M3 3JB. Telephone: 061-831 7111.

Merseyside (Cheshire, Merseyside) The Triad, Stanley Road, Bootle Merseyside L20 3PG. Telephone: 051-922 7211.

North West (Cumbria, Lancashire) Victoria House, Ormskirk Road, Preston PR1 1HH. Telephone: 0772-59321.

North East (Cleveland, Durham, Northumberland, Tyne & Wear) Arden House, Regent Farm Road, Gosforth, Newcastle-upon-Tyne NE3 3JN. Telephone: 091-2848448.

Scotland East (Borders, Central, Fife, Grampian, Highland, Lothian, Tayside, and the island areas of Orkney & Shetland) Belford House, 59 Belford Road, Edinburgh EH4 3UE. Telephone: 031-225 1313.

Scotland West (Dumfries and Galloway, Strathclyde, and the Western Isles) 314 St Vincent Street, Glasgow G3 8XG. Telephone: 041-204 2646.

APPENDIX 1

EDUCATION SERVICE ADVISORY COMMITTEE'S GUIDANCE DOCUMENT ON FIRST-AID PROVISIONS IN EDUCATIONAL ESTABLISHMENTS

This document offers practical advice on the implications for the Education Service of the Health and Safety (First-Aid) Regulations 1981.

INTRODUCTION

1 The Health and Safety (First-Aid) Regulations 1981 came into effect on the 1 July 1982. An HSE explanatory booklet HS(R) 11 entitled *First-Aid at Work* is available comprising an Approved Code of Practice and Guidance Notes to the Regulations. (HS(R) 11 can be obtained from HMSO or through booksellers, price £2.50 net.)

2 These Regulations cover all employees – both teaching and non-teaching staff – who work in schools, colleges, polytechnics and universities.

3 Although there is no statutory requirement under these Regulations for an employer to provide first-aid facilities for pupils or students, there is a continuing moral and civil duty to do so. First-aid facilities should also be available for visitors to educational establishments. In practice, many employers will wish to continue (or to establish) a combined system of first-aid provision for employees and pupils, students and visitors, whilst maintaining the level of provision required for employees by the Regulations.

SCALE OF PROVISION REQUIRED BY THE REGULATIONS

4 The Regulations are framed to allow employers considerable scope in deciding how provision can best be made for first-aid to suit the particular circumstances of a particular educational establishment. General advice on the criteria to be used by the employer for deciding what level of provisions will be appropriate is given in paragraphs 6–22 of the Approved Code of Practice is HS(R) 11.

5 In primary and secondary schools, which may be regarded as establishments with relatively low hazards, a first-aider would only be required where there are more than 150 employees and a first-aid room where there are more than 400 employees. As a consequence, the majority of schools will not require a first-aid room for employees (although many schools already have a medical room) and 'appointed persons' will be required rather than first-aiders. This does not prevent trained first-aiders being appointed in primary and secondary schools where this is considered appropriate.

6 In further and higher educational establishments, the hazards will vary greatly from department to department. Libraries, offices, teaching and lecture rooms may be regarded as areas with relatively low risks attracting a commensurate level of first-aid provisions. Research or teaching laboratories and workshops may be classified as areas with relatively higher risks requiring a higher level of first-aid provisions, such as more first-aiders. In establishments where special or unusual hazards exist, occupational first-aiders may be necessary, irrespective of the number of employees.

FIRST-AID BOXES AND KITS

7 The recommended contents of first-aid boxes and kits can be used by any employee, in the absence of a trained first-aider, without exacerbating the injury and until further help can be summoned, if necessary. Only the basic recommended contents which an untrained employee could use quickly and without risk should be kept in a first-aid box.

8 Access to the first-aid box should be available out of hours for persons such as cleaners and other persons who may have to work late.

9 If additional equipment, such as a special antidote or resuscitation apparatus, is necessary to deal with any special hazards, it should be kept in a safe place where it will be accessible if required. Any necessary training and/or instruction in the use of special antidote or resuscitation equipment should be given.

FIRST-AID ROOMS

10 The first-aid room should be sited within easy reach of all employees, but there may be sites where location in relation to hazardous areas is preferable. Care should be taken in the siting of first-aid rooms and should take account of such factors as access for ambulances and stretchers, concentrations of employment etc.

11 The main purpose of a first-aid room is to provide second aid for the treatment of cuts, bruises etc by trained first-aiders. In the case of remote work places, the first-aid room provides a safe and comfortable place to keep a casualty while awaiting an ambulance or medical care.

12 Adequate rooms, such as in Student Health Service or Occupational Health Service facilities, may already be in existence. Common rooms or rest rooms could be used as a safe place for a casualty to await in an emergency.

FIRST-AIDERS

13 The responsibility for selecting, appointing and training first-aiders rests with the employer.

14 First-aiders should be selected from among persons who will be within the building for a committed number of hours.

5 The training received by first-aiders must be on courses approved by HSE. Any organisation may apply to HSE for approval of their training courses. A number of universities and technical colleges have been approved. A list of approved organisations is contained in leaflet IND(G) 5 L which is available from HSE.

OUT OF HOURS WORKING

6 Out of hours working is common in many educational establishments. It is important that all educational establishments have written arrangements to cater for such situations and which, amongst other things, ensure that first-aid provisions are adequate. The nature of the hazards to which the individual may be exposed will help determine the level of first-aid provision required.

FIELD TRIPS

7 The planning of any field trip or expedition should include consideration of what first-aid provisions are required. Special training may be needed for those accompanying expeditions to remote locations away from the emergency services or where field trips involve specialised or unusual hazards, e.g. pot-holing, mountaineering or diving.

MEDICAL SCHOOLS

8 Universities occasionally have medical schools and hospitals associated with them. Employers should not assume that because qualified medical staff are present, no further consideration need be given to first-aid provisions. Medical practitioners have legal and ethical responsibilities and employers should comply with the individual wishes of the doctors concerned. Medical staff often have commitments which prevent them from being at their place of work during normal working hours. A practical approach might be to appoint lay first-aiders with a back-up system of doctors willing to be called on in an emergency.

HOSPITAL ACCIDENT AND EMERGENCY DEPARTMENTS

9 An employer may wish to use the facilities of an associated hospital accidents and emergency department as a part of the overall first-aid provisions. The facilities available should be determined and an agreed procedure for referral instituted. Accident and emergency departments are usually very busy and cannot be expected to give minor first-aid treatment which should be provided at the work place. Similarly, accident and emergency departments may not be able to attend to serious injuries in the work place.

FURTHER ADVICE

20 Advice about the application of the Regulations in any particular situation is available from the Area Offices of the HSE.

APPENDIX 2

THE INSPECTION OF EDUCATIONAL ESTABLISHMENTS

The following guidelines have been issued by the HSE concerning its approach to the inspection of educational establishments:

Inspection of large and complex establishments such as universities and the larger colleges of higher education will require initial visits by appointment to meet senior officials of the university or college and explain the purpose and arrangements for inspection and to determine the management structure and organisation of the establishment. The safety policy and the delegation of duties under the policy will be discussed at this stage. Before visiting establishments under the control of Local Education Authorities, inspectors will normally seek an appointment with the director of the department to determine the safety organisation of the department and the most efficient method of liaison concerning the programme of inspection.

2 The initial discussion will seek to determine the areas to be visited and identify the responsible persons to be contacted. Details of the trade union and staff association consultative arrangements and of safety representatives and committees will also be requested.

3 The first objective of inspection will be to ensure that each employing body has an adequate safety policy and has set up the necessary organisation for health and safety within its management structure. This will include a definition of the various levels of responsibility at which the duties described in the policy are to be carried out. The approach will be similar to that followed in other areas of employment but inspectors will seek to ensure that the arrangements for implementing the policy also cover the safety and health of non-employed persons, particularly students and pupils.

4 The safety policy statements should cover matters such as plant, machinery and electrical equipment. In addition, it should cover dangers arising from the activities carried on both inside the premises, e.g. engineering workshops, research laboratories and the use of ionising radiations, and outside the premises where field work is undertaken. It should set out the arrangements which have been made for occupational health and the procedure for identifying, recording, investigating and monitoring accidents, dangerous occurrences and cases of occupational disease. It should refer to the methods of control of dangerous or toxic materials and substances used in laboratories and the storage and use of flammable and explosive liquids and gases. Where appropriate the precautions should be set out in further detail in departmental safety policies and arrangements or rules or codes of practice. It is important that a senior member in the organisation should be appointed to co-ordinate the implementation of the policy and monitor its effectiveness.

5 In addition to being employees, a number of employed persons will, as in other spheres of activity, exercise managerial functions in varying degrees, or in the case of academic staff within departments or promoted teachers within schools exercise quasi managerial control and authority over other staff, students or pupils. It is accepted that in practical terms the employer who cannot be omni-present will need to delegate the performance of some of his [*sic*] function to others in respect of day to day matters. At the same time, it must be pointed out that it is not possible for him to delegate his overall responsibility. Where duties concerning health and safety are delegated within institutions or authorities, it should be made clear in any departmental or subsidiary safety policies to what extent duties have been further delegated and where these lie. Inspectors will pay particular attention to the way in which duties have been assigned to ensure compliance with the employer's overall responsibilities.

6 Because students and pupils greatly exceed the number of employees in educational establishments, inspectors will give particular attention to examining the measures taken to comply with the employer's responsibilities under Sections 3 and 4 of the Health and Safety at Work Act. They will, of course, bear in mind that the duty of care is not a concept new to educational establishments and is indeed implicit in the whole educational process. They will, however, wish to satisfy themselves for example that employers in education establishments have taken appropriate measures to ensure that any machinery or plant used by students or pupils is safe and that where necessary protective equipment, such as eye protection or respirators, is supplied and used.

7 Inspectors will also be concerned to examine the measures taken to protect teachers and

other employees from the hazards which could arise from the activities of students and pupils. They will, therefore, wish to establish that effective arrangements have been made for the health and safety of students and pupils and for their instruction, training and supervision in these matters and still expect to see a reference to these matters in the written safety policy.

8 A satisfactory level of health and safety training in educational establishments is considered to be of fundamental importance if everyone is to be made aware of the risks involved in his place of work and the precautions to be observed. There are four main areas of training, on the academic side the training of teachers in their duties to other employees as well as to students and pupils and the training of students and pupils themselves; and on the non-academic side the training of managers and supervisors of maintenance and other service departments and the training of service or supporting staff. Inspectors will seek to ensure that the standard of training in all these areas is of an acceptable level. The work of laboratory technicians, cleaners and security officers, particularly in research laboratories in universities and other further education establishments may expose them to special dangers. It is important that the arrangements for health and safety in such establishments should cover the special training needs of these workers.

9 In deciding whether to inspect with or without having given prior notice to the management, the Inspector will take account not only of the needs of effective inspection in the particular circumstances of the case, but also the need not to cause disruption which may adversely affect the teaching process. He will, as in the case of other premises, be guided by considerations, such as the purpose of his visit, the part of the premises to be inspected, the need to see one or more particular people in order to make the visit fully effective as well as his previous dealings with the establishment in question.

10 It is the intention of the HSE that employers in education establishments shall receive no less degree of protection against risk or injury or danger to health than persons in other areas of employment. The Inspectorate recognise, however, that financial and staff resources will not always be available to remedy immediately all the matters identified by the Inspector as requiring attention. As in the case of other employers, Inspectors will be prepared to discuss priorities with management with a view to phasing less urgent matters and will endeavour where possible to agree any programme with management. They will also discuss the matter with the trade union and staff associations. All matters of significance and any agreed programme of implementation will be confirmed in writing to both the management and employees' representatives.

11 Inspectors will establish contact with safety representatives when appointed and in the interim with shop stewards and other staff association representatives. However, in view of the complexity of the staff organisation in some establishments, Inspectors will seek to establish central points of contact for the disclosure of information in accordance with their duties under Section 28(8) of the HSW Act.

12 Inspectors will be familiar with many of the processes, hazards, plant and equipment found in education establishments and where appropriate will apply them to similar standards as in other premises. Certain guidance on health and safety precautions in the form of booklets, pamphlets, notes, rules or codes of practice already exists in universities, colleges of further education and schools. Where the DES, SED, Universities, Local Authorities or Professional Associations have issued technical guidance, this will not be queried at Area level. If Inspectors consider that this guidance is unsatisfactory either generally or in particular circumstances, they will refer the matter to the National Industry Group which will if necessary take it up centrally with the appropriate body. The aim will be to ensure that consistent standards of precautions and safety performance are achieved in all establishments. Where remedial measures are not covered by any national standard, it will be for the management to decide whether the implications of the problem are sufficiently important to merit the matter being referred through the normal channels to the Authority, Committee or appropriate Department of State concerned for discussion with the National Industry Group. It is intended that all standards

of technical guidance affecting the health, safety and welfare of persons employed in education establishments will eventually be reviewed by the Health and Safety Executive and discussed with the issuing body so that the standards can be agreed and recognised.

13 Some departments of universities and further education establishments are subject to inspection by HM Nuclear Installations Inspectorate. Factory Inspectors are aware of these designated premises and will work in close liaison with the Nuclear Installations Inspectors, so that duplication of inspection is avoided. The majority of premises where ionising radiations are used will be inspected by the Factory Inspectorate. Factory Inspectors may use the services of the National Radiological Protection Board for inspections in these premises on an agency basis as they do in factories.

14 Parts of educational establishments subject to the Factories Act or OSRP Act are designated under the Fire Precautions Act 1971 and fire certification and requirements for fire precautions are the responsibilities of the Fire Authority, with the exception of Crown educational establishments which are the responsibility of HM Inspectors of Fire Services of the Home Office and the Scottish Home and Health Department. In other parts which have not as yet been designated under the Fire Precautions Act, the Fire Authorities have traditionally advised on a goodwill basis and are also empowered under Section 10 of the Fire Precautions Act to apply to the courts for orders in cases of serious risk. Factory Inspectors will not examine the fire precautions nor will they inspect the structure of fittings of buildings other than the extent to which these may affect the process fire risk. If, however, matters of serious fire risk come to their attention, they will be brought to the notice of the management, the Fire Authority or the Inspector of Fire Services and employees' representatives as a matter of urgency.

15 Except for those with Crown status, education establishments will be subject to normal enforcement procedures provided for the HSW Act. The small number of Crown employers are being told separately of the special procedures that will apply to them. Inspectors will prefer to achieve health and safety standards by advice and recommendation but as in other areas of work activity will take enforcement action when the situation demands it.

16 The information available to date from the two pilot studies and from the feedback of information from the inspection programme already underway in HSE Areas suggest that there are many problems to be overcome. Measures to control health and safety in many educational establishments are in certain respects below those in industry. The occurrence of accidents, however, appears to be less than in industry from the accident information available and this seems to indicate that maintenance staff, technicians and ancillary workers such as cleaners, groundsmen and catering staff are more at risk than teaching staff or pupils. There is considerable variation in standards within establishments depending largely on the initiative of the head of department and between one similar establishment and another. From the examples of high standards found, it would seem that there is the know-how to achieve conditions which are safe and without risks to health inside all educational establishments providing performance can be equalised. The question of resources is raised repeatedly, but could be less significant than the correct deployment of existing resources.

17 Universities, colleges of further and higher education and local education authorities have in many cases taken the initiative to produce safety policies and a safety organisation before the HSE inspection programme began. The professional associations and trade unions representing teaching and non-teaching employees are being noticeably active in appointing safety representatives and in providing training for them to meet the Safety Representatives and Safety Committee Regulations. In response to this a number of employing bodies have organised management training courses and are discussing proposals for safety committees with the unions concerned. This interest and response is encouraging. A prime objective of the HSE will be the establishment of an effective organisation for health and safety covering each establishment. Inspection of individual establishments will measure the performance and effectiveness of that or-

ganisation. The HSE will take a part in the formulation of national standards for health and safety but in the main these standards can best be set by the many existing organisations in the education field.

2.8 GOVERNMENT AND MANAGEMENT

1 **The constitutional position**

The legal foundation of the government of colleges is in the instrument and articles of government. These documents establish the powers of and relationships between the elements in the government of colleges: the local education authority (LEA) for maintained colleges or the voluntary body (and/or trustees) for voluntary colleges; the governing body; the principal or director; and the academic board.

2 Instruments and articles are based on the Education (No. 2) Act 1968 and the guidance on its implementation issued by the Department of Education and Science (DES) in Circular 7/70. The act required that for every institution maintained by an LEA, both teacher training institutions and colleges of FE providing full-time education[1], there should be an instrument and articles of government. The circular included a model instrument and articles, and this model is broadly followed for most colleges. The Education (No. 2) Act 1968 and Circular 7/70 applied to maintained colleges, but the equivalent system has been applied to voluntary colleges since the Training of Teachers Regulations 1967 (Circular 4/67). (A brief outline of the constitutional position is given in this section; see the 1980 edition of *College Administration*, Waitt 1980, for a discussion of the Circular 7/70 model.)

3 Circular 7/70 adopted a hierarchical categorisation of colleges, depending on their proportions of advanced work: A – a substantial proportion of advanced work, and with most of their students full-time, over 18 years of age; B – a significant amount of advanced work; C – little or no advanced work, and most students 16–18 year old part-timers. It proposed that the A category should have most independence and C least (see below paragraphs 5–7 and 19–23). The fine distinctions have not been perpetuated, though differences sometimes show between A and C types, especially in the powers of academic board (see below paragraphs 6–7) and in the representation of students (see **3.5** 7–9).

4 **Instrument of government**

The instrument of government establishes a governing body and describes its composition. For maintained institutions, the instrument of government is made by order of the local education authority ; for teacher training institutions the instrument of government requires the Secretary of State's approval (though they no longer comprise a separate sector (see **1.1** 9–10). For voluntary colleges the instrument of government, which may be incorporated in a trust deed (see **1.2** Appendix 1 10–13), is made by the voluntary body.

5 The composition of the governing body typically includes, for a maintained college :

(i) Representatives of the LEA, in a minority, perhaps as low as a quarter of the membership. (There are differences in how far the LEA representatives have to be members of the council or education committee or hold particular posts in the council's committee structure. There is often a representative or two from neighbouring LEAs);

(ii) Representatives of industry, commerce and professions, employers and employees. (There are differences in how the representatives of industry etc are appointed ; in some cases they are appointed by named representative bodies, but in others they are coopted by the governing body. The latter in practice means they are coopted by those who take up their places first, that is the representatives of LEA, staff and maybe students (see below paragraph 28);

(iii) A member from another college, school or university;
(iv) The principal (and often deputy/ies);
(v) Representatives of teaching staff and, often, non-teaching staff;
(vi) Representatives of students where there is a substantial proportion of advanced or post-18 students (see **3.5** 7).

In a voluntary college there is typically a number of foundation governors (see **1.2** Appendix 1 10–13), instead of representatives of a maintaining LEA.

6 **Articles of government**

The articles of government set out the responsibilities of the LEA, governing body, director/principal and academic board. The articles of government require the approval of the Secretary of State. The wordings suggested in Circular 7/70 and commonly broadly followed are:
LEA – 'the general educational character of the college and its place in the local educational system';
Governing body – 'the general direction of the college';
Principal – 'the internal organisation, management and discipline';
Academic board – 'the planning, coordination, development and oversight of the academic work of the college'.

7 The more detailed statements of responsibilities of academic boards vary considerably. The major difference is whether they have decision-making powers, as they do in polytechnics and colleges with substantial amounts of advanced work (A category – see above paragraph 3) and many other colleges, or whether as is more likely in colleges in C category they are restricted to advising the principal. Where they have decision-making functions spelt out, these usually include responsibilities for admission of students, examination or assessment of students, and exclusion for unsatisfactory work, but there may also be statements about reviewing academic work, encouraging research, consultancy and staff development – the actual wordings are unique to institutions. A major difference is whether they have a role in financial decision-making or resource planning or allocation of staff and resources – these responsibilities are more likely in polytechnics and colleges with more advanced work. The membership of academic boards typically includes the principal and deputy/ies, heads of department and representatives of academic staff as well as chief/senior administrative officer and librarian.

8 Articles of government also set out procedures for: the appointment, promotion and dismissal of staff (see **2.4** and **2.5**); agreement of staff establishments; preparation and approval of annual estimates, and spending powers of the governing body; student discipline; representation of students (see **3.5** 7). The spending powers of the governing body are described in terms of their powers to spend up to a set figure on supplies and equipment and on repairs and maintenance and to exercise virement within (and, occasionally between) headings in the accounts (see **1.3** 85–88 and **1.6** 49–51) (see below paragraph 23). Articles often require colleges to use or consider the LA's central purchasing arrangements and to consult its Architect, as appropriate. Statements in articles of government differ from institution to institution (see the 1980 edition of *College Administration*, Waitt 1980).

9 In voluntary colleges the governing body typically includes the responsibilities given to the LEA in maintained colleges, though some aspects may be reserved to the trustees or voluntary body.

10 **Financial regulations**

The detailed provisions for the financial administration of colleges are set out in financial rules or regulations which Circular 7/70's model articles proposed should 'be made by the Authority after consultation with the Governors'. College financial regulations usually represent a compromise with the regulations applied to other local authority operations, though occasionally the same regulations are applied to colleges. The intention should be that the financial regulations implement the procedures outlined in articles of government, but in some instances the financial regulations restrict the college more than the articles of government. Financial regulations take many different forms; they include the role of the LA treasurer, the spending powers delegated to the principal, procedures for ordering, considering tenders and placing contracts, and procedures for record-keeping, reporting and audit.

11 **1986 Act**

The Education Act (No. 2) 1986 included sections relevant to college government, as to schools. Section 56 required a college governing body to make such reports and returns to the Secretary of State as she or he may require for the exercise of her or his functions. Section 62 enabled the Secretary of State to make regulations to extend the public's rights of access to governing body papers. Section 61 (1) prevented anyone under the age of 18 from serving as a governor unless they are a student at the college (though on school governing bodies no one under 18 may serve). However, Sections 61 (2) and (3) provided for regulations to restrict the participation of student governors: underage governors are excluded from voting on issues which involve the financial liability of the governing body; and all student governors have to withdraw when matters relating to staff (or prospective staff) are discussed, unless the instrument of government specifically allows them to be present. Section 43 placed a duty on all concerned in the government of institutions of further or higher education to secure, as far as reasonably practicable, freedom of speech within the law for members, students, employees and visiting speakers; this duty includes drawing up a code of practice on procedures and conduct for meetings (see **1.2** 30).

12 **Developments and clarifications**

Since they were first established following the 1968 (No. 2) Act, instruments and articles of government have been revised. There has not been a consistent pattern. Whereas there had been expectations that changes would create more independence for colleges, in some cases the changes have defined responsibilities more specifically and become more restrictive (Locke with Pratt, Silverman and Travers 1987).

13 The constitutional structure of college government has been upheld in law. For example, Mr Justice Slade in a case involving North East London Polytechnic and members of its Joint Education Committee (the LEA – see **1.6** 68) said: 'They (the JEC) purported to dictate elements of the Polytechnic's curriculum, which under its Articles was a matter not for the Joint Committee but for the Academic Board and the Director under the supervision of the Governors' (Royal Courts of Justice 2 May 1978).

14 Two major cases in schools have established the supremacy of the LEA as the employer. Bradford (in the case involving Ray Honeyford in 1985) and Brent (in the case involving Maureen McGoldrick in 1986 – (McGoldrick v Brent London Borough Council, Court of Appeal, 19 November 1986) local authorities have both established in the courts that they had the right to discipline headteachers, even though their governing bodies had wished not to proceed. There was a similar impact in Auld's advice to the Inner London Education Authority (ILEA) in his inquiry into the William Tyndale school that the LEA could not avoid exercising its power and duty over schools as laid down by the Education Act 1944 even though it had delegated them to other bodies (Auld 1976).

15 The law has not, however, resolved outstanding questions about the nature of the governing body by articles of government. One view – the better founded one, in the judgement of this writer – is that the powers ascribed to the governing body are original powers and not powers delegated from the local authority; thus the power of 'general direction' gives them the power to act on issues which are not specifically ascribed to the LEA or other bodies. A different interpretation is that the powers are actually delegated from the LEA; therefore issues which are not specifically ascribed to the governing body remain within the LEA's hands.

16 The instrument and articles of government do have legal force; the 1980 edition of *College Administration* described it as a 'codified domestic law' (Waitt 1980). But there remains a question about the kind of legal status which the governing body of a maintained institution has, whether it has a corporate nature in some aspects or is in law only a collection of individuals. The 1980 edition (Waitt 1980) said that the governing body 'may sue and be sued', implying that it has a legal personality in its own right; this view drew on opinion in the early 1970s and followed Locke (1972). But this view has not prevailed in public debate, and more usually it is thought that the governing body does not have a corporate nature and relies for the college's legal identity on the LEA (see **1.2** Appendix 1). The position is uncertain. If suing because of an event in a college, it might be advisable to join members of the governing body in the action, as well as the LEA; whether corporately or individually, governors can be answerable in law for carrying out their responsibilities as described in articles of government. It may also be thought, for instance, that in law the governing body would be seen as employers along with the local authority (though this could be as individuals like the managing body of an unincorporated association, rather than as a corporate body).

17 In colleges which are not maintained by an LEA the governors have some additional responsibilities, and, as the White Paper 1987 proposes that polytechnics and colleges of HE should cease to be maintained institutions, there are to be many more governors in this position. If the college is established under company law (as the polytechnics in the Inner London Education Authority and some voluntary colleges of higher education) the governing body is the board of directors, and the governors have the responsibilities in law of company directors. Where colleges are charitable bodies, the governors have trustee responsibilities, though this may depend on the particular arrangement and on some complex legal disputes (see **1.2** Appendix 1).

18 Governors in maintained and voluntary colleges have accumulated some responsibilities not put in instruments and articles of government. They have

responsibilities under Health and Safety legislation (see **2.7** in particular 12–14). The Education (No. 2) Act 1986 placed a responsibility for free speech (see above paragraph 11 and **1.2** 30). (See also **1.6** 8.)

19 **Constitutional issues**

The critical theme has been that of relationship between maintained colleges and their local education authorities. From the college side there is the push for more independence and freedom from LEA 'meddling' or from the way LA procedures permeate through a college's internal workings; and from the LEA side an assertion of their legal and political responsibilities for the institutions, which are in law part of the authority. The greatest concern has been for polytechnics and colleges of higher education; a longstanding concept is that advanced work required or deserved more independence (see White Paper 1956), and doubts have been current about LEAs' capability to manage colleges with substantial amounts of advanced level work (higher education). Polytechnics and a few colleges of HE also grew to be much the largest and most complex institutions managed by LEAs, seen sometimes as the cuckoo in the nest. Yet, these institutions have been part of the local educational service and legally and financially bound to their LEAs.

20 The pivot of the system for two decades was the Weaver Report (1966). The brief of the committee related only to colleges of education (teacher training institutions), but its report was applied to the whole of the FE sector. The report said:

> '. . . the problem was to strike the correct balance between the freedom which institutions of higher education should enjoy and the social control which democratically elected representative bodies are required to exercise' (paragraph 10).

It continued:

> '. . . no institution set in a complex democratic society can properly claim absolute freedom and . . . the ordering of its academic life is inevitably bound up with the management of its financial and administrative affairs' (paragraph 12).

And:

> 'So long as a local education authority maintains a college it feels itself in the last resort responsible for the college, for its general efficiency, for financing its expenditure, for its staff . . . and for its premises' (paragraph 14).

21 Weaver's solution was essentially to separate matters of an academic nature which should be the province of academic staff from financial matters which should be supervised by the LEA. It set the governing body as the body to reconcile these forces. Its objective was to provide:

> '. . . machinery and procedures designed to encourage close partnership between a maintained college and the authority responsible for it' (paragraph 117).

22 There was some resistance from LEAs generally to some of its proposals, but recommendations were adopted for the Education (No. 2) Act 1968 and Circular 7/70. They were of major significance in the designation of polytechnics, following the 1966 White Paper, and in Administrative Memorandum 8/67 the DES jumped the gun and it set a Circular 7/70-type structure of instruments and articles as a requirement for its designation of polytechnics (Locke 1974). It sought to ensure that polytechnics would have a large measure of autonomy.

23 There remained, however, widespread dissatisfaction in colleges with the relationship with local authorities so established. The methods of financial management exercised by local authorities were seen by colleges as unnecessarily bureaucratic and as impeding their chance of managing themselves. Bookkeeping and expenditure control procedures were often duplicated in

colleges and local authorities. Financial regulations undermined some of the intentions of articles of government to secure independence for colleges. Responsibilities for buildings and maintenance were often unclear. Colleges were required to use central purchasing arrangements more than they thought reasonable and educationally right. Colleges were often not given any choice about having the LA undertake central services, and these services sometimes did not provide value-for-money. Staff establishments were sometimes set by LAs without sufficient regard to the college's needs, and for non-teaching staff LAs often imposed their assessment of levels of staffing and gradings. Overall, there was a frustration and a feeling of energy wasted in resolving problems of the college – LA relationship (see, e.g., Locke with Pratt, Silverman and Travers 1987; Pratt and Gill 1987). Although this was felt throughout the public sector, the national debate concentrated on the problems of polytechnics and institutions of higher education, continuing the assumption that advanced work should be related to more independence in management.

24 The Oakes Report saw:

> '. . . a wide variety in the way in which institutions are in fact managed and it is a common complaint . . . that some local authorities intervene in the detailed management of their institutions so as to effectively prevent governing bodies exercising the responsibilities for management entrusted to them by their institutions' articles of government' (Oakes 1978).

The Select Committee in 1980 said:

> '. . . we believe that it will only be acceptable for local authorities to retain their stake in higher education if all of them can restrain themselves from excessive and unreasonable interference in the running of large developed polytechnics with the skills and competence to look after themselves. At the very least, duplication of bureaucracy is unacceptable' (Education, Science and Arts Committee 1980).

25 Another source of dissatisfaction within colleges was that the representative structures established in the instruments and articles of government had not generally produced the internal democracy which had been hoped for (see, e.g., Smith 1983 and NATFHE conference resolutions quoted in Waitt 1980). The hierarchical power of principals and heads of department continued to dominate decision-making, whether through executive control over resources or through weight of numbers on academic board (see below paragraphs 60–68). There was also some disillusion in colleges that the ideals of participation had often turned into byzantine structures of committees and subcommittees.

26 The system was also unsatisfactory for LEAs. In a draft report prepared, but not published, by a Review Group on College Government (1981) of the DES and Council of Local Education Authorities (CLEA) it was stated:

> 'CLEA's request for changes had been prompted by representations from member LEAs deeply concerned at the unsatisfactory constitutional position in which an authority rightly carried the responsibility for an action, or funding, or a contract, but lacked the means of controlling it; governors, in the exercise of their powers, could commit the LEA in some area where the LEA ought not, or would not wish, to be committed. Conversely, an LEA could be baulked by governors from achieving financial or manpower reductions in a college – for example, as part of an exercise to achieve economies assumed in the Public Expenditure White Paper or required through limitation of pooled expenditure. The Associations' conviction that change is needed has been strengthened by awareness of the LEAs' liabilities before the Courts and the Commissioners for Local Administration; . . . and by the need to take swift and drastic action to curtail expenditure at the time of, and in between, rate support grant settlements.'

27 The cuts in public expenditure during the 1970s and 1980s had thus accentuated the problems. LEAs, subject to the tightening control by central government over their finances, found it difficult, or impossible, to work on the basis of fixed annual estimates, drafted in the college, which was written into the Circular 7/70 model; the LEAs found it necessary to engage more closely in the budgeting process and, in some cases, to impose further cuts during the course of the financial year. (See **1.3** 76–91.)

28 Local authority control was not reduced as much as intended by the post-Weaver reforms. LAs intervened in financial administration and applied their procedures to the colleges (see above paragraph 23). LAs also in some cases retained a dominance on governing bodies: where independent members were coopted by the governors from the LA and the institution (see above paragraph 5), they could extend their interests through the cooptees, possibly even carving them up on party political lines. Above all, holding the purse strings gave local authorities more power than was written into articles of government. But local authorities regarded that as necessary to exercise their responsibilities. (See **1.6** 28–34 and 40–53.)

29 Other changes in the 1970s and 1980s accentuated the problems. First, the development of corporate management in local authorities, following the Bains Report (1972), meant that colleges had to deal with departments, such as Personnel and Architects, which (though expert in their own fields) had less understanding of educational institutions than had the Education Department (see **1.6** 9–12, 28–34 and 58–59). Second, the funding of public sector higher education increasingly operated on a national level. The National Advisory Body for Public Sector Higher Education (NAB) made recommendations to the Secretary of State for allocations from the AFE pool (see **1.3** 49–53) and so diminished the LEA role, even though the AFE pool was local authority money. The financial allocations to polytechnics and higher education increasingly were perceived as national funding in all but technical accuracy. Thirdly, the funding of work-related NAFE by the Manpower Services Commission (MSC) on the basis of plans negotiated with LEAs and colleges drew colleges and LEAs into a triangular relationship with the MSC which confused the constitutional lines of accountability from colleges to LEA (see **1.3** 43–45 and **1.7** 65–67). Fourthly, the post-1979 Conservative Governments under Prime Minister Margaret Thatcher heightened the pressures on local authorities and colleges by its centralisation of power (see **1.1** and **1.2**) and its commitment to shake up public services.

30 In 1985–86 NAB undertook a major inquiry on Good Management Practice which investigated the government and management of colleges. It explored the dissatisfactions noted above (see paragraphs 19–29) and judged that a greater separation between colleges and LEAs was needed to improve the effectiveness of college management. Its great problem was to decide whether this required that colleges be established with corporate status, that is a legal separation from LEAs, or whether a clarification of a constitutional position evolved from Circular 7/70 would serve both the colleges and the LEAs. The report was presented to NAB in March 1987 and so gained some currency, though it was not published then.

31 The report of the NAB Good Management Practice was outflanked by Conservative Secretary of State Kenneth Baker in publishing in April 1987 in readiness for the general election campaign the White Paper *Higher education:*

Meeting the challenge. This believed it could tackle the problems of college government by establishing colleges as corporate bodies (see **1.2** Appendix 1) and removing them from local authorities. It proposed that governing bodies should have strong representation of industry and commerce with the representation of local authorities much reduced. It saw the newly freestanding institutions as meeting the challenge of increasing student numbers without additional public funds, and of improving 'quality' and 'efficiency' (See below paragraphs 36–40) (see **1.1** Appendix 1).

32 **Operational issues**

The environment within which colleges are managed has changed considerably since the 1980 edition of *College Administration* was written (Waitt 1980), and this has stretched both the government system described in the first parts of this section and the established management structures of colleges.

33 **The policy environment**

The post-1979 Conservative Government of Prime Minister Margaret Thatcher changed the environment in which colleges operated (see **1.1** and **1.4**). Some of the changes were the culmination of the process of centralisation of funding and decision-making which had been taking place through the 1970s (see, e.g., Locke, Pratt and Burgess 1985). But this Government introduced new elements in its conviction that a commercial ethos would improve the effectiveness of public services and its attack upon what it saw as waste, bureaucracy and feather-bedding in the public services. It also reduced the financial base of local authorities and further education and tightened financial and legislative controls. It made central agencies stronger and more significant in the daily work of colleges: in non-advanced FE the Manpower Services Commission (MSC) (See **1.3** and **1.7**); in advanced FE the National Advisory Body (NAB) (See **1.3**).

34 The reduction in public expenditure took from colleges an important method of carrying out changes in colleges, that of incremental growth (See **1.3** 76–91). Traditionally, colleges had been able to develop their activities by adding on new activities without, broadly speaking, having to cut something to make room or resources for the growth. With little possibility of new resources, colleges were faced with more difficult decisions about how, when they wanted to develop new activities, to make savings from existing activities. Colleges, to different degrees in different local authorities, faced the problems of restricted public funding increasingly during the 1970s. The tightening of the screws financially in the 1980s set up the situation where colleges needed to generate new income, partly to compensate for the loss of public funding and keep an equilibrium, partly to provide some areas of growth and opportunity. These developments had considerable impact on the management structures and processes (See below paragraphs 51–77).

35 Colleges adapted to the external changes. FE has had a long tradition of responsiveness to changing environments, more so than other parts of the education service. However, some of the adaptations implied or effected during this Government conflicted with concerns for the quality of education and for the work and conditions of staff, raising dilemmas which went beyond simple entrepreneurial decisions into questions of professional conscience and political judgement.

36 **'Efficiency'**
The changes which affected colleges during this period went deeper than external pressures and financial restrictions. There were powerful statements of managerial principles on which colleges and staff were expected to work. The Audit Commission laid down the principles of the 'Three Es' – 'efficiency, economy and effectiveness' – which should guide public services. There has been much emphasis on 'value for money' and 'cost effectiveness'. (For NAB's measures intended to improve cost effectiveness, see Ball 1985 and Pratt 1982.) (See **1.3** 105–115 and **2.5** 19.)

37 The Audit Commission's approach was applied to further education in its report *Obtaining better value from further education* (1985) (See **1.3** 112 and **2.5** 20). This report suggested that 75,000 extra students could be provided with full-time further education without overstraining existing resources. It based this on notions of better marketing to create larger classes, putting teachers in front of classes for longer periods, recovering costs and billing more efficiently, and controlling non-teaching costs. The report served to illustrate the pressure to take up Audit Commission thinking, though there were doubts about its authority in education (e.g. *NATFHE Journal*, October 1985).

38 A considered approach to efficiency was taken by the DES-local authorities Joint Efficiency Study in non-advanced further education, the report of which was published in summer 1987[2] to be followed by a manual in spring 1988.

39 The White Paper 1987 *Higher education: Meeting the challenge* (See **1.1** Appendix 1) set out principles of 'quality' and 'efficiency'. 'Quality', it said, could be judged by looking at:

> 'academic standards as reflected by the design and content of courses, their fitness for purpose, what they require of students and how they meet the needs of employers;
> the quality of teaching;
> the achievements of students – both whilst in higher education and in subsequent employment;
> and the quality of research – pre-commitment scrutiny and subsequent evaluation of achievement' (paragraph 3.6).

The quality of teaching could be improved through 'staff training and development; staff appraisal; evaluation of the results achieved, including analysis of external examiners' reports and students' employment patterns' (paragraph 3.12). 'The pursuit of efficiency,' the White Paper said, 'is not just about saving money. It is about helping institutions and individuals to achieve more of what they should achieve with the money that is available' (paragraph 3.23). And it carried through this principle by proposing increases in student numbers without increases in public funding (See **1.3** 47–48).

40 Two innovatory methods were adopted by the White Paper 1987 to achieve 'quality' and 'efficiency'. It saw the process operating through efforts by individual members of academic institutions within systems through which the Government could ensure commitment and monitor results (White Paper 1987 paragraphs 3.5 and 3.23); this was consistent with the Government's ideology that it should legislate for a market framework within which individuals would make the choices the Government expected, unconstrained by public and collective bodies such as local authorities and unions. It also introduced a system of contracting between institutions and the Polytechnics and Colleges

Funding Council (PCFC) to fund public sector higher education. The intentions were to:

> 'encourage institutions to be enterprising in attracting contracts from other sources, particularly the private sector, and thereby to lessen their present degree of dependence on public funding;
> sharpen accountability for the use of public funds which will continue to be required;
> and strengthen the commitment of institutions to the delivery of the educational services which it is agreed with the (PCFC) they should provide' (paragraph 4.17).

The contracting principle would clearly have major impact on the internal management of institutions, but, at time of writing, it was unclear how far this would be implemented as written in the White Paper (See **1.3** 47–48).

41 **Accountability and evaluation**

A more general development was for improved accountability of educational institutions, spreading across different ideological and academic positions and affecting all levels of work. There was much talk of the need for accountability but not so much resolution of what form of accountability, to whom and for what. Broadly, approaches could be categorised into: bureaucratic and political forms; professional evaluation and appraisal; and market forces.

42 The traditional form of accountability for further education has been through political and bureaucratic structures. Such a model was used in the Weaver-Circular 7/70 system of college government. The college was accountable through its governing body to the LEA and the community. Within the college staff were accountable through executive structures to the head of department and principal and thence to the governing body, but they were also able to be represented in policies and decisions through academic board and its committee structure, and hence committed to them. The roots of the representative structures could be traced both through demands for employee or union representation and through concepts of 'participation' from the late 1960s (Locke 1976). Within this structure it was assumed that academic staff would have some degree of 'academic freedom' – probably, it would have been generally assumed, more in higher education than non-advanced FE, though this was not much tested in further education.

43 In practice, this model has been problematic. Governing bodies, the keystone of the structure, have seldom got a grip on matters of educational policy or programmes or had the capability to review the work of the college. Local authorities have tended to deal directly with the college, commonly through officers and administrative staff, and have used low-level bureaucratic devices to shape or impede developments (See above paragraphs 23–29). In an inquiry into the Polytechnic of North London Browne (1985) drew attention to problems of a governing body in relation to the institution. The inquiry saw factional differences on the governing body and problems of size and composition.

44 The methods of working established by the Council for National Academic Awards (CNAA) (See **3.1** 52–59) have been based on peer review of proposals, courses and institutions, though tending towards the bureaucratic (See Locke, Pratt and Spencer 1980).

45 Various forms of professional evaluation were developed. They used a variety of quantitative or qualitative techniques, committee-style reviews or performance indicators. A common approach was the monitoring or assessment of outcomes against some form of statement of aims or objectives, and much was based on second-hand ideas from behavioural theories or from 'Management by Objectives' (See **1.6** 10 and Waitt 1980). Ball (1985) remarked: '. . . in the absence of the competitive discipline of the market place, it is important for us to define explicit educational objectives so that evaluation of performance is possible'. Adelman and Alexander (1982a) suggested there were three distinct approaches to evaluation for course improvement: the appraisal of documented intentions; measurement of student learning outcomes against course objectives; and feedback on student and staff course experiences. There was development of college-based evaluation (e.g. FEU 1983, Challis 1983), of performance indicators (e.g. Kedney 1983), of an 'educational audit'[3] and of approaches in policy studies (See Pratt and Silverman 1988).

46 In higher education by 1987 the CNAA had moved towards self-validation (See **3.1** 54–59), thereby reinforcing processes already happening in some colleges, as well as, in terms of managerial impact, increasing the responsibility of the institution for its own affairs and heightening the importance of internal control and monitoring mechanisms. The case for self-evaluation by colleges was developed by Adelman and Alexander (1982b).

47 **Markets**

The Conservative Government and its agency the MSC in WRNAFE preferred accountability in terms of the customer–contractor principle. The MSC approved development plans from LEAs for its funding of WRNAFE and expected their implementation to be monitored – it was on that basis that it paid for college programmes.

48 The 'discipline of the market' was attractive to the Government and fitted the entrepreneurial approaches of many in FE. Its attractiveness was described by Williams (1986):

> 'The obvious weaknesses of collegial and bureaucratic models of organisational behaviour have led several observers to propose the market as a way of avoiding the inertia of the former and the conflict of the latter. The intellectual attraction of the market is that resource allocation decisions are taken out of the hands of both politicians and self-interested professionals. They are determined instead by independent decisions of many different consumers of educational services.'
> 'The main advantage claimed for the market is the incentive it provides to respond to changing external circumstances.'

(See Maynard 1982 for a discussion of the market in higher education.)

49 Colleges needed to be more entrepreneurial, both to compensate for loss of public funding and to find opportunities for growth. Some of this discussion overlooked the history of FE which had long prided itself on its entrepreneurialism and responsiveness (e.g. Robinson 1968). Colleges had long experience of entrepreneurial risk-taking in bringing together course approvals, validation, funding and students with an eye both to the public service and their own prosperity. In the urgency of the time, 'marketing' became a high priority (See **2.11**).

50 The markets for FE had traditionally been conceived in terms of meeting local employment needs and students' and employers' demands through full-time and part-time award-bearing courses. A major new market has been in full cost short courses, often contracted with employers, MSC and other agencies. Overseas students on full cost fees have also provided new income (See **1.3** 75 and **3.6** 1–5, 14–19 and 25–26). And colleges have marketed themselves to groups of potential students who had previously had made only limited use of further and higher education – thus widening access for, e.g., mature women and members of ethnic minorities. There have been added pressures to undertake more consultancy and research at full cost. The developments of the mid-1980s of contracting by MSC for WRNAFE and PCFC for HE meant that the mainstream educational programmes were to become founded on market principles and on customer–contractor accountability. There remained, however, a contradiction in that Government never actually let the market be free but retained its tight control over the scale and framework of the service. Ball (1985) (echoing the Education, Science and Arts Committee 1980) said 'the main engine in the planning of higher education should be *informed student demand* (his italics)' but no Government acted accordingly. Entrepreneurial activity by colleges was encircled by Government controls.

51 **Responses**

How have colleges responded? There have been few empirical studies, and what there have been have not indicated common patterns of development. Pratt and Gill (1987) showed that responses to financial restraint in polytechnics and colleges of HE were individual and related to local circumstances and histories, geography and cultures. Theodossin (1986) showed that it was difficult to specify key factors in responsive colleges; the 'Responsive College' project was continuing at the Further Education Staff College, Coombe Lodge, at time of writing.[4]

52 It is clear that a college's response to national policies is not a simple issue; a college does not usually just obey or adopt national policies. Management and staff in colleges treat national policies in terms of their perceptions of the policies and of their assumptions about their own institution, its academic profile, its experience, sense of mission and aspirations. (See Pratt and Gill 1987, for a case history of a college's response to NAB planning Bush and Goulding 1984, and for the response of colleges to the 1970s reorganisation Locke, Pratt and Burgess 1985.)

53 A working knowledge of the system suggested that the changes in the environment have changed part of the system of rewards and incentives within colleges with consequent impact on power relationships and management processes. In the traditional entrepreneurial model of FE a department (or the staff within it) commonly sought to build up student numbers, especially those on more advanced courses, and thereby to raise the 'points' of its department and hence raise the department's grading and increase its establishment of more senior posts (see, for example, Locke 1978, Tipton 1973). This was a slow process based on a bureaucratic rewards system. The changes, however, created a more direct relationship between work brought into the college and the institutional benefits. These benefits were more likely to be items which had become short because of the cuts in public expenditure, such as equipment, books and consumables, travel and other expenses, and short-term staff, rather than new appointments. The rewards were thus more direct and less prone to bureaucratic controls. Some were necessary to sustain an

adequate service, some constituted the 'extras' which could improve the working life of those staff who received them. The allocation of these benefits could lead to a system of feudal allegiances within colleges: course leaders and project leaders who produced the goods could attract colleagues into their domains. And it could be considered in the interests of the institution to allow this personal dispensation of patronage in order to give incentives to those who took successful initiatives. However, it could also undermine both more hierarchical patterns of management through heads of department (unless it was the heads of department who dispensed the patronage – but they probably were too busy to develop the new work) and representative or collegial systems.

54 Williams (1986) commented :

> '. . . there can be little doubt that the methods by which institutions receive their finance do affect the power relationships within them. This is most apparent in universities where a professor who secures large research grants can throw his weight around in a way denied to his less entrepreneurial colleagues. It is our hypothesis, however, that the same principles apply in educational institutions of all kinds. If a collegial model is working well, a professional ethos and high academic standards would be prominent. If working less well, the protection of vested interests within the institution is likely to be evident.'

55 So there have been questions about how far the changing environment has sustained the established combination of hierarchical leadership and representative structures or has developed more individual (or even collective) enterprise and about how far success in the environment is based on professional or commercial collegial or autocratic ways of working (see below paragraphs 60–67).

56 In creating corporate strategies for income generation in higher education Leyland (1986) saw that 'problems face the institutional manager in reconciling commercialisation with existing management systems and personal values of staff that are attuned to the provision of education and research as a public service, the aims of which are related to social need rather than financial gain'. But he found a difference between management styles which had been successful so far and what was needed for the future. He reported that for 'current market leaders' in higher education their success was based on factors which included: small to medium size corporate unitary institutions (more easy to control); a 'crisis situation requiring major short-term change and leading staff to acceptance of such change'; and directive management in by 'chief executives'. The 'chief executive' style consisted of personal attributes and strategies appropriate to the crisis. However, he argued, as the crisis continued the 'chief executive' style was less acceptable to staff, and a 'more deliberative and less cataclysmic' approach to institutional management would be appropriate. He commented :

> '. . . a key lesson should be learned from the management of large Japanese business enterprises, that a well thought-out strategy, honed through extensive staff participation, will be more effective and more rapidly implemented than the dictates of a management oligarchy.'

57 Sizer (1986) made a similar point, arguing that in the face of contraction managers need to see institutions through immediate crises but then to create the environment for individual initiative :

'High quality managers of appropriate academic standing are required who can overcome institutional inertia. These academic managers of change should not only be able to plan and control efficiently the allocation of resources to see their institutions through the short-term financial pressures, but also be able to motivate people to recognise the need for long-term change, and secure their participation in its planning and subsequent implementation . . . They will recognise that innovations in response to new needs and new opportunities are frequently created through the initiative of individuals. If they are to break the vicious circle they have to create an environment which motivates individuals and fosters rather than frustrates such initiatives.'

58 **Organisational structures**

Organisational structures within colleges could be seen to be crucial in the adaptation to the changing environment. The aspects of the organisation which could be seen to be most significant included the way courses and staff are organised into departments or other forms, the relationships between executive and representative forces, and the hierarchical order.

59 Parkes (1982b) characterised three major organisational options:

(i) Federal; some variation of courses organised in department, faculty or school – a subdivision of the whole.

(ii) Matrix; a splitting into responsibilities for what the students do and what the staff do, i.e. attend courses in the first case and teach subjects in the second.

(iii) Some variation of the matrix in preferring credit or modular based options from which the students construct their own course.

Various combinations of departments, within them perhaps divisions and above them faculties, or schools (which might be like large departments or like faculties) are evident in colleges. Matrices can be found within structures based on departments, faculties or schools and have become one of the established patterns. No one pattern has come to predominate or prove to be the most effective, and there is no common logic about these forms of organisation. (For a discussion of different concepts See Waitt 1980.)

60 Departmental structures in FE institutions have traditionally been formed on large and composite areas, rather than more narrowly delineated subjects. The latter form was more common in colleges of education and sometimes persists in colleges of HE formed from them. The incentives of the Burnham FE agreements worked towards large departments. The head of department could exert considerable power, helping or hindering the career development and working lives of staff through control of resources and timetables. The pressures of income generation (see above paragraph 53) and of marketing across departmental boundaries may be found to have undermined some of the power. The more representative structures of academic boards and their committees (see above paragraphs 6–8) have helped open out decision-making (see below paragraphs 66–67). Nonetheless, the department and the head of department remain the crucial elements in most colleges' organisational structures (see Parkes 1982).

61 There were pressures towards greater cooperation between departments – for marketing, for MSC programmes, for specialist short courses to meet the needs of clients, as well as for economic use of resources. An HMI report on a

college illustrated concerns about lack of cooperation between departments, e.g.:

> 'The present position of near independent departments without strong coordination on a college basis hinders the development of common approaches to such matters as: the availability of college computing facilities; the development of a student counselling service; policy for the handicapped and the establishment of subject groupings across departmental boundaries and curriculum development. It also affects the full utilisation of college resources and leads to variation in such matters as staff timetabling, staff responsibilities and the roles of course and personal tutors' (HMI 1984).

62 Pratt and Gill's (1987) study of responses to expenditure cuts showed that polytechnics and colleges of higher education in its case studies reorganised departments and faculties to widen and strengthen their resource bases. These reorganisations could be in response to growing or declining student markets. The study did not identify a trend towards greater centralisation in faculty/departmental structures. It found:

> 'In most cases, reorganisation of academic structures was justified on grounds of increasing efficiency and improving academic quality, although such policies clearly served a number of different purposes. New directors may begin restructuring in order to make their mark within the institutions or on the basis of hidden agendas which only become clear during the implementation of the policy. Since one institution was strengthening faculties at the same time as another was eliminating them, we cannot identify any particular direction for these restructuring policies and can only point to the felt need for change in whatever direction.'

63 For staff within colleges changes to the structure of faculties and departments sometimes seemed like 'change for the sake of change'. There was not a consensus about whether faculties or departments, or departments or matrices were more appropriate to institutions in the 1980s, and within one institution a change in one direction could be followed a couple of years later by its reverse. Typically, colleges have coped, whatever structure. Leech (1982) commented:

> 'The essence seems to be making it work whatever form of structure exists, and making it work well, which with a pyramidal hierarchical structure means effecting coordination, lateral operations as well as vertical operations.'

64 Other reorganisation involved senior management posts such as heads of faculty and assistant/deputy principals/directors (sometimes grouped into 'directorates') which increased and decreased without an obvious relationship to external events or internal effectiveness. However, reorganisation of posts and departments (in any direction) could serve as means of redeploying senior staff and encouraging retirements. In some colleges a 'senior management team' was formed to assist in coordination and a corporate approach.

65 A major theme in debates about the organisational structures of colleges was that of the relationship between executive and representative structures. Around the time of its publication Circular 7/70 was discussed mostly in terms of the impact of academic boards on the role of principals; it was wondered how principals could continue to carry out their responsibilities and leadership

role in tandem with a decision-making academic board. The experience of the operation of the Circular 7/70 system suggests that principals have not been diminished into being merely chairs for the academic board or ciphers for its decisions and that institutional pressures have sustained the executive power of the principal. Moreover, the introduction of a directorate or senior management team might have established a corporate executive body not mentioned in articles of government (except in so far as it might be said to be carrying out the responsibilities ascribed to the principal) but possibly in rivalry with the academic board as the locus of policy-formulation.

66 Intertwined with the issue of executive power and participation has been that of the development of the committees, subcommittees and working parties of the academic board. Leech (1982) commented:

> 'This (Circular 7/70) system has provided an opportunity for both Governors and College staff and students to participate more than previously in the formulation of College policy. If the system is operated in a reasonably workmanlike and expeditious manner it can be effective in stimulating the organisational health of an institution. However, without appropriate leadership it is all too easy for sub-committees and working parties to multiply and get out of control and be counter-productive . . .'

Probably such 'appropriate leadership' has not always been exercised, for anecdotal evidence has suggested that committee structures in some institutions have become a process for avoiding visible decisions.

67 As departments have remained the dominant form of organisation within colleges, heads of department have commonly continued to be identified as the 'boss', as discussed in the 1980 edition of *College Administration* (Waitt 1980). The operation of academic boards might have made more public – and so, in some ways, accountable – their work; it might have – through their numerical domination of the academic board – have confirmed their strength; there have been different views and different experiences. In a study of a CNAA visit to an institution Smith (1986) showed how the power of head of department could be applied differentially, giving space to junior staff to participate in educational matters but retaining control on questions of staffing and accommodation. He argued that professional authority 'pales into insignificance alongside the managerial and administrative tasks which have to be carried out in a period of contraction . . . Interaction between teaching staff and managers is minimised'. As suggested (See above paragraph 53), some of the hustling encouraged by the new entrepreneurialism has helped create informal power for some staff below heads of department status. However, as Hollyhock (1982) commented:

> 'Whatever arguments there may be for future changes in structure it must be admitted that the present structure has absorbed change and development in the seventies and also produced a range of courses which have at least partly coped with market demand.'

68 Organisational changes may not have fundamentally changed the hierarchical principle. In one case study of the development of initiative from the bottom-up, Woodrow (1983) showed how a principal could promote and facilitate course development by junior staff. She raised doubts as to how far the exercise was one of 'participative management', given that the hierarchical structure remained unchanged and the junior staff had in the course development process been dependent on senior management. Woodrow regarded this as

essentially a contingency approach to management but concluded that it showed the advantages of greater flexibility of structures and of equalisation of power.

69 **Resource management**

The contraction and the attempts to generate new income called for improved systems of financial management in colleges. Evidence was scanty on how they managed. At the Further Education Staff College, Coombe Lodge, the Resources Intelligence Unit was collecting breakdowns of costs at time of writing. Pratt and Gill (1987) reported how institutions developed their management information. (See below Appendix 1 for a review of management information systems.)

70 The need was recognised for financial management to support initiatives in income generation and marketing. The traditional processes of local authority administration of finances were seen as unsympathetic to the requirements of speed and flexibility for the new entrepreneurial activity. One vehicle in some institutions was to create a legally distinct limited company which could use, or mean to use, more commercial styles of financial management. (See **1.2** 29–30.)

71 The pressures towards on the one hand income generation and on the other hand efficiency promoted the concept of 'cost centres'. These could be established at faculty, departmental, division or course level and would expect the 'centre' to match its income to its expenditure, rather than, as was conventional in public institutions, to take little direct responsibility for either. However, this development required some devolution of decision-making within the institution, and other colleges responded to the external pressures, particularly the financial restraint, by centralising decision-making (Pratt and Gill 1987). (See **1.3** 98–103.)

72 **Staff management**

One of the unknown factors was how far the changes reduced and increased the individual effectiveness of staff. There was evidence, largely anecdotal, of reduced morale but also of – some – staff engaging enthusiastically in individual entrepreneurialism. It appeared, however, that the acceptance of, or resignation to, the changes was profound within the system. For most staff the job system had changed.

73 The changes were more difficult for staff for the tensions between the commercialisation of the system and the constitutional structures and administrative procedures and regulations which were based on local authority foundations. Legislation to promote or protect social justice, particularly equal opportunities (See **1.2** Appendices 2–3) and rights of employees (See **2.4**) also deployed legal and formal procedures, which had different values and processes than the new commercialism.

74 For college management there were competing, urgent pressures: the lack of growth or the contraction of services leading to pressures for reducing staff establishments; the need for energy and new blood to exploit new opportunities; the concern to improve equal opportunities in appointments and promotions. These pressures accentuated the problems of managing staff. There was a need to relate development plans for a college to its staffing requirements, to plan the deployment and development of staff (See **2.9**) and

to consider the design and specification of jobs more carefully than had been previously required. Where there were new posts, the processes of selection and induction had to be more precisely managed. But there were also the more personal, and sometimes hurtful, problems of the place – if any – of individuals in the changing institutions. There were problems of how to manage temporary and part-time staff taken on to teach on courses whose future funding was insecure. And all of these issues of corporate planning and individual interactions had to take place in a tenser framework of industrial relations.

75 Pratt and Gill (1987) concluded:

> 'We have detected widespread and serious effects on morale, especially among academic staff who are experiencing increased work loads, reduced resources affecting teaching quality, reductions in opportunities for advancement and a general lowering of expectations when compared with the recent phase of rapid expansion. Reductions in morale are also brought about by lack of recruitment of young staff and differential wastage of marketable staff who may also leave under voluntary schemes; age structures accordingly become unbalanced . . .
>
> 'There is a need for policies to increase the institutional commitment of staff by for example raising their status and relating staff development schemes to strategic objectives; to enable greater control of wastage by institutional managements by various new forms of early retirement and redundancy schemes, and to find ways of correcting unbalanced age structures by, for example, some form of "new blood" provisions.'

76 An HMI (1984) report illustrated the problem faced by many college managements:

> 'The College's response to the needs of the 16–19 age group, including the young unemployed, has been conditioned by the availability of resources, in particular, external sources of funding which often lack any long term (or even medium term) guarantee of continuity. A body of work largely dependent upon temporary staff appointments, temporary accommodation and funding is beginning to emerge in the college. The impermanent and tentative status of this group of courses inhibits the broad and vigorous approaches need in such matters as course and staff development and which are unlikely to come about without the support of a firm external policy framework.'

77 So, college managements somehow needed to find the strength of purpose to formulate the mission of the college and to involve staff in planning and in marketing, all the while in an environment which encouraged many staff to flight rather than fight.[5]

78 **Theory in use**

The analysis of college management in terms of responses to a tumultuous environment may tend to emphasise the ad-hocery and to neglect the steady progress in building up a body of knowledge and practice. Study, discussion and practice of college management has been developed by the Further Education Staff College (FESC) (See **3.1** 83–84), by the Further Education Unit (FEU) (See **3.1** 77–82) and the regional centres, as well as through such bodies as the British Educational Management and Administration Society (BEMAS), and the Association of Colleges for Further and Higher Education (ACFHE). The body of knowledge could be characterised as pragmatic good sense.

79 Training and theory in management tended to emphasise the development of personal and political skills, the better to cope on an individual level, and to avoid prescriptive theory. Theorising, such as that reported in the 1980 edition of *College Administration* (Waitt 1980), went out of fashion. Approaches which drew on theories of human relations and personal development had their application as justifying a kind of institutional natural selection, and 'garbage can' theories (March and Olsen 1979) fitted the prevailing pragmatism. But there was more interest in 'micropolitics' and plausible theories to fit changing situations. Bush and Goulding (1984), having investigated one college's reaction to proposed cuts, concluded:

> 'The validity of a number of different models as possible explanations of the management process in colleges has obvious implications for the managerial approach of senior managers. The often bland assumption of consensus within institutions is exposed by threatening situations . . . but is questionable even during periods of stability. Different models have greater or lesser validity according to the nature of the issue, the interests of the participants and the extent and nature of any planned or threatened change. Managers require an awareness of these variables if their managerial approaches are to be both relevant and acceptable.'

80 One body of theory acquired during the mid-1980s some broader acceptance, and that was to do with the pursuit of 'excellence'. It drew on fables of industrial achievement in the USA and was misleading for institutions concerned with collegial authority and public service. However, it was drawn into the thinking of the Thatcher Conservative Government and so became part of the ideological environment in which colleges had to manage.

NOTES

1 The Education (No. 2) Act 1968 actually referred to 'an institution . . . providing full-time education pursuant to a scheme of further education approved under section 42 of the Education Act 1944', though the use of Section 42 has lapsed (See **1.2** 15–16).

2 The Joint Efficiency Study was published as *Managing Colleges Efficiently* in the summer of 1987 and followed the HMI report *NAFE in Practice* (1987).

3 A study of 'educational audit' was at time of writing being directed by ACFHE and funded by FEU, led by McAllister (Blackpool and Fylde College).

4 The 'Responsive College' project was continuing at FESC at time of writing, led by Parkes (FESC).

5 For an exercise in such an approach See FEU (1987).

APPENDIX 1

MANAGEMENT INFORMATION

1 In the 1980s, local education authorities and individual college managements have been expected to come to grips with a welter of new management information systems. To some extent such systems have always existed; decisions have required methods of showing their probable and operational effects, and reporting on the outcome of past decisions has required some means of retaining and distilling information. Systems have developed for a number of reasons:

(i) The costs consciousness that is more apparent at times of financial stringency has meant that closer efforts have been made to establish expected costs and monitor expenditures. To discourage systematic over- or under-spending a variety of financial controls have been exerted, and these have encouraged managers to ensure that, when they come to accountancy periods, they know whether they will arrive on or near target. The District Audit has been a force in this direction.

(ii) A variety of techniques has been introduced for comparing the costs of activities or consumables. These techniques are often somewhat crude in their abilities to discriminate between legitimate and illegitimate cost differences, but they operate on the basis that it is possible to define certain activities or materials with sufficient precision to compare the cost of like with like, and hence to examine and eliminate the expensive end of the spectrum. Thus, much effort has been expended on comparing the costs of educating individual students undertaking broadly similar courses in the same disciplines but in different locations, or in different kinds of institution. Not all such comparisons are 'unit costs'. Comparisons are made of other performance indicators like staff : student ratios, or of the supply of materials. These methods owe much of their general origin to developments in accountancy and, in education, to the pioneering methodology in the context of the advanced further education pooling system undertaken in the late 1970s and early 1980s by the 'Steven Jones Group' in the DES. These initiatives have been considerably refined (and made more politically sensitive) by the National Advisory Body. (See **1.3** 54–65.)

(iii) A variety of questions have arisen in the lifetime of the Thatcher Conservative Government about 'value for money'. Questions are asked about what return there is for educational investment. If resources are regarded as inputs to the system, the issue arises as to what measurable outputs can be identified which provide quantitative judgements. Such outputs now routinely comprise student applications, admissions, completion (and drop-out) rates, and destination of those finishing courses.

(iv) The inexpensive availability of complex computers has enabled major breakthroughs in the technical capacity to count and measure performance. Many educational institutions already owned mainframe computers, but these were seldom used for management tasks other than payroll. In part that was a matter of their relative inconvenience and in part the absence of the right kinds of programme. The availability of 8-bit micro-processors, and more recently, of 16-bit micro-processors has made it feasible for managers to work with their own computerised information systems. The abundance of such machines has, in turn, meant that it has become commercially viable to write and market programmes (software) geared to the measurement of what is claimed to be educational performance.

The main management information systems customised for FHE are reviewed below but more general business programmes are in widespread use. Programmes like Supercalc (Computer Associates International, Inc), dBASE (Ashton-Tate, Inc), Lotus, Symphony and Visicalc (Lotus Development Corp) and the various Apple products (Apple Computer, Inc) provide businesses with powerful systems for recording data, making predictions on the basis of information recorded, varying the predictions by varying the input assumptions, and producing reports. The wide availability of these programmes has encouraged many public sector managers to use the techniques available.

2 **FEMIS**

The Further Education Management Information System (FEMIS) has been funded by the DES to create a computer-based information system which would enable educational managers in every college and LEA to deal with all aspects of resource management. To do so, it had to be cheap enough for all institutions to afford. The intentions of FEMIS were: to ensure that consistent and reliable information was instantly available to managers; to provide a basis for comparing the performance of similar courses and departments; to identify discrepancies and to indicate possible causes of variation; to provide a basis for planning and budgeting; and to help users get the maximum value out of the painstaking business of collecting, recording and using the data. The first phase of the project was operational in 1982, ran on a micro-processor and provided information on lecturer workloads, the data to which the DES, many LEAs, the Audit Commission and the MSC attached the greatest importance. By 1985 major new features of the programme were released which encompassed monitoring of space utilisation, unit costing, and a planning module. Thus, the first phase permitted development of staff : student ratio measurement, and the second phase refined this performance measure in the direction of unit costing. FEMIS I produces outputs on the basis of a summary and analysis of the timetable of each lecturer, the timetable of each course, an analysis of lecturer class contact hours and of student taught hours. It provides a computation of average class sizes, average lecturer hours, average student hours and staff : student ratios. The figures are computed for each term and the academic year, and can distinguish between grades of staff, poolable and non-poolable work, and advanced and non-advanced work. It could, for example, take account of the levels of work in any department, discipline, sections within a discipline and aggregate the information for the whole college. In these computations, the SSR is defined as:

$$\frac{\text{number of full-time equivalent students (FTEs)}}{\text{number of full-time equivalent lecturers (FTEs)}}$$

To arrive at the figures required, a system of weightings is used for different modes of attendance by students and a calculation of full-time staff up to and including heads of department plus a weighted system for part-time staff (weighted by level of work) (Birch 1984).

3 As FEMIS was introduced to colleges in 1982, they were advised to designate a senior member of the academic staff, usually known as the 'coordinator', to take responsibility for introducing the system. The Further Education Staff College advised that the coordinator should normally be at the vice-principal or chief administrative officer level. Although some of the management information gathering procedures were likely to be in place in colleges, it was thought prudent to take special pains to introduce the new system to staff. This was done by the coordinator instructing heads of department in the use of the system and its purposes, and later calling a meeting of staff in each department to explain the importance of using accurate data. Staff were to be involved by receiving data on themselves which they would then check for accuracy. Decisions had to be made on where the computer should be housed and who should have access to it. However, these exercises did not give rise to an unbridled repose of confidence, and in many colleges NATFHE sought collective agreements on the implementation of FEMIS. In general, agreements have identified the probability of additional administrative work for some staff and have sought to keep it within agreed bounds, and have tried to restrict the data to the kinds which have traditionally been collected even if not in computerised form. There has usually been an accord on access to the information generated, subject to realistic security arrangements. These early agreements have been somewhat elaborated by the later developments in FEMIS II, but the changes are largely to do with the scale of the operation rather than new issues of principle. The main characteristics of FEMIS II are set out above, and the increase in the scale of the administrative tasks for collecting data to be fed into the programmes has been the major cause of concern. The existence of performance information has not given rise to significant difficulties. There are, at present, no national agreements covering the use of management information systems.

4 **SRS and BCS**

Fretwell-Downing Data Systems developed college management systems based on their management programmes used in wider industry. By 1986 they had launched a management information system designed to deal with a number of labour intensive information collation tasks in colleges, the Student Records System (SRS). Information is input into four main files covering each student, course, employer and school with which a college has contact. Use of these files in combination can aid general data tasks but is also of use in dealing with tasks like fee computation, recoupment, student union funding allocations, etc. The programme is designed to handle records rapidly and provide means of interrogating data by use of programme utilities. It generates reports including statistical appreciations. An associated programme deals with college budgetary control. It provides means of analysing and interrogating budget data on the basis of cost centres determined by the user. The Budgetary Control System (BCS) makes a number of aspects of auditing more feasible for college managers who are not themselves specialists in audit technique.

5 NOMIS

Given the concern in college management with provision for unemployed people, and the need for accurate management information in this area, it is important to note the National On-Line Manpower Information System (NOMIS) facility installed at the University of Durham. A number of statistical sources generate data for small areas of the country (wards, postal code areas, etc), and these can provide a picture of larger areas – whole cities, counties, and so on. The problem has hitherto been the storage of the data and the capacity to interrogate it in appropriate ways. NOMIS is intended to assist in this process and is available to interested parties including educational institutions.

It is a permanent, on-line, interactive information system providing access to current and historical records of employment and unemployment from national to highly localised catchment areas. In the case of unemployed people, it deals with school leavers on a monthly basis. There is a cost in using NOMIS, aside from hardware costs, the rates being available from Room W807, Training Division, Manpower Services Commission, Moorfoot, Sheffield S1 4PQ (Telephone: 0742 703787).

2.9 STAFF APPRAISAL AND STAFF DEVELOPMENT

1 **Staff appraisal**

The introduction of staff appraisal in public sector further and higher education has become a highly charged industrial relations issue. One reason for this is that there are three basic approaches to the definition of appraisal and its role in college administration. These approaches are not compatible with each other, and the feasibility and desirability of each approach should be clarified before introducing a scheme of appraisal. Schemes in the private and public sectors using the three different approaches described below are described in Long (1986).

2 **Appraisal and pay or sanctions**

One approach to appraisal sees it as a method of pay or reward determination. In such schemes one of the outputs can be incremental progression (or its denial), promotion or transfer to a higher scale (or its denial) or the development of drastic action to remove the member of staff from their job on grounds of incompetency.[1] Such schemes are not common in Britain and tend to apply in very particular employment situations. Whilst the mechanisms exist for their introduction in further education by virtue of salary arrangements which, in theory, make scale transfer (Lecturer II to Senior Lecturer) partly dependent on efficiency (See **2.2** 51–52), and incremental credit dependent on satisfactoriness, in practice college managements have not used these mechanisms in dealing with teaching staff. There is little doubt that if they sought to do so industrial relations conflicts would soon develop. Hence, no known scheme of appraisal in education tries to link performance to pay. Equally, those schemes which do exist seek to isolate appraisal arrangements from either disciplinary matters or competency procedures.[2] The policy of the Conservative Government (which vacillated a little on this issue) has suggested that appraisal is necessary and should be pay related to a degree. The Secretary of State has powers under Section 49 of the Education (No. 2) Act 1986 to impose appraisal schemes on teachers in LEAs without acceptable arrangements. From time to time the Government has suggested that appraisal would enable the detection and reward of excellent performance. On other occasions Secretaries of State have eschewed the possibility of a direct link between appraisal and pay. In some employments pay and appraisal are directly linked. This has a potential cost disadvantage (as well, some would say, as cost and other advantages) since the pay bill under such a scheme can become wholly a function of the number of staff who are successfully appraised. For this reason most appraisal pay schemes provide a recommendation to promotion selection rather than automatic pay advancement. A scheme which has these features is that in use in the British Civil Service. One of the advocates of pay related schemes in education defines appraisal as:

> 'A regular, probably annual, system of assessing the performance of individuals in light of their innate abilities, application to the job and results achieved with a view to taking management decisions on training, promotion, posting and effective sanctions.'[3]

3 **Appraisal and staff development**

The second approach to appraisal is one which sees it as wholly related to staff development. The aim is to support staff by enabling them and their colleagues to appraise their development needs and arrange training and other development strategies to meet these needs. NATFHE favours this approach to appraisal and takes the view that such schemes should be introduced where the necessary funding of the staff development outcome has been determined. It is possible that NATFHE and the local authority associations will be able to agree a national framework for locally agreed schemes on this basis. Whether or not such schemes would meet the Conservative Government's objectives is less certain.

4 Staff development led appraisal schemes are not without their problems. They need to be trusted and carefully isolated from considerations of and the procedures relating to pay, promotion, competency and discipline. Again, if the presumptions are that development is primarily achieved through training courses and that all staff have development needs, the cost of resourcing the outcomes can be prohibitive. In personnel management terms it makes little sense to promise, if only implicitly, staff development which cannot, after appraisal, be delivered.

5 **Staff appraisal as good practice**

The third approach to appraisal emphasises the appraisal process (often called review rather than appraisal) as a good thing in itself. For example, Edwards (1984) defines appraisal as:

'An opportunity to review and discuss with each individual his/her past performance and, based on the conclusions reached, agree a plan of action and/or priorities for the forthcoming period.'

This approach has many merits. It doesn't presume that the outcome will always be costly staff development, nor does it create the industrial relations problems which pay related appraisal can cause. Its advocates claim it enables staff to feel they are valued. It may be particularly appropriate in employments where there are not complex hierarchies and where promotion opportunities are scarce rather than common. Recent changes in pay structure have meant that in advanced and non-advanced further education, significant numbers of entrants to the profession are unlikely to gain promotion during their careers. This appraisal approach enables a link to be made with other forms of evaluation (e.g. institutional and course evaluation) and through its action planning orientation it enables individuals and corporate objectives to be matched. Its dangers are that it can become routinised and token (as can the other approaches) and may leave some staff and their managers cynical precisely because it has no automatic rewards (staff development opportunities for example) or penalties, as outcomes.

6 **Appraisal in practice**

Education managers and administrators are under a number of imperatives to develop appraisal schemes, recent Government papers – not just those connected with pay but also those such as the 1987 White Paper (See **1.1** Appendix 1) – suggest that appraisal is the heart of good personnel management practice. This may be felt to be an exaggerated view and a more modest acclaim of appraisal as one amongst many instruments of personnel management is more appropriate. No appraisal scheme can compensate for difficulties in pre-entry training, selection, induction, disciplinary and competency procedure and so on.

7 However, Government intervention has generated a great deal of discussion

about appraisal, and a small crop of appraisal schemes are in various stages of development. Virtually all follow the staff development model – often one suspects as a device to ensure their acceptability – and most are at such an early stage of development that it is hard to assess their effectiveness. Few are college-wide, let alone LEA-wide and their scheme design features vary enormously.

8 A scheme which has existed for some time is the one at Gloucestershire College of Arts and Technology (GLOSCAT). This scheme came into being by decision of the Academic Board in June 1985. It aims at objective setting and the annual review considers individual and college needs in relation to the achievement of previously agreed objectives, teaching performance, staff development and career aspirations. A short written review covering the areas discussed is agreed by both participants. Based on the reviews, departments produce a profile of staff development needs for consideration by the College's In-Service Development Unit. The reviews are complementary to, and informed by, the course monitoring process. Proformas are used and appraisers are trained. Guidelines are published in a staff review procedures handbook.

9 There are three levels to the reviews: heads of schools review course teams; heads of department review heads of school; the senior management team reviews heads of department and are, in turn, reviewed by the departmental heads. Two elements are emphasised in GLOSCAT's approach. First, store is put on the two-way nature of the review interview. Secondly, an attempt is made to integrate staff appraisal with the general approaches to evaluation and monitoring of college performance. This requires an elaborate management information system (See Scribbins and Walton 1987).

10 **Designing an appraisal scheme**

The first question to decide in designing a scheme for full consultation is its intended outcomes (i.e. pay, sanction, development or action planning). Turner (1981) suggests a number of other scheme design decisions which managers should make (or more commonly negotiate) in advance of any launch of the scheme. Some of these items can be summarised:

(i) Should the scheme be voluntary or compulsory?
(ii) Is the reporting process through management or the academic board?
(iii) Are the methods used negotiable or fixed?
(iv) Are records to be kept and, if so, for what purpose?

11 **Who does what to whom**

A critical scheme design feature, dealt with separately here because of its highly charged character, is the direction of appraisal. In essence, there are five possibilities in education. *Line (or top-down) appraisal* involves a supervisor or manager appraising a member of staff in their charge. Sometimes this does not involve a direct stepping down but can provide that the appraiser should be two or more steps up the hierarchy compared to the appraisee. In organisations without attenuated hierarchies the burden thrown on those who are employed above the basic scale can be excessive. Appraisal interviews alone undertaken by the head of a big department (say 100 plus staff) could occupy a significant proportion of management time. Further, line appraisal is silent about who should appraise the head of the organisation (the Governors or LEA?). Schemes which don't provide for senior management appraisal are unlikely to have much credibility with the workforce. *Upward appraisal* in which junior staff review senior staff is sometimes advocated, as suiting organisations which require 'democratic' government. Again the absence of clear hierarchies can made this difficult and here the question of who appraises the most junior staff – the largest group of academic staff in most colleges – arises: *Peer appraisal* (often involving quality circle approaches) can appear as the least threatening method. However, peers can lack the power to implement the decided outcomes of the appraisal. Appraisal by *external experts* already takes place to some degree by HMI. The cost implications of LEAs routinising such arrangements will probably defeat such schemes and expert external appraisal can be difficult to integrate with other internal course and college evaluation processes. *Client or student appraisal* exists in some colleges (particularly advanced further education institutions), usually as part of course evaluation. All this approach provides is data. A peer or manager still has to decide what action is needed, if any, following receipt of the data. Finally, *self appraisal* is advocated as the least threatening form of performance review. It can, in isolation, also be the least effective method. However, as a preparation for second stage line, upward or peer appraisal it is indispensable.

12 Most of the approaches to the direction of appraisal can be combined together, as for example in the GLOSCAT scheme. The debate about the direction of appraisal may be felt to have generated more heat than light. What is important is that the direction relates to the purposes of the scheme. The purposes can be to appraise job related activities, personality, interpersonal relations, motivation, results achieved and many other items. Clearly some directions of appraisal will aid some of these purposes and not others.

13 Another critical issue relates to standards of performance. In some appraisal arrangements (e.g. those applying to sales people) these are easy to set. For professionals in an education context standards need to relate to the goals of the individual, the profession and the organisation. These standards may need to be personally negotiated or fall within a band of reasonable standards (see Oliver 1985). Again, in the education profession the method of standard settings is less important than the agreed existence of the standards. It is unlikely that agreement could be gained in education to the use of rating scales (e.g. marking performances in a number of aspects of the job from outstanding to unsatisfactory). Scribbins and Walton (1987) recommend a results orientated approach which enables performance review to be based on objectives agreed between the appraiser and appraisee. In this approach two forms are needed – one which aids self preparation for the appraisal interview and one which helps guide the appraisal. Whether or not classroom observation is a critical part of teacher performance review is a matter of argument. It is certainly resource intensive. The Suffolk study[4] sees classroom observation as central to appraisal in schools. In other cases it only arises if the appraisal interview suggests a need to set some objectives for changes in teaching/learning strategies.

14 **Appraisal training**

It is quite clear that many appraisal schemes fail because appraisers and appraisees have not been trained. There are many areas which training needs to cover in addition to appraisal interview skills. Amongst these areas are an explanation of the purposes and nature of the scheme, how to prepare for the appraisal, objective setting, counselling and feedback. If classroom observation is to be used training in techniques in this area will also be necessary. Some of this training can be done 'in-house'. Other aspects of it can best be covered by specialist courses run by the Further Education Staff College (See **3.1** 83–84) and other agencies.

15 **Some legal considerations**

Those devising appraisal schemes need to take care about aspects of employment law and agreements which may touch on the scheme. Four major areas of law need to be observed. They are the Sex Discrimination, Race Relations, Data Protection, and Employment Protection Acts (See **1.2** Appendices 2, 3 and 4 and **2.4**). Similarly, the national salary arrangements, probationary, disciplinary, dismissal and redundancy procedures (See **2.4** and **2.5**) as well as instruments and articles of government (See **2.8**), may impact on the design of particular schemes.

16 **Staff development**

The overlap between staff development and pedagogic training is particularly marked in further education largely because most initial (teacher) training is done on an in-service basis. In the schools' sector there is a requirement for teachers to have undergone a pre-service course of education and training leading to the award of qualified teacher status (QTS) prior to entering the teaching profession. By contrast the post-school sector has to recruit a very wide diversity of academic and professional staff, whose professional qualifications, training and work experience qualify them to enter the service, but whose pedagogic training has usually to be undertaken while employed as a teacher. There is therefore a backlog of training needs amongst serving teachers in further and higher education, and one important form of staff development takes the form of release to undertake pedagogic training, frequently on a day or block release basis.

17 **The present structure of education and training for academic staff**

Despite repeated attempts to establish a coherent national pattern of education and training opportunities for the further education sector the present system remains diffuse, with significant regional variations in opportunity. There are presently four major institutions in England, which provide courses of initial training on a pre-service basis wholly oriented to the needs of further and higher education.[5] They have concentrated on providing courses of initial training leading to the award of Certificate of Education (Cert Ed (FE)). These pre-service courses are for students who wish to be trained as teachers before seeking appointment. They last for one academic year and entrants must have a qualification in the subject they intend to teach; for example a university degree or diploma, a Higher BTEC certificate or diploma, full technological certificate of the City and Guilds (CGLI) or advanced Royal Society of Arts (RSA) certificate in shorthand and typing. Similar full-time pre-service courses are provided in Wales jointly by University College Cardiff, the University of Wales Institute of Science and Technology and the North East Wales Institute of Higher Education. A number of universities also offer a further education option within their PGCE courses which are, however, primarily orientated to training teachers for the schools sector.

18 The Haycocks Report (1975) recommended no increase in the number of centres providing pre-service courses. However, not only the four institutions mentioned above but also many other polytechnics and colleges now offer day and block release in-service courses, and there has been a considerable increase in the number of serving teachers taking part-time courses at local

centres which are either linked for validation purposes to one of the four institutions or are designated as a major regional centre in their own right.

19 The main routes therefore developed by the training institutions are full-time, sandwich or part-time courses of initial training leading to certification, and they are recognised for incremental purposes for certain grades of staff in further education. The major courses outside this pattern are City and Guilds 730 course for serving teachers and the Royal Society of Arts (RSA) courses with significant numbers of teaching studying office studies and the teaching of English as a foreign or second language. These are available almost exclusively via part-time day and/or evening routes in many colleges and represent the major alternative pattern by which existing teachers in further education receive pedagogic training.

20 **Haycocks and after**

The Haycocks Report, named after the Chair of the Committee, was approved by the Advisory Committee for the Supply and Training of Teachers (ACSTT) in June 1975 and published by the DES, together with Circular 11/77 The Training of Teachers for Further Education which formed the basis of the DES response, in September 1977. These were intended to create a framework for coherent national planning within the pattern of education and training for further education teachers. Amongst the main recommendations of the Haycocks Report were a target date for establishing a training requirement for all new entrants to full-time teaching in further education together with provision for induction arrangements for those new entrants who had already undergone pre-service training. The Government's strategy however in Circular 11/77 was one of delay and therefore major disappointment to those in the profession. It was unwilling to accept the target dates proposed but instead asked regional advisory councils (RACs) to submit plans to the Government to systematize the use of existing resources and training expertise within each region. It was the Government's view that priority should be given to the recommendation concerning systematic induction arrangements for teachers without previous teaching experience. Unfortunately the responses of the RACs, and the regional plans for further education teacher training, varied widely in quality and the extent of the provision they envisaged being undertaken in the region. The DES had no coherent scheme to propose and did little, other than by exhortation, to improve the proportion of staff undertaking training whether on a pre- or in-service basis. With no additional resources made available the impetus created by the publication of Haycocks and Circular 11/77 died away. Wide variations still exist between local authorities as to the proportion of teachers released for training, the numbers proceeding to full certification (normally requiring two years part-time study), and the modest target of 3% of the teaching force being released for initial training by 1981, proposed in Haycocks Report, has never been achieved nationally.

21 **Developments in the 1980s; towards a new pattern of in-service training and staff development**

The Advisory Committee on the Supply and Education of Teachers (ACSET) (the successor to ACSTT – see above paragraph), following its reconstitution in the late 1970s, began to reconsider the issue of in-service training for teachers, including teachers in further education. This reflected widespread concern throughout the education service at the failure to establish a fully comprehensive pattern of in-service education and training whether for schools or FE. It also took cognisance of the fact that, for the first time, the

Secretary of State announced in September 1982 his intention to introduce a scheme of direct grants to fund in-service teacher training in order to ensure that areas which he accorded particular importance would receive priority. In 1984 for the first time the national in-service training grants scheme was extended to include further education teachers. Each local authority was allocated a maximum grant based on an estimate of the number of 16 years old full-time equivalent (FTE) students in non-advanced further education in each local authority area. Support for the in-service training of lecturers in advanced further education continued to be met from the advanced further education (in-service education and training – INSET) pool. From 1983/4 the scheme of specific grants directed to particular national priorities for schools and further education was expanded each year both in the level of funding and the number of programmes supported, until it was superseded by the introduction of new arrangements which commenced on 1 April 1987.

22 **Local education authority training grants scheme**

The new scheme has replaced the INSET pooling arrangements[6] which were administered by the DES on behalf of LEAs, the TVEI related in-service training scheme (TRIST) (See **3.1** 4–9) and the in-service training grants scheme under DES Circulars 3/85 and 1/86. It has completely changed the basis of funding for staff development and in-service training. It was announced in March 1985 following widespread consultations on two reports from the ACSET Committee, one concerned with in-service training for schools and the other recommending new proposals for in-service training for teachers in further education. At the same time as the announcement of the new funding scheme, the Secretary of State also established arrangements for the interim two year period (1985/86 and 1986/87) during which additional resources were made available to promote developments across the curriculum of the kind particularly related to the Technical and Vocational Educational Initiative (TVEI). The TRIST scheme was administered by the Manpower Services Commission (MSC) with the involvement and cooperation of the Secretaries of State for Employment and Education and Science. It funded in-service training for teachers in both schools and further education. It was yet a further dimension of the increasing trend towards greater centralisation of funding and control of staff development and in-service provision, which in the case of further education emanates not only from the DES but also from the involvement of the MSC in the provision made by the further education sector.

23 The new scheme provides for two levels of funding; those elements of in-service which are designated national priority areas will receive grant aid at the level of 70%, while a further grant allocation will be earmarked to each LEA to fund locally determined priorities but these will only be grant aided at the level of 50%. The national and local priority areas for 1987/88 are set out below in Appendix 1 together with those eligible for training under the scheme. Although the main financial resources will now be made available from central government, it is clear that significant local resources will also be needed; moreover, there has been a significant loss of local autonomy to determine in-service priorities, since the new scheme is heavily weighted in favour of national priorities.

24 Of the £200 m available in 1987/88 for in-service training across schools and further and higher education, it is estimated that only some £25–30 m is actually 'new', i.e. additional, money and at the same time new categories of staff, not hitherto included in the education INSET budget, have been incorporated

in the framework of the new scheme. It represents a very significant change in the funding and control of in-service education and does not fulfil the criteria laid down in the original ACSET Report which called for a substantial increase in resources and significant involvement of individual schools and colleges and their academic staff in the determination of their professional needs for staff development and in-service training.

25 Local authorities, following the pattern established by the TRIST Scheme, were required to make 'bids' for funding both for the national and local priorities by mid October 1986, outlining their staff development plans, their consultation procedures for determining training priorities, the basis of collaboration with major higher education institutions providing in-service training opportunities in their area and their proposals for monitoring and evaluating their proposed scheme.

26 It should also be noted that advanced FE (AFE) is a national priority area in its own right. The major institutions of higher education (those involved are listed specifically in Circular 6/86) have an earmarked allocation of resources to fund their staff development programmes, and they are to determine their own priorities for training and staff development. It is also open for them to be included in the bids for funding under one of the other national or locally determined priority areas by mutual agreement with their LEA. As far as institutions of higher education are concerned, many here received considerably less funding than they had previously claimed via the INSET pool which has been abolished as from 31 March 1987.

27 One effect of the new scheme will be to establish a clear picture of the actual levels of expenditure on in-service education and staff development and to assess the variations in local practice and priorities. It will, for example, become possible to assess what authorities are spending on initial pedagogic training of FE lecturers as compared to secondments for professional updating or shorter courses of in-service training and curriculum development on a local basis. It is too early to assess what those patterns will be and whether the first bids for funding under the new scheme will establish a pattern or change markedly as the planning process develops. Certainly the national priorities are being reviewed annually. Whether significant changes occur will no doubt depend upon the extent to which the planning and evaluation process is taken seriously not only by local authorities themselves but also by the DES. The staffing committed to the evaluation procedures nationally (i.e. for evaluating the bids from LEAs) is limited to date and this in itself may prove an obstacle. There is little doubt that the new scheme could become an important foundation for introducing a greater measure of coherence into staff development and in-service training although with the present resource levels, few of them earmarked specifically for further and higher education, it seems unlikely that significant inroads will be made to the backlog of training needs while there are so many competing demands for staff development provision in many institutions.

28 **Other agencies and major schemes relevant to staff development**

Manpower Services Commission

As a result of changes which have occurred in Government policy in the education and training of the 16–19 age group particularly that organised and delivered via the MSC, involving first the Youth Opportunities Programme (YOP) scheme followed by the one year and subsequently two year Youth

Training Scheme (YTS) programme (See **1.7**), staff development needs in FE increased sharply. It became clear that many staff were being either asked to teach new skills and curricula or use existing skills to teach the wholly new client groups coming into colleges. In acknowledgement of this, the MSC did release funds, for the first time, specifically to fund staff development needs. In particular it was to aid the developments needed for the YOP. This funding, which became known as the 'Robertson shilling', was a block payment to LEAs based on a formula related to the number of YOP trainees and the number of staff involved in the programme.

29 Subsequently funding for the development of Accredited Training Centres (ATCs) became the major route via which MSC exerted its influence in the area of staff development. Under the timetable for the development of YTS the first nine centres became operational early in 1983 and by the end of 1983 fifty-five ATCs had been identified and established. Approximately 50% were based in colleges and 50% in private training agencies. Originally entirely supported by MSC funding the intention was to become self-supporting. By the end of 1986 this had not been achieved although the funding base of the ATCs changed during that year and funding is now given for training and training services provided whereas hitherto it had included significant sums for development work and overheads.

30 There are now two main strands to MSC's involvement and concern with staff development and in-service training of those involved in the delivery of further education. The first emanates from the Training Development Section whose overall remit includes the training and development of all 'trainers', a term which embraces all those working in the educational sector, (e.g. tutor, lecturer, staff development officer, head of department) who have a role in helping the learning process.

31 The second strand is more specific and arises from MSC's involvement in the purchasing and delivery of NAFE (See **1.3** 44–45 and **1.7**). The NAFE Guidance Handbook makes it clear that local education authorities are expected to produce a development plan which includes priorities for in-service training and staff development initiatives for further education. At the same time MSC has retained a central reserve to 'assist in achieving improvements in the responsiveness of work related NAFE to employment needs'. It is anticipated that development projects in this area will include elements of staff development and training. Thus, MSC is broadly concerned with the development of those in FE who are fulfilling the role of trainers and specifically concerned with the staff development and in-service training of those responsible for the delivery of NAFE.

32 *Professional, Industrial and Commercial Updating (PICKUP)*

The programme of Professional, Industrial and Commercial Updating (PICKUP) was launched by the DES in 1982 covering England and Wales with an allied programme in Scotland (see **3.1** 66). PICKUP aims to help colleges, polytechnics and universities to improve and increase the work they do in meeting adult training and retraining needs. Almost from the beginning it was recognised that staff development programmes would also be needed for those not primarily accustomed to working with adults and unused to identifying training needs, or marketing courses or learning programmes. A substantial expansion of the PICKUP INSET programme is now underway; Circular 5/86, for example, committed a further £800,000 in educational support grants to support PICKUP via 'pump priming' money for such activities as market research, course development and marketing. PICKUP funded projects in higher education have seen a major expansion with £3 million allocated to development projects via the National Advisory Body (NAB), some of which have made an important contribution to staff development. In 1987 a joint FEU/PICKUP Staff Development programme was published to assist staff development in support of PICKUP. Finally PICKUP has been sponsoring a scheme to stimulate staff development via the interchange of staff between colleges and industry and business.

33 *Education Support Grants*

The Education (Grants and Awards) Act 1984 empowered the Secretaries of State for Education and Science and Wales to pay education support grants to LEAs. These grants support a range of locally devised training places and programmes with staff replacement costs, course fees and travel being eligible expenditure under these programmes. Education Support Grants are currently to continue alongside the new GRIST scheme. (See **1.3** 28–31.)

NOTES

1 Curtis (1981/82) describes very elaborate arrangements which exist in the British Columbia Institute of Technology for taking drastic action of this sort. They can involve an obligation on the employer to find the employee another post.

2 Scribbins and Walton (1987) show how the absence, until recently, of disciplinary and incompetency arrangements in education have induced caution about the role and introduction of staff appraisal.

3 This definition was proposed by Roy Walker, then an Under Secretary in the DES, in November 1986 when he addressed a conference at the Further Education Staff College.

4 This most elaborate study of performance appraisal in education can be found in Suffolk Education Department *Those Having Torches, 1985*. As well as classroom observation that study suggests, amongst other items, that understanding of the system, a scheme applying to all staff, mutually agreed and up-dated job descriptions and training in appraisal are all critical to implementing and running an acceptable scheme.

5 Bolton Institute of HE, Wolverhampton Polytechnic, Huddersfield Polytechnic and Garnett College (merging with Thames Polytechnic).

6 The INSET scheme set out guidelines for approved expenditure and all LEAs contributed to central funding on an agreed national formula and recouped eligible expenditure according to training undertaken.

APPENDIX 1

NATIONAL PRIORITY AREAS – FROM CIRCULAR DES 6/86

SUMMARY LIST

School Teachers

(i) Training in organisation and management in the context of the responsibilities of head teachers and other senior teachers in schools
(ii) Training in the teaching of mathematics
(iii) Training to meet the special educational needs of pupils with learning difficulties in schools
(iv) Training related to industry, the economy and the world of work
(v) Training in the teaching of science

(vi) Training in the teaching of craft, design and technology (CDT)
(vii) Training in teaching and the planning of the curriculum in a multi-ethnic society
(viii) Training in the teaching of microelectronics and in the uses of microelectronics across the curriculum
(ix) Training in the teaching of religious education

Further Education Teachers
(x) Training related to industry, the economy and the world of work
(xi) Training to develop competence in the teaching of technical, commercial or professional subjects in the light of recent developments in industry, commerce or the professions
(xii) Training in organisation and management in the context of the responsibilities of teachers in further education
(xiii) Training to meet the special educational needs of further education students with learning difficulties
(xiv) The training of teachers engaged mainly or entirely in the provision of advanced further education (AFE) in polytechnics and certain other institutions
(xv) Training in the teaching of microelectronics and in the uses of microelectronics across the curriculum

School and Further Education Teachers
(xvi) Training for the General Certificate of Secondary Education (GCSE)

School and Further Education Teachers and Youth and Community Workers
(xvii) Training to help combat misuse of drugs
(xviii) Training for youth and community workers
(xix) The training of educational psychologists

ELIGIBLE TRAINING
The scheme applies to the training of full-time and part-time teachers in schools and in further, higher and adult education and to others in the specific categories below:
(i) The further training as teachers of qualified teachers, whether or not they are currently employed as such;
(ii) The initial or further training as teachers of persons who do not hold qualified teacher status but who are employed as teachers by an authority, by the Governors of an aided school or by a local authority assisted institution of further, higher or adult education;
(iii) The training of qualified teachers or any teacher specified in category (ii) above as: youth and community workers; educational psychologists; education authority inspectors; or education advisers;
(iv) The initial or further training of those employed
As youth and community workers[1] working to discharge a statutory function of an education authority, whether or not they are on the staff of that authority (authorities may therefore propose for grant aid eligible expenditure incurred by them in respect of the training of those in this category who are employed by voluntary organisations); as educational psychologists; as education authority inspectors; or by an authority as education advisers.
Eligible training may include any activity directed to the purpose of the scheme so as to contribute to the development, expertise or effectiveness of one or more of the specified types of trainees; this may include school or college based training, training courses, secondments to industry and commerce, and secondments of teacher trainers to schools.

NOTE
1 For the purposes of this scheme a 'youth and community worker' is any person in any category of employment connected with leisure-time facilities of a kind which local authorities have a duty to provide under sections 41(b) and 53(1) of the 1944 Education Act except those employed in a solely administrative, secretarial, clerical or manual capacity.

2.10 INDUSTRIAL RELATIONS

1 'Industrial relations are about the relationships between employers and the people they employ – their aspirations, expectations, achievements, successes and failures. The satisfaction of the employee in doing a good job contributes to the successful implementation of the policies of the employer and the effectiveness of his undertaking. Conversely the anxieties, frustrations and failures of employees in their working environment can diminish the effectiveness of the organisation. Employers and employees therefore have a mutual interest in maintaining and developing good industrial relations.'

This definition of industrial relations was provided by the Local Authorities' Conditions of Service Advisory Board (LACSAB) in a guide for local authority chief officers and managers published in 1978. This section addresses the practices and procedures that facilitate good industrial relations at college level. Clearly, however, the context is much broader involving state regulation, and national and local authority level policy, collective bargaining and agreement.

2 Industrial relations are essentially the transactions occurring between employer and employee. They involve power relationships regulated through the mechanisms of collective bargaining and consultation. At college level the employer/employee nexus will generally be conducted through, for example, the college principal, employee representative and the trade union.

3 Employer responsibilities for maintained establishments of further, higher and adult education, attach to individual local education authorities. The colleges and institutions themselves are not the employers except in the case of the five Inner London polytechnics (see paragraph 8 below).

4 The major employers/employee relationship here is that between local education authority and the organisational unit of the trade union covering the LEA area – for lecturers, the NATFHE Liaison Committee, and for other occupations, the union Branch which is often authority-wide and Joint Works Committee.

5 Employer responsibility located in the LEA has been the dominant form in post-school public sector education. This will no longer be the case if higher education is reorganised as projected in the 1987 White Paper (See **1.1** Appendix 1 and **1.2** Appendix 1). The granting of corporate status to a substantial number of institutions will entail a transfer of employer power from LEA or joint education committee (in the case of establishments maintained by more than one authority) to the governing bodies of the incorporated institutions. Here the employer/employee relationship will be akin to that pertaining in voluntary or grant-aided establishments which are usually constituted as employers in their own right. One can anticipate that the director or principal of the new higher education institutions will have a major role in industrial relations. The unions will have to adopt their forms of representation to accommodate a changed public sector higher education structure and new bargaining arrangements will clearly be necessary both locally and nationally. Recent DES proposals for other further education colleges could also entail changes in the location of certain employer responsibilities.

6 In the current national negotiating machinery (See **2.1** and **2.5**) agreements

are concluded, binding in honour upon all LEAs and upon all levels of union organisation. The provisions of the Burnham FE document (See **2.1** 5) continue to have statutory force unless and until they are amended in the National Joint Council (See **2.1**). In respect of lecturers there is some scope for determination of certain matters at LEA level; both national and local agreements may leave scope for discussion on implementation to the college level. In respect of non-teaching staff variation will occur at Provincial Council and LEA Level.

7 The actors in industrial relations at college level are therefore constrained by agreements made elsewhere (See **2.1**) and by legal regulation (See **2.4**). For college management there is also the overriding constraint that the level of financial resources (whether for accommodation, staffing or equipment and materials) is determined outside the college (See **1.3**).

8 Governing bodies are responsible 'for the general direction of the college' (DES Circular 7/70). Their powers are determined by the articles (and instrument) of government for the college concerned (See **2.8**). (In reorganised higher education the memoranda and articles of association are to lay down the power of the governing body (See **1.2** Appendix 1); this is currently already the case in the five Inner London Education Authority polytechnics. In the case of LEA institutions, the LEA may expressly delegate some of its employer powers and responsibilities to the governing body and college level discussions must have regard to this. On the whole, however, industrial relations are better handled through other channels. Similarly, college academic boards are not a satisfactory vehicle for the ventilation of industrial relations issues.

9 In industrial relations matters the principal of a local authority institution is a manager acting on behalf of the LEA. The principal is 'responsible to the Governors for the internal organisation, management and discipline of the college' (DES Circular 7/70). His or her immediate aides in these functions are the vice-principal and administrative officer. Within the governing body of which the principal is a member, he or she has a responsibility to ensure that all governors are aware of the work of the college, its policies and principles, the physical environment and resources, and its aspirations. The principal's role as an educational initiator will also have an impact upon industrial relations within the college.

10 As an administrator the principal has a responsibility to see that the college operates smoothly; that staff and students know the rules, regulations, and procedures of the college and the LEA. The identification of clear procedures for handling industrial relations questions and a clear understanding of both the procedures themselves and the role of those involved in operating them are central to a good industrial relations environment. The observance or non-observance of procedures is frequently an issue in industrial relations matters that become the subject of legal process.

11 The majority of further education staff belong to trade unions which seek to promote and defend their members' interests as employees, representing them both collectively, and individually where necessary. The lecturers' unions regard themselves as also having a professional association role with the representation of members' views and interests in respect of educational policy as an important area of activity.

12 The major negotiating bodies for adult, further and higher education staff cover: lecturers; administrative, professional and technical staff; and manual workers. The trade unions nationally recognised for these groups are as follows:

(i) *Lecturers* NATFHE, Association of Agricultural Education Staffs, Association of Principals of Colleges and National Society for Education in Art and Design (most further education members of these three specialist organisations are also members of NATFHE. The Association of Polytechnic Teachers is recognised by the government but not by employers or employees.

(ii) *Administrative, Professional, Technical and Clerical* (APT&C) National and Local Government Officers Association (NALGO), General, Municipal, Boilermakers and Allied Trades Union (GMB), National Union of Public Employees (NUPE), Transport and General Workers Union (TGWU), Confederation of Health Service Employees (COHSE).

(iii) *Manual Workers* GMB, NUPE, TGWU.

13 At college level staff are generally represented through their Branch or shop steward or other workplace representative. NATFHE rules give specific responsibility to the Branch (or Coordinating Committee in institutions with more than one NATFHE Branch) to make representations to the principal/director and governing body. The three groups of unions may have formed a Joint Union Committee (JUC) in the college to coordinate policies and action on matters of common concern, and it may be appropriate on occasion for JUC representatives to meet college management. Occasionally a union will involve a full-time official in representations to management. More usually the representatives will be lay officers of the union, usually drawn from the college staff.

14 A national agreement on trade union facilities concluded in 1976 (See **2.5** 28–30) provided for arrangements to be made to enable accredited representatives of recognised teachers' unions to carry out their industrial relations responsibilities. The precise nature of these facilities is specified in agreements concluded at LEA level.

15 Students of industrial relations have suggested that attitudes and behaviour of those involved in this arena are influenced by their own particular frame of reference. Two distinctive frames of reference are generally identified – the unitary frame of reference which suggests that the interests of employer and employee are broadly the same, and the pluralist which suggests that industrial relations are a reflection of a large number of interests and divisions in society. In education there is a communality of interest in providing the best educational provision to clients of the service but it is as well to recognise that the perceptions, interests and aspirations of parties to the system may conflict from time to time and that resolution of differences will entail negotiation, agreement and sometimes compromise.

16 Consultation and negotiation are the two key processes in industrial relations. Consultation has generally been seen as concerning matters which management sees as its responsibility which it is not prepared to share but on which it is prepared to give notice of action intended or envisaged, and receive representations. Consultation may lead to modification or even abandonment of plans but the decision is seen to rest with management. Occasionally consulta-

tion may be statutorily prescribed, for example, where redundancies are projected. Negotiations concern matters mutually accepted by employer and union/s as suitable for collective bargaining, the outcome of which is expected to be a collective agreement freely entered into and binding in honour upon the parties involved. In practice the distinction between consultation and bargaining can be an artificial one, and it is common for items reserved for the consultative process to shift into the bargaining arena. Indeed, trade unions often seek to secure such movement.

17 Both consultation and negotiation can take place at college level providing that any agreements reached are restricted to matters where college management has power to decide: otherwise agreements have to be confirmed at local authority level and may of course be repudiated there.

18 Good communications and clear procedures for consultation and negotiations are essential ingredients in good industrial relations. In most working environments problems occur that could be avoided with adequate attention to communication and discussion. Any delegation of managerial responsibilities for industrial relations should be clearly defined. In particular, the power to hire and fire part-time staff should be explicitly assigned, if assigned at all (at least one large LEA forbids the termination of part-time teachers' contracts by staff other than the principal).

19 Disclosure of information is an important aspect of collective bargaining. The Employment Protection Act 1977 imposes a general duty on employers to disclose information to representatives of independent, recognised trade unions for the purpose of all stages of collective bargaining. The Act does not specify what information should be disclosed. A union may complain to the Central Arbitration Committee if information requested is refused and the CAC will order disclosure if it finds the complaint well founded. The Code of Practice 1977 from the Advisory Conciliation and Arbitration Service (ACAS) gives examples of information which could be relevant in certain collective bargaining situations. LACSAB has recommended that LEAs should reach an information procedure agreement with unions as envisaged in the ACAS code.

20 Almost any matter of concern within the college may be identified as requiring discussion of some sort between management and union. It is important to distinguish those which are capable of resolution at college level from those in which the LEA has a clear role.

21 Examples of issues for discussion at college level include the following:

(i) *Staffing levels* Current establishments of full-time staff, their deployment within the college and between departments; future estimates of staffing requirements for submission to the local education authority; and departmental and other staffing patterns (it is helpful for any changes to have been discussed before they are implemented).

(ii) *Staff selection and development* Procedures within the college for the: appointment of staff; promotion of staff; and staff development. Note: Any such college procedures will naturally have to satisfy the requirements of procedures at authority level, but these usually incorporate scope for variation.

(iii) *Timetabling* The teachers' conditions of service agreement requires access to timetables on request for representatives of the recognised trade unions.

(iv) *Working conditions* Variations to daily starting times for classes; (for technicians) the timetabling of laboratory use to permit access for preparatory work; provisions of working space outside teaching areas. Note: there may well be 'welfare' issues more suitably considered by a college Safety Committee established within the purview of the Health and Safety at Work etc. Act 1974 (See **2.7**).

(v) *Matters affecting individual staff.*

22 Procedures for management/trade unions discussion will depend on the nature of the issues involved. Matters affecting individual staff (known as 'casework' by NATFHE) may be urgent and necessitate access to a designated member of college management by a union representative without undue formality. Other matters merit pre-arranged meetings with defined agenda. A proper record of such meetings should be available to the representatives of both parties. A reliance on 'ad hoc' meetings is seldom satisfactory and a regular calendar of meetings (which can always be cancelled if there is no business) is mutually beneficial and facilitates adjustments to lecturing timetables which do not adversely affect students.

23 The national scheme of conditions of service for lecturers sets out a model procedure for handling grievances (See **2.5** 26–27). This procedure is commended to all LEAs and contains informal and formal stages for dealing with individual grievances or disputes. Arrangements for resolving collective disputes are laid down nationally (See **2.5** 34) and there are also national procedures for discipline, suspension and dismissal which must be incorporated into local procedures (See **2.5** 13–17). Each of these procedures specify arrangements to be followed at establishment level. There are comparable procedures governing non-teaching staff.

24 Good industrial relations at college level is not just as a one-way process involving a management decision followed by its willing and successful implementation: to paraphrase LACSAB: good industrial relations involve give and take with the staff, through their unions influencing the decisions. With good industrial relations, this influence is of benefit to the college, and thus to the authority. With indifferent or bad industrial relations, important decisions may be deferred, or if taken, may be impossible adequately to implement.

APPENDIX 1

UNIONS IN NORTHERN IRELAND

1 In further education there are three recognised lecturers unions; NATFHE, The association of Principals of Colleges and the National Association of Schoolmasters/Union of Women Teachers. Approximately 80% of college lecturing staff are NATFHE members.

2 *Irish Congress of Trade Unions (ICTU)*
The ICTU was formed in 1959, bringing together in one organisation the Irish Congress of Trade Unions and the Irish Trade Union Congress. An umbrella organisation for trade unions throughout Ireland, the ICTU has an affiliated membership of 670,000 (Republic of Ireland 446,066; Northern Ireland 224,377)

3 *Northern Ireland Committee of the Irish Congress of Trade Unions (NIC-ICTU)*
In 1942 the Irish Trade Union Congress formed the Northern Ireland Committee to deal with trade union and related matters in Northern Ireland. The Committee was retained upon the formation of the ICTU. NIC-ICTU has an annual meeting and certain functions relating to Northern Ireland are devolved to the Northern Ireland Committee. In particular, it is NIC-ICTU that deals with Government in Northern Ireland and makes appointments to various bodies. For example, it appoints to the manpower Council, which has an advisory role with the Department of Economic Developments and The Department of Education (there is no equivalent to the Manpower Services Commission in Northern Ireland). NIC-ICTU, and ICTU maintain close links with the Trades Union Congress in Great Britain.

4 *Council of Education Unions (CEU)*
The CEU exists to develop links between, and coordinate the actions of, all the teacher unions affiliated to the ICTU. The membership, therefore, consists of representatives from NATFHE, Irish National Teachers Organisation, Teachers Union of Ireland, Irish Federation of University Teachers, Association of Secondary Teachers Ireland. The Association of University Teachers recently affiliated to the ICTU but has yet to join the CEU.

5 *Agricultural Colleges and Prison Education*
The Department of Agriculture in Northern Ireland is responsible for the provision of agricultural education and training, including the three colleges of agriculture. The Department also provides staff and facilities for the Faculty of Agriculture and Food Science at Queens University Belfast. The teaching staff are employees of the Department of Agriculture on salary scales negotiated for Civil Servants in Northern Ireland. The Education service in Northern Ireland's prisons operates under the auspices of the Northern Ireland Office. Teaching staff are employees of the Northern Ireland Office and paid on Civil Service salary scales.

2.11 MARKETING

1 There are comments almost on a monthly basis that something is wrong with the marketing of further and higher education. The Government said so in *Training for Jobs* (See **1.1** 28); the Audit Commission has said so in *Obtaining Better Value from Further Education* (See **1.3** 112–113); HMI say so; and the 1987 White Paper *Higher Education: Meeting the Challenge* (See **1.1** Appendix 1) has declared marketing to be a key management task for higher education institutions. The Manpower Services Commission (MSC) has made the apparent weakness of marketing in FE one of its major platforms and after several years of seeking to change NAFE's marketing record still felt moved in June 1987 to issue a press release headlined NAFE Needs Better Marketing. The interesting thing about all these criticisms, apart from the fact that they come from powerful quarters and on that account alone need attention, is that none of them are based on a concerted study of how colleges, local education authorities (LEAs), or the Government markets further and higher education. There has been some glancing study of how colleges sell or promote their courses but, as every first year student of marketing knows, marketing involves much more than just selling. Inevitably some of the mud has stuck. If only for this reason those who work in further and higher education need to understand marketing in order to be able to refute unjustified accusations of marketing inadequacy more positively. A marketing perspective has enabled many FE staff to make sense of the awkward decisions facing colleges in terms of what to provide and for whom in a time of significant economic, social and technological change.

2 What, then is marketing and how might further education be changed if it adopted marketing as a management perspective? How challenging is marketing to our current ways of doing things?

3 **The marketing perspective**

It is often said that marketing is very easy to talk about but very difficult to do. Fortunately marketing has no complex theories but is rather an assembly of straightforward concepts, perspectives and techniques. The classic definition is that marketing is the management process responsible for identifying, anticipating and satisfying customer requirements profitably. Given that further education is a public service we must justifiably question the word 'profitably'. If we substitute words such as 'cost effectively' we are perhaps nearer a definition which applies to the marketing of a public service.

4 The following elementary marketing propositions enable us to assess the effects of adopting a marketing approach to further education:

(i) For any product or service there needs to be an appropriate *marketing mix*. A marketing mix is a balance of the features of the *product*, its *price*, its *place* of delivery and its *promotion* (the famous four 'p's of marketing).

(ii) Generally products and services go through a life cycle which can be illustrated as in Figure 1. Over time, any product or service has a low initial demand, increases it, reaches a peak and then declines. Depending on the nature of the product or service, the cycle may last as little as a few weeks or as long many years. Eventual decline is inevitable, however, unless there is an appropriate change in the 'marketing mix'. As many have found to their cost, even changing the mix cannot guarantee

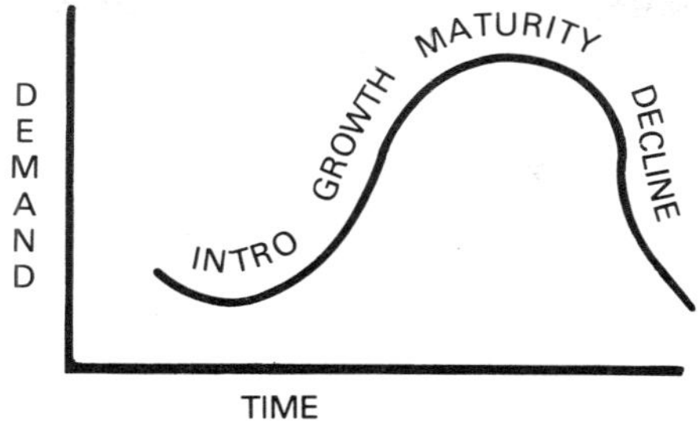

Figure 1: Life cycle of products and services.

that the decline does not become terminal. To expect market penetration to be as successful in the introductory stage as in the maturity stage is to expect the unattainable in the case of most products and services. Different levels of marketing expenditure are appropriate to different levels of the life cycle. Expenditure often needs to be at its maximum in the introductory phase or before the service is launched. Significant marketing expenditure on a declining service may simply waste resources which could be used elsewhere to more benefit to potential students.

(iii) Marketing decisions, on for example the appropriate marketing mix for any product; how much to charge for it; how to promote (e.g. advertise) it; are assisted if they are based on some basic *marketing information*. Such information has to be obtained by marketing research and involves knowing, for example, the following kind of things about the market:
Its demographic character;
The geographical distribution of customers;
The distributive channels;
The market shares of competitors;
The availability of support facilities:
Consumer wants and needs.

(iv) No market consists of a uniform mass of people, Instead it is split into market *segments*. The segments are clusters of purchasers with a common identity in terms of features such as class, age, sex, employment etc. Different segments need to be approached in different ways. This is especially true in relation to promotion of a product or a service. Each segment will therefore demand a different marketing mix if it is to be fully satisfied with any product or service. This is the essence of marketing.

5 The marketing perspective and FHE

The propositions outlined above have a deceptive simplicity. When they are applied to the management of further and higher education some problems arise. Take, for example, the marketing mix. What are the *products* of education? One is tempted to conclude that they are courses. Indeed, if we examine most colleges' promotional literature (prospectuses and leaflets) they are concerned primarily with the features of courses as if they were *product*. The front cover usually leads with the name of the college and the course rather than any benefit which may accrue to the student. But the customers need to know what benefits the service can give. For example, will the service help find a job; will it, for employers, make them more competitive if their staff are trained; will it, for parents, provide a good education and job opportunities for their children? Further and higher education is in the business of providing learning opportunities. Promoting a service requires greater subtlety than promoting a product – for you can see and touch a product; a service is intangible.

6 What of *price*? For most courses FE colleges are not free to fix price. Indeed, there is a question of what the price equivalent is for the service. Is it course fees? If it is, we know very little about the relationship between fees and demand. How elastic is that relationship? We do know that some parts of the community cannot afford further and higher education. We also know that for some areas the fees may be very low in comparison to private provision. Consider, for example, management education. Some believe that the relatively low price charged by FHE actually attaches a stigma to the provision, i.e. low price suggests poor quality to the prospective customer. Some argue that price is not, or not only, fees but the matriculation requirements imposed on courses. Why does FHE have entry requirements? Clearly they have a pedagogic value but in marketing terms they turn prospective customers away. Hence FHE could widen access by varying the traditional entry routes for certain market segments. Of course, for many parts of the FE curriculum, the price is fixed by a decision external to the college. The fact colleges often have to market courses and qualifications they have not designed at prices (fees and entry qualifications) they have not fixed makes marketing a very difficult task for colleges.

7 The third of the four P's – *place* – offers perhaps more hope. Are colleges the retail outlets of the further education business? If they are, ways to achieve more flexible delivery arrangements become apparent: distance learning is one example; outreach work another; and on-the-job training a third. Are colleges convenient retail outlets? From the customer's point of view the answer is often no. People buy further education by enrolling on courses. In many cases it is very difficult even to find out what is on offer and whether it is possible to obtain an off-the-peg course which will satisfy the particular education or training need a customer has. Try phoning or calling in to any college and making an enquiry from the point of view of a customer with particular needs. The chances of being put through to the right person, in the right section of the right department of the right building can be quite low in some colleges. Even if the query is answered, most customers then will still have to go through a cumbersome enrolment procedure. So, if 'place' is about how and where customers buy and the enrolment victual is the major selling device used by most colleges, it is not surprising that FE has been criticised for its apparent disinclination to accept the 'sovereignty of the customer'.

8 Finally, what do we know of *promotion*? There are various types of promotional media in marketing. Promotional literature, personal selling, advertising, videos, exhibitions, editorial coverage in the mass media etc. Many colleges use all these devices. Central to the promotional efforts of all colleges is promotional literature. This usually takes two forms: the ubiquitous prospectus and course leaflets. The marketing perspective requires study of how effective these devices are in achieving recruitment. Most colleges spend the lion's

share of their promotional budget in producing promotional literature. Does it actually produce more customers? The indications are that often it is not very cost effective. This could be for a variety of reasons. First, it may be an inappropriate vehicle. Secondly it may just be of inferior design. Thirdly, the distribution may be wrong. To put it another way, either the medium or the message or both may be defective in relation to the required impact on the target market.

9 **Promotional literature**

Existing evidence suggests that many college customers make decisions to purchase as a result of word of mouth publicity, counselling, parental influence, peer group influence and the attitudes of their employers. Few are turned on to further education by seeing promotional material. Many students see the material, if at all, after they have already decided to enrol or are close to such a decision.

10 How good is the material by marketing standards? Much of the literature is 'product oriented' (it advertises a course) and does not sell benefits. In some cases the literature varies arbitrarily in its design from department to department and even section to section. In other words it doesn't promote a professional and consistent corporate image. Marketing people talk of 'AIDA' – the need to write persuasively by using promotional literature to arouse *attention*, develop *interest*, shape *desire* and give rise to *action*. Much college literature fails to do that. It sometimes starts with an outline of entry requirements – tantamount to trying to sell a luxury car by first telling the customer about its price. It often goes on to list 'objectives', 'methods', exam regulations and the like. There is frequent use of abbreviations and jargon which may be commonly understood in education circles which most people are unable to comprehend. In particular, promotional literature in FE fails to recognise that the type of leaflet appropriate to one market segment (e.g. young adults) is unlikely to appeal to others (e.g. their parents or employers).

11 What of the prospectus? Is it an appropriate vehicle? Perhaps for employers, and training officers and counsellors it is. For other customers it may not be. More often than not its main use may be as a reference book rather than as a sales brochure. Despite the above remarks, it is evident that the quality and professionalism of the promotion of the FE service has improved enormously in recent years. This has taken place with budgets which when compared with those of other organisations are woefully inadequate.

12 **Organising for marketing**

An increasing number of colleges are trying to develop an organisational framework to aid marketing. In some cases this takes the form of appointing a marketing officer (usually below the senior management team). Whilst this often helps to improve specific activities in market research, industrial liaison or publicity, it can have the disadvantage of separating the marketing function from other management areas. In some cases a member of the senior management team is given charge of marketing. This can aid decision making but not, necessarily, implementation. In the most developed cases both these solutions and the development within departments or sections of a marketing team and a salesforce, have been attempted.

13 In yet other cases the LEA has taken on the responsibility of organising marketing across the service it provides through its colleges.

14 The particular organisational form is perhaps less important than the fact that some organisation of marketing comes to exist. Any arrangement will bear on academic and non-academic staff alike and raises training and development needs for both groups of staff. These needs vary from consciousness raising to specific skill development, for example, in personal selling, customer reception, writing promotional literature, designing exhibitions and so on. Many colleges have found that these needs can be met cost effectively by in-house and other forms of training.

15 **Improving a college's marketing**
In recent years a number of guides have been written which seek to help staff who manage college marketing. The most comprehensive work is an American one: *Strategic Marketing for Educational Institutions* by Philip Kotler and Karen Fox (1985). Three recent British publications are *Marketing Further and Higher Education – A Handbook* (Davies and Scribbins 1985), *Taking Education Further* (Megson and Barber 1986) and *In Search of the Responsive College* (Theodossin 1986). These and other texts set out practical exercises which colleges can undertake in judging their effectiveness at marketing. They also provide a wide range of checklists for improving marketing research, promotion, media relations and other aspects of marketing. In the paragraphs which follow some of these exercises and checklists are reviewed.

16 **Consumer responsiveness**
Kotler and Fox (1985) suggest that responsive educational institutions are characterised by top management support for marketing, effective organisation, providing marketing training and using staff recruitment and induction techniques which emphasise marketing. They propose a simple grid which colleges can use to categorise their degree of consumer responsiveness, which is shown in Table 1.

Table 1
Grid of consumer responsiveness

	Unresponsive	*Casually Responsive*	*Highly Responsive*
Complaint System	No	Yes	Yes
Surveys of Satisfaction	No	Yes	Yes
Surveys of needs and preferences	No	No	Yes
Customer Oriented Personnel	No	No	Yes

Source: Kotler and Fox (1985) pp 28–34

17 **The college's image**
Kotler and Fox (1985) outline a method of analysing the college's overall image in two dimensions: familiarity (the degree to which it is known by prospective customers) and favourability (the degree to which it is liked by them). Familiarity can be assessed on the dimensions shown in Table 2. It is quite possible to score badly on both counts – i.e. some colleges will have an unfavourable image coupled with widespread ignorance of their services. If a college adopts a committed marketing strategy, 'before' and 'after' studies using the above approach can help to monitor its effectiveness.

Table 2
Dimensions of familiarity

*	*	*	*	*
Never heard of	*Heard of*	*Know a little*	*Know a fair amount*	*Know well*
Favourability can be analysed in the following way:				
*	*	*	*	*
Very Unfavourable	*Somewhat Unfavourable*	*Indifferent*	*Somewhat Favourable*	*Very Favourable*

Source: Kotler and Fox (1985) pp. 38–43

18 **The college's portfolio**
Strategy involves the selection of a target market, the choice of a competitive position and the development of an effective marketing mix to reach and serve the chosen market. The first step is to evaluate the college's current offerings and markets: its 'portfolio'. Should these be maintained, built up or dropped? A commonly used technique for analysing the state of an organisation's portfolio is the Boston Consulting Group Matrix which relates market share to market size and growth rate as shown in Table 3. 'Star' courses are those for which a college has market share dominance in a growing market. Heavy investment is needed in this area. 'Cash cows' are courses for which the general demand is low and not growing but in respect of which the college has a dominant position. These usually require small scale investment but produce a steady revenue which can be invested in the stars or stimulate the question marks. For 'question marks' – courses for which the demand is generally high but of which the college has a small share – a decision to increase investment or terminate the endeavour will be necessary. The aim of investment is to make the question marks into stars. 'Dogs' are probably best killed reallocated off unless there are good policy reasons for their maintenance. For example, it might be decided not to terminate a declining course that is the last provision for a depressed industry in a college's locality.

Table 3
Matrix for portfolio analysis

		Market Share	
		High	*Low*
Market Size/Growth Rate	High	STARS	QUESTION MARKS
	Low	CASH COWS	DOGS

19 **A comprehensive audit**
The most sophisticated and developed technique for judging the effectiveness and efficiency of an institution's marketing is the so-called marketing audit. It is intended to be *comprehensive,* covering all the marketing related issues facing an institution; *systematic*, involving an orderly sequence of diagnostic steps; *independent*, usually involving outside consultants; and, *periodic,* not just when a crisis looms. Applied to a college, or any other organisation, it

usually involves four elements, as shown in Table 5. The generation of detailed answers to questions along the lines indicated should enable an organisation to assess its own *strengths* and *weaknesses* and the *opportunities* and *threats* which face it. This can assist the generation of policies to counteract the latter and exploit the former.

Table 5
Marketing audit

1 Strategic profile	What 'business' are we engaged in? Who are our existing and potential customers? How do we relate to them? How do we see ourselves?
2 External environment	What are the political, social, economic, technological and educational developments which affect us?
3 Resource audit	What are the capabilities of our staff, buildings and equipment? What is our present and potential financial position? How are we organised and managed in relation to the marketing function?
4 Current strategy	What are our current strategies for marketing, production, finance and personnel, and do they relate clearly to each other and to an overall corporate strategy?

20 **Marketing information**

The increased attention being given in FE to the gathering and analysis of market information is largely a response to the demands of external agencies such as the DES, LEAs and in particular, the MSC. The marketing approach mean that an efficient and effective system of market intelligence is essential if colleges are to make sensible judgements about:

(i) The size of the potential market for their services;
(ii) The range and size of potential client groups;
(iii) The amount of potential demand from each group;
(iv) Whether that demand is expanding or contracting.

From this colleges may judge the extent to which they are meeting demand and the extent to which is being met by others. Overall this helps to identify the scope and the direction of future policy.

21 There are two main types of data – secondary and primary. Secondary data already exists somewhere in one form or another. Primary data is original information collected to address the problem at hand. It is therefore liable to be much more expensive to obtain. The FE service has available to it an enormous supply of secondary data. Many colleges may gain a more significant benefit from a more effective analysis and utilisation of existing data than by committing scarce resources to primary research. The main categories of information likely to be needed by any college are:

(i) Demographic/socio-economic details: a profile of potential customers broken down by age, sex, income group, occupational, social status, etc.

(ii) Geographical distribution of potential consumers;
(iii) Transport facilities;
(iv) Economic and employment information, e.g. employment trends in the area, training needs of employers, the level of and structure of unemployment etc;
(v) Details of voluntary organisations and pressure groups within the local community;
(vi) The activities of competing institutions and organisations;
(vii) The availability to potential customers of ancillary services (creches, libraries, etc).

Much of the above information will be easier to obtain and utilise if there is an effective college record system. Some form of student and employer database is necessary for this. Increasingly databases are being computerised in order to handle large volumes of data effectively on a college-wide rather than a departmental or course basis.

22 The main sources of *secondary data* of relevance to FE are:
(i) *Central Government* – the DES produce detailed educational statistics which should allow colleges to compare their performance in particular programme areas against national trends. The Department of Employment produces quarterly estimates of employees in employment in all industries and services as well as a whole range of other employment information.
(ii) The Manpower Services Commission is in the process of establishing more detailed Local Labour Market Intelligence (LLMI) and in mapping Travel to Work Areas (TTWA).
(iv) Reports of professional associations and trade unions.
(v) Studies undertaken by specialised bodies such as the detailed forecast by industry broken down to regional level undertaken by the Institute for Employment Research at Warwick University.
(vi) Information from the prospectuses, annual reports, etc., of competing organisations.
(vii) Trade journals and technical publications.

23 **Improving promotional effectiveness**

The main channels which are available to colleges for communicating with actual and potential customers are:
(i) Leaflets; prospectuses.
(ii) Direct Mail.
(iii) Advertising (the media which can range from newspapers to bus panels and beer mats).
(iv) Media relations.
(v) Personal selling.
(vi) Exhibitions, Open days, etc.
(vii) Public relations.

As with other parts of marketing, Colleges have found that the key to success is to identify the different characteristics of different groups in the market place and to target them accordingly. The more the message and the media are tailored to the wants and needs of a particular target group the more likely it is that promotional efforts will be successful.

24 A useful checklist for devising promotional campaigns is:
(i) Identify the market segments at which the campaign is aimed.

(ii) Tailor the message and select the medium which are most likely to appeal to those markets.
(iii) Lead with benefits not courses (a course is a means to an end for most prospective students – the names of the college and the courses are unlikely to be intrinsically interesting to potential customers who are not already committed to education).
(iv) Overall a successful promotional campaign needs to engage the *attraction* of potential customers, *interest* them in what is offered, stimulate a *desire* in them to acquire the benefits arising from what is offered and allow them to take *action* swiftly and easily to acquire the service on offer. This gives use to the so called *AIDA* principle.
(v) Jargon words, long sentences, long words and initials which may be meaningless to the potential customer are best avoided. The aim is to give the minimum information necessary to the stage which the customer has reached in considering enrolment.
(vi) Good design is essential: it uses white space, photographs and illustration to advantage.
(vii) Establish an attractive and consistent corporate image which is recognisable to the public and conveys the essential 'mission' of the organisation.
(viii) The effectiveness of any promotional strategy is improved if expenditure is monitored carefully. This can be achieved by such devices as identifiable and returnable coupons in advertisements and leaflets, and pre- and post-testing of promotional material in order to assess public recognition and response.

25 **Using the media**

Contrary to generally held beliefs, regular coverage of college activities in local press and radio is not difficult to obtain, provided certain rules are observed. Editorial – as opposed to paid for – exposure in the media also has far more impact on the public. The facts and opinions which are recorded have far more effect than when they appear in advertisements.

26 It therefore pays colleges to pursue a consistent coherent and positive media strategy. As with the writing of other promotional material, copy supplied to the media should appeal to the benefits which are sought by the public and the media professionals. A story will usually only be judged newsworthy if it is about *people* – stories which are really about *courses* therefore need to be given a strong personal angle and a headline that will appeal to the journalist or news editor. The media does not exist to give colleges free advertising. In order to enjoy a good working relationship with journalists it is necessary to be aware of and respect the demands of their profession. Hence it is necessary to be able to deal with journalists about the stories and incidents which reflect badly, as well as those that reflect well, on the college.

27 A critical part of any media relations strategy is via the press (or media) release and, on occasion, through a press (or media) conference. This is not the only form of media relations. Letters to the press, writing features, running or assisting with phone-in programmes, getting to know the editors and education correspondents; all these and other devices play an important part. However, the media release is the heart media relations. Badly produced releases not only fail to get coverage but worse still can get the wrong sort of coverage and create the image of the college or LEA as amateurish in the eyes of the media.

28 Some hints on writing media releases (adapted from Davies and Scribbins 1985) are:

(i) The release must have a good headline which attracts immediate interest. This is the only part of many releases which is actually read, prior to their consignment to the waste bin! To avoid this fate the headline must be eye-catching and sum up the item in question. It is important to remember that the headline is not written for inclusion in the paper; that is the sub-editor's job. The purpose of the headline is to catch the editor's attention.

(ii) The release needs an angle. Make it people-centred and locally orientated, especially for the local and regional press, radio and TV.

(iii) The first paragraph is crucial. In many cases only the first paragraph will be used so it should contain the bones of the message. In general, the bottom sections of a release are more likely to be cut than the top sections.

(iv) The first paragraph should state *who* the information is about, *what* you are publicising, *why* (if it is an event) the event has occurred, *where* and *when* it has happened, or will happen, and (if it is a course) *when* it will start.

(v) The release should be short (rarely over one page) with wide margins and double spacing.

(vi) The release should be succinct and contain a quote or quotes from an individual, whether it is the principal, head of department, member of staff or a student.

(vii) A clear black and white photo with a caption will always increase the chance of publication, particularly if the caption points out 'local' people.

(viii) Any embargo should be clearly marked at the top of the release. The end of the release should be marked by the words 'ENDS' at the bottom, and the day and night telephone number of a contact for further information should be given. It is necessary to make sure that this contact is available when the journalist receives the release.

(ix) The release should be submitted in good time to meet the media's deadline. This is particularly important for weekly papers and journals.

Section 3

HIGHER EDUCATION

3.1 CURRICULUM AND CURRICULUM AGENCIES

1 The range of curriculum in further education is immense. It stretches from an overlap with schools, to vocational preparation to 16–18 year olds, to 'vocational' education from operative through craft technician to graduate and professional qualifications, to 'non-vocational' adult education and to postgraduate programmes. It includes the development of knowledge and skills in almost all areas of human endeavour; only a few academic subjects are not studied somewhere in the FE system. There are many approaches to the design and delivery of the curriculum and many sources of initiative for its development. The scene shifts continually, and many different agencies have an impact on the curriculum.

2 SCHOOL-LEAVING AND VOCATIONAL PREPARATION

At one end of its range further education overlaps with school education. Though the two systems have different regulations and are characterised by different approaches to curricula, there is no clear dividing line in terms of different courses or sets of qualifications. The increasing concern for vocational relevance in school education has drawn colleges and schools together both in courses and qualifications and collaboration between institutions. For the under-16s age group the growth of linked courses (See below paragraph 3) has been accelerated by the Technical and Vocational Education Initiative (TVEI) (See below paragraphs 4–9) and the Certificate of Pre-Vocational Education (CPVE) (See below paragraphs 10–15) and Pre-Vocational Programmes (PVP) and the development of those new programmes has demanded collaboration between schools and FE. For the 16–19 age group the young people themselves are – in most local education authorities (LEAs) – in a position to choose whether to progress through the school or FE systems. The courses available to them include GCE A levels (supplemented by AS levels) (See paragraphs 21–27 below), CPVE and additional or resits of GCSE (See paragraphs 16–20 below), vocational courses leading to qualifications of the Business and Technician Education Council (BTEC) (See below paragraphs 44–49), City and Guilds of London Institute (CGLI), (See below paragraphs 33–39) Royal Society of Arts (RSA) (See below paragraphs 40–43), and others within the scope of the National Council for Vocational Qualifications (See below paragraphs 50–57). Some of the lower levels of these qualifications are available in schools as well as FE, though part-time modes are usually only available in FE, and FE is more likely than schools to offer vocational as well as academic subjects and qualifications. In some LEAs provision for the 16–19 age group has been reorganised into a single system of tertiary colleges, integrating schools and FE (See below paragraphs 28–31). The development of the Youth Training Scheme (YTS) into the major stage through which 16 and 17 year olds pass in the transition from full-time education to employment (and unemployment) has laid another dimension over the pattern of FE qualifications (See **1.7** 7–27). Although tertiary reorganisation and local reviews and planning have introduced elements of rationalisation into the education and training of the 16–19 age group and, increasingly, the 14–16 age group, the overall situation is very complex and looks likely to remain so. How far this complexity represents a useful network of opportunities for young people and a valuable responsiveness to social and market forces and how far it forms a maze which confuses and impedes young people, their employers and their advisers are matters of continuing debate.

3 **Linked courses**

Linked courses (links between schools and colleges) enable school pupils to attend a college for one or one and a half days per week. Most courses are pre-vocational and since they provide insights into occupational areas are sometimes referred to as 'sampling' or 'taster' courses. Some courses lead to a qualification, such as under the Mode III of the old Certificate of Secondary Education (CSE) which could be used, for example, as a route into a City and Guilds of London Institute (CGLI) craft course. Linked courses facilitate cooperation and liaison between schools and colleges, and can also assist in the transition between schools and work.

4 **The Technical and Vocational Education Initiative**

The Technical and Vocational Education Initiative, funded by MSC (TVEI), was announced by the Prime Minister in November 1982, initially on a pilot basis with 14 projects in September 1983; a further 48 in September 1984, and further 12 in September 1985; the 74 projects were based in 73 LEAs. The 1986 White Paper *Working Together – Education and Training* announced the Government's intention to extend TVEI pilots into a national scheme from autumn 1987 at a cost of around £900 million over a period of ten years. The main aim of TVEI is to test methods of organising and managing the education of 14–18 year olds across the ability range 'to improve the provision of technical and vocational education in a way which will widen and enrich the curriculum and prepare young people for adult and continuing life' (*Working Together – Education and Training*, paragraph 3.1).

5 By 1985, over 400 schools and 100 colleges were involved in TVEI. For the 62 projects started in 1983 and 1984, there were 19 sixth from colleges, 8 tertiary colleges, plus 75 colleges of FE and 19 other FE establishments. LEAs submit schemes to MSC for funding (See **1.7** 61–63). Participating LEAs have to look closely at 14–16 and 16–18 provision, requiring close working relationships between schools and colleges. Guidance issued by the TVEI Unit emphasises that when 16–18 provision is school-based there should be evidence that FE involvement has been carefully considered; and similarly when FE based there should be evidence that school involvement has been considered.

6 TVEI programmes are designed over a 4-year period to provide for individual students a balance of general, technical and vocational education. Pupils are often able to choose TVEI options in addition to common or core elements. All programmes must include careers and educational guidance and counselling and planned work experience. All programmes offer some form of technology, craft and design, business studies, or a related area. Many have some options of particular local interest, e.g. media studies, agriculture, and horticulture. TVEI criteria emphasise equal opportunities for boys and girls; and individual projects have explored ways of overcoming sex stereotyping. TVEI projects have examined ways of developing a broad and relevant curriculum and of improving collaboration between education and industry.

7 Projects are also introducing changes in teaching styles, geared towards providing students with the opportunity to develop initiative, motivation, problem-solving skills, and other personal qualities which are frequently assessed as part of their record of achievement. Various methods used include: assign-

ment of work, where students undertake projects; hands-on experience and practical application of knowledge; and the involvement of students in clarifying their objectives.

8 The decision to extend TVEI pilots into a national scheme was taken before completion of TVEI pilot projects and any major evaluation. MSC has publicly expressed concern that funding might not be sufficient to achieve the aim of every secondary school having the opportunity to provide a TVEI option.

9 TVEI for 16–18 year olds has led to the development of closer links between examining bodies such as CGLI, BTEC, and RSA which have modified existing courses to fit more closely the requirements of individual schemes and have devised new modules/units.

THE CERTIFICATE FOR PRE-VOCATIONAL EDUCATION

10 Following the Government's policy in *17+ – a New Qualification* (DES 1981b) the Joint Board for Pre-Vocational Education was set up under the auspices of the Business and Technician Educational Council (BTEC) and CGLI 'to establish joint arrangements for a system of pre-vocational education on a national basis including the 17+ qualification'. The Joint Board, after issuing a consultative document in 1984, published details of the new Certificate of Pre-Vocational Education (CPVE) in January 1985. CPVE is a national framework for pre-vocational education; and provides a qualification which is available to those who have undertaken an approved one-year full-time programme of study and related activities after the end of compulsory schooling. It is designed to assist young people in the transition from general schooling to vocational education, training and employment. The first courses began in Autumn 1985.

11 CPVE replaced the vocational preparation courses run by CGLI, RSA, and BTEC (See below paragraph 15) and the Certificate of Extended Education (CEE). CEE, which commenced as a pilot project in 1972, was designed as a single subject examination for students in schools who had gained, broadly, grades 2–4 in Certificate of Secondary Education (CSE). In 1979 the Keohane Report reviewed the pilot schemes and recommended that CEE should be established nationally. However, in a Green Paper (DES 1980b) the Government rejected Keohane's arguments in favour of a qualification which was structured as a programme (rather than single subjects) and included a range of skills to prepare students for a general field of employment. The Government's arguments preferred the approach of the FEU's *A basis for choice* (1979) which recommended national recognition and common elements for vocational preparation courses, having surveyed the variety of such courses which had grown up locally in FE.

12 This approach was confirmed in *17+ — A New Qualification* (DES 1981b) which described the new qualification as 'a key element in a set of Government policies designed to improve the vocational relevance of education and training for young people and to rationalise the confusing pattern of qualifications available to them'. It saw single subject examinations – CEE and additional or resit GCE O levels – as not sufficiently practical for its target group of young people of 'modest examination achievements at 16+ who have set their sights on employment rather than higher education, but have not yet formed a clear idea of the kind of job they might tackle successfully, or are not

yet ready to embark on a specific course of vocational education or training'. The Government thought about 80,000 young people a year would at first take CPVE, which, it reckoned, would be about half the target group.

13 There are three components of the CPVE framework: the core; vocational studies; additional studies. The core and vocational studies amount to some 75% of course time. The core covers a range of experiences and competences in ten areas: personal and career development; industrial social and environmental studies; communication; social skills; numeracy; science and technology; information technology; creative development; practical skills; problem solving. Vocational studies have been organised using a modular approach into five main categories covering: business and administrative services; technical services; production; distribution; services to people. Additional studies are intended to provide time for community activities and leisure recreation and for reflection; and to cater for particular educational needs. The development of CPVE locally has often been carried out by the use of local consortia – usually consisting of one college and several schools. In the CPVE pilot programmes, for example, school pupils usually spent between a half and two days per week at a local college. The use of consortia is likely to become an increasingly important feature of CPVE schemes and underlies again the close links between colleges and schools. For the 1985 start, the Joint Board received 657 submissions covering 459 individual schools or colleges, and 198 consortia covering 785 schools or colleges.

14 The place of CPVE in relation to TVEI and YTS is as yet unclear. The option of CPVE being offered as a third year of TVEI is being explored; and those completing CPVE are able to embark on the second year of YTS. The feasibility of developing the part-time CPVE as part of YTS is being explored. Without incorporation into YTS and TVEI there is a serious risk that CPVE will be squeezed out between a national TVEI scheme covering four years with schools needing to plan carefully for progression and cohesion over the four year period and the YTS, in which young people receive a trainee allowance.

15 The CPVE has entered a field already occupied by a variety of 'foundation' and 'gateway' courses and by RSA and CGLI vocational preparation courses and BTEC General awards. The Government intended CPVE to be a single framework covering all young people wanting a pre-vocational qualification. However, this plan was upset by BTEC's precipitate announcement of a new First Award for this group of young people. The resolution of this confusion and of the relationship with YTS has not been helped by rivalries between examination boards.

16 **The General Certificate of Secondary Education**

The Secretary of State announced in June 1984 that the GCSE would be introduced to replace GCE O level, CSE, and Joint 16+ examinations and that the first GCSE certificate would be awarded in Summer 1988. Pupils would no longer have to choose between O levels and CSE and such a bewildering variety of syllabuses. The announcement brought to an end a period of uncertainty about the future of 16+ examinations. A White Paper in 1978 stated the Government's intention to introduce one examining system for 16+, following the advice of the Waddell Report (1978). However, the special needs of mature students, many of whom study part-time, have caused the FE service to press the case for alternative arrangements, shorter course lengths etc., as a feature of the GCSE. Whilst most Examining Boards have sought to accommodate such student groups, the crucial test is the extent to which the HE system accepts these modified courses as of equal value to more traditional school based study. In general the position facing mature students is fluid and uncertain, not just because of the changes in GCSE provision but also arising out of the growth of alternative forms of adult provision such as access courses, and the evaluation of work, experience, and training (see below paragraphs 63–65 and **3.2** 7–11).

17 The Secondary Examinations Council (SEC) and Joint Council of GCE and CSE Boards worked closely together to establish and revise the final forms of the national criteria statements. These criteria make clear in subject terms what candidates may broadly be expected to experience, learn, and do in courses based on syllabuses bearing a particular title. They cover inter-disciplinary, integrated or modular syllabuses as well as the more traditional single subjects.

18 The GCSE is a single system of examinations with a single scale of grades. Pupils do not however follow the same class work and examination questions. In the final examination in many subjects there is a choice of papers and questions to give all the pupils the chance to show what they can do. Successful pupils are awarded a grade on a single scale from A to G. Grades A to C have standards which reflect equivalence to former O level A to C grades and CSE Grade 1. Similarly grades D to G have standards approximating to CSE grades 2 to 5. Although GCSE is mainly aimed at 16 year old pupils, the examinations are open to students of any age whether in school or college.

19 The launch of the GCSE with the first courses starting in Autumn 1986 were dogged with problems; the 1985/6 schools teachers' dispute affected the attendance of school teachers on in-service courses, though not for the pilots in FE. There were also criticisms of inadequate preparation time and doubts about requirements for assessment which raised questions about the size of teaching groups and supply of teachers. There were seen to be insufficient resources for text books and equipment, although the newly appointed Secretary of State provided additional resources in 1986–87 and made a commitment to do so in 1987–88.

20 The nineteen GCE and CSE boards in England and Wales have joined together into five examining groups (plus one in Northern Ireland). Each group is offering a full range of subjects; and schools may choose any syllabus from any of the groups. The groups are:

Northern Examining Association
GCE: Joint Matriculation Board
CSE: Associated Lancashire Schools Examining Board; North Regional Examinations Board; Yorkshire and Humberside Regional Examinations Board.
Midland Examining Group
GCE: Cambridge University Local Examinations Syndicate; Oxford and Cambridge Schools Examinations Board; Southern Universities' Joint Board
CSE: East Midlands Regional Examinations Board; West Midlands Examinations Board
London and East Anglian Group
GCE: University of London Schools Examinations Board

CSE: East Anglian Examinations Board; London Regional Examining Board
Southern Examining Group
GCE: Oxford Delegacy of Local Examinations, Associated Examining Board
CSE: Southern Regional Examinations Board, South Western Examinations Board, South East Regional Examination Board
Wales
GCE and CSE: Welsh Joint Education Committee
Northern Ireland
GCE and CSE: Northern Ireland Schools Examinations Council

21 **GCE A Levels**

In spite of many proposed changes e.g., the debate over N (Normal) and F (Further) levels, the GCE A level examinations have remained. Ministers are publicly committed to their retention. The SEC took over from the Schools Council which had monitored examination provision at A level through a programme of syllabus approval and scrutiny (See below paragraphs 72–76). In 1984–85 SEC approved 40 new or substantially amended syllabuses.

22 The GCE Boards have introduced common core at A level. In some subjects these are no more than common aims and objectives; in others common core statements cover aims, assessment objectives, and certain defined topics or aspects of the content of the syllabus.

23 In 1986, the Secretary of State for Education and Science agreed to a number of changes to the A level grading system designed to resolve the long-standing problem of the narrow range of marks constituting grade C. Under the revised system the five A level pass grades A to E would be retained; the 'O' grade be replaced with a 'N' grade denoting a narrow failure and an unclassified performance be identified by the letter 'U' but not certificated. The A/B grade borderline would be established on the basis of Board's existing practices including examiners' judgement on quality; the B/C and E/N borderlines should be established by reference to examiners' judgement of quality and by using methods to ensure fairness and reliability at these crucial points; and the mark between the B/C and E/N grade borderlines should be divided into three equal intervals and these assigned respectively to grades C, D and E with the same interval assigned to grade N.

24 SEC has announced a major review of A levels in the light of the changes at 16+. It is likely that the review will seek greater emphasis on oral work and on work undertaken at school or college. Also that greater emphasis will be given to candidates understanding processes rather than learning facts.

25 **Advanced Supplementary Level**

The March 1985 White Paper *Better Schools* introduced Advanced Supplementary (AS) Level Examinations. The new examinations were in response to longstanding concern that A level studies were undesirably narrow – students have had to abandon subjects taken at O level or CSE to pursue a limited range of A levels. This has meant that students concentrating on arts subjects, for example, have had little opportunity to continue with mathematical, scientific and technical studies, and science students have had to discontinue studies in humanities and foreign languages.

26 AS levels are designed to broaden A level students' studies by providing the opportunity for them to continue with more of the subjects that they have studied up to the age of 16 or to take on new ones. GCE boards and the SEC developed and approved the first AS level syllabuses for courses to start in September 1987.

27 Courses are intended to occupy half of the teaching and private study time of an A level. Thus students can take two A levels and two AS levels instead of three A levels. AS level passes will be graded A/E with grade standards related to A level grading and each grade counted as half that of the corresponding A level grade. At the time of writing, the future of AS levels remains uncertain. The potential take-up in schools and colleges depends very much on the views of higher education institutions, and of teachers and students.

28 **Tertiary reorganisation**

By September 1986 there were 36 tertiary colleges in 21 LEAs and there were proposals for secondary reorganisation including tertiary colleges in a further 8 LEAs (Parliamentary Answer – 9 July 1986). The steady increase in tertiary reorganisation can be attributed to educational and economic arguments. The belief has grown that the principle of comprehensive education should be extended to 18, and that there should be no separation into 'academic' and 'vocational' categories at 16. Alongside this, school rolls have fallen, and many schools have been unable to maintain the size of sixth form capable of sustaining a developing range of courses. Furthermore the cost effectiveness of setting up tertiary colleges and sixth form colleges is attractive (See DES Statistical Bulletin 6/87, Macfarlane 1980 and Arthur Young 1981). (See **1.6** 54.)

29 Liaison between tertiary colleges and secondary schools is well established. In addition there is often direct liaison between tertiary colleges and other FE colleges to ensure that students can be offered the complete range of vocational courses available through the FE examining bodies.

30 In August 1986 the Education Secretary issued draft guidance to LEAs on the pattern of organisation up to age 19 (Draft DES Circular *Providing for Quality – the Pattern of Organisation to Age 19*, DES August 1986). The draft circular emphasised the need to plan provision for the 16–19 age group as a whole in both schools and non-advanced further education, as well as covering the organisation of schools alone in respect of the 5–16 age group. The draft circular invited each LEA, in the light of the considerations and guidance of the circular, 'to review, plan and take the necessary action to organise their 16–19 provision in order to maximise educational effectiveness and value for money'. In carrying out these reviews, authorities will 'need to consider, inter alia, the size and type of institutions, the area each is to serve, and the type of courses each is to provide; staffing policies; including where appropriate target student-staff ratios; and target levels of space utilisations within institutions.' Although the draft guidance makes no firm recommendations, it is likely that more LEAs will be persuaded of the arguments in favour of reorganisation which creates a break at 16. The NATFHE policy document *Planning for Change in Further Education* (1986b) notes: 'The tertiary sector should encompass the whole of post-school provision and training (other than higher education) and should preferably take place within a system of tertiary colleges. Such a pattern would eliminate the arbitrary institutional barriers to would-be students which are often perceived to exist at present. A tertiary sys-

tem should also facilitate a highly flexible and responsible pattern of courses, with greater opportunities for the provision of minority subjects.'

31 Overall the position on tertiary reorganisation seems in doubt given the uncertainties of the detail of Government's plans to afford 'schools' an opportunity to remove themselves from LEA control. Clearly the decisions of individual boards of governors, and the subsequent response of Ministers to any such applications, poses what at the present time are unanswerable questions about strategic reorganisations by LEAs. Almost certainly the presence of an apparently popular sixth form in a school will be an important factor in possible votes by parents and governing bodies.

VOCATIONAL QUALIFICATIONS

32 Many bodies offer vocational qualifications in FE; Locke and Bloomfield (1982) listed about 50 bodies which certificated 16–19 year-olds, the majority specific to a trade or profession; and there is no established pattern of equivalences and correspondences between most of them. However, FE is dominated by three major examining bodies for vocational qualifications : City and Guilds of London Institute (CGLI), Royal Society of Arts (RSA), and Business and Technician Education Council (BTEC), each of which has systems of qualifications internally interrelated and with broadly accepted comparabilities. The establishment of the National Council for Vocational Qualifications is to increase cooperation among these bodies (See below paragraphs 50–51).

33 **City and Guilds of London Institute**

The City and Guilds of London Institute (CGLI or 'City and Guilds') provides colleges and schools with national structures of curricula and qualifications in technical and pre-vocational education. Established as the 'City and Guilds of London Institute for the Advancement of Technical Education' by the Corporation and Livery Companies of the City of London in 1878, the Institute has concerned itself from its foundation with the improvement of instructional facilities and of standards of knowledge and skill. Its activities apply to students of all ages from 14 to mature years and to all levels from secondary to professional post-graduate.

34 The Institute is an independent body providing a public service under the authority of a Royal Charter granted in 1890 and accountable to the Privy Council. Its membership comprises:

(i) Founder Members – the Corporation and Livery Companies of London;

(ii) Corporate Ordinary Members – firms and public corporations, employers associations and trade unions, and other organisations.

(iii) Ex-officio Members – individuals appointed by virtue of their offices, e.g. the Lord Mayor of London, the President of the Royal Society, and others;

(iv) Honorary Members – individuals appointed by the Institute in recognition of their eminence in education and training and their contributions to City and Guilds work. Many past and present teachers in further education are Honorary Members of the Institute.

35 The Institute is a registered charity which receives no Government or other public funding. Corporate Members subscribe annual amounts of £50 to £3,000 to the Institute of their discretion. The Institute's main source of income is examination fees.

36 The Governing Body of the Institute is its Council, the majority of whose 76 members are elected by the membership of the Institute or co-opted. Each of the 10 Regional Advisory Councils for Further Education is represented. The Council, and its supporting structure of Committees including National Advisory Committees for each major sector of industry or educational activity, are all assisted by Assessors from the Department of Education and Science and the Manpower Services Commission. The constitution of all City and Guilds Committees provides for a member (or members) nominated by NATFHE. The Institute's Committee structure involves some 8,000 individuals who contribute their advice and expertise voluntarily.

37 City and Guilds courses in colleges of further and higher education and in schools are followed annually by some 1½ million students: the related exams produce over 500,000 candidate entries annually. A further 50,000 entries annually are received for skills tests and other types of examination 'on demand'. Altogether some 2,500 educational and industrial training establishments in Britain and throughout the world act as centres for City and Guilds exams in approximately 300 different vocational and educational subjects. More than 5,000 subject specialists are appointed annually by the Institute as examiners, assessors and moderators.

38 Administrative and teaching staff of colleges have contact with the Institute through course provision, and the administration of assessments and examinations. All colleges maintained by local education authorities in Britain are recognised as approved centres for City and Guilds courses and exams. Registrars, chief administrative officers and examinations officers act as Local Examinations Secretaries to correspond with the Institute's Examinations Secretary on all matters concerning the administration of City and Guilds exams, including results and prizes.

39 The main areas of educational activity for which City and Guilds provides and publishes schemes of curricula including regulations for its qualifications and syllabuses for examination are:

(i) *Secondary* (in partnership with the Business and Technician Education Council (BTEC) (See paragraph 47 below);
14–16: Pre-vocational courses associated with the Technical and Vocational Education Initiative (TVEI) (See paragraphs 4–9 above);
16 plus: The Certificate of Pre-Vocational Education (CPVE), through the Joint Board for Pre-Vocational Education, jointly administered by City and Guilds and BTEC (See paragraphs 12–14 above).

(ii) *Non-Advanced Further Education*
Specified Vocational Preparation This is the Institute's principal area of activity. It includes Certificates at Operative, Craft, Advanced Craft and Technician Level each aimed at students preparing for industrial careers. The schemes are classified as:
Level 1 – Occupational Preparation;
Level 2 – Industrial Competence; and
Level 3 – Preparation for specialization or Supervisory Management.
Career Extension Certificates of success in further study to broaden

technical skill and equip the individual for greater responsibilities for products, processes and personnel.

Licentiateship of City and Guilds The Institute's highest award for progression through vocational courses and qualifications and the attainment of occupational experience, carrying the post-normal letters LCG and replacing the former Full Technological Certificate.

(iii) *Post-Experience*

City and Guilds Insignia Award in Technology The Warrant of the Award, which carries the post-nominal letters CGIA, is conferred upon individuals in senior line or research management who have been successfully assessed by the Institute on project reports on aspects of technology or industrial practice not hitherto specifically studied.

Prince Philip Medal A gold medal conferred once annually by Prince Philip as President of the Institute in recognition of outstanding achievement in industry or public service by the attainment of a senior management appointment, starting from the workshop floor and based originally on City and Guilds certification.

(iv) *Higher Education*

Associateship Diplomas of Associateship carrying the post-nominal letters ACGI are conferred upon students successfully completing undergraduate courses at City and Guilds College, which comprises the Engineering and Computing Departments of Imperial College of Science and Technology, University of London

Fellowship Diplomas of Fellowship – FCGI – are conferred upon Associates who have achieved particular eminence in the engineering profession, either in industry or as academics.

40 **The Royal Society of Arts**

The Royal Society for the Encouragement of Arts, Manufactures and Commerce was established in 1754 and has been conducting public examinations since 1856.

41 The Society's activities are under the general direction of its Council and matters relating to examinations are the responsibility of the Examinations Board. Membership is drawn from a variety of categories representative of the Board's activities – from local authorities and public bodies to teachers' and professional associations, including NATFHE. Seven Advisory Committees, each with its sub-structure of subject committees and specialist working groups, report to the Examinations Board. In 1987 the RSA Examinations Board was established as a separate company limited by guarantee with charitable status.

42 RSA qualifications are established nationally and internationally in the secretarial, business and commercial field. RSA activities have diversified considerably to cover schemes in languages, computer studies, English as a Foreign Language, and the operational management of Road Transport as well as a number of teaching qualifications in office skills and languages. Schemes are also available on a Mode 3 basis, and RSA is willing to respond to any new initiatives by way of trial or experimental schemes.

43 By far the largest numbers of candidate entries, 600,000 a year, are for Single Subjects at Stages I, II and III. Many of the Single Subject schemes continue to follow the conventional pattern with a syllabus covering a prescribed range of objectives and a final examination. Recent developments have seen a grow-

ing trend towards the use of continuous assessment procedures, without a requirement for a final examination and leading to profile based certification. Continuous assessment features in the range of integrated schemes such as the Vocational Certificates (Clerical) and (Distribution) and the Diplomas and Certificates in Office Procedures and Retail Distribution; assessment is carried out through task-based assignments. Higher level schemes above the Stage III level such as the Diploma for Personal Assistants and Diploma for Bilingual Secretaries are also moving towards continuous assessment. Teachers' Diplomas in Office Skills and English as a Foreign Language have existed for some time, mainly to complement student level schemes. Recent diversification has extended to schemes covering computer and information technology teaching, additional languages qualifications, drama teaching and, for trainers, in general assessment procedures. RSA is associated with the Southern Examining group for GCSE within which a number of RSA schemes will attract dual certification.

44 **Business and Technician Education Council**

The Business and Technician Education Council (BTEC) was set up in 1983 by the formal merger of the Business Education Council (BEC) and the Technician Education Council (TEC), which were established on the recommendation of the Haslegrave Report (1969). It is a company limited by guarantee and a registered educational charity. The Chairman and up to 25 members of the Council are appointed by the Secretary of State for Education and Science to serve in a personal capacity for a period of three years; reappointment is possible. The Council itself may appoint a further three members. The Chief Executive is a member, ex officio. The new Council of BTEC was established from the 1 October 1986.

45 The Council has summarised its remit as 'to advance the quality and availability of a wide range of employment-related education, to the mutual benefit of the students, their current and future employers, and the national interests'. To achieve this it:

(i) Establishes educational qualifications;
(ii) Determines the criteria for awarding those qualifications;
(iii) Approves centres with appropriate staff, equipment and learning resources, to operate the courses and programmes of study leading to qualifications; and
(iv) Validates specific courses which lead to BTEC qualifications.

46 The Council inherited responsibility for all courses and qualifications previously operated under the aegis of BEC and TEC including those formerly designated BEC/TEC and DATEC. Over 180,000 new students registered each year with BTEC between 1983 and 1986 on courses leading to BTEC qualifications and Certificates of Achievement. The majority of students are in the age range 16–23 and of technician and equivalent potential. The Continuing Education programme provides updating, retraining and education for all age groups. All categories of students may study full-time or part-time.

47 The Council is also involved in pre-vocational education. In 1983 BTEC, together with the City and Guilds of London Institute, accepted responsibility from the Secretary of State for the establishment of a Joint Board for Pre-Vocational Education which would oversee the development of the Certificate of Pre-Vocational Education (CPVE) See paragraphs 10–15 above). Other pre-vocational developments, also in cooperation with the City and

Guilds and Guilds of London Institute, have been for the 14–16 age group. These grew out of a need to provide an appropriate curriculum for pupils in the first two years of the four-year TVEI programme for 14–18 (See above paragraphs 4–9). However, they are not limited to schools participating in TVEI. Pupils under-taking in these programmes also have the opportunity to undertake studies leading to GCSE (See paragraphs 16–20 above).

48 The Council's qualifications include: BTEC First Certificates and Diplomas; BTEC National Certificates and Diplomas; BTEC Higher National Certificates and Diplomas; BTEC Continuing Education Certificates and Diplomas. Students may also undertake studies for individual units or groups of units which amount to less than a full qualification. The nine Board areas of BTEC are: Agriculture; Business and Finance; Computing and Information Systems; Construction; Design; Distributive, Hotel and Catering and Leisure Services; Engineering; Public Administration; Science (including the caring professions).

49 At each level and for each employment area, BTEC publishes guidelines indicating the curriculum and vocational approach to be adopted. From these, in most instances, at First and National level, the Council produces the detailed curriculum for the units, which set out in objective form. For Higher National Certificates and Diplomas in almost all areas of work the Council asks centres to design their own programmes to meet BTEC specifications. Assessment is both in-course and end-of-unit or course examinations prepared and marked by the approved centres to BTEC standards. There are no BTEC externally set examinations (since BTEC General was phased out). All courses are subject to moderation by BTEC appointed moderators. BTEC both selects and trains its moderator force, the majority of whom are employed in the further and higher education sectors.

50 **National Council for Vocational Qualifications**

In accepting the recommendations of the Review (MSC/DES 1986) of Vocational Qualifications (RVQ) the Government has, with the establishment of a National Council for Vocational Qualifications (NCVQ), put in position a significant element in a programme of change which began with the White Paper, *A New Training Initiative: A Programme for Action*, in 1981. In the RVQ Report the Review Group recommended that:

> Vocational qualifications in England and Wales should be brought within a new national framework to be called the National Vocational Qualification (NVQ).
>
> A new National Council for Vocational Qualifications (NCVQ) should be set up to secure necessary changes, to develop the NVQ framework and to ensure standards of competence are set.

These recommendations, made in May 1986, were incorporated into the White Paper, *Working Together – Education and Training*, in July 1986 and the new National Council met for the first time in October 1986. (See below for the membership of NCVQ and the terms of reference.)

51 By March 1987, the Council had published its first policy statement, *The NVQ Framework*, which set out the objectives and criteria for the reform of vocational qualifications. The framework sets out a design for arranging all vocational qualifications to be identified within four levels: basic, standard, advanced, and higher ranging from programmes which prepare for entry into

employment such as YTS, to those which are presently covered by the Higher National Awards. The underlying premise is that all qualifications shall, in future, by based on standards of competence as determined by industry-led bodies such as industrial training boards (ITBs)[1]. At time of writing, the theoretical model as represented by the framework is being tested in eight projects designed to map existing qualifications against new criteria. The occupations concerned are agriculture, travel and tourism, retail/distribution, engineering and clerical. The results of these projects were expected in Autumn 1987 along with a consideration of the feasibility of instituting a process of credit accumulation within the system. This latter initiative would heighten interest in the modularisation of courses, a process which the NVQ framework clearly favours. A third development, also taking place at time of writing, was the announcement of the first accreditation of existing qualifications which, in the opinion of the Council, fall within the proposed criteria.

HIGHER EDUCATION

52 **The Council for National Academic Awards**

The CNAA was established by Charter in 1964, following a recommendation in the Robbins Report (1963) on *Higher Education*. The principal purpose of the CNAA is to validate higher education courses and award degrees and diplomas to students in maintained institutions outside the university sector. The Council also awards degrees based on research. It took over the role of the National Council for Technological Awards, and had from the outset a much wider scope than its predecessor. The scope of the CNAA has continued to expand with, for example, its more recent responsibilities for teacher education courses and, following amalgamation in 1974 with the National Council for Diplomas in Art and Design, its responsibility for the award of degrees in art and design. The CNAA is also responsible for Diploma in Management Studies (DMS) courses.

53 CNAA has hitherto operated to a considerable extent through its subject boards and panels, which include teachers from both the public sector of higher education and the universities. Nominations are invited from university departments, from polytechnics and public sector institutions offering degree courses in the subject area, and for teacher education courses, from the relevant teacher associations. The CNAA system has achieved a considerable degree of flexibility and variety in course patterns and modes of study (including part-time and modular), in promoting more flexible entrance requirements, and developing assessment techniques. Throughout its existence it sought an evolutionary relationship with institutions as they themselves developed greater maturity and expertise in the whole process of assessment and validation.

54 In the early 1980s, partly as a result of criticism that institutions were not allowed sufficient flexibility to design and monitor courses and that the CNAA procedures were not only bureaucratic, but expensive and time consuming for institutions, the Government announced in April 1984 the establishment of a Committee of Inquiry to review procedures for the validation of degree courses in polytechnics and colleges in public sector higher education. The Committee, under the chairmanship of Sir Norman Lindop, was given the following terms of reference:

'To identify and examine key issues for the effective and efficient maintenance and improvement of academic standards in the way those responsible for the academic validation of first and higher degree level courses in the public sector in Great Britain discharge their responsibilities, having regard to the validation arrangements of subdegree higher education courses in the public sector, and distinguishing as necessary between different branches of learning; and to recommend changes as appropriate.'

55 The Committee reported in April 1985 and set out three broad options for the Government's consideration. Option one would have retained the CNAA for all public sector institutions not validated by universities, but envisaged a range of validating arrangements including continued external validation of courses in many colleges and 'accreditation' for others. Broadly speaking accreditation would leave an institution free to validate and approve its own course proposals and review its existing courses, subject to procedures laid down by the accrediting body and subject also to periodic review by that body. Option two would have abandoned a national system of external validation so any institution not granting its own degrees would have to seek validation from another that did. The third option would involve designation by the Secretary of State of some public sector institutions as fit to award their own degrees independently, but with the CNAA and universities still validating the majority of institutions under a system based on option one. Of these options the Lindop Committee recommended option three.

56 There was a lengthy delay between the publication of the Lindop Report and the final response by Government to its recommendations. In the interim the CNAA formulated its own response to the Lindop Report indicating it had itself become convinced, as a result of the success with which public sector higher education had developed, that major changes to the Council's Charter and Statutes were necessary to delegate the power of course approval to institutions through accreditation, and to empower institutions to confer degrees and other awards in their own name. CNAA then established both a review of Council's own structures and procedures, with a view to rationalising the number and format of existing committees, boards and panels, and while working on a long term model for achieving patterns of accreditation it decided to allow a limited number of experimental 'institutional agreements' to operate. This allowed, following agreement between the CNAA and the institution, considerably more delegated power and authority for the institution to operate its own internal review and assessment of courses, and to modify them as it thought appropriate.

57 The Government finally responded to the Lindop Report in March 1986. The response indicated that the Government was not persuaded, at present, that to achieve the objective of maintaining and improving standards certain polytechnics or colleges needed to be granted full autonomy in validation with powers to award their own degrees as the Lindop Committee proposed in Option three. Instead, the response welcomed the changes that CNAA had already made in enabling institutions greater responsibility for validation and review of their courses and, subject to the necessary amendment to CNAA's Charter and Statutes, the authority in approved cases to award degrees in the name of the institution. The Government indicated an intention to monitor these developments before coming to a final decision on Option three. The CNAA undertook further consultations, and in October 1986 it issued a consultative document *Quality and Validation: Future Relationships with Institutions.*

58 Following these consultations, the CNAA's decision that it would accredit approved institutions was announced in February 1987 with the anticipation that the first accreditations would be made in autumn 1987. The basis for accreditation would be the CNAA's assessment of the internal validation and monitoring arrangements. The CNAA set out these features for the new arrangements: a review of all courses every five to seven years by the institutions by groups including participants from industry, commerce or the professions as well as academics (but no obligation to include CNAA nominees); a strengthening of the external examiner system; the CNAA's right to intervene at any time if there was cause to believe standards were at risk; a review arranged by CNAA at regular intervals to decide whether institutions should remain accredited, with the CNAA's right to withdraw accreditation at any time. The CNAA would act as a national centre and focus for information on course design, good practice in teaching and student assessment. These arrangements were seen by CNAA as building on its system of peer review whilst encouraging institutions to develop as (in its Chief Officer's words) 'strong, cohesive and self-critical academic communities', and recognising the maturity of institutions without losing the means of ensuring standards comparable across the country. The necessary changes to its charter were approved by the Queen in Council in March 1987.

59 At time of writing the detailed pattern of validation for degree and postgraduate awards in the public sector had not yet been determined but the broad outlines of the future shape of the system became clear. The CNAA expected that institutions responsible for some three-quarters of its students would become accredited. The variety of awards is likely to increase, but the quality assurance, which is the hallmark of the CNAA system, will remain, although it will be implemented in a variety of ways according to the maturity and experience of the different institutions within public sector higher education. Whether this would produce a hierarchy of esteem among institutions remained a question.

60 **Teacher training and related qualifications**

There were major changes in teacher training qualifications during the 1970s and early 1980s which had an impact on the whole of PSHE provision. The 1972 White Paper *Education: A framework for expansion* led to the phasing out of the Certificate of Education, a sub-degree route into qualified teacher status, and its replacement by BEds, validated by the CNAA and by some universities. BEds were commonly structured in modules, frequently sharing modules with other first degrees, thus broadening students' experience and economising on resources, and encouraged by DES policy on both grounds. The diversification of colleges of higher education out of teacher training into general higher education, following the 1972 White Paper, mostly adopted this approach, and patterns of modular programmes provided a substantial part of degree level work in CHEs and in polytechnics, particularly in humanities and social studies. The White Paper had also proposed the introduction of the Diploma in Higher Education (DipHE) as an important stage within the new structure, offering a qualification equivalent to the first two years of a first degree and providing students with the possibility of leaving HE at that point or changing tracks. In practice, the DipHE in most institutions came to be merely a qualification for dropping-out, though in some institutions it made feasible flexible entry and broader access and did constitute a fresh approach to higher education.

61 The policies of the 1972 White Paper were, however, found by the Government in the 1980s to have not produced the teacher quality which it sought. It preferred, particularly for secondary school teachers, a structure of first degrees topped off with a Postgraduate Certificate in Education and it preferred the students to have concentrated on the subjects which they would teach in schools. And it preferred BEds which were kept separate from other first degrees so as to concentrate on teacher training. It established the Council for the Accreditation of Teacher Education (CATE) to validate teacher training qualifications (See Appendix 2).

62 **National Advisory Body**

The work of the National Advisory Body (NAB) was primarily concerned with the allocation of funds to PSHE and with resolving its formulae for equitable distribution of limited finances (See **1.3** 54–65). These distributive mechanisms were bound to have a conservative effect on educational provision. However, NAB also sought to promote specific innovations and invited institutions to submit proposals for funding in 'special initiatives' to meet national needs. In 1987–88 these are in seven defined areas:

(i) Improvement of teacher supply in mathematics, physics and technology, including in particular the development of specially-designed initial and in-service teacher training courses;
(ii) Conversion courses to prepare students for entry to advanced courses in engineering and technology;
(iii) Postgraduate conversion courses in advanced manufacturing technology;
(iv) Pilot undergraduate and higher diploma courses in engineering design;
(v) Extension of research initiative from previous years;
(vi) Enhancement of technician staff;
(vii) Development of continuing education (PICKUP) courses.

For the second of these initiatives NAB set up the Higher Introductory Technology and Engineering Conversion Courses (HITECC) to encourage school-leavers without science qualifications and over-21 year-olds without A levels but with appropriate work experience or other qualification to join a one-year course which will lead to a degree or HND course in engineering and technology; HITECC students were eligible to receive grants from MSC under its Wider Opportunities Training Programme (See **1.7** 36).

63 **Adult and continuing education**

The further education system includes non-vocational adult education, a service offering education for leisure, time out-of-work and retirement and for personal development without recognised qualifications, for the most part, and without vocational goals – though the distinctions between vocational and non-vocational study could never be sharp and with high levels of unemployment are more blurred. The service is run by LEAs in collaboration with the 'responsible bodies', the Workers' Educational Association (WEA), university extramural departments and Welsh National Council of Young Men's Christian Associations. Within LEAs' own provision, non-vocational adult education is, variously, organised within FE colleges as separate institutions, such as evening institutes, and in some places combined with secondary education in 'community schools' (though that nomenclature in itself does not necessarily imply there is education for adults in the school). Course provision includes both traditional leisure pursuits and innovations in curricula for special needs, minority interests and personal development. Innovations include courses for Return to Study and Fresh Start and programmes of basic literacy and numeracy. The service develops through local initiatives on a course by course basis largely uncoordinated nationally except through professional networks and some limited national interventions. Thus the level and nature of the service is very different across the country. The general tendency has been for non-vocational adult education to be cut relatively more severely than other aspects of the education service, and the economic state of the service contrasts with its potential or aspirations: a body of thinking has developed on how the non-vocational adult education service could be the basis for 'lifelong' education, incorporating 'outreach' into the community and some degree of 'deschooling' and use of non-educational establishments. (See **1.6** 55–56.)

64 The National Institute of Adult Continuing Education, established in 1949, is the principal national advisory body, bringing together in its governing council local authorities associations, universities, voluntary organisations and other bodies. Under its aegis is the Adult Literacy and Basic Skills Unit (ALBSU) (which succeeded the Adult Literacy Unit established in 1978 which in turn succeeded the Adult Literacy Resource Agency established in 1975 to help LEAs and other agencies tackle problems of illiteracy) and the Unit for the Development of Adult Continuing Education (UDACE). (See **1.1** 34–36.)

65 Significant changes have taken place in recent years in relation to access by adults to higher education. Both the NAB and the UGC produced major reports on Continuing Education in 1984. A transbinary NAB/UGC Continuing Education Standing Committee has been established. The entry of non-traditional students into higher education is being increasingly encouraged and the number of school leavers is declining until the mid-1990s. Special Access Courses are being developed by HE and FE institutions to facilitate this process. Other routes into higher education and alternative modes of attendance are being promoted and schemes of credit transfer and the accreditation of prior learning are emerging. Major pieces of research have been or are being undertaken by the CNAA and the DES to assess the impact of Access students on HE institutions and to compare their performance with that of traditional students; most of the research to date demonstrates that non-standard students perform at least as well as their traditional counterparts (e.g. Bourner and Hamed 1987). (See **3.2** 7–10.)

EMPLOYMENT AND UNEMPLOYMENT

66 In 1982 the DES launched the Professional, Industrial and Commercial Updating Programme (PICKUP). The aim was to help colleges, polytechnics and universities to increase and improve the work they do in meeting adult training and updating needs. The main features are that the programme is: specifically vocational; for people in employment; updating, post-experience; collaborative between colleges and employers; short, part-time, flexible and cost-effective; self-financing. PICKUP acts as a catalyst for change. It does not pay directly for courses or training activities, though it makes grants to LEAs to coordinate and advance the work. PICKUP operates through regional agents, a wide range of projects on learning materials, staff development programmes for updating teachers and projects bringing together employers and trainers with shared funding with the MSC. The 1987 White Paper on *Higher Education: Meeting the Challenge* commended the approach promoted by PICKUP for 'continuing education'. (See **2.9** 32.)

67 The MSC (see below paragraphs 85–86 and **1.7**) has two main adult training programmes – the Job Training Programme (JTP) directed to meeting local and national labour market requirements and the Wider Opportunities Training Programme (WOTP) aimed at helping unemployed people improve their basic skills and retain employability. There are several schemes within the programmes, including the Job Training Scheme, which replaces TOPS (See **1.7** 33–35). The WOTP has replaced the TOPS Preparatory Courses and mainly provides part-time opportunities for the unemployed on a fees-only basis with trainees remaining on benefit under the 21 hours rule (See **1.7** 31–36). Further opportunities for adult training are provided through the Community Programme (See **1.7** 46–57), the Voluntary Projects Programme (See **1.7** 59), and the Restart Programme (See **1.7** 41–42) which is part of the new in-depth interview and counselling scheme for the long-term unemployed. Restart involves the provision of short one week Restart courses at local colleges, adult education centres, or with other training providers. Information about training and employment opportunities are also to be made available through Training Access Points (TAPs). These, assuming they get beyond the current feasibility study, will be databases which can be accessed by the public through job centres, libraries, and even shops and supermarkets.

68 The College-Employer Links Projects (CELP) began in 1984 with a pilot scheme in Hertfordshire and plans for eight further projects. The aim was to review and improve the relevance of NAFE to the needs of industry and commerce. Projects are set these tasks : to test the adequacy of links between FE colleges and the world of employment; to identify good practice and problem areas; to disseminate good practice; to develop and implement programmes for dealing with the problems. Hence, investigations concern employers' needs, liaison machinery, structure of courses and qualifications, and deployment of staff, equipment and other resources.

CURRICULUM DEVELOPMENT AGENCIES

69 **Schools Council for Curriculum and Examinations**

The Schools Council for Curriculum and Examinations was an independent body established in 1964 to promote education by research and by reviewing curricular methods and examinations in schools. It was subject to several reviews during its 20-year existence. The last was carried out by Nancy Trenaman in 1981 at the request of the Secretary of State for Education and Science. Her report emphasised the key role played by the Schools Council and recommended that it should continue its work, albeit with some organisational changes. The overwhelming majority of the submissions to Trenaman supported a continuation of the Council's work. However, in April 1982, to the dismay of the education world, the Secretary of State for Education and Science announced the winding up of the Schools Council and its replacement with two separate bodies, the covering curriculum development and one covering examinations. In spite of protests that it was educationally unsound to separate examinations from curriculum planning, the Schools Council formally closed in March 1984.

70 **The School Curriculum Development Committee**

The School Curriculum Development Committee (SCDC) was set up in December 1983 with a budget of over £2m provided equally by the local education authorities (under section 56 (9) of the Local Government Planning and

Land Act 1980) and the DES. Its main role is to support curriculum development relevant to the needs of schools in England and Wales. SCDC has a separate committee for Wales. It is empowered to co-operate and exchange information and ideas with a wide range of bodies including further education. The Committee is made up of representatives from local authority associations, industry and the teaching profession. Teacher unions and other trade unions are not directly represented.

71 SCDC has worked closely with FEU in encouraging increased participation of FE institutions in TVEI pilot schemes and in evaluating the CPVE pilot programmes. SCDC representatives act in an advisory role and undertake joint projects and publications. They also serve on other national bodies involved in curriculum development including FEU, the Joint Board for Pre-Vocational Education, MSC bodies and subject associations. By these means SCDC keeps close links with what is happening in FE. SCDC projects with relevance to the FE sector include career development of girls and young women, equal opportunities in education, and the School Curriculum Industry Partnership.

72 **Secondary Examinations Council**

The Secondary Examinations Council (SEC) held its first meeting in May 1983. It was set up to promote involvements in the systems of examination and assessment in England and Wales designed principally for pupils in secondary education. The particular functions in the Council are:

(i) With regard to the activities of the GCE and CSE boards: to ensure that syllabuses and procedures for assessment at 16+ are in accordance with the national criteria; to approve new A level syllabuses and revisions to existing syllabuses; to monitor the comparability of standards at both 16+ and 18+ examinations.

(ii) To advise the Secretaries of State on the validity of national criteria for examinations at 16+.

73 The Council's members, appointed by the Secretary of State after consultation with the interests involved, cover industry, education, examining bodies and the local authority associations, but teachers are appointed rather than nominated by teacher unions.

74 In its first years, SEC oversaw a number of key initiatives. The reform of examinations at 16 (the GCSE) has been a high priority, and SEC has set up GCSE subject committees to advise it on the implementation of the national criteria. The major task for these committees will be the approval of Mode 1 syllabuses, and the monitoring of GCSE examinations.

75 On the new or amended A levels the Council has established twelve 18+ committees charged with making reports and recommendations to Council on existing and proposed A level examinations administered by GCE boards. Any new or amended syllabus at A level is given detailed attention by the relevant subject committee, which then recommends to the Examinations Committee of the Council whether the syllabus merits approval or whether further work is needed to make it acceptable.

76 SEC is also undertaking development work on the Advanced Supplementary (AS) level examinations announced in the March 1985 White Paper *Better Schools*.

77 **The Further Education Unit (FEU)**

The FEU is an advisory, intelligence and development body for further education in the United Kingdom. It was set up within the Department of Education and Science (DES) in 1977 as the Further Education Curriculum Review and Development Unit, but adopted its present title in January 1983 when it became a limited company independent of, but still funded by, the DES.

78 The objects for which the unit is established are to promote, encourage and develop the efficient provision of further education in the United Kingdom and for that purpose:

(i) To review and evaluate the range of existing further education curricula and programmes and to identify overlap, duplication, deficiencies and inconsistencies therein;

(ii) To determine priorites for action to improve the provision of further education and to make recommendations as to how such improvements can be effected;

(iii) To carry out studies in further education and to support the development of further education curricula and to contribute to the evaluation of initiatives in further education;

(iv) To disseminate and publish information about recommendations for and experiments and developments in further education.

79 The Unit has its own Board of Management, comprising representatives of teachers, employers' organisations, local and national education authorities, the Manpower Services Commission, examining bodies and the DES, including Her Majesty's Inspectorate.

80 While the Unit's activities concentrated on prevocational education in its early years, the range now also includes: mainstream vocational FE; adult education and training; special needs; curriculum development for a multicultural society; FE management and marketing; curriculum evaluation, innovation and change; new technology. Under the terms of its remit, FEU also accepts commissions from other organisations in relevant areas of work. Such work includes a programme of curriculum development projects forming part of the DES Professional Industrial and Commercial Updating (PICKUP) programme (See above paragraph 66). FEU also manages the network of PICKUP regional development agents. The DES also commissions the Unit to undertake curriculum development as part of its REPLAN programme for the adult unemployed.

81 Much of the FEU's work takes the form of research and development projects. Some 400 have so far been initiated and many have resulted in project reports, staff development manuals or occasional papers, mostly published by FEU and offered to the FE system at no charge. Projects are chiefly carried out in FHE institutions, but sometimes by other educational bodies, or by consultants. The Unit supports a significant publishing programme, issuing some 40 major titles per year, some published commercially in partnership with Longman Group UK Ltd.

82 The future of the FEU was reviewed in 1986 by the DES and in the early Spring of 1987 its existence as a separate entity enjoying a measure of functional independence was confirmed. Geoff Stanton was appointed Chief Executive of the Unit following the retirement of Jack Mansell.

83 **Further Education Staff College**
The Further Education Staff College, now known by its acronym FESC rather than as 'Coombe Lodge' (after one of its buildings), is the national management training centre for the post-compulsory education sector. It is based in two buildings located at Blagdon in the Country of Avon, although courses organised by FESC are increasingly sited at various places elsewhere in the country. FESC is funded by local authorities throughout the United Kingdom and is therefore committed to provide courses, conferences and consultancy services in each of the different FE systems which make up the UK. As with the Further Education Unit, FESC reviewed its activities and in 1986 published a joint statement setting out the respective missions of both. At time of writing the governing body of FESC is in the process of considering the extent to which the college should seek to discharge a role in AFE if the responsibility for the service is removed from the local authorities (See **1.1** Appendix 1).

84 In recent years the activities of FESC have moved in the direction of a greater involvement in research and development work notably from Government Departments and the MSC. In 1986 R & D and consultancy accounted for 30% of all income. Approximately half the income of the college is derived from the block grant funding to LEAs, thus enabling lower and, in effect, subsidised course fees to participants in the college's programme.

85 **MSC**
The main impact of the Manpower Services Commission (MSC) on curriculum development, other than through TVEI, has been through the indirect use of resources to stimulate and generally influence behaviour in colleges. It laid down a set of objectives for itself and the whole system in its consultative document *A New Training Initiative* (1981). (See **1.7** in particular 72–73 and **3.2** 17.)

86 A notable example of the MSC's approach has been the funding by MSC of the Responsive College Project (RCP), launched in 1985 and involving LEAs in England, Wales and Scotland. The Project is administered by staff seconded from the FE Staff College and is guided by a National Steering Group consisting of industrial, professional and LEA representatives. Running in a somewhat parallel manner to the RCP are a number of projects initiated by the MSC, involving Colleges and LEAs and using resources 'held back' from the switch of RSG money transferred under the arrangements announced in the White Paper, *Training for Jobs*, in 1984. These projects resemble RCP in that they are based upon the unsuccessful bids by LEAs for inclusion in RCP. Use of the central reserve (or 'hold-back') money by MSC has reflected a desire by the Commission that it should be able to stimulate a number of curricular-related activities in colleges beyond those set out in individual LEA development plans.

87 **Commentary**
The focus in this section has been mainly descriptive and has aimed at providing a concise account of the curriculum as it was half-way through 1987. One difficulty which recurs throughout the text is that the pace of change is such that any such descriptive account will be overtaken by events. A key illustration of this is the uncertainty of how far and at what speed the newly established National Council for Vocational Qualifications would develop during 1987. In order to achieve an effective position statement of the curriculum in FHE it has been necessary to include a significant amount of material on the

structure within which curriculum development is largely generated. That is another reason why the prospect of uncertainty as to the changing nature of bodies such as the NCVQ or FEU directly affects the content of what is covered by the institutions of FHE.

88 The main and as yet unresolved tension within the section is clearly between the contrasting and perhaps competing traditions of the schools-academic sector and that of the FE-vocational world. When the 1980 edition of *College Administration* was written this tension was of course apparent but in those pre-TVEI and pre-RVQ days it was not as sharp as today. Nor was it the case that the vocationalist ethos of the FE world had penetrated the compulsory school sector as was first dramatically achieved by government fiat in 1982 when TVEI was launched. The quieter days of the old Schools Council Industry Project, when curriculum change was assumed to be predicated on the gradual achievement of consensus among *all* the partners involved, now seems a long time ago. Finally the sharpening of the demographic impact on the 16–19 age group may stifle and dampen down the urgency with which youth unemployment has been treated and also seems to intensify the competition between the two sectors.

89 Whether or not the tension between the two traditions come closer to resolution will largely depend upon political and economic forces mainly outside the organisations and agencies described in this chapter or, in the case of the MSC, elsewhere in this book. However, it seems clear that given the rapidity of curriculum development in the last five years at least, both the names and the remits of those described here now, will undergo significant transformation.

NOTE

1 NATFHE set out concerns of the detail of the NVQ Framework, which it welcomed, in *The NVQ Framework and NATFHE's Response*, Briefing Document 12/87.

ANNEX 1

THE NATIONAL COUNCIL FOR VOCATIONAL QUALIFICATIONS

Terms of Reference
Secure standards of occupational competence and to ensure that vocational qualifications are based upon them
Design and implement a new national framework for vocational qualifications
Approve bodies making accredited awards
Obtain comprehensive coverage of an occupational section
Set up effective liaison with bodies awarding vocational qualifications
Establish a national data base for vocational qualifications
Undertake or arrange to be undertaken research and
Development to discharge these functions
Promote vocational education, training and qualifications.

Membership
Chair: H. G.(Oscar) de Ville, CBE
Derek Birley, Vice Chancellor, University of Ulster
Clive Brain Principal, Swindon College

Gerald Brinsdon, Director of Education, Sandwell, MBC
Robert Cant, Chair, Staffordshire County Council Education Committee
Harvey Davies, Executive Director Administration, British Aerospace
Ken Graham, Deputy General Secretary, TUC
Sheila Green, Group Head of Personnel, Unigate
Geoffrey Hall, Director, Brighton Polytechnic
William Hughes, Chair, Grampian Holdings
Peter Reay, Group Personnel, Director, Cadbury Schweppes
Ms Steve Shirley, Group Managing Director, F. International
Owen Thomas, Director of Personnel, J. Sainsbury
John Walkerdine, Director, Centre for Educational Resources for Construction Industry.

Chief Executive
Professor Peter Thompson

Address
222 Euston Road, London NW1 2BZ; Tel 01-387 9898

APPENDIX 1

EQUAL OPPORTUNITIES

1 There has been marked growth in organisational responses to racism and sexism by LEAs, maintained and voluntary colleges and in NATFHE, the National Union of Teachers (NUT) and National Union of Students (NUS). This has occurred alongside a growth in published research, policy guidance and practical advice. A full review would be impossible here but some indication of developments is important (See **1.2** Appendices 2 and 3).

2 *Anti-racism*
A growing proportion of LEAs and individual institutions describe themselves in advertisements and prospectuses as 'equal opportunity employers', and it has become common to see either staff advertisements or student recruitment literature encouraging application from members of ethnic minorities. In many cases, employers have limited policy statements dealing with advertisements but few elaborated policies beyond this.

3 There are, however, an increasing number of metropolitan LEAs which have produced policy statements, and these are often replicated in appropriate form in individual institutions. Although varied in content, most expound policy on recruitment, interview, training, promotion, grievance (in which they reflect Section 2.3 of the Scheme of Conditions of Service in FE which recommends recourse to the agreed grievance procedure where an employee considers he or she is being discriminated against), and discipline. Some deal with the curriculum offer and the content of teaching materials and text books where racial stereotyping may appear.

4 Not all authorities with policy statements have structures to deliver policies or means of monitoring delivery. In an increasing number arrangements have been made either by placing specialist staff in all the main operational departments or by providing a specialist unit to advise the operational departments. Where arrangements exist, reports from officers to authorities reflect a higher level of monitoring in respect of objectives, although there can be practical problems in ethnic monitoring and developmental work is being undertaken to meet anxieties. HM Inspectorate has a growing role in the development of equal opportunities access, multicultural and, more recently, anti-racist curricula.

5 An FEU (1985a) study showed 'a serious information gap between college and communities, and . . . this constitutes for many black people the major barrier to their take-

up of FE'. It pointed to the need for a 'public relations exercise to create better understanding of the nature of further education' and for intensive marketing. But it also argued that increased take-up by ethnic minority groups would imply: rethinking of current provisions; consultation over course design; and reallocation of resources. There was, the report said, evidence of apparent discrimination in, for example, concentrations of ethnic groups in particular subject areas and their absence from others, though it did not reach conclusions about how far this was attributable to young people's preference or to institutional racism. In November 1986 the FEU, commissioned by the MSC, began an exploration of integrating the review and development of multicultural curriculum into the planning by LEAs and MSC of work-related NAFE. (See also Gibson 1986 and FEU 1987.)

6 The Commission for Racial Equality (CRE) has assisted colleges to draw up equal opportunities policies and has published reports on youth and employment issues (see CRE 1987). It became concerned about the possibility of discrimination in admissions to HE. It also undertook a survey of equal opportunities policies in HE. The CRE endeavoured to keep in local authorities' minds their duty under Section 71 of the Race Relations Act 1976 to make arrangements to ensure that their functions are carried out with due regard for the need to eliminate racism and to promote equality of opportunity and good relations between people of different racial groups. Some initiatives, TVEI and CPVE, have made a limited amount of use of equal opportunities objectives in course and curriculum stuctures.

7 *Anti-sexism*

Some LEAs and institutions have given a high profile to policy initiatives for anti-sexism and have set timetables for implementation. Some policies tend to emphasise aspects of the content and design of courses, the production of anti-sexist and elimination of sexist materials and the allocation of responsibilities for staff and course development. Others have concentrated on employment and student recruitment practices, on the procedures which might discriminate in staff recruitment, retention and promotion, and on student numbers, focusing on managerial endeavour to eliminate discrimination. However, it remains hard to judge progress in that relatively little monitoring takes place. It may be that monitoring has been made harder by the lack of distinction made between issues upon which LEAs can effectively intervene, those which they may more marginally influence and those upon which their impact can be only small or non-existent. (See also **1.8** 9–10 and 20.)

8 Some national initiatives, TVEI and CPVE, have made a limited amount of use of equal opportunities objectives in course and curriculum structures. Monitoring was designed into, for example, the pilot year of the Certificate of Pre-Vocational Education (CPVE) which included evaluation criteria involving gender, race and perceived ability. However, no piloted LEA stated that gender issues had been a factor in planning CPVE schemes and that they now monitored the issue in their internal evaluations. None acknowledged any discrimination, or could provide information on incidents of discrimination. In later follow-up studies it was discovered that lecturers and students were concerned about the curriculum, teaching and learning strategies, job recruitment, access to vocational options, to work experience, on counselling, guidance and student support, and on the recruitment and development of lecturers (FEU 1985b). A broadly similar picture exists for the Technical and Vocational Education Initiative (TVEI) where patterns of option choices within courses remain traditional and where options tend to lead to stereotypical gendered choices.

9 A systematic process of reappraisal of curriculum content and delivery and of college ethos and style was proposed by the FEU (1985b) to develop equal opportunities. Its ideas included: the preference for a negotiated/learner-centred curriculum over a rigid, predetermined syllabus; conversion modules; 'women only' bridging course; women's studies for consciousness-raising; timetabling to avoid reinforcing stereotypical choice. It called for a variety of procedures to enable greater flexibility in careers and learning programmes, including ways of accrediting prior learning and experimental learning. The report also commented on the 'invisibility' of women in the management of FE –

the percentage of women among principals, vice-principals and heads of department has declined in recent years.

APPENDIX 2

TEACHER TRAINING

Initial teacher training (ITT) has always held a unique position within higher education as far as planning is concerned. In the early 1980s the Secretary of State had statutory responsibility for four aspects of ITT planning:
(i) Approval of specific courses
(ii) Professional registration, i.e. the award of qualified teacher status (QTS)
(iii) Manpower planning, i.e. the number of qualified people produced, and
(iv) Content of courses
Prior to 1985 the Secretary of State exercised these functions through a variety of agencies which offered advice. Much of the detailed work in the field of manpower planning was undertaken by DES officials. They would offer advice on detailed institutional allocation of places, whereas advice on the overall size and shape of the training system would normally be tendered by a national advisory committee. (In the 1980s, this was the Advisory Committee on the Supply and Education of Teachers ACSET.) The validating bodies and HMI were the main sources of advice and/or decision on course content and course approval.

Manpower Planning
The Secretary of State took final decisions on overall teacher supply in March 1985 and then invited the National Advisory Body (NAB) (See **1.3** 54–65) to offer advice on the distribution of places to training institutions for 1986/89 and to do so by Summer 1985. NAB had already assumed a 'formal' responsibility for planning teacher education, including in-service provision, but this was the first occasion on which it was asked to undertake a major review of training places. NAB submitted its advice in Summer 1985 but the advice did not find favour with the current Secretary of State, Sir Keith Joseph, who felt insufficient rationalisation was proposed. He therefore announced an interim allocation of places for 1986 (to allow colleges to proceed with recruitment from the Autumn) and in October asked NAB to submit revised advice for 1987/9 by May 1986. He also indicated that should the NAB decline to do so he would return the planning of ITT to the DES and instruct his officials to set the process in hand immediately.
The problems with ITT planning stemmed in part from the different time constraints then affecting the planning process. When NAB was first formed, ITT was not specifically included in its planning brief and the time-cycle for the major NAB planning exercise, undertaken every three years, was not consistent with the three year planning cycle for ITT. When NAB was asked in 1985 to undertake a major ITT allocation, this was again out of phase with its three year planning cycle for all other courses, including in-service training.
The problems were exacerbated in the mid-1980s by the fact that major increases in the number of ITT places were needed and many in NAB, faced with declining resources for the system as a whole, felt that the Secretary of State was involving them in a pre-emptive planning process which favoured teacher education at the expense of places on other courses and programmes. This feeling was compounded when it became known that the University Grant Committee (UGC) had refused to allocate teacher education places for more than a single year (1986) because it was not prepared to commit the university system to increasing places until the resources for 1987 and beyond were made known.
In the event the NAB Committee declined to undertake a new round of planning consultations and therefore allocations for 1987/89 were made following advice from the DES. With the decision to wind up NAB from Summer 1988 (See **1.1** Appendix 1), the responsibility for planning ITT places remains with the DES. Whether it will transfer to the new Polytechnics and Colleges Funding Council (PCFC) is unclear at time of writing.

Approval of Courses

In 1984 the Secretary of State announced the establishment of a new body, the Council for the Accreditation of Teacher Education (CATE) to advise the Secretaries of State for Education and Science and for Wales on the approval of ITT courses both in the university and public sector. It was intended to review all existing and proposed courses of training leading to the award of QTS, the review to be completed within three to four years. The Council was given operational guidelines and criteria for course approval in DES Circular 3/84 (Welsh Office Circular 21/84) *Initial Teacher Training: Approval of Courses*. The timescale for the completion of the review has proved over-optimistic but the first courses to be approved were notified in 1986. Several institutions were required to make changes and resubmit courses for approval. By Autumn 1987 no courses had failed absolutely to be given approval though many are still in the process of review. It is not known if the CATE machinery will continue in existence after a full review cycle has been completed.

3.2 ADMISSIONS AND ACCESS

1 Since the mid-1970s there have been major developments in individual access routes into public sector further and higher education. Whilst it remains the case that a great many courses are entered by conventional patterns of qualification (or by no qualification), a number of developments have occurred. The traditional standards of qualification for entry to courses continue to underpin the grading standards by which courses in FHE are categorised under the Grading of Courses system (See **2.2**), but more recent developments owe their origin to three major forces. First, increased student applications and admissions in higher education, together with the planning system for allocating student numbers and resources, have meant that greater efforts have been put into the planning of access itself. Second, there has been a growing effort to encourage non-traditionally qualified students into higher education by routes other than GCE A levels, particularly where local education authorities are concerned by under-representation of women and members of ethnic minorities on courses. Third, there are new pressures on people between 16 and 18 to enter some form of education or training, and these pressures seem certain to have impact on methods of allocating individuals to courses.

2 **The Polytechnics Central Admissions System (PCAS)**
The Polytechnics Central Admissions System (PCAS) mechanism was established in 1984 to provide a service broadly similar to that provided for the universities by the University Central Council on Admissions (UCCA). Originally established by the Committee of Directors of Polytechnics (CDP) on a Department of Education and Science grant of £210,000, it was intended to deal with increasing numbers of prospective students, a proportion of whom withdraw shortly before courses start. This tendency was regarded as unfair to both applicants and institutions. The polytechnics, also, operated widely differing admissions procedures, which made it difficult for prospective students, careers advisers, schools and FE colleges to judge how best to proceed.

3 The PCAS arrangements are compatible with those of the UCCA, and applicants may submit forms through both in the same application cycle. PCAS covers all full-time and sandwich first degree and Diploma of Higher Education (DipHE) in polytechnics other than those leading to qualifications in Art and Design. The system imposes some order on this area of activity but does not promote or recruit on behalf of polytechnics. Applicants complete single application forms in the autumn of the year before proposed entry and return them to PCAS who, in turn, sends them to the polytechnics named by the applicant. Up to four courses may be selected. No order of preference is sought. Polytechnics normally make their decisions by 31 March for applications received before 15 December, and not later than 30 April for applications received by 31 March.

4 Polytechnics make either conditional or unconditional offers or reject candidates. Conditionality is usually specified in terms of examination results. Once a place is offered, a commitment is made unless the applicant declines the offer or does not satisfy the conditions. Applicants are asked to reply to the polytechnic through PCAS within a fortnight, and by firmly accepting, applicants effectively declare the offer to be the preferred offer received or which may be received. The offer may not be subsequently declined. If unconditional, it is assumed that is the polytechnic to which the applicant will go. If

conditional, the outcome is resolved by receipt by the institution of evidence that the condition is fulfilled. In fact, applicants may hold two offers at once but must indicate a binding preference by 15 May at the latest – the second offer becoming 'insurance' against failure to fulfil what may be tougher conditions attached to the preferred offer.

5 PCAS also invites applicants who are without offers to choose courses at up to four polytechnics in which they are interested. PCAS forwards this further application to one of them on the basis of information that the institution is considering further applications, and it may also send the application to any other polytechnic which is making further considerations. This is known as the Continuing Application Procedure (CAP). In September a clearing scheme comes into operation, and applicants with suitable qualifications but no place are put into contact with institutions with places. Applicants receive details of the September Clearing Scheme in the previous June.

6 **Art and Design Admissions Registry (ADAR)**

The Art and Design Admissions Registry continues to operate outside the PCAS machinery. Practitioners in the field of art and design argued that ADAR was very efficient and had a proven track record in handling access to such courses. Despite the use of the UCCA computer, PCAS does not seem likely to meet the same standards of efficiency. Given the initial focus on polytechnics, it was argued that PCAS was unable to deal with non-polytechnic and non-degree courses. As PCAS enlarges its scope of operation, these objections look to be less viable but no change is envisaged for a number of years to come. Applicants apply, paying a £5 fee, for two courses among the 58 BA courses and similar number of Higher Diploma courses. If unsuccessful in both of these, they may be placed in a pool system should they so wish.

7 **Access or Preparatory Courses**

The term 'access' to denote an alternative route into a degree or diploma course first appeared in about 1977. In 1978 the Department of Education and Science sought the assistance of eight authorities in piloting courses with an emphasis of drawing members of ethnic minorities into higher education. The original intention was directed to but not exclusively concerned with recruitment to initial teacher training. A set of access courses were evaluated by the Director of the DES Evaluation Project in 1984 (Millins 1984). As a method of enhancing access, such courses have now become central to aspects of National Advisory Body (NAB 1984a) thinking.

8 Access courses have tended to concentrate outside science and technology, although this is changing gradually. The curriculum offered almost wholly within further education colleges is determined by the 'receiving' institutions although there is much negotiation of the curriculum offer between the colleges involved in practice. In many schemes it is possible to find patterns based on traditional academic excellence tightly defined in disciplinary terms and examined on the basis of acquired knowledge, combined with student centred processes and skills. By July 1984, the CNAA were in a position to publish an entire booklet listing 90 existing or proposed courses (CNAA 1984) in over 50 LEAs. A great deal of development has been encouraged by the Forum for Access Studies (FAST) and through the channels of its journal 'Forum', based at the Roehampton Institute of Higher Education.

9 In December 1986, the Centre for Access Studies at Roehampton published a study (Yates and Davies 1986) funded by the Nuffield Foundation making its final report on the progress of the students originally described in 1978 by the DES as those 'who have valuable experience but lack the qualifications required and who have special needs which cannot be met by existing educational arrangements'. It followed the Millins Report (1984) and sought to show how access students did in higher education in terms of completion of courses, differential performance in different kinds of course, and end qualification. Broadly, and subject to sampling criteria, three-quarters of access students were shown to be proceeding to or having completed higher education courses with a qualification, about one-fifth withdrawing either because of failure in assessed work or for other reasons. Women fare relatively better than men. The best completion rates were in vocational subjects or social studies and the least satisfactory rates in technology and engineering sciences. The study emphasises some of the practical (often family reasons) for those who deferred study during their course, showing the very reason, perhaps, that access is such a valuable mode of entry. In research terms, there is little as yet that shows the position of ethnic minority students.

10 Strategies for promoting access courses, establishing and maintaining quality, and providing an element of 'social engineering' by promoting positive action for groups traditionally denied a route into higher education, have been under constant review since 1978. These courses were viewed as giving substance to the Robbins (1963) principle which argued that those who were qualified for, could benefit from and wished to undertake higher education courses should do so, by slightly modifying that principle to assert that such courses should be available for all those who could benefit from them and wished to do so (NAB 1984b). The Secretary of NAB urgently stressed that strategies require mechanisms to accomplish them and identified

(i) General advice – a weak but environment-promoting mechanism;
(ii) Identification and promulgation of good practice – a mechanism fostering creative emulation;
(iii) Planning intervention – which in either general or interventionist form takes a decisive step beyond simply having a 'policy'; and
(iv) Sending financial 'signals' – which can have the result of encouraging specific allocation of resources to objectives particularly when there are overall cuts.

11 **The Central Register and Clearing House (CRCH)**

The Clearing House started nearly 50 years ago under the auspices of the Association of Teachers in Colleges and Departments of Education (ATCDE), one of the two organisations that formed NATFHE. It was a response to the need in the 1920s to rationalise the system by which students applied to individual teacher training institutions, which for their part offered places without knowing what one another were doing. Initially, the principals devised a system so that admissions were considered one college at a time. The ATCDE were then asked to administer the scheme from their offices, and the CRCH was formed. Two governing principles guided the operation of the CRCH: applicants had a right to choose the colleges they wished to apply to; and colleges had a right to select. Starting with limited numbers of both applicants and colleges, the scheme grew to embrace over 190 institutions and 23,000 applicants (1960). In the early 1960s, the CRCH was asked by the Conference of Heads of University Departments of Education to run a central admissions procedure for those seeking entry to postgraduate courses of teacher training in university departments. In 1961 the Graduate Teacher Training Registry (GTTR) was formed to facilitate recruitment to all teacher training postgraduate courses in England and Wales. Such was the pattern of growth that by 1962 the ATCDE concluded that these bodies justified existence as independent corporations with appropriate articles of incorporation and status as own profit-making private companies. The Central Register and Clearing House Ltd was formed, the shares largely owned by ATCDE (later NATFHE) nominees. Members of the Council of Management are drawn widely from the profession.

12 The CRCH Registry deals with applications for entry to undergraduate and some specialist one year certificate courses at institutes and colleges of higher education or polytechnic departments of education in England and Wales. Additionally, it deals with other undergraduate courses and the DipHE offered in institutes and colleges of higher education. Thus, it provides a wide field of selection and eases the process of application for individuals. There is an application form upon which applicants can initially specify three institutions. The form is submitted from 1 September in the year prior to entry to a course. Although there is no formal closing date, it is advisable to apply early and certainly not later than 15 December. The three institutions receive the application simultaneously. Decisions are sent to the applicants by the CRCH as soon as all decisions have been received. One offer may be accepted and another held in reserve if, for example, it has less stringent conditions attached to it. Applicants who receive no offers initially are invited by the CRCH to have their application sent to other institutions by whom they would like to be considered.

13 The Graduate Teacher Training Registry (GTTR) deals with applications for one year postgraduate courses in initial teacher training offered by university or polytechnic departments of education or institutes or colleges of higher education in England and Wales. Its purposes are broadly the same as the CRCH. The application forms (accompanied by a booklet) are issued on 1 September in the year preceding application and allow nomination of four institutions. The forms are circulated in the order of the institutions named until all possibilities are exhausted, applicants being informed throughout.

14 **Initial Teacher Training**

From 1980 the non-graduate Certificate of Education was replaced by degree or postgraduate courses, to which further requirements were added in 1984 to the effect that there must also be demonstrable competences in English language understanding and use, and in mathematics. As shown above, certain access courses also provide entry to courses of initial teacher training[1]. Certain additional criteria have been developed over the years so that judgements can be made about the likely medical suitability of candidates for posts in schools. Thus, before admission, medical examinations are required and the initial onus fall on the College or Department of Education when deciding whether or not to accept an applicant for training. The Secretary of State does not become concerned until individuals complete their training and wish to take up a teaching appointment. College medical officers are, however, given the links between taking up the college place and likely occupation, advised to consult the DES (or Welsh Office) before arriving at decisions in instances of uncertainty about either suitability for training or ultimate teaching employment. This is especially advised with applicants with histories of epilepsy, psychiatric disorder, or with particular physical, visual or aural disabilities which might affect efficiency as a teacher. A full medical report, including a specialist's report, should be sent in confidence to the Medical Adviser to the Department in such circumstances. When special reports are considered necessary by the examining medical officer or by a candidate appealing against a decision of a potential training institution, they should be obtained from a specialist selected by the candidate (normally on the advice of the family physician) and approved by the examining medical officer. It is always as well to take all these steps in good time. It is possible that unsuitability at one college does not disbar acceptance elsewhere and adequate time is needed to clarify such possibilities with the permission of the candidate.

15 The arrangements for access for trainee school teachers do not affect the provision of certificate courses for the training of further education teachers.

16 The Secretary of State for Education has jurisdiction over instances of misconduct of teachers. If a teacher is convicted of a criminal offence, the DES may refuse to allow her or him to continue in teaching employment. In arriving at a decision, the DES may require medical reports. The teacher is entitled to have written reasons for the decision and there exists a right of appeal heard before a senior official of the Department, according to the Education (Teachers) Regulations 1982 and Administrative Memorandum 4/87, *Misconduct of Teachers*. These powers also extend to persons proposing to become teachers, for if such persons have behaved in ways which would render them liable to exclusion from the teaching profession in a school, then they should not be admitted to training. When doubts exist on this issue, it should be discussed in confidence with the DES.

17 **Adult Training Access**

In 1984-85 the Manpower Services Commission (MSC) phased out the Training Opportunities Scheme (TOPS) to replace it with a Job Training Scheme to cover occupational training for unemployed people (See **1.7** 33–35). It was said to be designed to focus more closely on meeting the known needs of employers and employees (MSC *Annual Report 1984-85*) and formed part of the Adult Training Strategy. TOPS, in its last year, enrolled 87,690 people of whom 75,380 completed training in colleges of further education, skillcentres, commercial training establishments and on employers' premises. (An account of TOPS strategy is to be found in the 1980 edition of *College Administration.*) The Adult Training Strategy has been designed, according to the MSC's Corporate Plan, to encourage employers and others to value adult training more highly and help in its development. Access has, therefore, to be flexible, efficient and responsive to client needs. Close collaboration is needed with education authorities and with the Open Tech programme. The MSC has also contributed to the DES REPLAN programme to develop educational support for the adult unemployed. Thus, schemes are fostered where access is intended to be easy and where what are said to be rigidities in delivery of the curriculum are overcome. In general, the strategies for fostering access are closely related to the mode of training adopted and the objectives which are expressed as the rationale for the scheme. It is said by some critics of this approach that many of the values of traditional adult and continuing education make a more viable and fulfilling contribution. The argument is supported by the contention that the traditional forms were based upon readily available access.

18 **Further Education Information Service**
The Further Education Information Service (FEIS) is operated by the DES local FEIS advisory officers to inform intending students about the courses available in the further education system. It was introduced to overcome difficulties in the spread of information across institutional boundaries. The service is operational in August and September when schools are closed. LEAs are asked to supply the names and addresses of local advisory officers to all the secondary schools in their areas as early as possible so that publicity can be provided and school leavers will know how to use the service before they have left school. A network of addresses is centrally maintained so as to assist students who may move to new areas.

19 **Issues about access**
Whilst policies on access to the variety of courses and institutions necessarily vary considerably, the practice almost always involves central and departmental procedures in institutions to ensure that all features of the process are covered. There should be procedures on publicity, and colleges should be able to provide clear information on courses and procedures (See **2.11**). Information on grants, entry exemptions and other material data are required by intending students; clear guidance is needed on enrolment procedures; detailed course information should be supplied; and the provision of information on college and student union facilities (See **3.4** and **3.5**) is generally regarded as good practice. (It should be noted that it is not unknown for disaffected students to resort to litigation.) In the background to all these activities, the establishment of access mechanisms should be supported by effective record-keeping. All such matters may be appropriately monitored by the academic board and by committees liasing with student unions. External liaison with validating bodies and the regional advisory councils (See **1.6** 65–66) is essential so that accurate information on access – recruitment and admission – flows in both directions. The introduction of common formats for recording data has made these processes both easier and more bureaucratic.

20 These activities make the role of the academic admissions tutors, the registry and other administrative staff all the more important. In institutions, other than the smallest, staff specifically allocated should be at institutional and departmental levels, coordinated by a senior member of academic staff. Such coordination includes the calling of appropriate meetings, setting key timetables, establishing written procedures, and training all staff involved. The functions should be integrated with the welfare, counselling and careers advisory services (See **3.4**) as well as the student union (See **3.5**). Where admissions policies are designed to afford greater opportunity to disadvantaged groups, these objectives should be widely understood and accepted by all staff involved, and they should be trained in the objectives and operational elements.

21 However, not all courses or institutions have this degree of formality in their operation. Where students are contacted in their home or working environments or are drawn into study by outreach workers, it may be inappropriate to discuss access procedures in the ways suggested above. Indeed, the concept of a 'course' is not always an appropriate term. In more informal circumstances, access tends to be thought of as enabling the individual to gain and retain contact with the education or training process.

22 **Other 'clearing houses'**
A number of professional bodies other than those mentioned above deal with access to particular professional courses which provide the membership of, or qualifications for membership of, professional groups (See Addresses below).

NOTE

1 For example, North Hulme Community Education Centre runs an Access Course linked to the Manchester Polytechnic BEA.

ADDRESSES

The Art and Design Admissions Registry (ADAR), Penn Hse, 9 Broad St, Hereford HR4 9AP
The British Association of Occupational Therapists (Occupational Therapy Training Clearing House), 20 Rede Pl, London W2 4TV
The Central Council for Education and Training in Social Work, Derbyshire Hse, St Chad's St, London WC1H 8AD
The Central Register and Clearing House (CRCH), 3 Crawford Place, London W1H 2BN
The Chartered Society of Physiotherapy, 14 Bedford Row, London WC1R 4ED
The Graduate Teacher Training Registry (GTTR), 3 Crawford Place, London W1H 2BN
The Polytechnics Central Admissions System, PO Box 67, Cheltenham, Gloucestershire GL50 3AP
Roehampton Institute of Higher Education, Southlands College, Wimbledon Parkside, London SW19 5NN
The Royal Institute of Chartered Surveyors, 12 St George St, London SW1
The Society of London Chartered Accountants (Students Induction Service), 18 Bedford Sq, London WC1

FURTHER READING

The principal directories setting out courses and access requirements are:
The Directory of First Degree Courses CNAA, 244-54 Gray's Inn Rd, London WC1X 8BP
The Compendium of Advanced Courses in Colleges of Further and Higher Education Regional Advisory Councils for Further Education
The Handbook of Degree and Advanced Courses NATFHE/Linneys ESL, 27 Britannia St, London WC1

3.3 GRANTS

1 Local authorities have a legal obligation under the Education Acts 1962 and 1975 to make an award (i.e. grant) to every student in their area who satisfies the conditions of the regulations. Regulations made under the Acts deal with the implementation of this legal obligation and themselves have the force of law. The amounts of awards are subject to annual review, and payment must be made at the prescribed rate and include the payment of tuition fees. The regulations concerning grants are complex, and they are dealt with here only in outline. However, as it may be necessary for colleges to advise students of their grant entitlements, reference should be made to the sources cited at the end of this sub-section.

2 **Mandatory Awards**

A student is entitled to a mandatory award if they meet the following conditions:

They are attending a 'designated' course;
They are 'ordinarily resident' in the UK;
They have not previously attended a course of advanced further education of more than two years duration;
They are not an 'assisted student';
They have not shown themselves to be 'unfitting to hold an award';
They have applied for an award by the due date.

(i) *Designated Courses*

First degree courses of a United Kingdom university, the CNAA or the Cranfield Institute;
Diploma in Higher Education;
Higher National Diploma (including those of the Business and Technician Education Council);
Initial teacher training (including the Postgraduate Certificate of Education and other part-time day courses designated by the Secretary of State);
Other qualifications specifically prescribed as being comparable to a first degree.

The Department of Education and Science can provide a list of all designated courses.

(ii) *Ordinary Residence* The requirements of this clause are broadly speaking:

The student has been ordinarily resident in the British Isles (UK, Channel Islands, Isle of Man) for at least three years before the first day of January, April or September whichever is closest to the first day of the course.

The purpose of residency must not have been wholly or mainly to receive full-time education.

These requirements apply to everyone irrespective of nationality or immigration status (See **1.2** 26). There are a few exceptions, notably refugees/asylees and their families; some European Community nationals and their families.

(iii) *Previous Courses* The mandatory award system is designed for those undertaking an initial course in higher education. If a student has attended a course of advanced further education of more than two years duration (including comparable part-time courses), they are disallowed from claiming a further award (a period of up to one term being disregarded).

There are some exceptions; grants are awarded in the case of: those taking a PGCE; those who attended a course at a Long Term Residential College.

Where a previous course was a designated course of two years or less or was a non-designated course of exactly two years, a student may receive a mandatory award. However, it may be restricted, i.e. not available for the full duration of the course.

There are exceptions, e.g. where the subsequent course is a BEd in a shortage subject.

The previous courses rule is very inflexible; for example that the student did not receive a grant is not a ground for exemption.

(iv) *Assisted Students* A student may not receive a mandatory award if they are receiving (or will receive) a scholarship or sponsorship by an employer – equal to the equivalent of the students' fees and maintenance requirements. Students following a course of teacher training on a part-time basis in some instances may be exempted from this rule.

(v) *Unfitting to hold an award* The interpretation of 'unfitting to hold an award' is entirely at the discretion of the LEA.

(vi) *Dates of Application* Failure to abide by closing dates will result in no award being made for the whole duration of the course.

3 The award

(i) *The payment of the grant* is usually made termly through the college. It is made up of a number of elements (depending on the student's circumstances) but as a minimum tuition fees to the college are paid on behalf of the student.

(ii) *Differential rates* relate to circumstance. These are, in descending order of the size of sum paid: students living in hall/lodgings attending London area establishments; students living in hall/lodgings attending establishments outside London; students living in the parental home; students on teacher training courses provided with full board and lodging. The providing LEA may apply the parental home rate instead of a higher rate if it considers that the student could conveniently attend the course from the parental home, except where the student is married or has satisfied an independent status condition or on the recommendation of the academic authorities that the student lives in a hall of residence. Special arrangements apply to students provided by their college with free board and lodging.

(iii) *The determination of the student's resources* represents a means test for the calculation of grant. A student in receipt of private income or unearned income will have these contributions deducted. In determining the residual value of income, the student is allowed to retain an initial amount, and certain other sources of income are disregarded. These sources are: scholarship and sponsorship sums up to a maximum figure; disability pensions not subject to taxation; forces bounties; family allowances; DHSS benefits; earnings; tax and national insurance contributions; and earnings by sandwich course students resulting from periods of industrial or other experience.

(iv) *The grant is reduced* by an amount calculated on parental income (except for independent students, see below paragraph 4). There is no obligation on parents to make their contributions although if they neglect to do so the student's resources will be less than her or his assessed needs. Contributions are not expected from parents who cannot be traced. Only actual or legally adoptive parents are subject to a means test. Step-parents are not subject to such a test. To calculate parental contribution, deductions are made from the gross income in the financial year preceding the academic year for which the grant is being assessed. Allowable deductions to determine this residual income are: sums for dependent adults and other dependent children; interest payments for which income tax relief is given; contribution to a dependant's income tax relieved pension scheme; and half the gross amount of any life assurance premium allowed for tax relief; in some circumstances, and up to a prescribed maximum, the wage cost of domestic assistance; a discretionary extra allowance where the parents live outside the UK; and an allowance against gross income which may be made for parents who are themselves in receipt of a grant. Once the parental residual income has been established, parental contribution is calculated on a sliding scale. Special arrangements apply: where two or more children in the family are eligible for awards; to sandwich course students (because no maintenance grant is paid for any year in which there are no periods of full-time study); to students on part-time initial teacher training courses; to 'assisted' students (for example, students given paid leave from employment to attend a course); to students married before the course but whose marriage has terminated; and to members of religious orders.

(v) *An additional maintenance grant* may be claimed by students, where appropriate. These additional allowances are added to the student's maintenance requirements and are for: permissible travelling expenses over a certain amount for students on course prior to 1984; special equipment expenditure for students on course prior to 1986; required course attendance in excess of 30 weeks and three days of the academic year; vacation hardship; disabled students; the maintenance of two homes; mature students who have earned £12,000 over the three years prior to the course commencement and aged over 26; and dependants' allowances. Some of these allowances are made at the LEA's discretion, although most are obligatory. Students ineligible for dependant's allowance payments may qualify under separate regulations administered by the Students' Unit of the Department of Health and Social Security at Blackpool, for which application forms are available from LEAs. Additional grants in certain cases are also available for any expenditure resulting from study away from the college during term time, up to a prescribed maximum (normally by application to the college); for vacation study, payable by the LEA only in colleges not wholly maintained out of public funds and otherwise by the institution; for students required to study abroad, including the cost of medical insurance, and determined according to whether or not the country is classified as one of high cost; and for students whose marriage has terminated.

4 Independent status

A student will not be assessed for a parental contribution if they have reached the age of 25 before the beginning of the appropriate academic year (this means a student can become 'independent' mid-course) or the student has been self-supporting from earnings for a total of three years prior to the beginning of the course.

The calculation of the three years can include: periods of unemployment;

some training schemes; periods in which the student received sickness benefit, invalidity pension, maternity allowance and some other state benefits; holding of an award previously.
Married students will be assessed on their spouse's income (similar conditions to the assessment of parental contribution) *unless* the student is regarded as being dependent on their parents or has a son/daughter who is an award holder for whom a parental contribution is assessed.

5 **Discretionary awards and awards for non-advanced courses**
Courses of non-advanced further education and all non-designated courses do not attract mandatory awards. Financial support is discretionary in these cases.
The LEA is the grant awarding body for discretionary awards. The level of award varies considerably according to the individual authority and type of course studied. It is advisable to get hold of a copy of the authority's regulations when dealing with individual cases. The discretionary nature of awards gives rise to problems and anomalies; what may be common practice in one authority may be the exception in another. The absence of national regulations makes appealing against the non-award of a grant difficult, and each LEA has a different appeals procedure. There are two main types of award available:

Educational Maintenance Award (EMAs)
Discretionary Awards

6 **Educational maintenance awards**
EMAs are also called Intermediate or Minor Awards by some authorities. Usually EMAs are only available to students under the age of 19 and may be payable to their parent(s) instead of the student. If the LEA gives EMAs they are usually:

Awarded to students on NAFE courses (i.e. CSE, O level, Ordinary BTC, A level, RSA, etc).
Means tested on parental income which usually has to be low, i.e. Supplementary Benefit level, in order to qualify for a full award;
On average £6.91 per week, maximum of about £9.44 (Source: *No Choice at 16* (1983) published by the Child Poverty Action Group);
Exclusive of travel or other costs (such as out-of-county fees) – so the LEA will insist that a student should study at the nearest institution (which may be a school instead of an FE College).

7 **Discretionary awards**
Discretionary awards are available to students on some NAFE courses (such as resits of 'A' levels), although some LEAs will not make awards for NAFE courses to students over 19 or 21. Mostly discretionary awards are available to students on some DES designated courses.

(i) *Qualifying for an award* Students who are studying on designated courses but who do not fulfil the conditions for a mandatory award (e.g. because of the residential requirements or previous study) may apply for a discretionary award, which if awarded must be at mandatory rates and conditions, including conditions as to means-testing.
Students on non-designated advanced course should apply to their local education authority for a discretionary award. The value of a discretionary grant for this type of course is determined by the local authority and varies from one LEA to another.
There are no mandatory grants available for part-time students and

assistance on a discretionary basis from LEAs is becoming rarer. Supplementary/Unemployment Benefit may be available to such students.

Each local authority has its own rules and policies about considering applications. ILEA, for instance, require candidates to have been resident in their area for three years prior to the beginning of the course. Competition for limited resources can be intense and examination results and other factors will have to be taken into account. Students may be expected to study locally if a course similar to the one they want to take is available. For these reasons it is very important to apply early for a discretionary grant.

(ii) *Discretionary dependants' allowances* Being discretionary, the award of these allowances depends on the attitude of the Local Education Authority. There are therefore no clear guidelines that can be easily given. Meeting the criteria below is therefore no guarantee of being given an allowance.

Students who fulfil the conditions of independence are in receipt of an LEA discretionary award and were married prior to the commencement of the course may be given allowances under the same conditions and rates as for LEA mandatory awards. Students who do not fulfil these conditions but are married and have a child born within six months of the start of the course may be able to persuade the LEA to make allowances to them at the mandatory rate.

Students not on mandatory awards are not eligible for assistance under the Hardship Scheme operated by the DHSS Students Unit.

(iii) *Appeals* Students who have been refused discretionary awards can appeal. There is no legal right of appeal but it is possible to request the LEA to reconsider the decision to refuse an award and most authorities do have established machinery to consider appeals. When appealing, the student needs to make a very full statement of application stressing the exceptional nature of their case. If any student in the area in similar circumstances has been given a grant, then their case can be used as a precedent, though the LEA will not necessarily recognise it as such. If possible new information should be introduced at the appeal stage. Stress should be laid upon academic and educational arguments in an appeal.

Contacting MPs and the DES is unlikely to be productive in individual cases. Students could, however, approach local councillors (particularly those on the Education Committee) to enlist their support and take advice from the National Union of Students (NUS) and Citizens Advice Bureaux.

8 Other financial assistance

(a) Students ineligible for either a mandatory or a discretionary award are responsible for their own fees and maintenance.

Some industrial organisations and some government departments have schemes whereby subsidies are afforded to promising students. Details of these schemes can be found in *Sponsorships* published by the Careers and Occupational Information Centre.

(b) Students following full-time advanced courses are ineligible for Supplementary Benefit (SB) whilst on course. The only exceptions to this are a single parent with a dependent child under 16; a student with a disability who is unlikely to obtain employment within a reasonable period of time; a student who is one of an unmarried couple and whose partner is not a student and who has a child dependent on the student or where the partner is unable to work through illness.

(c) At the non-advanced level, the eligibility of students for benefit depends upon their age and, in some cases, upon their having passed a preliminary qualifying period.

(i) Students aged 16–18 who are in full-time non-advanced further education cannot claim SB either in term time or in vacations unless they fall into one of the five categories mentioned below. Instead, such students attract Child Benefit which is paid to their parents (primarily their mother).

As exceptions to this rule, a student may claim SB where she or he:

Has a child for whom she or he is responsible and who is a member of the same household;

Has a mental or physical disability which (if she or he were not in full-time education) would render her/him unlikely to obtain employment within the next twelve months;

Has no parents and there is no person acting in the place of a parent;

Is living away from and is estranged from her/his parent(s) or any person acting in place of her/his parents;

Is taking or has terminated a course under the 21 hours rule.

Students who fall into any of these categories are not required to register for work (if aged 16 or 17) and do not have to register as unemployed or be 'available for work'.

(ii) Certain students aged 19 are in the same position as students referred to in paragraph (a) above. These 'dependent 19 year olds' are people who: are aged 19; are attending a course of full-time secondary education; attained the age of 19 on or after the first day of the autumn term of the college or school year applicable to the course;

during the whole of the two years immediately preceding the beginning of the course were not in full-time work or available for employment; and

do not fall into any of the five category exceptions referred to in paragraph (i) above.

Students who fall into this category of 'dependent 19 year olds' are in effect on the same footing as 16–18 year olds. These 19 year olds are described as 'dependent' because the effect of the regulation excluding them from SB in their own right is also to include them in an Assessment Unit with their parent(s).

(iii) Students in NAFE who are 20 or over or who are aged 19 and do not fall within the scope of paragraph (b), are treated in all respects on the same footing as students in advanced education.

Students following courses in dental hygiene, occupational therapy, physiotherapy, radiography, remedial gymnastics and the postgraduate Certificate of Qualification in Social Work (CQSW) may be eligible for a discretionary award from the Department of Health and Social Security. Contact DHSS, Branch P202, Friar House, 157–168 Blackfriars Road, London, SE1 8EU.

9 Postgraduate

For Postgraduate study there are two main types of awards – Bursaries and the State Studentship Scheme

The Bursaries Scheme is administered by the DES and is college-based. A full list of the areas of study and its applicability is available from the

DES Postgraduate Awards Section, Honeypot Lane, Canons Park, Stanmore, Middlesex.
State Studentships are administered by the various research councils, and for humanities by the British Academy (see Annex 1). Students should contact the appropriate body for advice on eligibility and so on.

10 **Adult residential colleges**

State bursaries for adult education are available from the Residential Colleges Council for England and the Welsh Office in Wales for students attending one year or two year full-time courses of liberal adult education at certain long-term residential colleges. These bursaries are not available where students are eligible for LEA discretionary awards. The eligibility requirements are: to be over 20 at the start of the course; to have been offered a place and recommended for a bursary by the college; and to have satisfied the UK residence requirements. Application is made to the college on form SBAE1, and the form is forwarded by the college to the RCC. The grant is payable at the same rate as for students taking first degree of comparable courses and includes tuition fees. Additional grants may be made for married students; widows, widowers, divorced and separated students; vacations; and travelling expenses. No parental contribution is expected from students aged 25 or who have supported themselves by the beginning of the course for at least three years (including up to six months of registered unemployment). A student's and spouse's income may result in the value of the bursary being reduced.

FURTHER READING

Sources of Law
Education Act 1962 Chapter 12 HMSO
Education Act 1975 Chapter 2 HMSO
Education Act 1976 Chapter 81 HMSO
Local Government Act 1974 Chapter 7 HMSO
The Education (Mandatory) Awards Regulations 1986. Statutory Instruments 1986 No 1306 HMSO
The Postgraduate etc Courses (Exclusion from Discretionary Awards) Regulations 1973 Statutory Instruments 1973 No. 1232 HMSO
The Education (Students Dependants Allowances) Regulations 1983 No. 1183 HMSO
The Education (Students Dependants Allowances (Amendment) Regulations SI 1986 No. 1325 HMSO

Government Publications
Grants to Students; a Brief Guide DES
Guide to Postgraduate Awards 1 State bursaries for postgraduate study on designated professional and vocational courses 1986
Guide to postgraduate studentships for study in the humanities 1986
Guide to Postgraduate Awards – Information science studentships and fellowships 1986
Postgraduate awards for librarianship and information science
All these publications available from the Department of Education and Science Publications Despatch Department. Honeypot Lane, Canons Park, Stanmore, Middlesex, except for the *Guide to studentships for study in the humanities 1986* which is available from the British Academy, Postgraduate Studentships Office, Spur 15, Block 1, Government Buildings, Honeypot Lane, Stanmore, HA7 1AZ.
The handbooks on grants for postgraduate study/or other subjects are available from the respective research councils addresses
Adult Education Bursaries 1986 handbook is available from the Awards Officer, Adult Education Bursaries, c/o Ruskin College, Oxford OX1 2HE

Grants to Students 1986/87 (in Northern Ireland) Department of Education for Northern Ireland, Rathgael House, Balloo Road, Bangor, Co Down
Sponsorships Careers and Occupational Information Service, MSC, Moorfoot, Sheffield S1 4PQ

Publications by Non-Governmental Organisations
Student Welfare Manual 1987
Local Education Authority Awards Survey 1986 NUS
Undergraduate Income and Expenditure Survey 1984 NUS
National Union of Students (NUS) also publishes a series of information leaflets on awards and benefits for students which is available from NUS, Nelson Mandela House, 461 Holloway Road, London N7 6LJ
Charities Digest Family Welfare Association, 501/505 Kingsland Road, London E8
Directory of Grant Making Trusts Charities Aid Foundation
Grants for Higher Education Barrie and Jenkins for the Advisory Centre for Education (out of print)
The Grants Register Macmillan
Study Abroad UNESCO

ADDRESSES

Agricultural and Food Research Council
Studentship Section, Agricultural and Food Research Council, 160 Great Portland Street, London W1N 6DT

Economic and Social Research Council
Postgraduate Training Division, Economic and Social Research Council, 1 Temple Avenue, London EC4Y 0BD

Medical Research Council
Training Awards Group, Medical Research Council, 20 Park Crescent, London W1N 4AL

Natural Environment Research Council
University Support Section, Natural Environment Research Council, Polaris House, North Star Avenue, Swindon, Wilts, SN2 1EU

Science and Engineering Research Council
Postgraduate Training Support Section, Science and Engineering Research Council, Polaris House, North Star Avenue, Swindon, Wilts, SN2 1ET

Postgraduate Studentship Office,
The British Academy, Block 1, Spur 15, Government Buildings, Honeypot Lane, Stanmore, Middx HA7 1AZ

Central Council for Education and Training in Social Work (CCETSW), Student Grant Office, 261 Grays Inn Road, WC1 8QT

3.4 STUDENT WELFARE

1 Standards and provision of student services vary greatly among colleges and polytechnics, though all have a student services offer at some level. This section deems accommodation, health, finances/funding, counselling and support service, equal opportunities, religious and college life as the key areas.

2 **Accommodation**

A breadth of issues need to be covered, comprising lists of vacant properties within the private and public sectors, tenancy rights, housing benefit queries, recruitment of vacant properties, investigating the possibility of head-tenancy schemes, liaison with local authorities and the ever-increasing issue of homelessness. However, accommodation offices are usually under-resourced and under-staffed. Accommodation officers are often unable to view prospective properties before being able to recommend them to students, a desirable factor which is at present negligible.

3 Institutions of higher education commonly cannot even offer all first year entrants residential places in halls of residences, so that students have to go into the private and public sector, often with little or no choice of property in which to live. Academic institutions should continue to take responsibility for providing advice and support for students who live outside of the college residences. The majority of FE students either choose or are forced to remain within the parental home. Accommodation services should provide support for these students, including advice on their rights under the benefits system, regarding 'the irreconcilable breakdown of family relations' and its implications.

4 **Health**

Advice on doctor, dentist and optical registration should be handed to students (including overseas students), together with advice on how to find out the type of practice available to them within the locality.

5 Residential colleges or halls of residence ideally should provide a nursing facility with a well equipped sick bay or, at the very least, several members of staff, wardens, or students who are qualified in first aid (i.e. holding a qualification certificate). All accidents whether major or minor should be recorded and reports copied to the Health and Safety adviser of the institution, be it the college, hall of residence, student union etc.

6 Colleges could invite a local doctor to hold a surgery at the college at least once a week. Where the doctor is a man, arrangements should also be made for a woman doctor to attend either the same and/or an alternative surgery. The Area Health Authority has the power to decide whether or not this is possible. All students are also entitled to register (with their NHS card) at a practice of their choice.

7 A college medical or student service should be able to supply students with resources, covering all areas, including medical services specifically for women, gay men, black groups, and ethnic groups. Advisory publications should include contraception advice, abortion advice, AIDS information[1] and drug abuse publications, as well as information on typical student illnesses such as glandular fever and hepatitis B.

8 If a student on a sandwich course is obliged to undertake a medical examination, they are eligible to reclaim the costs. (This does not apply to PGCE students).

9 **Finances**
Advice should be readily available on all elements of student financial support, including grants, benefits, social security, disability allowances, general allowances, child benefit, and legal aid. This should be updated regularly as regulations change often. Publicity should be given to the existence of any form of hardship fund, and colleges without such a facility should examine the feasibility of establishing one, both for home and overseas students. Lists of local charities and postgraduate and research awards should also be provided.

10 **Counselling and support services**
College support services play an integral part in the institution, linking into course planning, careers advice and systems of courses. They should be well publicised, and their confidentiality should be highlighted. There are differences between advice and counselling which should be made clear.

11 Counselling should be carried out by professionally trained and qualified personnel. A minimal requirement could be considered to be one counsellor to every 600 students. Whilst institutions of HE are establishing counselling facilities, in other colleges provision is not so easily available though an everyday FE student faces additional factors. As a short term measure, until a counsellor is appointed, it may be acceptable for trained individuals to work with a group of others and to devolve this role.

12 Counselling should be seen as integral to the college and involved in the planning of the institution Counselling. Staff should be seen as full members of its academic composition, taking into account the individual counsellor's wishes about how their role is viewed. If counsellors see problems in the institution that may be exacerbating the problems of students, they should have recourse to the college or LEA authorities with whom the power of reform lies.

13 Personal tutors may be required to fulfil a small part of a counsellor's role. However, this can make it impossible for them to take individual responsibility for disciplinary action against a student who as of right should be able to change their personal tutor if they so wish. It may be viewed as incompatible for staff who retain a disciplinary function within the college to act as a counsellor.

14 Counselling should be undertaken on a one-to-one basis, or in group sessions if appropriate, and should be held on a well publicised college-wide basis. Both counselling and advice should be seen as recognising a need and finding a solution (by the individual themself) to that need or problem, rather than being moralistic or judgmental. Confidentiality must be maintained at all times, including the referral function that a counsellor may be required to perform

15 **Equal opportunities**
Colleges should have become more conscious of women, black and ethnic group students, and lesbians and gay men; support services should reflect their needs and wishes and should include the provision of women, lesbians, gay men and black ethnic group staff, to whom students can turn, bringing in

external specialist bodies if so required. Literature should also reflect these needs, and it is desirable, for example, that it is produced in mother tongue languages as well as English.

16 **Religion**

Information on local religious communities should be readily available, including the possibility of religious leaders coming to the college if students of that religion so wish. Liaison with religious leaders and information of their activities is desirable and should be publicised and available at all times.

17 **College life**

Current movements within further and higher education reflects a need for institutions to become more involved in and reflect the needs of the community. Colleges have become more prepared to resource community-based activities such as adult education courses, access courses, improvement in training and the new Job Training Schemes (See **1.7** 33–35). Colleges may also be seen as community colleges, assessing their facilities in relation to the community, e.g. careers advisory services for the unemployed. Liaison with the local education authority is required if access is to be accelerated, with the opening of facilities both during the evenings and weekends. Colleges, as well as drawing in the local community, may also market themselves externally, be it in the form of local community action involvement, environmental issues, local planning issues etc. This also requires increased funding and resources as well as liaison with the LEA.

18 Not all students wish to fully integrate themselves into college life, including perhaps part-time students, mature students, postgraduate students. Their wishes should be respected as long as it is their choice and not the lack of provision for them that makes them do so.

19 **Commentary**

In the current economic and political climate, the welfare provision of students is not high on the political agenda, and this is one of the major factors in the differing standards of welfare provision for students within the UK. Provision, however, is in no way a reflector of need. Nor is it helpful to argue that provision of welfare services by the students union and external bodies duplicates provision by the institution itself. Very little duplication of services actually occurs; each body has its own distinct role to play. If we think of the average consumer as aged about 18, we can see that they need the resources of the institution to provide permanent services to meet the depth and range of students' requirements.

NOTE

1 Guidance on AIDS and sources of further information is given in DES (1987) AIDS – *Some Questions and Answers* Department of Education and Science.

3.5 RELATIONS WITH STUDENT UNIONS

1 A basic structure for student self organisation now exists in the great majority of colleges and polytechnics. Whilst universities have had a student union organisation for many years, the growth of student unions within the public sector institutions can be dated back to around 1970. In that year, the Department of Education and Science issued Circular 7/70 (See **2.8**) which included advice on student representation. It included in its model articles:

'The Governors shall make arrangements for the Students' Union or other body representing the students to conduct and manage its own affairs and funds in accordance with a constitution approved by the Governors'.

With the growth of student unions throughout the 1970s and the 1980s, there exists a miriad of differing structures and internal organisations of student unions ranging from vast, highly professional, commercial ventures to three people working from a cupboard. Having said that, basic principles can be outlined. This chapter reviews the overall rationale behind student unions and offers guidance on relations with student unions.

2 **Constitution**

The constitution of a student union (approved by the Governors) provides the legal basis for the existence of the union.[1] By and large, it includes the functions of the union as providing social, recreational, welfare facilities for its members and as representing the views of its members to other bodies both internal and external to the college. Added to these constitutional functions can be the recognition of the value to young people of being able to develop their own capacities for responsibility, participation and self government.

3 **Finances**

Changes made to the financing of student unions in the early 1980s have brought some semblance of order to the system. However, institutions of higher education sector are still generally much better funded than other colleges in the public sector. A student union is responsible for drawing up its own budget and conducting its own negotiations concerning its fees. The college is involved in this process and establishes its own policy of whether and how to support, and to what extent to support, the student union submission. Liaison with the local education authority (LEA) is essential. The student union requires details from the college to help with its budget submission; this may include advice on the date by which college estimates need to be drawn up and therefore the timing within the college's own timetable for submission of the budget to Governors' meetings. During the negotiations the student union may very well lobby some staff, governors, local authority officials and elected representatives. As the estimates have to be ultimately considered by the local authority, the student union may well request support from the college authorities and information as to the people to approach at this final stage of its submission. Where the matter of a student union submission is a subject of college disagreement, it is important for college administrators not only to have fulfilled their duties under the provisions of college government and to the students and employers, but also to be seen to be acting fairly. (This observation may be extended from the topic of fees to all matters involving student unions' submissions to governing bodies and local authorities.)

There is a variety of union fees and of methods of payment:

(i) *Registration Fee* This is a common source of income for many student unions. When the college collects individual student registration fees some or all of such moneys may be passed to the student union. In some colleges the fees are passed to a student welfare fund. The student union often has no control over the money, and the college is under no obligation to give income details to the union. In many cases, where money is given to the union the college reserves supervisory rights.

(ii) *Block Grant* This is by far the most common method of financing student unions. Once a budget for the student union has been agreed the income for the student union will be paid directly from the college. The block grant may be handed over in one lump sum at the beginning of the year but more commonly it will be made available to the student union in instalments throughout the academic year.

(iii) *Fee* This system is mainly operated in some colleges with mostly non-advanced work. On enrolling at a college the individual student pays a fee direct to the student union. There are many different forms this system takes; these include the college or local authority guaranteeing a certain amount of money to the student union if it can attract union fees from a certain proportion of the students involved at a college.

In many LEAs a standard fee per student is agreed between groups of colleges (usually through the National Union of Students) and is paid direct to the student union or via college authorities. In these instances Liaison Committees may be approached by the local organisation of the National Union of Students (NUS) for assistance in their claim for a union fee.

4 Structures

Decision-making structures within student unions follow a broadly similar pattern. At its core it has a system of general meetings which are open to all members of the student union to attend, speak and vote. The general meeting decides policy for the student union which the elected representatives of the union carry out. By and large the elected representation is on the basis of an executive committee headed normally by a president (though a general secretary is becoming more common). The executive committee will be charged with the day to day running of the students union and they will be primarily the people college administrators and members of staff will deal with.

5 Sabbaticals

One of the major demands within colleges from student unions is for funds to enable the president of the student union to take a sabbatical year from their studies. The NUS has put forward this demand over the years. It was supported by one of NATFHE's predecessor bodies, the Association of Teachers in Colleges and Departments of Education (ATCDE): 'The contribution which a good student union president can make to the relationship between the college authorities and the student union is inestimable . . . We feel that colleges and student unions should seek to provide for optimum conditions for this difficult and demanding job.' College authorities are advised against laying down specific academic commitments as a precondition for granting sabbatical leave to student union officers and are advised to ensure that adequate financial support is made available to a person via union funds.

6 Relationships with staff unions

There are instances where the student union decides to take action on an issue within the college. While such action should not interfere with the traditional concerns of trade unions within the establishment, staff unions should not seek to curtail such action. Where a relationship has been built up between staff unions and a student union, advance warning of any action should ensure that the rights of staff members are not diminished. The NUS has produced guidance in association with various college based unions for procedures in the event of any dispute. Each local institution should seek local agreements to ensure each body's rights are protected.

7 **Student representation**

Circular 7/70 advised in the case of colleges with a substantial proportion of advanced work, or a substantial proportion of adult students (whether or not they are following advanced courses) that in the establishment of membership of governing bodies 'consideration should be given to the inclusion of students appointed through the students' union' (See **2.8**). The circular stated that authorities might wish to consider the representation of students in other cases, and indicated that where specific provision was not made that the general power of co-option could be used. However, the circular advised LEAs when determining the articles of government of a college to have regard in matters of representation to the age composition of the student body, and the proportions of full-time, sandwich, and part-time day or evening students. The statement that governors 'shall also make arrangements whereby representation on matters of proper concern to the student may be made by their representatives to the Governors, the Academic Board or the Principal as may be appropriate' was intended to apply to full-time students.

8 In determining representation matters the issues are: the numbers of students involved and their voting rights; where and at which levels representation occurs, and what policies are implemented concerning reserved business. Representation should mean that there are at least two student representatives upon any body upon which they serve, and that they ought to have voting rights; other students designated by the union may attend as observers (and in the case of business of some committees it may be appropriate for representation to consist of observers only). Student representatives should be selected by the union, not by the college.

9 Representation on bodies dealing with the business of the college, such as the academic board and its committees, is not the whole issue, however. As students are the consumers of education, and may also be able to make contributions to its progress, it can be argued that their representatives' involvement should extend beyond business, disciplinary, and social and welfare matters to academic representation – that is to be involved in the designing, preparation and review of courses. Such representation may be most appropriate in a college where the union enjoys the services of an academic affairs office, but there can be benefits to students and all kinds of colleges of student academic representation, the nature of which may depend on the courses and their levels. It may be necessary for there to be reserved business in certain college committees. However, this business ought to be as limited as possible, refer only to matters of absolute confidentiality and not to be a device to limit student participation. The designation of agenda into parts A and B, for example, where part B requires student withdrawal, can allow items to be discussed under the cloak of confidentiality which properly belong to an open agenda. In considering any system of student representation, whatever the nature of the college, it is important that it fits the needs of the students and allows a form of representation for all students. For example, in the case of students on sandwich courses, machinery should exist for their representation during the times at which they are away from college; and in the case of part-time stu-

dents whose direct participation is impractical, maximum efforts should be made to represent their views. Structures in such cases may be difficult to devise, especially in the case of evening students, but in all colleges, no matter the ages of the students, representation should exist and be as full as possible. Such representation should extend to sub-committees of the academic board and governing body. It is necessary for there to be careful examination of the means by which students aged under 18 are represented.

NOTE

1 The nature of the legal status of student unions is not entirely clear in law. They have been treated as unincorporated associations, rather than, say, as deriving (in maintained colleges) a corporate status from the LEA or (in colleges which are corporate bodies) from the college. But it may be thought that they do derive their status from the college (and maintained colleges in turn from the LEA). As unincorporated associations, the members of student union executive would carry personal responsibility for the finances. The functions of student unions make them charitable bodies, and in their actions student unions have been held in law to be restricted to these charitable functions (See **1.2** Appendix 1.)

3.6 OVERSEAS STUDENTS

1 Overseas student policy underwent a major change when 'full-cost' fees were introduced for the 1980/81 academic year.[1] Transitional arrangements and special provisions for European Community (EC) students apart, the change had a swift and major effect on applications and admissions which reduced overall numbers of overseas students by a third in four years. In the public sector, overseas students on non-advanced further education (NAFE) courses dropped by over two-thirds in the same period.

2 In 1983, recognising the damage that had been caused, not least to British foreign relations, a limited, targeted set of measure was introduced by the then Foreign Secretary, Francis Pym. Inevitably known as the 'Pym package', various scholarship schemes and fee payment arrangements (notably for Hong Kong and Cypriot students) were introduced to mitigate the severest effects of the 'full cost' fee policy. These arrangements have been extended and refined and, along with an expanded technical cooperation training programme run by the Overseas Development Administration, they remain the principal methods by which a targeted policy of subsidy is implemented.

3 Central government no longer sets tuition fees levels, though it indirectly sets minima which are recommended by the Council for Local Education Authorities (CLEA) for the public sector 'after discussions with the Secretary of State'. Local authorities and their institutions of F and HE determine actual levels with CLEA's recommendations as guidelines. Behind this approach is an implicit wish for fee levels to be determined at local level, which may be reinforced by current changes in funding arrangements for higher education institutions in the public sector (See **1.3** 75–76).

4 The broad picture is that the public sector has been 'slow off the mark' in recovering from the overseas fee increase in 1980, perhaps by a combination of lack of interest, initiative and direct financial incentive and as a consequence of the public sector's bearing the brunt of the peak in demand from British students. However, the opportunities and benefits afforded by the presence of overseas students has been increasingly recognised, and, as this has been translated into positive politicies and active recruitment, so numbers have begun to pick up again. Institutions in the public sector have also been able to learn from both good and bad practice in the university sector in the early 1980s. 'Responsible recruitment' are now the watchwords.

5 Students from the European Community (EC) have not figured greatly in the debates about overseas students in recent years, particularly while finance has been the dominant issue in these discussions. With EC students paying 'home' fees (and many now having them paid for them, see below paragraph 17) there has been little financial incentive for institutions to recruit actively from the EC, except perhaps to make up 'NAB numbers' (See **1.3** 55–56). However, with educational arguments coming to the fore, exchange agreements on the increase and the new ERASMUS scholarship programme being approved by member states, there are prospects for greater student mobility amongst EC countries. The needs and provisions these developments generate also require consideration by institutions and authorities alike.

ADMISSIONS AND RECRUITMENT

6 **Immigration regulations**

Overseas students from countries other than member states of the EC must satisfy certain criteria laid down by the Immigration Act 1971 (See 1980 edition of *College Administration*, Waitt 1980). Most students must first obtain entry clearance at the British Embassy or High Commission in their own country. They will have to demonstrate that:

(i) They have been accepted for a full-time course of study at a bona fide college or school;

(ii) The course will occupy the whole or most of their time (usually defined as 15 hours of full-time, organised day-time study at one institution);

(iii) They can meet the cost of the tuition fees, their maintenance and the maintenance of any dependants they may bring with them;

(iv) They intend to leave the UK at the end of their course.

The countries whose nationals *require* entry clearance are listed below. However, even where this is not a requirement (e.g. in most but not all Commonwealth countries) entry clearance is strongly advised, and institutions would need to point this out to prospective students. Similarly, prospective students should be informed that coming as a *visitor* in the first instance could lead to difficulties in extending their stay later. Intending students who have not finalized all the admission arrangements or who wish to visit a number of institutions before deciding where to enrol can come as *intending* students.

7 Detailed immigration regulations and advice on Home Office practice are available from the UK Council for Overseas Student Affairs (UKCOSA). There is, however, no substitute for having a copy of the actual immigration rules (HMSO). The specialist organisations offering advice to individuals and representation where necessary at immigration appeals are:

(i) UK Immigrants Advisory Service, 7th Floor, Brettenham House, Savoy Street, London WC2; Tel 01-240 5176

(ii) Joint Council for the Welfare of Immigrants, 115 Old Street, London EC1V 9JR; Tel 01-251 8706

8 **Responsible recruitment**

Because of the financial pressures and incentives for the recruitment and admission of overseas students since 1980, and particularly in the public sector from the mid 1980s, institutions, sometimes on their own, sometimes jointly and, in the case of many polytechnics, through the British Council Education Counselling Service (ECS) (See below paragraph 13), have engaged in active recruitment overseas.

9 Arising out of the experience – good and bad – of institutions and organisations UKCOSA has developed a model for an institutional code of good practice. This provides a framework within which an institution can develop its own policy and has gained independent backing from educational and government bodies. (It is reproduced in full in Appendix 1.)

10 **The role of the British Council**

The British Council offers a number of services to institutions and to individual students, as well as being responsible for the award holders under such programmes as the Technical Cooperation Training Programme.

11 Overseas the British Council Information Service is open to prospective students who need general educational or practical advice about coming to the UK (a list of British Council Offices overseas is available). The Council also produces a handbook for overseas students, *How to Live in Britain* (1987), which is updated annually.

12 While the British Council cannot meet overseas students at airports or book accommodation in advance, any student needing help in finding temporary hotel accommodation in London on arrival should write to Arrivals Group, 10 Spring Gardens, London SW1A 2BN, giving the flight number of the aircraft and the expected date and time of arrival. The Group will arrange for a courier to meet the student at the British Council Arrivals office at Victoria Railway Station and the courier will book a single room in a central London hotel. In addition, the Council's Accommodation Unit will help any full-time overseas student to find long-term accommodation in London provided he or she can produce evidence of student status, evidence of financial status and a recommendation from the appropriate embassy/high commission or other responsible organisation in Britain.

13 In addition to providing specialist services in the fields of English Language teaching, testing and advice, through the English Teaching Information Service, and equivalence of qualifications, through the National Academic Recognition Information Centre, the British Council has recently embarked on a new venture to promote British university and polytechnic education in collaboration with the institutions themselves, in a programme called the Education Counselling Service, operating initially in Singapore, Hong Kong and Malaysia. This service, funded by subscriptions from institutions, seeks to guide prospective students into appropriate courses in the UK. The service carries out functions and has developed promotional activities which are of wider interest and application, i.e. in other countries and offices of the British Council and in other sectors of the education system. Expansion of the scheme in these directions looks inevitable, though whether government on institutions will be asked to foot the bill is open to question.

14 **Fees and Awards Regulations**

While it is no longer possible for most overseas students to qualify for home fees or a local education authority grant simply by virtue of being in the country for three years before a particular course, such is the power and mythology of 'the three year period', that institutions need to be aware of the need both to implement the regulations fairly and to explain them fully. While institutions are responsible only for interpretation of the fee regulations, they should be ready and equipped to give guidance on criteria of eligibility for awards too.

15 The main common element to the rules for fees and awards is that in addition to the period of ordinary residence (normally three years) required prior to a specified date just before the start of the course, a student must also be able to establish that he/she has not been here mainly or wholly for the purpose of full-time study for any part of that period (See **1.2** 26).

16 As far as fees are concerned, there are five main additional ways in which a student can qualify for the 'home' rate of fees by:

(i) Possessing refugee status, or 'exceptional leave' to remain, granted by the British Government;

(ii) Settlement in Britain, within the three years before a course begins, i.e.

if he/she has been given permanent residence or residence without restriction during that three year period;

(iii) Virtue of being a national of a European Community (EC) country who has been ordinarily resident in an EC country for the three years before the course, as long as that residence was not solely for educational purposes;

(iv) Evidence that he or she cannot fulfil the three year rule only because he/she or his/her parent or spouse was temporarily working abroad;

(v) Being a student in Britain as part of a formal exchange agreement when there is one-to-one reciprocity with the overseas institutions.

17 In general the awards regulations are more restrictive, except for the common element referred to in paragraph 15. However, a recent development is the use of the awards criteria in enabling EC students on designated courses to have their fees paid for them by the British Government. This arrangement began in 1986/87 and seems likely to be extended to other levels of study.

18 For detailed guidance on regulations governing fees and awards criteria information produced by UKCOSA and the National Union of Students (in their *Welfare Manual*) provide the best analysis of a complex subject, while the Department of Education and Science have produced a helpful set of notes of interpretation of the awards regulations.

19 It is perhaps worth bearing in mind that the difference between the home and overseas rates of fee is such (well over £3,000 at undergraduate level) that classification as one or the other may be a deciding factor in whether a student takes up a place on a course. Fee assessments must therefore be fair and seen to be fair and made as early as possible in the admission process by people qualified to make that assessment. There is nothing so disruptive and deflating to a student's progress if told one day he/she is a 'home' student and the next classified as an 'overseas' student.

INSTITUTIONAL SUPPORT SYSTEMS

20 It is widely acknowledged that the key to a proper 'all through' support service to overseas students is a co-ordinated network with a sufficiently senior person overseeing the arrangements and a designated committee to develop policy and improve practice.

21 Accommodation

Where overseas students live, particularly in their first year, is of critical importance to their well-being. Institutions with halls of residence might therefore ensure that priority goes to overseas students in making their allocation (See **3.4** 2–3). As there is often a demand from married overseas students for family accommodation it is important for there to be access to such housing or for prospective students to be warned of the difficulties in locating suitable accommodation. The problems and some solutions are highlighted in a report on accommodation for overseas students in London published by the London Conference on Overseas Students (LCOS 1986).

22 A particular difficulty for overseas students in halls is that some LEA-run halls close down in the vacation periods or are given over to conference bookings. In this situation it is important for institutions to retain some hall accommoda-

tion for overseas students staying on, particularly over the short vacations, or to make alternative arrangements. Hospitality schemes such as those run under the auspices of the Victoria League at Christmas are welcome opportunities for students to see other parts of the UK, but it would be equally appreciated by many students if local hospitality arrangements were made by the student's institution.

23 **Welfare**

Whether Student Services consist of a team of counsellors or one Student Services Officer, it is only through a network of care which also includes academic staff with a personal tutoring role, an active student union, a sensitive administration and a concerned director/principal that overseas students will feel welcome, understood and listened to. Student Services must obviously give a lead and it is frequently by the planning, running and evaluation of an orientation/induction course for new overseas students that much is learnt, by students and staff, about communication and cooperation (see UKCOSA's guide on Orientation – 1985).

24 In this context it is often helpful to have a designated staff member, either within Student Services or from the academic staff, who will 'take the lead' on overseas student support issues, part of whose job is keeping up to date on changes in regulations, new scholarship opportunities and particular national crises affecting groups of students, and sharing this information or alerting relevant people in the institution or authority. A number of models of good practice for institutional handling of difficulties facing individuals and groups is given in *Containing Crises: The response to overseas student group in hardship* (UKCOSA 1985b).

25 **Finance**

With such large sums of money being paid in tuition fees by overseas students many institutions set aside sums of money for remission of fees or for loans or grants in cases of hardship. The wise use of such funds depends to some extent on there being good links between Student Services, Registry and Finance Department. Whatever the system for payment of fees – in advance, on enrolment or upon later invoicing – flexibility on the institution's part is often needed to preserve the student's academic career and to retain the possibility of money arriving and outstanding fees being paid.

26 Many financial difficulties faced by overseas students – though not just by overseas students – are caused by bad budgeting and it would be helpful if institutions, in both their pre-arrival literature and in their briefing to newly arrived students, gave guidance on both overall costs and wise spending patterns. The annual 'cost of living' letter produced by the London Conference on Overseas Students and the publication *How to Live in Britain* (British Council 1987) are useful in this respect, but there is no substitute for institutional, local advice.

27 **UK Council for Overseas Student Affairs (UKCOSA)**

Institutions seeking information, models of good practice, specialist training or advice on how to handle a difficult case can find these services and others offered by UKCOSA to its members. As an umbrella organisation, UKCOSA is the main forum for the exchange of information and ideas on overseas student issues and works with institutions, local authorities and central government to ensure high professional standards in the recruitment and support of overseas students. It also offers a management consultancy service to institutions wishing to assess and improve their academic, administrative and welfare provisions for overseas students.

28 Specialist advice on refugee and development issues is provided by World University Service. Recent WUS reports include *It Ain't Half Sexist, Mum* (1985 Goldsmith and Shawcross jointly with UKCOSA) and *The Forgotten Overseas Students: Towards a policy for refugees* (1986).

LOOKING AHEAD

29 A clutch of reports and surveys have emerged during 1986 and 1987 which make important recommendations for Government and institutions and which may herald further policy developments, though major changes to the framework (See above paragraphs 1–5) seem unlikely.

30 The Overseas Students Trust, which has produced and commissioned a series of influential reports in recent years, has set out in *The Next Steps: Overseas Student Policy into the 1990s* (OST 1987) a blueprint for further action by Government, in the fields of specific award schemes (which would have substantial application in the public sector), promotion of further and higher education, and institutional policy in more flexible entry criteria, better language and pastoral provision, and comprehensive, fixed fees.

31 Another volume combining forward thinking and 'state of the art' contributions is *Overseas Students – Destination UK?* (Shotnes 1987), while a revealing insight into how current overseas students view Britain as a host nation – warts and all – is given in essays by overseas students in *Overseas Students – At Home in Britain?* (Bristow and Shotnes 1987).

NOTE

1 Differential fees for overseas students were first announced in December 1966 by Secretary of State Anthony Crosland, and further increases were introduced during the 1970s.

COUNTRIES WHOSE NATIONALS REQUIRE VISAS FOR ENTRY TO UK

Afghanistan, Albania, Angola, Argentina, Bangladesh, Benin, Bhutan, Bulgaria, Burma, Burundi, Cameroon, Comoras, Cape Verde, Central African Republic, Chad, China, Congo, Cuba, Czechoslovakia, Djibouti, Egypt, Equatorial Guinea, Ethiopia, Gabon, Germany (Democratic Republic), Ghana, Guinea, Guinea-Bissau, Hungary, Indonesia, India, Iran, Iraq, Jordan, Kampuchea (formerly Cambodia), Korea (North), Laos, Lebanon, Liberia, Libya, Madagascar, Mali, Mauritania, Mongolia, Mozambique, Nepal, Nigeria, Oman, Pakistan, Philippines, Poland, Romania, Rwanda, Soa Tome e Principe, Saudi Arabia, Senegal, Somali Democratic Republic, Soviet Union, Sri Lanka, Sudan, Syria, Thailand, Togo, Upper Volta, Vietnam, Yemen (North), Yemen (South), Zaire,

ADDRESSES

British Council, 10 Spring Gardens, London SW1A 2BN. There are several British Council offices elsewhere in London, also an office or officer in each of Aberdeen, Belfast, Birmingham, Brighton, Bristol, Cambridge, Cardiff, Dundee, Edinburgh, Exeter, Glasgow, Hull, Leeds, Leicester, Liverpool, Manchester, Newcastle upon Tyne, Nottingham, Oxford, Reading, Sheffield, Southampton and Swansea

UK Council for Overseas Students Affairs (UKCOSA), 60 Westbourne Grove, London W2 5SH

World University Service (WUS), 20 Compton Terrace, London N1 2UN

FURTHER READING

Bristow, R. and Shotnes, S. (eds) (1987) *Overseas Students – At Home in Britain?* Essays and analysis of the overseas student experience. UKCOSA
British Council (1987) *How to Live in Britain 1987*, Macmillan
DES (1986) *Notes of Guidance on Awards* Department of Education and Science
Goldsmith, J. and Shawcross, V. (1985) *It Ain't Half Sexist, Mum* WUS/UKCOSA
HMSO (1983, 1985, 1986) *Statement of Immigration Rules* HMSO
London Conference on Overseas Students (1987) *Cost of Living Letter 1987/88*, LCOS.
London Conference on Overseas Students (1986) *Report of a Working Party on Some Accommodation Problems of Overseas Students in London* LCOS
National Union of Students (1986) *Welfare Manual 1986/87* NUS.
Overseas Students Trust (1987) *The Next Steps: Overseas Student Policy into the 1990s* OST
Shotnes, S. (ed) (1987) *Overseas Students – Destination UK?* UKCOSA
UKCOSA (1986) *Containing Crisis: The Response to Overseas Student Groups in hardship* A Report by the UKCOSA Working Party on Crisis and Hardship Arrangements for Overseas Students (CHAOS) UKCOSA
UKCOSA (1985) *Orientation: A Practical Guide* UKCOSA
UKCOSA (1987) *Notes for Students* UKCOSA
UKCOSA (1987) *Responsible Recruitment : a model for a code of practice for institutions involved in the education of students from overseas* UKCOSA
Williams, G., Kenyon, M. and Williams, L. (1987) *Readings in overseas Student Policy*. A collection of essays commissioned by the Overseas Students Trust
WUS (1986) *The Forgotten Overseas Student: Towards a Policy for Refugees* World University Service

APPENDIX 1

RESPONSIBLE RECRUITMENT – A MODEL FOR A CODE OF PRACTICE FOR INSTITUTIONS INVOLVED IN THE EDUCATION OF STUDENTS FROM OVERSEAS (UKCOSA)

Principles and Policy

1 The institution should have a clearly stated policy on the recruitment of overseas students, which is endorsed by the governing body and is openly communicated to all staff. Academic and administrative staff who will be affected by the recruitment of overseas students should be consulted on the development and promulgation of the policy. The policy should include the institution's aims and objectives in relation to the recruitment and education of overseas students, including intake and market targets. This policy should be taken into account in the institution's planning and budgeting, and consideration should be given to the allocation of fees income to support those areas of institutional activity concerned with international education. Resource allocation should be sufficient to ensure that the principles and practices outlined in this document can be consistently maintained.

2 The operational aspects of this policy, as it affects the overseas students themselves, should cover the nature and quality of pre-offer information and pre-departure briefing and extend to the care of students on arrival in the UK right through to their departure from the institution.

3 Any institution which actively engages in recruiting overseas students should accept responsibility for the information and services it provides to such students and for any deficiencies in its provision.

4 In order to ensure the effective implementation of a coherent policy, a senior member of staff should be made coordinator of recruitment activities and given responsibility for ensuring that the institution's policy in recruitment is followed and its results monitored. The coordinator should have the backing of other senior officers and a coordinating committee if appropriate to the size of the institution.

5 Staff engaged in active recruitment overseas should be briefed on institutional policy by the coordinator and report to the coordinator at regular intervals. The coordinator's briefing should stress the role of marketing the institution and the need to judge performance in terms of the quality as well as the quantity of overseas students who respond.

6 Entry standards, admission requirements and teaching provision should be such as to maintain the institution's academic standards and to ensure a high success rate amongst overseas students.

7 Active recruitment should be seen as part of an institution's work in international education and not as a separate activity.

8 Therefore the institution should ensure that communication between all staff and departments affected by the recruitment of overseas students is effective and that staff and departments work cooperatively.

9 Appropriate training and staff development is part of responsible recruitment and should be provided for all staff in regular contact with overseas students, as part of the recruitment policy. Where in-house training cannot be provided effectively, support should be made available for staff to attend regional and national training events provided by organisations concerned with the welfare of overseas student affairs such as UKCOSA and regional organisations.

10 Any institution engaged in active recruitment should consider being a member of UKCOSA and thus benefiting from their information and training services.

11 Responsible recruitment should ensure that institutional policies and provision do not discriminate against individuals on grounds of gender, race, religion, sexual orientation or disability.

12 In addition, institutions should be aware of and sensitive to the varying experience and expectations of students from other cultures and have particular regard for the special needs of female students, of students with families and of their spouses.

Guidelines on Good Practice

Policy

13 Have a clearly stated policy on recruitment, to include why recruitment is a necessary and important activity, how many students the institution aims to recruit and from which countries, what services will be provided and how the policy will be monitored and evaluated.

14 Make a senior member of staff responsible for coordinating and overseeing the implementation of the recruitment policy.

15 Designate a central unit or coordinating committee to assist in the coordination, implementation and monitoring of the recruitment policy.

16 Involve welfare services and the student union, as well as administrative and academic staff, in the discussion of recruitment issues.

17 Calculate the cost of a recruitment programme in advance, including the extra demand students recruited may make on staff time. Only recruit if the institution has the means and willingness to devote the necessary resources to the programme and its follow-through

Marketing

18 Conduct a comprehensive analysis of the student market in any targeted countries and make an honest and realistic evaluation as to whether the institution can meet the identified needs.

19 Be clear about what can be offered both in terms of quantity, e.g. the number of course places, accommodation places, etc and quality, e.g. areas of excellence, standard of student services, etc.

20 Investigate the various different means of accessing the desired market and their relative merits before launching recruitment initiatives. British Council surveys are available for useful information in certain countries.

21 Use specialised marketing and recruitment staff who know the institution well and who are sensitive to the needs of prospective overseas students.

22 Investigate the possibility of joint ventures with other institutions in the area. A consortium can offer a broad range of language and other access courses followed by undergraduate, postgraduate or specialised training courses which will attract students who wish to follow a complete academic progression and not move from area to area.

23 Prepare promotional visits carefully, refer to available market surveys or education profiles, set clear objectives and ensure that the personnel are well briefed.

24 Consult the British Council on local conditions and the timing and staging of recruitment visits.

25 Ensure that promotional visits have regard to the UK admissions timetable and to the overseas examination cycle.

26 Find out about and be sensitive to the needs, assumptions, expectations and conventions of the prospective students.

27 Establish agreements with overseas schools and colleges on the frequency, timing, content and conduct of liaison and promotional visits.

Information

28 Send out comprehensive and easily comprehensible information for potential students, written specifically for the purpose.

29 Consider translations for appropriate student groups and/or parents of prospective students.

30 Review information regularly to check accuracy.

31 Make sure information provided for prospective students states clearly the cost of studying and living in the UK in sufficiently detailed form for students to make an accurate estimate of their ability to pay.

32 Use students already in the institution to help prepare information for prospective new students.

33 Use returned students to help brief prospective new students.

34 Ensure that the qualifications offered in UK are clearly defined and understood.

35 Make clear to prospective students what financial regulations will apply to them, including arrangements for the payment of fees, and in the event of non-payment of fees.

36 Ensure prospective students are fully aware of the immigration conditions for entry to the UK.

37 Provide information on language testing requirements and the level of proficiency required.

38 Ensure that detailed records are kept on entry levels, failure and withdrawal rates and examination results for overseas students for evaluation purposes.

Academic and Non-Academic Support Services

Academic

39 Consider the need to provide access courses for students who will need a bridging course or who would benefit from a preliminary course of this kind.

40 Ensure that proficiency tests are given to students whose first language is not English, wherever possible.

41 Assess student's likely need for language tuition and support and establish arrangements for pre-sessional and on-going instruction as necessary.

42 Integrate language teaching with the course structure as far as possible.

43 Inform students of the availability of access courses and language support within the institution or arranged by the institution, with an explanation of the advantages of such courses.

44 Provide basic training for students on equipment and machinery with which they may not be familiar.

45 Look at assessment and examination procedures, identify any difficulties they may present for overseas students and consider ways in which students can be prepared for such procedures.

46 Be aware that assessment and reporting procedures may have to be adapted to take account of the expectations of overseas students and the stipulations of their sponsors.

47 Consider whether the courses offered can be made more relevant to the needs of overseas students and the countries from which they come.

48 Consider the use of flexible course structures, e.g. modular courses, course transfer and split courses to attract overseas students whose requirements and/or qualifications may not fit into a 'standard' course.

49 Be sensitive to the high value many overseas students place on the relationship with those teaching them and consider the appropriateness of academic and personal tutorial arrangements in this context.

Non-Academic

50 Use incentives in ways which encourage responsible recruitment and which ensure that the supporting infrastructure of both Departments and Central Services can respond adequately to an increase in numbers.

51 Consider ways of using income generated by recruitment to enhance support services as well as rewarding academic departments.

52 Provide staff development courses/opportunities for all staff working with overseas students.

53 Before places are offered, ensure that clear and honest information is given to students about the availability and cost of accommodation on campus and off campus and the extent to which the institutions accommodation service is able to help students find accommodation. Make special reference to the level of or lack of accommodation for married students and families.

54 Make some arrangements for short term emergency accommodation for newly arrived students.

55 Provide an orientation programme that is relevant to new overseas students and which provides them with the information and introductions they need, whether or not it is held separately from a general orientation even for all new students.

56 Consider the use of special arrangements such as peer-pairing to help students feel welcome and settle in.

57 Ensure catering services meet the need for special diets among overseas students.

58 Consider the potential for an International House or Overseas Student Centre.

59 Ensure that staff are sensitive to and aware of potential problems of racism on campus. Set up channels for complaints and be prepared to take prompt and positive action if necessary.

60 Examine the needs of overseas students for accommodation, child care, health care, personal security.

61 Provide support and preparation for students moving on to a new institution to undertake new studies.

62 Provide support and preparation for students about to return to their own country, including reorientation for possible reverse culture shock, and information on seeking employment where possible.

63 At all times be sensitive to the different cultural backgrounds from which students come which may affect their requirements at every level including diet, family housing, privacy and the place that women students or the wives of male students take in the home and society.

Note: UKCOSA's practical manual on *Orientation and Pre-Arrival Information* gives detailed guidance and models of good practice on the above points.

3.7 SPECIAL EDUCATIONAL NEEDS

1 This chapter is in two parts. The first is a necessarily extended scene-setting: work for students with special needs is a new field within the post-school education service, and consequently many administrators are unfamiliar with the rapid and continuing developments. The second part considers how the administrator at college level can introduce, establish, maintain, and improve the quality of education available to meet special educational needs.

2 *Definitions* In 1980 the World Health Organisation (WHO) defined the general terms impairment, disability, and handicap in words commonly accepted internationally as standard definitions:

> '*Impairment* Any loss or abnormality of psychological, physiological or anatomical structure or function.
>
> *Disability* Any restriction or lack (resulting from an impairment) of ability to perform an activity in the manner or within the range considered normal for a human being.
>
> *Handicap* A disadvantage for a given individual, resulting from an impairment or disability, that limits or prevents the fulfilment of a role that is normal, depending on age, sex, social and cultural factors for that individual' (WHO 1980).

3 Such definitions suggest that 'handicap' is not an objective fact but a social construct imposed on individuals as a result of other people's perceptions of disability. Thus, the working assumption of this section is that handicap can – and should be – largely eliminated within colleges (or any other educational environment): disadvantage inescapably associated with a particular disability or group of disabilities can be minimised; disadvantage resulting from social and cultural factors – often attitudes and prejudices arising from ignorance – should be eliminated.

4 The definitions need closer examination; handicap, disability, and impairment are not inseparable.

> *Learning difficulty* does not necessarily result from impairment or psychological abnormality in other than a statistical sense. The Education Act 1981 defined special educational needs in relative terms. A child (the Act did not turn its attention to education beyond school) had 'special educational needs' if there was a learning difficulty calling for special educational provision to be made; a learning difficulty for a child meant either significantly greater difficulty than the majority of children of that age *or* a disability preventing or hindering the normal use of educational facilities generally provided in schools within the area.
>
> *Special needs* within the definition of the Manpower Services Commission has a more extensive meaning still, encompassing not only learning difficulty and disability but also forms of socially constructed disadvantage such as gender, ethnic background, socioeconomic background and even residence in areas of especially high unemployment.

5 The emphasis in policy formation with regard to special *educational* needs has changed from classifying people according to their particular disabilities towards analysing the needs which are special to each individual. This has meant that the statistics which used to show the response of the education service across the board at primary and secondary stage to pupils with special

3.7

Table 1

To illustrate the variety of Special Educational Needs

Data extracted from the relevant Table (A22/83) are reproduced from DES 1983 *Statistics of Education* in order to illustrate the variety of needs, together with comparable data from the Inner London Education Authority's 1984 Special Schools Survey (published in *Educational Opportunities for All?* Fish 1985), which uses more modern terminology.

DES 1983						*ILEA 1984*	
		No	*%*	*No*	*%*		
Educationally Sub-Normal – mild	(ESN(M))	69174	44½	2519	31	Moderate Learning Difficulties	(MLD)
Educationally Sub-Normal – severe	(ESN(S))	30050	19½	1381	17	Severe Learning Difficulties	(SLD)
Maladjusted	(Mal)	22241	14½	1289	16	Emotional and Behavioural Difficulties	(EBD)
Physically Handicapped		13642	9	473	6	Motor Impaired	
Deaf and Partially Hearing		7308	4½	528	6½	Hearing Impaired	
Delicate		4603	3	1172	14½	Delicate	
Blind and Partially Sighted		2956	2	367	5	Visually Impaired	
Speech Defect		3024	2	110	1½	Language Units	
Autistic		1063	½	122	1½	Autistic	
Epileptic		892	½	–	–		
		–	–	106	1	Hospital	
		154953	100	8067	100		

needs are no longer present; one effect of the 1981 Act has been that the Department of Education and Science's *1983 Statistics of Education* were the last to subdivide pupils having special needs by the old school categories.

6 Table 1 shows the:

Range of impairments, disabilities and special learning needs which have been historically recognised by the education service as requiring special provision within the school system;

Overwhelming preponderance of children with learning difficulties among the school pupils who have been recognised as having special needs;

Relatively small numbers (even in a large authority like ILEA) of children with particular physical or sensory disabilities (and, since the tables show the whole age range of school education, less than a tenth of the pupils will be 15 years old at any given time, with the implied curriculum needs associated with school-leaving);

Variation between the situation in individual local education authority areas and the national pattern, both in provision and (by extension) in need. (As with other public services, expressions of need may remain private in the absence locally of provision to satisfy them.)

7 The ILEA Committee of 1984–85, set up to review provision to meet special educational needs and chaired by John Fish, formerly HM Inspector for Special Education, entitled its report *Educational Opportunities for All?* The question mark was intended to cast doubt not on the objective but on the extent to which it was being attained. The Fish Report (1985) set out certain basic principles which apply in colleges, polytechnics, universities, and other establishments for the education of adults just as much as in schools:

'1.1.22 The long term aims of education for all children and young people include the achievement of responsible personal autonomy and full participation in the communities in which they live. These aims are expressed practically in terms of employment, independent living and adequate financial and other arrangements which allow an acceptable range of opportunities, choices and life styles. The aims of education for children and young people with disabilities and significant difficulties are the same as those for all children and young people. They should have opportunities to achieve these aims, to associate with their contemporaries, whether similarly disabled or not, and have access to the whole range of opportunities in education, training, leisure and community activities available to all. Disabilities and significant difficulties do not diminish the right to equal access to, and participation in society.

1.1.23 Equal access to and participation in society demands respect for children and young people with disabilities and difficulties and their families. Wherever they are educated, work and enjoy their leisure, these children and young people, like all others, whatever their race, class and gender, must be acknowledged as participants with current and potential abilities to contribute to society.

1.1.24 All those responsible for providing services to children and young people, whether or not they have specific responsibilities for those with disabilities and significant difficulties, should accept the aim of integration for all. Provision of services that are additional to or different from those available to all should be directed towards this aim.

1.1.25 It follows from these considerations that our definition of handicap is a dynamic and relative one. Disabilities and difficulties become more or less handicapping depending on the expectations of others and on social contexts. Handicaps thus arise from the mismatch between the intellectual, physical, emotional and social behaviour and aspirations of the individual and the expectations, appropriate or otherwise, of the community and society at large. Individuals with disabilities or significant difficulties may be handicapped by their own attitude to them and by the attitudes of others. Of equal significance, the degree to which the individual is handicapped is determined by the educational, social, physical and emotional situations which he or she encounters. Handicapping effects will vary from situation to situation and may change over time.

1.1.26 Most children and young people are expected to move from stage to stage through education and training in a fixed chronological sequence and time scale. The handicapping effects of some disabilities can be increased if educational and social arrangements do not allow for flexibility in the time over which goals in development can be achieved.

1.1.27 It is also important to recognise that integration in society is a process not a state. It is not simply a question of placement in the same groups and institutions as others. It is a process which requires continued and planned interaction with contemporaries and freedom to associate in different groups. The potentially adverse effects of isolation and segregation in whatever context, including comprehensive institutions, are now well known, including the risks to social competence and to the development of a positive self-identity. The process of integration should be actively developed wherever the individual lives, learns, works and enjoys leisure activities. Placement in the wider group or same institution as non-handicapped contemporaries, although an essential prerequisite to effective integration, does not necessarily result in the process being actively developed. The process of integration should form an essential element in all education wherever it takes place.'

8 These basic principles have operational implications. In 1975 HM Inspectorate undertook a national survey of the extent to which the further education system responded to a special educational need; little activity could be reported, though the survey process itself stimulated greater consideration of such needs within colleges. The Warnock Report (1978) accelerated this process with a series of recommendations which may be summarised (as they affected the post-school service):

The 'designated person'. Every institution of further education should designate a member of staff as responsible for the welfare of students with special needs in the college and for briefing other members of staff. Warnock advocates a 'named person' to whom an individual might turn to for help and advice, the concept applying from birth and through education. In post-school education, this person for Warnock's purposes is the careers officer.

The report recommends the necessity of skilled careers advice, particularly for those with special needs and the need for early assessment. Effective counselling is also advocated.

Every institution of further and higher education should formulate and publicise a policy on the admission of and provision for students with special educational needs.

A range of link and other courses which colleges might offer is recommended. Similarly emphasis is placed on the links between the employment prospects of people with disabilities and their education and training.

It is emphasised that progress will occur by the devoted attention of teaching staff in developing or adapting appropriate courses. Further ancillary staff are recommended to assist this process.

There should be a number of additional facilities such as accommodation and the provision of special units.

All initial teacher education should include a special educational element and there should be extensive provision of in-service education.

The report also sets out ways in which people with disabilities can take advantage of increased opportunities to become teachers.

The report emphasises the need for research to be undertaken. Post-sixteen education and training, and the development of teacher education and training, were areas which should receive high priority for action.

9 No central government commitment to action which would involve increased public expenditure has followed, and the remodelling of special education at school level which was required by the Education Act 1981 bypassed the post-school service. The implications of the Warnock Report have, however, had some impact on post-school provision. The legal duty on LEAs to secure educational facilities for young people up to the age of 19 in full-time education is enshrined in the Education Act 1944, and applies to young people with special educational needs just as much as to any one else. No test case has been necessary to establish this right, which has been confirmed more than once in answer to Parliamentary questions.

10 **Provision**

In autumn 1985 the Department of Education and Science commissioned the National Bureau for Handicapped Students[1] to undertake a further national survey of public sector colleges of further and higher education in England. The postal questionnaire attracted the very high response rate of 93%, and the Bureau's findings can therefore be regarded as authoritative. The following summary of findings is of necessity selective – the full report *Catching Up* (NBHS 1987) repays careful study. (Asterisks against particular figures indicate that they have been adjusted appropriately to allow for non-response.)

8,400* students were on school-college link courses associated with special schools, which represented fewer than one in four of all pupils aged 14 or over in special schools nationally; about half the 454 colleges in the sample ran at least one such course.

About 3600* trainees with special educational needs attended college through the Youth Training Scheme (YTS). One-third of the colleges surveyed ran a college-based YTS scheme for students with special needs, catering in total for a little over 3,000 students; the remainder were in off-the-job provision within college for other managing agents.

Over 6,000* students enrolled for the 370 full-time or major part-time courses described as pre-vocational or 'transition' courses.

Just over 2,900 students were on mainstream courses at every level of further and higher education. Of them 573 (about 20%) were studying on degree or other higher education courses; others were on a variety of courses, the largest number (35%) being on non-advanced further education courses leading to a recognised qualification. Half of the students with special educational needs on mainstream courses were over 19 years of age; fewer were found on part-time courses in comparison with the total student population.

An estimated 4,600* students were attending part-time minor courses (one-third of whom attend evening courses, most of them over 19), chiefly courses in adult literacy and basic education, or else leisure pursuits.

Just over 3,800 students were on adult-link courses established with adult training entres and (less often) hospitals.

More than 13,000* students were catered for outside the colleges, by outreach arrangements in adult training and day centres and long-stay hospitals; the curriculum mirrored the part-time minor and adult-link courses taking place on college premises.

Students with moderate learning difficulties were the majority group among students on school-link, special YTS, and full-time pre-vocational and 'transition' courses, but few were able to progress to mainstream courses. (Only 21% of colleges provided support to assist students with learning difficulties on mainstream courses.)

Students with severe learning difficulties benefited from more than 60 full-time courses specially designed for them, and from the bulk of adult-link and outreach provision.

Students with physical disabilities had little provision specifically for themselves: 38% of colleges provided additional support to such students on mainstream colleges.

More than one quarter of colleges had some part of their college buildings specially adapted for use by students with mobility problems. However, almost half of all teaching blocks were said to have no adequate access, although 30% of all colleges could offer some measure of access to all of their teaching buildings. Nonetheless, more than 60% of colleges believed they might have to deny a place on a chosen course to a student with a physical disability because of access problems or because of the lack of necessary support.

Students with sensory disabilities benefited from the occasional school-link course and a very few YTS schemes: fewer than one-third of colleges provided support to hearing-imparied students on mainstream courses, and only some 100 colleges to visually-impaired students. A significant minority of part-time minor courses offered training in skills specifically related to disability, e.g. lip-reading, braille, etc.

Fewer than one in seven colleges provided support to students with emotional or behavioural difficulties, who emerged as the group most handicapped by lack of provision.

The level of special course provision showed a considerable regional variation. Provision was consistently greater in the East Midlands, the North-West, and Yorkshire and Humberside, for example, in comparison with East Anglia, the South-East, or the South-West of England. Provision of special courses is also relatively less in Greater London than in the counties or in the other metropolitan areas.

One half of all colleges had run staff development courses to raise awareness of special educational needs among staff generally; slightly more had held in-house staff development courses for the 1,500 teaching staff (nationally) engaged in teaching students with special educational needs as their main teaching commitment.

11 Policies

There is little expressed policy from central government. The Warnock Committee recommended that post-school provision, teacher education, and work for the under 5s were the highest priority areas for development – colleges are well-placed to pioneer in all three. But the Education Act 1981 concentrated on schools. During 1986 two circulars from the DES included policy by implication: Circular 5/86 included, among the possibilities for Educational Support Grant, money for the provision of micro-electronic equipment for the use of students in further education with physical and/or sensory handicaps enabled thereby to participate effectively in mainstream college courses. A condition of grant was an effective assessment procedure to determine the equipment required by individual students and the provision of training in its use. Circular 6/86 (See **2.9** Appendix 1) included among the national priorities for in-service training grants the organisation and management of special needs provision within colleges, and this has been followed up by an official report *A Special Professionalism* (DES 1987a) which contains the recommendations of a working party chaired by David Stafford on teacher training needs for further (including higher and adult) education staff in respect of special educational needs.

12 National statements have otherwise been left to the Further Education Unit and the Manpower Services Commission, which has gone beyond statements to include permanent additional funding for the disabled (PAFD) in its funding arrangements for the two-year Youth Training Scheme from 1985 onwards, and which has a considerable record of specific programmes for young people with moderate learning difficulties within earlier schemes. In the training context, MSC also makes specific grants to individuals for training aids and other equipment. Frequent changes to both the form and substance of MSC programmes means that current detail should be sought both from MSC Area Offices and from the National Bureau for Handicapped Students, which monitors MSC policies at national level.

13 One national constraint is the absence of explicit recognition within successive Burnham FE reports and NJC FE agreements of the demands of work to meet special educational needs, for modified staffing, grading and conditions of service arrangements. The NBHS publication on the subject bore the title *Burnham: the Biggest Barrier of All?* (1986) and outlined remedial action (See below paragraph 20).

14 Local education authority policies are variable and seldom explicit. The degree of corporate concern between education and social services departments, and between either or both and the local health authorities is also variable.

15 **Developing the service**

At LEA level one area for development is the clarification of policies. Administrators from colleges would then be enabled to put forward professional concerns and to advocate policies in association with pressure groups of parents, voluntary organisations and workers; provision for special needs is often an area of political sensitivity and concern. Policy areas which are essentially for decision at LEA rather than institutional level include:

Resourcing levels in respect of teaching staff, support staff, equipment and materials, extra-institutional support (e.g. specialist careers services, peripatetic speech therapists);

Construction or major adaptation of buildings: the Chronically Sick and

Disabled Persons Act 1970 was amended by the Disabled Persons Act 1981 so that 'appropriate provision' should be made for the needs of disabled people on education premises; this is difficult to enforce, and the DES (1984) issued a revised Design Note 18 on the subject;
Transition from school to college at what age, under what arrangements for advice and choice, with what staffing and funding support;
School-college link courses with what staffing, funding and transport arrangements;
Choice of residential or day education under what policy criteria, with what budgetary consequences, with what arrangements for advice and student or parental choice;
Access to the 'mainstream' curriculum whether individual colleges are to be designated 'specialist' with consequent weakening of access to mainstream curriculum opportunities only available elsewhere; whether specialist support should (or can) be made available to meet all forms of disability throughout the whole service (or in the case of students with mobility problems throughout the whole of an individual college);
Awards and other financial support surprising anomalies may exist unless there is careful consideration (e.g. large expenditures if residential education is chosen but no special financial support at all to attend a local college as a full-time student; or conversely an insistence on attendance at a less suitable local college course rather than a more expensive but more suitable course at a residential college);
Age limits for support and access as already mentioned, there is a duty to provide full-time education 'in school or elsewhere' to the age of 19 (See above paragraph 9); after that only a power, but a consensus of informed opinion believes that the duty should be extended to meet special needs up to the age of 25 if their severity warrants. The continuation of transport arrangements regarded as normal during school age often seems particularly hard for LEAs to arrange;
Education and training for adults what facilities are to be offered through the LEA's general provision, and what facilities are to be offered in cooperation with health authorities, social services departments, and the MSC; in both cases, with what special support and/or financial arrangements;
Staff development what arrangements are to be made and funded for both specialist and mainstream staff (both teaching and support staff); what management development is required for post-school provision to meet special educational needs; the extent to which necessary arrangements can be provided 'in-house' within institutions and LEAs or require inter-LEA cooperation, and through what channel;
Administrative structures and systems the requirements of a maturing approach to the meeting of special educational needs across traditional sectors (schools, continuing education), across departments and between authorities, and in procedurally innovating ways to meet needs hitherto unrecognised.

16 At college level the responsiveness of the post-school education service to newly expressed and changing educational needs is recognised by most LEAs: people with special educational needs approach colleges, and initiatives by and within colleges seek to respond. A consensus view has emerged since the mid-1970s that colleges should adopt clear statements of policy regarding the admission and support of students with special educational needs, and should

designate from their staff a special needs coordinator in order to ensure implementation of the policy; examples are given in a short guide to good practice in FHE entitled *Handicap, Disability and Special Learning Needs* (NATFHE, 1985b). It is possible in the light of experience to go beyond statements of intent and initial staff appointments to the identification of two major principles of informing policy and three major fields for development programmes.

17 The first principle is that of ensuring the widest possible access to the curriculum offered by the post-school education service, in all institutions and at all academic levels. The consensus is that normal entry criteria to any course should apply. Also that flexibility should extend to applicants with special needs in the same way as to others who have been unable to follow traditional academic routes into post-school education, supported as necessary by special arrangements (and sometimes by special courses). The second principle is that of ensuring progression to more advanced courses, such that students with special educational needs are not offered a more restrictive curriculum than others.

18 **A course development programme**

The first field for a development programme is course development. Colleges need to satisfy themselves that either within their own institution or (accessibly) elsewhere there is introductory course provision for students with:

Moderate Learning Difficulties (both education-based and through the Youth Training Scheme)

Severe Learning Difficulties (both education-based and by outreach or link arrangements with hospitals and social services centres)

Emotional and Behavioural Difficulties

Motor Impairments

Hearing Impairments

Visual Impairments

Colleges also need to satisfy themselves that any other group of potential students in the area with a disability or disabilities in common who could benefit from specific course provision has access to that. That is often the first field for development, and produces consequential needs for both experienced staff and appropriate resources, which can also be used to support the next phase of development, proceeding in parallel.

19 **A support system development programme**

An effective college programme will follow through the cycle for individual students to identify support needs. Stages in the cycle include

Initial contacts through effective prospectus and publicity material; effective contacts with schools, careers advisers, social services and health service workers, voluntary organisations active in the area, etc;

Admission and induction incorporating diagnosis of special needs and necessary support, whether applications are for special or for mainstream courses;

Student services during the course incorporating the various supplementary provisions for staff, equipment and materials discussed below;

Assessment and examinations where special arrangements may well need to be negotiated in advance with validating bodies if physical or sensory disability impedes or slows normal assessment processes;

Progression recognising the especial obligation colleges have to their own students either to facilitate progression within the college or to negotiate admission to appropriate mainstream courses elsewhere; *Destinations* recognising again an especial obligation to support and (where possible) maintain contact with former students as they grapple with employment (sheltered or open), further education or training, or what has been called 'significant living without work'. Destination surveys are particularly important for students with special educational needs, and modifications to courses may become necessary as facts replace assumptions about students' destinations.

20 **A Resources Development Programme**

This third field of development interacts with, supports, and makes possible the other two. Experience suggests that fully developed programmes take time to establish and that priorities are largely determined by local factors which (by definition) vary. However, the necessary and desirable costs of particular developments can be identified, funding sources investigated, and progress maintained. The following provide a basis for colleges to discuss with LEAs (and others):

Teaching Staff A Special Needs Coordinator at Senior or Principal Lecturer grade is generally recognised as a desirable early step for most colleges (See NATFHE 1985, NBHS 1985). Special courses each need a course tutor of at least Lecturer II grade, with sufficient staffing allocation to provide both an effective course team capable of withstanding staff absence and for average group sizes of not more than 50% – 60% of normal. Special courses for students with certain needs require additional teaching support: six blind students will keep a support teacher busy full-time; a class of students with hearing impairment requires attention from both a support teacher and a speech therapist (neither necessarily full-time); a group of students with emotional and behavioural difficulties will require 1–2 hours a week of tutorial support for each student. Few experienced teachers are likely to be obtainable for such work below Lecturer II grade.

Support staff The establishment of a network of any size would require, administrative/clerical support comparable with that of a college department; large numbers of students with disabilities require reconsideration of the load upon examinations administration as negotiations with validating bodies multiply. Courses for students with moderate learning difficulties benefit from direct classroom assistance by volunteers or care assistants; for those with severe learning difficulties a course can hardly work without care assistants. Courses and programmes for students with motor and other physical impairments often require attendants to assist individual students, either through paid support or by volunteers. Courses and programmes for students with visual impairment require braillers and other technician support to prepare special learning materials. Courses and programmes for students with hearing impairment require both speech therapists and special learning materials.

Equipment The design and manufacture of new equipment proceeds apace, and any attempt to specify needs would quickly date. The National Bureau for Handicapped Students can recommend sources of authoritative information and advice.

Premises The conversion of whole buildings for access (and for swift and certain egress in the event of fire) by students with mobility problems is both expensive and technical, and will require action at LEA rather than college level. The conversion of individual rooms to provide bases for students with particular disabilities may be possible for colleges to undertake within their own resources; and this would be highly desirable. (See **4.3** 58–62.)

Staff Development A DES Working Party has considered issues identified by the official Advisory Committee. Needs analysis points to regional and LEA conferences for managerial staff within and between colleges, for extended training support for special needs coordinators on a regional basis, and for considerable 'in-house' support for teaching and support staff concerned, whether in a large or in a small way, with students who have special needs. This requires planning, careful timetabling, and budgeting.

21 **Conclusion**

At the time of writing, provision for students with special educational needs is gaining ground very considerably in further education, though remaining static in most of higher and adult education as the result of resource constraints. It is an exciting time; while it took the best part of a century to build the framework of special education (largely on a segregated basis) for children of compulsory school age, the further education system is attempting to build an equivalent framework (on a largely integrated basis from the start) within a decade.

NOTE

1 The National Bureau for Handicapped Students is a Government supported cooperative network of educational institutions, authorities and organisations, bodies concerned with disability, student organisations and individuals which maintains an information and advice service for students, intending students, and educational bodies.

FURTHER READING

After 16: The Education of Young People with Special Needs – A Public Campaign. Available from National Bureau for Handicapped Students

Cooper, D (1987) *Developing Effective Policy Statements.* National Bureau for Handicapped Students

Darnbrough Ann, and Kinrade Derek, *Directory for the Disabled: A Handbook of Information and Opportunities for Disabled and Handicapped People*. Royal Association for Disability and Rehabilitation

DES (1984) *Access for Disabled People to Educational Buildings (Design Note 18)* Department of Education and Science (Architects and Buildings Section)

Education Act 1981 HMSO

FEU (1982) *Skills for living: a curriculum framework for young people in FE with moderate learning difficulties.* Further Education Unit

FEU (1982) *Stretching the System: FE and related responses to Students with Special Needs*. Further Education Unit

FEU (1984) *Learning for independence.* Longman Group UK Ltd for Further Education Unit

FEU (1984) *Routes to Coping: implementing teaching programmes for students with moderate learning difficulties*. Further Education Unit

FEU (1986) *A College Guide: Meeting Special Educational Needs.* Longman Group UK Ltd for Further Education Unit

FEU (1986) *Special Needs Occasional Papers: (1) Skills and self-confidence* (Buckinghamshire C H E); *(2) Opening the doors* (Southwark College, London); *(3) Open and accessible* (Liverpool LEA). Longman Group UK Ltd for Further Education Unit

FEU (1986) *Special Needs Occasional Papers : (4) Succeeding with the deaf student in college* (National Association for Teaching Education for the Deaf). Longman Group UK Ltd for Further Education Unit.
FEU/FESC (1986) *Provision for Students with Special Needs* (Coombe Lodge Report, vol. 18, nos 10 and 11) Further Education Staff College
Fish J. (Chair) (1985) *Educational Opportunities for All?* Inner London Education Authority
Hutchinson David (1982) *Work Preparation for the Handicapped*. Croom Helm
MSC (1985) *Code of Practice on the Employment of Disabled People*. Manpower Services Commission
NATFHE (1985) *Handicap, Disability and Special Learning Needs: A Guide to Good Practice in FHE*. National Association of Teachers in Further and Higher Education
NBHS (1986) *Burnham: the Biggest Barrier of All?* National Bureau for Handicapped Students
NFER (1985) *From Coping to Confidence*. (A multi-media pack) National Foundation for Educational Research
QEFD (1984) *Directory of Opportunities for School Leavers with Disabilities*. Queen Elizabeth's Foundation for the Disabled, Leatherhead, Surrey KT22 0BN
Stowell, R (1987) *Catching Up? Provision for students with special educational needs in further and higher education*. National Bureau for Handicapped Students
TUC *Guide on the Employment of Disabled People*. Trades Union Congress
Warnock M (Chair) (1978) *Special Educational Needs: report of the Committee of Enquiry into the education of handicapped children and young people* (Cmnd 7212). HMSO
Wiltshire County Council *COPE: Compendium of Post-16 Education in Residential Establishments for Handicapped Young People*. Available from National Bureau for Handicapped Students, 336 Brixton Road, London SW7 7AA

Section 4

BUILDINGS

4.1 PROCEDURES FOR EDUCATIONAL BUILDING AND MAINTENANCE

1 National capital allocations (i.e. normally permission to raise loans) are made to local education authorities for building programmes undertaken at colleges. Within this allocation specific provision is made for any major building projects costing £200,000 or more, exclusive of professional fees, furniture and equipment, which have been included in a major building programme previously announced by the DES.

2 Periodically authorities are asked to submit proposals for new major building projects. Normally the DES tries to announce major building programmes up to two years in advance of when the work would start. The final decision is made by the Secretary of State who receives advice from the appropriate branches of the Department, including the Architects and Building Branch.

3 In order to gain a slot in the major works programme, authorities have to satisfy the DES or Welsh Office that the numbers and types of students to be enrolled at a college cannot be properly accommodated in the buildings as they exist. Institutions are expected, as a first step, to assess the capacity of their existing buildings and to compare this notional capacity, based on area or number of workplaces, with the actual or forecast student numbers.

4 Design Notes 37 and 45 published by the Architects and Building Branch of the DES shows how to calculate the notional capacity of existing buildings. In all cases the resultant notional capacity is expressed in Space Full Time Equivalent (SFTE) students. The conversion formula for an SFTE student is shown in Table 1.

In the normal way, the maximum number of full-time and sandwich students present at any time during the academic year should be entered here. However, it is recognised that this formula, designed to help in the physical planning process, may not always adequately reflect the complex attendance patterns of non-traditional FE students, and amendments to it were being considered at time of writing.

5 Design Note 37 suggests two methods whereby the capacity of non-advanced further education buildings may be assessed. The first method, Method A, requires the total gross floor area of the institution to be known, and for this area to be divided by one of three factors, according to the type of activity predominantly undertaken. For a normal college with an average spread of large and small scale activities, the divisor should be 10 square metres. If the buildings are used mainly for general education and humanities, the divisor should be 7 square metres, and if they are used mainly for large scale activities (e.g. drama, building, and heavy engineering), the divisor should be 13 square metres.

6 Method A is quick and easy and does not require inspection of individual rooms; it has been tested and found to be reasonably accurate. Utilisation levels (See **4.4** 5–9) for students enrolled based on 80% frequency and 80% occupancy have been assumed. The area standards are those considered suitable for average mixes of student disciplines within the given categories and

Table 1
Conversion formula for an STFE Student

Students enrolled	*Count as*
Full-time and sandwich	1
Part-time day	0.22
Part-time day and evening	0.22
Block release	0.33
Short course	0
Evening only	0

assume that the accommodation mixes are also average. The method is useful for showing in general terms whether an institution has spare capacity or not.

7 The second method suggested in Design Note 37, Method B, aims to give a more accurate assessment of the number of students it is possible to accommodate in an institution, and it is based on the numbers of workplaces provided. The method calculates the number of workplaces available in each category of teaching accommodation, and adjusts the final figure according to local circumstances:

Basic procedural steps

(i) Establish a schedule of teaching spaces, and for each space, identified by name or number, give its area, measured to internal face of walls.
(ii) Decide on the primary use of each space, relating it to the list of space types shown in Appendix 1, Design Note 37.
(iii) Visit each space and assess the number of workplaces.
(iv) Divide the area of each space by the appropriate area standard.
(v) Compare the capacity given by (iii) with the capacity given by (iv). If the former is within 10% of the latter, take it as the capacity of the area. If not, take the capacity given by (iv).
(vi) Record the total capacity in workplaces for each space type and add together.
(vii) Apply the adjustment relating to utilisation, and any of the following as appropriate.

Utilisation
Multiply the total number of workplaces in the college by 64%.

Storage Where it is considered necessary to reduce the area of teaching spaces by a factor to allow for large and fixed internal storage, the scale as in Table 2 is suggested.

Table 2
Teaching Space/Storage Scale

*For space types**	*Multiply area by*
1, 2, 3, 5	90%
4, 6, 7	85%
8, 9	70%

*See Appendix 1, Design Note 37

Non-teaching accommodation If the proportion of teaching to non-teaching accommodation, including balance area, *exceeds* the appropriate ratio of 65% teaching area to 35% non-teaching area, the capacity may be further adjusted:

(i) Calculate the actual ratio of teaching area to non-teaching area.
(ii) Compare it to the 65:35 ratio.
(iii) Decrease the workplace capacity by one percentage point for every percentage point difference between (i) and (ii).

Separate sites
Utilisation levels may be lower on sites more than five minutes' walk away from the main site (and which are not operating in a self-contained way) because of, for example, timetabling difficulties and inappropriate accommodation mixes. It may be appropriate to adjust their workplace capacity by applying a utilisation factor of around 55–60%, rather than 64%. Also, the adjustment factor concerning the ratio of teaching to non-teaching accommodation will be particularly appropriate.

8 Method B allows for local judgement to be allied to the use of area standards and makes it possible to identify excess or deficit capacity in different space types. It can also provide guidance for management decisions on space use, involving, for example, the adaptation of buildings and adjustments to space allocation methods in order to achieve a closer match between student numbers, courses and accommodation.

9 For advanced further education buildings, the fundamentals of Methods A and B apply also, with some allowances being made for the different nature of work and for the variations in size found across some institutions.

10 Thus, Method A suggests three divisors for institutions with 5,000 or more SFTE students, 14.5, 10.5 and 17.5 square metres. For institutions with fewer than 5,000 SFTEs, the suggested divisors are 15, 11, and 18 square metres.

11 In relation to Method B, it is suggested that the basic procedure be carried out both for teaching and learning accommodation. To cover such spaces as libraries, seminar rooms, and project rooms, the recommended ratio among teaching, learning and other accommodation is 50:20:30. Adjustments should be made if the ratio of teaching plus learning accommodation exceeds 70:30.

12 In all cases it is important to be realistic about the primary use of the spaces under scrutiny so that the area standards applied are not too generous. All the area standards used in these calculations derive from design notes giving recommendations for new buildings (Design Notes 33 and 44) (See **4.2**).

13 The amount and mix of existing accommodation are not the only factors taken into account in deciding whether a major project should be approved or not. The Secretary of State will wish to pursue the Government's current policy objectives. Thus the 1986 DES letter to chief education officers states that priority will be given to projects falling into one or more of the following categories:

> Approved local reorganisation of 16–19 education;
> Meeting the expanding needs of science and technology, and for vocational education in response to employment needs at local and national level;

Rationalisation of sites and buildings with a view to achieving revenue savings;
Emergency renewal and replacement of defective buildings.

14 Until recently all successful bids for major projects had to be closely vetted by the professional staff of the DES. Following an efficiency scrutiny of the Architects and Building Branch however, it was decided that this procedure could be greatly streamlined and that only a few items of information need be supplied, the most important of which is an undertaking that the proposed project conforms to the DES constructional standards. The new streamlined procedures are explained in DES Administrative Memorandum 1/86 and the requirements of the constructional standards are outlined in DES Administrative Memorandum 2/85.

15 To summarise, in general no submission of particulars is required in respect of the approval of minor works, i.e. those costing less than £200,000. For major works up to £2 million, form ABBX should be completed, giving identifying particulars, a short description of the project, and the undertaking of conformity with the Department's recommended constructional standards. For major works over £2 million, the existing forms ABB25 and ABB24 should be used, together with sketch plans, as soon as the appropriate information is available.

16 In any case, it is recommended that any request for exemption from the Department's constructional standards should be made as early as possible, and that a regular dialogue should continue to take place between DES building professionals undertaking territorial duties and the staff of individual LEAs on the content of the authority's building programmes and the design issues arising from particular projects. This will provide an opportunity for the exchange of information and ideas and a contribution in support of the achievement of value for money. Thus the Department's territorial architects and quantity surveyors remain available for consultation and advice.

FURTHER READING

Department of Education and Science.
Design Note 37. 1984 *Assessing the Capacity of Further Education Buildings* DES Architects and Building Branch.
Design Note 44. 1985 *Area Guidelines for Advanced Further Education Institutions* DES Architects and Building Branch.
Design Note 45. 1985 *Assessing the Capacity of Public Sector Higher Education Buildings* DES Architects and Building Branch.
Administrative Memorandum 2/85 *Constructional standards for maintained educational building in England* 13 September 1985. Department of Education and Science.
Administrative Memorandum 1/86 *Modification of approval procedures for LEA school and further education building projects* 2 January 1986. Department of Education and Science.

4.2 CONSTRUCTION, ACCOMMODATION AND DESIGN STANDARDS

1 Construction and design standards for all colleges are recommended by the DES through administrative memoranda, procedural notes, circulars, and the publications of the Department's Architects and Building Branch. Without the specific agreement to exemption of the Secretary of State, all educational building must conform with the constructional standards outlined in Administrative Memorandum 2/85. These standards are drawn from Schedule 1 to the Buildings Regulations (SI 1985 No. 1065), from other 'approved documents' and from relevant documents published by the Architects and Building Branch.

2 The legal position is complex. Colleges are subject in the matter of buildings to a variety of statutory provisions, among which are the Public Health Acts 1936 and 1961, Gas Act 1972, and the Offices, Shops and Railway Premises Act 1963. Each of these acts, inter alia, has a direct application in certain circumstances. The Health and Safety at Work etc Act 1974 means that where statutory regulations do not exist reference must then be made to relevant codes of practice and other advice (See **2.7** 4). Although it is a matter ultimately for the courts to determine, it may be generally held that good cause would have to be shown why relevant advice was not followed where it is considered that duties under the Health and Safety at Work etc. Act were not fulfilled. This would involve the question of reasonable practicability where the determinant is that of cost balanced against the likelihood of injury. (It is notable thus that whereas DES recommended standards have risen, and in many cases are higher than statute, cost provision has not, for building programme allocations have been subject to governmental restraint on public expenditure.)

3 General statutory provision concerning college premises is made by the Further Education Regulations 1975. However, all that the Regulations require is that 'effective and suitable provision' should be made, particularly regarding: lighting, heating, sanitation, and ventilation; the safeguarding against danger from fire and accident; the maintaining of the premises and the equipment of the premises in good repair and with regard to their cleanliness. The reason for this general statutory requirement only is that whereas authorities have a duty to make arrangements for schools, provision of further and higher education is discretionary. The burden, therefore, of ensuring satisfactory standards in premises which are provided by discretion falls on the provider. That education has been included in the scope of the Health and Safety at Work etc. Act means that further education is subject to general duties and to such standards as are relevant; but it is difficult in many cases to state what these standards are, except where they are imposed by statute, such as the Factories Act. DES advice on standards, therefore, ought not to be lightly ignored, although the norms will in practice be varied according to the circumstances of a college, its use, and the nature of courses it operates.

4 The requirements of 'effective and suitable' provision, in terms of the amount and type of space to be provided in a new further education building are described in Design Notes 33 and 44. Environmental energy and welfare considerations are covered by other documents published by DES and other

bodies (see **4.3**). Most of these documents were designed to be applied in the case of new buildings. For a discussion of the use of existing buildings see **4.4**.

5 The area standards they suggest are based on two approaches: the first concerns teaching accommodation and gives the amount of area which should be provided for one workplace in a particular subject at a particular level. (The number of workplaces to be provided will depend on a formula which takes account of numbers and sizes of groups, numbers of hours of teaching, desirable and achievable levels of utilisation, length of teaching week and so on.) The second approach, where the idea of workplaces is inappropriate (as in the provision of administrative and communal accommodation) suggests the area which should be provided for each SFTE.

6 The Design Notes categorise accommodation as being of three basic types: teaching, learning, and other. Teaching accommodation includes all those areas used for traditional, formal, timetabled teaching; learning accommodation covers those areas, becoming increasingly important, where students carry out individual projects, study privately, and supplement their formal activities through untimetabled activities. These activities will vary considerably across different types of colleges. Other areas, also known as non-teaching areas (a reference back to previous documents before the category of learning area was instituted), include the accommodation necessary to support the teaching and learning process, e.g. administration, staff workrooms, and communal and catering accommodation.

7 In addition, these three types of accommodation need to be balanced by appropriate areas for circulation and other common services. The three basic accommodation types plus the balance areas constitute the gross area of an institution. For a summary of what should be provided in an institution of further education, useful for general planning and costing purposes, see Table 1 in Design Note 20. The following paragraphs extract the most important recommendations of Design Notes 33 and 44.

8 **Non-advanced further education**

Teaching Area Timetabled teaching area and total teaching area are assessed by first establishing the required number of spaces and then deciding the respective area of each space. The aggregation of these will give the total teaching area.

9 The number of teaching spaces can be estimated by combining various assumptions in the following formula. The use of the word 'spaces' is intended to avoid implying any particular design solution.

$$\text{Number of spaces} = N \times \frac{T}{L} \times \frac{100}{F} \text{ where}$$

N = number of timetabled teaching groups per week in the category of accommodation being considered.

T = average hours/periods per week timetabled in that type of accommodation.

L = the total number of hours/periods per week assumed to be available in the timetable.

F = a factor representing the likely frequency of use of the teaching spaces.

The number of timetabled teaching groups (N) can be estimated with various degrees of precision. The number of students attending should be expressed on a common basis, SFTEs, see **4.1**. The best prediction is likely to take account of a number of variables related to the assumed organisation of the college, the availability of specialist staff, and the popularity of examination subjects. (For further information see Arthur Young 1982.)

The teaching time (T), measured in hours or periods per week per teaching group, should be established separately for each category of teaching accommodation required.

The length of the weekly timetable (L) is the number of hours or periods available in the weekly timetable. (L) must be measured in the same units as (T).

The frequency of use factor (F) is a measure of likely space usage over time. An overall target figure of between 70 and 80% is likely to be appropriate.

10 The size of teaching spaces depends on the maximum group size to be accommodated and the area standards appropriate to the activities to be accommodated.

Table 3
Teaching Area Standards and Storage Allowances

Space type	*Area standard m^2 per student*
General teaching	
Lecture theatres: close seating arrangements	1.0
Students seated at tables or in informal groups	1.8–2.1
Demonstration facilities (e.g. for music); students seated at large tables (e.g. for geography)	2.5–3.0
Science and technology	
Non-advanced laboratories	3.0–4.6
Commerce and business studies	2.7–3.2
Crafts	
Home economics, dressmaking; workshops with benches (e.g. carpentry, plumbing, electronics)	4.5–5.6
Art and design studios (up to foundation level); drawing offices	3.2–5.6
Catering; hairdressing	6.5–8.4
Heavy crafts with large machines and/or equipment (e.g. for welding, motor vehicle work, construction, installation trades)	7.5–8.4

Suggested standards for teaching storage and service areas are expressed as a percentage of the teaching space which they serve:	*Storage allowance*
General teaching (only a proportion of the rooms); geography; language laboratories	10%
Science and commerce (including preparation rooms, model office)	15%
Home economics; dressmaking; art and design; music	20%
Craft workshops (e.g. electrical, motor vehicle, carpentry)	25%
Hairdressing (including laundry, dispensary, reception areas)	40%
Catering (including reception, bar/restaurant, preparation areas)	40%

11 **Learning areas**

These will include library and social areas, and possibly some large spaces, so long as these are appropriately used for a variety of purposes.

Table 4
Library accommodation

SFTEs	Bookstacks	Support[2]	Floor area (m^2) Reader[3]	Total
250	50	70	63	183
500	88	80	125	293
1000	138	95	250	483
2000	238	125	500	863
3000	338	155	750	1243

A minimum of 0.2 m^2 to 0.3 m^2 of social space should be designated overall per SFTE. If alternative large spaces are not available nearby, a minimum of two large spaces should be provided in each college. See Table 5.

Table 5
Large Spaces

Multi-purpose hall	250m^2
Assembly hall	250m^2
Gymnasium	250m^2–280m^2 (sports hall 500m^2)
Drama studio	120m^2–150m^2
Lecture theatre	100^2–120m^2

12 **Non-teaching areas**

For academic staff it is suggested that 2.9 m^2 (including storage) should be provided for each staff workplace, and for non-academic staff it is suggested that work places may be provided out of the allowances for storage and service areas. For staff social provision, 1.2 m^2 should be provided for each full-time staff member. Administrative accommodation should be provided as in Table 6.

Table 6
Administrative accommodation

SFTEs	Total administrative area (m^2)
250 or fewer	220
500	255
1000	330
1500	395
2000	450
2500	495
3000	530

No specific recommendations are made concerning catering, since requirements will vary widely, particularly according to what is otherwise available locally.

13 **Balance area**

The balance area provides for circulation, support services, medical room, lavatories, changing rooms, cloakrooms, and lockers. The previous categories of accommodation should be increased by an allowance for the balance area as in Table 7.

Table 7
Balance Area

Type of accommodation	*Percentage increase*
Storage	0
Catering accommodation	10
Workshops	25
Learning areas, staff social areas	25
Large space requirements	25
Teaching spaces and areas (other than workshops)	40
Staff workrooms	45
Administration	50

14 **Advanced further education**

Timetabled teaching areas The method for calculating the numbers of spaces required and the resulting total area is the same as for non-advanced further education, but the area standards per workplace, the allowances for ancillary and storage space, and for balance areas should be derived from Table 8.

15 **Learning areas**

Space for the library, to include areas for book and periodicals storage, readers and support services, should be provided according to Table 9.
Accommodation for other learning activities, taking place in resource centres, computer centres and project spaces should usually be provided out of the allowances for teaching areas.

16 Non-teaching accommodation should be provided according to Table 10.

17 There is no detailed information for further education concerning sites and playing fields. General points are made in Design Notes 33 and 44, and other guidance is contained in Building Bulletin 28.

18 The standards outlined in the preceding paragraphs were established in the context of designing new buildings. They have already been adapted to be applicable in the context of assessing the capacity of existing buildings (see **4.1** 4–12). Increasingly authorities and institutions are having to rationalise and adapt what they already own, and many of the design principles outlined in the Design Notes already mentioned, as well as in other documents[6] are relevant to this process.

Table 8
Teaching Area Standards

1. Space type used for	*2. m² per student workplace*	*3. Ancillary and storage space Add to values in column 2*	*4. Balance area Add to total of columns 2 and 3*
(i) General teaching			
Lecture theatres; close seating arrangements	1.0	nil	40%
Teaching at tables in informal groups	1.8–2.1	nil	40%
Teaching at tables or desks	2.3–2.5	nil	40%
Teaching with demonstration facilities students seated at large tables	2.5–3.0	nil	40%
(ii) Specialised teaching			
a. small scale			
Information technology	2.7–3.2	10%	40%
Science[4]	5.6	25%	40%
Art and design (studios and drawing offices)	4.0–5.6	10%	40%
b. large scale[5]			
Engineering	5.6	25%	40%
Science and technology	5.6	25%	40%
Art and design (specialist areas)	5.6–8.4	10%	40%

19 Among the changes which are occurring in advanced and non-advanced further education it is possible to identify the following, each with its implications for the design and management (see **4.4**) of accommodation: the closure of courses; the development of modular and similar courses; a reduction in formal teaching hours; an increase in tutorial/seminar group sizes; the development of computer facilities; the development of learning packages; increases in project work; more private teaching staff activities; a wider range of training courses and post-experience vocational education and open learning. These changes are due to a change in emphasis in teaching methods and to an efficiency-led drive towards rationalisation and a tighter student:staff ratio.

20 Colleges should consider making adaptations along the lines suggested (see below paragraphs 30–40). Lecture theatres for groups of around 70 to 100 students are increasingly required, as teaching group sizes tend to the larger and smaller ends of the range. Groups of up to about 60 students may be successfully accommodated in flat floor spaces, but above that size, appropriate teaching areas need to contain raked seating. Very successful conversions have been made from underused specialist laboratories, workshops, studios, assembly halls, and gymnasia (of which there may be a surplus in ex-teacher training colleges). Conventional lecture theatres may be unsuitable for the informal discussion-type activities which are more and more required in informal teaching, in which case it may be more appropriate to provide U-shaped lecture spaces, where the participants can all see each other, and where the lecturer can position himself/herself nearer to or further away from the students.

Table 9
Total Usable Library Area

Level of work	*Basic net area (m^2) up to 250 SFTEs*	*Area per SFTE (m^2) to be added to column (2) (no. of SFTEs)*						
(1)	*(2) 250*	*(3) 251–500*	*(4) 501–1000*	*(5) 1001–2000*	*(6) 2001–3000*	*(7) 3001–4000*	*(8) 4001–5000*	*(9) 5001+*
Over 90% advanced work	328	1.00	0.86	0.72	0.66	0.55	0.49	0.43
60–90% advanced work	270	0.76	0.64	0.56	0.52	0.46	0.42	0
30–60% advanced work	227	0.59	0.51	0.47	0.42	0.42	0	0

Table 10
Area Guidelines for Administrative, Communal and Catering Accommodation

Space type used for	*Area per SFTE* m^2	*Area per person* m^2	*Area per meal served* m^2	*Balance area per cent*
Administration				
up to 3000 SFTEs	0.50			50
3001 + SFTEs	0.36			50
Academic staff		5.46		50
Non-academic staff		4.00		40
Communal				
up to 3000 SFTEs	1.72			30
3001–5000 SFTEs	1.47			30
5001 + SFTEs	1.22			30
Catering				
3 main meals			0.45	25
2 main meals			0.40	25
1 main meal			0.30	25
cooked snacks			0.20	25
coffee/sandwich service			0.10	25

21 In any case attention must be paid to good mechanical ventilation, sound amplification and insulation, projection and blackout facilities and the location of appropriate chalkboards, overhead projection screens and so on – these are important features of any satisfactory teaching space. Air conditioning may be justified if lecture theatres are in almost continuous use. The provision of standard projection/amplification facilities in all appropriate rooms may be found to be cheaper than having large numbers of technicians constantly moving equipment about.

22 Rooms used for teaching smaller groups may be combined with academic staff rooms, so that the mixture of private academic work and general teaching makes the best use of the accommodation, and so that group sizes are appropriately matched to room sizes.

23 When using partitioning to form extra staff rooms in existing buildings, great attention must be paid to the need for natural light, noise insulation, adequate ventilation, and to the difficulties of interfering with existing light fittings, radiators, and sound insulation. Flexibility must be maintained for future adaptations.

24 Computing facilities should be available locally in the same way as other specialist facilities, as well as existing as a centralised provision for those studying computing as such, and for the central administration. As their environmental requirements become less demanding they can generally be accommodated without major modifications to the existing buildings, either in adapted teaching spaces or, for example, in unfilled areas, or on mezzanine floors (given proper attention to floor loading).

25 There are now several sources of general information on the use of visual display units (VDUs)[7], but the following points might be considered in connection with installations in further and higher education:

Assess the purpose of each unit. Is it for group teaching, for individual use in and/or outside the timetable, as back-up to other equipment, as a resource tool, for administration etc.? Many computing facilities will have more than one purpose and the priorities must be worked through at the planning stage.
The area of each workplace can be estimated from the appropriate guidelines. Actual layouts will vary according to room shapes and large rooms are often more economical than small ones.
If the facilities are to be used for group work, between 12 and 20 units is a reasonable number to site in one place. It is helpful if most students can see the teaching position easily, while students sitting next to each other often learn from one another. Space behind the operator for one or more people to see the screen is a useful asset.
Microcomputers or terminals may also be sited in workshops or laboratories. Facing a blank wall behind the screen may not be the most satisfactory position for prolonged sessions, but the wall might be given some visual interest to provide relief from the screen.
Other points to consider include glare and reflections on the screen, the ability to adjust the positions of the screen and keyboard to suit individual tastes, and well designed seating. Many units are used both for group and individual work, and a set of reference manuals must be provided for each group of units.

26 There is an increasing use of individually-based resource centres; institutions need to clarify their policy and to allocate sufficient resources in their budget to implement it. In addition, if materials are to be made available at less usual times, the cost of this availability may have to include adjusting security and access arrangements by modifying appropriate parts of the building.

27 The use of specialist laboratories by science, engineering and technology students is expected to increase, particularly as proportions in these disciplines are planned to grow. However, because of their costs such spaces must be prime targets for rationalisation, both within and across institutions. The equipment may not need to be as massive as previously. In many cases old-fashioned items, perhaps expensive to run, can be replaced by stimulation provided by computers and local computing facilities should be provided where possible.

28 Most science laboratories in further and higher education take about 20 students. In order to achieve tighter student:staff ratios, institutions may wish to increase group sizes, particularly in the early stages of courses; however, care must be taken to ensure that health and safety requirements are not thereby breached.

29 The relocation or creation of laboratories requires special attention to be paid to such matters as fume extraction, waste disposal and the weight of equipment, which may make modifications expensive. When costs are so high, flexibility is particularly important, in order to provide for the ever-changing proportions of teaching, project and research work and when laboratories have to be moved from one side to another according to the process of rationalisation. The labkit trolley, the labkit workstation system and the mobile fume extraction cabinet developed by the Laboratories Investigation Unit of DES[8] enable such relocations and changes of use to occur with maximum speed and efficiency, and with minimum cost and inconvenience.

30 Different methods of adaptation may be appropriate in different circumstances, according to requirements and the nature of the existing buildings. In any case, care should be taken to ensure that no modification in itself forestalls subsequent alterations as they become necessary. If flexibility, as all too often, was not built into the original buildings, at least it should not be further diminished. A relatively small job may help to relieve an institution-wide log-jam caused by inappropriate accommodation in one sector.

31 The experience of the Architects and Building Branch of the DES suggests that expenditure of much more than half the cost of equivalent new building should not be justified unless there are special circumstances.

32 Some institutions have managed to create additional usable space by filling in the open spaces left between the pilotis which are such a feature of many 1960s buildings. These infills can produce useful classroom, laboratory and workshop accommodation, and extensions to provide additional space in existing rooms. The main item of cost in such modifications is often the provision of heating and lighting.

33 Some institutions have also taken advantage of the height of existing entrance halls, workshops and specialist laboratories to construct mezzanine floors. Although access may prove difficult, and adaptations may not be as cheap as first thought, mezzanines have been built to give extra offices, work spaces and stores. It is unlikely that more than half of an existing floor area can be given over to providing a mezzanine. Structural considerations are particularly important.

34 At the same time as carrying out such modifications, institutions may want to reexamine the servicing and zoning arrangements in their buildings. All further and higher education institutions have various activities taking place in the evening. In the past such activities have not necessarily been concentrated into particular parts of the institution so that whole buildings have had to be heated for the sake of one or two rooms. As this is uneconomic, institutions have had to consider either restricting classes to a few evenings a week or concentrating evening classes in as few buildings or parts of buildings as possible.

35 Another approach is to reexamine the heating system, assessing the life of the major components and whether it is possible to install heating controls which allow better zoning. In some cases a central boiler plant may be at the end of its useful life and institutions have reorganised into having a separate boiler plant for each building, often on the roof. Moves of this type may not only improve the heating but may enable spaces vacated by plant to be put to other uses, such as staff offices.

36 When modifying existing buildings it is important to ensure that existing arrangements for fire control are not upset and that health and safety requirements are met. When erecting partitions or building mezzanine floors, egress/access for fire escape/control must be considered. When specialist accommodation is created or moved the stringent regulations relating to the use and storage of dangerous materials should be observed. Even if the only change is to make more use of specialist accommodation, the consequences should be assessed carefully. Some workshops are laid out in such a way that to use them to the capacity suggested by the number of machines installed would be dangerous unless it were certain that only a few machines were in use at once[9].

37 For accounting and control purposes revenue expenditure on maintenance and capital expenditure on improvements are separately identified. However, there is no barrier to spending revenue monies on capital work. Since in practice coordination is essential, it is desirable for authorities to allow discretion within an overall budget so that minor adaptations can be carried out while the need for essential maintenance work is respected. When this greater responsibility is allowed to institutions, through procedures agreed with the local authority, there is evidence of greater value for money: institutions can react quickly to changing circumstances, and can complete building work in a relatively short period such as the summer vacation.

38 It is no longer appropriate for authorities and institutions to follow detailed, long-term development plans which were posited on a continued growth of student numbers and resources. Rather institutions should prepare a development strategy, which need be only a sample statement of principles together with a short-term programme. The base for the strategy will be the total student numbers likely to be generated by the courses to be offered. The numbers may be broken down into disciplines and faculties but great care must be taken not to overestimate potential numbers since this fault has made many past efforts almost useless.

39 The main steps in preparing a building strategy might be:

(i) Assess total gross area (using Table 1 of Design Note 20[10] or Method A of Design Notes 37 or 45[11]), to be compared to student numbers;

(ii) Assess capacity on a site by site basis (using Method B of Design Notes 37 or 45[11]) to identify excess/shortfall in different accommodation categories;

(iii) Monitor utilisation of teaching and non-teaching accommodation, to establish match/mismatch of types and sizes of spaces (and equipment) against activities[12];

(iv) Establish the degree to which teaching and non-teaching accommodation is adequate/inadequate;

(v) Assess the possibilities for optimising the use of accommodation and equipment.

40 The programme to support the above procedure should cover about two years' work, while keeping in hand a reserve list of agreed projects. The programme could involve changes to the total estate of the institution, the relocation or regrouping of areas of work and the improvement of the general environment of the accommodation.

NOTES

[1] The space needed by the teacher for traditional teaching methods remains the same and thus smaller rooms need proportionately more space per student than larger rooms. For some optimum layouts See *Educational Furniture for the 16–19 Age Group: Space standards.* Architects and Building Branch, DES, 1984.

[2] Includes counter and catalogue space, librarian's office, workroom, photocopying, bookstore and area for audiovisual aids and other resources.

[3] Provides for private study, browsing and periodicals.

[4] Most science laboratories.

[5] Where there is a requirement for particular conditions of work, it may be justified to increase this figure.

[6] See particularly Design Note 41 and all the publications of the Laboratories Investigation Unit (Architects and Building Branch, DES).

[7] See Health and Safety Executive 1983, Institute for Consumer Ergonomics 1984, SED 1984 (see **FURTHER READING**).

[8] See *Profile of the LIU* (DES). Further information is available from the DES.

[9] *Health and Safety in Schools and Further Education Establishments. Pilot Study* Health and Safety Executive. 1978.

[10] Design Note 20. *Polytechnics: planning for change.* DES Architects and Building Branch.

[11] Design Note 37. 1984 *Assessing the Capacity of Further Education Buildings.* DES Architects and Building Branch; Design Note 45. 1985 *Assessing the Capacity of Public Sector Higher Education Buildings.* DES Architects and Building Branch.

[12] See section **4.4** and *Managing Space in Colleges*, by G. Kenny and K. Foster, Management in Colleges Series No. 1, FE Staff College, 2nd Edition, 1986.

FURTHER READING

SI 1985 1065 *Building Regulations* HMSO

Department of Education and Science
Design Note 8. 1972. *Polytechnics: planning for development.* Architects and Building Branch
Design Note 9. 1972. *Designing for Further Education.* Architects and Building Branch
Design Note 20. 1979. *Polytechnics: planning for change.* Architects and Building Branch.
Design Note 22. 1980. *Accommodation for the 16–19 age group – NAFE: designing for change.* Architects and Building Branch
Design Note 23. 1980. *Accommodation for the 16–19 age group: from colleges in 1980.* Architects and Building Branch
Design Note 24. 1981. *Compliance with constructional standards.* Architects and Building Branch
Design Note 30. 1982. *Educational furniture for the 16–19 age group: specification and design.* Architects and Building Branch
Design Note 33. 1983. *Area guidelines for Sixth Form, Tertiary and NAFE Colleges.* Architects and Building Branch
Design Note 35. 1983. *Accommodation for the new training courses.* Architects and Building Branch
Building Bulletin 28. 1983. *Playing Fields and Hard Surface Areas.* Architects and Building Branch
Design Note 37. 1984. *Assessing the capacity of further education buildings.* Architects and Building Branch
Design Note 39. 1984. *Educational furniture for the 16–19 age group: space standards.* Architects and Building Branch
Design Note 40. 1984. *Maintenance and renewal in educational buildings: needs and priorities.* Architects and Building Branch
Design Note 41. 1985. *Accommodation for changes in Public Sector Higher Education.* Architects and Building Branch

Administrative memorandum 2/85. 1985. *Constructional standards for maintained educational building in England*
Design Note 44. *Area Guidelines for Advanced Further Education Institutions*. Architects and Building Branch
Design Note 45. 1985. *Assessing the capacity of public sector higher education buildings*. Architects and Building Branch
Building Bulletin 64. 1986. *Adaptable facilities in further education for business and office studies*. HMSO
Building Bulletin 65. 1986. *Adaptable teaching kitchens in further education*. HMSO
Profile of the Laboratories Investigation Unit. 1986
Scottish Education Department. 1984. *Computer rooms: making room for information technology*. SED

Department of Employment
Health and Safety in Schools and Further Education
Health and Safety Executive. 1978. *Establishments*. Pilot study 1978. HMSO
Health and Safety Executive. 1983. *Visual display units*. 1983. HMSO

FEU. 1985. *Towards the Electronic Office*. Further Education Unit
Donovan, K. 1981. *Learning Resources in Colleges: their organisation and management*. Council for Educational Technology
Kenny, G. and Foster, K. 1986. *Managing space in colleges*. Management in Colleges Series, No. 1, Second Edition, Further Education Staff College
BS8205. *British Standard Code of Practice for determining the design of learning spaces where audio-visual equipment will be used*. 1985

4.3 ENVIRONMENT, ENERGY CONSERVATION AND WELFARE

1 **Acoustics**

In every part of a further education building the acoustic conditions and the insulation against disturbance by noise should be appropriate to the normal use of that part. The aim is, either in designing new buildings or in adapting existing ones, that the users of the building should hear clearly what they need to hear without this being swamped, or their attention distracted, by intruding noise. Successful acoustic design is achieved in three main ways: by planning, by adopting measures for noise control, and by giving the spaces suitable reverberant characteristics. Detailed explanations of criteria and methods of calculation are given in *Acoustics in Educational Buildings*, Building Bulletin 51.

2 The following table, giving recommended maximum Background Noise Levels (BNL), is taken from *Guidelines for Environmental Design and Fuel Conservation in Educational Buildings*, Design Note 17 where more details can be found.

Table 1
Maximum Background Noise Levels

Type of space	*BNL*
Music and drama spaces	25
Teaching groups of more than 35 people (communication distance of over 8m)	25
Large lecture rooms; Language laboratories	30
Teaching groups of between 15 and 35 people (communication distance of not more than 8m) Small lecture rooms; Presentation rooms; Offices; Medical inspection rooms; Seminar rooms	35
Teaching groups of less than 15 people (communication distance of not more than 4m)	40
Sports Halls (subject to the requirements of multiple use); Resource areas; Libraries; Individual study areas (large area containing a number of small groups); Practical areas; Workshops (equipment not in use); Circulation areas	45

3 **Lighting**

The main recommendations of Design Note 17 are:

Each room or other space should have lighting appropriate to the normal use to which it is designed.

In daytime, daylight should be the main source of light in working areas except in special circumstances. Every teaching space should have a window area of at least 20% of the internal elevation of the external wall, and through which an adequate view out can be obtained.

The lowest level of maintained illumination, whether daylight or electric light, at any point on a working plane should be not less than 150 lux and where fluorescent lighting is used the general level of illumination should not be less than 300 lux.

The glare index for electric lighting should not be more than 19 in educational spaces, and due regard should be paid to the control of glare from daylight.

In the design of lighting regard should also be paid to the need to conserve energy.

4 The section dealing with educational premises in the latest *CIBS Code for Interior Lighting* gives recommendations as in Table 2.

Table 2
Standard Service Illuminance

Type of Space	*Standard Service Illuminance (lx)*
Assembly halls	
(General)	300
(Platform and stage)	as appropriate
Teaching spaces	
(General)	300
Lecture theatres (General)	300
(Demonstration benches)	500
Seminar rooms	500
Art rooms	500
Needlework rooms	500
Laboratories	500
Libraries	300
Music rooms	300
Sports halls	300
Workshops	300

5 **Thermal environment**
The main recommendations of Design Note 17 are:

Heating The system should be capable of heating a minimum of 10m^3 of fresh air per person per hour and the following resultant temperatures at a height of 0.5m above floor level should be maintained during normal hours of occupation when the external temperature is −1°C: 21°C in areas where occupants are lightly clad and inactive (e.g. medical inspection rooms)
18°C in areas where there is an average level of clothing and activity (e.g. classrooms)
15°C in dormitories
14°C in areas where the occupants are lightly clad and where activity is vigorous (e.g. gymnasia)
The temperature in circulation spaces should not be more than 3°C below the temperature of the spaces they serve.

Ventilation All working areas, halls, sick rooms and dormitories should be capable of being ventilated at a minimum rate of 30m^3 of fresh air per hour for each person normally occupying these areas, or such higher rates as may be necessary to maintain comfortable conditions.

Adequate measures should be taken to prevent condensation in, and to remove noxious fumes from, every kitchen and other room in which there may be steam or fumes.

All lavatory accommodation, changing areas and cloakrooms in which adequate cross ventilation to give at least 6 air changes per hour cannot be achieved by natural means should be mechanically ventilated.

6 *Energy conservation* The education service has to face the simple practical issue that as the costs of energy rise, so budgetary considerations in an institution may result in there being fewer resources available for direct educational provision. Conservation measures may result in the present balances being maintained; but there may be circumstances where energy saving could release monies for other educational uses. It may also be the case that an LEA might wish to use such 'saved' money for purposes other than education.

7 Resources have been allocated by the Department of Energy to local authorities for energy conservation measures in educational and other non-domestic buildings. These allocations, in later years, will, it is estimated, be recovered from the savings made; or else set against the amounts available for school building and FE minor works. However, the allocations also include some deductions from previously planned expenditure by way of enforced savings. The details will be settled within the context of the annual rate support grant negotiations and in actual capital allocations. Although it remains open to authorities to use their allocations (including additional provision for the employment and training of staff in energy matters) as they see fit, Government advice suggested that priority be given to heating control installation, insulation, and the better management of buildings (DoE Circular 56/78). It was expected that part of an authority's energy manager's job would be to advise principals on building management. Government estimates on energy saving suggested that improved management can result in an up to 20% saving, and heating controls result in a further saving of up to 15%.

8 When considering the real cost of a building over a life span of, for example, forty years, the total costs are approximately 20% to design and furnish and 80% to operate. Thus, despite the concentration in building programme decisions on the initial capital costs, it is appropriate to consider in the design of any new building or the adaptation of existing premises how the total operating cost can be reduced, even though that may entail incurring extra costs at the design and construction stages.

9 In a pilot monitoring scheme in a district of one authority, it was discovered that buildings ranged from 50% below target fuel consumption to over 900% above (Hamlyn 1978). The over-consumption was not caused by mismanagement alone: much could be attributed to plant malfunction and faulty building design. When a good housekeeping campaign was implemented, fuel consumption dropped by 19.6% (£41,500). It is estimated that substantial improvement can be attained, and that at a conservative estimate at least 20% of the authority's fuel bill could be saved – representing over £600,000 at current prices. The authority exceptionally for a two-year period decided to return the net savings from the fuel monitoring scheme to the relevant committees in order to assist their budgeting problems in a period of severe restraint.

10 Fuel monitoring is required of authorities in any case in return for their

resource allocation. It may well be that individual institutions will be required to furnish the authority with detailed fuel use information. Whether or not this is the case, monitoring of fuel consumption can include information on the use of its buildings. This would include the total number of hours and days when the institution is open for normal use as well as special uses, including evening, social, weekend and vacation use. Full monitoring requires professional expertise and will usually be the responsibility of an LEA. Required data will include full details of construction, design and engineering; weather information; and fuel consumption as well as user information.

11 The advice of the DES in the matter of fuel conservation is published in Design Note 17 and Building Bulletin 55. The remainder of this sub-section provides a digest of the matters discussed, though specific reference on technical matters ought to be made to these publications.

12 The aim of saving energy must be achieved in ways which are cost effective. Cost effectiveness is generally determined in the DES publications as being the ways by which any capital outlay is recouped within a short period. The riders must be added therefore that total cost provisions should be considered and that cost effectiveness is subject to rapid change: fuel price increases will render further savings measures appropriate which previously were too expensive. Any conservation policy also needs to have regard to the purpose of the buildings: varied patterns of use and intermittent occupancy require consideration, and so do educational needs. The nature of the building largely dictates many conservation practices.

13 **Good management**

Good housekeeping can achieve dramatic savings and provide a quick return for little expenditure. Many authorities have issued advice regarding fuel saving by good management. The DES offers the following general advice:

Teaching staff and students

(i) As supplementary heaters, such as electric fires, are costly to run, they should be used only in exceptional circumstances, for example, during cold spells outside the normal heating season when the main heating system is not in use, or when a room is occupied after the main heating period.

(ii) Lights and electrical appliances should be switched off when no longer needed, and nor should lights be used in rooms with blinds or curtains after the need for such facilities has passed. The minimum necessary number of lights and appliances should be used when people are working late.

(iii) Heating systems should be adjusted when rooms become overheated during the heating season. Ventilation should be used only in exceptional circumstances and then at minimal levels. Excess ventilation will usually activate thermostats so that more heat is supplied.

(iv) Subject to the needs for hygiene and cleanliness, hot water should be used economically.

(v) Heat can be conserved overnight by up to 20% by preventing loss through windows if blinds and curtains are closed at dusk (or when it is clear that artificial lighting will be required for the rest of the working day). Maximum use should be made of daylight for both lighting and heating purposes, by fully drawing back blinds and curtains during the day.

(vi) Clothing appropriate to the temperatures at which the institution is necessarily maintained ought to be worn.
(vii) Rooms should be allocated in such a way, where separate areas of a building can be heated independently, to allow economical use whereby heat and light are not supplied to unused areas.
(viii) Windows should be closed overnight, and external doors kept closed as much as possible during cold spells.
(ix) High power consumption equipment ought not to be used during the winter months in circumstances whereby the accumulation of other electrical demands will lead to loads in excess of the Maximum Demand Tariff (See below paragraphs 14–15).

Maintenance and caretaking staff
(i) Thermostats should be set to provide the appropriate heat for the various uses of the premises.
(ii) Hot water thermostats should be set to the lowest acceptable temperature, but hot water should be stored at 60°C and circulated at at least 50°C in order to control legionnaire's disease, and where warmer water is required, consideration should be given to the provision of 'topping up' or a separate supply.
(iii) There should be immediate replacement of faulty washers, especially in hot taps.
(iv) Windows should be closed at night, and external doors kept shut as much as possible.
(v) Cleaners should be instructed to use lights sparingly and to extinguish them when no longer required.
(vi) To avoid heating the whole building, rooms used for evening, weekend or vacation use should wherever possible be those which can be heated independently.
(vii) Although heating can usually be turned off before people have vacated a building, where automatic controls are not available to guard against weather damage, a temperature of about 5°C or 6°C (or higher if there is a serious condensation problem) will be necessary to afford protection against frost.
(viii) The times at which heating comes into operation will need to be varied: it should be started no earlier than is necessary to achieve normal working temperatures and consequently later during mild weather.
(ix) Plant maintenance is essential: boilers should be maintained in good working order and operated at their designed temperature; thermal insulation should be regularly checked; the heating load should be supplied by the minimum number of boilers; and boilers not in operation, where practicable, isolated from the heating system.

14 Electricity tariffs are a complex topic, but some brief explanation will be useful. There are twelve Electricity Boards serving different areas of the country. Each board operates its own practices and tariffs. Thus, although these are broadly similar, it will be necessary for a college itself to ascertain its particular position. Maximum Demand Tariffs are only a part of a range of tariffs. In general, the Maximum Demand Tariff will be the highest demand recorded in the premises in a month or year, according to the particular rate at which an establishment is charged, and this will determine a part of the charge for the electricity used. The amount may be significant. To give examples, there is a rate charged by the London Electricity Board which comprises a demand charge and a unit charge: the demand charge consists of the maximum

demand which has occurred over a twelve months period; and the unit charge consists of the price of the number of kilowatt hours used over monthly periods. At another rate, the demand charge comprises the maximum demand incurred during the month. Consumers of electricity can, within reason, choose the rates at which they are charged. Each rate has its specific rules, and some tariffs are available only from particular electricity boards.

15 Consequences for colleges can be considerable. The college and LEA can review existing electricity consumption, and discuss with the relevant electricity boards other rates of charge which might be applied. It follows that staff and students should be informed of the consequences of any proposed changes in the nature of electricity supply, and that the ways in which electricity might be saved are fully discussed. To provide a final illustration, a Maximum Demand operated by the London Electricity Board demonstrates the need for good housekeeping, at least: 'the maximum demand in kilowatts at any point of supply in any month shall be deemed to be twice the largest number of units supplied in any half hour in that month. Where the supply to the premises is metered at more than one point the maximum demand in any month shall be deemed to be the arithmetical sum of the maximum demands at any of those points in that month.'

16 Users of colleges should be made fully aware of conservation advice; responsibilities need to be defined. It is also important, and relevant to the general duties imposed by the Health and Safety at Work etc. Act, that there is no unauthorised alteration of a college heating or any other power supply system.

17 **Energy conservation and the design of buildings**
Items discussed here are relevant to new buildings and to the adaptation of existing premises. Although the main elements of the conservation of energy – ventilation, lighting, insulation, and heating – will be discussed separately, overall conservation clearly depends on the interaction of those elements.

18 *Ventilation* Where a building is well insulated, about one-third of the total heat loss is due to ventilation. Control of ventilation is therefore important. In either the design of new buildings or in improvements to existing buildings it is appropriate to consider the following, subject to cost effectiveness limitations:

(i) Draught stripping can be fitted to ill-fitting external doors and windows. Either, or both, door closers and draught lobbies can be installed where external doors are used frequently. Joints between, for example, walls and window frames or in panelling may result in heat loss and the problem therefore remedied by the use of draught exclusion materials.

(ii) Where buildings are exposed to a prevailing wind, it may be appropriate to provide screening by tree or hedge planting, or even the construction of walls or earth barriers.

(iii) In older buildings, although many window frames may be suitable for the use of draught stripping, others may require replacement. This may not be cost effective. Double glazing for energy conservation purposes alone is not at present considered cost effective.

(iv) The use of mechanical ventilation by such means as air extractors will be necessary in certain parts of a college. Use of a warning device or time switch may be appropriate however in ensuring that an extractor is not left to operate unnecessarily.

(v) If costs continue to rise, it will be necessary to consider the benefits of heat recovery whereby ducted air systems are adapted to transfer heat from extracted air to incoming fresh air; these systems are now becoming cost-effective.

19 *Lighting* Although colleges constructed during the past three decades have generally made full use of daylight, consideration of the following is appropriate:

(i) Economic use of electric lighting can be assisted if lights in a room can be operated independently: thus, lights furthest from a source of daylight can be switched on independently.

(ii) Research is perfecting the automatic controlling of lighting to eliminate abrupt and annoying changes of level. This control of lighting is achieved by a photoelectric process whereby an on/off switch or dimming device is activated, causing the lights to come on or be raised or lowered in accordance with given illumination requirements and the incidence of daylight. However, such systems can be expensive.

(iii) Ease of maintenance of any lighting system is relevant, as is the choice of the most efficient sources and lighting fittings.

(iv) In new buildings factors to be taken into account include the advantage of a southerly orientation, the full exploitation of daylight and the cost effectiveness against fuel consumption of more glazed areas, including side windows and roof lights.

(v) In older colleges built with very large windows which cause large winter heat loss and summer overheating the situation could be remedied by: reduction of loss by means of refitting or reglazing using opaque material; use of blinds and curtains; and the sealing of some windows where the original provision of opening windows was excessive.

20 *Insulation* Although the effectiveness of thermal insulation depends on where it is placed, its cost effectiveness increased as fuel prices rose. In general, the most effective measures are roof or ceiling insulation, according to conditions. Wall insulation has also become important. Double glazing, however, becomes economic only where a high cost fuel such as electricity is used. The purpose of thermal insulation is to retain as much heat, from whatever source, as is possible. Insulation can also reduce condensation, and in this respect the following points should be considered:

(i) The insulation should not be by-passed by cold air entering a cavity behind it, nor allowed to become wet.

(ii) It is cheapest and easiest to insulate pitched roofs with large, accessible voids. Problems arise with flat roofs, however, and the high humidity conditions prevailing in kitchens and swimming baths demand a careful consideration of any insulation decision. In some circumstances it may be appropriate to cover or add to an existing roof an additional insulation, such as expanded plastic board; or to add a suspended ceiling under a flat roof. At present, however, these methods are not considered to be cost effective.

21 *Heating* Opportunities occur naturally to change the type of fuel used, since the efficient life of a heating system is of about twenty years' duration. Where old or inefficient systems are reaching the end of their period of useful existence, they should be replaced. In this instance, planned maintenance programmes are often available. Changing of a fuel system at any time is appropriate if sufficient cost effectiveness can be achieved. At present, coal is the cheapest fuel, closely followed by gas. Oil is the next cheapest fuel, and electricity decidedly expensive. It may be that market forces will operate to

narrow the gap between oil and solid fuel prices, whereas the electricity price differential is likely to continue. In selecting a heating system it may be worthwhile to consider: the advantages of a warm air system, particularly in lightly constructed buildings, as it provides a short heat-up period; the recovery of heat from exhaust air; and the benefits of utilising solar radiation where appropriate.

22 Installation of heating control systems usually repays the investment. To keep temperature fluctuations to a minimum is the main requirement for a control system: a rise in room temperatures of 1°C can mean an increase of fuel consumption of 10%. Space heating controls should be reliable, fully automatic, accessible only to responsible personnel and be proof against unauthorised interference. Overall control alone has been found to be economic only in small premises, and controls which respond to localised heat changes are recommended instead. For example, local controls would respond to sudden temperature rises caused by sunshine and obviate the need for ventilation which would entail heat loss. Control devices known as optimum programmers or optimum start controllers give frost protection and also allow for the most efficient pre-occupation heating of a building. Any controls used must be properly maintained and regularly checked to ensure the most efficient operation. User manuals should be available, the LEAs and their colleges should ensure that all appropriate staff are fully conversant with the operation and controls of all heating and ventilation plant.

23 **General improvements and modifications**

Consideration of the following is also worthwhile:

(i) Where a choice of heating system exists, an option should be kept open to allow change from one type of fuel to another in accordance with price developments. Systems whereby heat is conveyed by warm air or hot water could be converted to coal, gas, oil or electricity. Of the alternative energy sources currently available, and then only after further research, heat pumps and passive solar design are likely to prove cost effective.

(ii) Temporary buildings, such as concrete framed huts, timber huts and 'portakabins' have high running costs. The DES advises their removal or replacement with a permanent building as soon as possible. Where this is not possible, efforts should be made to save energy by cost effective means.

(iii) Water consumption can be reduced and energy saved by up to 50% by the use of spray taps in wash basins but these may not be suitable for heavy educational use. Modifications to the plumbing system can also reduce water consumption. Spray nozzles in showers are much more economical than roses but are less effective.

(iv) Advice is not yet available on energy savings which can be made in kitchens. While awaiting the advice, however, it will be worthwhile considering what measures may be appropriate.

24 **Welfare**

Where activities carried on in a college are such that they are relevant to the provisions of statute governing such practices, then their environmental and welfare standards must be observed. Thus, kitchens are subject to the Food Hygiene Regulations, and administrative areas to the Offices, Shops and Railway Premises Act. Workshops are directly subject to the Factories Act only if in them articles are made or adapted for sale in the course of employment. However, under the Health and Safety at Work etc. Act, the standards set in the Factories Act apply to those college activities and workplaces which are construed as carrying out factory activities. The same conditions apply concerning the Offices, Shops and Railway Premises Act. This will remain the case until regulations specific to education are made under the Health and Safety at Work etc. Act. There are no indications that this will occur soon. In practical terms, the situation can be summed up as meaning that the welfare provisions of the Factories Act and Offices, Shops and Railway Premises Act apply directly where relevant, and otherwise through the Health and Safety at Work etc. Act. Thus colleges possess a statutory welfare standard base, albeit one which is qualified. However, if standards are not adequate, and the statute under which that is determined is the Health and Safety at Work etc. Act, the matter can be determined only by the courts and under the powers of the Health and Safety Executive (HSE) and its inspectorate. Only the HSE can institute criminal proceedings. Subject to regulations which might be made under the Health and Safety at Work etc. Act, breach of that Act cannot result in a civil action. Therefore, although standards required by the Act can be enforced, personal redress for injury or loss resulting from inadequate provision can be obtained only at civil law, such as under the Occupier's Liability Act (See **4.5** 1–3). Rather than deal separately with factory and offices legislation, it will be convenient in this sub-section to investigate in turn the various areas of welfare provision.

25 **Cleanliness**

The Factories Act requires that places of work are kept clean and free from smells. Rubbish and dirt must be removed daily; floors cleaned weekly; inside walls and ceilings be washed every fourteen months, and white or colour washed every fourteen months or else painted every seven years. Severe problems have been experienced in some colleges regarding air extraction, especially with regard to fumes, dust and where woodworking is being carried out. Common examples are: the explosion risk arising from wood dust, and the dangers from toxic fumes used in glass fibre moulding (used, for instance, in the repair of canoes). There is a need in many cases for a thorough review of air extraction provision. As the brushing of dust and waste can create considerable air pollution, it is preferable that such cleaning be undertaken outside working hours.

26 Under the Offices, Shops and Railway Premises Act there are only general requirements requiring cleanliness. The premises, equipment and fittings have to be kept clean; there should be no accumulation of rubbish or dirt, and steps and floors have to be cleaned weekly.

27 **Cooking and eating areas**

Kitchens are subject to the Food Hygiene Regulations. There are cases in which the Public Health Act itself may be relevant, as well as statute relating to the supply of energy. Where food is stored, prepared or handled, then there has to be compliance with the standards laid down in the Food Hygiene Regulations, and the areas in which food is kept or prepared are subject to the inspection of the public health inspectors. The main provision of the Food Hygiene (General) Regulations is that no food business (i.e. preparation, storing and handling) is to be conducted at insanitary places, or where the condition, situation or construction of premises are such as to expose food to the risk of contamination. Food must be hygienically handled, and contamination avoided. Persons engaged in food handling are required to maintain a standard of cleanliness. There must be provision of a constant water supply and washing facilities. Arrangements for the proper disposal of waste materials must be made. Certain foods are to be kept at specified temperatures.

28 Those engaged in food business are required as far as reasonably practicable to keep clean all parts of their persons and clothing likely to come into contact with food; to cover cuts and abrasions with suitable waterproof dressings; and to refrain from smoking and spitting. There are special regulations which apply to persons suffering from certain infections.

29 Sanitary conveniences must be suitably sited, not communicate directly with any room where open food is handled, and be equipped with hand washing notices. Washing facilities must be suitable, efficient, and equipped with a constant hot and cold water supply, wash basins, soap, nail brushes, towels or other drying facilities.

30 First aid materials must be available. There must be accommodation for clothing. Food and equipment washing facilities must be suitable and adequate. Food rooms must be suitably and sufficiently lit, ventilated, kept in good order, and be of a repair and condition such as to allow effective cleaning and prevent – as far as reasonably practicable – infestation by rats, mice or insects. Waste storage and disposal facilities must be adequate, and no refuse is to be deposited or allowed to accumulate except where unavoidable. As well as persons working with food, those with management responsibilities for the activity can be guilty of an offence if all reasonable steps have not been taken to prevent contravention of the food hygiene regulations.

31 It has been found on occasion that college kitchens have been substandard. In some cases the wrong sorts of fabrics have been used in construction: porous walls and ceiling fabrics have allowed germ retention to occur. Laminated work surfaces have been found to be unhygienic: when the laminate has worn, it too has allowed germ retention. The remedy is to ensure that stainless steel is used on all food preparation surfaces, and similarly on all serving or counter surfaces. Floors have been found to be both dangerous and unhygienic. The regulations require that catering premises are cleaned frequently and regularly; floor surfaces should be non-slip.

32 There have been cases where kitchens have been closed because ventilation was inadequate or insufficient. This circumstance can arise when staff interfere with the ventilation provided. It is important for staff to be made aware, therefore, of both the need for ventilation and the possible penalties which an institution can suffer where this is tampered with. That consideration will be appreciated to be applicable in other catering circumstances. By way of example, reference may be made to the provisions of the Gas Act. The Gas Corporation is empowered to cease to supply gas where there is improper use by a consumer, or interference with the supply. Should an unauthorised alteration be made to the supply, pipes, meter or fittings then the person wilfully, fraudulently or by culpable negligence perpetrating the action will be guilty of an offence and may be fined.

33 **Thermal environment**

The general requirement of the Factories Act that there be 'reasonable' temperature (subject to certain specific stated levels in special circumstances) and the similar requirement of the Offices, Shops and Railway Premises Act (except that here there should be a minimum temperature of 16°C after one hour's work, and a thermometer be available to check this) means that in practice reference should be made to the DES standards (See paragraph 5 onwards). Similar recourse may be taken in the matter of ventilation. However, it should be noted that the Factories Act requires not only adequate ventilation but that all practicable measures should be taken to give protection against fumes and dust; and that ventilation implies the supply of fresh air.

34 **Working space provisions and facilities**
The Factories Act requires that there should be 400 cubic ft. (11.32m^3) of space allocated for each worker, and that there should not be overcrowding which will cause risk of injury or to health. The Act requires the posting of a notice specifying the number of people who may be employed in the workroom. Students and staff, where their activities are construed as being the same as would obtain in a factory, are subject to this requirement.

35 Both the Factories Act and the Offices, Shops and Railway Premises Act require seating facilities to be provided wherever work can be satisfactorily undertaken when seated. Where a large proportion of work may be so undertaken, seating must be of a design, size and construction suitable for both the work and the person; and where necessary for comfort, a footrest has to be provided.

36 **Cloakrooms, lavatories and washrooms**
Under the Factories Act and the Offices, Shops and Railways Premises Act there is an obligation to provide suitable and adequate cloakroom space for clothing not worn during working hours, and arrangements for drying wet clothes. While it is not easy to define 'suitable' or 'adequate', such provision should include space for changing of clothing and footwear, adequate lighting and ventilation, separate pegs or lockers, and a high standard of cleanliness. There may be grounds for action if provision is inadequate under the Occupier's Liability Act (See **4.5** 1–3) or other law.

37 Requirements concerning lavatories made by the Factories Act and Offices, Shops and Railway Premises Act and regulations made under them are similar, with the exception that the latter Act requires that a suitable and effective means of disposal of sanitary towels be provided where the total number of women exceeds ten. Incinerators must be constantly maintained, and the contents of bins suitably and regularly disposed of. There is no such provision in the Factories Act. Main statutory provisions common to both Acts may be summarized:

(i) If conveniences for men and women adjoin, the approaches must be clearly indicated and separate. Lavatories for each sex must be so screened or placed in order that, although the door may be open, the interior is not visible where persons of the other sex have either to pass or work.

(ii) There must be at least one suitable convenience for every 25 employees of each sex. In the case of men, this suitability does not include urinals. Where college activities under the Health and Safety at Work etc. Act would be subject to Factories Act provisions, then where there are over 100 male persons so engaged in such activities and sufficient urinal accommodation is provided, one seated convenience may be supplied for every 25 men up to the first 100, and thereafter one for every extra 40.

(iii) There must be sufficient ventilation and, except through the open air or an intervening ventilated space, a lavatory must not communicate directly with any workroom.

(iv) Except for urinals, every lavatory must be covered and partitioned to allow privacy and have an adequate, locking door. Urinals must be so screened and sited for them not to be visible from elsewhere in the workplace. Lavatories must be easily accessible.

There must be a supply of clean, running, hot and cold water. Means of cleaning and drying must be supplied, a provision which includes soap and clean towels. One wash basin for every 20 employees is recommended by the HSE inspectorate. For colleges of FHE the recommendations of Design Notes 33 and 44 may be more appropriate.

38 **Medical rooms and first aid**

As regulations made under the Factories Act require that medical rooms have to be provided in certain industries where the numbers employed in most circumstances are 500 or more, larger colleges undertaking activities which include building, metalwork, woodworking, and work with chemicals appropriate to regulations will probably on aggregation of numbers be required to comply with these provisions. Similarly, when a college is engaged in these activities, a responsible person must be readily available during working hours to call an ambulance or other means of transport.

39 The Factories Act requires that an accessible first aid box or cupboard must be provided and maintained by a responsible person. Where more than 150 people are employed (including in the case of colleges any persons engaged in activities subject to the Act), an additional box must be provided for every additional 150. Where there are more than 50 employees or persons in colleges protected by the Act, there must be a person in charge of first aid who is trained in the subject. Notices must be provided in each work area giving the person's name, and that person must be readily available during working hours. He or she must undergo further training of a refresher course every three years and have her or his certificate renewed. While that person is undergoing further training, the post must be filled by a suitably trained replacement.

40 **Asbestos**

In 1986 a joint administrative memorandum, *The Use of Asbestos in Educational Establishments*, was issued drawing the attention of education authorities to the dangers of asbestos in educational buildings. The potential dangers from asbestos materials arise when asbestos fibres are released from them into the air. Measurements made in buildings in normal use, including schools and colleges, suggest that the risk arising from typical levels of exposure in buildings in the UK is very small. In general, fibres are not released unless asbestos materials are disturbed or damaged,and undisturbed materials in good condition present little risk. However, asbestos fibres can be released when asbestos products deteriorate over time or are damaged, either accidentally or during maintenance and repair. As there is no known threshold level for exposure to asbestos below which there is no risk, it is important always to take whatever steps are necessary to reduce exposure from any form of asbestos to the lowest reasonably practicable level. The aim should be to prevent the inhalation of asbestos dust by pupils, students, or staff.

41 Exceptionally, the working of asbestos products may be necessary in some scientific and technical courses of further education which cover specialised processes and operations in which asbestos products continue to be used. In all such instances course members should be instructed in the safe use of asbestos, and the observation of safe practices. Where such use of asbestos products is necessary, drilling, filing or sawing should be kept to an absolute minimum and carried out under efficient local exhaust ventilation with the exhaust effectively filtered before discharge. Ventilation equipment used for the extraction of dust which may contain asbestos should be subject to frequent inspection.

42 Asbestos has been used in some equipment found in schools and colleges. The mere presence of asbestos in equipment does not present a hazard, and it is only when asbestos materials are in a damaged and pliable condition, or when the equipment is being modified, removed or demolished that there is likely to be significant fibre release. Some pottery and enamelling kilns may contain asbestos for insulating purposes. Furnaces and scientific equipment are also sometimes insulated with asbestos. Care should be taken to ensure that the asbestos is properly sealed where this is possible. Where the equipment cannot be treated, it will be necessary to assess the likelihood of fibre release into the air to decide whether replacement is necessary. Kilns and furnaces should be replaced with asbestos-free installations at the end of their useful lives. Readers should refer to the Memorandum for more information on the use of asbestos in teaching.

43 For detailed guidance on the use of asbestos in buildings, including educational buildings, authorities and others concerned should consult *Asbestos Materials in Buildings* (DoE 1986). The booklet describes the main types of asbestos found in buildings, explains the controls on their use, and presents the results of studies on the effect on health of asbestos. It sets out a general control strategy for dealing with asbestos in buildings:

(i) Identify the presence of asbestos, its extent, type and location
(ii) Assess the potential for fibre release in the light of an examination of the type, integrity, location and assessibility of the asbestos
(iii) Decide what remedial action is necessary, and in what order of priority.

44 The choice of an appropriate remedial strategy depends on the circumstances of each case but the guiding principle should be to avoid the release of dust. Work involving the removal, repair or disturbance of asbestos insulation or coating, other than short-term repair or maintenance should normally only be carried out by licensed contractors under the Asbestos (Licensing) Regulations 1983 and in accordance with the statutory requirements and guidance. Air monitoring will be needed to decide when a building can be re-occupied following extensive removal of asbestos.

45 **Fire precautions**

Advice from the DES and local fire officers centres on the personal safety of users. Parts of colleges are subject to the Fire Precautions Act 1971 in the case of means of escape and safety provision under the Health and Safety at Work etc. Act is also relevant. Otherwise, maintained colleges are exempt from local bye-laws but subject to certain arrangements made under DES Administrative Memoranda and to parts of the DES Building Bulletin 7 *Fire and the*

Design of Schools as well as other DES safety advice. The Building Bulletin is designed in places to achieve uniformity with the Building Regulations. In the matter of structural fire precautions, the provisions contained in the Building Bulletin apply with statutory force. A further consideration applies in that insurance companies are now becoming increasingly interested in the resistance of buildings' fabrics to fire. The companies' reasons for this are purely financial, but there are clear implications for colleges and LEAs.

46 This sub-section provides a summary of DES recommendations and discusses fire precautions issues. DES recommendations do not apply to residential accommodation. This is considered by the Department on an individual basis. As design responsibilities rest with an authority rather than its colleges, and are an adjunct to a college building programme rather than its purpose, emphasis is placed here mainly on the precautions for occupants.

47 In considering means of escape, precautions have to be taken against smoke and fumes as well as flame and heat. Therefore there should be no 'dead end' corridors if at all possible – escape should be possible in both directions. Corridors should have appropriate surfaces. Stairs should be fire-resisting and surrounded by fire-resistant walls or partitions. Self-closing fire doors are recommended. To enable occupants to evacuate quickly, large rooms should have more than one exit. The number of room exits should relate to the size, occupancy and purpose of the room. Where halls are licensed for public assembly, it will be necessary for the approval of the local licensing authority to be sought regarding fire precaution arrangements. It may be necessary to install emergency lighting. Extra stairways in buildings over two storeys are preferable to external fire escapes. Escape distances and door opening widths are subject to standard recommendations. No alterations without professional advice should be made to any structure which may afford a means of escape. It is inadvisable to seek the advice of a fire officer without LEA officers being present at the meeting.

48 It is impossible to give even general advice on matters such as room planning for, while they may follow DES recommendations, much will depend on the nature and purpose of the college. There is, however, a method of numbers calculation used to determine the maximum number of students using a stairway. These figures are used in the planning of minimum stairway widths according to the height of a building in storeys. The number of students may be taken as 80% of the maximum full-time equivalent student capacity of the accommodation on the upper floors.

49 In the case of structural fire precautions, colleges are subject to Schedule 1 of the Building Regulations as interpreted in Appendix 2 of Building Bulletin 7, and as modified by the appendix to Administrative Memorandum 2/85. Compliance with the standards is essential to life, but also limits damage to property. In general, the necessary precautions deal with limiting the spread of fire from building to building, the restriction of spread of smoke and flame, the use of fire resistant construction, and limiting the use of combustible materials. Recommendations here do apply to residential accommodation.

50 Fire warning systems should preferably be such that, once activated, they continue to sound an alarm. They should be tested weekly, the results recorded, and any fault immediately rectified. The DES considers it preferable for such installations to be uniform throughout an institution and, if possible, through-

out a local authority's area. The alarm sound should be distinctive to avoid confusion with any other sound devices, and operating power should be from an independent source. Call-points are recommended to be in prominent positions; within 30m walking distance on every floor; of the 'break-glass release' type; and provided in or near every boiler room, kitchen, laboratory, workshop, housecraft and craft room, and assembly hall. Indicator boards which show the points from which warning has been given may be necessary in some colleges. There should be an extinguisher adjacent to every call-point.

51 Water supply and ready means of access to the building for the fire brigade are necessary. Dry risers or internal hydrants may be necessary in special circumstances and where the building is of over four storeys. Consultations between the chief fire officer, the authority, and college are required at the planning stage.

52 All the Department's recommendations in Building Bulletin 7 concerning fire fighting and fire prevention by a building's occupants are relevant to colleges. The usual types of fire fighting equipment are hosereels, portable fire extinguishers, buckets of sand and fire blankets. Consultation with the chief fire officer regarding the types of equipment suitable in each circumstance will be necessary, but it must also be borne in mind that equipment should generally be such as to allow effective use with little training. Extinguishers expelling water or soda-acid are suitable for fires involving ordinary combustible materials. Foam, carbon dioxide or dry powder extinguishers are suitable for fires which involve flammable liquids such as cooking fats, oils, and solvents. Extinguisher provision should be of the type suitable to the circumstances, and instruction given to ensure the use of the appropriate means of effective extinguish. Almost all laboratory fires can be dealt with by the use of either or both extinguishers or sand. Blankets of either asbestos or glass fibre can be used to smother small fires which involve flammable liquids, and are recommended in dealing with persons whose clothing is alight (they should be wrapped and rolled in the blanket). If the presence of live electricity is thought or known, fire fighting equipment must not be used. It is recommended that the equipment should be standardised throughout an institution in accordance with the relevant British Standard, be maintained and recharged according to the manufacturers' instructions, and positioned well away from heat sources.

53 The DES recommends that in the following high risk areas there should be:
(i) A water or soda-acid extinguisher in every craft room, workshop and assembly hall stage;
(ii) A foam, carbon dioxide or dry powder extinguisher in every laboratory, housecraft room and kitchen, except that dry powder or carbon dioxide may be preferable in laboratories where there are volatile liquids or fragile equipment, and that those extinguishers may similarly be where cooking takes place and there is no fixed frying equipment; and
(iii) A foam extinguisher in every boiler room where oil fuel is used.

54 In the event of fire the DES recommends: safety of occupants always takes precedence over fire fighting; however small the fire, the fire brigade should immediately be called; and although small fires may be fought by occupants, evacuation procedures agreed with the chief fire officer should be carried out. The first step must always be to evacuate the building. The combustion of certain materials may emit lethal gasses (see DES Safety in Education Bulletin No. 5).

55 A variety of everyday precautions is recommended by the Department:

(i) Lockable doors across escape routes must be unlocked while the building is occupied. Exit doors should not be obstructed and be capable of being opened during occupation of the building from within. The purpose of fire and smoke doors is to contain fire and smoke within an area and so allow escape into a safer place.

(ii) Stairways should be kept clear, in good repair, and not have accumulated in their enclosures any combustible material. Storage cupboards, for example, should not be set up in stair-wells or on landings.

(iii) Materials, furniture and fixed equipment should not be allowed to block escape routes, especially in open areas.

(iv) Combustible rubbish and waste material should not be allowed to accumulate. All flammable materials should be stored carefully. Intending arsonists ought not be aided by the accessible storage of combustible materials outside the building.

(v) Heating appliances should be protected against misuse. Open fires should have the relevant British Standard specified guard. The Department strongly recommends regular maintenance.

(vi) Only the correct fuse wire should be used to repair blown fuses. Wiring work should be undertaken only by a qualified electrician. There should be regular inspections of flexible cable to electric fittings. The cable should be as short as possible and replaced if worn immediately.

(vii) In laboratories, it is recommended that dangerous experiments do not take place near doors. Further reference is recommended to DES Safety Series 2, *Safety in Science Laboratories*.

(viii) Petrol storage on the premises should be limited. Not more than 14 litres may be stored, and then in separate half-litre containers. Other dangerous liquids and gases are mentioned in DES Safety in Education Bulletin No. 5.

(ix) Where irons are used, the Department recommends that guidance is given on their nature and use; they should have pilot lights, efficient stands, and be put away only when cool, and without damage to the cable by winding it around the appliance while hot.

(x) Furnishings and equipment should be fire retardant where possible. Materials should be selected for their fire resistance, and advice sought where appropriate.

(xi) Smoking should be discouraged in all teaching areas. It should be confined to social and staff areas where sufficient ashtrays should be provided.

(xii) Where premises are used by the public, information should be supplied concerning fire escape routes and procedures. Before a building is locked for the night the premises should be thoroughly checked.

56 It is worth noting in addition that fire and safety precautions are sometimes held to be an obstacle in making provision for the handicapped. Resolution of the problem may not be too difficult: escape routes should be clearly marked and have been made known. In the event of a fire where a handicapped person requires assistance, there must be a person responsible for such help, for example, is assisting their movement down stairs. There may be extreme circumstances where this would be difficult, but fire precautions need not be a pretext for inaction where a handicapped student is being considered for admission. Clear management procedures regarding assistance for a handicapped person in the event of fire are necessary.

57 Among the periodic actions recommended by the Department are the regular inspection of the premises and fire drills. Inspections may be made by fire brigade officers or other competent persons. Safety representatives, who may in any case wish to operate their own procedures, must be informed if an inspection is to be made. Recommendations for fire drill procedure should be agreed with the chief fire officer.

58 **Access for disabled people**

A joint circular was issued in April 1982, *Re: Disabled Persons Act 1981*, drawing attention to the relevant act and reminding all local authorities of the importance of bearing in mind the needs of disabled people in discharging all their functions. The new Section 29B of the Act places a duty on local planning authorities when granting permission for educational buildings covered by Section 8 of the Chronically Sick and Disabled Persons Act 1970, to draw the attention of developers to the relevant provisions of the 1970 Act, and to Design Note 18 *Access for the Physically Disabled to Educational Buildings*. The Design Note identifies seven essential areas of provision (minimum requirements) which will allow disabled people to enter and move around in a building and to have access to wc facilities designed for their use.

59 *Arrival, departure and parking*

For all disabled persons brought to and from the site, a setting down area or collecting bay must be provided which is level, suitably sized, clearly defined, adequately lit, and in a convenient position close to the most appropriate point of entry to the building. For disabled persons arriving or departing in their own vehicles, or as passengers in other vehicles remaining on site, there must be reserved parking space, which is level, clearly defined, adequately lit and close to the point of entry to the building. Minimum parking bay widths are required as follows: vehicles for ambulant disabled persons – 2.8m; vehicles for wheelchair users – 3.2m. General design considerations include providing good signposting, sheltered/covered areas of waiting, well designed and slip resistant surfaces, and suitably ramped kerbs (gradients not exceeding 1:10).

60 *Approach and entrance*

A level approach clearly defined, adequately lit, and not less than 1,200 mm wide must be provided to at least one entrance to a building. Exceptionally where the provision of a level approach is not practicable, a ramp with a gradient not exceeding 1:12 is acceptable. Minimum requirements for external ramps are as follows. Gradients and lengths must not exceed those given in Table 4

Table 4
External Ramps

Length	*Maximum gradient*
Not exceeding 3m	1:12
Over 3m but not exceeding 6m	1:16
Over 6m but not exceeding 10m	1:20

Widths

To facilitate passing a width of not less than 1,200 mm is required.

Platforms
A level platform of minimum dimensions 1,200 mm × 1,500 mm, unobstructed and clear of any gate or door swing, is required at the head and foot of each ramp (and where necessary at intermediate points).

Handrails
Suitably designed handrails are required for each side of ramps which exceed 1:20 in gradient (other than ramps for negotiating kerbs).

Balustrades and kerbs
Upstanding kerbs not less than 100 mm high are required to all exposed sides of ramps, unless safety balustrades are incorporated.

Surfaces
All surfaces must be firm, well drained and slip resistant.

Lighting
All ramps, landings and passing bays must be adequately lit. General design considerations include providing weather protection, passing bays, temporary ramps if necessary and colour contrast.

The design of *external steps* should comply with these minimum requirements:

Dimensions
Step goings of not less than 280 mm and step risers not exceeding 150 mm are required. Each flight of consecutive steps must not exceed a total rise of 1,200 mm. Step goings and step risers must be uniform.

Handrails
Suitably designed handrails are required to each side of steps.

Surfaces
All surfaces must be well drained and slip resistant.

Lighting
All steps and associated landings must be adequately lit. General design considerations include avoiding single steps if possible and providing splayed (not projecting or open) risers, weather protection and colour contrast.

The design of *handrails* has the following minimum requirements:

Handrails must be continuous and unbroken at landings where possible and must always extend horizontally, not less than 300 mm at the top and bottom of any ramp or staircase.

For ramps, handrails must be fixed so that the top of the rail is not more than 1,000 mm above the ramp surface.

For steps, handrails must be fixed so that the top of the rail is not more than 850 mm above the line of step nosings, nor more than 1,000 mm above finished ground or landing level.

General design considerations include providing more handrails, on wider routes, lower handrails for young children, and handrails which are easy to grip (circular section of 40–55 mm preferred).

61 *Doors and doorways*
Minimum requirements are:

Openings
A clear opening width per single leaf of not less than 800 mm is required for entrance doors and 750 mm for internal doors leading to spaces intended to be accessible to wheelchair users.

Wall space
A clear wall space of not less than 300 mm is required to the side of the door by the door handle to aid the wheelchair user when approaching and opening the door.

Lobbies
Unobstructed circulation space is required within all lobbies accessible to wheelchair users. General design considerations include giving particular attention to manoeuvring space in circulation areas, providing vision panels at the appropriate height, avoiding raised thresholds, placing door handles at the appropriate height (830 mm–1,040 mm), protecting doors with kicking plates, making sure door mats are flush, and providing sliding doors and automatically opening doors where appropriate.

62 **Internal changes of level**

Internal access
Where access for disabled persons is likely to be needed to accommodation above or below the entrance level of the building, internal ramps or lifts will be required. All stairs to such accommodation must be suitable for use by ambulant disabled persons.

Internal ramps
Gradients and lengths must not exceed these:

Length	*Gradient*
Not exceeding 3m	1:12
Over 3m but not exceeding 6m	1:16
Over 6m but not exceeding 10m	1:20

Widths
To facilitate passing, a width of not less than 1,200 mm is required.

Platforms
A level platform of minimum dimensions 1,200 mm by 1,500 mm, unobstructed and clear of any door swing is required at the head and the foot of each ramp (and where necessary at intermediate points).

Handrails
Suitably designed handrails are required to each side of ramps.

Balustrades and kerbs
Kerbs not less than 100 mm high are required to all exposed sides of ramps, unless safety balustrades are incorporated.

Surfaces
All surfaces must be slip resistant, whether wet or dry and must be adequately illuminated at all times during the occupation of the building.

Lifts
Minimum requirements are:
Car size: lift cars are to accommodate at least one wheelchair user plus an adult attendant. Minimum clear internal car plan dimensions of 1,400 mm depth and 1,100 mm width are required.

Doors: a clear opening width of not less than 800 mm is required for lift car and landing doors.

Landings: a clear landing space in front of the lift doors (on all levels accessible to wheelchair users) of not less than 1,800 mm deep and 1,500 mm wide is required.
General design considerations will include locating lifts near the point of building entry and main circulation routes, choosing the appropriate type (not home lifts, counterweight lifts, stair lifts or pater nosters), placing controls at the right height (1,000–1,400 mm), providing internal handrails and resistant surfaces, making sure the lifts operate smoothly and covering emergency needs.

Internal staircases
Dimensions: stair goings of not less than 250 mm and stair risers not exceeding 163 mm are required; each flight of consecutive stairs must not exceed a total rise of 1,800 mm; stair goings and risers are to be uniform.
Handrails: suitably designed handrails are required to each side of stairs.
Surfaces: all staircase heads and landing surfaces must be slip resistant and must be adequately illuminated at all times during the occupation of the building.

63 **Lavatory accommodation**
WC compartments: the minimum requirements are that at least one WC compartment accessible to a person in a wheelchair is required, and that the internal plan dimensions of the WC compartment must not be less than 1,400 mm by 1,750 mm. General design considerations will include modifying normally sized WC compartments for ambulant disabled users, locating the compartment centrally but with due regard to privacy, ensuring the door opens outwards or slides, providing a WC pan at a height of 450 mm–475 mm and locating it in such a way as to allow 750 mm either side, placing lavatory basins at a height of around 750 mm and making sure they are easy to approach and operate, providing support rails and appropriate normal (accessible) and additional fittings.

64 **Facilities for medical inspection and treatment**
A room suitable for consultation, treatment and withdrawal and accessible to wheelchair users must be provided. General design considerations will include locating the room near a wheelchair user's WC, and providing a telephone for emergency use.

65 **Means of escape**
The minimum requirements are that adequate and appropriate arrangements must be made for the emergency escape of disabled persons wherever access is provided. For general principles of design and management, reference should be made to *Fire and the Design of Schools*, Building Bulletin 7. General design considerations include possibly modifying escape routes, making proper use of fire doors, smoke-stop doors and door closers, and working out suitable methods for escape from, particularly, multi-storey buildings.

FURTHER READING

Legislation
Factories Act 1961, Chapter 34, HMSO
Food Act 1984, HMSO
Gas Act 1972, HMSO
Offices, Shops and Railway Premises Act 1963, HMSO
Public Health Act 1936, HMSO
Public Health Act 1961, HMSO
The Health and Safety at Work etc. Act 1974, HMSO
Fire Precautions Act 1971, HMSO

SI 1985 1086 *The Building Regulations 1985*, HMSO
SI 1976 No. 2007 *The Fire Precautions Act 1971 (Modifications) Regulations 1976*, HMSO

Department of Education and Science
Building Bulletin 7. 1987 *Fire and the Design of Schools* Sixth edition, HMSO

Administrative Memorandum 2/85 *Constructional Standards for Maintained and Direct Grant Educational Buildings in England* 13 September 1985
DES 1985 *Safety in Practical Studies* Department of Education and Science Safety Series, HMSO
DES 1987 *Fire Safety in Education* Department of Education and Science Safety Series. HMSO

Acoustics
Department of Education and Science Building Bulletin 51. 1975 *Acoustics in Educational Buildings*, HMSO

Lighting
CIBS 1984 *CIBS Code for Interior Lighting* The Chartered Institute of Building Services
CIBS *Lighting Guide to Lecture Theatres* The Chartered Institute of Building Services
CIBS *Lighting Guide to Libraries* The Chartered Institute of Building Services

Energy conservation
Department of Education and Science Building Bulletin 55. 1981 *Energy Conservation in Buildings*, HMSO
Design Note 17. 1981 *Guidelines for Environmental Design and Fuel Conservation in Educational Buildings* Second edition Architects and Building Branch
Department of Energy Circular 1/75 *Energy Conservation*, HMSO
Department of the Environment Circular 56/78 *Energy Conservation Measures* (DES Circular 10/78; Welsh Office Circular 100/78)
BRE 1975 *Energy Conservation*. Current Paper S6/75. Building Research Establishment Working Party Report
BRE 1976 *Energy Consumption and Conservation in Buildings* Building Research Establishment Digest 191 181 in 1980 ed.), HMSO
British Standards Institution
BSI 1985 *Code of practice for energy efficiency in buildings* BS 8207, British Standards Iinstitution
BSI 1985 *Energy Design Guide to BS 8207*, British Standards Institution

Welfare
SI 1970 No. 1172 *Food Hygiene (General) Regulations*, HMSO
SI 1978 No. 1927 *The Materials and Articles in Contact with Food Regulations*, HMSO
Department of Employment/Health and Safety Executive Guidance Notes:
No. 2 1970 *Canteens, messrooms and refreshment services,* HMSO
No. HS(G) 10 0000 *Cloakroom Accommodation and Washing Facilities*, HMSO

First aid
Department of Employment/Health and Safety Executive Guidance Notes:
No. 36 0000 *First Aid in Factories*, HMSO
No. 48 0000 *First Aid in Offices, Shops and Railway Premises*, HMSO

Asbestos
SI 1969 No. 690 *The Asbestos Regulations*, HMSO
SI 1983 No. 1649 *The Asbestos Licensing Regulations* HMSO
SI 1985 No. 910 *The Asbestos (Prohibitions) Regulations*, HMSO
Department of Education and Science. Administrative Memorandum 3/86 *The use of asbestos in educational establishments* (Administrative Memorandum 1/86 Welsh Office) 15 August 1986
Department of the Environment. DoE 1986 *Asbestos materials in buildings*, HMSO
Department of Employment:
Health and Safety Executive Guidance Notes on Asbestos:
MS 13 *Asbestos* (under revision)

EH 10 *Asbestos: control limits, measurement of airborne dust concentrations and the assessment of control measures*
EH 35 *Probable asbestos dust concentrations at construction processes*
EH 36 *Work with asbestos cement*
EH 37 *Work with asbestos insulating board*
EH 41 *Respiratory protective equipment for use against asbestos*

Disabled people
Department of Education and Science Design Note 18. 1984 *Access for Disabled People to Educational Buildings* Second edition, Architects and Building Branch
Department of Education and Science Circular 2/82: *Re: Disabled Persons Act 1981* April 1982
BSI 1979 *Code of Practice for Access for the Disabled to Buildings* BS 5810. British Standards Institution
IOS 1981 *Needs of the Handicapped in Buildings*, International Organisation for Standardisation
NATFHE 1985 *Handicap, disability and special learning needs: A guide to good practice in the FHE*, National Association of Teachers in Further and Higher Education

Fire
SI 1976 2007 *The Fire Precautions Act 1971 (Modifications) Regulations, 1976* HMSO
Elder, J. *Guide to the Building Regulations* The Architecture Press
Department of Education and Science, Administrative Memorandum 2/85 *Constructional Standards for Maintained and Direct Grant Educational Buildings in England* HMSO
Department of Education and Science, Safety in Education Bulletin No. 5, 1987 *Fire Safety* DES
Department of Education and Science, Building Bulletin 7, 1988 *Fire and the Design of Schools* Seventh edition, HMSO

4.4 ACCOMMODATION USE AND ALLOCATION

1 Section 4.1 outlined a method which addressed the static capacity of a set of buildings. This section describes how to make an assessment of the dynamic use of buildings, and how to improve this use if it is felt not to be acceptable. In either case, an essential prerequisite of accurate monitoring is a comprehensive, and frequently updated, space inventory; this will provide details of total areas currently used by different departments and for different activities (See Kenny and Foster 1986). Such an inventory can be computerised. In any educational establishment, costs related to premises are the second most important element in the budget, after teaching staff costs, and they may account for between 20 and 25% of annual expenditure (See Kedney 1984). These costs are to a certain extent fixed, unless premises can be taken out of use, so that if the use of existing accommodation can be improved and if the numbers of users can be increased, the premises-related costs for each student using the buildings will be reduced.

2 It is not only the financial economies and diseconomies of intensifying space use which should be assessed but the implications for the educational and social activities of an establishment must be carefully considered. Although they are more difficult to measure it may be that welfare benefits outweigh financial costs or, and this is more likely nowadays, that financial savings will overrule welfare costs. Thus, a clear improvement to the overall institution will result if the use of a certain number of teaching rooms can be increased by moving classes from other less suitable rooms, thereby freeing accommodation for other purposes (e.g. for use as staff workrooms or local social bases). On the other hand overall institutional welfare will suffer if all teaching rooms are used so heavily that there are no gaps for the occasional ad hoc meeting or extra external lecture. Equally, increasingly heavy use of accommodation makes special demands on environmental support systems, whether human (maintenance personnel and cleaners) or mechanical (ventilation).

3 **Activity surveys**

Colleges should, so far as it is possible with their management resources, carry out periodic surveys of the activities taking place within their buildings. Ideally these activities would encompass both non-timetabled and timetabled activities, but it is recognised that in most cases it will be possible to examine only timetabled activities. In any case it has been found that the most accurate way of carrying out such surveys is to count the numbers of people present in the designated spaces, as often as possible, over a predetermined period. Other methods, such as using annotated timetables or diaries, or asking people to complete forms which have been left in rooms, have been tried and have been found profoundly wanting. For the purposes of comparability and as the result of years of discussion, it is generally accepted that counts taken each hour from 9 to 17 from Monday to Friday inclusive, giving 40 counts for each room, are perfectly adequate.

4 **Untimetabled activities**

The use of accommodation, such as refectories, libraries and common rooms, for non-timetabled activities can reflect interesting perceptions and habits. It has often been found for instance that refectories are perceived as being more over-crowded than they actually are, giving rise to an underutilisation of accommodation provided. Equally, what may appear to an adult to be unbearable overcrowding may be tolerable or even enjoyable to students, particularly if the periods involved are not too long. There is some evidence that students prefer studying in an atmosphere of movement and some noise and that quiet areas may be shunned. Ideally a college would provide a range of such areas, so that all tastes may be met.

5 **Timetabled activities**

Each room used for timetabled activities within a college should be identified, allocated a primary use and therefore a potential capacity (see **4.1**), and visited 40 times during a typical teaching week. Colleges usually choose to carry out such surveys during the middle of the Autumn term when student attendance is at its highest level for the year, and when other statistics are being gathered. From the array of data collected it is possible to calculate a wide range of results, either by hand or by using the Room Utilisation Module in the computerised Further Education Management Information Systems (FEMIS) developed by the Further Education Staff College.

5 For each room in the survey and for groups of rooms aggregated by type, site, department or other characteristics, and for all rooms together it is possible to calculate overall utilisation, together with the constituent factors of utilisation, frequency, and average occupancy. The definition of the three factors is as follows:

$$\text{Frequency} = \frac{\text{room hours used}}{\text{room hours available}} = \frac{20}{40} = 50\%$$

$$\text{Average occupancy} = \frac{\text{seats used on average}}{\text{seats available (capacity)}}$$

$$= \frac{(60 \times 10) + (80 \times 10)}{20} /100 = 70\%$$

$$\text{Utilisation} = \text{Frequency} \times \text{Average Occupancy} = 50 \times 70 = 35.$$

In addition it is possible to calculate and show graphically the numbers of people involved in timetabled activities across the week. It is possible to compare average group sizes with average room sizes and, with a bit of manipulation, group size distributions with room size distributions.

7 In the above example, based on one conceptual room, the utilisation factor is 35%, and it has to be stated that over a range of space use surveys, dating from the late 1960s and including universities and advanced and non-advanced further education, this figure has seldom been exceeded. Empirical and theoretical studies have shown that it is possible to increase this figure, so that it is important to try to understand why institutions sometimes feel under pressure even when achieving such low overall utilisation levels. (Equally it is very important to question the assumptions underlying any proffered figure, to find out how the information was gathered and to examine separately all the constituent factors.)

8 There are two main reasons for low utilisation levels, one physical and therefore not amenable to improvement without physical adaptations, and one managerial and therefore capable of being adjusted. In most colleges, in most

disciplines, the group size distribution lies consistently below the room size distribution: groups are too small for the rooms which they have to use and therefore the average occupancy is bound to be low. Without recruiting more students and teaching in larger groups or partitioning existing spaces (all of which it is possible but difficult to do), utilisation will remain low. One issue is that as SSRs are enlarged there are more teaching groups at the larger end of the range so that, although there are plenty of rooms for groups of 10 to 12, there are not enough for groups of over 70. A buildings officer can keep an eye on such trends and plan accordingly (see **4.2**).

9 The second main reason for low utilisation is the problem of peaking: it has been shown in some cases that the number of rooms made available for classes at the most popular time of the week could be halved if the classes could be spread evenly across a 40 hour week. This not uncommon situation has the disadvantage of producing the same sort of mythical overcrowding (see **4.4**.4). At the most popular time of the week there are perhaps 150 staff members clamouring for rooms, unaware of the 50 rooms empty on average for the rest of the week. Quite apart from providing accurate monitoring and planning statistics, space use surveys have the well proved advantage of dispelling perceived overcrowding.

10 In order to overcome these problems of mismatch and peaking it is important to examine the current timetabling system and to see whether it can be improved. There is a continuing debate about the merits or otherwise of central timetabling. There is no doubt that for maximum efficiency and assuming that the large amounts of data can be easily handled (this is a very important proviso, and can only really be met by using a computerised system), a centralised timetable is preferable. However, people often feel easier if decisions are taken close to the user, and if a certain amount of slack can be provided for individual and short order departmental activities. A college or authority may be willing to accept some such decentralisation so long as the implications for overall space use can be spelled out, and so long as some mechanism allows 'horse-trading' to go on among departments as required. In many institutions a compromise between central and local timetables exists, with the balance varying as priorities change.

11 When colleges find that they are becoming unable to carry out their required curriculum within their existing buildings, it may be time to consider setting up the computerised space allocation and timetabling program which has been developed for institutions of FHE. Its unique characteristic is that it carries out two processes which are normally separate – timetabling and space allocation – simultaneously. Thus all the problems which come from trying to match one rigid structure, the timetable, to another, a set of buildings, are overcome. The system allocates student groups and teaching staff to the most appropriate space and time slot, while respecting any physical, managerial or personal considerations the user may wish to stipulate. The system's objectives are:

(i) To improve space use and provide an effective solution to an institution's timetabling problem by coordinating space use at the institutional level whilst maintaining the personal choices usually included at the departmental level.

(ii) To provide a wide range of statistics on space utilisation and on movement patterns generated by the timetable, thus enabling any under- or over-provision of various kinds of space to be recognised and the necessary action taken.

(iii) To enable explicit assessment to be made of the impact of new policy decisions on patterns of space use.
(iv) To enable administrators and academics alike to understand the effects of personal and departmental preferences on space use and space provision.
(v) To provide detailed information to assist in the planning of new accommodation and the adaptation of existing buildings. Space provision can be directly related to the projected pattern of activity requirements.

12 Each institution should try to manage space as efficiently as possible and Design Note 12 suggests as potential ways towards improvement:

'Those measures falling within the purview of management seem to be:
(i) To place as much accommodation as possible in a common pool for timetabling, to be shared between departments or, in large institutions where distances are great, between groups of departments;
(ii) To classify rooms by their basic size, shape and facilities so that all potential uses are revealed;
(iii) To examine carefully the customs that have grown up in the timetabling of events and the use of rooms in order to see which are essential and which may be altered with advantage;
(iv) To spread scheduled activities as far as possible throughout the day, week, term and year so that unnecessary peaking is avoided, bearing in mind that the hours of opening of non-teaching areas such as cafeterias may have a considerable effect on the timetable.

Measures that should be considered during the process of design (or adaptation) should include:
(i) Developing sites and buildings so that working links between different facilities can be developed easily;
(ii) Surrounding departments that require an identifiable core or nucleus by spaces which are shared in a way that allows the departments to expand or contract their activities by using shared spaces for more or less time;
(iii) Avoiding the use of schedules of accommodation consisting of rooms tailor-made to a single activity – rooms should be grouped into the broadest possible categories and particular functions should be provided for by furniture and services that can be altered easily to meet likely alternative uses;
(iv) Making sure that buildings contain a variety of room sizes suitable for a wide range of different teaching groups so that changes in courses and teaching methods can be accommodated principally by timetabling, and thus the amount of moving of partitioners that is required can be limited.

In the fields both of management and of design it is necessary to keep a continual check on the demand for, and the supply of, space and facilities.'

FURTHER READING

Daff, I. 1984 'Room for college improvement' *Education* Vol. 163. No. 20

Kenny, G. 1985 'Space and facilities' in Lockwood, G. and Davies, J.L. eds. *The Management Challenge* London, NFER–Nelson

Kenny, G. and Foster, K. 1986 *Managing space in colleges*, Management in Colleges series, No. 1, Second Edition, Further Education Staff College

Kenny, G. and Wickham, D. 1984 *Making Effective Use of Space in Colleges* Coombe Lodge Information Bank No. 1971. Further Education Staff College

Kedney, R.J. 1984 *SFTEs, standards and effectiveness: the use of FE buildings* Coombe Lodge Information Bank Working Paper No. 2141, Further Education Staff College

Kedney, R.J. and Kenny, K. 1983 'How to make space for FE', *Education*, vol. 161, No. 9, pp 167–8

Pryor, A. E. M. 1976 *The Use of Teaching Accommodation: An investigation at Harlow Technical College during the week 2–6 February 1976*. Coombe Lodge Information Bank No. 1137, Further Education Staff College
Ridings, K. 1975 *A detailed investigation into the utilisation of accommodation at Stockport College of Technology during the period 1974–January 1975*. Coombe Lodge Information Bank No. 1059. Further Education Staff College
Wagner, X. 1983 *Progress report on the accommodation needs of FE Colleges* Coombe Lodge Working Paper Information Bank No. 1856. Further Education Staff College
Wickham, D. 1975. *FEMIS Room Utilisation Module: a description*, Coombe Lodge FEMIS paper No. 2077. Further Education Staff College

Department of Education and Science
Design Note 12. 1974 *Space Utilisation in Universities and polytechnics*, UGC DES Architects and Building Branch (University Building Note)
Architects and Building Branch Paper 4, 1979 *Accommodation for the 16–19 age group: Stockton Sixth Form College space utilisation survey*
Architects and Building Branch Paper 6, 1980 *Accommodation for the 16–19 age group: Hounslow Borough College space utilisation survey*
Architects and Building Branch 1977 *Space Allocation and Timetabling System for Tertiary Institutions of Education*

4.5 BUILDINGS-RELATED LAW

1 **Occupier's liability**
Every occupier of premises owes a duty to have reasonable care for the safety of lawful visitors on those premises, and the matter is covered by the Occupier's Liability Act 1957. For most purposes the occupier of further and higher education colleges is the local education authority. There may, however, be two occupiers at the same time if part of the buildings is handed over to contractors or when rooms are hired out for occasional use by another body. (See 1980 edition **5.7**.)

2 The occupier's duty is defined: 'The common duty of care is a duty to take such care as in all the circumstances of the case is reasonable to see that the visitor will be reasonably safe in using the premises for the purposes for which he is invited or permitted by the occupier to be there'. If a visitor exceeds the area of invitation or permission, he or she may become a trespasser, to whom the 1957 Act affords no rights.

3 Most, if not all, students enter a college in virtue of a contract. Most, if not all, LEAs make it clear, in their conditions of acceptance of students to their courses, that the authority will not be liable for any loss or injury to students' personal belongings. Acceptance of that condition by students makes them, in the eye of the law, willing parties to the arrangement, even though they have no alternative but to accept; the same principle applies to the personal belongings of members of staff.

4 **Use of premises**
Colleges may be used for the purposes of the Representation of the People Act 1983, under section 95(3), which refers to 'meeting rooms situated in the constituency the expense of maintaining which is payable wholly or mainly out of public funds or out of any rate, or by a body whose expenses are so payable'. If in complying with its duties under the Act, the authority has prepared in its area lists of meeting rooms which candidates in any constituency are entitled to use and the list includes rooms in a college, then that college may be so used. This provision relates to parliamentary elections only. This entitlement is restricted to the times between the receipt of the writ and the date of the poll, and it can be exercised only where reasonable notice is given.

5 Section 5 of the Public Order Act 1936 makes it an offence for any person in a public place or at a public meeting to use threatening, abusive or insulting words or behaviour or distribute or display any writing, sign or visible representation which is threatening, abusive or insulting with intent to provoke a breach of the peace or whereby a breach of the peace is likely to be occasioned. The public place is defined as including any 'highway or any other premises or place to what at the material time the public have or are permitted to have access'. If a principal or member of the college feels that persons gathering outside the college premises are likely to cause a breach of the peace, the police should be contacted immediately (see **1.2**).

6 Practices vary with regard to lettings. Normally authorities and/or governors issue guidance and instructions, and set levels of fees. These generally reflect the status and function of the outside user: no or very low charges are made to cultural or educational organisations; a higher charge is made to users who are

non profit-making but have no direct links with the college; the highest rate is charged to profit-making organisations, particularly if they are engaged in fund-raising activities. It remains to be seen whether the enabling of FE institutions to engage in commercial activities will lead to more revenue from outside lettings being retained by individual institutions. The Further Education Act 1985 empowers 'local education authorities to supply goods and services through further education establishments', and Section 1 (1)b states that goods are supplied through a further education establishment if they result from 'the use of its facilities'. In any case it is important to ensure that the appropriate insurance and licensing regulations are met, and that identifiable subsidies (as for students' meals) are not passed on to inappropriate outside users.' (See **1.2** 28.)

7 Section 8 of the Misuse of Drugs Act 1971 makes it an offence for an occupier or person concerned in the management knowingly to permit or suffer the production or supply of any controlled drug on the premises or the smoking of opium or cannabis.

FURTHER READING

Public Order Act 1936 HMSO
Occupier's Liability Act 1957 HMSO
Misuse of Drugs Act 1971 HMSO
Unfair Contract Terms Act 1977 HMSO
Representation of the People Act 1983 HMSO
Further Education Act 1985 HMSO

DES 1977 *Polytechnics: The Shared Use of Space and Facilities* Department of Educaiton and Science

4.6 SECURITY

1 It is a common perception that problems of security are increasing and that colleges and LEAs are having to spend growing sums on the repair of damaged buildings and facilities and on replacing damaged or stolen equipment. In fact, the supporting evidence is scanty; it may be that individual institutions and localities suffer more than others, and it tends to be the worst hit who generate the most publicity. Because of problems of definition, and because of many authorities' understandable reluctance to admit to high levels of crime and vandalism on educational premises, it is difficult to get a clear picture of the level and types of crime prevalent in schools and colleges.

2 Authorities individually, however, have undertaken a wide range of procedures to combat what they see as their local difficulties, as it is obviously important to fit any solution as nearly as possible to individual problems. The Department of Education and Science hopes at the time of writing to prepare a report on the current level of buildings-related crime in educational establishments and on its real cost. A guidance document on targeted design and management strategies will then be published.

3 It is possible to identify various general aspects of a building's design and use which, all things being equal, should keep crime to a minimum. The following suggestions are taken from *Crime Prevention in Schools: building-related aspects*, and divide into two types of approach, one aimed at the building itself, physical strategies, and the other aimed at the organisation of building use, management strategies.

4 **Physical strategies**

Target hardening is the procedure most quickly thought of and most easily put into practice. It involves protecting or removing particularly vulnerable targets such as the finance office where money may be kept, or classrooms and workshops where valuable equipment is used and stored. Floor safes and strong storage cabinets may be appropriate, although it is essential to balance carefully the needs of security against the wish of staff and students, and outside users, to have easy access to frequently used equipment. There is little point in setting up a 'walk-in' computer workshop if potential users cannot get in because the key holder has disappeared. Equally some equipment storage systems are so heavy and bulky that they may not be used. Another form of target hardening is to make sure that the most resilient materials are used for vulnerable doors and windows.

5 Access control is another commonly used method; it consists primarily in restricting access to the college site or buildings by keeping the number of entry points to a minimum and making sure that these are controlled. Additionally it may be necessary to put a physical barrier around the site, and to supplement this by planting shrubs and flowerbeds in such a way as to keep people at a distance from vulnerable points of the buildings; these may be entry points previously used by intruders, made easier to reach often by conveniently placed flat roofs. All these points should be examined and made more secure. As part of access control, intruder alarms are often fitted; again the evidence as to their deterrent effect is inconclusive, particularly taking into account any tendency to go off accidentally and the wide range of costs that

they may incur. Speed of response from the suppliers and real cost effectiveness are essential.

6 As well as providing hardware, the college should ensure that surveillance of premises is easy at all times, and it would appear that often the most effective deterrent is a resident caretaker who has a good view of buildings and site, but a caretaker may be expensive. Particularly vulnerable areas may be under electronic surveillance or floodlit; this will help casual passers-by and neighbours to join in the surveillance task. The introduction of outside users into the college premises may be welcomed as an extension of the establishment's role within the local community; some would argue that such increased outside use improves casual surveillance and lessens crime, while others would argue, from equally valid evidence, that outside users are potential burglars sizing up the target.

7 Finally it is often argued that keeping the buildings and site in good order develops an atmosphere of care and involvement which naturally discourages vandalism, particularly in the form of graffiti. Again, the evidence is inconclusive for educational buildings; it may not be possible for a college to spend as much as it would like on the long-term, let alone the day to day, maintenance and cleaning of buildings.

8 **Management strategies**

Colleges are expected increasingly to collect full information on all aspects of their operation. In the context of vandalism and crime it is essential to have as much detailed information as possible on each incident so that remedial action can be taken immediately, so that trends may be identified and so that scarce resources can be concentrated where they will produce the best effect: *Vandalism in schools and colleges: Some possible ways of reducing damage* has a useful checklist.

9 Such information should be analysed by all the parties who may have an interest, from LEA to Fire Service to Police Force to Students' Union, with a view to a properly cooperative effort being made against the crime or vandalism problem. Such cooperation becomes essential when action has been decided upon and has to be implemented and evaluated. The ideal process is a series of steps – information gathering, problem analysis, choice of measures, implementation and evaluation – which will be repeated as necessary by those agencies who are most closely concerned with the safety and security of FE colleges and their users.

FURTHER READING

Clarke, R. V. G. 1978 *Tackling vandalism* HMSO
Poyner, B. 1983 *Design against crime* Butterworths

Home Office 1980 *Coordinating crime prevention efforts* Home Office Research Study No. 62, HMSO
Home Office 1982 *Burglary in Schools: the prospects for prevention* Research and Planning Unit Paper 11

Department of Education and Science
Circular 1/81 *Crime Prevention*
Building Bulletin 1987 *Vandalism, Arson and Theft in Schools: Guidelines on Prevention* Architects and Building Branch
DES 1983 *Vandalism in schools and colleges* Broadsheet 12 Architects and Building Branch
DES 1986 *Crime prevention in schools: building-related aspects* Discussion Paper Architects and Building Branch

REFERENCES

References

ACAS 1977 *Disclosure of Information to Trade Unions for Collective Bargaining Purposes* Advisory Conciliation and Arbitration Services.

ACC 1987 *Understanding Block Grant: Guide and Glossary* Association of County Councils

ACSTT 1975 *the Training of Teachers for Further Education: A Report by the Sub-Committee on the Training of Teachers for Further Education relating to the Training of Full-time teachers in Further Education* Advisory Committee for the Supply and Training of Teachers

Adelman, C and Alexander, R 1982a 'Internal evaluating and external validation' *Higher Education Review* 14.2 Spring 1982

Adelman, C and Alexander, R 1982 b *The self-evaluating institution* Methuen

Arthur Young McClelland Moore 1981 *Costing Educational provision for the 16–19 Age Group* Department of Education and Science

Audit Commission 1984 *The Impact on Local Authorities' Economy, Efficiency and Effectiveness of the Block Grant Distribution System* HMSO

Audit Commission 1985 *Obtaining better value from further education* HMSO

Auld, R 1976 *William Tyndale Junior and Infants School Public Inquiry* Inner London Education Authority

Baines, M A (chair) 1972 *The New Local Authorities: Management and Structure* HMSO

Ball, C 1985 *Fitness for Purpose* Society for Research into Higher Education and National Foundation for Educational Research – Nelson

Bell, R (ed) 1983 *Education in Great Britain and Ireland: A Source Book* RKP

Birch, D 1982 *FEMIS 1: a systems specification (outline)* Coombe Lodge FEMIS Working Paper 1BN 1687 Further Education Staff College

Bolam, R, Smith G, and Cantor, H 1976 *Local Education Authority Advisers and Educational Innovation* University of Bristol

Bourner, T and Hamad, M 1987 *Entry qualifications and degree performance* Development Services Publication No. 10 Council for National Academic Awards

Bristow, R and Shotnes, S (eds) 1987 *Overseas Students – at Home in Britain* United Kingdom Council on Overseas Student Affairs

British Council 1987 *How to live in Britain* Macmillan

Browne, S (chair) 1985 *Report of the Polytechnic of North London Committee of Inquiry 1985* Polytechnic of North London

Burgess, T 1981 'Do as I say, not as I do' *The Guardian* 31 July 1981

Bush, T and Goulding, S 1984 'The National Advisory Body and college management' *Educational Management and Administration* 12.1 Spring 1984

Carr, R (chair) 1957 *Training for skill: Recruitment and training of young workers in industry* HMSO

Challis, B 1983 *College-based Course Evaluation* Further Education Unit

Chapman, P G and Tooze M J 1987 *The Youth Training Scheme in the United Kingdom* Avebury

CIPFA 1979 *Financial Information systems for Institutions of Further and Higher Education in the Maintained Sector* Chartered Institute of Public Finance and Accountancy

CIPFA 1984a *Performance Indicators in Education Service* Chartered Institute of Public Finance and Accountancy

CIPFA 1984b *Guide to Local Authority Finance* Chartered Institute of Public Finance and Accountancy

CNAA 1984 *Access/Preparatory Courses* Council for National Academic Awards

CNAA 1986 *Quantity and validation: Future relationships with institutions* Council for National Academic Awards

Coopers and Lybrand 1985 *A Challenge to Complacency: changing attitudes to training* Manpower Services Commission/National Economic Development Office

CRE 1987 *Annual Report 1986* Commission for Racial Equality
Crispin, A and Marsten-Wilson, F 1984 'Extent of Central Control: LEA Responses to the 1981 Block Grant' *Educational Management and Administration* 21.1 Spring 1984
Crowther, G (chair) 1959 *15–18* Report of the Central Advisory Council for Education 2 Vols HMSO
Curtis, J R A 1981/1982 *Managing Marginal Performane* I, II and III IBN 1700, 1701, 1701 Further Education Staff College
Davies, P and Scribbins, K 1985 *Marketing Further and Higher Education: A Handbook* Longman
DED/DENI 1986 *Youth Training Programme: Cohort Study: Third Stage* Policy Planning and Research Unit Department of Economic Development
DENI 1983 *The Youth Training Programme and Further Education Colleges: The first Year 1982–83* Department of Education Northern Ireland
DENI 1980 report of the sub-committee of the Advisory Committee on the Supply and Training of Teachers (ACSTT) Department of Education Northern Ireland
Department of Education and Science
DES Annual *Education Statistics of the United Kingdom* HMSO
DES Annual *Statistics of education* Department of Education and Science
DES 1977 *The management of non-university higher education* Report on Education 90. Department of Education and Science
DES 1978a *Non-advanced further education* Report on Education 94. Department of Education and Science
DES 1978b *Higher education into the 1990s* Department of Education and Science
DES 1979 *Future trends in higher education* Department of Education and Science
DES 1980a *Report of the Monitoring of Student: Staff Ratios* Department of Education and Science
DES 1980b *Examinations 16–18* Department of Education and Science
DES 1981a *The legal basis of further education* Department of Education and Science
DES 1981b *17+ – A New Qualification* HMSO
DES 1981c *Higher education in England outside the universities: Policy, funding and management* Department of Education and Science
DES 1983 *Future demand for higher education in Great Britain* Report on Education 99. Department of Education and Science
DES 1985 *The development of higher education into the 1990s* Cmnd 9524. HMSO
DES 1986 *The Department of Education and Science – A brief guide* Department of Education and Science
DEE 1987a *A Special Professionalism* Department of Education and Science
DES 1987b *Maintained Further Education: Financing, Governance and Law* Consultative paper. Department of Education and Science
DES Circulars
Circular 4/87 *Training of Teachers Regulations* Department of Education and Science
Circular 7/70 *Government and conduct of establishments of further education* Department of Education and Science
Circular 8/73 *Organisation of the Department* Department of Education and Science
Circular 11/77 *The Training of Teachers for Further Education* Department of Education and Science
Circular 3/84 *Initial Teacher Training – Approval of Courses* Department of Education and Science
Circular 3/85 *The In-Service Teacher Training Grants Scheme* Department of Education and Science

Circular 1/86 *The In-Service Teacher Training Grants Scheme* Department of Education and Science
Circular 5/86 *Education Support Grants* Department of Education and Science
Circular 3/87 *Providing for Quality – The Pattern of Education to Age 19* Department of Education and Science
DES and LAA 1987 *Managing Colleges Efficiently* HMSO
DES and WOED 1983 *The work of HM Inspectorate in England and Wales* Department of Education and Science/Welsh Office
DES and WOED 1985 *The educational system of England and Wales* Department of Education and Science/Welsh Office
DOE 1986 *Paying for Local Government* Cmnd 9714. HMSO
Education, Science and Arts Committee 1980 *The Funding and Organisation of Courses in Higher Education* HMSO
Edwards, C 1984 *Performance Appraisal* Industrial Society
Elder, A J 1986 *Guide to the Building Regulations 1985* The Architectural Press
Farley, M and Clayton G 1980 'Humberside: Is Mr Carlisle failing to uphold the 1944 Act? *Education* 31 October 1980
FEU 1979 *A Basis for Choice* Further Education Curriculum Review and Development Unit
FEU 1985 *Marketing FE: A Staff Development Initiative* Further Education Unit
FEU 1985a *Black Perspectives on FE* provision Further Education Unit
FEU 1985b *Changing the Focus: Women and FE* Further Education Unit
FEU 1985c *CPVE in Action* Further Education Unit
FEU 1986 *A Fragmented View* Further Education Unit
FEU 1987 *FE in Black and White* Longman
Fish, J (chair) 1985 *Educational opportunities for all?* Inner London Education Authority
Fletcher, M C 1986 *The Further Education Act 1986: Commerical activities in Further Education* IBN 2207 Further Education Staff College
Gibson, A with Barrow, J 1986 *The Unequal Struggle* The Centre for Caribbean Studies
Gillies, J F and White, O M 1982 *Technical Education in Northern Ireland: An Historical Study* Ulster Polytechnic
Goldsmith, J and Shawcross, V 1985 *It ain't half sexist, mum* World University Service United Kingdom Council on Overseas Student Affairs
Grant, M 1986 *Rate capping and the Law* Association of Metropolitan Authorities
Hamlyn, G 1978 'Prospects for Change' *County Councils Gazette* December 1978
Harbinson, J 1985 *The role of the Vice-Principal: A View From Northern Ireland* Coombe Lodge Report Vol 18 No 6 Further Education Staff College
Haslegrove, H L (chair) 1969 *Technician courses and examinations* National Advisory Council on Education for Industry and Commerce HMSO
Haycocks, N (chair) 1975 *The Training of Teachers for Further Education: a report by the sub-committee on the training of teachers for further education relating to the training of future teachers in Further Education* ACSTT Department of Education and Science
Heald, O 1983 *Public Expenditure* Martin Robertson
Henley, D Holtham, C Likierman, A and Perrin, J 1986 *Public Sector Accounting and Financial Control* Van Nostrand Reinhold
Henniker-Heaton, C (chair) 1986 *Day Release* HMSO
HMI 1984 *Report by HM Inspectors on Abingdon College of Further Education* Department of Education and Science
HMI 1987 *NAFE in Practice* HMSO
Holland Report 1977 *Young People and Work* Manpower Services Commission
Hollyhock, N 1982 'Middle Management' in Parkes 1982a

Holtham, O 1986 in Henley et al 1986
Home Office 1975 A Guide to the Sex Discrimination Act 1975
Home Office 1985 *the Data Protection Tribunal Rules* HMSO
Houghton, Lord C H (chair) 1974 *The Pay of Non-unionist Teachers* Cmnd 5848 HMSO
Howard G 1985 *The Steps to Registration* Video Arts
HSE 1978 *Pilot Study, Health and Safety in Schools and Further Education Establishments* HMSO/Health and Safety Executive
James Lord of Rusholme (chair) 1971 *Teacher Education and Training Report by a Committee of Inquiry* HMSO
Kedney, R J 1983 *Performance Indicators in FE* IBN 1815 Further Education Staff College
Kedney, R J 1984 *SFTE, Standards and Effectiveness: The Use of FE Buildings IBN 2141. Further Education Staff College*
Kenny, G and Foster, K 1986 *Managing Space in Colleges* Further Education Staff College
Keohane, K W (chair) 1979 *Proposals for a Certificate of Extended Education* Cmnd 7755 HMSO
Kotler, P and Fox K 1985 *Strategic Marketing for Educational Institutions* Prentice-Hall
LACSAB 1977 *The LACSAB Employee Relation Handbook* Local Authorities' Conditions of Service Advisory Board
LACSAB 1978 *Employee Relations Reference Guide for Chief Officers and Managers in Local Authorities* Local Authorities Conditions of Service Advisory Board/ Local Government Training Board
Layfield, F (chair) 1976 *Local Government Finance* Cmnd 6453 HMSO
LCOS 1986 *Some Accommodation Problems of Overseas Students in London* London Conference on Overseas Students
Leech, M 1982 'College Government and Organisation' in Parkes 1982a
Leyland, D G 1986 'Commercialism and corporate strategy in British Higher Education *Higher Education Review* 19.1 Autumn 1986
Liell, P and Saunders J B 1987 *The Law of Education* Ninth Edition. Butterworths
Lindop, N (chair) 1985 *Academic Validation in Public Sector Higher Education* Cmnd 9501 HMSO
Locke, M 1972 *College Government: The Law and the Issues* Coombe Lodge Report 5.3 Further Education Staff College
Locke, M 1974 'Government' in Pratt and Burgess 1974
Locke, M 1978 *'Traditions and Controls in the Making of a Polytechnic:* Woolwich Polytechnic 1890–1970 Thames Polytechnic
Locke, M and Bloomfield, J 1982 *Mapping and reviewing the patterns of 16–19 education* Pamphlet 20 Schools Council
Locke, M, Pratt, J and Burgess, T 1985 *The colleges of higher education 1972–1982: The central management of organic change* Critical Press
Locke, M Pratt, J and Spencer, A 1980 *the CNAA Quinquennial Visit to North East London Polytechnic: Monitoring the Polytechnic's Performance* Centre for Institutional Studies North East London Polytechnic
Locke, M with Pratt, J, Silverman, S and Travers, T 1987 *Polytechnic Government* Committee of Directors of Polytechnics
Long, P 1986 *Performance Appraisal Revisited* Institute of Personnel Management
Loughlin, M 1986 *Local Goverment in the modern state* Sweet and Maxwell
Macfarlane, N (chair) 1980 *Education for 16–19 year olds* A review undertaken for the Goverment and Local Authority Associations Department of Education and Science
Mallaby, G (chair) 1967 *Staffing of Local Goverment* Ministry of Housing and Local

References

Government

MSC Training Services Agency 1975 *The vocational preparation of young people* Manpower Services Commission

MSC 1981 *A New Training Initiative: A Consultative Document* Manpower Services Commission

MSC 1981 *A New Training Initiative: an agenda for action* Manpower Services Commission

MSC 1982 *Youth Task Group Report* Manpower Services Commission

MSC/NEDO 1984 *Competence and Competition* Manpower Services Commission/ National Economic Development Office.

MSC/Local Authority Associations 1985 *Work related Non-Advanced Further Education* Report by Policy Group MSC

MSC/DES 1986 *Review of Vocational qualification in England and Wales* A report by the working group HMSO

March, J G and Olsen J P 1979 *Ambiguity and Choice in Organisations* Universities forlagets Bergen

Marsh, D 1982 *The Provision for Further Education in Northern Ireland* Coombe Lodge Information Bank 1767 Further Education Staff College

Maynard, A 1982 'Privatisation and Market Mechanisms' in Morris and Sizer 1982

McNair, A Sir (chair) 1944 *Teachers and Youth Leaders Report of the Committee appointed by the President of the Board of Education to consider the supply, recruitment and training of teachers and youth leaders* HMSO

Megson, C and Barber, M 1986 *Taking Education Further* MSE

Millins, K 1984 *ACCESS Studies to Higher Education* Department of Education and Science

Morris, A and Sizer, J (eds) 1982 *Resources and Higher Education* Society for Research into Higher Education

NAB 1984a *Report on Continuing Education* National Advisory Body for Public Sector Higher Education

NAB 1984b *A Strategy for Higher Education in the Late 1980s and Beyond* National Advisory Body for Public Sector Higher Education

NAB 1986 *Planning for 1987–88: Programme Balance* Board Paper 4/86 National Advisory Body for Public Sector Higher Education

NAB 1987 *Management for a Purpose: The Report of the Good Management Practice Group* National Advisory Body for Public Sector Higher Education.

NATFHE 1981 *Further Education in Northern Ireland: Policy Statement* National Association of Teachers in Further and Higher Education.

NATFHE 1985a 'The Audit Commission Report' *NATFHE Journal* October 1985

NATFHE 1985b *Handicap, disability and special learning needs* National Association of Teachers in Further and Higher Education

NATFHE 1986a *NATFHE against Racism* National Association of Teachers in Further and Higher Education

NATFHE 1986b *Planning for change in further education* National Association of Teachers in Further and Higher Education

NATFHE 1987 *The NVQ Framework and NATFHE's Response* Briefing Document 12/87 National Association of Teachers in Further and Higher Education

NCVQ 1987 *The NVQ Framework* National Council for Vocational Qualifications

NBHS 1987 *Catching Up* National Bureau for Handicapped Students

NBHS 1986 *Burnham: The biggest barrier of all?* National Bureau for Handicapped Students

NJC *Conditions of Service for Further Education Teachers in England and Wales* National Joint Council for Teachers in Further Education in England and Wales (updated regularly listed 1981)

NUS 1986 *Welfare Manual 1986/7* National Union of Students

Oakes, G (chair) 1978 *The Management of Higher Education in the Maintained Sector* HMSO
O'Hara, R (1985) *Unit costs at NELP: An unfair basis of comparison* CIS Commentary Series 28, North East London Polytechnic
Oliver, J E 1985 'Performance Appraisals that Fit' Personnel Journal
OST 1987 *The Next steps: Overseas Students Policy into the 1990s* Overseas Students Trust
Parkes, D 1982a (ed.) *The Changing Face of FE* Further Education Curriculum Review and Development Unit
Parkes, D 1982b 'The Changing Face of FE' in Parkes 1982a
Percy, Lord (chair) 1948 *Higher technological education* HMSO
PFOG 1987 *Polytechnic Expenditure: Actual 1985–86* Polytechnic Finance Officers Group
Plowden, W (chair) 1961 *The Control of Public Expenditure* Cmnd 1432 HMSO
Pratt, J 1982 'Resource Allocation within the Public Sector' in Morris and Sizer
Pratt J and Burgess, T (1974) Polytechnics: *A report* Pitman
Pratt, J and Gill, J (1987) *Responses to financial constraint in Public sector higher education institutions* Report to the Department of Education and Science
Pratt, J and Silverman 1988 *Responding to Constraint* Open University Press
Redcliffe-Maud, J P Lord (chair) 1969 *Royal Commission Local Goverment in England* 1966–1969 Vol 1 and 2 Cmnd 4040 HMSO
Robinson, E *The New Polytechnics: The People's Universities* Penguin
Robbins, Lord (chair 1963) *Higher education* Cmnd 2154 HMSO
Russell, Sir L (chair) 1973 *Adult Education: A Plan for Development* HMSO
Scribbins, K 1986 *Data Protection and Further Education* Further Education Staff College
Scribbins, K and Walton F 1987 *Staff Appraisal in Further and Higher Education* Further Education Staff College
SEO 1977 *The Position of the Education Service Following Local Government Reorganisation* Society of Education officers
Shattock, M and Rigby, O 1983 *Resource Allocation in British Universities* Society for Research into Higher Education
Shotnes, S (ed) 1987 *Overseas Students—Destination UK?* United Kingdom Council for Overseas Students Affairs
Sizer, J 1986 'Efficiency and Scholarship: Uncomfortable or Compatible Bedfellows?' *Higher Education Review* 18.2 Spring 1986
Smith, T J 1986 'Faculty Governance – Professionals and Bureaucrats' Educational *Management and Administration* 14.3 Autumn 1986
Smith, V J E 1983 'College Democracy: It isn't working' *NATFHE Journal* March/April 1983
Statutory instruments SI 1975/1054 Education (Further Education) Regulations HMSO.
SI 1980/917 Education (Areas to which pupils belong) regulations 1980 HMSO
SI 1981/1086 The Education (Schools and Further Education) regulations 1981 HMSO
SI 1982/106 Education (Teachers) regulations 1982 HMSO
SI 1983/262 Education (Schools and further education) (Amendment) regulations 1983 HMSO
SI 1983/973 Education (Fees and awards) regulations 1983 HMSO
SI 1985/1065 The Building Regulations, 1985 HMSO
SI 1972/1263 The Education and Libraries (Northern Ireland) Order HMSO
Suffolk Education Department 1985 *Those Having Torches* Suffolk Education Department
Sutherland, M 1983 'Education in Northern Ireland' in Bell 1983

References

Taylor T (chair) 1977 *A New Partnership for our schools* HMSO
Theodossin, E 1984 *Management in an FE College* Further Education Staff College
Theodossin, E 1986 *In Search of the Responsive College* Further Education Staff College
Tipton, B F A 1973 *Conflict and change in a Technical College* Hutchinson
Treasury 1986a *The Government's Expenditure Plans 1986–87 to 1988–89* Cmnd 9702. HMSO
Treasury 1986b *United Kingdom National Accounts* HMSO
Treasury 1987 *The Government's Expenditure Plans 1987–88 to 1989–90* Cmnd 56-II. HMSO
Turner, C 1981 'Appraisal Systems' *Coombe Lodge Report* Vol. 15 No 7 Further Education Staff College
UKCOSA 1985a *Orientation – 1985* United Kingdom Council for Overseas Student Affairs
UKCOSA 1985b *Containing Crises: The Responses to Overseas Student Groups in Hardship* United Kingdom Council for Overseas Student Affairs
Ulster Year Book 1985 Northern Ireland Services HMSO
Waddell, Sir J (chair) 1978 *School examination* Cmnd 7281, HMSO
Waitt. I (ed) 1980 *College Administration* National Assocation of Teachers in Further and Higher Education
Walton, F (editor) (annaul) *Encyclopaedia of Employment Law and Practice* Professional Publishing Ltd
Warnock, M 1978 *Special educational needs: Report of the Committee of Inquiry into the Education of Handicapped Children and Young People* Cmnd 7212 HMSO
Weaver T (chair) 1966 *College Government* HMSO

WHITE PAPERS
Ministry of Education 1943 *Educational reconstruction* Cmnd 6458 HMSO
Ministry of Education 1956 *Technical education* Cmnd 9703 HMSO
Ministry of Education 1961 Better opportunities in technical education Cmnd 1254 HMSO
Ministry of Education 1966 A plan for polytechnics and other colleges Cmnd 3006 HMSO
DES 1972 Education: A framework for expansion Cmnd 5174 HMSO
DES 1978 Secondary school examinations: A single system at 16-plus Cmnd 7368 HMSO
Department of Employment 1981 *A new training initiative: A programme for action* Cmnd 8455 HMSO
DES 1983 *Teaching Quality* Cmnd 8836 HMSO
DES 1984 *Training for Jobs* Cmnd 9135 HMSO
DES/Department of Employment/DTI 1985 Education and training for young people Cmnd 9482 HMSO
Department of Employment 1985 *Employment – The challenge for the nation* Cmnd 9474 HMSO
DES 1985 *Better Schools* Cmnd 9469 HMSO
DES 1986 *Working together – Education and training* Cmnd 9823 HMSO
DES 1987 Higher education – Meeting the challenge Cmnd 114 HMSO
DTI 1987 *Intellectual property and innovation* Cmnd 9712 HMSO

Waddell, Sir J (chair) 1978 *School Examinations* Cmnd 7281 HMSO
WHO 1980 *International Classification of Impairment, Disabilities and Handicaps (ICDH)* World Health Organisation, Geneva
Widdicombe, D (chair) 1986 *The Conduct of Local Authority Business* Cmnd 9797 HMSO

Wilson, J A 1983 'Development in Secondary and Further Education in Northern Ireland' *Northern Teacher* 14 (i) Autumn 1983
Williams, G 1986 'Changing Patterns of Educational Finance and Their Anticipated Effects on Institutional Behaviour and Educational Outcomes: A programme of Research' Conference of the British Educational Management and Administration Society 24–25 April 1986
Woodrow, M 1983 'New courses: New management' *Educational Management and Administration* 11.3 October 1983
Yates, J and Davies, P 1986 *The Progress and Performance of Former Access Students in Higher Education* 1984–86 Roehampton Institute of Higher Education.
WUS 1986 *The Forgotten Overseas Students – Towards a Policy for Refugees* World University Service

EDITORIAL ADVISORS

NOTES ON CONTRIBUTORS

John Baillie, MA, DipFE, FBIM, FRSA. Has over twenty-five years' teaching experience in six London colleges. He is now Principal of Newham Community College, and Co-Chair of the National Bureau for Handicapped Students. He was Chair of the national Further Education Teachers' Panel (1977–80) and a member of the Further Education Unit's Board of Management (1980–86).

Paul Bennett, MA has worked in the Research Department of the General and Municipal Workers Union, and since 1972 has served as the Education Officer of the ATTI and subsequently NATFHE. He has written a number of articles on various topics.

Derek Betts, BSc has taught mathematics in both secondary schools and further education. He joined NATFHE as a Regional Official in 1977 and has, since 1984, held the post of Assistant Secretary, Further Education.

Jean Bocock, BA has lectured in politics and sociology at Kingston Polytechnic, Brunel University and Sheffield University. She joined the ATTI as a Regional Official in 1974 and since 1976 has held the post of Assistant Secretary, Higher Education, NATFHE. In 1987–88 she spent the year as part of the Directorate team at the Polytechnic of the South Bank, on secondment from her post at NATFHE.

Linzi Brand, aged 24, graduated from the Polytechnic of the South Bank in 1984. In 1984–85, she held the post of Education and Welfare Officer for the student's union. In 1985–86 she was elected to the National Union of Students National Executive and held joint responsibility for the Women's, Lesbian and Gay and Anti-Racism campaign. Since leaving NUS in 1986, she has written a variety of freelance pieces for Harrow CRC, University of London Union and *Time Out* publications. She is now the Youth Director at West London Synagogue.

Rupert Bristow BA, DipFE, Dip Counselling and Guidance, after teaching overseas worked for twelve years at the UK Council for Overseas Student Affairs (UKCOSA), becoming its second Executive Secretary in 1980. He has been Head of Student Services at South Bank Polytechnic since 1983, a year in which he was also specialist adviser to the Overseas Development Subcommittee of the Foreign Affairs Committee of the House of Commons in its investigation on overseas students. He has written articles, chaired working parties and edited publications on overseas student and other education issues.

Peter Davies, BA, Cert Ed, MSc worked for eight years with British Rail, mainly in marketing, and subsequently with the Business Education Council, the Business and Technician Education Council, and the Further Education Unit. He is currently a staff tutor at the Further Education Staff College and, with Keith Scribbins, is the author of *Marketing Further and Higher Education* (Longman for FEU and FESC, 1985)

Jim Doran, BA (Politics) joined the NATFHE Salaries Department in 1986. Prior to that, he was the full-time National Secretary of the National Union of Students.

Lynton Gray, BA MA (Ed) MSc MBIM has taught in schools, a college of education and for the last nine years at the North East London Polytechnic where he is Head of the Education Management Service. He has written on a wide range of education management issues, is an Associate Tutor at the Further Education Staff College, and currently is chairman of the newly formed Marketing Network for Further & Higher Education.

Frank Griffiths, BSc, MSc, is the Education Secretary and one of two Deputy General Secretaries of (NATFHE) and as such is responsbile for overseeing the development of Association policy on the entire range of post-compulsory schooling. Before this he was a Senior Lecturer at Teesside Polytechnic involved in teaching and research in the field of socio-medical studies. Prior to taking up employment with NATFHE he held elected office including being Chair of the Association's Higher Education Committee and serving as a teacher representative on Cleveland Education Committee. He is a member of the National Advisory Body for Public Sector Higher Education and a number of its sub-groups include a joint standing Committee with the University Grants Committee on Continuing Education. Additional activities include participating in various research projects most notably a national study the industrial and commerical responsiveness of FE Colleges.

Grace Kenny, BA, PhD, LèsL has worked as a researcher at University College London, in the Department of Political Economy and at the Bartlett School of Architecture where the Unit for Architectural Studies examined space use in complex organisations, including polytechnics and universities. Since 1975, she has worked in the Architects and Building Branch of the Department of Education and Science where she is Senior Research Officer. She writes and lectures on efficient space, management, advises on educational building research and promotes UK building-related educational exports.

Paula Lanning, BSc (Econ) read industrial relations at University College, Cardiff, has been a training officer in an engineering company, and worked for the National Union of Public Employees and as Research Officer for Industrial Relations Review and Report and Industrial Relations Law Reports. She has been the Information Officer for NATFHE (and its predecessor, the ATTI) since 1974 with responsibility for the Association's public relations, publications, communications and library. She holds a specialist journalist qualification and has lectured and written widely on labour law, industrial relations, women and employment and public relations.

Michael Locke, BA is Senior Research Fellow in the Centre for Institutional Studies at North East London Polytechnic. He has worked on a number of research projects on policy and management in further and higher education, including studies of college government, multi-site institutions, the reorganisation of colleges of education, the impact of financial restraint, and corporate status for polytechnics. He is author of *Your Local Education* (with John Pratt, Tyrrell Burgess and Ralph Allemano) (Penguin, 1973), *Power and Politics in the School System* (Routledge and Kegan Paul, 1974), *A Guide to Learning After School* (with John Pratt) (Penguin, 1979), *How to run Committees and Meetings* (MacMillan, 1980), *The Colleges of Higher Education 1972 to 1982* (with John Pratt and Tyrrell Burgess) (Critical Press, 1985) and many reports and articles. He is Editor of *Educational Management and Administration*. He also works as a researcher, consultant and trainer on the development of voluntary and community organisations.

Gerry McAleavy, BA, MEd, Ed, DASE is Lecturer in the University of Ulster at Jordanstown. He taught for fifteen years in a variety of FE institutions in Northern Ireland. Presently he is Senior Course Tutor of the Advanced Diploma in Education (FE) at the University of Ulster. Current research interests: self-evaluation in colleges of FE.

John McAleer, BA, MA, MSc, Cert Ed (FE) is Senior Lecturer in the University of Ulster at Jordanstown. He worked in the United States for ten years in a variety of lecturing posts before returning to Ireland in the early 1980s when he joined the Ulster Polytechnic. His present position is Director of the Northern Ireland Regional Curriculum Base. Current research interests: management of staff development.

James McKeown, BA, lectures in trade union studies at Belfast College of Technology. He is Northern Ireland Regional Secretary of NATFHE. Before entering teaching he was a Post Office engineer and active in the Post Office Engineering Union (now the N.C.U.). He is a member of the Northern Ireland Further Education Negotiating Committee and the Northern Ireland Colleges of Education Negotiating Committee.

Geoffrey Melling, MA after teaching for ten years in FE joined HM Inspectorate (Further Education) from which he was seconded into the Department of Education and Science as the founding Director of the Further Education Unit. He later became Regional Staff Inspector for the North of England before being appointed to the post of Director of The Further Education Staff College in 1984.

Alison Mitchell, BA, an Assistant Organising Officer for NALGO since 1977, prior to that she was a Research Officer with NALGO and with Incomes Data Services. For most of her period as a national officer she has had responsibility for NALGO's membership in schools, colleges and polytechnics.

Clive Norris, MA, is an Assistant Secretary in the Department of Employment. He returned recently from a three-year secondment as adviser on education, training and youth policy to the Commission of the European Communities.

Rory O'Hara, BA, works in the Department of management and Education in the Public Sector at North East London Polytechnic and lectures in different aspects of public finance, particularly local government finance. He has written on educational finance and on the approaches developed by the National Advisory Body as well as the implications for polytechnic and college management.

Keith Scribbins, BSc, MA, was educated at Goldsmith's college, where he read sociology, and at Sussex University and the LSE where he studied philosophy. Following teaching in further education in London and Worcester he became a full-time official for NATFHE working as a regional official. Salaries Officer, and finally, as an Assistant Secretary responsbile for salaries and employment law. His consultancy work has taken him to the South Pacific and he has taught in Africa and in a large number of UK polytechnics, universities and colleges on various aspects of personnel management, industrial relations and marketing. He has published widely on employment law, the position of women and education, the statutes and regulations effecting further and higher education. His most recent publications include *Marketing Further and Higher Education* (Longman, 1985, with Peter Davies) and *Staff Appraisal in Education* (FESC, forthcoming, with Frank Walton). He is a member of the Industrial Tribunals for England and Wales. He joined the Further Education Staff College in 1984 and, in 1986 became its first Director of External Services.

Janet Shuter, is an information management consultant now working primarily in the field of public access information systems, particularly in the field of education and training information. She completed two years funded research in the teaching of library management, and has taught in library schools at Ealing, University College and Hammersmith and West London College. She is chairperson of the Society of Indexers.

David Triesman formerly a semi-professional footballer and journalist, went to the University of Essex. Undertook postgraduate research at the Universities of Cambridge and London. Responsible for aspects of drug addiction research at the Institute of Psychiatry (1970–73), working for ASTMS the following year. Became a Senior Lecturer in Social Sciences at the Polytechnic of the South Bank (1975–85), holding two visiting professorships at American universities during this peiod. Having chaired the Burnham FE Teachers' Panel, became national Negotiating Secretary of NATFHE in 1985, responsible for the Association's industrial relations activities. Widely published on drug epidemiology, the economic and social organisation of sport and the structure of inner city labour markets.

Ian Waitt, BA, PhD, MBIM, has taught in schools, at a college of education and at the North East London Polytechnic where he has lectured in education management and co-ordinated a range of overseas activities. He is currently responsible for international development at NELP. He is a governor of an educational charity and acts as academic adviser to the Shashoua Foundation. He has published extensively, in the educational press and in a number of books, his most recent publication being on technical education in East Asia in the 1987 *World Year Book of Education.*

Frank Walton compiles and edits *The Encyclopaedia of Employment Law and Practice* (Professional Publishing Ltd, part of the International Thomson Organisation) and is nationally recognised as an expert and adviser on the practical application of employment law. He was previously Deputy Secretary of the Local Authorities' Conditions of Service Advisory Board. He is an Associate Tutor at the Further Education Staff College. He contributes regularly to a number of publications including *Employment Bulletin* and *IR Digest.*

Index

Introductory Note

This index is intended to provide an alternative subject approach to the text. It includes no personal names, except for major committee reports known by the name of the chairperson. Names of reports, white papers and institutions are only included where these are of significance to modern college administration. Because of space constraints, some very specific topics have had to be omitted.

Notes: 'App' indicates appendix and 'n' indicates endnote.

The index is arranged alphabetically word by word, and conforms to the provisions of the British Standards BS3700 1976 (as revised 1988 and BS1749 1985).

SECRET LONDON

ISBN - 978-1-0686720-0-2

MIX
Paper | Supporting responsible forestry
FSC® C022913
FSC www.fsc.org

PROUD TO BE PRINTED IN ENGLAND

The Painted Hall

GREENWICH | **EDITOR'S PICK** | SEE P108

Stepping into The Painted Hall in Greenwich is a breathtaking spectacle. Known as Britain's 'Sistine Chapel', this masterpiece in the heart of the Old Royal Naval College, offers a visual feast that rivals the greatest European frescoes.

Marylebone Village

MARYLEBONE | **EDITOR'S PICK** | SEE P26

Marylebone Village, with its tree-lined streets and chic boutiques, is a jewel in London's West End. This tranquil enclave, just a stone's throw from the hustle of Oxford and Baker Street, offers a blend of first-rate dining and stylish shopping.

Spitalfields

CITY OF LONDON | **EDITOR'S PICK** | SEE P54

Spitalfields, a dynamic enclave in East London, is a canvas of creativity, hosting a diverse community of artists and a Bangladeshi population. The area's heart beats along Brick Lane, famous for its curry houses and rich street art, while...

Maison Assouline

PICCADILLY | **EDITOR'S PICK** | SEE P194

Maison Assouline in London is more than a bookstore, it is an inviting and sophisticated retreat in the heart of Piccadilly. This enclave of intellect and style stands as a tribute to the art of living well, offering an excellent selection of books...

Leadenhall Market

CITY OF LONDON | **EDITOR'S PICK** | **SEE P44**

Leadenhall Market, found on Gracechurch Street in London, combines historical charm with modern vitality beneath its distinctive Victorian roof. This architectural gem, with its glazed façade, domed walkways, and atmospheric lighting...

The Holly Bush

CAMDEN | **EDITOR'S PICK** | **SEE P98**

In the heart of Hampstead, The Holly Bush gastropub invites patrons to indulge in a diverse menu that ranges from classic British pub fare to innovative global dishes. Believed to occupy the former stables of artist George Romney's house...

Regent's Canal

REGENT'S CANAL | **EDITOR'S PICK** | **SEE P84**

Regent's Canal, a waterway threading through central London, offers a tranquil escape from the city's frenetic pace. This historic canal, once the lifeline for Victorian London's commerce, is now a cherished route for weekend walks along...

Gods Own Junkyard

WALTHAMSTOW | **EDITOR'S PICK** | **SEE P72**

God's Own Junkyard is a dazzling treasure trove of handmade neon signs, lighting up an old warehouse in Walthamstow. Curated by third-generation neon artisan Marcus Bracey, it doubles as an art gallery, Instagram hotspot, signage...

Helix at The Gherkin

The Gherkin, 30 St Mary Axe, EC3A 8BF

Searcys Helix restaurant and Iris bar, located on floors 39 and 40 of The Gherkin, offer unparalleled views across London. Guests can savour afternoon tea, fine dining, or cocktails high above the city. The menus, crafted with seasonal British ingredients, feature dishes such as sweet roast pumpkin velouté with caraway toast, miso cod loin with roast cauliflower, and white chocolate cremeux with passionfruit. These ever-changing menus celebrate the best of London's markets like Borough and Billingsgate. For a dining experience with stunning 180-degree views from one of London's most recognised skyscrapers, Helix Restaurant is the place to be.

1

The Walbrook Club

37A Walbrook, EC4N 8BS

Enviably located in the heart of the Square Mile, this discreet and elegant members' club neighbours the Mansion House, NM Rothschild, Bloomberg's European Headquarters, and the Bank of England. With interiors by the late Mark Birley and kitchens once overseen by Albert Roux, the club brings style and fine dining to a traditionally under-served area, featuring a Bar, Dining Room, and two private rooms. Family-run, the club boasts a warm atmosphere, with each decor piece telling a story. Its townhouse style encourages member interaction, complemented by a renowned guest speaker series.

2

The British Museum

Great Russell St, WC1B 3DG

Discover a treasure trove of human history at the British Museum, where the ancient and modern worlds collide under one roof. Founded in 1753 with Sir Hans Sloane's collection, it first welcomed visitors in 1759. Today, marvel at over 13 million artefacts, including the enigmatic Rosetta Stone and majestic Parthenon sculptures. Journey through over 60 free galleries, spanning Ancient Greece to Medieval Europe, all radiating from the stunning Great Court. While admission is free, some special exhibitions may require a ticket. Booking in advance is recommended to ensure entry to this monumental repository of global cultures.

3

QUEEN ELIZABETH II AD 2000 THIS GREAT COURT
Charmed lives in Greece Ghika, Craxton, Leigh Fermor
Rodin and the art of ancient Greece
and let thy feet
millenniums hence
be set in midst of knowledge

The Staircase at Heal's

196 Tottenham Court Rd, Bloomsbury, W1T 7LQ

Designed by Cecil Brewer in 1916 and refurbished in 2013, the spiral staircase at Heal's on Tottenham Court Road is a stunning feature composed of concrete and wood. It leads customers to the Mansard Gallery, with an impressive Bocci chandelier cascading through its centre. This photogenic staircase, adorned with a bronze cat sculpture, has been a charming element of the store for over a century. Restored to its former glory, the staircase continues to add a touch of elegance to Heal's, making it a must-see for visitors in London.

4

Coal Drops Yard

Stable St, N1C 4DQ

Based within King's Cross, Coal Drops Yard blends Victorian industrial heritage with contemporary flair, offering an excellent retail and dining experience. Once the throbbing heart of London's coal distribution, built in the 1850s, these brick viaducts have transitioned from historic coal stores to quirky cultural spaces. Today, beneath their restored iron and brick arches, over 50 boutiques, galleries, and eateries thrive, offering everything from designer fashion at Paul Smith to innovative technology at Samsung and gourmet indulgence at Alain Ducasse's Le Chocolat. This unique canal-side hub not only captivates with its blend of historic and modern design but also entices with a lively calendar of events, including the regular artisan Lower Stable Street market.

5

Searcys St Pancras

St Pancras International Station, N1C 4QL

Searcys St Pancras, ensconced in the St Pancras International Station, offers a luxurious retreat amidst the throng of London's travel nexus. Its setting is unparalleled as one of the city's premier champagne bars, with its location providing a grand vista of the station's Victorian architecture. Patrons are invited to indulge in a selection of the finest champagnes, accompanied by a curated assortment of European cuisine, with blankets to wrap around for comfort in the colder months. The elegance of the space, combined with the ceremonial precision of the service, transports guests to an era of timeless sophistication.

6

Credit - Elena Shamis

St Pancras Hotel

Euston Rd. NW1 2AR

The St Pancras Renaissance Hotel stands as a masterpiece of Victorian design, an imposing landmark that captures London's architectural heritage. This grand edifice, originally opened in 1873, has been meticulously restored to its former glory, offering guests a blend of historical elegance and contemporary luxury. Its towering gothic façades and ornate interiors are a testament to the opulence of a bygone era, while its modern amenities ensure a stay of unmatched comfort. Located within St Pancras International Station, the hotel provides direct access to some of the world's most exciting destinations. Whether it's dining in its exquisite restaurants, unwinding in the sumptuous spa, or simply marvelling at the building's majestic architecture, a stay at the St Pancras Renaissance Hotel is an invitation to enjoy the unparalleled charm of London's past, melded seamlessly with the demands of modern luxury travel.

7

Credit - Elena Shamis

Afternoon Tea at the Hansom

Euston Rd., NW1 2AR

Afternoon tea at The Hansom in King's Cross St Pancras offers a modern, stylish setting to enjoy elegant sandwiches, decadent pastries, and endless loose-leaf tea. The venue honours British heritage through its décor and menu, creating a perfect location for this classic tradition. The menu changes with the seasons, featuring delightful sweet and savoury treats. Start with dainty sandwiches, followed by freshly baked scones with clotted cream and strawberry jam. Save room for exquisite pastries like berry mousse and dark chocolate mousse. Choose between the classic or Champagne afternoon tea, with a selection of exceptional teas available.

8

Daunt Books

84 Marylebone High St, W1U 4QW

Daunt Books in Marylebone is a sanctuary for book lovers. Housed in a light-infused Edwardian building, it boasts a rich selection of travel literature, fiction, and non-fiction. The store's architectural beauty, with its herringbone parquet floors and a galleried interior, adds to the charm of exploring its vast collection. It's a haven for browsers, where time slows, and the scent of pages old and new fills the air. The knowledgeable staff offer tailored recommendations, embodying their passion for literature.

9

ATLAS
WORLD

Marylebone Village

Marylebone High Street is W1U 2QQ

Marylebone Village emerges as a harmonious enclave of urban sophistication and bohemian charm in London's West End. This chic area captivates with its elegant Georgian streets, tree-lined avenues, a mix of independent boutiques, first-rate dining, and artisanal cafés. Renowned for its diversity, from Granger & Co.'s famed breakfasts to Ottolenghi's Middle Eastern delights, it's a place where culture, wellness, and gastronomy meet, offering a refined slice of city life away from the nearby bustle. For those drawn to the finer things, Marylebone Village is an essential experience.

10

MARYLEBONE
HIGH STREET W1
CITY OF WESTMINSTER
ORRERY EPICERIE
ORRERY EPICERIE

Marylebone

Marylebone Lane, W1U 2QG

Marylebone Village, with its tree-lined streets and chic boutiques, is a jewel in London's West End. This tranquil enclave, just a stone's throw from the hustle of Oxford and Baker Street, offers a blend of first-rate dining and stylish shopping. As you wander its cafe-dotted pavements, it's easy to see why icons like Madonna and Paul McCartney have called it home. From the foodie delights of Moxon Street to the unique boutiques of Marylebone Lane, Marylebone Village is ripe for exploration, blending the buzz of the city with the charm of village life.

11

Le Relais de Venise
L'ENTRECÔTE
CALDESI
IN MARYLEBONE
ITALIAN DINING
CROSS KEYS
CLOSE W1

Mount Street

Mount Street, W1K 2RX

Traversing the historical expanse of Mount Street in Mayfair, one encounters a tableau of architectural marvels and luxury living. This grandiose thoroughfare, stretching from Park Lane to Davies Street, has been a cornerstone of high-end shopping since Mayfair's inception. Originating from the English Civil War's fortifications, Mount Street hosts landmark hotels like The Connaught and The Biltmore Mayfair, alongside heritage institutions such as James Purdey & Sons and Scott's Seafood Restaurant. A stroll here is not just a journey through a shopping street but a walk through history, amidst luxury and legacy.

12

MARCHESI
PASTICCERIA MARCHESI
117
117
MARCHESI

Annabel's

46 Berkeley Square, Mayfair, W1J 5AT

Annabel's, a distinguished members' club at 46 Berkeley Square in Mayfair, London, occupies a grand Georgian townhouse. While its lavish interior, designed by Martin Brudnizki, is exclusively for members, the exterior often dazzles passersby with vibrant floral displays. Opened in 1963 by Mark Birley and named for his wife, Lady Annabel Vane-Tempest-Stewart, Annabel's has transformed from a traditional Sloane retreat to a bold, eclectic space. Despite its dramatic makeover, which some describe as a mix of whimsical and flamboyant styles, Annabel's continues to be a popular nigh-time haunt.

13

The Royal Arcade

28 Old Bond St, Mayfair, W1S 4DR

The Royal Arcade, built in 1879, connects Old Bond Street with Albemarle Street in Mayfair, London. This Victorian-era shopping arcade, designed by Archer & Green, showcases a saddled glass roof, richly adorned stucco arches, curved glass shop fronts, and elegant Ionic columns. As the city's oldest purpose-built shopping arcade, it retains its original features, offering a glimpse into 19th-century design. Home to fine silverware, art, bespoke shoes, and chocolates, The Royal Arcade remains a charming and historic destination. Conveniently located near Green Park tube station, it invites visitors to experience a piece of Victorian elegance in the heart of London.

14

THE
TROTTER

The Foreign Office

King Charles St, Whitehall, SW1A 2AH

This imposing government building, home to the Foreign Secretary's team, sits in the heart of Westminster, with Downing Street as its closest neighbour. The Italianate style is particularly striking inside, where a grand marble staircase adorned with a plush red carpet and glistening chandeliers creates an impressive centrepiece. Designed by George Gilbert Scott, this historic Whitehall building features murals in the long gallery at the head of the staircase, painted during the First World War. These murals form an allegorical narrative of Britain's growth as an imperial power, depicting the arts of peace and war through youthful and graceful figures.

15

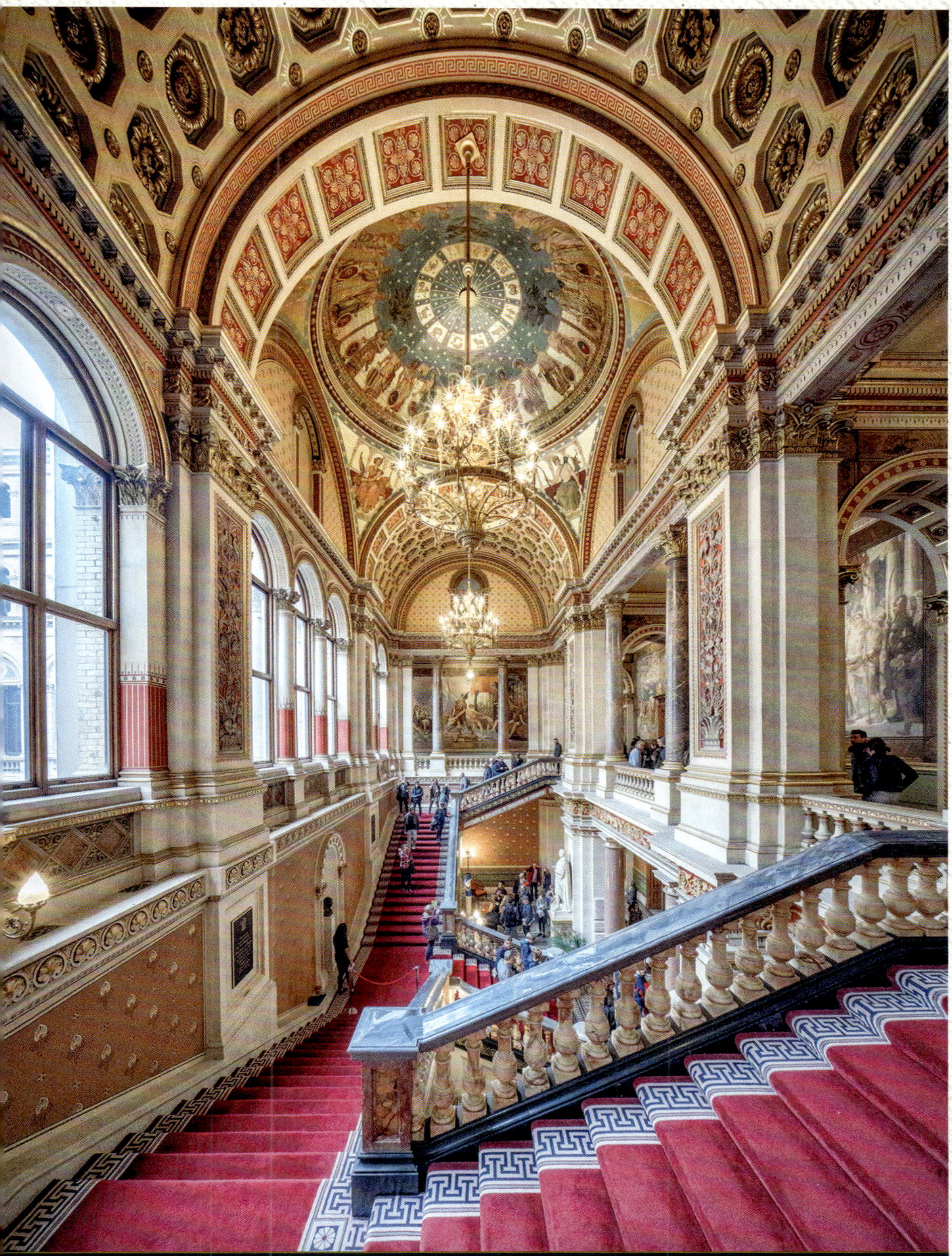

Exmouth Market

Exmouth Market, EC1R 4QB

Since the late 1800s, Exmouth Market has thrived as a busy marketplace. Today, it transforms into a trendy lunchtime food market, flanked by an enticing array of independent shops, cafés, and bars with a plethora of outside seating. Lacking its own tube station only enhances its appeal as a somewhat concealed treasure, despite its widespread recognition. Conveniently situated north of Farringdon, south of Angel, with Old Street to the east and Russell Square to the west, its central location offers easy access from virtually anywhere. Notable spots such as Café Kick, offering table football alongside your coffee, and Santore, a family-run pizzeria echoing the flavours of Naples, highlight the market's diverse quirky appeal.

16

EXMOUTH
MARKET E.C.1
BRIKI

Smithfields Meat Market

220 Smithfield, EC1A 9LH

Smithfield, described in 1174 by William Fitzstephen as a marketplace for fine horses and livestock, has a rich history. Its name likely comes from the Saxon "smeth field," meaning smooth field. In 1327, Edward III granted market rights to the City of London, establishing it as a key trade hub. The Smithfield Market Removal Act of 1852 relocated the live cattle market to Islington, making way for new buildings. Designed by Sir Horace Jones, the East and West Market buildings were completed in 1868. Today, these refurbished structures house diverse, temperature-controlled units, preserving Smithfield's legacy as a bustling marketplace.

17

The Charterhouse

Charterhouse Square, Barbican EC1M 6AN

The Charterhouse in Farringdon, dating back to the 14th century, is a remarkable complex of medieval and Tudor buildings. Originally a Carthusian priory founded in 1371, it later became one of Tudor London's grand courtyard houses. In 1611, Thomas Sutton transformed it into an almshouse and school. Today, the almshouse remains, and the site, in partnership with the Museum of London, offers a new museum, educational programmes, and a beautifully landscaped square. Visitors can explore the Charterhouse's rich history, from its origins on a Black Death burial ground to its present-day community. Opened to the public in January 2017, it's a hidden gem in the heart of London.

18

W E

Leadenhall Market

Gracechurch St, EC3V 1LT

Leadenhall Market, found on Gracechurch Street in London, combines historical charm with modern vitality beneath its distinctive Victorian roof. This architectural gem, with its glazed façade, domed walkways, and atmospheric lighting, harks back to the 14th century, making it one of London's oldest markets. Evolving from its origins in trading meat and poultry to a bustling hub for luxury and tradition, Leadenhall is a place where history meets commerce, offering a unique shopping and dining experience amidst its rich heritage. An enchanting retreat, the market offers everything from fashion to gourmet foods, all within an impressive atmospheric setting.

19

THE PEN SHOP
WINE BAR
Brokers
Wine Bar
YOUNGS

The Whispering Gallery

St. Paul's Churchyard, EC4M 8AD

St. Paul's Cathedral, an architectural masterpiece by Sir Christopher Wren, is home to the Whispering Gallery, a marvel of acoustics and design. Situated 30 metres above the cathedral floor, reached by a climb of 259 steps, this gallery fascinates with its ability to carry whispered conversations across its curve with crystal clarity. Visitors are drawn not only to test the gallery's unique sound properties but also to experience the breathtaking views of the cathedral's vast nave. The Whispering Gallery, enveloped in discreet netting, also offers an intimate view of Sir James Thornhill's dramatic monochrome depictions of St Paul's missionary travels. Emerging at the gallery's east, visitors are greeted by the vivid scene of Paul's conversion, enhancing the gallery's allure as a place of both acoustic wonder and historical contemplation.

20

Credit - Camille Kenny-Ryder

Fortnum's at The Royal Exchange

Royal Exchange, EC3V 3LR

Fortnum & Mason at The Royal Exchange blends London's historic elegance with modern dining luxury, serving seasonal, contemporary menus in the architectural marvel of its central courtyard. Celebrated as 'The Most Instagrammable Restaurant in London' by The Evening Standard, it offers an unparalleled, memorable visit where past and present unite. Esteemed for refined British classics and afternoon tea, under the grand vaulted ceiling, it combines tradition with contemporary flair.

21

FORTNUM & MASON

The Barbican Conservatory

Silk St, EC2Y 8DS

The Barbican Conservatory, an unexpected oasis amidst the architectural marvel that is the Barbican Centre, offers a serene respite from the urban whirl of London. The city's second largest conservatory is home to a lush array of tropical flora, towering palms, and exotic fish, creating an enchanting and soothing environment. As visitors wander through this botanical wonderland, they encounter a harmonious blend of art, nature, and architecture, a testament to the Barbican's visionary design ethos. The conservatory also hosts a myriad of cultural events, making it a dynamic hub for those who appreciate the arts in all its forms.

22

Old Spitalfields Market

16 Horner Square, E1 6EW

Since 1638, Old Spitalfields Market has evolved from a rural trading post, sanctioned by King Charles I, to a bustling centre of contemporary commerce and culture on the edge of London's East End. Following its re-establishment by King Charles II in 1682, the market has become integral to the fabric of the area, now encapsulated by Grade II listed Victorian architecture. Today, it offers a mix of fashion, art, crafts, and gastronomy seven days a week. With the addition of 'The Kitchens', it also boasts one of the city's finest street food experiences, surrounded by a myriad of independent shops. Just a short walk from Liverpool Street Station, Spitalfields is a magnet for those seeking East London's unique blend of heritage and hip.

23

KINGS STORES
WHITE COURT
LUXTRIPPER
DISCOVER YOUR UNIQUE
KINGS STORES
KEEP SMILING
HONEST
BURGERS
WE ARE

Spitalfields

Number 4 Princelet Street Spitalfields E1

Spitalfields, a dynamic enclave in East London, is a canvas of creativity, hosting a diverse community of artists and a Bangladeshi population. The area's heart beats along Brick Lane, famous for its curry houses and rich street art, while quirky shops and trendy bars pepper the streets. The historic Spitalfields Market, dating back to the 1600s and rebuilt in 1876, is a treasure trove of crafts, fashion, and local creatives. With a mix of well-known brands and independent gems, plus a bustling array of street food in The Kitchens, Spitalfields is a feast for the senses, offering everything from art exhibitions at Christ Church to lively markets and unique dining experiences.

24

St Dunstan in the East

St Dunstan's Hill, EC3R 5DD

St Dunstan in the East, a historic London site with 900-year-old origins, symbolises the city's resilience. Initially damaged in the Great Fire of London in 1666 and later in the 1941 blitz during World War II, it now stands as a serene public garden amidst the city's hustle and bustle. Sir Christopher Wren's architectural legacy is evident in the remaining tower, around which nature has woven a verdant tapestry of trees and vines, offering a tranquil retreat. This blend of medieval architecture and lush greenery against the modern skyline highlights London's capacity for renewal. It's a peaceful oasis where visitors can reflect on the beauty that emerges from history's trials, embodying the city's enduring spirit and its continuous transformation.

25

The Sky Garden

Sky Garden Walk, EC3M 8AF

The Sky Garden, perched 155 metres above London in the distinctive Walkie-Talkie building, offers breathtaking panoramic views through its three-storey glass walls. This urban oasis features lush indoor gardens, two elegant bars, and two exceptional restaurants, creating a unique dining experience amidst greenery. Visitors can enjoy stunning sights such as St. Paul's Cathedral and Tower Bridge. Free to enter with advance booking required, the Sky Garden is a popular destination. It's open daily, with tickets available up to three weeks in advance. For a memorable start to the weekend, enjoy cocktails, live bands, and house DJs in this spectacular setting.

26

Brick Lane

Brick Lane, E1 6PU

Brick Lane, a dynamic and much-loved area, evolving from its humble beginnings to a cultural and culinary hub, offers an array of options. From exploring markets and independent galleries to indulging in the many famed curry houses that earned it the nickname "Curry Capital of the UK," Brick Lane is a mosaic of London's diverse heritage and contemporary flair. Whether tracing the historical cobbled lanes or sampling the myriad tastes that define its present, a journey down Brick Lane is a memorable way to spend an afternoon in East London.

27

JONOJIBON

The Young V&A

Cambridge Heath Rd, Bethnal Green ,E2 9PA

The Young V&A in Bethnal Green, evolving from the esteemed V&A Museum of Childhood, stands as a fascinating extension of the Victoria and Albert Museum, the United Kingdom's national treasure of applied arts. Situated in London's trendy East End, this institution specialises in a unique collection of objects designed by and for children, offering a rich tapestry of childhood through the ages. The venue is an intriguing space where curiosity leads the way, inviting young minds to delve into the realms of creativity, design, and history. Through interactive displays and innovative workshops, the Young V&A nurtures the imaginations of its visitors, making it a cornerstone for those who seek to inspire and be inspired by the endless possibilities of youth and art combined.

28

Credit - Mariana Martins

Columbia Road Flower Market

Columbia Rd, E2 7RG

Columbia Road Flower Market, originally a Saturday market, was moved to Sundays by Act of Parliament to accommodate local Jewish traders and allow Covent Garden and Spitalfields vendors to sell leftover stock. Every Sunday, Columbia Road becomes a picturesque haven from 8am-3pm, filled with stunning flowers, houseplants, herbs, bulbs, and shrubs. For a serene visit, come early at 8am for the best selection. For bargains, visit around 2pm when prices drop. A photographer's delight, the market boasts bouquets, lush greenery, and charming shop fronts. Nearby, discover The Lily Vanilli Bakery, Campania & Jones, and street art on Wellington Row.

29

CASH ONLY
TOP QUALITY
EX-LARGE
DRIED
NATURAL PERFUMED
ENGLISH
LAVENDER
£10
A BUNCH

Libreria Bookshop

65 Hanbury St, E1 5JL

Second Home's mission is to foster creativity and innovation, reflected in their Libreria bookshop designed by Spanish architects SelgasCano. Libreria is crafted to spark discovery and interdisciplinary thinking, curating books to maximise serendipity. Shelves are arranged by themes like 'Wanderlust', 'Enchantment for the Disenchanted', and 'The City', encouraging encounters with unexpected titles. Spanning 830 square metres with over 6,000 titles, Libreria opposes algorithmic recommendations, offering freedom to explore. Technology is forbidden; no smartphones or Wi-Fi, allowing visitors to immerse themselves in stories without digital distractions. It's a celebration of analogue, inviting you to lose yourself in a world of books.

30

Redchurch Street

Redchurch Street E2 7DL

Redchurch Street in Shoreditch stands as London's hidden jewel, known only to those with an insider's eye. This discreet spot veers away from the usual tourist paths, capturing the contemporary cool that Shoreditch is famous for. A paradise for fashion aficionados, it's dotted with cutting-edge boutiques, concept stores, and secret places for coffee or cocktails, offering a fresh dimension to London's varied scene. Hosting some of the city's most creative fashion talents, Redchurch Street has evolved into a lively centre of creativity and style, much like New York's Meatpacking District, showcasing London's expansion into new creative territories.

31

Credit - Camille Kenny-Ryder

Labour and Wait

85 Redchurch St, East End

Established by designers Rachel Wythe-Moran and Simon Watkins, this unique collection features timeless household items, hardware, stationery, accessories, and clothing. With backgrounds in menswear, they collaborate with specialist makers globally to create products that embody functionality, quality, and honesty. Their curated selection blends new and vintage items that are both familiar and ready to be discovered. Celebrating a simple, honest approach to design, these everyday classics are built to withstand the test of time and will only improve with age, making them suitable for both traditional and contemporary settings.

32

85
LABOUR AND WAIT
LABOUR AND WAIT
FUNCTIONAL PRODUCTS FOR HOUSEHOLD KITCHEN AND GARDEN
SINCE 2000
OPEN

Gods Own Junkyard

Unit 12, Shernhall St, E17 9HQ

God's Own Junkyard is a dazzling treasure trove of handmade neon signs, lighting up an old warehouse in Walthamstow. Curated by third-generation neon artisan Marcus Bracey, it doubles as an art gallery, Instagram hotspot, signage recycler, and prop shop for films and photo shoots. The collection includes thousands of signs and figures, from cheerful diner and hotel emblems to neon-trimmed religious images and retro Soho-inspired displays. This psychedelic paradise is the legacy of the late Chris Bracey, the 'Neon Man', who started making signs for Soho's clubs before Hollywood directors like Kubrick and Burton took notice. Entry is free, with donations encouraged.

33

GLORY
Hot
Sexy
MONEY
CLUB
PAWN SHOP
Neon is My Favourite Colour
SACRED
Let's get naked
THIS IS IT
APPLAUSE
THRILLS
Cocktails & Dreams

Walthamstow Wetlands

2 Forest Rd, N17 9NH

Walthamstow Wetlands, opened in October 2017, is Europe's largest urban wetland reserve, spanning 211 hectares and managed by Thames Water. This vital 160-hectare reservoir supplies water to 3.5 million people and serves as an internationally significant nature reserve. It hosts a variety of wildlife, including rare wildfowl, peregrine falcons, bats, and amphibians. The Wetlands offer diverse habitats, from dense scrub-lined banks to expansive city views, and house London's largest fishery. Recognised as a Site of Special Scientific Interest and part of the Lee Valley Special Protection Area, it is a haven for both wildlife and nature enthusiasts.

34

Hoxton

8 Hoxton Square, Hackney, N1 6NU

Hoxton and Shoreditch, in the heart of London, are buzzing with creativity and character. Graffitied disused tube carriages and witty street art decorate the neighbourhood, bringing smiles to those who appreciate these colourful images. This area boasts a mix of hip pubs, cafes, edgy galleries, and popular nightclubs. Head to Boxpark for trendy pop-up shops or explore the diverse restaurants and bars off Shoreditch High Street. Known for its rich history, Hoxton was first recorded in the Domesday Book and has evolved from a rural part of Shoreditch parish to a lively cultural hub.

35

LETS
ADORE And EN
UNCERTAIN SUBJECTS
UNCERTAIN SUBJECTS
SAUDIA AD-DIRIYAH E-PRIX
FIAFormulaE.com/ad-diriyah
saudia.com

Highgate

Swain's Lane, N6 6PJ.

Highgate, a leafy enclave in North London, melds Georgian elegance with cultural richness and excellent wining and dining opportunities. Famous for its distinguished residents past and present, from George Eliot and Karl Marx to celebrities like George Michael, this area boasts historic tea rooms, gastropubs, and remarkable 18th-century architecture. Walking tours are available around the fascinating Highgate Cemetery, with its ornate tombs amid wild foliage, while nearby Waterlow Park offers restful duck feeding spots. Lauderdale House, amidst this greenery, hosts exhibitions and concerts, encapsulating Highgate's blend of historical legacy and contemporary flair and adding to the locale's charm.

36

HIGHGATE AVENUE, N.
LEADING
SOUTHWOOD

Highgate Cemetary

Swain's Ln, N6 6PJ

Highgate Cemetery, a captivating destination in London, offers a glimpse into the past with its grand avenues and notable occupants. This Victorian necropolis, consecrated in 1839, is part of the 'Magnificent Seven' cemeteries established to address the overcrowding of inner-city graveyards. Highgate is the final resting place for over 850 notable figures, including poets, painters, and princes, with perhaps its most famous resident being Karl Marx. The cemetery's creation was prompted by a surging population and health concerns from outbreaks of cholera and typhoid, leading city authorities to close inner-city churchyards to new burials.

37

Alexandra Palace

Alexandra Palace Way, N22 7AY

Alexandra Palace, or "Ally Pally," is a Grade II listed entertainment and sports venue in North London, between Wood Green and Muswell Hill. Built in 1873 by John Johnson and Alfred Meeson, it was rebuilt after a fire shortly after its opening. Known as "The People's Palace," it was designed as a centre for recreation and education. Acquired by local authorities in 1900, it remains a public trust. Home to the BBC's first regular television service in 1936, its radio mast still stands. Today, it hosts exhibitions, concerts, and offers a pub, ice rink, and stunning views of London.

38

WHAT'S ON

Regent's Canal

New Wharf Rd, N1 9RT

Regent's Canal, a waterway threading through central London, offers a tranquil escape from the city's frenetic pace. This historic canal, once the lifeline for Victorian London's commerce, is now a cherished route for weekend walks along its towpath, cycling, and boating. Cafés and pubs dot the route, providing charming stops for refreshment, making the canal a beloved urban oasis for both Londoners and visitors alike, eager to discover a different facet of the metropolis and a more leisurely pace of life.

39

Credit - Elena Shamis

The Sherlock Holmes Museum

221b Baker St, NW1 6XE

The Sherlock Holmes Museum, a truly unique London destination, stands as the world's first museum dedicated exclusively to the legendary fictional detective Sherlock Holmes. Situated at 221B Baker Street, this privately run establishment pays tribute to the enduring legacy of Sir Arthur Conan Doyle's celebrated creation. Inside, visitors are transported into the meticulously recreated Victorian world of Holmes and his faithful companion Dr. Watson. Each room, artefact, and piece of memorabilia has been lovingly assembled to ignite the imagination, allowing fans and newcomers to step into the shoes of the famed detective.

40

THE SHERLOCK HOLMES
SOUVENIRS BOOKS ANTIQUES AND
Open

Camden's Punks

Camden Lock, NW1 8AL

Camden Town, since the late 1970s, has been the heart of London's punk scene, embodying the rebellious spirit and energy of the movement. It's a place where music, fashion, and attitude converge around the streets and canal, drawing in a global community of musicians, fans, and artists alike. Camden teems with market stalls selling an array of food, jewellery and vintage punk attire. Look out for its graffiti and eccentric shop signage, all a nod to defiance, and spot venues like the Electric Ballroom and The Underworld, which maintain the legacy of punk, making Camden a living monument to the genre. More than music, punk's influence on Camden's art, fashion, and lifestyle creates a community that continues to inspire and challenge norms, celebrating the ethos of individuality and rebellion.

41

on Zoo (via canal)
5 mins
nt's Canal Towpath
GORDO

Primrose Hill

Primrose Hill Road, Camden, NW3 3NA

Primrose Hill, part of Regent's Park and north of Camden, offers panoramic views of London from its 63-metre high summit. This tranquil spot is a favoured escape from the buzz of the city, providing a unique perspective on landmarks like the Shard and the London Eye. Beyond its views, Primrose Hill serves as a community hub for picnics, walks, and fitness activities, with its open spaces and tree-lined paths inviting visitors to relax and connect with nature. It draws people throughout the year to enjoy its peaceful mornings, stunning sunsets, or the city's illuminated skyline by night. Primrose Hill exemplifies London's ability to blend urban life with greenery, offering a serene retreat from the urban pace of life.

42

The British Library

96 Euston Rd, NW1 2DB

Beside London's St. Pancras Station, the British Library stands as a magnificent repository of the United Kingdom's literary and historical wealth. Created in 1973 and housed in a modern complex since 1997, this national treasure secures over 170 million items, ranging from ancient manuscripts to contemporary digital works. It boasts diverse collections like the Oriental and India Office Collections and the National Sound Archive, attracting scholars and visitors worldwide. Previously dispersed, including within the renowned British Museum Reading Room—a sanctuary for notables such as Karl Marx and Virginia Woolf—the library now offers unified access to its extensive holdings. With a narrative marked by resilience, expansion, and adaptation, the British Library continues to enchant and educate, bridging the past with the future in London's literary landscape.

43

Camden Town

Camden High Street NW1 0RR.

Camden Town, with its eclectic vibe, is a melting pot of creativity and culture, just 2.5 miles from Charing Cross. Famous for its sprawling markets, live music venues, and energetic street performers, Camden also offers serene escapes like the picturesque canal and tranquil green spaces. Explore the diverse stalls of Camden Market, unwind by Camden Lock, or take a leisurely boat ride to Little Venice. Animal lovers can even visit nearby London Zoo. With everything from vintage finds at The Stables to ethical fashions at Buck Street container market, Camden is a true urban adventure every day of the week.

44

COURAGE
ELEPHANTS HEAD
A.S.K
Tattoo
&
Piercing
LONDON SOUVENIRS
FULL ENGLISH BREAKFAST
FISH & CHIPS SPECIAL

The Elephants Head

224 Camden High St, NW1 8QR

In the heart of Camden Market, this unique tile-fronted pub captivates with its unusual corner shape. The name likely hails from the Marquess of Camden's coat of arms, featuring an elephant's head, now part of Camden's emblem. Though the Marquess lived in Chislehurst, his connection to Camden is reflected in the similar road names between the areas. This mid-19th-century pub, located at Camden High Street and Hawley Crescent, boasts a distinctive tiled shopfront and curved corner window. Close to Camden Lock and the Roundhouse, it's a popular weekend spot, offering a lively atmosphere amid historic charm.

45

THE ELEPHANTS HEAD
224
BOY

The Holly Bush

22 Holly Mount, NW3 6SG

In the heart of Hampstead, The Holly Bush gastropub invites patrons to indulge in a diverse menu that ranges from classic British pub fare to innovative global dishes. Believed to occupy the former stables of artist George Romney's house, this Grade II-listed pub exudes charm with its 18th-century wood panelling, cask ales, and cosy fireplaces. As modern renovations claim other local pubs, The Holly Bush's allure only grows. With three intimate bar areas, excellent pints, and an impressive selection of wines, it also hosts a Supper Club featuring Michelin-starred chefs in the Romney and Lady Hamilton rooms.

46

The Holly Bush

Hampstead Heath Swimming Ponds

Hampstead Heath, NW5 1QR

Hampstead Heath offers three swimming ponds: men's, women's, and a mixed pond, welcoming swimmers year-round. Children aged eight to 15 must be supervised. The men's pond, once featuring a diving tower, now has a low board, showers, and sunbathing areas. The men's and women's ponds are off Millfield Lane, while the mixed pond is a short walk from Hampstead Heath railway station and South End Green. Managed by the City of London Corporation, these ponds, originally dammed clay pits, are undergoing essential flood protection work. Despite the chilly waters, they remain a beloved spot for swimmers.

47

Abbey Road Studios

3 Abbey Rd., NW8 9AY

Abbey Road Studios, the world's most famous recording studio, is celebrated for its creativity and technological innovation. For 90 years, it has been home to musical legends like The Beatles, Pink Floyd, Ella Fitzgerald, Radiohead, and Adele. The studio's story is the story of recorded music, beginning in 1929 when the Gramophone Company transformed a St John's Wood house into the first purpose-built recording studio. Abbey Road is also a premier destination for film scoring, with credits including Raiders of the Lost Ark, the Lord of the Rings series, and Black Panther. The studio boasts a Dolby Atmos Mix Stage, making it the UK's only facility for both scoring and post-production. The famous zebra crossing, immortalised by The Beatles, was designated a Grade II listed site by English Heritage in 2010, and remains a popular photo spot.

48

Abbey Road Studios

Maltby Street Market

Arch 46, Ropewalk, Maltby St, SE1 3PA

Maltby Street Market, a Bermondsey treasure since 2010, has quickly become a favourite weekend spot for locals and savvy visitors. Expect hipsters, local Londoners, and in-the-know food lovers drawn by the rich aromas and bustling atmosphere. And, of course, the food. Did we mention the food? Don't miss Bar Tozino, a hidden Spanish Jamón and wine bodega under a railway arch. This market is where passionate street food traders launch their visions, some going on to open their own establishments, while others stay, charmed by SE1's Ropewalk. Named after a nearby 18th-century ropewalk owned by eccentric Robert Rich, the area was transformed by the 1836 London to Greenwich railway. The viaduct now houses Maltby Street Market and other Bermondsey traders.

49

DUCK FRITES
DUCK FRITES
All you need is Duck
RACLETTE CHEESE
DUCK FRITES
All you need is Duck
DUCK FRITES
All you need is Duck

The Wallace Collection

Hertford House, Manchester Square, W1U 3BN

Located in Marylebone, The Wallace Collection of fine and decorative arts is a cultural jewel. This grand mansion, a gift from the 19th century to the modern world, hosts masterpieces from Titian to Velázquez and includes the curious smile of Hals' Laughing Cavalier. Its lavish rooms abound with paintings, furniture, gleaming suits of armour and French porcelain, inviting you into a world where beauty and history converge. Described by The Guardian newspaper as, "One of the sexiest collections in Europe," The Wallace Collection is an immersion into an age of splendour, designed to evoke the lives and tastes of its founders, making it a must-see for any lover of art and history.

50

Credit - Mariana Martins

The Painted Hall

Old Royal Naval College, SE10 9NN

Stepping into The Painted Hall in Greenwich is a breathtaking spectacle. Known as Britain's 'Sistine Chapel', this masterpiece in the heart of the Old Royal Naval College, offers a visual feast that rivals the greatest European frescoes. Conceived in the early 18th century by Sir James Thornhill, the Hall's ceiling and walls are adorned with allegories celebrating England's naval power and political ascendancy. The intricacy of Thornhill's work is staggering, each brushstroke a testament to an era when art served power, and beauty was a public statement. As you wander through this opulent space, the tales of gods and monarchs painted overhead transport you back to a time of ambition and intrigue. The recent restoration, a meticulous labour of love, has breathed new life into Thornhill's vision, revealing the original vibrancy of his palette.

51

Credit - Elena Shamis

Greenwich Park

SE10 8QY

Greenwich Park, the largest royal expanse in southeast London, is packed with historical and natural heritage. Overlooking the Thames, and close to the famous Cutty Sark ship, it offers breathtaking views that stretch to the capital's modern skyline, juxtaposing the old with the new. This park, a UNESCO World Heritage site, is also home to the Royal Observatory and the prime meridian line. Whether it's witnessing the marvel of time at the Greenwich Meridian, enjoying the floral diversity in the herb garden, or spotting the Queen Elizabeth Oak dated to 1290, Greenwich Park invites visitors on a journey through nature and time, offering discoveries at every turn.

52

Credit - Mariana Martins

Herne Hill

Herne Hill, SE24

Herne Hill, a thriving locale in South London, offers a delightful blend of community spirit and urban flair. Known for its weekend market, the area teems with artisan stalls, gourmet eateries, and independent shops. Once overshadowed by the districts of Brixton and Dulwich, Herne Hill now stands out individually with its community spirit and quaint high streets. A community-run monthly street fair transforms the area into a centre of cultural and foodie delights. With excellent rail links and just a 20-minute walk from the heart of Brixton, its highlights include a Grade II listed lido, a farmers market and some of the city's finest gelato.

53

Llewelyn's

Hay's Galleria

1 Battle Bridge Ln, SE1 2HD

Hay's Galleria, once the "Larder of London" in the 1850s, has transformed from a bustling trade depot into an elegant fusion of retail and leisure under a snaking, vaulted glass and steel canopy. This architectural gem in London's mercantile past now houses shops, cafés, and restaurants within its revitalised historic walls. At its heart, David Kemp's captivating kinetic sculpture pays homage to the site's industrial roots. An architectural feat, Hay's Galleria symbolises London's knack for blending history with modernity, offering a scenic spot along the Thames for dining or contemplation, bridging past and present.

54

CAFE ROUGE

Dulwich Village

Dulwich Village SE21 7AL

Known for its green spaces and cultural gems, Dulwich boasts the Dulwich Picture Gallery, the world's first purpose-built public art gallery. Founded in 1811 and designed by John Soane, it houses masterpieces by Rembrandt, Gainsborough, and Rubens. Rembrandt's portrait of Jacob De Gheyn III, infamously stolen four times, highlights the gallery's allure. Dulwich Park, established in 1890, offers 29 acres of tranquillity, featuring a boating lake and the Grade II-listed Queen Mary Gate. Despite historical ties to Camberwell, Dulwich remains distinct, partly due to Dulwich College, founded in 1619 by Edward Alleyn. Notably, Margaret Thatcher once resided in this exclusive enclave.

55

Credit - Camille Kenny-Ryder

Shad Thames

Shad Thames, Southwark, , SE1 2YT

Shad Thames, a picturesque riverside street by Tower Bridge, is steeped in London's trading past. Once the city's warehouse heartland, this Bermondsey area thrived as the 'larder of London' with vast depots of tea, spices, and dried fruits at Butler's Wharf. The area's name, a twist on 'St John at Thames', nods to its medieval roots. Today, Shad Thames has transformed, with its historic warehouses now hosting chic cafés, bars, and shops under the original overhead goods gantries. Although the Design Museum has moved to Kensington, the architectural charm of this district continues to captivate visitors and locals alike.

56

INDIAN
RESTAURANT
OPEN
LOUNGE
&
GRILL
BETFRED
the bonus king
BETFRED
the bonus king
more yoga
more yoga

Borough Market

Southwark Street, SE1 1TL

Borough Market, London's premier food destination, is a feast for the senses, celebrating 25 years of bustling retail. This historic market, dating back over 1,000 years, offers an endless parade of treats from freshly made chutneys to bubbling paella, giant cheese wheels, and exotic emu burgers. Whether you're a coffee enthusiast eager to visit the famed Monmouth Coffee or a foodie craving a taste of Roast Restaurant's British dishes, Borough Market caters to all. Located beside Southwark Cathedral, it's not just a market but a hub of gourmet food and culture. With over 100 stalls, it promises a rich tapestry of flavours and aromas, drawing food lovers and chefs alike.

57

BAO
13
ELLIOT'S
WRIGHT BROTHERS
OYSTER & PORTER HOUSE
SPECIALIST SHOP
刈包專門店
內用

Horsleydown Stairs

48 Shad Thames, SE1 2LY

Horsleydown Stairs, nestled near Tower Bridge on the Thames, is a historic relic from when London's river was a thriving hub of activity. These worn stone steps, once a lifeline for goods and passengers, embody London's river commerce and community through the ages. Now a tranquil spot offering views of the flowing Thames and the city skyline, Horsleydown's history is rich with tales of sailors, merchants, and adventurers, as evidenced by the many artefacts found on the riverbed at low tide. Legends of secret meetings, romantic rendezvous, and smugglers' nocturnal activities add mystique, suggesting the stairs were more than just a physical connection to the river but also a backdrop to countless personal stories embodying the dynamic history and transformation of London itself.

58

Shad Thames

Shad Thames, , SE1 2YT

Shad Thames, along London's South Bank, embodies a transformation from the heart of the capital's historic docklands to a chic urban area. Its Victorian warehouses and cobbled streets, once alive with the commerce of tea, coffee, and spices, now host sleek apartments and trendy restaurants. The architecture, with overhead walkways and brick façades, tells stories of past trade and labour. Echoes of dock workers hint at the area's bustling past. Now, the Design Museum adds cultural vibrancy, combining design innovation with the area's rich history, making Shad Thames a unique blend of the old and the new in London's riverside landscape.

59

BENGAL
CLIPPER
INDIAN
RESTAURANT
0207 357 9001
BENGAL
CLIPPER
CANTINA
DELIVERIES

Waterloo

Roupell Street, Waterloo, SE1

Waterloo, just a mile east of Charing Cross in central London, is far more than a gateway for commuters and travellers. This lively district, rejuvenated in recent years, brims with cultural hotspots—from the Old Vic and Young Vic theatres to the cinematic giant BFI IMAX. Beyond its famous train station, Britain's busiest, Waterloo offers a slice of London life with trendy coffee shops, quality food markets, and bustling pubs and bars. Whether you're taking a spin on the London Eye or exploring the South Bank, Waterloo is a hub of activity and excitement in the heart of the city.

60

JOY THROUGH CAKE

Battersea Power Station

Circus Rd W, Nine Elms, SW11 8DD

Once a beacon of industrial might on the Thames, Battersea Power Station has emerged from its ashes as a dazzling phoenix in London's skyline. Redesigned by luminaries such as Frank Gehry and Foster + Partners, this colossal brick edifice now hosts an array of shops, bars, restaurants, and leisure venues, welcoming the public for the first time in decades. Amid its historic walls, the transformation includes luxurious apartments and the innovative Electric Boulevard, a pedestrian high street that breathes new life into the area. The addition of award-winning roof gardens, crafted by Andy Sturgeon, offers a serene oasis within its imposing setting.

61

Battersea Park

SW11 4NJ

Battersea Park, a 200-acre Victorian green space in London, offers both historic and contemporary gardens. Enjoy the Promontory Garden with its river views, or the sub-tropical garden. Designed by renowned landscape gardener Russell Page, the park boasts a riverside promenade, a large lake, notable trees, and ecological areas. Opened in 1858, Battersea Park features a children's zoo, a boating lake, a bandstand, and sports facilities, including tennis courts and football pitches. The Grade II listed Pump House Gallery, housed in a Victorian tower, and the London Peace Pagoda, erected in 1985, are notable landmarks. Wander through the Woodland Walk to find the bronze statue commemorating the Brown Dog affair.

62

Northcote Road

Northcote Rd, SW11 6QB

Situated in the heart of 'Nappy Valley' between Battersea and Wandsworth in South London, Northcote Road boasts an eclectic mix of cafes, bars, independent shops, and restaurants. The colourful facades reflect the street's lively atmosphere, which even includes a summer festival. Located near Battersea Rise and Clapham Junction, this area offers a diverse range of cuisines for any occasion. Home to a historic food market dating back to the 1860s and an indoor antiques market, Northcote Road has it all.

63

BYRON
PROPER HAMBURGERS

Elizabeth Street

Elizabeth Street SW1W 9NZ

Elizabeth Street in Belgravia epitomises London's elegance and history with its Victorian facades and bespoke boutiques, echoing the affluence of its past. This street showcases a blend of class and modern flair, with shops offering artisanal goods and designer wear that reflect centuries of craftsmanship. The ambience, enriched by the scent of coffee and flowers, invites leisurely strolls. Beyond its charm, Elizabeth Street has evolved from an aristocratic enclave to a cosmopolitan hot spot. Intriguingly, rumours of secret tunnels used by historical figures beneath the street add a mysterious depth, making it a fascinating blend of tradition and tales of yore.

64

See and be scene

Motcomb Street

Motcomb Street SW1X 8LB

Motcomb Street, situated in the heart of Westminster's Belgravia, is a serene bastion of luxury and history. Known for its high-end fashion boutiques, including the original sites of Jimmy Choo and Christian Louboutin, this street exudes classic elegance with its Georgian architecture and cobblestoned charm. A short stroll from Hyde Park, it boasts a curated selection of fashion, food, and beauty shops amid quaint courtyards and mews. Once home to the pioneering Pantechnicon department store, Motcomb Street today offers a unique shopping experience, blending illustrious history with contemporary luxury in one of London's most coveted locales.

65

See
and be
scene
Belgravia
MAYHEW NEWSAGENTS
MAYHEW
NEWS

Brixton Village

Coldharbour Lane. Brixton..SW9 8PS

Brixton Village, found in the historic market arcades of Brixton, South London, has transformed from a traditional retail market into a lively centre for diverse eateries, shops, and creative spaces. This evolution into a foodie hotspot has revitalised the neighbourhood, attracting food lovers for its wide range of global cuisines. Its covered lanes buzz with the world's flavours, from Caribbean to Asian, Italian, and beyond, each stall and restaurant weaving tales of migration and innovation. Nearby to film lovers' destination, the acclaimed Ritzy Picturehouse, Brixton Village not only celebrates the area's multicultural heritage through authentic dishes but also showcases the community spirit, making it a dynamic part of London's cultural and gastronomic landscape.

66

THE JOINT
BRIXTON
KRAFT
Unisex
Public
Toilet
LOST IN BRIXTON
NHS
DISCOUNT
20%
Brunch

The Design Museum

224-238 Kensington High St, W8 6AG

The Design Museum in Kensington is a compelling centre for creativity, offering a deep dive into design's ever-changing influence on society. Relocated in 2016, this architectural beauty, a revamped Commonwealth Institute, champions contemporary design through its diverse exhibitions. Covering fashion, furniture, graphics, and more, it aims to demystify design for professionals and enthusiasts alike. With a multitude of programmes, workshops, and the Design of the Year Award, it invites visitors to consider design's role in everyday life, promoting innovation and thoughtful analysis of our surroundings.

67

MAKER
CONTEMPORAR
Barbie
MARI

The Artist Residence

52 Cambridge St, Pimlico, SW1V 4JD

In Pimlico, London, Artist Residence stands out as a boutique hotel with a twist, thanks to its creative flair and welcoming atmosphere. Launched from a unique vision by co-founder Justin, this hotel, part of a select chain, brings together original art and cosy comfort. Situated conveniently between Chelsea, Tate Britain, and Westminster, it offers 10 individually decorated rooms. The on-site Clubhouse bar, open from morning till late, serves a range of drinks and a breakfast menu that includes dishes like eggs Florentine and smoked haddock kedgeree.

68

Credit - Camille Kenny-Ryder

Venn Street Market

Venn St, SW4 0AT

Every Saturday, Venn Street Market transforms the heart of Clapham Common into a thriving hub of local commerce, celebrating the finest in seasonal and locally sourced goods. This community-centric food market connects customers directly with the farmers and artisans behind the produce, embodying a commitment to quality, fairness, and sustainability. Garnering high praise for its vibrant atmosphere, Venn Street stands out not just for its foodie offerings but as a cornerstone of community interaction, making it a noteworthy mention for anyone seeking an authentic local experience. Open from 10 am to 3 pm, it's a weekly event that invites exploration, discovery, and the joy of meeting the makers behind each carefully crafted product.

69

BERBERÈ
Pizzeria
BELLE BIRRE · VINI NATURALI

The Library at the V&A

Cromwell Road SW7 2RL

The Victoria and Albert Museum in South Kensington stands as a sentinel to the world's creativity and is an unparalleled treasure trove in the heart of London. Within its walls lies an exhaustive celebration of creativity that spans continents and centuries. From the delicate intricacies of Renaissance sculptures to the bold statements of contemporary fashion, the V&A is a testament to human ingenuity and craftsmanship. It's a place where every exhibit tells a story, weaving a rich tapestry that captures the imagination. Whether marvelling at the detail of Islamic art, taking in the latest photography exhibition or exploring the innovative designs of modern furniture, there is something for everyone and visitors are invited on a journey that transcends time and geography.

70

Credit - Elena Shamis

The Royal Albert Hall

Kensington Gore, South Kensington, SW7 2AP

Proudly standing in Kensington, the Royal Albert Hall is one of London's most renowned music and performance venues. Its distinctive Italianate red brick exterior houses a unique oval-shaped hall, hosting diverse events from gala evenings and award ceremonies to ballet performances and rock concerts. Built in 1871 with proceeds from the 1851 Great Exhibition organised by Prince Albert, this iconic venue features a domed amphitheatre adorned with Minton tiles. Known for its rich history and royal connections, visitors can explore its fascinating past and stunning architecture through various guided tours, including a popular one-hour grand tour.

71

ROYAL ALBERT HALL

Richmond Green

The Green, Richmond TW9 1LX

Richmond Green, in Richmond upon Thames, is a historical expanse that marries the peace of the English countryside with community life. Once a Tudor hunting ground, it now serves as a communal hub, resonating with centuries of history from jousts to community festivals. This green tapestry of leisure and tradition is flanked by Georgian and Victorian homes and pubs enriching its charm. With the acclaimed Richmond Theatre and various eateries nearby, it's a cultural and social focal point. Intriguing legends abound with whispers of secret tunnels and ghostly figures at dusk, blending Richmond Green's historical depth with the mystique of local folklore.

72

THE CRICKETERS
CRICKETERS

Bramble and Moss

64 Hill Rise, Richmond TW10 6UB

In Richmond, Surrey, Bramble & Moss emerges as a cherished independent florist, gracing one of the most picturesque shop fronts in London. This quaint store crafts exquisite arrangements, blending classic British flowers like roses and peonies with unique touches of feathers and fruits. Their speciality in seasonal blooms and artful dried bouquets adds a lasting, whimsical elegance to any setting, showcasing nature's unparalleled beauty with every carefully curated piece.

73

Credit - Camille Kenny-Ryder

The Royal Botanic Gardens

Kew, Richmond, TW9 3AE

Kew Gardens, on London's outskirts, is a homage to botanical diversity, evolving from a modest 18th-century garden to what is now a 300-acre site with the world's largest botanical collections. Initially a royal garden, it's now a centre for scientific research and conservation, featuring much-loved structures like the tropical Palm House and the Treetop Walkway for soothing canopy views. The stunning Pagoda reflects Eastern fascination, and the Marianne North Gallery displays 832 botanical paintings, illustrating the garden's rich history and demonstrating its enduring commitment to preserving nature's variety.

74

Richmond Park

Richmond Park, Surrey, TW10 5HS

Richmond Park, London's largest Royal Park, established by Charles I in the 17th century, remains a sprawling sanctuary of heaths, ancient woodlands, and herds of Red and Fallow deer. Its 2,500 acres mirror the changing seasons, from winter's frost to autumn's warm palette, encapsulating centuries of history with each oak and pathway. The park houses the Mound, a possible Bronze Age burial site. Notably, the view from King Henry's Mound to St Paul's Cathedral connects the present with the historical landscape, offering a timeless glimpse into the city's heritage. It's not only a refuge for wildlife and those seeking peace away from urban life but also a testament to London's natural and royal past.

75

Richmond

Richmond TW9 1EP

For a taste of country life in London, the leafy Thames-side suburb of Richmond is a perfect escape. Just 30 minutes from central London, Richmond offers favourites like Richmond Park, Kew Gardens, and Richmond Riverside. The riverside area exudes a laid-back charm, making it a popular spot for summer afternoons. With an array of bars, restaurants, and attractions, it's perfect for any length of visit. Don't miss Richmond Bridge, the oldest surviving Thames bridge, dating back to 1776. Enjoy a leisurely stroll along the Riverside, hire paddle boats, or catch a riverboat to central London or Hampton Court.

76

Wimbledon Village

High Street, Wimbledon, SW19 5BY

Wimbledon is a delightful area to explore, offering the green expanses of Wimbledon Common and the quaint charm of Wimbledon Village. During the Wimbledon Lawn Tennis Championships, catch a game or visit the Wimbledon Lawn Tennis Museum. Other attractions include the iconic Wimbledon Windmill and the serene Buddhapadipa Temple. History buffs will appreciate the Iron Age fort remains on the Common and the 19th-century windmill. Several 16th-century properties reflect Wimbledon's royal past. The village flourished in the 18th century along the stagecoach route between Portsmouth and London, with the Dog and Fox pub's riding school as a notable remnant.

77

The Buddhapadipa Temple

14 Calonne Road, SW19 5HJ

The Buddhapadipa Temple, the first Thai Buddhist temple in the UK, relocated from East Sheen to Wimbledon in 1976. Open to all, it offers a serene space for Buddhist worship and community gatherings. Under Thai royal patronage, this temple welcomes visitors daily from 9 am to 5.30 pm, though its Uposatha Hall opens only on weekends or by appointment. Located at 14 Calonne Road, SW19 5HJ, near Wimbledon Park station, admission is free. Discover more about its events and teachings on their website.

78

Kingly Court

Kingly St, Carnaby, W1B 5PW

Venture through an unassuming archway off trendy Carnaby Street or navigate a slender passageway on Beak Street to discover a secluded courtyard in the heart of Soho. Kingly Court, Carnaby's famed three-storey gastronomic paradise of alfresco dining amidst London's West End. Home to 21 distinguished international eateries, bars, and cafés, this enclave offers a tapestry of global flavours within a fabulous setting. The courtyard, bathed in the open air during summer and warmly sheltered in winter, pulses with life, inviting food enthusiasts to revel in its diverse offerings.

79

SEÑOR CEVICHE
BARBECUE
SEÑOR CEVICHE
Imad's
BURGERS
PLEASE TAKE CARE OF YOUR BAGS AND VALUABLES

Chinatown

Gerrard St, W1D 6JD

Chinatown, a stone's throw from Leicester Square in London, is a fusion of Eastern culture, cuisine, and history, marked by red and gold flags, pagodas, embellished dragons and Qing dynasty gates. It's a portal to the East, where tradition and modernity meet, offering tales of distant lands and migrant dreams. More than a place for dim sum, bubble tea or Chinese New Year celebrations, Chinatown represents a dynamic and thriving community where diverse dialects fill the air, and patrons spill from popular eateries. It provides a window into the rich cultural heritage of one of the world's oldest civilisations, right in London's core.

80

MACCLESFIELD
STREET W1
麥高田街
金滿樓
LOTUS
GARDEN
DIM SUM DAILY
精美點心 粵式小菜

Floral Street

44 Floral St WC2E 9DG

In the heart of Covent Garden lies Floral Street, named after its bygone market trade, and now the epitome of London's shopping elegance and style. Parallel to King Street and a stone's throw from the iconic Market Building, this destination marries the charm of open-air shopping with the allure of high-end fashion, jewellery, and fragrance. Beyond its chic boutiques, including the likes of Paul Smith, lies the hidden gem of Floral Court, offering a serene escape. With the Royal Ballet School adding a touch of grace and the innovative Bridge of Aspiration connecting it to the Royal Opera House.

81

KECHERS
TED BAKER
Paul Smith

Choosing Keeping

21 Tower St, WC2H 9NS

In 2012, amidst the charm of East London's Columbia Road, known for its flower market and quaint boutiques, Choosing Keeping emerged as a sanctuary for stationery enthusiasts. Its inception was a nod to the timeless allure of handwritten notes and the tactile pleasure of pen and paper in an increasingly digital world, echoing memories of the first fountain pens and cherished notebooks. Fast forward to 2018, and the store found a new home in Covent Garden. The space, meticulously adorned with handcrafted cabinetry and displays, elevates the presentation of its curated collection of writing instruments, paper goods, and art supplies. Quarterly "exhibitions" and eagerly anticipated Christmas showcases reflect Choosing Keeping's commitment to the art of stationery.

82

SEVEN DIALS
TOWER COURT WC2
PING
STATIONERY · PAPETERIE
21

Mariage Frères

38 King Street, Covent Garden, WC2E 8JS

Mariage Frères, the prestigious tea purveyor, graces Covent Garden within a Georgian townhouse dedicated to the world of tea. As France's oldest tea house, this flagship store is a sanctuary for tea lovers, offering a global collection from rare vintage blends to aromatic infusions. It features an elegant restaurant where tea-infused cuisine transforms dining into art, a museum showcasing tea's heritage, and private spaces for intimate events. Mariage Frères is a journey into sophisticated brewing traditions, making it a unique destination in the heart of London.

83

MAISON DE THÉ
FRÈRES
ROSE D'HIMALAYA

Neal's Yard

Neals Yard, , WC2H 9DP

Neal's Yard, a hidden gem in Covent Garden, London, dazzles with its colourful façades and shops. This quaint courtyard offers everything from skincare to artisanal foods. Known for its commitment to sustainability and holistic well-being, Neal's Yard is home to pioneers like Neal's Yard Remedies. With cafés and eateries serving organic fare, it offers a healthful dining experience in a delightful setting. Neal's Yard stands as a testament to London's dedication to environmental consciousness and ethical consumerism, drawing both locals and tourists to its quirky charm and bustling atmosphere.

84

HAIR BY FAIRY
john masters organics
NEAL'S YARD
meeting rooms
FIRE EXIT
14
Chi nails
HAIRCUT
BLOW DRY
BALAYAGE
LADIES £38
GENTS £26
PLEASE BE AS QUIET AS POSSIBLE & ENJOY THE PEACE

The Royal Opera House

Bow St, WC2E 9DD

The Royal Opera House in Covent Garden stands as a pillar of cultural heritage in central London, housing The Royal Opera, The Royal Ballet, and their acclaimed orchestra. Since its inception in 1728, following John Rich's commission of The Beggar's Opera, this stunning venue has been at the forefront of the performing arts. By 1735, it had premiered numerous operas by George Frideric Handel, cementing its reputation as a premiere destination for opera and ballet. Over the centuries, despite devastating fires and reconstructions, it has maintained its architectural beauty and its esteemed creative position, continuing to offer groundbreaking performances in opera, ballet, and beyond, making it an essential visit for anyone captivated by the performing arts.

85

Seven Dials

Seven Dials, WC2H 9HD

Seven Dials, a junction within the St Giles district of Camden, made famous by novelist Agatha Christie, presents a fascinating slice of London's history, artfully blending its 17th-century origins with modern Covent Garden with its theatres and eateries. At its heart, there's a column bearing six sundials, with the column serving as the seventh, set in the convergence of seven historic streets. The area, once a monastic land turned royal possession and later a hub for the West End, retains much of its original street plan with several Stuart houses, now elegantly refaced. Managed by The Seven Dials Trust in collaboration with local stakeholders, it stands as a testament to London's ability to preserve its rich heritage. A nearby time plaque explains the area's unique story, from its early development to its time as one of London's most notorious slums, and its role in the social and political movements that have shaped the city.

86

GREENE KING
THE CROWN
THE CROWN
CAFFÈ

Somerset House

Strand, WC2R 1LA

Overlooking the Thames near Waterloo Bridge, Somerset House, an imposing Neoclassical complex in central London, is a classical gem with a modern twist. Conceived by Sir William Chambers in 1776 with Victorian expansions, it epitomises London's architectural heritage and now it's a hub for the UK's creative community, promoting art, technology, and enterprise. Its ethos, 'Step Inside, Think Outside', encourages exploration and collaboration, making it a site not just of historical importance but of contemporary cultural engagement. From ice skating in winter to open-air cinema in summer, Somerset House offers a space where innovation and tradition intersect, hosting memorable events that inspire within an unforgettable setting.

87

The Nomad Hotel

28 Bow St, WC2E 7AW

NoMad London, featured among the World's 50 Best Hotels, breathes new life into the historic grade II listed Bow Street Magistrates' Court in Covent Garden. This artistic endeavour, a collaboration with Roman and Williams, bridges the cultural vibrancy of London and New York, paying homage to figures like Oscar Wilde with its bohemian and romantic interiors. Transforming former judicial offices and even jail cells into luxurious, sunlit rooms, NoMad stands out with its eclectic restaurant set in a greenhouse-like atrium and subterranean speakeasy-style Common Decency bar.

88

Credit - Camille Kenny-Ryder

Seven Dials Market

Seven Dials Market WC2H 9AU

Discover Seven Dials Market, London's culinary playground in the heart of Covent Garden. Created by street food mavens, KERB, this food haven hosts over 20 independent traders within the storied walls of Thomas Neal's Warehouse, serving an irresistible array of global street food, from ramen and bao buns to a pioneering revolving cheese restaurant. The market's lively atmosphere is enhanced by original touches like a sculptural banana, celebrating its heritage as a former banana storage warehouse. It's a bustling, social space where London's food lovers converge seven days a week, complete with two bars.

89

ARNABEET

Stanfords Bookshop

7 Mercer Walk, WC2H 9FA

Stanfords, the UK's leading specialist in maps and travel books, has been a beloved destination since 1853. Recently relocated to Mercer Walk in Covent Garden after 118 years at Long Acre, Stanfords offers an unrivalled collection of maps, globes, and maritime charts. It has even provided cartography for the British Army and James Bond films. An essential stop for adventurers and armchair travellers alike, Stanfords boasts a distinguished clientele, including Amy Johnson, David Livingstone, Captain Scott, Ernest Shackleton, Florence Nightingale, Ranulph Fiennes, Bill Bryson, Michael Palin, and even Sherlock Holmes. Explore and let your imagination wander.

90

Stanfords
EST. 1853
WORLD OF
WELLINGTON ST

Old Bond Street

Old Bond Street, W1S 4QB

Old Bond Street, in the heart of London's Mayfair, epitomises luxury and sophistication. Established in the 18th century, it attracts fashion aficionados and discerning shoppers worldwide, boasting flagship stores of elite designers and jewellers such as Chanel, Burberry, and Cartier. Its architecture reflects a rich history and commitment to luxury, with its elegant storefront façades. More than a shopping destination, Old Bond Street is a cultural landmark where fashion, art, and history merge. It represents an enticing mix of tradition and contemporary luxury, drawing in discerning shoppers and art enthusiasts globally, making it a part of London's prestigious landscape.

91

Cartier
Cartier
Cartier
Cartier
Cartier
Cartier
CHAUMET

Burlington Arcade

51 Piccadilly, W1J 0QJ

Since 1819, Burlington Arcade has been a landmark of luxury in London, offering upscale shopping from Piccadilly to Bond Street. Designed by Samuel Ware for Lord George Cavendish, it aimed to provide a civilised shopping atmosphere, away from the city's chaos. Its serene interior boasts a glass roof and polished stone floors, housing over 40 independent retailers that specialise in fine jewellery, bespoke tailoring, luxury leather goods, and more, reflecting its commitment to quality and craftsmanship. The presence of Beadles, dressed in Regency-era uniforms and enforcing traditional regulations which include no running or humming, adds to the Arcade's unique English charm.

92

Fortnum & Mason

181 Piccadilly, St. James's,W1A 1ER

Steeped in over three centuries of tradition, Fortnum & Mason, a gem on Piccadilly, remains a bastion of British luxury. From its humble beginnings with William Fortnum's ingenious candle wax venture, it has blossomed into a symbol of opulence, famous for its pioneering speciality teas and sumptuous hampers, cherished at prestigious events like Ascot and Wimbledon. Awarded royal warrants and celebrated for its contribution to British armed forces, Fortnum's seamlessly blends its rich history with modern allure, from the acclaimed tea counter to the retro charm of the Soda Fountain. A £24 million refurbishment in 2007, marking its 300th anniversary, ensured that Fortnum's continues to redefine elegance while honouring its heritage.

93

Credit - Camille Kenny-Ryder

Maison Assouline

196A Piccadilly, St. James's, W1J 9EY

Maison Assouline in London is more than a bookstore, it is an inviting and sophisticated retreat in the heart of Piccadilly. This enclave of intellect and style stands as a tribute to the art of living well, offering an excellent selection of books that span the realms of art, fashion, design, and gastronomy. Beyond its literary treasures, Maison Assouline is a sanctuary for those who seek the refined and the rare, with its curated artefacts and sumptuous furnishings. The space itself, designed with an eye for elegance and comfort, invites visitors to linger, whether to enjoy a crafted cocktail at its distinguished bar or to engage in quiet contemplation amidst its wealth of knowledge.

94

Credit - Elena Shamis

The Wolseley

160 Piccadilly, St. James's, W1J 9EB

One of London's most famous restaurants, The Wolseley on Piccadilly, boasts a grand Art Deco interior with marble pillars and archways, ideal for all-day European dining. Known for its elegant setting and lively atmosphere, it serves classic European dishes with impeccable service. The extensive menu features top-quality seafood, from clams and oysters to crevettes and caviar. Dessert lovers will relish choices like apple strudel and assorted coupes. Founded by restaurant impresarios Chris Corbin and Jeremy King, this former 1920s car showroom, with its marble floors, Japanese panels, and leather banquettes, exudes timeless glamour next to the Ritz.

95

WOLSELEY

Lina Stores

18 Brewer St Soho, W1F 0SH

Since 1944, Lina Stores in Soho has been a flagship of authentic Italian cuisine in London. Founded by Lina, a Genovese woman with a formidable reputation, this delicatessen has become a culinary landmark, dedicated to delivering a slice of Italy with its artisanal fare and carefully sourced ingredients. The store buzzes daily with the creation of fresh pasta and sandwiches, filling the bustling Soho streets with enticing aromas. Lina Stores is an immersion into Italian culture with every item, from its aged Parmigiano Reggiano to its Prosciutto di Parma and antipasti, epitomising Italy's gastronomic excellence but in the heart of London.

96

VENTRICINA
£3.00
PANCETTA
£2.50
MARRONS GLACES

Liberty London

Regent St, Soho, W1B 5AH

Liberty London is to the English capital what Bergdorf Goodman and Neiman Marcus are to New York. This Regent Street gem offers six floors of designer treasures, each marked by unmatched quality. Renowned for its imaginative patterns and prints, Liberty's collections stand out. The store is famous worldwide for its bold, floral fabrics and close connection to art and culture. The vast mock-Tudor building also features men's, women's, and children's fashion, beauty products, and homewares from both high-end and emerging brands.

97

LIBERTY

Goodwin's Court

Goodwins Court, , WC2N 4LL

Nestled in London's heart, Goodwin's Court is an enchanting alleyway reminiscent of a bygone era, and could be taken from the pages of Harry Potter with its gas-lit path and Georgian windows. This Dickensian nook offers a glimpse into the city's rich history and architectural beauty, tucked away from the modern pavements of the city. It serves as a silent homage to London's past, inviting visitors to delve into its mystery and charm, and imagine the myriad stories etched into its very stones.

98

Credit - Elena Shamis

Foster Books

183 Chiswick High Rd., Chiswick, W4 2DR

Visitors to Chiswick High Road are transported to a bygone era upon stepping through the doors of its oldest shop, a charming 18th-century bookshop. The bright green bay window, dating back to 1790, overflows with vintage books, while outside, £1 paperbacks and maps evoke the charm of a Dickensian curiosity shop. This enchanting establishment, owned by Stephen Foster since 2007, has been in his family for nearly 50 years. Foster, previously a Marylebone bookseller for 25 years, shifted focus to collectors' items in response to the changing book market, ensuring a treasure trove for bibliophiles.

99

183
FOSTER BOOKS
183

Brompton Cemetery

Fulham Rd, SW10 9UG

Over 200,000 souls rest in Brompton Cemetery, commemorated by stunning memorials, from grieving angels to ornate mausoleums. Amidst these gothic monuments, the cemetery brims with life, with birds, butterflies, and bats among the wildflowers. Explore its avenues and discover graves of notable figures like suffragette leader Emmeline Pankhurst and pioneering doctor John Snow. The cemetery's architecture, including the spectacular Great Circle and elegant Central Avenue, is as impressive as its residents. Unwind at the café or seek guidance at the Information Centre. Brompton Cemetery, part of the 'Magnificent Seven,' remains a serene urban oasis and a living testament to history.

100

ALSO OF
JAMES WHITTAKER BURGESS
HUSBAND OF THE ABOVE
DIED OCTOBER 25. 1937
AGED 91 YEARS.

Hammersmith

101 Queen Caroline St, W6 9BN

Hammersmith has preserved some architectural gems, especially along the riverside, despite mid-20th-century urbanisation. Notable arts venues include the Lyric, a 19th-century theatre encased in concrete, the Apollo, a former cinema now hosting major gigs and comedy shows, and Riverside Studios, a cinema and performing arts venue. Hammersmith Bridge, designed by William Tierney Clark in 1827, was the first suspension bridge over the Thames and remains the lowest at just under 4 metres above the water. The area also boasts the world's first underground line, the Hammersmith and City. Sports fans can visit Chelsea F.C.'s Stamford Bridge, one of three major clubs in this compact borough. Remarkably, Gandhi lived here in the 1880s while studying law.

101

Lidgates Butchers

110 Holland Park Ave, W11 4UA

Lidgate's family butcher's boasts five generations of expertise at its renowned shop in Holland Park, west London. Chefs, dedicated carnivores, and locals flock here for everything from lunchtime sausage rolls to magnificent ribs of grass-fed beef. Known for top-quality meat and innovative recipes, Lidgate's offers classics like chicken and ham pie and Cornish pasties, alongside new creations such as gourmet kebabs. Founded by Charles Lidgate in 1850, the shop is now run by Danny Lidgate, who, with his father David, personally selects organic and grass-fed meats from free-range farms.

102

LIDGATES
110 LIDGATE 110
SANDERSONS
LONDON
Local Expertise Global Connections
Q AWARD
C. LIDGATE
Free Range & Organic Meats & Poultry
020 7727 8243
www.lidgates.com
Free Range & Organic Meats & Poultry
GRASS FED & ORGANIC
BEEF

The Peninsula

1 Grosvenor Pl, SW1X 7HJ

Located near Hyde Park Corner and Wellington Arch, The Peninsula London is nestled in the heart of one of the UK's most exclusive areas, boasting the prestigious SW1X postcode alongside other luxury establishments like Mandarin Oriental Hyde Park, The Berkeley, and The Lanesborough. Echoing the elegance of its custom-built Brewster green Rolls Royce Phantoms, The Peninsula Hotels operate with flawless precision, transforming every visit into a memorable journey. Few entry points to a city promise the grandeur found here.

103

Credit - Camille Kenny-Ryder

The Serpentine Galleries

Kensington Gardens, W2 3XA

Nestled within London's picturesque Kensington Gardens, the Serpentine, with its two contemporary art galleries, serves as a haven for modern art enthusiasts. Just a short stroll across a bridge spanning the Serpentine Lake, the galleries—Serpentine South and Serpentine North—host an array of compelling exhibitions and public programmes. Notably, each summer since 2000, Serpentine has commissioned a temporary pavilion designed by an international architect, making it a highlight of London's cultural calendar. Admission is free, inviting up to 1.2 million visitors annually to engage with pioneering art and architecture set against the tranquil backdrop of the gardens. Open Tuesday to Sunday, the Serpentine continues to push the boundaries of contemporary art.

104

St Lukes Mews

St Lukes Mews, W11 1DF

St Luke's Mews, tucked away in the charming enclave of Notting Hill, is a picturesque street that seems lifted from the pages of a storybook. With its row of pastel coloured houses and cobbled pathways, it offers a tranquil contrast to the busy city life just beyond its confines. Known to many through its cinematic appearances, the mews have a magical quality, with climbing roses and wisteria framing the quaint facades of its historic homes during summer. For those who stumble upon St Luke's Mews, it's an enchanting, serene discovery, showcasing the enduring charm of London's lesser-known quarters.

105

Credit - Mariana Martins

Alice Antiques

86 Portobello Rd, W11 2QD

Alice Antiques, situated on the world famous Portobello Road, offers an enchanting array of antique furnishings, china, curios, and toys. Its theatrical ambience and flamboyant exterior make it a standout in London's famed market, reminiscent of "The Greatest Showman." This shop is a treasure trove, with each piece—from Edwardian porcelain to Victorian mirrors—telling a story of bygone days. Captivating both curious browsers and serious collectors alike, Alice Antiques blends the charm of the past with the allure of discovery.

106

DENBIGH CLOSE, W11
PREVIOUSLY DENBIGH MEWS
ESTD 1887
ALICE'S
ALICE'S
THE BEST VALUE IN THE BRITISH ISLES
SCHOOL FRIEND

Electric Cinema

191 Portobello Rd, W11 2ED

The Electric Cinema in Notting Hill, London, first opened on 24 February 1910 and is one of Britain's oldest working film theatres. It became Britain's first black-owned cinema in 1993, remaining so until 2000. Originally designed for motion pictures and among the first buildings in the area with electricity, the cinema has a storied past. After a turbulent 1980s, it was transformed, replacing its 240 seats with 98 luxurious leather armchairs. A bar was also installed, serving cocktails, pints of lager, and bottles of wine, creating a unique atmosphere for film lovers.

107

HONEST
WELCOME TO
NOW SHOWING FURIOSA A MAD MAX SAGA
THE COSTMONGERS
63/64 THE MARKET STALLS
NOTTING HILL
LONDON W11 2ED
PORTOBELLO BURGER,

The Secret Sandwich Shop

103 Talbot Rd, W11 2AT

Their sandwiches are inspired by the Japanese Wanpaku sandwich, which means cheeky or naughty. These sandwiches boast glorious stacks of colourful layers and varying textures from meat, cheese, eggs, and fresh vegetables, all nestled in pillowy Japanese shokupan bread. Open every day from 8 am to 3 pm, their offerings include the Signature Sando, filled with avocado, tomato, mayo, and a variety of vegetables, the T.L.T. with all the turkey, and the popular Honey Mustard Chicken.

108

GLOBE

Little Venice

Blomfield Road, , W9 2PF

Little Venice, the area where the Grand Union and Regent's Canals meet, is a tranquil retreat in London, famed for its Regency architecture and houseboats. Rumoured to be named by poets like Robert Browning or Lord Byron, "Little Venice" mirrors the scenic charm of its namesake city and has long been a muse for artists and writers. Today, it's a tightly knit community. Towpaths and waterside cafes offer serene spots to unwind, Canal boats transport tourists to London Zoo or Camden Market, while venues like the Puppet Theatre Barge and Canal Café Theatre contribute to its cultural richness.

109

Cœur de Lion

Paddington Station

Praed St, W2 1HU

Isambard Kingdom Brunel envisioned a grand terminus for the Great Western Railway at Paddington, near the Grand Junction and Regent's canals. However, soaring construction costs forced Brunel to create a temporary station using the arches of Bishop's Bridge Road. Opening on 4 June 1838, this provisional station served until the line reached Bristol and required expansion. In 1850, Brunel designed a permanent station inspired by the Crystal Palace, featuring a vast wrought iron and glass roof. The station's three spans were the largest train shed roof globally. Today, Paddington Station is a key London hub, serving Great Western Railway and Heathrow Express, with Underground connections on several lines. Additionally, Paddington Bear fans can find themed gifts at the station.

110

1
Welcome to
Paddington Station
Connect to
Free Station WiFi

Word on the Water

Regent's Canal Towpath, N1C 4LW

Word on the Water, London's floating literary bookshop, offers a novel retreat on the serene waters of the Regent's Canal. This 1920s Dutch barge has been transformed into a unique treasure trove of literature, where shelves brim with books from riveting bestsellers to timeless classics. As you step aboard, the intimate charm of this floating mobile bookstore envelops you. With regular live music and poetry readings, this bibliophilic barge is more than just a place to purchase books; it's an unforgettable cultural venue that celebrates the joy of reading in one of the city's more unusual and picturesque settings.

111

Credit - Mariana Martins

TEN OF LONDON'S BEST

PARKS & GARDENS

1. Hyde Park
Hyde Park, London, W2 2UH

2. Regent's Park
Regent's Park, London, NW1 4NR

3. Richmond Park
Richmond Park, Richmond, TW10 5HS

4. Greenwich Park
Greenwich Park, London, SE10 8XJ

5. Hampstead Heath
Hampstead Heath, London, NW3 7JR

6. St. James's Park
St. James's Park, London, SW1A 2BJ

7. Kensington Gardens
Kensington Gardens, London, W2 2UH

8. Victoria Park
Victoria Park, Grove Road, London, E3 5TB

9. Battersea Park
Battersea Park, London, SW11 4NJ

10. Bushy Park
Bushy Park, Hampton Court Road, Hampton, TW12 2EJ

FIFTEEN OF LONDON'S BEST

BOOKSHOPS

BookBar, 166 Blackstock Road, N5 1HA

Bookshop on the Heath, 74 Tranquil Vale, Blackheath, SE3 0BW

Brick Lane Bookshop, 166 Brick Ln, E1 6RU

Gay's the Word, 66 Marchmont Street, WC1N 1AB

Hatchards, 187 Piccadilly, St James's, W1J 9LE

Kirkdale Bookshop, 272 Kirkdale, Sydenham, SE26 4RS

London Review Bookshop, 14-16 Bury Pl, WC1A 2JL

Newham Bookshop, 743-745 Barking Rd, E13 9ER

Nomad Books, 781 Fulham Rd, SW6 5HA

Primrose Hill Books, 134 Regent's Park Rd, NW1 8XL

Skoob Books, 66 The Brunswick, Off Marchmont Street, WC1N 1AE

The Atlantis Bookshop, 49A Museum St, WC1A 1LY

The L & R Bookshop, 21 Kensington Park Road, W11 2EU

The Notting Hill Bookshop, 13 Blenheim Cres, W11 2EE

Treadwell's Books, 33 Store St, WC1E 7BS

WOODEN and CARTY
The BEST AMERICAN MYST
JOHN SANDFORD
PIGAL
OXFORD
Simulation for the Social Sc
James Branch Cabell · BREWER
CATCH A FALLING SPY
LIPPINCOTT
Very Sincerely Yours
UNION
ALLAN NEVINS
THE VANISHED POMPS OF YESTERDAY
BEN BOVA

FIVE OF LONDON'S BEST

CINEMAS

The Chiswick Cinema , 94-96 Chiswick High Road, Chiswick, W4 1SH

The Cinema at Selfridges - 40 Duke Street, W1U 1AT

Electric Cinema Portobello - 191 Portobello Road, W11 2ED

Everyman Cinema - Where? 5 Holly Bush Vale, NW3 6TX

BFI Southbank - Belvedere Rd, SE1 8XT

NINE OF LONDON'S BEST

CHRISTMAS MARKETS

Covent Garden Christmas Village
The Market Building, London WC2E 8RF

Canopy Christmas Market at King's Cross
Granary Square, London N1C 4BH

Borough Market at Christmas
Southwark St, London SE1 1TL

Christmas At Flat Iron Square
45 Southwark St, London SE1 9HP

Christmas by the River, Bankside
London SE1 2RR

Greenwich Christmas Market
Greenwich Market, London SE10 9HZ

Kingston Christmas Market
Kingston upon Thames KT1 1JT

Maltby Street Night Market
Arch 46, Ropewalk, Maltby St, London SE1 3PA

Chelsea Physic Garden Christmas Fair
66 Royal Hospital Rd, London SW3 4HS

FIVE OF LONDON'S BEST

COCKTAIL BARS

The Connaught Bar - Carlos Place, W1K 2AL

Scarfes Bar - Rosewood London, 252 High Holborn, WC1V 7EN

Coupette - 423 Bethnal Green Road, E2 0AN

Lyaness - 20 Upper Ground, South Bank, SE1 9PD

The Nest - 14-15 Langham Pl, London W1B 2QS

TEN OF LONDON'S BEST

CHRISTMAS LIGHTS

1. Oxford Street : Oxford Street, London, W1D 1BS
2. Regent Street : Regent Street, London, W1B 5AH
3. Covent Garden : Covent Garden, London, WC2E 8RF
4. Carnaby Street : Carnaby Street, London, W1F 9PS
5. Bond Street : Bond Street, London, W1S 1SR
6. South Bank : South Bank, London, SE1 9PX
7. King's Cross : King's Cross, London, N1C 4AX
8. Sloane Square : Sloane Square, London, SW1W 8AQ
9. Marylebone Village : Marylebone High Street, London, W1U 4NP
10. Leicester Square : Leicester Square, London, WC2H 7LU

Oxford

THE BEST OF
LONDON
DISCOVER LONDON'S BEST PLACES TO VISIT

Coming Soon...

The Best of London App

SECRET
LONDON
101 OF LONDON'S BEST PLACES TO VISIT
BEST
LONDON
FOOD GUIDE
101 OF LONDON'S BEST PLACES TO EAT
BEST
LONDON
PUB GUIDE
101 OF LONDON'S BEST PLACES TO DRINK
INN
THE BULL AND LAST
BEST OF BRITAIN

A-Z Index

USE OUR HANDY

GOOGLE MAP

We have marked each location featured in this book on a Google Map, allowing you to plan your route and discover nearby attractions. Please visit the website below to access the map.

WWW.BESTOFENGLAND.COM/LONDON-MAP

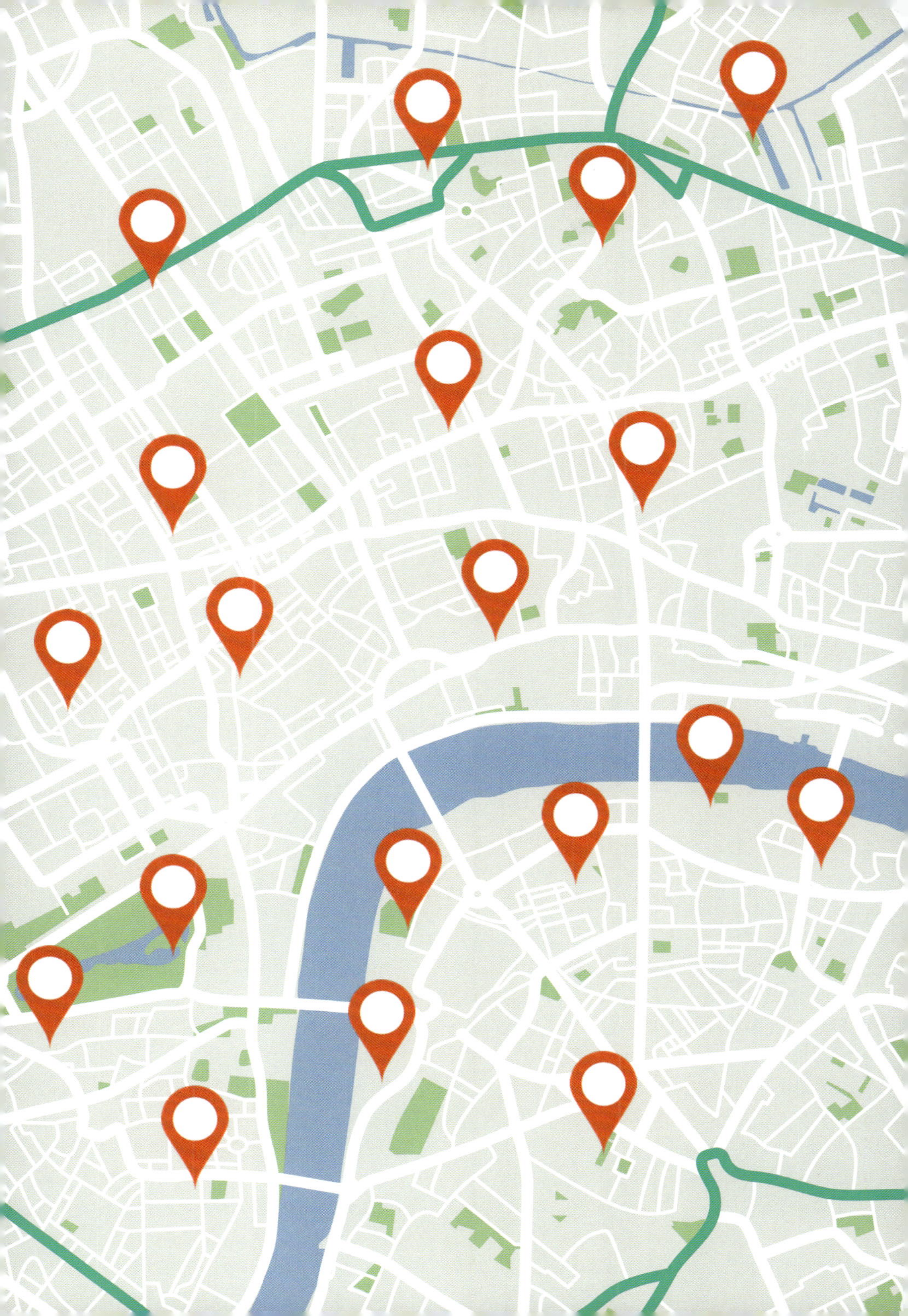